Green type indicates global example

MACROECONOMICS

IN MODULES

THIRD EDITION

MACROECONOMICS

IN MODULES

Paul Krugman • Robin Wells

Princeton University

WORTH PUBLISHERS

A Macmillan Higher Education Company

Vice President, Editing, Design, and Media Production: Catherine Woods

Vice President, Editorial—Sciences & Social Sciences: Charles Linsmeier

Publisher, Social and Behavioral Sciences: Kevin Feyen

Associate Publisher, Economics & Geography: Steven A. Rigolosi

Executive Development Editor: Sharon Balbos

Development Editor: Mary Walsh

Editorial Assistant: Fay Kelly

Marketing Manager: Thomas Digiano

Marketing Assistant: Tess Sanders

Executive Media Editor: Rachel Comerford

Media Editor: Lukia Kliossis

Director of Development for Print and Digital: Tracey Kuehn

Product Owner—LaunchPad: Marie McHale

Managing Editor: Lisa Kinne

Project Editor: Liz Geller

Art Director: Babs Reingold

Cover Designers: Lyndall Culbertson and Babs Reingold

Interior Layout: Paul Lacy

Interior Design: Charles Yuen

Photo Editor: Cecilia Varas

Photo Researcher: Elyse Rieder

Production Manager: Barbara Anne Seixas

Supplements Production Manager: Stacey Alexander

Supplements Project Editor: Edgar Bonilla

Composition and Illustration: TSI Graphics

Printing and Binding: RR Donnelley

See page vii for credits information. Page vii is an extension of this copyright page.

ISBN-13: 978-1-4641-3905-5

ISBN-10: 1-4641-3905-9

Library of Congress Control Number: 2014932841

Printed in the United States of America

First printing

Worth Publishers

41 Madison Avenue

New York, NY 10010

www.worthpublishers.com

ABOUT THE AUTHORS

Paul Krugman, recipient of the 2008 Nobel Memorial Prize in Economic Sciences, is Professor of Economics at Princeton University, where he regularly teaches the principles course. In the summer of 2015 he will join the faculty of the Graduate Center, City University of New York, and become a distinguished scholar at the Graduate Center's Luxembourg Income Study Center. Krugman received his BA from Yale and his PhD from MIT. Prior to his current position, he taught at Yale, Stanford, and MIT. He also spent a

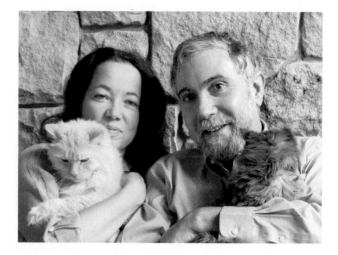

year on the staff of the Council of Economic Advisers in 1982–1983. His research is mainly in the area of international trade, where he is one of the founders of the "new trade theory," which focuses on increasing returns and imperfect competition. He also works in international finance, with a concentration in currency crises. In 1991, Krugman received the American Economic Association's John Bates Clark medal. In addition to his teaching and academic research, Krugman writes extensively for nontechnical audiences. He is a regular op-ed columnist for the *New York Times*. His latest trade books, both best sellers, include *End This Depression Now!*, a look at the recent global financial crisis and recovery, and *The Return of Depression Economics and the Crisis of 2008*, a history of recent economic troubles and their implications for economic policy. His earlier books, *The Conscience of a Liberal, Peddling Prosperity*, and *The Age of Diminished Expectations*, have become modern classics.

Robin Wells was a Lecturer and Researcher in Economics at Princeton University. She received her BA from the University of Chicago and her PhD from the University of California at Berkeley; she then did postdoctoral work at MIT. She has taught at the University of Michigan, the University of Southampton (United Kingdom), Stanford, and MIT. The subject of her teaching and research is the theory of organizations and incentives.

To beginning students everywhere,
which we all were at one time.

BRIEF CONTENTS

CONTENTS

Section 3
Macroeconomic Measurement 95

Section 4
Unemployment and Inflation 131

Section 7
Income and Expenditure   241

Section 8
Aggregate Demand and
Aggregate Supply   273

Section 11
Monetary Policy

Section 12
Policy Responses to Unemployment and Inflation

PREFACE

"It is not how much empty space there is, but rather how it is used. It is not how much information there is, but rather how effectively it is arranged."

—*Edward R. Tufte*

An Innovative Modular Format

For a long while, we have been hearing from instructors who wanted to use the Krugman/Wells text in their principles course, but needed a less comprehensive version: a book that was shorter overall, with a focus on the essential principles of economics, and with less in the way of theory and analytics. We've responded to these requests, and you are holding the result in your hands.

Macroeconomics in Modules **is a streamlined textbook that incorporates an innovative format geared toward how students learn today.** Instead of tackling 24 chapters of about 25 to 40 pages each, students encounter 6- to 10-page *modules* designed to be read in a single sitting. What exactly is a module? We think users and reviewers have come up with the best definition. They consistently describe modules as "short, digestible chunks" of text that students actually read. We should also add that shorter does not mean taking shortcuts. Although each module is a short, easy-to-manage reading assignment, each is also informative and thorough, with adequate rigor.

This text includes carefully crafted pedagogy that works within the modular format to enhance the student learning experience. The modular format offers a unique opportunity for structured learning and assessment. Each module concentrates on a specific topic using a learning-objectives approach and then concludes with three types of self-assessment questions: "Check Your Understanding" and multiple-choice questions that allow students to test their comprehension of module content, followed by critical-thinking questions that encourage reflection and analysis. Answers to these questions appear at the end of the book, so students can actually see how well they've mastered concepts.

There is additional opportunity for assessment at the end of each section (a section is a grouping of modules): thoughtful problems that test related concepts across all of the modules in a section, encouraging students to make connections among ideas as well as apply and practice what they've learned.

We've refined the modular structure in this edition to offer even greater flexibility. We've added six new sections to help unpack some of the more module-heavy sections. The result: more focused sections with fewer modules in each. Important topics are contained within their own sections, making it easier for instructors to navigate through the book and assign the topics they want to teach without breaking chapters apart (often done with non-modular texts), which can undermine narrative flow and diminish comprehension.

The Science Behind Modules

We see it for ourselves, we have heard it from reviewers, and the research confirms it: students are reading less, for shorter periods of time, and they continue to struggle with comprehension. So, when we began thinking about the idea of developing a more streamlined principles text, we also thought a lot about the best way to format it.

The modular format, which is popular in other disciplines, appealed to us. It was in keeping with the findings of cognitive psychologists who have demonstrated that comprehension is best attained when material is "chunked" into smaller reading assignments, reinforced with frequent questioning (the "testing effect"), and incentivized by a sense of accomplishment earned from completing discrete reading tasks. These findings are at the heart of the modular format of this text and its pedagogy.

Comments from users confirm the benefits of this new way of presenting economic concepts. Each user reported an almost identical story: students were actually completing their reading assignments, something that was rare when traditional textbook chapters were assigned. Overall, they found students coming to lectures better prepared. And, each of these users couldn't imagine returning to a textbook with a more traditional format.

This result makes intuitive sense. Why wouldn't students prefer to read short modules instead of long chapters? Of course it would enrich the learning experience if students could check their comprehension more frequently, at the end of short modules.

For a closer look at the text's format and feature set, see the walkthrough on pages xxiv–xxxi.

About the Revision

This edition of *Macroeconomics in Modules* represents a major revision. We had three goals in mind as we worked: adding important new content, improving the organization of sections, and updating examples and data to keep the book current and relevant. We even added a new feature.

Decisions about many of the changes were made with the help of feedback from a devoted group of adopters and reviewers—all fans of the modular format who offered us excellent suggestions for how we could make the text an even better match for their principles courses. Here is an overview of the major revisions.

New Coverage of the Keynesian Cross

This was an omission that prompted the most vocal response from instructors and we've remedied it in this edition with **new Module 26, "The Income-Expenditure Model."** The new module offers a detailed look at the aggregate-expenditure model and presents the famous 45-degree diagram for those who cover this material. We worked hard to keep this module focused and free of unnecessary complexity.

New Modules and Organizational Improvements

In addition to the new module on the Keynesian cross, we've included two new modules on topics that mean a lot to us and, that we hope, will allow you to enrich your own teaching. **Module 8, "International Trade,"** has been included for those who wish to delve deeper into trade topics than is possible with the coverage of comparative advantage and trade presented in Module 3.

Module 42, "Crises and Consequences," offers a unique look at the financial crisis of 2008, examining the aspects of the banking system that allowed the crisis to happen, the reasons why banking crises are so bad for so many, and the role that government and regulation play in crises.

Organizational Improvements We made the following changes in this edition. But for those who prefer to teach using a different order, the sections and modules remain completely flexible.

Many new sections: We've already touched on the benefits of more sections. Those of you familiar with the second edition will notice that we've virtually doubled the number of them, a structural change that alters the look of our table of contents, we think, for the better. Material that had been submerged previously, such as ADAS (Section 8), Fiscal Policy (Section 9), and Money, Banking, and the Fed (Section 10), is now prominent. Some modules have moved to accommodate the new structure, resulting, overall, in a more logical flow of ideas.

New early growth coverage: Following the section on unemployment and inflation is an early, all-new section devoted to economic growth (Section 5). This early coverage allows us to emphasize the idea that economic growth, along with low unemployment and stable inflation, are important policy goals. In addition, early coverage of long-run economic growth in real GDP helps students understand why the business cycle involves fluctuations around an upward trend. And we are now able to highlight the role that the markets and institutions covered next, in Section 6, play in economic growth.

New Feature: Business Case Studies

Now, more than ever, students need a strong understanding of economic principles and their applications to business decisions. To meet this need, virtually every section now concludes with a real-world business case that illustrates how the economic principles just covered play out in the world of entrepreneurs and bottom lines.

The cases are wide-ranging and provide insight into business decision making. They include an examination of how lean production techniques at Boeing and Toyota increased efficiency at both companies and led to a worldwide manufacturing revolution. (Section 1: "Efficiency, Opportunity Cost, and the Logic of Lean Production"). Another case looks at the changing job market during a recession, examined through the lens of companies like Monster Worldwide and its competitors (Section 4: "A Monster Slump"). One of our favorites is the case addressing the role of gift cards in secondary markets and the value of *breakage* when individual consumers fail to pay down their gift cards completely (Section 10: "The Perfect Gift: Cash or a Gift Card?").

Each case concludes with "Questions for Thought" that help students engage more deeply with economic concepts by seeing them applied in actual business situations. A list of the new Business Cases appears on the inside front cover.

Extensive Updates

This edition includes 15 new "Economics in Actions" (formerly called "In Real Life"). Many of those not replaced outright have been updated to include recent developments and research. Virtually every module includes at least one "Economics in Action" feature. In addition, all but two of our section-opening stories are new to this edition, for a grand total of 12 new openers. We have also undertaken a thorough updating of examples, data, and applications.

It is important to us to emphasize currency and to use stories from real life and the news. This makes every revision a work-intensive endeavor, but we believe that currency drives student interest.

A Closer Look at the Table of Contents and Feature Set

The annotated table of contents that follows shows how the modular format works and explains the focus of each section. Although the sections are grouped into building blocks in which conceptual material learned at one stage is built upon and then integrated into the next stage, the coverage is also flexible enough to allow instructors to organize content to best meet their needs.

Following the table of contents is a visual tour of our feature set that clarifies how well the content of this text is supplemented by real-world examples and ample opportunity for practice and review (pages xxiv–xxvii).

Annotated Table of Contents . . .
A Closer Look at Content and Format

The text contains 14 sections with two to five modules in each.

An introduction to basic economic principles that will help students develop an understanding of economic modeling and the nature of markets.

Each component of the supply and demand model is covered in its own module, allowing students to master the model incrementally. The section includes a **new module** on international trade.

Introduces macroeconomics and explains how macroeconomic aggregates are measured.

A **new** stand-alone section examining unemployment, how it's measured, and the problems posed by inflation.

NEW TO THIS EDITION Early treatment of long-run growth. The section looks at sources of economic growth and explains why some countries have been more successful than others.

An introduction to the financial system with the background students will need to tackle upcoming topics such as monetary policy and international capital flows.

NEW TO THIS EDITION Coverage of Keynesian cross analysis in **new Module 26.** It is preceded by a look at the logic of the multiplier and determinants of consumer and investment spending.

A thorough treatment of AD–AS focusing on the aggregate price level using the traditional approach to AD–AS, with coverage on the ability of economies to recover in the long run.

The addition of six new section divisions on major topics in macroeconomics, like fiscal policy and monetary policy, means fewer modules in each section and more flexibility.

A **new** stand-alone section devoted to how fiscal policy can be used to manage the ups and downs of the business cycle, with an in-depth look at discretionary fiscal policy and automatic stabilizers.

This section examines the roles of money, money creation, and the structure and role of the Federal Reserve System—including historical background on the evolution of money and monetary institutions.

A **new** stand-alone section examining the use of monetary policy in the face of recession or inflation, with a close look at the Fed's role in driving interest rates and aggregate demand.

This section addresses the causes and consequences of inflation, deflation, and the dangers of disinflation. **NEW TO THIS EDITION** Module 42 on financial crises, offering a detailed and up-to-date look at the recent crisis and its aftermath.

Analyzes the special issues raised by an open economy: a weak dollar, foreign accumulation of dollar reserves, and debates about the euro.

A unique overview of the history of macroeconomic thought set in the context of changing policy concerns and current macroeconomic debates.

These appendices offer a helpful review of graphing skills and easy access to select macroeconomic data for reference.

Solutions allow students to independently test their mastery of concepts.

Tools for Learning . . .
Getting the Most from
This Book

Each section consists of interrelated modules with a consistent set of features and pedagogy. Each module is self-contained giving students discrete reading assignments to complete. Instructors have the freedom to assign only those modules that are important to their course.

SECTION 2

The **SECTION-OPENING OUTLINE** offers a quick opening preview of the modules in each section.

Supply and Demand

BLUE JEAN BLUES WORLD VIEW

SECTION-OPENING STORY Each section begins with a compelling story that often extends through the modules. The opening stories are designed to illustrate important concepts, to build intuition with realistic examples, and then to encourage students to read on and learn more.

If you bought a pair of blue jeans in 2011, you may have been shocked at the price. Or maybe not: fashions change, and maybe you thought you were paying the price for being fashionable. But you weren't—you were paying for cotton. Jeans are made of denim, which is a particular weave of cotton, and by December 2010, the price [...] h had hit a 140-year high, the highest [...] cords began in 1870.

[...]ton prices so high?
[...]and for clothing of all kinds was surg-
[...]s the world struggled with the effects
[...] nervous consumers cut back on cloth-
[...]y 2010, with the worst apparently over,
[...] force. On the supply side, Pakistan,
[...]rgest cotton producer, was hit by dev-
[...]put one-fifth of the country underwa-
[...]troyed its cotton crop.
[...]umers had limited tolerance for large increases in the price of cotton clothing, apparel makers began scrambling to find ways to reduce costs. They adopted changes like smaller buttons, cheaper linings, and—yes—polyester, doubting that consumers would be willing to pay more for cotton goods. In fact, some experts on the

cotton market warned that the sky-high prices of cotton in 2010–2011 might lead to a permanent shift in tastes, with consumers becoming more willing to wear synthetics even when cotton prices came down.

At the same time, it was not all bad news for everyone connected with the cotton trade. In the United States, cotton producers had not been hit by bad weather and were relishing the higher prices. American farmers responded to sky-high cotton prices by sharply increasing the acreage devoted to the crop. None of this was enough, however, to produce immediate price relief.

Wait a minute: how, exactly, does flooding in Pakistan translate into higher jeans prices and more polyester in your T-shirts? It's a matter of supply and demand—but what does that mean? Many people use "supply and demand" as a sort of catchphrase to mean "the laws of the marketplace at work." To economists, however, the concept of supply and demand has a precise meaning: it is a *model of how a market behaves*.

In this section, we lay out the pieces that make up the *supply and demand model*, put them together, and show how this model can be used to understand how many—but not all—markets behave.

35

WHAT YOU WILL LEARN

1 What a competitive market is and how it is described by the supply and demand model

What the demand curve is

The difference between movements along the demand curve and changes in demand

The factors that shift the demand curve

Each module begins with WHAT YOU WILL LEARN, a numbered list of learning objectives in an easy-to-review format that alerts students to critical concepts in the pages ahead.

Supply and Demand: A Model of a Competitive Market

Cotton sellers and cotton buyers constitute a *market*—a group of producers and consumers who exchange a good or service for payment. In this section, we'll focus on a particular type of market known as a *competitive market*. Roughly, a **competitive market** is a market in which there are many buyers and sellers of the same good or service. More precisely, the key feature of a competitive market is that no individual's actions have a noticeable effect on the price at which the good or service is sold. It's important to understand, however, that this is not an accurate description of every market.

For example, it's not an accurate description of the market for cola beverages. That's because in the market for cola beverages, Coca-Cola and Pepsi account for such a large proportion of total sales that they are able to influence the price at which cola beverages are bought and sold. But it *is* an accurate description of the market for cotton. The global marketplace for cotton is so huge that even a jeans maker as large as Levi Strauss & Co. accounts for only a tiny fraction of transactions, making it unable to influence the price at which cotton is bought and sold.

It's a little hard to explain why competitive markets are different from other markets until we've seen how a competitive market works. For now, let's just say that it's ... ets. When taking an exam, it's ... r questions. In this book, we're ... etitive markets.

A **competitive market** is a market in which there are many buyers and sellers of the same good or ... of whom can influence the ... which the good or servic...

The **supply and deman...** a model of how a compe... works.

KEY TERMS Every key term is defined in the text and then again in the margin, making it easier for students to study and review important vocabulary.

... l described by the **supply and** ... itive, the supply and demand

BEATING THE TRAFFIC

All big cities have traffic problems, and many local authorities try to discourage driving in the crowded city center. If we think of an auto trip to the city center as a good that people consume, we can use the economics of demand to analyze anti-traffic policies.

One common strategy is to reduce the demand for auto trips by lowering the prices of substitutes. Many metropolitan areas subsidize bus and rail service, hoping to lure commuters out of their cars. An alternative is to raise the price of complements: several major U.S. cities impose high taxes on commercial parking garages and impose short time limits on parking meters, both to raise revenue and to discourage people from driving into the city.

A few major cities—including Singapore, London, Oslo, Stockholm, and Milan—have been willing to adopt a direct and politically controversial approach: reducing congestion by raising the price of driving. Under "congestion pricing" (or "congestion charging" in the United Kingdom), a charge is imposed on cars entering the city center during business hours. Drivers buy passes, which are then debited electronically as they drive by monitoring stations. Compliance is monitored with automatic cameras that photograph license plates.

The current daily cost of driving in London ranges from £8 to £10 (about $13 to $16). And drivers who don't pay and are caught pay a fine of £120 (about $195) for each transgression.

Not surprisingly, studies have shown that after the implementation of congestion pricing, traffic does indeed decrease. In the 1990s, London had some of the worst traffic in Europe. The introduction of its congestion charge in 2003 immediately reduced traffic in the London city center by about 15%, with overall traffic falling by 21% between 2002 and 2006. And there was increased use of substitutes, such as public

GLOBAL STAMPS identify features that are global in focus.

ECONOMICS IN ACTION This feature, which appears in every module, provides a compelling real-life application of major concepts covered in the module. Students experience an immediate payoff when they can apply concepts they've just read about to real phenomena.

There are ...
- The *deme...*
- The *supp...*
- The set o... cause the...
- The *mar... quantity*
- The way ... shifts

To explain... in turn. In th...

The De...

How many ... around the w... answer this c... around the w... make a pair ... question, bec... cotton—cons...

When the ... higher price... switching co... linen. In gen... want to buy, ... people want ... purchase.

So the ans... to buy?" depe... price will be, ... would want to ... *schedule*. Thi... elements of th...

The Dem...

A **demand sc...** want to buy a... demand sche... world deman...

According ... will want to p... is $1.25 a po... $0.75 a pound... price, the few... the price rise... willing to buy...

The graph ... (For a refresh... vertical axis s... quantity of co... tries in the ta... curve is a gra... the relationsh...

Each module concludes with a unique set of REVIEW QUESTIONS.

Check Your Understanding

1. Explain whether each of the following events represents
(i) a *change in demand* (a *shift of* the demand curve)
or (ii) a *change in the quantity demanded* (a *movement*

that customers are willing to pay
on rainy days.

, a long-distance telephone
ered reduced rates on weekends,
nd calling increased sharply.

c. People buy more long-stem roses the week of
Valentine's Day, even though the prices are higher
than at other times during the year.

d. A sharp rise in the price of gasoline leads many
commuters to join carpools in order to reduce their
gasoline purchases.

CHECK YOUR UNDERSTANDING
review questions allow students to
immediately test their understanding of
a module. By checking their answers
with those found in the back of the book,
students will know when they need to
reread the module before moving on.

Multiple-Choice Questions

1. Which of the following would increase demand for a
normal good? A decrease in
   a. price.
   b. income.
   price of a substitute.
   sumer taste for a good.
   price of a complement.

   ease in the price of butter would most likely
   se the demand for
   garine.
   els.
   c. jelly.
   d. milk.
   e. syrup.

3. If an increase in income leads to a decrease in demand,
the good is
   a. a complement.
   b. a substitute.
   c. inferior.
   d. abnormal.
   e. normal.

**MULTIPLE-CHOICE
QUESTIONS** offer students
additional opportunity to
practice what they've learned.

4. Which of the following will occur if consumers expect
the price of a good to fall in the coming months?
   a. The quantity demanded will rise today.
   b. The quantity demanded will remain the same today.
   c. Demand will increase today.
   d. Demand will decrease today.
   e. No change will occur today.

5. Which of the following will increase the demand for
disposable diapers?
   a. a new "baby boom"
   b. concern over the environmental effect of landfills
   c. a decrease in the price of cloth diapers
   d. a move toward earlier potty training of children
   e. a decrease in the price of disposable diapers

Critical-Thinking Question

correctly labeled graph showing the demand for
On your graph, illustrate what happens to the de-
or apples if a new report from the Surgeon General
at an apple a day really *does* keep the doctor away.

CRITICAL-THINKING QUESTIONS
offer students an opportunity to
think more deeply about content in
the module.

PITFALLS

DEMAND VERSUS QUANTITY DEMANDED

? Consider how the term *demand* is used in the following
sentence. Why is the sentence incorrect?

If the price of the good goes up then people will buy
less and this will lead to a fall in demand which shifts the
demand curve to the left.

> THIS STATEMENT MISTAKES A CHANGE IN QUANTITY
DEMANDED FOR A CHANGE IN DEMAND. WHEN DOING ECO-
NOMIC ANALYSIS, IT IS IMPORTANT TO MAKE THE DISTINCTION
BETWEEN CHANGES IN *DEMAND*, WHICH MEAN SHIFTS OF THE
DEMAND CURVE, AND CHANGES IN *QUANTITY DEMANDED*.
When economists say "an increase in demand," they mean
a rightward shift of the demand curve, and when they say
"a decrease in demand," they mean a leftward shift of the
demand curve—that is, when they're being careful. In or-
st people, including professional econ-
rd *demand* casually. For example, an
ay "the demand for air travel has dou-
fifteen years, partly because of falling
r she really means that the *quantity de-*
led. The key point to remember is that
causes a *movement along the demand*
ift of the demand curve.

Figure 5.3 for an illustration of a movement
ve versus a shift of the demand curve. For an
rence, see pages 38–40.

NEW The **PITFALLS** feature,
appearing at the end of select
modules, helps students come to a
better understanding of commonly
misunderstood concepts, using a
question-and-answer format.

Solutions to all module-review questions can
be found at the back of the book.

BUSINESS CASE • The Chicago Board of Trade

Around the world, commodities are bought and sold on "exchanges," markets organized in a specific location, where buyers and sellers meet to trade. But it wasn't always like this.

The first modern commodity exchange was the Chicago Board of Trade, founded in 1848. At the time, the United States was already a major wheat producer. And St. Louis, not Chicago, was the leading city of the American West and the dominant location for wheat trading. But the St. Louis wheat market suffered from a major flaw: there was no central marketplace, no specific location where everyone met to buy and sell wheat. Instead, sellers would sell their grain from various warehouses or from stacked sacks of grain on the river levee. Buyers would wander around town, looking for the best price.

In Chicago, however, sellers had a better idea. The Chicago Board of Trade, an association of the city's leading grain dealers, created a much more efficient method for trading wheat. There, traders gathered in one place—the "pit"—where they called out offers to sell and accepted offers to buy. The Board guaranteed that these contracts would be fulfilled, removing the need for the wheat to be physically in place when a trade was agreed upon.

This system meant that buyers could very quickly find sellers and vice-versa, reducing the cost of doing business. It also ensured that everyone could see the latest price, leading the price to rise or fall quickly in response to market conditions. For example, news of bad weather in a wheat-growing area hundreds of miles away would send the price in the Chicago pit soaring in a matter of minutes.

The Chicago Board of Trade went on to become the world's most important trading center for wheat and many other agricultural commodities, a distinction it retains to this day. And the Board's rise helped the rise of Chicago, too. The city, as Carl Sandburg put it in his famous poem, "Chicago," became:

Questions for Thought

1. In Module 6 we mention how prices can vary in a tourist trap. Which market, St. Louis or Chicago, was more likely to behave like a tourist trap? Explain.

2. What was the advantage to buyers from buying their wheat in the Chicago pit instead ... e advantage to sellers?

... ned from this case, explain why the online auction site eBay ... as it been so successful as a marketplace for second-hand ... composed of various flea markets and dealers?

SECTION **2** REVIEW

Summary

Demand

1. The **supply and demand model** illustrates how a **competitive market,** one with many buyers and sellers of the same product, works.

2. The **demand schedule** shows the **quantity demanded** at each price and is represented graphically by a **demand curve.** The **law of demand** says that demand curves slope downward, meaning that as price decreases, the quantity demanded increases.

3. A **movement along the demand curve** occurs when the price changes and causes a change in the quantity demanded. When economists talk of **changes in demand,** they mean shifts of the demand curve—a change in the quantity demanded at any given price. An increase in demand causes a rightward shift of the demand curve. A decrease in demand causes a leftward shift.

4. There are five main factors that shift the demand curve:
   - A change in the prices of related goods, such as **substitutes** or **complements**
   - A change in income: when income rises, the demand for **normal goods** increases and the demand for **inferior goods** decreases
   - A change in tastes
   - A change in expectations
   - A change in the number of consumers

Supply and Equilibrium

5. The **supply schedule** shows the **quantity supplied** at each price and is represented graphically by a **supply curve.** Supply curves usually slope upward.

6. A **movement along the supply curve** occurs when the price changes and causes a change in the quantity supplied. When economists talk of **changes in supply,** they mean shifts of the supply curve—a change in the

quantity supplied at any given price. An increase in supply causes a rightward shift of the supply curve. A decrease in supply causes a left ...

7. There are five main factors tha ...
   - A change in **input** prices
   - A change in the prices of rela ...
   - A change in technology
   - A change in expectations
   - A change in the number of p ...

8. The supply and demand mode ... ple that the price in a market n ... **price,** or **market-clearing pr** ... the quantity demanded is equ ... plied. This quantity is the **equil** ... the price is above its market-clearing level, there is a **surplus** that pushes the price down. When the price is below its market-clearing level, there is a **shortage** that ...

Cha ...

9. ...

10. S ...

Key Terms

Competitive market, p. 36
Supply and demand model,

Movement along the demand
curve, p. 39

Supp ...
Supp ...

Problems

1. A survey indicated that chocolate ice cream is America's favorite ice-cream flavor. For each of the following, indicate the possible effects on the demand and/or supply, equilibrium price, and equilibrium quantity of chocolate ice cream.

   a. A severe drought in the Midwest causes dairy farmers to reduce the number of milk-producing cows in their herds by a third. These dairy farmers supply cream that is used to manufacture chocolate ice cream.

   b. A new report by the American Medical Association reveals that chocolate does, in fact, have significant health benefits.

   c. The discovery of cheaper synthetic vanilla flavoring lowers the price of vanilla ice cream.

   d. New technology for mixing and freezing ice cream lowers manufacturers' costs of producing chocolate ice cream.

   a. the market for newspapers in your town

   Case 1: The salaries of journalists go up.

   Case 2: There is a big news event in your town, which is reported in the newspapers, and residents want to learn more about it.

   b. the market for St. Louis Rams cotton T-shirts

   Case 1: The Rams win the championship.

   Case 2: The price of cotton increases.

   c. the market for bagels

   Case 1: People realize how fattening bagels are.

   Case 2: People have less time to make themselves a cooked breakfast.

5. Find the flaws in reasoning in the following statements, paying particular attention to the distinction between changes in and movements along the supply and demand curves. Draw a diagram to illustrate what actually hap-

---

NEW BUSINESS CASES appear at the end of virtually every section, applying key economic principles to real-life business situations in both American and international companies. Each case concludes with critical-thinking questions.

END-OF-SECTION REVIEW AND PROBLEMS
In addition to the opportunities for review at the end of every module, each section ends with a brief but complete summary of concepts, a list of key terms, and a comprehensive problem set that includes concepts from across all of the modules in the section.

Supplements and Media

Worth Publishers is pleased to offer an enhanced and completely revised supplements and media package to accompany this textbook. The package has been crafted to help instructors teach their principles course and to give students the tools to develop their skills in economics.

For Instructors

Instructor's Resource Manual with Solutions Manual

The Instructor's Resource Manual, revised by Nora Underwood, University of Central Florida, is a resource meant to provide materials and tips to enhance the classroom experience.

The Instructor's Resource Manual provides the following:

- Module objectives
- Module outlines
- Teaching tips and ideas that include:
  - Hints on how to create student interest
  - Tips on presenting the material in class
- Discussion of the examples used in the text, including points to emphasize with your students
- Activities that can be conducted in or out of the classroom
- Hints for dealing with common misunderstandings that are typical among students
- Web resources (includes tips for using LaunchPad)
- Solutions manual with detailed solutions to all of the end-of-section problems from the textbook

The files for the Instructor's Resource Manual will be available for download by adopting instructors.

Test Bank

The Test Bank, coordinated by Doris Bennett, Jacksonville State University, provides a wide range of questions appropriate for assessing your students' comprehension, interpretation, analysis, and synthesis skills. The Test Bank offers multiple-choice, true/false, and short-answer questions designed for comprehensive coverage of the text concepts. Questions have been checked for continuity with the text content, overall usability, and accuracy.

The Test Bank features include the following:

- To aid instructors in building tests, each question has been categorized according to its general *degree of difficulty*. The three levels are: *easy, moderate,* and *difficult.*
  - *Easy* questions require students to recognize concepts and definitions. These are questions that can be answered by direct reference to the textbook.
  - *Moderate* questions require some analysis on the student's part.
  - *Difficult* questions usually require more detailed analysis by the student.

- Each question has also been categorized according to a *skill descriptor*. These include: *Fact-Based, Definitional, Concept-Based, Critical Thinking,* and *Analytical Thinking.*
  - *Fact-Based* questions require students to identify facts presented in the text.
  - *Definitional* questions require students to define an economic term or concept.
  - *Concept-Based* questions require a straightforward knowledge of basic concepts.
  - *Critical Thinking* questions require the student to apply a concept to a particular situation.
  - *Analytical Thinking* questions require another level of analysis to answer the question. Students must be able to apply a concept and use this knowledge for further analysis of a situation or scenario.

- To further aid instructors in building tests, each question is conveniently cross-referenced to the appropriate topic heading in the textbook. Questions are presented in the order in which concepts are presented in the text.

- The Test Bank includes questions with tables that students must analyze to solve for numerical answers. It also contains questions based on the graphs that appear in the book. These questions ask students to use the graphical models developed in the textbook and to interpret the information presented in the graph. Selected questions are paired with scenarios to reinforce comprehension.

The Diploma Computerized Test Bank and software is available in CD-ROM format for both Windows and Macintosh users. With this program, instructors can easily create and print tests and write and edit questions. Tests can be printed in a wide range of formats. The software's unique synthesis of flexible word-processing and database features creates a program that is extremely intuitive and capable.

Lecture PowerPoint Presentation

Created by Tori Knight, Carson-Newman University, these PowerPoint presentation slides are designed to assist with lecture preparation and presentations. The slides are organized by topic and contain graphs, data tables, and bulleted lists of key concepts suitable for lecture presentation. Key figures from the text are replicated and animated to demonstrate how they build. These slides can be customized to suit your individual needs by adding your own data, questions, and lecture notes.

Dynamic PowerPoint Presentation

This dynamic set of slides, designed by Solina Lindahl, CalPoly San Luis Obispo, is available as an alternative to the traditional lecture outline slides. The slides are brief, interactive, and visually interesting to keep students' attention in class. The slides utilize additional graphics and animations to demonstrate key concepts. The slides include additional (and interesting) real-world examples. The slides include hyperlinks to other relevant outside sources to illustrate real world examples and key concepts (including links to videos!). The slides also include opportunities to incorporate active learning in your classroom.

For Students

Study Guide

Prepared by Elizabeth Sawyer Kelly, University of Wisconsin–Madison, the Study Guide reinforces the topics and key concepts covered in the text. For each module, the Study Guide is organized as follows:

Before You Read the Module

- Summary: an opening paragraph that provides a brief overview of the module.

- Objectives: a numbered list outlining and describing the material that the student will learn in the module. These objectives can be easily used as a study tool for students.

- Key Terms: a list of boldface key terms with their definitions—including room for note-taking.

After You Read the Module

- Tips: numbered list of learning tips with graphical analysis.

- Worked Problems: A set of worked-out problems that take the student step-by-step through a particular problem/exercise.

- Problems and Exercises: a set of comprehensive problems.

Before You Take the Test

- Module Review Questions: a set of multiple-choice questions that focus on the key concepts students should grasp after reading the module. These questions are designed for student exam preparation.

Answer Key

- Answers to Problems and Exercises: detailed solutions to the Problems and Exercises in the Study Guide.

- Answers to Module Review Questions: solutions to the multiple-choice questions in the Study Guide—along with thorough explanations.

Online Offerings

sapling learning
www.saplinglearning.com
Sapling Learning provides the most effective interactive homework and instruction that improves student-learning outcomes for the problem-solving disciplines.

Sapling Learning offers an enjoyable teaching and effective learning experience that is distinctive in three important ways:

- **Ease of Use:** Sapling Learning's easy-to-use interface keeps students engaged in problem-solving, not struggling with the software.

- **Targeted Instructional Content:** Sapling Learning increases student engagement and comprehension by delivering immediate feedback and targeted instructional content.

- **Unsurpassed Service and Support:** Sapling Learning makes teaching more enjoyable by providing a dedicated Masters- or PhD-level colleague to service instructors' unique needs throughout the course, including content customization.

CoursePacks

Plug our content into your course management system. Registered instructors can download cartridges with no hassle, no strings attached. For more information, go to http://worthpublishers.com/catalog/Other/Coursepack.

Further Resources Offered

CourseSmart eTextbooks
http://www.coursesmart.com/ourproducts
CourseSmart textbooks offer the complete book in PDF format. Students can save money, up to 60% off the price of print textbooks. With the CourseSmart textbook, students have the ability to take notes, highlight, print pages, and more. A great alternative to renting print textbooks!

Worth Noting
Worth Noting keeps you connected to your textbook authors in real time. Whether they were just on CNBC or published in the *New York Times*, this is the place to find out about it. Visit Worth Noting at http://blogs.worthpublishers.com/econblog/.

i>clicker
Developed by a team of University of Illinois physicists, i>clicker is the most flexible and reliable classroom response system available. It is the only solution created *for* educators, *by* educators—with continuous product improvements made through direct classroom testing and faculty feedback. You'll love i>clicker, no matter your level of technical expertise, because the focus is on *your* teaching, *not the technology*. To learn more about packaging i>clicker with this textbook, please contact your local sales rep or visit www.iclicker.com.

Dismal Scientist
A high-powered business database and analysis service comes to the classroom! Dismal Scientist offers real-time monitoring of the global economy, produced locally by economists and professionals at Economy.com's London, Sydney, and West Chester offices. Dismal Scientist is *free* when packaged with the Krugman/Wells textbook. Please contact your local sales rep for more information or go to www.economy.com.

ECONPORTAL IS NOW LAUNCHPAD

Because Technology Should Never Get in the Way

LaunchPad
http://www.worthpublishers.com/launchpad
LaunchPad is an online homework, e-Book, and teaching and learning system that can be used as a stand-alone course management system or integrated into many campus course management systems such as Blackboard, Canvas, Desire2Learn, and others. And now, drawing on what we've learned from thousands of instructors and hundreds of thousands of students over the past several years, we are proud to introduce a new generation of Macmillan's Portals—*LaunchPad*.

LaunchPad features include:

- **LaunchPad Units** that provide the ability to build a course in minutes. LaunchPad offers selected resources compiled into ready-to-use teaching units, complete with problem sets, activities, e-Book sections, and state-of-the-art online homework and testing. Instructors can quickly set up their course using precreated LaunchPad units. They can also enhance LaunchPad units or create their own original assignments, adding selections from our extensive resource library of questions and activities, and their own materials as well.

- **LearningCurve:** A popular student resource, LearningCurve is an adaptive quizzing engine that automatically adjusts questions to the student's mastery level. With LearningCurve activities, each student follows a unique path to understanding the material. The more questions a student answers correctly, the more difficult the questions become. Each question is written specifically for the text and is linked to the relevant e-Book section. LearningCurve also provides a personal study plan for students as well as complete metrics for instructors. Proven to raise student performance, LearningCurve serves as an ideal formative assessment and learning tool. For detailed information, visit http://learningcurveworks.com.

- **Clear, consistent interface:** LaunchPad integrates and unifies a consistent series of resources—LaunchPad units, the e-Book, media, assessment tools, instructor materials, and other content—to a degree unmatched by other online learning systems.

- **Robust, interactive e-Book:** The e-Book offers powerful study tools for students and easily customizable features for instructors. Our simple note-taking tool allows instructors to post notes, hyperlinks, content and more with a few simple clicks. Students can also take their own notes and can view all notes within each module to allow for easy study and review. Students can also highlight, access a glossary, and enlarge images within the text.

- **Powerful online quizzing and homework:** In addition to the LaunchPad units, instructors can create their own assignments using their own questions or drawing on quiz items within LaunchPad, including:

- **The complete test bank** for the textbook for use in creating exams, quizzes, or homework problems. Instructors can use built-in filters and settings to ensure the right questions are chosen and displayed to their preferences.

- **The end-of-section problem sets** are carefully edited and available in a self-graded format—perfect for in-class quizzes and homework assignments.

- **Electronically gradable graphing problems** using a robust graphing engine. Students will be asked to draw their response to a question, and the software will automatically grade that response. Graphing questions are tagged to appropriate textbook sections and range in difficulty level and skill.

Get your feet wet with our graphing tools: Let's imagine a market for Tabloid Newspapers.

Part 1: Select the Line tool and draw a downward-sloping line. Label it "Demand 1". Next, using the same tool, draw an upward-sloping line that intersects "Demand 1" and label it "Supply 1".

Part 2: Use the Double Drop Line tool to identify the price and quantity where the two lines intersect. Label it "Equilibrium 1".

Part 3: With the Line tool, draw a new downward-sloping line that is to the LEFT of "Demand 1". Label it "Demand 2". Use the Double Drop Line tool to show the new equilibrium price and quantity in the global market for this Alien Bigfoot journalism. Label this point "Equilibrium 2."
Feel momentarily happy that demand for sensational stories has fallen, then remember that it's only because of the rise in demand for substitute goods like reality TV.

Continue to play with the graph if you like. We know you are an economist, after all.

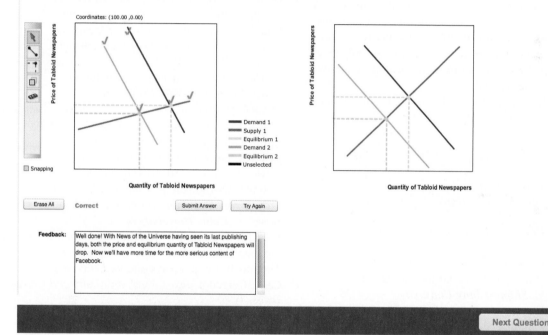

ACKNOWLEDGMENTS

Our deep appreciation and heartfelt thanks go out to Margaret Ray, University of Mary Washington, and David Anderson, Centre College, for their hard work on the previous edition of this text. Their efforts and innovations, inspired by many years of working with students in the classroom, provided us with a foundation for the modular approach that we have extended and built upon in this third edition. Thank you, Margaret and Dave, for doing such an exceptional job.

We must also thank Nora Underwood, University of Central Florida, for her extensive contributions during every stage of this revision. Nora was involved with planning this edition, helping us make important decisions about sequencing and adding new content. This was a major revision, with numerous additions and updates. Nora's contributions were invaluable, as was her role in putting the final touches on the book in the page-proof stage. Her efforts helped us craft a third edition that is current and has even broader appeal.

We would also like to thank the following instructors who helped us with the revision of the third edition. Your enthusiasm for this project has been infectious.

Giuliana Campanelli Andreopoulos, *William Paterson University*
Becca Arnold, *San Diego Mesa College*
Margaret apRoberts-Warren, *University of California–Santa Cruz*
Robert Baden, *University of California–Santa Cruz*
Bryce Casavant, *University of Connecticut*
Dixie Dalton, *College of the Low Country*
Julie Gonzalez, *University of California–Santa Cruz*
Janet Koscianski, *Shippensburg University*
Sang Lee, *Southeastern Louisiana University*
Bill McLean, *Oklahoma State University*
Christopher McMahan, *University of Colorado–Boulder*
Joan Nix, *Queens College*
Dimitrios Pachis, *Eastern Connecticut State University*
Matthew S. Rutledge, *Boston College*
Robert Schlack, *Carthage College*
Fahlino Sjuib, *Framingham State University*
Bryan Snyder, *Bentley University*
Cheryl Wachenheim, *North Dakota State University*

We are indebted to the following reviewers, focus group participants, and other consultants for their suggestions and advice on earlier editions of this book.

Miki Brunyer Anderson, *Pikes Peak Community College*
Myra L. Moore, *University of Georgia*
Elizabeth Sawyer-Kelly, *University of Wisconsin, Madison*
Carlos Aguilar, *El Paso Community College*
Terence Alexander, *Iowa State University*

Morris Altman, *University of Saskatchewan*
Farhad Ameen, *State University of New York, Westchester Community College*
Christopher P. Ball, *Quinnipiac University*
Sue Bartlett, *University of South Florida*
Scott Beaulier, *Mercer University*
David Bernotas, *University of Georgia*
Marc Bilodeau, *Indiana University and Purdue University, Indianapolis*
Kelly Blanchard, *Purdue University*
Emily Blank, *Howard University*
Anne Bresnock, *California State Polytechnic University*
Douglas M. Brown, *Georgetown University*
Joseph Calhoun, *Florida State University*
Douglas Campbell, *University of Memphis*
Kevin Carlson, *University of Massachusetts, Boston*
Andrew J. Cassey, *Washington State University*
Shirley Cassing, *University of Pittsburgh*
Sewin Chan, *New York University*
Mitchell M. Charkiewicz, *Central Connecticut State University*
Joni S. Charles, *Texas State University, San Marcos*
Adhip Chaudhuri, *Georgetown University*
Eric P. Chiang, *Florida Atlantic University*
Hayley H. Chouinard, *Washington State University*
Kenny Christianson, *Binghamton University*
Lisa Citron, *Cascadia Community College*
Steven L. Cobb, *University of North Texas*
Barbara Z. Connolly, *Westchester Community College*
Stephen Conroy, *University of San Diego*
Thomas E. Cooper, *Georgetown University*
Cesar Corredor, *Texas A&M University and University of Texas, Tyler*
Jim F. Couch, *University of Northern Alabama*
Daniel Daly, *Regis University*
H. Evren Damar, *Pacific Lutheran University*
Satarupa Das, *Montgomery College, Takoma Park*
Antony Davies, *Duquesne University*
Greg Delemeester, *Marietta College*
Patrick Dolenc, *Keene State College*
Christine Doyle-Burke, *Framingham State College*
Ding Du, *South Dakota State University*
Jerry Dunn, *Southwestern Oklahoma State University*
Robert R. Dunn, *Washington and Jefferson College*
Ann Eike, *University of Kentucky*
Tisha L. N. Emerson, *Baylor University*
Hadi Salehi Esfahani, *University of Illinois*
William Feipel, *Illinois Central College*
Rudy Fichtenbaum, *Wright State University*
David W. Findlay, *Colby College*
Mary Flannery, *University of California, Santa Cruz*

Robert Francis, *Shoreline Community College*
Shelby Frost, *Georgia State University*
Frank Gallant, *George Fox University*
Robert Gazzale, *Williams College*
Seth Gitter, *Towson University*
Robert Godby, *University of Wyoming*
Michael Goode, *Central Piedmont Community College*
Douglas E. Goodman, *University of Puget Sound*
Marvin Gordon, *University of Illinois at Chicago*
Kathryn Graddy, *Brandeis University*
Mike Green, *College of Southern Maryland*
Yoseph Gutema, *Howard Community College*
Alan Day Haight, *State University of New York, Cortland*
Mehdi Haririan, *Bloomsburg University*
Clyde A. Haulman, *College of William and Mary*
Richard R. Hawkins, *University of West Florida*
Michael Heslop, *Northern Virginia Community College, Annandale*
Mickey A. Hepner, *University of Central Oklahoma*
Michael Hilmer, *San Diego State University*
Tia Hilmer, *San Diego State University*
Jane Himarios, *University of Texas, Arlington*
Jim Holcomb, *University of Texas, El Paso*
Don Holley, *Boise State University*
Alexander Holmes, *University of Oklahoma*
Julie Holzner, *Los Angeles City College*
Robert N. Horn, *James Madison University*
Steven Husted, *University of Pittsburgh*
John O. Ifediora, *University of Wisconsin, Platteville*
Hiro Ito, *Portland State University*
Mike Javanmard, *Rio Hondo Community College*
Robert T. Jerome, *James Madison University*
Shirley Johnson-Lans, *Vassar College*
David Kalist, *Shippensburg University*
Lillian Kamal, *Northwestern University*
Roger T. Kaufman, *Smith College*
Herb Kessel, *St. Michael's College*
Rehim Kiliç, *Georgia Institute of Technology*
Grace Kim, *University of Michigan, Dearborn*
Michael Kimmitt, *University of Hawaii, Manoa*
Robert Kling, *Colorado State University*
Sherrie Kossoudji, *University of Michigan*
Andrew Kozak, *St. Mary's College of Maryland*
Charles Kroncke, *College of Mount Saint Joseph*
Reuben Kyle, *Middle Tennessee State University (retired)*
Katherine Lande-Schmeiser, *University of Minnesota, Twin Cities*
David Lehr, *Longwood College*
Mary Jane Lenon, *Providence College*
Mary H. Lesser, *Iona College*
Solina Lindahl, *California Polytechnic State University, San Luis Obispo*
Haiyong Liu, *East Carolina University*
Jane S. Lopus, *California State University, East Bay*
María José Luengo–Prado, *Northeastern University*
Rotua Lumbantobing, *North Carolina State University*
Ed Lyell, *Adams State College*
Mireille Makambira, *Montgomery College, Rockville*

John Marangos, *Colorado State University*
Ralph D. May, *Southwestern Oklahoma State University*
Wayne McCaffery, *University of Wisconsin, Madison*
Dennis McCornac, *Anne Arundel Community College*
Bill McLean, *Oklahoma State University*
Larry McRae, *Appalachian State University*
Mary Ruth J. McRae, *Appalachian State University*
Ellen E. Meade, *American University*
Meghan Millea, *Mississippi State University*
Norman C. Miller, *Miami University (of Ohio)*
Khan A. Mohabbat, *Northern Illinois University*
Myra L. Moore, *University of Georgia*
Jay Morris, *Champlain College in Burlington*
Akira Motomura, *Stonehill College*
Kevin J. Murphy, *Oakland University*
Robert Murphy, *Boston College*
Ranganath Murthy, *Bucknell University*
Anthony Myatt, *University of New Brunswick, Canada*
Randy A. Nelson, *Colby College*
Charles Newton, *Houston Community College*
Daniel X. Nguyen, *Purdue University*
Dmitri Nizovtsev, *Washburn University*
Thomas A. Odegaard, *Baylor University*
Constantin Oglobin, *Georgia Southern University*
Charles C. Okeke, *College of Southern Nevada*
Terry Olson, *Truman State University*
Una Okonkwo Osili, *Indiana University and Purdue University, Indianapolis*
Chris Osuanah, *J. Sargeant Reynolds Community College, Downtown*
Maxwell Oteng, *University of California, Davis*
P. Marcelo Oviedo, *Iowa State University*
Jeff Owen, *Gustavus Adolphus College*
James Palmieri, *Simpson College*
Walter G. Park, *American University*
Elliott Parker, *University of Nevada, Reno*
Michael Perelman, *California State University, Chico*
Nathan Perry, *Utah State University*
Dean Peterson, *Seattle University*
Ken Peterson, *Furman University*
Paul Pieper, *University of Illinois at Chicago*
Dennis L. Placone, *Clemson University*
Michael Polcen, *Northern Virginia Community College*
Raymond A. Polchow, *Zane State College*
Linnea Polgreen, *University of Iowa*
Michael A. Quinn, *Bentley University*
Eileen Rabach, *Santa Monica College*
Matthew Rafferty, *Quinnipiac University*
Jaishankar Raman, *Valparaiso University*
Margaret Ray, *Mary Washington College*
Helen Roberts, *University of Illinois, Chicago*
Jeffrey Rubin, *Rutgers University, New Brunswick*
Rose M. Rubin, *University of Memphis*
Lynda Rush, *California State Polytechnic University, Pomona*
Michael Ryan, *Western Michigan University*
Sara Saderion, *Houston Community College*
Djavad Salehi-Isfahani, *Virginia Tech*
Elizabeth Sawyer-Kelly, *University of Wisconsin, Madison*

Jesse A. Schwartz, *Kennesaw State University*
Chad Settle, *University of Tulsa*
Steve Shapiro, *University of North Florida*
Robert L. Shoffner III, *Central Piedmont Community College*
Joseph Sicilian, *University of Kansas*
Judy Smrha, *Baker University*
John Solow, *University of Iowa*
John Somers, *Portland Community College*
Stephen Stageberg, *University of Mary Washington*
Monty Stanford, *DeVry University*
Rebecca Stein, *University of Pennsylvania*
William K. Tabb, *Queens College, City University of New York (retired)*
Sarinda Taengnoi, *University of Wisconsin, Oshkosh*
Henry Terrell, *University of Maryland*
Rebecca Achée Thornton, *University of Houston*
Michael Toma, *Armstrong Atlantic State University*
Brian Trinque, *University of Texas, Austin*
Boone A. Turchi, *University of North Carolina, Chapel Hill*
Nora Underwood, *University of Central Florida*
J. S. Uppal, *State University of New York, Albany*
John Vahaly, *University of Louisville*
Jose J. Vazquez-Cognet, *University of Illinois at Urbana-Champaign*
Daniel Vazzana, *Georgetown College*
Roger H. von Haefen, *North Carolina State University*
Andreas Waldkirch, *Colby College*
Christopher Waller, *University of Notre Dame*
Gregory Wassall, *Northeastern University*
Robert Whaples, *Wake Forest University*
Thomas White, *Assumption College*
Jennifer P. Wissink, *Cornell University*
Mark Witte, *Northwestern University*
Kristen M. Wolfe, *St. Johns River Community College*
Larry Wolfenbarger, *Macon State College*
Louise B. Wolitz, *University of Texas, Austin*
Gavin Wright, *Stanford University*
Bill Yang, *Georgia Southern University*
Jason Zimmerman, *South Dakota State University*

In the past, we always trusted Andreas Bentz and his indefatigable eye for detail while we focused on big-picture issues in the sections. We count ourselves extremely fortunate that Michael Reksulak, Georgia Southern University, stepped in when Andreas was unavailable to devote as much time to this project as in the past. Andreas was a helpful advisor during early stages of the revision. Michael turned out to be more than capable of providing expert-level guidance in the page-proof stage, when tending to accuracy and details is paramount. Michael's efforts as accuracy checker and coordinator were supported by the invaluable contributions of accuracy checkers Dixie Dalton, Southside Virginia Community College, Matthew S. Rutledge, Boston College, Sang Lee, Southeastern Louisiana University, Becca Arnold, San Diego Mesa College, Janet Koscianski, Shippensburg University, Stephanie Riche, North Carolina State University, and Cheryl Wachenheim, North Dakota State University. Many thanks to Solina Lindahl, California Polytechnic State University, who provided expert guidance on the media program associated with the textbook, and to Scott Houser, California State University, for his involvement.

We must also thank the many people at Worth Publishers for their contributions. Elizabeth Widdicombe and Catherine Woods for their role in planning this revision. Charles Linsmeier, who ably oversaw the revision and contributed throughout, and now Steve Rigolosi, who will have an important role to play post publication. A special thanks to Craig Bleyer, our original publisher and now national sales manager, who put so much effort into making all of our textbooks a success. And to Scott Guile, associate director of digital marketing, who recognized a need for a more streamlined version of our text and whose enthusiasm for the modular format helped to bring an innovative approach to fruition.

Once again, we have an incredible production and design team. Thank you all: Tracey Kuehn, Lisa Kinne, Barbara Seixas, and Liz Geller for producing this book; Babs Reingold, Lyndall Culbertson, Chuck Yuen, Diana Blume, and Paul Lacy for their beautiful interior design, layout, and cover; Deborah Heimann for her thoughtful copyedit; Cecilia Varas and Elyse Rieder, who work so hard and with lightning speed to get photos permissioned and just right; Stacey Alexander and Edgar Bonilla for coordinating the supplemental materials; Mary Walsh, associate editor, who made invaluable editorial contributions to this revision; and Fay Kelly, editorial assistant, who did a fine job preparing the manuscript for production.

Many thanks to Lukia Kliossis and Marie McHale for devising and coordinating the impressive collection of media and supplements. With each edition you've shown how far we've come in supporting instructors who choose to adopt our textbook. Thanks to the incredible team of writers and coordinators who worked with Lukia and Marie on the supplements and media package.

Thanks to Tom Digiano, marketing manager, and to Tom Acox for his many contributions. We must also extend our heartfelt thanks to the many members of the sales force, some who have been with us from the beginning, on your tireless efforts in promoting our book.

And most of all, special thanks to Sharon Balbos, executive development editor on each of our editions. Much of the success of this book is owed to Sharon's dedication and professionalism; in this edition, perhaps more so than most. Sharon, we're not sure we deserved an editor as good as you, but we're sure that everyone involved as well as our adopters and their students have been made better off by your presence.

Paul Krugman   Robin Wells

MACROECONOMICS
IN MODULES

Basic Economic Concepts

ANY GIVEN SUNDAY

It's Sunday afternoon in the spring of 2013, and Route 1 in central New Jersey is a busy place. Thousands of people crowd the shopping malls that line the road for 20 miles, all the way from Trenton to New Brunswick. Most of the shoppers are cheerful—and why not? The stores in those malls offer an extraordinary range of choice; you can buy everything from sophisticated electronic equipment to fashionable clothes to organic carrots. There are probably 100,000 distinct items available along that stretch of road. And most of these items are not luxury goods that only the rich can afford; they are products that millions of Americans can and do purchase every day.

The scene along Route 1 on this spring day is, of course, perfectly ordinary—very much like the scene along hundreds of other stretches of road, all across America, that same afternoon. And the discipline of economics is mainly concerned with ordinary things. As the great nineteenth-century economist Alfred Marshall put it, economics is "a study of mankind in the ordinary business of life."

What can economics say about this "ordinary business"? Quite a lot, it turns out. What we'll see in this book is that even familiar scenes of economic life pose some very important questions—questions that economics can help answer. Among these questions are:

- How does our economic system work? That is, how does it manage to deliver the goods?

- How is the performance of the economy as a whole measured?

- Why are there ups and downs in the economy? That is, why does the economy sometimes have a "bad year"?

- Finally, why is the long run mainly a story of ups rather than downs? That is, why has America, along with other advanced nations, become so much richer over time?

In this section we discuss the study of economics and the difference between microeconomics and macroeconomics. We also introduce the major topics within macroeconomics and the use of models to study the macroeconomy. Finally, we present the production possibility frontier model and use it to understand basic economic activity, including trade between two economies.

1 The Study of Economics

iStockphoto

Economics is the study of scarcity and choice.

Individual choice is decisions by individuals about what to do, which necessarily involve decisions about what not to do.

An economy is a system for coordinating a society's productive and consumptive activities.

In a market economy, the decisions of individual producers and consumers largely determine what, how, and for whom to produce, with little government involvement in the decisions.

Individual Choice: The Core of Economics

Economics is the study of scarcity and choice. Every economic issue involves, at its most basic level, **individual choice**—decisions by individuals about what to do and what *not* to do. In fact, you might say that it isn't economics if it isn't about choice.

Step into a big store such as Walmart or Target. There are thousands of different products available, and it is extremely unlikely that you—or anyone else—could afford to buy everything you might want to have. And anyway, there's only so much space in your home. Given the limitations on your budget and your living space, you must choose which products to buy and which to leave on the shelf.

The fact that those products are on the shelf in the first place involves choice—the store manager chose to put them there, and the manufacturers of the products chose to produce them. The **economy** is a system that coordinates choices about production with choices about consumption, and distributes goods and services to the people who want them. The United States has a **market economy,** in which production and consumption are the result of decentralized decisions by many firms and individuals. There is no central authority telling people what to produce or where to ship it. Each individual producer makes what he or she thinks will be most profitable, and each consumer buys what he or she chooses.

Market economies are able to coordinate highly complex activities and to reliably provide consumers with the goods and services they want. Indeed, people quite casually trust their lives to the market system: residents of any major city would starve in days if the unplanned yet somehow orderly actions of thousands of businesses did not deliver a steady supply of food. Surprisingly, the unplanned "chaos" of a market economy turns out to be far more orderly than the "planning" of a command economy.

In 1776, in a famous passage in his book *The Wealth of Nations*, the pioneering Scottish economist Adam Smith wrote about how individuals, in pursuing their own interests, often end up serving the interests of society as a whole. Of a businessman whose pursuit of profit makes the nation wealthier, Smith wrote: "[H]e intends only his own gain, and he is in this, as in many other cases, led by an invisible hand to promote an end which was no part of his intention." Ever since, economists have used the term **invisible hand** to refer to the way a market economy manages to harness the power of self-interest for the good of society.

All economic activities involve individual choice. Let's take a closer look at what this means for the study of economics.

Resources Are Scarce

You can't always get what you want. Almost everyone would like to have a beautiful house in a great location (and help with the housecleaning), two or three luxury cars, and frequent vacations in fancy hotels. But even in a rich country like the United States, not many families can afford all of that. So they must make choices—whether to go to Disney World this year or buy a better car, whether to make do with a small backyard or accept a longer commute in order to live where land is cheaper.

Limited income isn't the only thing that keeps people from having everything they want. Time is also in limited supply: there are only 24 hours in a day. And because the time we have is limited, choosing to spend time on one activity also means choosing not to spend time on a different activity—spending time studying for an exam means forgoing a night at the movies. Indeed, many people feel so limited by the number of hours in the day that they are willing to trade money for time. For example, convenience stores usually charge higher prices than larger supermarkets. But they fulfill a valuable role by catering to customers who would rather pay more than spend the time traveling farther to a supermarket where they might also have to wait in longer lines.

Why do individuals have to make choices? The ultimate reason is that *resources are scarce*. A **resource** is anything that can be used to produce something else. Lists of the economy's resources usually begin with land, labor (the time of workers), physical capital (machinery, buildings, and other man-made productive assets), and human capital (the educational achievements and skills of workers). A resource is **scarce** when there's not enough of the resource available to satisfy all the ways a society wants to use it. There are many scarce resources. These include natural resources—resources that come from the physical environment, such as minerals, lumber, and petroleum. There is also a limited quantity of human resources—labor, skill, and intelligence. And in a growing world economy with a rapidly increasing human population, even clean air and water have become scarce resources.

Just as individuals must make choices, the scarcity of resources means that society as a whole must make choices. One way for a society to make choices is simply to allow them to emerge as the result of many individual choices. For example, there are only so many hours in a week, and Americans must decide how to spend their time. How many hours will they spend going to supermarkets to get lower prices rather than saving time by shopping at convenience stores? The answer is the sum of individual decisions: each of the millions of individuals in the economy makes his or her own choice about where to shop, and society's choice is simply the sum of those individual decisions.

For various reasons, there are some decisions that a society decides are best not left to individual choice. For example, the authors live in an area that until recently was mainly farmland but is now being rapidly built up. Most local residents feel that the community would be a more pleasant place to live if some of the land were left undeveloped. But no individual has an incentive to keep his or her land as open space, rather than sell it to a developer. So a trend has emerged in many communities across the United States of local governments purchasing undeveloped land and preserving it as open space. Decisions about how to use scarce resources are often best left to individuals but sometimes should be made at a higher, community-wide, level.

The **invisible hand** refers to the way in which the individual pursuit of self-interest can lead to good results for society as a whole.

A **resource** is anything that can be used to produce something else.

Resources are **scarce**—not enough of the resources are available to satisfy all the various ways a society wants to use them.

.shock/Dreamstime

Opportunity Cost: The Real Cost of Something Is What You Must Give Up to Get It

It is the last term before you graduate, and your class schedule allows you to take only one elective. There are two, however, that you would really like to take: Intro to Computer Graphics and History of Jazz.

Suppose you decide to take the History of Jazz course. What's the cost of that decision? It is the fact that you can't take the computer graphics class, your next best alternative choice. Economists call that kind of cost—what you must give up in order to get an item you want—the **opportunity cost** of that item. So the opportunity cost of taking the History of Jazz class is the benefit you would have derived from the Intro to Computer Graphics class.

The concept of opportunity cost is crucial to understanding individual choice because, in the end, all costs are opportunity costs. That's because every choice you make means forgoing some other alternative. Sometimes critics claim that economists are concerned only with costs and benefits that can be measured in dollars and cents. But that is not true. Much economic analysis involves cases like our elective course example, where it costs no extra tuition to take one elective course—that is, there is no direct monetary cost. Nonetheless, the elective you choose has an opportunity cost—the other desirable elective course that you must forgo because your limited time permits taking only one. More specifically, the opportunity cost of a choice is what you forgo by not choosing your next best alternative.

You might think that opportunity cost is an add-on—that is, something *additional* to the monetary cost of an item. Suppose that an elective class costs additional tuition of $750; now there is a monetary cost to taking History of Jazz. Is the opportunity cost of taking that course something separate from that monetary cost?

Well, consider two cases. First, suppose that taking Intro to Computer Graphics also costs $750. In this case, you would have to spend that $750 no matter which class you take. So what you give up to take the History of Jazz class is still the computer graphics class, period—you would have to spend that $750 either way. But suppose there isn't any fee for the computer graphics class. In that case, what you give up to take the jazz class is the benefit from the computer graphics class *plus* the benefit you could have gained from spending the $750 on other things.

Either way, the real cost of taking your preferred class is what you must give up to get it. As you expand the set of decisions that underlie each choice—whether to take an elective or not, whether to finish this term or not, whether to drop out or not—you'll realize that all costs are ultimately opportunity costs.

Sometimes the money you have to pay for something is a good indication of its opportunity cost. But many times it is not. One very important example of how poorly monetary cost can indicate opportunity cost is the cost of attending college. Tuition and housing are major monetary expenses for most students; but even if these things were free, attending college would still be an expensive proposition because most college students, if they were not in college, would have a job. That is, by going to college, students *forgo* the income they could have earned if they had worked instead. This means that the opportunity cost of attending college is what you pay for tuition and housing plus the forgone income you would have earned in a job.

It's easy to see that the opportunity cost of going to college is especially high for people who could be earning a lot during what would otherwise have been their college years. That is why star athletes like LeBron James and entrepreneurs like Mark Zuckerberg, founder of Facebook, often skip or drop out of college.

AP Photo/Paul Sakuma, FILE

Mark Zuckerberg understood the concept of opportunity cost.

The real cost of an item is its **opportunity cost**: what you must give up in order to get it.

Microeconomics versus Macroeconomics

We have presented economics as the study of choices and described how, at its most basic level, economics is about individual choice. The branch of economics concerned with how individuals make decisions and how these decisions interact is called

microeconomics. Microeconomics focuses on choices made by individuals, households, or firms—the smaller parts that make up the economy as a whole.

Macroeconomics focuses on the bigger picture—the overall ups and downs of the economy. When you study macroeconomics, you learn how economists explain these fluctuations and how governments can use economic policy to minimize the damage they cause. Macroeconomics focuses on **economic aggregates**—economic measures such as the unemployment rate, the inflation rate, and gross domestic product—that summarize data across many different markets.

Table 1-1 lists some typical questions that involve economics. A microeconomic version of the question appears on the left, paired with a similar macroeconomic question on the right. By comparing the questions, you can begin to get a sense of the difference between microeconomics and macroeconomics.

> **Microeconomics** is the study of how people make decisions and how those decisions interact.
>
> **Macroeconomics** is concerned with the overall ups and downs in the economy.
>
> **Economic aggregates** are economic measures that summarize data across many different markets.
>
> In a **self-regulating** economy, problems such as unemployment are resolved without government intervention, through the working of the invisible hand.

TABLE 1-1

Microeconomic versus Macroeconomic Questions

Microeconomic Questions	Macroeconomic Questions
Should I go to business school or take a job right now?	How many people are employed in the economy as a whole this year?
What determines the salary offered by Citibank to Cherie Camajo, a new MBA?	What determines the overall salary levels paid to workers in a given year?
What determines the cost to a university or college of offering a new course?	What determines the overall level of prices in the economy as a whole?
What government policies should be adopted to make it easier for low-income students to attend college?	What government policies should be adopted to promote employment and growth in the economy as a whole?
What determines whether Citibank opens a new office in Shanghai?	What determines the overall trade in goods, services, and financial assets between the United States and the rest of the world?

As these questions illustrate, microeconomics focuses on how individuals and firms make decisions, and the consequences of those decisions. For example, a school will use microeconomics to determine how much it would cost to offer a new course, which includes the instructor's salary, the cost of class materials, and so on. By weighing the costs and benefits, the school can then decide whether or not to offer the course. Macroeconomics, in contrast, examines the *overall* behavior of the economy—how the actions of all of the individuals and firms in the economy interact to produce a particular economy-wide level of economic performance. For example, macroeconomics is concerned with the general level of prices in the economy and how high or low they are relative to prices last year, rather than with the price of a particular good or service.

Macroeconomics: Theory and Policy

To a much greater extent than microeconomists, macroeconomists are concerned with questions about *policy*, about what the government can do to make macroeconomic performance better. This policy focus was strongly shaped by history, in particular by the Great Depression of the 1930s.

Before the 1930s, economists tended to regard the economy as **self-regulating:** they believed that problems such as unemployment would be corrected through the working of the invisible hand and that government attempts to improve the economy's performance would be ineffective at best—and would probably make things worse.

The Great Depression changed all that. The sheer scale of the catastrophe, which left a quarter of the U.S. workforce without jobs and threatened the political stability of many countries—the Depression is widely believed to have been a major factor in the Nazi takeover of Germany—created a demand for action. It also led to a major

According to **Keynesian economics,** economic slumps are caused by inadequate spending, and they can be mitigated by government intervention.

Monetary policy is the government's use of changes in the quantity of money to alter interest rates, which in turn affects the overall level of spending.

Fiscal policy is the use of changes in taxes and government spending to affect overall spending.

A **model** is a simplified representation used to better understand a real-world situation.

effort on the part of economists to understand economic slumps and find ways to prevent them.

In 1936 the British economist John Maynard Keynes (pronounced "canes") published *The General Theory of Employment, Interest, and Money,* a book that transformed macroeconomics. According to **Keynesian economics,** a depressed economy is the result of inadequate spending. In addition, Keynes argued that government intervention can help a depressed economy through monetary policy and fiscal policy. **Monetary policy** uses changes in the quantity of money to alter interest rates, which in turn affect the level of overall spending. **Fiscal policy** uses changes in taxes and government spending to affect overall spending.

In general, Keynes established the idea that managing the economy is a government responsibility. Keynesian ideas continue to have a strong influence on both economic theory and public policy. In 2008 and 2009, the U.S. government took steps to fend off an economic slump that were clearly Keynesian in spirit, as described in the following Economics in Action.

ECONOMICS ▶ IN ACTION
WORLD VIEW

FENDING OFF DEPRESSION

In 2008 the world economy experienced a severe financial crisis that was all too reminiscent of the early days of the Great Depression. Major banks teetered on the edge of collapse; world trade slumped. In the spring of 2009, two economists, Barry Eichengreen and Kevin O'Rourke, reviewing the available data, pointed out that "globally we are tracking or even doing worse than the Great Depression."

But the worst did not, in the end, come to pass. The first year the two crises were indeed comparable with obvious dips in production. But, fortunately, during the "Great Recession," the now widely used term for the slump that followed the 2008 financial crisis, world production leveled off and turned around. Why?

At least part of the answer is that policy makers responded very differently. During the Great Depression, it was widely argued that the slump should simply be allowed to run its course. Attempts to mitigate the ongoing catastrophe were actively resisted. In the early 1930s, some countries' monetary authorities actually raised interest rates in the face of the slump, while governments cut spending and raised taxes—actions that, as we'll see in later modules, deepened the recession.

In the aftermath of the 2008 crisis, by contrast, interest rates were slashed, and a number of countries, the United States included, used temporary increases in spending and reductions in taxes in an attempt to sustain spending. Governments also moved to shore up their banks with loans, aid, and guarantees.

Many of these measures were controversial, to say the least. But most economists believe that by responding actively to the Great Recession—and doing so using the knowledge gained from the study of macroeconomics—governments helped avoid a global economic catastrophe.

The Use of Models in Economics

To answer microeconomic and macroeconomic questions, economists use models. A **model** is any simplified version of reality that is used to better understand real-world situations. But how do we create a simplified representation of an economic situation? One possibility is to find or create a real but simplified economy. For example, economists interested in the economic role of money have studied the system of exchange that developed in World War II prison camps, in which cigarettes became a universally accepted form of payment, even among prisoners who didn't smoke.

Another possibility is to simulate the workings of the economy on a computer. For example, when changes in tax law are proposed, government officials use *tax models*—

large mathematical computer programs—to assess how the proposed changes would affect different groups of people.

Models are important because their simplicity allows economists to focus on the effects of only one change at a time. That is, they allow us to hold everything else constant and to study how one change affects the overall economic outcome. So when building economic models, an important assumption is the **other things equal assumption,** which means that all other relevant factors remain unchanged. Sometimes the Latin phrase *ceteris paribus,* which means "other things equal," is used.

But it isn't always possible to find or create a small-scale version of the whole economy, and a computer program is only as good as the data it uses. (Programmers have a saying: garbage in, garbage out.) For many purposes, the most effective form of economic modeling is the construction of "thought experiments": simplified, hypothetical versions of real-world situations. And as you will see throughout this book, economists' models are very often in the form of a graph. In the next module, we will look at the *production possibility frontier,* a model that helps economists think about the choices every economy faces. But first we will define the different types of questions asked by economists, so we can better understand what our economic models will be used for.

The **other things equal assumption** means that all other relevant factors remain unchanged. This is also known as the *ceteris paribus* assumption.

Positive economics is the branch of economic analysis that describes the way the economy actually works.

Normative economics makes prescriptions about the way the economy should work.

Positive versus Normative Economics

Economic analysis, as we will see throughout this book, draws on a set of basic economic principles. But how are these principles applied? That depends on the purpose of the analysis. Economic analysis that is used to answer questions about the way the world works, questions that have definite right and wrong answers, is known as **positive economics.** In contrast, economic analysis that involves saying how the world *should* work is known as **normative economics.**

Imagine that you are an economic adviser to the governor of your state and the governor is considering a change to the toll charged along the state turnpike. Below are three questions the governor might ask you.

1. How much revenue will the tolls yield next year?

2. How much would that revenue increase if the toll were raised from $1.00 to $1.50?

3. Should the toll be raised, bearing in mind that a toll increase would likely reduce traffic and air pollution near the road but impose some financial hardship on frequent commuters?

There is a big difference between the first two questions and the third one. The first two are questions about facts. Your forecast of next year's toll revenue without any increase will be proved right or wrong when the numbers actually come in. Your estimate of the impact of a change in the toll is a little harder to check—the increase in revenue depends on other factors besides the toll, and it may be hard to disentangle the causes of any change in revenue. Still, in principle there is only one right answer.

But the question of whether or not tolls should be raised may not have a "right" answer—two people who agree on the effects of a higher toll could still disagree about whether raising the toll is a good idea. For example, someone who lives near the turnpike but doesn't commute on it will care a lot about noise and air pollution but not so much about commuting costs. A regular commuter who doesn't live near the turnpike will have the opposite priorities.

This example highlights a key distinction between the two roles of economic analysis and presents another way to think about the distinction between positive and normative analysis: positive economics is about description, and normative economics

Should the toll be raised?

is about prescription. Positive economics occupies most of the time and effort of the economics profession.

Looking back at the three questions the governor might ask, it is worth noting a subtle but important difference between questions 1 and 2. Question 1 asks for a simple prediction about next year's revenue—a forecast. Question 2 is a "what if" question, asking how revenue would change if the toll were to change. Economists are often called upon to answer both types of questions. Economic *models,* which provide simplified representations of reality such as graphs or equations, are especially useful for answering "what if" questions.

The answers to such questions often serve as a guide to policy, but they are still predictions, not prescriptions. That is, they tell you what will happen if a policy is changed, but they don't tell you whether or not that result is good. Suppose that your economic model tells you that the governor's proposed increase in highway tolls will raise property values in communities near the road but will tax or inconvenience people who currently use the turnpike to get to work. Does that information make this proposed toll increase a good idea or a bad one? It depends on whom you ask. As we've just seen, someone who is very concerned with the communities near the road will support the increase, but someone who is very concerned with the welfare of drivers will feel differently. That's a value judgment—it's not a question of positive economic analysis.

Still, economists often do engage in normative economics and give policy advice. How can they do this when there may be no "right" answer? One answer is that economists are also citizens, and we all have our opinions.

When and Why Economists Disagree

Economists have a reputation for arguing with each other. Where does this reputation come from?

One important answer is that media coverage tends to exaggerate the real differences in views among economists. If nearly all economists agree on an issue—for example, the proposition that rent controls lead to housing shortages—reporters and editors are likely to conclude that there is no story worth covering, and so the professional consensus tends to go unreported. But when there is some issue on which prominent economists take opposing sides—for example, whether cutting taxes right now would help the economy—that does make a good news story. So you hear much more about the areas of disagreement among economists than you do about the many areas of agreement.

It is also worth remembering that economics is, unavoidably, often tied up in politics. On a number of issues, powerful interest groups know what opinions they want to hear. Therefore, they have an incentive to find and promote economists who profess those opinions, which gives these economists a prominence and visibility out of proportion to their support among their colleagues.

Although the appearance of disagreement among economists exceeds the reality, it remains true that economists often *do* disagree about important things. For example, some highly respected economists argue vehemently that the U.S. government should replace the income tax with a *value-added tax* (a national sales tax, which is the main source of government revenue in many European countries). Other equally respected economists disagree. What are the sources of this difference of opinion?

One important source of differences is in values: as in any diverse group of individuals, reasonable people can differ. In comparison to an income tax, a value-added tax typically

THE GLASS IS HALF FULL.

HALF EMPTY.

ECONOMISTS

THE CONSUMER IS HALF ALIVE. —

falls more heavily on people with low incomes. So an economist who values a society with more social and income equality will likely oppose a value-added tax. An economist with different values will be less likely to oppose it.

A second important source of differences arises from the way economists conduct economic analysis. Economists base their conclusions on models formed by making simplifying assumptions about reality. Two economists can legitimately disagree about which simplifications are appropriate—and therefore arrive at different conclusions.

Suppose that the U.S. government was considering a value-added tax. Economist A may rely on a simplification of reality that focuses on the administrative costs of tax systems—that is, the costs of monitoring compliance, processing tax forms, collecting the tax, and so on. This economist might then point to the well-known high costs of administering a value-added tax and argue against the change. But economist B may think that the right way to approach the question is to ignore the administrative costs and focus on how the proposed law would change individual savings behavior. This economist might point to studies suggesting that value-added taxes promote higher consumer saving, a desirable result. Because the economists have made different simplifying assumptions, they find themselves on different sides of the issue.

Most such disputes are eventually resolved by the accumulation of evidence that shows which of the various simplifying assumptions made by economists does a better job of fitting the facts. However, in economics, as in any science, it can take a long time before research settles important disputes—decades, in some cases. And since the economy is always changing in ways that make old approaches invalid or raise new policy questions, there are always new issues on which economists disagree. The policy maker must then decide which economist to believe.

The important point is that economic analysis is a method, not a set of conclusions.

MODULE 1 Review

Solutions appear at the back of the book.

Check Your Understanding

1. You make $45,000 per year at your current job with Whiz Kids Consultants. You are considering a job offer from Brainiacs, Inc., which would pay you $50,000 per year. Which of the following are elements of the opportunity cost of accepting the new job at Brainiacs, Inc.? Answer yes or no, and explain your answer.

   a. the increased time spent commuting to your new job

   b. the $45,000 salary from your old job

   c. the more spacious office at your new job

2. Which of the following questions involve microeconomics, and which involve macroeconomics? In each case, explain your answer.

   a. Why did consumers switch to smaller cars in 2008?

   b. Why did overall consumer spending slow down in 2008?

   c. Why did the standard of living rise more rapidly in the first generation after World War II than in the second?

   d. Why have starting salaries for students with geology degrees risen sharply of late?

   e. What determines the choice between rail and road transportation?

   f. Why has salmon gotten cheaper over the past 20 years?

   g. Why did inflation fall in the 1990s?

3. Identify each of the following statements as positive or normative, and explain your answer.

   a. Society should take measures to prevent people from engaging in dangerous personal behavior.

   b. People who engage in dangerous personal behavior impose higher costs on society through higher medical costs.

Multiple-Choice Questions

1. Which of the following is an example of a resource?

   I. petroleum

   II. a factory

   III. a cheeseburger dinner

   a. I only

   b. II only

   c. III only

   d. I and II only

   e. I, II, and III

2. Which of the following situations represent(s) resource scarcity?

   I. Rapidly growing economies experience increasing levels of water pollution.

   II. There is a finite amount of petroleum in the physical environment.

   III. Cassette tapes are no longer being produced.

   a. I only

   b. II only

   c. III only

   d. I and II only

   e. I, II, and III

3. Suppose that you prefer reading a book you already own to watching TV and that you prefer watching TV to listening to music. If these are your only three choices, what is the opportunity cost of reading?

   a. watching TV and listening to music

   b. watching TV

   c. listening to music

   d. sleeping

   e. the price of the book

4. The other things equal assumption allows economists to

   a. avoid making assumptions about reality.

   b. focus on the effects of only one change at a time.

   c. oversimplify.

   d. allow nothing to change in their model.

   e. reflect all aspects of the real world in their model.

5. Which of the following statements is/are normative?

   I. The price of gasoline is rising.

   II. The price of gasoline is too high.

   III. Gas prices are expected to fall in the near future.

   a. I only

   b. II only

   c. III only

   d. I and III only

   e. I, II, and III

6. Which of the following questions is studied in microeconomics?

   a. Should I go to college or get a job after I graduate?

   b. What government policies should be adopted to promote employment in the economy?

   c. How many people are employed in the economy this year?

   d. Has the overall level of prices in the economy increased or decreased this year?

   e. What determines the overall salary levels paid to workers in a given year?

Critical-Thinking Question

In what type of economic analysis do questions have a "right" or "wrong" answer? In what type of economic analysis do questions not necessarily have a "right" answer? On what type of economic analysis do economists tend to disagree most frequently? Why might economists disagree? Explain.

The Production Possibility Frontier Model

UPI/Alan Marts/Boeing/Landov

A good economic model can be a tremendous aid to understanding. In this module, we look at the *production possibility frontier*, a model that helps economists think about the *trade-offs* every economy faces. The production possibility frontier helps us understand three important aspects of the real economy: efficiency, opportunity cost, and economic growth.

Trade-offs: The Production Possibility Frontier

One of the important principles of economics we introduced in Module 1 was that resources are scarce. As a result, any economy—whether it contains one person or millions of people—faces trade-offs. You make a **trade-off** when you give up something in order to have something else.

Consider Boeing's newest jet, the 787 Dreamliner. The plane, which took its historic first test flight in 2009, was the result of an aerodynamic revolution—a superefficient airplane designed to cut airline operating costs and the first to use superlight composite materials. The jet underwent over 15,000 hours of testing that resulted in subtle design changes that improved its performance, making it 20% more fuel efficient and 20% less pollutant emitting than existing passenger jets. But, no matter how lightweight the Boeing Dreamliner is, and no matter how efficient Boeing's assembly line, producing Dreamliners means using resources that therefore can't be used to produce something else.

To think about the trade-offs necessary in any economy, economists often use the **production possibility frontier** model. The idea behind this model is to improve our understanding of trade-offs by considering a simplified economy that produces only two goods. This simplification enables us to show the trade-offs graphically.

You make a trade-off when you give up something in order to have something else.

The **production possibility frontier (PPF)** illustrates the trade-offs facing an economy that produces only two goods. It shows the maximum quantity of one good that can be produced for each possible quantity of the other good produced.

11

Suppose, for a moment, that the United States was a one-company economy, with Boeing its sole employer and aircraft its only product. But there would still be a choice of what kinds of aircraft to produce—say, Dreamliners versus small commuter jets.

Figure 2-1 shows a hypothetical production possibility frontier representing the trade-off this one-company economy would face. The curve—the dark-blue line in the diagram—shows the maximum quantity of small jets that Boeing can produce per year *given* the quantity of Dreamliners it produces per year, and vice versa. That is, it answers questions of the form, "What is the maximum quantity of small jets that Boeing can produce in a year if it also produces Dreamliners that year?"

There is a crucial distinction between points *inside* or *on* the production possibility curve (the shaded area) and *outside* the curve. If a production point lies inside or on the curve—like point *C*, at which Boeing produces 20 small jets and 9 Dreamliners in a year—it is feasible. After all, the curve tells us that if Boeing produces 20 small jets, it could also produce a maximum of 15 Dreamliners that year, so it could certainly make 9 Dreamliners. However, a production point that lies outside the curve—such as the hypothetical production point *D*, where Boeing produces 40 small jets and 30 Dreamliners—isn't feasible.

In Figure 2-1 the production possibility curve intersects the horizontal axis at 40 small jets. This means that if Boeing dedicated all its production capacity to making only small jets, it could produce 40 small jets per year. The production possibility curve intersects the vertical axis at 30 Dreamliners. This means that if Boeing dedicated all its production capacity to making Dreamliners, it could produce a maximum of 30 Dreamliners per year.

The figure also shows less extreme trade-offs. For example, if Boeing's managers decide to make 20 small jets this year, they can produce at most 15 Dreamliners; this production choice is illustrated by point *A*. And if Boeing's managers decide to produce 28 small jets, they can make at most 9 Dreamliners, as shown by point *B*.

Thinking in terms of a production possibility frontier simplifies the complexities of reality. The real-world U.S. economy produces millions of different goods. Even Boeing produces more than two different types of planes. Yet it's important to realize that even in its simplicity, this stripped-down model gives us important insights about the real world.

By simplifying reality, the production possibility frontier helps us understand some aspects of the real economy better than we could without the model: efficiency, opportunity cost, and economic growth.

FIGURE **2-1**   **The Production Possibility Frontier**

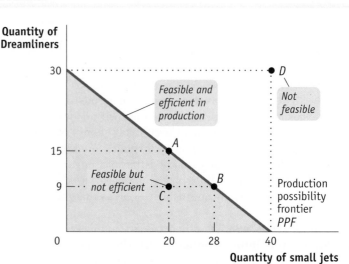

The production possibility frontier illustrates the trade-offs Boeing faces in producing Dreamliners and small jets. It shows the maximum quantity of one good that can be produced given the quantity of the other good produced. Here, the maximum quantity of Dreamliners manufactured per year depends on the quantity of small jets manufactured that year, and vice versa. Boeing's feasible production is shown by the area *inside* or *on* the curve. Production at point *C* is feasible but not efficient. Points *A* and *B* are feasible and efficient in production, but point *D* is not feasible.

Efficiency

The production possibility frontier is useful for illustrating the general economic concept of efficiency. An economy is **efficient** if there are no missed opportunities—meaning that there is no way to make some people better off without making other people worse off. For example, suppose a course you are taking meets in a lecture hall or classroom that is too small for the number of students—some may be forced to sit on the floor or stand—despite the fact that a larger space nearby is empty during the same period. Economists would say that this is an *inefficient* use of resources because there is a way to make some people better off without making anyone worse off—after all, the larger space is empty. The school is not using its resources efficiently.

When an economy is using all of its resources efficiently, the only way one person can be made better off is by rearranging the use of resources in such a way that the change makes someone else worse off. So in our classroom example, if all larger classrooms or lecture halls were already fully occupied, we could say that the school was run in an efficient way; your classmates could be made better off only by making people in the larger classroom worse off—by moving them to the room that is too small.

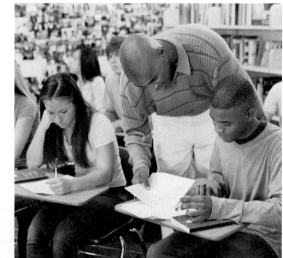

Crowded classrooms reflect inefficiency if switching to a larger space would make some students better off without making anyone worse off.

Returning to our Boeing example, as long as Boeing operates on its production possibility curve, its production is efficient. At point *A*, 15 Dreamliners are the maximum quantity feasible given that Boeing has also committed to producing 20 small jets; at point *B*, 9 Dreamliners are the maximum number that can be made given the choice to produce 28 small jets; and so on.

But suppose for some reason that Boeing was operating at point *C*, making 20 small jets and 9 Dreamliners. In this case, it would not be operating efficiently and would therefore be *inefficient:* it could be producing more of both planes.

Another example of inefficiency in production occurs when people in an economy are involuntarily unemployed: they want to work but are unable to find jobs. When that happens, the economy is not efficient in production because it could produce more output if those people were employed. The production possibility frontier shows the amount that can *possibly* be produced if all resources are fully employed. In other words, changes in unemployment move the economy closer to, or further away from, the PPF. But the curve itself is determined by what would be possible if there were full employment in the economy. Greater unemployment is represented by points farther below the PPF—the economy is not reaching its possibilities if it is not using all of its resources. Lower unemployment is represented by points closer to the PPF—as unemployment decreases, the economy moves closer to reaching its possibilities.

Although the production possibility frontier helps clarify what it means for an economy to be efficient in production, it's important to understand that efficiency in production is only *part* of what's required for the economy as a whole to be efficient. Efficiency also requires that the economy allocate its resources so that consumers are as well off as possible. If an economy does this, we say that it is *efficient in allocation*.

To see why efficiency in allocation is as important as efficiency in production, notice that points *A* and *B* in Figure 2-1 both represent situations in which the economy is efficient in production, because in each case it can't produce more of one good without producing less of the other. But these two situations may not be equally desirable. It may be more desirable to have more small jets and fewer Dreamliners than at point *A;* such as 28 small jets and 9 Dreamliners, corresponding to point *B*. In this case, point *A* is inefficient from the point of view of the economy as a whole: it is possible to move from point *A* to point *B*, and have some be made better off without making anyone else worse off.

This example shows that efficiency for the economy as a whole requires *both* efficiency in production and efficiency in allocation. To be efficient, an economy must produce as much of each good as it can, given the production of other goods, and it must also produce the mix of goods that people want to consume.

An economy is **efficient** if there is no way to make anyone better off without making anyone else worse off.

Opportunity Cost

The production possibility frontier is also useful as a reminder that the true cost of any good isn't the money it costs to buy, but what must be given up in order to get that good—the *opportunity cost*. If, for example, Boeing decides to change its production from point *A* to point *B*, it will produce 8 more small jets but 6 fewer Dreamliners. So the opportunity cost of 8 small jets is 6 Dreamliners—the 6 Dreamliners that can't be produced if Boeing produces 8 more small jets. This means that each small jet has an opportunity cost of $^6/_8 = ^3/_4$ of a Dreamliner.

If Boeing decides to produce more small jets, the opportunity cost is the Dreamliners it must forego producing.

Is the opportunity cost of an extra small jet in terms of Dreamliners always the same, no matter how many small jets and Dreamliners are currently produced? In the example illustrated by Figure 2-1, the answer is yes. If Boeing increases its production of small jets from 28 to 40, the number of Dreamliners it produces falls from 9 to zero. So Boeing's opportunity cost per additional small jet is $^9/_{12} = ^3/_4$ of a Dreamliner, the same as it was when Boeing went from 20 small jets produced to 28. The fact that the opportunity cost is always the same number—$^3/_4$ in this case—is just one possible assumption we could make in this case. Anytime we make the assumption that the opportunity cost of an additional unit of a good doesn't change regardless of the output mix, the production possibilities curve is drawn as a straight line, as it is in Figure 2-1.

Moreover, as you might have already guessed, the slope of a straight-line production possibility curve is equal to the opportunity cost—specifically, the opportunity cost for the good measured on the horizontal axis in terms of the good measured on the vertical axis. In Figure 2-1, the production possibility curve has a *constant slope* of $-^3/_4$, implying that Boeing faces a *constant opportunity cost* for 1 small jet equal to $^3/_4$ of a Dreamliner. (A review of how to calculate the slope of a straight line is found in Appendix A at the back of the book.) This is the simplest case, but the production possibility frontier model can also be used to examine situations in which opportunity costs change as the mix of output changes.

Figure 2-2 illustrates a different assumption, a case in which Boeing faces *increasing opportunity cost*. Here, the more small jets it produces, the more costly it is to

FIGURE 2-2   **Increasing Opportunity Cost**

The bowed-out shape of the production possibility frontier reflects increasing opportunity cost. In this example, to produce the first 20 small jets, Boeing must give up producing 5 Dreamliners. But to produce an additional 20 small jets, Boeing must give up manufacturing 25 more Dreamliners.

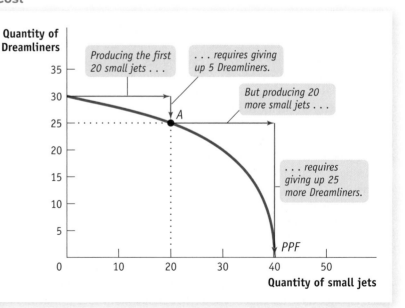

produce yet another small jet in terms of reduced production of a Dreamliner. For example, to go from producing zero small jets to producing 20, Boeing has to give up producing 5 Dreamliners. That is, the opportunity cost of those 20 small jets is 5 Dreamliners. But to increase its production of small jets to 40—that is, to produce an additional 20 small jets—it must produce 25 fewer Dreamliners, a much higher opportunity cost. And the same holds true in reverse: the more Dreamliners Boeing produces, the more costly it is to produce yet another Dreamliner in terms of reduced production of small jets. As you can see in Figure 2-2, when opportunity costs are increasing rather than constant, the production possibility curve is bowed outward rather than a straight line.

Although it's often useful to work with the simple assumption that the production possibility curve is a straight line, economists believe that in reality, opportunity costs are typically increasing. When only a small amount of a good is produced, the opportunity cost of producing that good is relatively low because the economy needs to use only those resources that are especially well suited for its production. For example, if an economy grows only a small amount of corn, that corn can be grown in places where the soil and climate are perfect for growing corn but less suitable for growing anything else, such as wheat.

So growing that corn involves giving up only a small amount of potential wheat output. Once the economy grows a lot of corn, however, land that is well suited for wheat but isn't so great for corn must be used to produce corn anyway. As a result, the additional corn production involves sacrificing considerably more wheat production. In other words, as more of a good is produced, its opportunity cost typically rises because well-suited inputs are used up and less adaptable inputs must be used instead.

Economic Growth

Finally, the production possibility frontier helps us understand what it means to talk about *economic growth*, which economists describe as creating *a sustained rise in aggregate output.* Economic growth is one of the fundamental features of the economy. But are we really justified in saying that the economy has grown over time? After all, although the U.S. economy produces more of many things than it did a century ago, it produces less of other things—for example, horse-drawn carriages. In other words, production of many goods is actually down. So how can we say for sure that the economy as a whole has grown?

The answer, illustrated in Figure 2-3, is that economic growth means an *expansion of the economy's production possibilities:* the economy *can* produce more of everything. In it, we assume again that our economy is only made up of Boeing, and therefore, our economy only produces two goods, Dreamliners and small jets. For example, if Boeing's production is initially at point A (20 small jets and 25 Dreamliners) economic growth means that Boeing could move to point E (25 small jets and 30 Dreamliners). Point E lies outside the original curve, so in the production possibility frontier model, growth is shown as an outward shift of the curve.

What can lead the production possibility curve to shift outward? There are basically

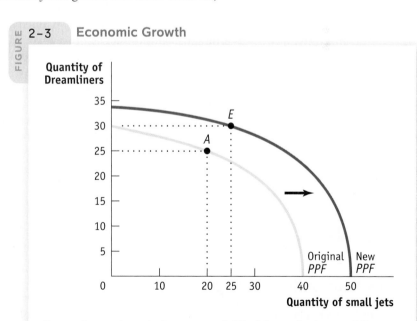

FIGURE 2-3   Economic Growth

Economic growth results in an *outward shift* of the production possibility curve because production possibilities are expanded. The economy can now produce more of everything. For example, if production is initially at point A (25 Dreamliners and 20 small jets), economic growth means that the economy could move to point E (30 Dreamliners and 25 small jets).

The four factors of production: land, labor, physical capital, and human capital.

two sources of economic growth. One is an increase in the economy's **factors of production,** the resources used to produce goods and services. Broadly speaking, the main factors of production are the resources land, labor, physical capital, and human capital. As you learned in Module 1, land is a resource supplied by nature; labor is the economy's pool of workers; physical capital refers to created resources such as machines and buildings; and human capital refers to the educational achievements and skills of the labor force, which enhance its productivity.

To see how adding to an economy's factors of production leads to economic growth, suppose that Boeing builds another construction hangar that allows it to increase the number of planes—small jets or Dreamliners or both—it can produce in a year. The new construction hangar is a factor of production, a resource Boeing can use to increase its yearly output. We can't say how many more planes of each type Boeing will produce; that's a management decision that will depend on, among other things, customer demand. But we can say that Boeing's production possibility curve has shifted outward because it can now produce more small jets without reducing the number of Dreamliners it makes, or it can make more Dreamliners without reducing the number of small jets produced.

The other source of economic growth is progress in **technology,** the technical means for the production of goods and services. Composite materials had been used in some parts of aircraft before the Boeing Dreamliner was developed. But Boeing engineers realized that there were large additional advantages to building a whole plane out of composites. The plane would be lighter, stronger, and have better aerodynamics than a plane built in the traditional way. It would therefore have longer range, be able to carry more people, and use less fuel, in addition to being able to maintain higher cabin pressure. So in a real sense Boeing's innovation—a whole plane built out of composites—was a way to do more with any given amount of resources, pushing out the production possibility curve.

But even if, for some reason, Boeing chooses to produce either fewer Dreamliners or fewer small jets than before, we would still say that this economy has grown, because it *could* have produced more of everything. At the same time, if an economy's production possibility curve shifts inward, the economy has become smaller. This could happen if the economy loses resources or technology (for example, if it experiences war or a natural disaster).

The production possibility frontier is a very simplified model of an economy. Yet it teaches us important lessons about real-world economies. It gives us our first clear sense of what constitutes economic efficiency, it illustrates the concept of opportunity cost, and it makes clear what economic growth is all about.

Factors of production are resources used to produce goods and services.

Technology is the technical means for producing goods and services.

MODULE **2** Review

Solutions appear at the back of the book.

Check Your Understanding

1. True or false? Explain your answer.

   a. An increase in the amount of resources available to Boeing for use in producing Dreamliners and small jets does not change its production possibility curve.

   b. A technological change that allows Boeing to build more small jets for any amount of Dreamliners

   built results in a change in its production possibility curve.

   c. The production possibility frontier is useful because it illustrates how much of one good an economy must give up to get more of another good regardless of whether resources are being used efficiently.

Multiple-Choice Questions

Refer to the accompanying graph to answer the following questions.

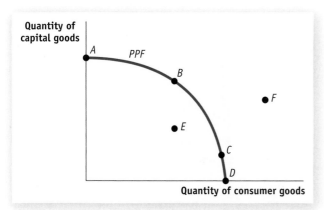

1. Which point(s) on the graph represent efficiency in production?

   a. *B* and *C*

   b. *A* and *D*

   c. *A*, *B*, *C*, and *D*

   d. *A*, *B*, *C*, *D*, and *E*

   e. *A*, *B*, *C*, *D*, *E*, and *F*

2. For this economy, an increase in the quantity of capital goods produced without a corresponding decrease in the quantity of consumer goods produced

   a. cannot happen because there is always an opportunity cost.

   b. is represented by a movement from point *E* to point *A*.

   c. is represented by a movement from point *C* to point *B*.

   d. is represented by a movement from point *E* to point *B*.

   e. is only possible with an increase in resources or technology.

3. An increase in unemployment could be represented by a movement from point

   a. *D* to point *C*.

   b. *B* to point *A*.

   c. *C* to point *F*.

   d. *B* to point *E*.

   e. *E* to point *B*.

4. Which of the following might allow this economy to move from point *B* to point *F*?

   a. more workers

   b. discovery of new resources

   c. building new factories

   d. technological advances

   e. all of the above

5. This production possibility curve shows the trade-off between consumer goods and capital goods. Since capital goods are a resource, an increase in the production of capital goods today will increase the economy's production possibilities in the future. Therefore, all other things being equal, producing at which point today will result in the largest outward shift of the PPF in the future?

   a. *A*

   b. *B*

   c. *C*

   d. *D*

   e. *E*

Critical-Thinking Question

Assume that an economy can choose between producing food and producing shelter at a constant opportunity cost. Graph a correctly labeled production possibility curve for the economy. On your graph:

a. Use the letter *E* to label one of the points that is efficient in production.

b. Use the letter *U* to label one of the points at which there might be unemployment.

c. Use the letter *I* to label one of the points that is not feasible.

Comparative Advantage and Trade

Kees Metselaar/Alamy

Gains from Trade

A family could try to take care of all its own needs—growing its own food, sewing its own clothing, providing itself with entertainment, and writing its own economics textbooks. But trying to live that way would be very hard. The key to a much better standard of living for everyone is **trade,** in which people divide tasks among themselves and each person provides a good or service that other people want in return for different goods and services that he or she wants.

The reason we have an economy is that there are **gains from trade:** by dividing tasks and trading, two people (or 7 billion people) can each get more of what they want than they could get by being self-sufficient. Gains from trade arise, in particular, from this division of tasks, which economists call **specialization:** each person engages in a different task that he or she is good at performing.

The advantages of specialization, and the resulting gains from trade, were the starting point for Adam Smith's 1776 book *The Wealth of Nations,* which many regard as the beginning of economics as a discipline. Smith's book begins with a description of an eighteenth-century pin factory where, rather than each of the 10 workers making a pin from start to finish, each worker specialized in one of the many steps in pin-making:

One man draws out the wire, another straights it, a third cuts it, a fourth points it, a fifth grinds it at the top for receiving the head; to make the head requires two or three distinct operations; to put it on, is a particular business, to whiten the pins is another; it is even a trade by itself to put them into the paper; and the important business of making a pin is, in this manner, divided into about eighteen distinct operations. . . . Those ten persons,

In a market economy, individuals engage in **trade:** they provide goods and services to others and receive goods and services in return.

There are **gains from trade:** people can get more of what they want through trade than they could if they tried to be self-sufficient. This increase in output is due to **specialization:** each person engages in the task that he or she is good at performing.

therefore, could make among them upwards of forty-eight thousand pins in a day. But if they had all wrought separately and independently, and without any of them having been educated to this particular business, they certainly could not each of them have made twenty, perhaps not one pin a day. . . .

The same principle applies when we look at how people divide tasks among themselves and trade in an economy. The economy, as a whole, can produce more when each person *specializes* in a task and *trades* with others.

The benefits of specialization are the reason a person typically focuses on the production of only one type of good or service. It takes many years of study and experience to become a doctor; it also takes many years of study and experience to become a commercial airline pilot. Many doctors might have the potential to become excellent pilots, and vice versa, but it is very unlikely that anyone who decided to pursue both careers would be as good a pilot or as good a doctor as someone who specialized in only one of those professions. So it is to everyone's advantage when individuals specialize in their career choices.

Markets are what allow a doctor and a pilot to specialize in their respective fields. Because markets for commercial flights and for doctors' services exist, a doctor is assured that she can find a flight and a pilot is assured that he can find a doctor. As long as individuals know that they can find the goods and services that they want in the market, they are willing to forgo self-sufficiency and are willing to specialize.

"I hunt and she gathers—otherwise, we couldn't make ends meet."

Comparative Advantage and Gains from Trade

One of the most important insights in all of economics is that there are gains from trade—that it makes sense to produce the things you're especially good at producing and to buy from other people the things you aren't as good at producing. This would be true even if you could produce everything for yourself: even if a brilliant brain surgeon *could* repair her own dripping faucet, it's probably a better idea for her to call in a professional plumber.

How can we model the gains from trade? Let's stay with our aircraft example and once again imagine that the United States is a one-company economy where everyone works for Boeing, producing either large or small jets. Let's now assume, however, that the United States has the ability to trade with Brazil—another one-company economy where everyone works for the Brazilian aircraft company Embraer, which is, in the real world, a successful producer of small commuter jets.

Both countries could produce either kind of jet. But as we'll see in a moment, they can gain by producing different things and trading with each other. Let's return to the simpler case of straight-line production possibility curves. America's production possibilities are represented by the production possibility curve in panel (a) of Figure 3-1, which is similar to the production possibility curve in Figure 2-1 (page 12). According to this diagram, the United States can produce 40 small jets or 30 large jets, or some combination of the two. Recall that this means that the slope of the U.S. production possibility curve is $-3/4$: its opportunity cost of 1 small jet is $3/4$ of a large jet.

Panel (b) of Figure 3-1 shows Brazil's production possibilities. Like the United States, Brazil's production possibility curve is a straight line. Brazil's production possibility curve has a constant slope of $-1/3$. Brazil can't produce as much of anything as the United States can: at most it can produce 30 small jets or 10 large jets. But it is relatively better at manufacturing small jets than the United States. While the United States sacrifices $3/4$ of a large jet per small jet produced, for Brazil the opportunity cost of a small jet is only $1/3$ of a large jet. Table 3-1 summarizes the two countries' opportunity costs of small jets and large jets.

Now, the United States and Brazil could each choose to make their own large and small jets, not trading any airplanes at all. Let's suppose that the two countries start out this way and make the consumption choices shown in

TABLE 3-1

U.S. and Brazilian Opportunity Costs of Small Jets and Large Jets

	U.S. Opportunity Cost		Brazilian Opportunity Cost
One small jet	¾ large jet	>	⅓ large jet
One large jet	⁴⁄₃ small jets	<	3 small jets

FIGURE **3-1**   Production Possibilities for Two Countries

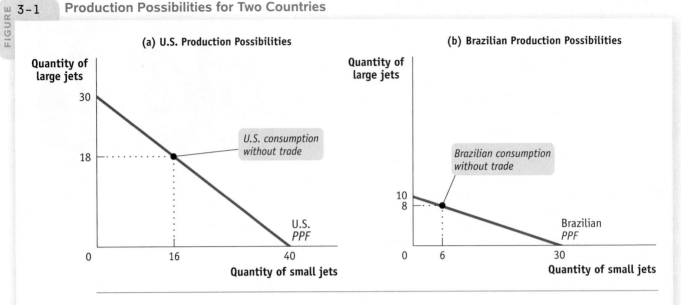

Here, both the United States and Brazil have a constant opportunity cost of small jets, illustrated by a straight-line production possibility curve. For the United States, each small jet has an opportunity cost of ¾ of a large jet. Brazil has an opportunity cost of a small jet equal to ⅓ of a large jet.

Figure 3-1: in the absence of trade, the United States produces and consumes 16 small jets and 18 large jets per year, while Brazil produces and consumes 6 small jets and 8 large jets per year.

But is this the best the two countries can do? No, it isn't. Given that the two producers—and therefore the two countries—have different opportunity costs, the United States and Brazil can strike a deal that makes both of them better off.

Table 3-2 shows how such a deal works: the United States specializes in the production of large jets, manufacturing 30 per year, and sells 10 to Brazil. Meanwhile, Brazil specializes in the production of small jets, producing 30 per year, and sells 20 to the United States. The result is shown in Figure 3-2. The United States now consumes more of both small jets and large jets than before: instead of 16 small jets and 18 large jets, it now consumes 20 small jets and 20 large jets. Brazil also consumes more, going from 6 small jets and 8 large jets to 10 small jets and 10 large jets. As Table 3-2 also shows, both the United States and Brazil reap gains from trade, consuming more of both types of plane than they would have without trade.

Both countries are better off when they each specialize in what they are good at and trade. It's a good idea for the United States to specialize in the production of large jets because its opportunity cost of a large jet is smaller than Brazil's: ⁴⁄₃ < 3. Correspondingly, Brazil should specialize in the production of small jets because its opportunity cost of a small jet is smaller than the United States: ⅓ < ¾.

TABLE 3-2

How the United States and Brazil Gain from Trade

		Without Trade		With Trade		Gains from Trade
		Production	Consumption	Production	Consumption	
United States	Large jets	18	18	30	20	+2
	Small jets	16	16	0	20	+4
Brazil	Large jets	8	8	0	10	+2
	Small jets	6	6	30	10	+4

FIGURE 3-2 Comparative Advantage and Gains from Trade

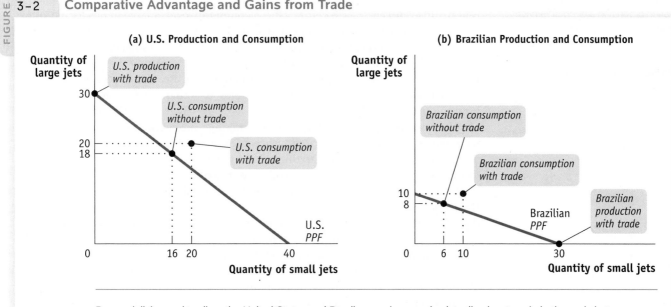

By specializing and trading, the United States and Brazil can produce and consume more of both large jets and small jets. The United States specializes in manufacturing large jets, its comparative advantage, and Brazil—which has an *absolute* disadvantage in both goods but a *comparative* advantage in small jets—specializes in manufacturing small jets. With trade, both countries can consume more of both goods than either could without trade.

What we would say in this case is that the United States has a comparative advantage in the production of large jets and Brazil has a comparative advantage in the production of small jets. A country has a **comparative advantage** in producing something if the opportunity cost of that production is lower for that country than for other countries. The same concept applies to firms and people: a firm or an individual has a comparative advantage in producing something if its, his, or her opportunity cost of production is lower than for others.

One point of clarification before we proceed further. You may have wondered why the United States traded 10 large jets to Brazil in return for 20 small jets. Why not some other deal, like trading 10 large jets for 12 small jets? The answer to that question has two parts. First, there may indeed be other trades that the United States and Brazil might agree to. Second, there are some deals that we can safely rule out—one like 10 large jets for 10 small jets.

To understand why, reexamine Table 3-1 and consider the United States first. Without trading with Brazil, the U.S. opportunity cost of a small jet is ³⁄₄ of a large jet. So it's clear that the United States will not accept any trade that requires it to give up more than ³⁄₄ of a large jet for a small jet. Trading 10 large jets in return for 12 small jets would require the United States to pay an opportunity cost of 10/12 = 5/6 of a large jet for a small jet. Because 5/6 > ³⁄₄, this is a deal that the United States would reject. Similarly, Brazil won't accept a trade that gives it less than ¹⁄₃ of a large jet for a small jet.

The point to remember is that the United States and Brazil will be willing to trade only if the "price" of the good each country obtains in the trade is less than its own opportunity cost of producing the good domestically. Moreover, this is a general statement that is true whenever two parties—countries, firms, or individuals—trade voluntarily.

While our story clearly simplifies reality, it teaches us some very important lessons that apply to the real economy, too.

First, the model provides a clear illustration of the gains from trade: through specialization and trade, both countries produce more and consume more than if they were self-sufficient.

A country has a comparative advantage in producing a good or service if its opportunity cost of producing the good or service is lower than other countries'.

A country has an **absolute advantage** in producing a good or service if the country can produce more output per worker than other countries. Likewise, an individual has an absolute advantage in producing a good or service if he or she is better at producing it than other people. Having an absolute advantage is not the same thing as having a comparative advantage.

Second, the model demonstrates a very important point that is often overlooked in real-world arguments: each country has a comparative advantage in producing something. This applies to firms and people as well: *everyone has a comparative advantage in something, and everyone has a comparative disadvantage in something.*

Crucially, in our example it doesn't matter if, as is probably the case in real life, U.S. workers are just as good as or even better than Brazilian workers at producing small jets. Suppose that the United States is actually better than Brazil at all kinds of aircraft production. In that case, we would say that the United States has an **absolute advantage** in both large-jet and small-jet production: in an hour, an American worker can produce more of either a large jet or a small jet than a Brazilian worker. You might be tempted to think that in that case the United States has nothing to gain from trading with the less productive Brazil.

But we've just seen that the United States can indeed benefit from trading with Brazil because *comparative, not absolute, advantage is the basis for mutual gain.* It doesn't matter whether it takes Brazil more resources than the United States to make a small jet; what matters for trade is that for Brazil the opportunity cost of a small jet is lower than the U.S. opportunity cost. So Brazil, despite its absolute disadvantage, even in small jets, has a comparative advantage in the manufacture of small jets. Meanwhile the United States, which can use its resources most productively by manufacturing large jets, has a comparative *dis*advantage in manufacturing small jets.

If comparative advantage were relevant only to airplane manufacturers, it might not be that interesting. However, the idea of comparative advantage applies to many activities in the economy. Perhaps its most important application is in trade—not between individuals, but between countries. So let's look briefly at how the model of comparative advantage helps in understanding both the causes and the effects of international trade.

ECONOMICS ▶ IN ACTION — WORLD VIEW

RICH NATION, POOR NATION

Try taking off your clothes—at a suitable time and in a suitable place, of course—and take a look at the labels inside that say where the clothes were made. It's a very good bet that much, if not most, of your clothing was manufactured overseas, in a country that is much poorer than the United States is—say, in El Salvador, Sri Lanka, or Bangladesh.

Why are these countries so much poorer than the United States? The immediate reason is that their economies are much less *productive*—firms in these countries are just not able to produce as much from a given quantity of resources as comparable firms in the United States or other wealthy countries. Why countries differ so much in productivity is a deep question—indeed, one of the main questions that preoccupy economists. In any case, the difference in productivity is a fact.

But if the economies of these countries are so much less productive than ours, how is it that they make so much of our clothing? Why don't we do it for ourselves?

The answer is "comparative advantage." Just about every industry in Bangladesh is much less productive than the corresponding industry in the United States. But the productivity difference between rich and poor countries varies across goods; there is a very great difference in the production of sophisticated goods such as aircraft but not as great a difference in the production of simpler goods such as clothing. So Bangladesh's position with regard to clothing production is like Brazil's position with respect to producing smaller jets. While Brazil is not as good as the United States at making either small or large jets, producing smaller jets is what Brazil does comparatively well.

Although less productive than American workers, Bangladeshi workers have a comparative advantage in clothing production.

Although Bangladesh is at an absolute disadvantage compared with the United States in almost everything, it has a comparative advantage in clothing production. This means that both the United States and Bangladesh are able to consume more because they specialize in producing different things, with Bangladesh supplying our clothing and the United States supplying Bangladesh with more sophisticated goods.

Comparative Advantage and International Trade, in Reality

Look at the label on a manufactured good sold in the United States, and there's a good chance you will find that it was produced in some other country. On the other side, many U.S. industries sell a large fraction of their output overseas.

Should all this international exchange of goods and services be celebrated, or is it cause for concern? Politicians and the public often question the desirability of international trade, arguing that the nation should produce goods for itself rather than buy them from foreigners. Industries around the world demand protection from foreign competition: Japanese farmers want to keep out American rice, American steelworkers want to keep out European steel. And these demands are often supported by public opinion.

Economists, however, have a very positive view of international trade. Why? Because they view it in terms of comparative advantage. As we learned from our example of U.S. large jets and Brazilian small jets, international trade benefits both countries. Each country can consume more than if it didn't trade and remained self-sufficient. Moreover, these mutual gains don't depend on each country being better than other countries at producing one kind of good. Even if one country has, say, higher output per worker in both industries—that is, even if one country has an absolute advantage in both industries—there are still gains from trade.

Thomas Lenne/Alamy

Sources of Comparative Advantage

International trade is driven by comparative advantage, but where does comparative advantage come from? Economists who study international trade have found three main sources of comparative advantage: international differences in *climate*, international differences in *factor endowments*, and international differences in *technology*.

DIFFERENCES IN CLIMATE In general, differences in climate play a significant role in international trade. Tropical countries export tropical products like coffee, sugar, bananas, and shrimp. Countries in the temperate zones export crops like wheat and corn. Some trade is even driven by the difference in seasons between the northern and southern hemispheres: winter deliveries of Chilean grapes and New Zealand apples have become commonplace in U.S. and European supermarkets.

DIFFERENCES IN FACTOR ENDOWMENTS Canada is a major exporter of forest products—lumber and products derived from lumber, like pulp and paper—to the United States. These exports don't reflect the special skill of Canadian lumberjacks. Canada has a comparative advantage in forest products because its forested area is much greater compared to the size of its labor force than the ratio of forestland to the labor force in the United States.

Forestland, like labor and capital, is a *factor of production:* an input used to produce goods and services. Due to history and geography, the mix of available factors of production differs among countries, providing an important source of comparative advantage.

Consider world trade in clothing. Clothing production is a labor-intensive activity: it doesn't take much physical capital, nor does it require a lot of human capital in the form of highly educated workers. So you would expect labor-abundant countries such as China and Bangladesh to have a comparative advantage in clothing production. And they do.

DIFFERENCES IN TECHNOLOGY In the 1970s and 1980s, Japan became by far the world's largest exporter of automobiles, selling large numbers to the United States and the rest of the world. Japan's comparative advantage in automobiles wasn't the result of climate. Nor can it easily be attributed to differences in factor endowments: aside from a scarcity of land, Japan's mix of available factors is quite similar to that in other advanced countries. Instead, Japan's comparative advantage in automobiles was based on the superior production techniques developed by its manufacturers, which allowed them to produce more cars with a given amount of labor and capital than their American or European counterparts.

Japan's comparative advantage in automobiles was a case of comparative advantage caused by differences in technology—the techniques used in production. (See the upcoming Business Case for more on these techniques.)

The causes of differences in technology are somewhat mysterious. Sometimes they seem to be based on knowledge accumulated through experience—for example, Switzerland's comparative advantage in watches reflects a long tradition of watchmaking. Sometimes they are the result of a set of innovations that for some reason occur in one country but not in others. Technological advantage, however, is often transitory. American auto manufacturers have now closed much of the gap in productivity with their Japanese competitors. In addition, Europe's aircraft industry has closed a similar gap with the U.S. aircraft industry. At any given point in time, however, differences in technology are a major source of comparative advantage.

MODULE 3 Review

Solutions appear at the back of the book.

Check Your Understanding

1. In Italy, an automobile can be produced by 8 workers in one day and a washing machine by 3 workers in one day. In the United States, an automobile can be produced by 6 workers in one day, and a washing machine by 2 workers in one day.

   a. Which country has an absolute advantage in the production of automobiles? In washing machines?

   b. Which country has a comparative advantage in the production of washing machines? In automobiles?

   c. What type of specialization results in the greatest gains from trade between the two countries?

2. Using the numbers from Table 3-1, explain why the United States and Brazil are willing to engage in a trade of 10 large jets for 15 small jets.

Multiple-Choice Questions

Refer to the graph below to answer the following questions.

1. Use the graph to determine which country has an absolute advantage in producing each good.

	Absolute advantage in wheat production	Absolute advantage in textile production
a.	Country A	Country B
b.	Country A	Country A
c.	Country B	Country A
d.	Country B	Country B
e.	Country A	Neither Country

2. For Country A, the opportunity cost of a bushel of wheat is

a. ½ units of textiles

b. ⅔ units of textiles

c. 1⅓ units of textiles

d. 1½ units of textiles

e. 2 units of textiles

3. Use the graph to determine which country has a comparative advantage in producing each good.

	Comparative advantage in wheat production	*Comparative advantage in textile production*
a.	Country A	Country B
b.	Country A	Country A
c.	Country B	Country A
d.	Country B	Country B
e.	Country A	Neither Country

4. If the two countries specialize and trade, which of the choices below describes the countries' imports?

	Import Wheat	*Import Textiles*
a.	Country A	Country A
b.	Country A	Country B
c.	Country B	Country B
d.	Country B	Country A
e.	Neither Country	Country B

5. What is the highest price Country B is willing to pay to buy wheat from Country A?

a. ½ units of textiles

b. ⅔ units of textiles

c. 1 unit of textiles

d. 1½ units of textiles

e. 2 units of textiles

Critical-Thinking Questions

Refer to the table below to answer the following questions. These two countries are producing textiles and wheat using equal amounts of resources.

	Weekly output per worker	
	Country A	**Country B**
Bushels of Wheat	15	10
Units of Textiles	60	60

1. What is the opportunity cost of producing a bushel of wheat for each country?

2. Which country has the absolute advantage in wheat production?

3. Which country has the comparative advantage in textile production? Explain.

PITFALLS

? Back in the 1980s, when the U.S. economy seemed to be lagging behind that of Japan, commentators often warned that if we didn't improve our productivity, we would soon have no comparative advantage in anything. What is wrong with this statement?

> IT IS INACCURATE; THOSE COMMENTATORS MISUNDERSTOOD COMPARATIVE ADVANTAGE. It happens all the time. Students, pundits, and politicians confuse *comparative* advantage with *absolute* advantage. What the commentators meant was that we would have no *absolute* advantage in anything— that there might come a time when the Japanese were able to produce more goods in an absolute sense than we were. (It didn't turn out that way, but that's another story.) And they had the idea that in that case we would no longer be able to benefit from trade with Japan.

A country has an absolute advantage in producing a good or service if the country can produce more output per worker than other countries. Likewise, an individual has an absolute advantage in producing a good or service if he or she is better at producing it than other people. Having an absolute advantage is not the same thing as having a comparative advantage.

Just as Brazil, in our example, is able to benefit from trade with the United States (and vice versa) despite the fact that the United States may be able to produce absolutely more goods than Brazil, in the real-world nations will still gain from trade even if they are less productive in all industries than the countries with whom they trade

To learn more, see pages 21–22, including Figure 3-2.

BUSINESS : **Efficiency, Opportunity Cost, and**
CASE : **the Logic of Lean Production**

In the summer and fall of 2010, workers were rearranging the furniture in Boeing's final assembly plant in Everett, Washington, in preparation for the production of the Boeing 767. It was a difficult and time-consuming process, however, because the items of "furniture"—Boeing's assembly equipment—weighed on the order of 200 tons each. It was a necessary part of setting up a production system based on "lean manufacturing," also called "just-in-time" production. Lean manufacturing, pioneered by Toyota Motors of Japan, is based on the practice of having parts arrive on the factory floor just as they are needed for production. This reduces the amount of parts Boeing holds in inventory as well as the amount of the factory floor needed for production—in this case, reducing the square footage required for manufacture of the 767 by 40%.

Boeing had adopted lean manufacturing in 1999 in the manufacture of the 737, the most popular commercial airplane. By 2005, after constant refinement, Boeing had achieved a 50% reduction in the time it takes to produce a plane and a nearly 60% reduction in parts inventory. An important feature is a continuously moving assembly line, moving products from one assembly team to the next at a steady pace and eliminating the need for workers to wander across the factory floor from task to task or in search of tools and parts.

Toyota's lean production techniques have been the most widely adopted of all manufacturing techniques and have revolutionized manufacturing worldwide. In simple terms, lean production is focused on organization and communication. Workers and parts are organized so as to ensure a smooth and consistent workflow that minimizes wasted effort and materials. Lean production is also designed to be highly responsive to changes in the desired mix of output—for example, quickly producing more sedans and fewer minivans according to changes in customers' demands.

Toyota's lean production methods were so successful that they transformed the global auto industry and severely threatened once-dominant American automakers. Until the 1980s, the "Big Three"—Chrysler, Ford, and General Motors—dominated the American auto industry, with virtually no foreign-made cars sold in the United States. In the 1980s, however, Toyotas became increasingly popular in the United States due to their high quality and relatively low price—so popular that the Big Three eventually prevailed upon the U.S. government to protect them by restricting the sale of Japanese autos in the United States. Over time, Toyota responded by building assembly plants in the United States, bringing along its lean production techniques, which then spread throughout American manufacturing.

Questions for Thought

1. What is the opportunity cost associated with having a worker wander across the factory floor from task to task or in search of tools and parts?

2. How does lean manufacturing improve the economy's efficiency in allocation?

3. How will the shift in location of Toyota's production from Japan to the United States alter the pattern of comparative advantage in automaking between the two countries?

SECTION 1 REVIEW

Summary

The Study of Economics

1. Everyone has to make choices about what to do and what *not* to do. **Individual choice** is the basis of **economics**—if it doesn't involve choice, it isn't economics.

2. The **economy** is a system that coordinates choices about production and consumption. In a **market economy,** these choices are made by many firms and individuals. The **invisible hand** refers to the way individual self-interest leads to good results for society as a whole.

3. The reason choices must be made is that **resources**—anything that can be used to produce something else—are **scarce.** Individuals are limited in their choices by money and time; economies are limited by their supplies of resources.

4. Because you must choose among limited alternatives, the true cost of anything is what you must give up to get it—all costs are **opportunity costs.**

5. **Microeconomics** is the branch of economics that studies how people make decisions and how those decisions interact. **Macroeconomics** is concerned with the overall ups and downs of the economy, and focuses on **economic aggregates** such as the unemployment rate and gross domestic product, that summarize data across many different markets.

6. Macroeconomics has a strong policy focus: **Keynesian economics,** which emerged during the Great Depression, advocates the use of *monetary policy* and *fiscal policy* to fight economic slumps. Prior to the Great Depression, the economy was thought to be **self-regulating.**

7. Almost all economics is based on **models,** "thought experiments" or simplified versions of reality, many of which use analytical tools such as mathematics and graphs. An important assumption in economic models is the **other things equal (*ceteris paribus*) assumption,** which allows analysis of the effect of change in one factor by holding all other relevant factors unchanged.

8. Economists use economic models for both **positive economics,** which describes how the economy works, and for **normative economics,** which prescribes how the economy *should* work. Positive economics often involves making forecasts. Economics can determine correct answers for positive questions, but typically not for normative questions, which involve value judgments. Exceptions occur when policies designed to achieve a certain prescription can be clearly ranked in terms of efficiency.

9. There are two main reasons economists disagree. One, they may disagree about which simplifications to make in a model. Two, economists may disagree—like everyone else—about values.

The Production Possibility Frontier Model

10. One important economic model is the **production possibility frontier,** which illustrates the **trade-offs** facing an economy that produces only two goods. The PPF illustrates three elements: opportunity cost (showing how much less of one good must be produced if more of the other good is produced), **efficiency** (an economy is efficient in production if it produces on the production possibility curve and efficient in allocation if it produces the mix of goods and services that people want to consume), and economic growth (an outward shift of the production possibility curve).

11. There are two basic sources of growth in the production possibility frontier model: an increase in resources and improved **technology.**

Comparative Advantage and Trade

12. There are **gains from trade:** by engaging in the **trade** of goods and services with one another, the members of an economy can all be made better off. Underlying gains from trade are the advantages of **specialization,** of having individuals specialize in the tasks they are comparatively good at.

13. **Comparative advantage** explains the source of gains from trade between individuals and countries. Everyone has a comparative advantage in something—some good or service in which that person has a lower opportunity cost than everyone else. But it is often confused with **absolute advantage,** an ability to produce more of a particular good or service than anyone else. This confusion leads some to erroneously conclude that there are no gains from trade between people or countries.

Key Terms

Problems

1. Which of the following questions are relevant for the study of macroeconomics and which for microeconomics?

   a. How will Ms. Martin's tips change when a large manufacturing plant near the restaurant where she works closes?

   b. What will happen to spending by consumers when the economy enters a downturn?

   c. How will the price of oranges change when a late frost damages Florida's orange groves?

   d. How will wages at a manufacturing plant change when its workforce is unionized?

   e. What will happen to U.S. exports as the dollar becomes less expensive in terms of other currencies?

   f. What is the relationship between a nation's unemployment rate and its inflation rate?

2. Describe some of the opportunity costs of the following choices.

   a. Attend college instead of taking a job.

   b. Watch a movie instead of studying for an exam.

   c. Ride the bus instead of driving your car.

3. Use the concept of opportunity cost to explain the following situations.

   a. More people choose to get graduate degrees when the job market is poor.

   b. More people choose to do their own home repairs when the economy is slow and hourly wages are down.

   c. There are more parks in suburban areas than in urban areas.

   d. Convenience stores, which have higher prices than supermarkets, cater to busy people.

4. A representative of the U.S. clothing industry recently made this statement: "Workers in Asia often work in sweatshop conditions earning only pennies an hour. American workers are more productive and, as a result, earn higher wages. In order to preserve the dignity of the American workplace, the government should enact legislation banning imports of low-wage Asian clothing."

   a. Which parts of this quotation are positive statements? Which parts are normative statements?

   b. Is the policy that is being advocated consistent with the statement about the wages and productivities of American and Asian workers?

   c. Would such a policy make some Americans better off without making any other Americans worse off? That is, would this policy be efficient from the viewpoint of all Americans?

   d. Would low-wage Asian workers benefit from or be hurt by such a policy?

5. Are the following statements true or false? Explain your answers.

   a. "When people must pay higher taxes on their wage earnings, it reduces their incentive to work" is a positive statement.

   b. "We should lower taxes to encourage more work" is a positive statement.

   c. Economics cannot always be used to determine what society ought to do.

   d. "The system of public education in this country generates greater benefits to society than the cost of running the system" is a normative statement.

   e. All disagreements among economists are generated by the media.

6. Evaluate this statement: "It is easier to build an economic model that accurately reflects events that have already occurred than to build an economic model to forecast future events." Do you think that this is true or not? Why? What does this imply about the difficulties of building good economic models?

7. Suppose Atlantis is a small, isolated island in the South Atlantic. The inhabitants grow potatoes and catch fish. The accompanying table shows the maximum annual output combinations of potatoes and fish that can be produced. Obviously, given their limited resources and available technology, as they use more of their resources for potato production, there are fewer resources available for catching fish.

Maximum annual output options	Quantity of potatoes (pounds)	Quantity of fish (pounds)
A	1,000	0
B	800	300
C	600	500
D	400	600
E	200	650
F	0	675

   a. Draw a production possibility curve with potatoes on the horizontal axis and fish on the vertical axis, and illustrate these options, showing points A–F.

   b. Can Atlantis produce 500 pounds of fish and 800 pounds of potatoes? Explain. Where would this point lie relative to the production possibility curve?

   c. What is the opportunity cost of increasing the annual output of potatoes from 600 to 800 pounds?

   d. What is the opportunity cost of increasing the annual output of potatoes from 200 to 400 pounds?

   e. Explain why the answers to parts c and d are not the same. What does this imply about the slope of the production possibility curve?

8. Two important industries on the island of Bermuda are fishing and tourism. According to data from the World Resources Institute and the Bermuda Department of Statistics, in the year 2009 the 306 registered fishermen in Bermuda

caught 387 metric tons of marine fish. And the 2,719 people employed by hotels produced 554,400 hotel stays (measured by the number of visitor arrivals). Suppose that this production point is efficient in production. Assume also that the opportunity cost of one additional metric ton of fish is 2,000 hotel stays and that this opportunity cost is constant (the opportunity cost does not change).

a. If all 306 registered fishermen were to be employed by hotels (in addition to the 2,719 people already working in hotels), how many hotel stays could Bermuda produce?

b. If all 2,719 hotel employees were to become fishermen (in addition to the 306 fishermen already working in the fishing industry), how many metric tons of fish could Bermuda produce?

c. Draw a production possibility curve for Bermuda, with fish on the horizontal axis and hotel stays on the vertical axis, and label Bermuda's actual production point for the year 2009.

9. In the ancient country of Roma, only two goods, spaghetti and meatballs, are produced. There are two tribes in Roma, the Tivoli and the Frivoli. By themselves, the Tivoli each month can produce either 30 pounds of spaghetti and no meatballs, or 50 pounds of meatballs and no spaghetti, or any combination in between. The Frivoli, by themselves, each month can produce 40 pounds of spaghetti and no meatballs, or 30 pounds of meatballs and no spaghetti, or any combination in between.

a. Assume that all production possibility curves are straight lines. Draw one diagram showing the monthly production possibility curve for the Tivoli and another showing the monthly production possibility curve for the Frivoli.

b. Which tribe has the comparative advantage in spaghetti production? In meatball production?

In A.D. 100, the Frivoli discovered a new technique for making meatballs that doubled the quantity of meatballs they could produce each month.

c. Draw the new monthly production possibility curve for the Frivoli.

d. After the innovation, which tribe had an absolute advantage in producing meatballs? In producing spaghetti? Which had the comparative advantage in meatball production? In spaghetti production?

10. In recent years, the United States used 124 million acres of land for wheat or corn farming. Of those 124 million acres, farmers used 50 million acres to grow 2.158 billion bushels of wheat, and 74 million acres of land to grow 11.807 billion bushels of corn. Suppose that U.S. wheat and corn farming is efficient in production. At that production point, the opportunity cost of producing one additional bushel of wheat is 1.7 fewer bushels of corn. However, farmers have increasing opportunity costs, so additional bushels of wheat have an opportunity cost greater than 1.7 bushels of corn. For each of the production points described below, decide whether that production point is (i) feasible and efficient in production, (ii) feasible but not efficient in production, (iii) not feasible, or (iv) uncertain as to whether or not it is feasible.

a. From their original production point, farmers use 40 million acres of land to produce 1.8 billion bushels of wheat, and they use 60 million acres of land to produce 9 billion bushels of corn. The remaining 24 million acres are left unused.

b. From their original production point, farmers transfer 40 million acres of land from corn to wheat production. They now produce 3.158 billion bushels of wheat and 10.107 billion bushels of corn.

c. From their original production point, farmers reduce their production of wheat to 2 billion bushels and increase their production of corn to 12.044 billion bushels. Along the production possibility curve, the opportunity cost of going from 11.807 billion bushels of corn to 12.044 billion bushels of corn is 0.666 bushel of wheat per bushel of corn.

11. The Hatfield family lives on the east side of the Hatatoochie River, and the McCoy family lives on the west side. Each family's diet consists of fried chicken and corn-on-the-cob, and each is self-sufficient, raising their own chickens and growing their own corn. Explain the conditions under which each of the following statements would be true.

a. The two families are made better off when the Hatfields specialize in raising chickens, the McCoys specialize in growing corn, and the two families trade.

b. The two families are made better off when the McCoys specialize in raising chickens, the Hatfields specialize in growing corn, and the two families trade.

12. According to the U.S. Census Bureau, back in July 2006 the United States exported aircraft worth $1 billion to China and imported aircraft worth only $19,000 from China. During the same month, however, the United States imported $83 million worth of men's trousers, slacks, and jeans from China but exported only $8,000 worth of trousers, slacks, and jeans to China. Using what you have learned about how trade is determined by comparative advantage, answer the following questions.

a. Which country has the comparative advantage in aircraft production? In production of trousers, slacks, and jeans?

b. Can you determine which country has the absolute advantage in aircraft production? In production of trousers, slacks, and jeans?

13. Peter Pundit, an economics reporter, states that the European Union (EU) is increasing its productivity very rapidly in all industries. He claims that this productivity advance is so rapid that output from the EU in these industries will soon exceed that of the United States and, as a result, the United States will no longer benefit from trade with the EU.

a. Do you think Peter Pundit is correct or not? If not, what do you think is the source of his mistake?

b. If the EU and the United States continue to trade, what do you think will characterize the goods that the EU exports to the United States and the goods that the United States exports to the EU?

SECTION 2

Supply and Demand

BLUE JEAN BLUES W☉RLD VIEW

If you bought a pair of blue jeans in 2011, you may have been shocked at the price. Or maybe not: fashions change, and maybe you thought you were paying the price for being fashionable. But you weren't—you were paying for cotton. Jeans are made of denim, which is a particular weave of cotton, and by December 2010, the price of a pound of cotton had hit a 140-year high, the highest cotton price since records began in 1870.

And why were cotton prices so high?

On one side, demand for clothing of all kinds was surging. In 2008–2009, as the world struggled with the effects of a financial crisis, nervous consumers cut back on clothing purchases. But by 2010, with the worst apparently over, buyers were back in force. On the supply side, Pakistan, the world's fourth-largest cotton producer, was hit by devastating floods that put one-fifth of the country underwater and virtually destroyed its cotton crop.

Fearing that consumers had limited tolerance for large increases in the price of cotton clothing, apparel makers began scrambling to find ways to reduce costs. They adopted changes like smaller buttons, cheaper linings, and—yes—polyester, doubting that consumers would be willing to pay more for cotton goods. In fact, some experts on the cotton market warned that the sky-high prices of cotton in 2010–2011 might lead to a permanent shift in tastes, with consumers becoming more willing to wear synthetics even when cotton prices came down.

At the same time, it was not all bad news for everyone connected with the cotton trade. In the United States, cotton producers had not been hit by bad weather and were relishing the higher prices. American farmers responded to sky-high cotton prices by sharply increasing the acreage devoted to the crop. None of this was enough, however, to produce immediate price relief.

Wait a minute: how, exactly, does flooding in Pakistan translate into higher jeans prices and more polyester in your T-shirts? It's a matter of supply and demand—but what does that mean? Many people use "supply and demand" as a sort of catchphrase to mean "the laws of the marketplace at work." To economists, however, the concept of supply and demand has a precise meaning: it is a *model of how a market behaves.*

In this section, we lay out the pieces that make up the *supply and demand model,* put them together, and show how this model can be used to understand how many—but not all—markets behave. We'll also see what happens when governments step in and either try to control prices in competitive markets or dictate the quantity of goods bought and sold. The section concludes with a look at the economics of international trade.

Thinkstock

Supply and Demand: A Model of a Competitive Market

Cotton sellers and cotton buyers constitute a *market*—a group of producers and consumers who exchange a good or service for payment. In this section, we'll focus on a particular type of market known as a *competitive market*. Roughly, a **competitive market** is a market in which there are many buyers and sellers of the same good or service. More precisely, the key feature of a competitive market is that no individual's actions have a noticeable effect on the price at which the good or service is sold. It's important to understand, however, that this is not an accurate description of every market.

For example, it's not an accurate description of the market for cola beverages. That's because in the market for cola beverages, Coca-Cola and Pepsi account for such a large proportion of total sales that they are able to influence the price at which cola beverages are bought and sold. But it *is* an accurate description of the market for cotton. The global marketplace for cotton is so huge that even a jeans maker as large as Levi Strauss & Co. accounts for only a tiny fraction of transactions, making it unable to influence the price at which cotton is bought and sold.

It's a little hard to explain why competitive markets are different from other markets until we've seen how a competitive market works. For now, let's just say that it's easier to model competitive markets than other markets. When taking an exam, it's always a good strategy to begin by answering the easier questions. In this book, we're going to do the same thing. So we will start with competitive markets.

When a market is competitive, its behavior is well described by the **supply and demand model.** Because many markets *are* competitive, the supply and demand model is a very useful one indeed.

A **competitive market** is a market in which there are many buyers and sellers of the same good or service, none of whom can influence the price at which the good or service is sold.

The **supply and demand model** is a model of how a competitive market works.

There are five key elements in this model:

- The *demand curve*
- The *supply curve*
- The set of factors that cause the demand curve to shift and the set of factors that cause the supply curve to shift
- The *market equilibrium,* which includes the *equilibrium price* and *equilibrium quantity*
- The way the market equilibrium changes when the supply curve or demand curve shifts

To explain the supply and demand model, we will examine each of these elements in turn. In this module we begin with demand.

The Demand Curve

How many pounds of cotton, packaged in the form of blue jeans, do consumers around the world want to buy in a given year? You might at first think that we can answer this question by looking at the total number of pairs of blue jeans purchased around the world each day, multiply that number by the amount of cotton it takes to make a pair of jeans, and then multiply by 365. But that's not enough to answer the question, because how many pairs of jeans—in other words, how many pounds of cotton—consumers want to buy depends on the price of a pound of cotton.

When the price of cotton rises, as it did in 2010, some people will respond to the higher price of cotton clothing by buying fewer cotton garments or, perhaps, by switching completely to garments made from other materials, such as synthetics or linen. In general, the quantity of cotton clothing, or of any good or service that people want to buy, depends on the price. The higher the price, the less of the good or service people want to purchase; alternatively, the lower the price, the more they want to purchase.

So the answer to the question "How many pounds of cotton do consumers want to buy?" depends on the price of a pound of cotton. If you don't yet know what the price will be, you can start by making a table of how many pounds of cotton people would want to buy at a number of different prices. Such a table is known as a *demand schedule*. This, in turn, can be used to draw a *demand curve*, which is one of the key elements of the supply and demand model.

The Demand Schedule and the Demand Curve

A **demand schedule** is a table showing how much of a good or service consumers will want to buy at different prices. On the right side of Figure 4-1, we show a hypothetical demand schedule for cotton. It's hypothetical in that it doesn't use actual data on the world demand for cotton and it assumes that all cotton is of equal quality.

According to the table, if a pound of cotton costs $1, consumers around the world will want to purchase 10 billion pounds of cotton over the course of a year. If the price is $1.25 a pound, they will want to buy only 8.9 billion pounds; if the price is only $0.75 a pound, they will want to buy 11.5 billion pounds; and so on. So, the higher the price, the fewer pounds of cotton consumers will want to purchase. In other words, as the price rises, the **quantity demanded** of cotton—the actual amount consumers are willing to buy at some specific price—falls.

The graph in Figure 4-1 is a visual representation of the information in the table. (For a refresher on graphs in economics, see Appendix A at the back of the book.) The vertical axis shows the price of a pound of cotton and the horizontal axis shows the quantity of cotton in pounds. Each point on the graph corresponds to one of the entries in the table. The curve that connects these points is a **demand curve.** A demand curve is a graphical representation of the demand schedule, another way of showing the relationship between the quantity demanded and the price.

A **demand schedule** shows how much of a good or service consumers will want to buy at different prices.

The **quantity demanded** is the actual amount of a good or service consumers are willing to buy at some specific price.

A **demand curve** is a graphical representation of the demand schedule. It shows the relationship between quantity demanded and price.

4-1   The Demand Schedule and the Demand Curve

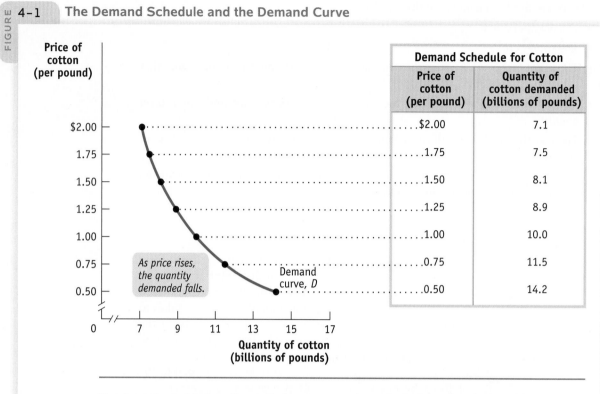

Demand Schedule for Cotton	
Price of cotton (per pound)	Quantity of cotton demanded (billions of pounds)
$2.00	7.1
1.75	7.5
1.50	8.1
1.25	8.9
1.00	10.0
0.75	11.5
0.50	14.2

The demand schedule for cotton yields the corresponding demand curve, which shows how much of a good or service consumers want to buy at any given price. The demand curve and the demand schedule reflect the law of demand: as price rises, the quantity demanded falls. Similarly, a fall in price raises the quantity demanded. As a result, the demand curve is downward sloping.

The **law of demand** says that a higher price for a good or service, all other things being equal, leads people to demand a smaller quantity of that good or service.

Higher prices for jeans will reduce the quantity demanded.

Note that the demand curve shown in Figure 4-1 slopes downward. This reflects the general proposition that a higher price reduces the quantity demanded. For example, jeans-makers know that they will sell fewer pairs when the price of a pair of jeans is higher, reflecting a $2 price for a pound of cotton, compared to the number they will sell when the price of a pair is lower, reflecting a price of only $1 for a pound of cotton. In the real world, demand curves almost always *do* slope downward. (The exceptions are so rare that for practical purposes we can ignore them.) Generally, the proposition that a higher price for a good, all other things equal, leads people to demand a smaller quantity of that good is so reliable that economists are willing to call it a "law"—the **law of demand.**

Shifts of the Demand Curve

Even though cotton prices in 2010 were higher than they had been in 2007, total world consumption of cotton was higher in 2010. How can we reconcile this fact with the law of demand, which says that a higher price reduces the quantity demanded, all other things being equal?

The answer lies in the crucial phrase all other things being equal. In this case, all other things weren't equal: the world had changed between 2007 and 2010, in ways that increased the quantity of cotton demanded at any given price. For one thing, the world's population, and therefore the number of potential cotton clothing wearers, increased. In addition, the growing popularity of cotton clothing, as well as higher incomes in countries like China that allowed people to buy more clothing than before, led to an increase in the quantity of cotton demanded at any given price. Figure 4-2 illustrates this

FIGURE **4-2**   **An Increase in Demand**

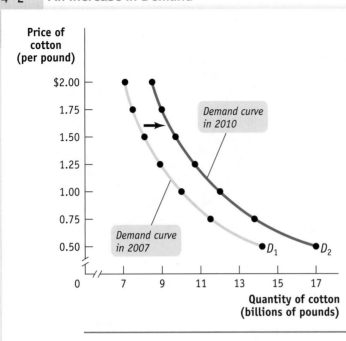

Demand Schedules for Cotton		
Price of cotton (per pound)	Quantity of cotton demanded (billions of pounds)	
	in 2007	in 2010
$2.00	7.1	8.5
1.75	7.5	9.0
1.50	8.1	9.7
1.25	8.9	10.7
1.00	10.0	12.0
0.75	11.5	13.8
0.50	14.2	17.0

An increase in the population is one factor that generates an increase in demand—a rise in the quantity demanded at any given price. This is represented by the two demand schedules—one showing demand in 2007, before the rise in popu- lation, the other showing demand in 2010, after the rise in population—and their corresponding demand curves. The increase in demand shifts the demand curve to the right.

phenomenon using the demand schedule and demand curve for cotton. (As before, the numbers in Figure 4-2 are hypothetical.)

The table in Figure 4-2 shows two demand schedules. The first is the demand sched- ule for 2007, the same as shown in Figure 4-1. The second is the demand schedule for 2010. It differs from the 2007 demand schedule due to factors such as a larger popula- tion and the increased popularity of cotton clothing, factors that led to an increase in the quantity of cotton demanded at any given price. So at each price the 2010 schedule shows a larger quantity demanded than the 2007 schedule. For example, the quantity of cotton consumers wanted to buy at a price of $1 per pound increased from 10 bil- lion to 12 billion pounds per year, the quantity demanded at $1.25 per pound went from 8.9 billion to 10.7 billion, and so on.

What is clear from this example is that the changes that occurred between 2007 and 2010 generated a *new* demand schedule, one in which the quantity demanded was greater at any given price than in the original demand schedule. The two curves in Figure 4-2 show the same information graphically. As you can see, the demand sched- ule for 2010 corresponds to a new demand curve, D_2, that is to the right of the demand schedule for 2007, D_1. This **change in demand** shows the increase in the quantity de- manded at any given price, represented by the shift in position of the original demand curve D_1 to its new location at D_2.

It's crucial to make the distinction between such changes in demand and **movements along the demand curve,** changes in the quantity demanded of a good that result from a change in that good's price. Figure 4-3 illustrates the difference.

The movement from point *A* to point *B* is a movement along the demand curve: the quantity demanded rises due to a fall in price as you move down D_1. Here, a fall in the price of cotton from $1.50 to $1 per pound generates a rise in the quantity demanded from 8.1 billion to 10 billion pounds per year. But the quantity demanded can also rise when the price is unchanged if there is an *increase in demand*—a rightward shift

A **change in demand** is a shift of the demand curve, which changes the quantity demanded at any given price.

A **movement along the demand curve** is a change in the quantity de- manded of a good that is the result of a change in that good's price.

FIGURE 4-3   Movement Along the Demand Curve versus Shift of the Demand Curve

The rise in quantity demanded when going from point A to point B reflects a movement along the demand curve: it is the result of a fall in the price of the good. The rise in quantity demanded when going from point A to point C reflects a shift of the demand curve: it is the result of a rise in the quantity demanded at any given price.

of the demand curve. This is illustrated in Figure 4-3 by the shift of the demand curve from D_1 to D_2. Holding the price constant at $1.50 a pound, the quantity demanded rises from 8.1 billion pounds at point A on D_1 to 9.7 billion pounds at point C on D_2.

When economists talk about a "change in demand," saying for example "the demand for X increased" or "the demand for Y decreased," they mean that the demand curve for X or Y shifted—*not* that the quantity demanded rose or fell because of a change in the price.

Understanding Shifts of the Demand Curve

Figure 4-4 illustrates the two basic ways in which demand curves can shift. When economists talk about an "increase in demand," they mean a *rightward* shift of the demand curve: at any given price, consumers demand a larger quantity of the good or service than before. This is shown by the rightward shift of the original demand curve D_1 to D_2. And when economists talk about a "decrease in demand," they mean a *leftward* shift of the demand curve: at any given price, consumers demand a smaller quantity of the good or service than before. This is shown by the leftward shift of the original demand curve D_1 to D_3.

What caused the demand curve for cotton to shift? We have already mentioned two reasons: changes in population and a change in the popularity of cotton clothing. If you think about it, you can come up with other things that would be likely to shift the demand curve for cotton. For example, suppose that the price of polyester rises. This will induce some people who previously bought polyester clothing to buy cotton clothing instead, increasing the demand for cotton.

Economists believe that there are five principal factors that shift the demand curve for a good or service:

- Changes in the prices of related goods or services
- Changes in income
- Changes in tastes
- Changes in expectations
- Changes in the number of consumers

FIGURE 4-4   Shifts of the Demand Curve

Any event that increases demand shifts the demand curve to the right, reflecting a rise in the quantity demanded at any given price. Any event that decreases demand shifts the demand curve to the left, reflecting a fall in the quantity demanded at any given price.

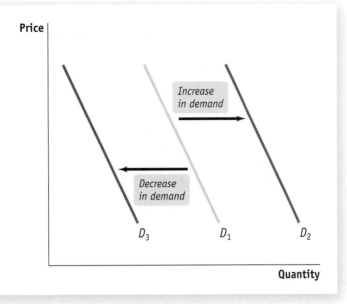

Although this is not an exhaustive list, it contains the five most important factors that can shift demand curves. So when we say that the quantity of a good or service demanded falls as its price rises, all other things being equal, we are in fact stating that the factors that shift demand are remaining unchanged. Let's now explore, in more detail, how those factors shift the demand curve.

CHANGES IN THE PRICES OF RELATED GOODS OR SERVICES While there's nothing quite like a comfortable pair of all-cotton blue jeans, for some purposes khakis—generally made from polyester blends—aren't a bad alternative. Khakis are what economists call a *substitute* for jeans. A pair of goods are **substitutes** if a rise in the price of one good (jeans) makes consumers more willing to buy the other good (khakis). Substitutes are usually goods that in some way serve a similar function: concerts and theater plays, muffins and doughnuts, train rides and air flights. A rise in the price of the alternative good induces some consumers to purchase the original good *instead* of it, shifting demand for the original good to the right.

But sometimes a rise in the price of one good makes consumers *less* willing to buy another good. Such pairs of goods are known as **complements.** Complements are usually goods that in some sense are consumed together: computers and software, cappuccinos and croissants, cars and gasoline. Because consumers like to consume a good and its complement together, a change in the price of one of the goods will affect the demand for its complement. In particular, when the price of one good rises, the demand for its complement decreases, shifting the demand curve for the complement to the left. So, for example, when the price of gasoline rises, the demand for gas-guzzling cars falls.

CHANGES IN INCOME When individuals have more income, they are normally more likely to purchase a good at any given price. For example, if a family's income rises, it is more likely to take that long-anticipated summer trip to Disney World—and therefore also more likely to buy plane tickets. So a rise in consumer incomes will cause the demand curves for most goods to shift to the right.

Two goods are substitutes if a rise in the price of one of the goods leads to an increase in the demand for the other good.

Two goods are complements if a rise in the price of one good leads to a decrease in the demand for the other good.

Sweatpants are also a substitute for jeans.

Thinkstock

When a rise in income increases the demand for a good—the normal case—it is a **normal good**.

When a rise in income decreases the demand for a good, it is an **inferior good**.

Why do we say "most goods," not "all goods"? Most goods are **normal goods**—the demand for them increases when consumer income rises. However, the demand for some products falls when income rises. Goods for which demand decreases when income rises are known as **inferior goods.** Usually an inferior good is one that is considered less desirable than more expensive alternatives—such as a bus ride versus a taxi ride. When they can afford to, people stop buying an inferior good and switch their consumption to the preferred, more expensive alternative. So when a good is inferior, a rise in income shifts the demand curve to the left. And, not surprisingly, a fall in income shifts the demand curve for inferior goods to the right.

One example of the distinction between normal and inferior goods that has drawn considerable attention in the business press is the difference between so-called casual-dining restaurants such as Applebee's or Olive Garden and fast-food chains such as McDonald's and KFC. When their incomes rise, Americans tend to eat out more at casual-dining restaurants. However, some of this increased dining out comes at the expense of fast-food venues—to some extent, people visit McDonald's less once they can afford to move upscale. So casual dining is a normal good, while fast-food appears to be an inferior good.

CHANGES IN TASTES Why do people want what they want? Fortunately, we don't need to answer that question—we just need to acknowledge that people have certain preferences, or tastes, that determine what they choose to consume and that these tastes can change. Economists usually lump together changes in demand due to fads, beliefs, cultural shifts, and so on under the heading of changes in *tastes* or *preferences*.

As tastes change, styles come and go.

For example, once upon a time men wore hats. Up until around World War II, a respectable man wasn't fully dressed unless he wore a dignified hat along with his suit. But the returning GIs adopted a more informal style, perhaps due to the rigors of the war. And President Eisenhower, who had been supreme commander of Allied Forces before becoming president, often went hatless. After World War II, it was clear that the demand curve for hats had shifted leftward, reflecting a decrease in the demand for hats.

Economists have relatively little to say about the forces that influence consumers' tastes. (Marketers and advertisers, however, have plenty to say about them!) However, a *change* in tastes has a predictable impact on demand. When tastes change in favor of a good, more people want to buy it at any given price, so the demand curve shifts to the right. When tastes change against a good, fewer people want to buy it at any given price, so the demand curve shifts to the left.

CHANGES IN EXPECTATIONS When consumers have some choice about when to make a purchase, current demand for a good is often affected by expectations about its future price. For example, savvy shoppers often wait for seasonal sales—say, buying next year's holiday gifts during the post-holiday markdowns. In this case, expectations of a future drop in price lead to a decrease in demand today. Alternatively, expectations of a future rise in price are likely to cause an increase in demand today. For example, as cotton prices began to rise in 2010, many textile mills began purchasing more cotton and stockpiling it in anticipation of further price increases.

Expected changes in future income can also lead to changes in demand: if you expect your income to rise in the future, you will typically borrow today and increase your demand for certain goods; if you expect your income to fall in the future, you are more likely to save today and reduce your demand for some goods.

CHANGES IN THE NUMBER OF CONSUMERS As we've already noted, one of the reasons for rising cotton demand between 2007 and 2010 was a growing world population.

Because of population growth, overall demand for cotton would have risen even if the demand of each individual wearer of cotton clothing had remained unchanged.

Let's introduce a new concept: the **individual demand curve,** which shows the relationship between quantity demanded and price for an individual consumer. For example, suppose that Darla is a consumer of cotton blue jeans; also suppose that all pairs of jeans are the same, so they sell for the same price. Panel (a) of Figure 4-5 shows how many pairs of jeans she will buy per year at any given price. Then D_{Darla} is Darla's individual demand curve.

The *market demand curve* shows how the combined quantity demanded by all consumers depends on the market price of that good. (Most of the time, when economists refer to the demand curve, they mean the market demand curve.) The market demand curve is the *horizontal sum* of the individual demand curves of all consumers in that market.

> An **individual demand curve** illustrates the relationship between quantity demanded and price for an individual consumer.

FIGURE 4-5   Individual Demand Curves and the Market Demand Curve

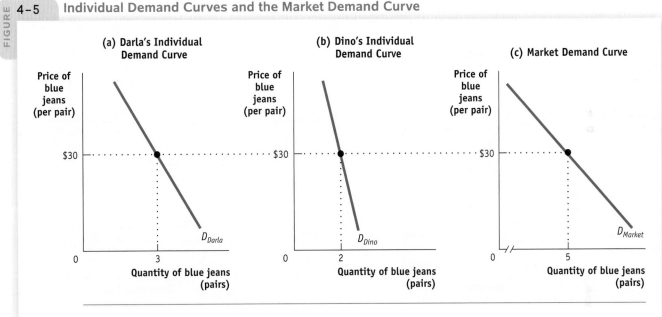

Darla and Dino are the only two consumers of blue jeans in the market. Panel (a) shows Darla's individual demand curve: the number of pairs of blue jeans she will buy per year at any given price. Panel (b) shows Dino's individual demand curve. Given that Darla and Dino are the only two consumers, the *market demand curve*, which shows the quantity of blue jeans demanded by all consumers at any given price, is shown in panel (c). The market demand curve is the *horizontal sum* of the individual demand curves of all consumers. In this case, at any given price, the quantity demanded by the market is the sum of the quantities demanded by Darla and Dino.

To see what we mean by the term *horizontal sum*, assume for a moment that there are only two consumers of blue jeans, Darla and Dino. Dino's individual demand curve, D_{Dino}, is shown in panel (b). Panel (c) shows the market demand curve. At any given price, the quantity demanded by the market is the sum of the quantities demanded by Darla and Dino. For example, at a price of $30 per pair, Darla demands 3 pairs of jeans per year and Dino demands 2 pairs per year. So the quantity demanded by the market is 5 pairs per year.

Clearly, the quantity demanded by the market at any given price is larger with Dino present than it would be if Darla were the only consumer. The quantity demanded at any given price would be even larger if we added a third consumer, then a fourth, and so on. So an increase in the number of consumers leads to an increase in demand.

For a review of the factors that shift demand, see Table 4-1.

TABLE 4-1

Factors That Shift Demand

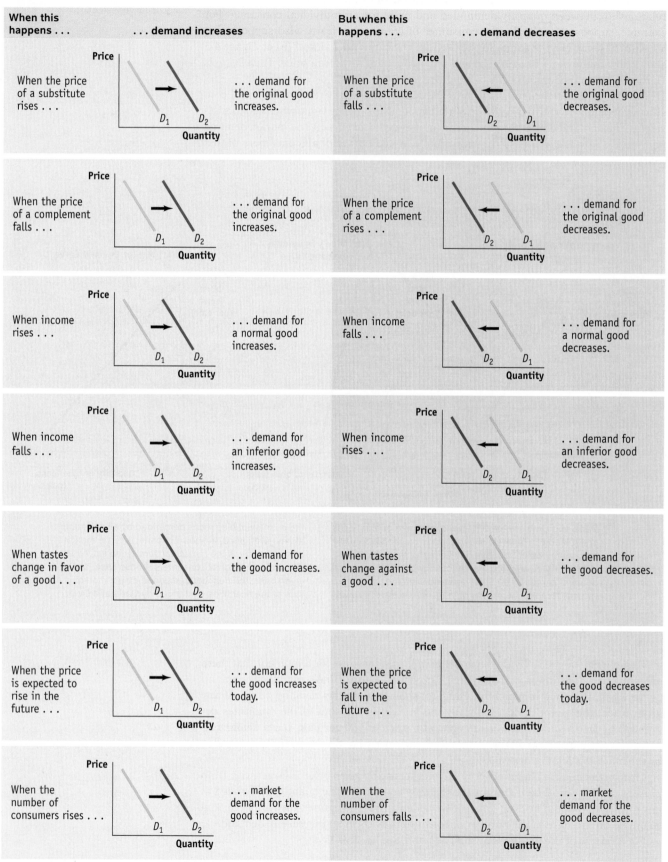

ECONOMICS ▶ IN ACTION

WORLD VIEW

BEATING THE TRAFFIC

All big cities have traffic problems, and many local authorities try to discourage driving in the crowded city center. If we think of an auto trip to the city center as a good that people consume, we can use the economics of demand to analyze anti-traffic policies.

One common strategy is to reduce the demand for auto trips by lowering the prices of substitutes. Many metropolitan areas subsidize bus and rail service, hoping to lure commuters out of their cars. An alternative is to raise the price of complements: several major U.S. cities impose high taxes on commercial parking garages and impose short time limits on parking meters, both to raise revenue and to discourage people from driving into the city.

A few major cities—including Singapore, London, Oslo, Stockholm, and Milan—have been willing to adopt a direct and politically controversial approach: reducing congestion by raising the price of driving. Under "congestion pricing" (or "congestion charging" in the United Kingdom), a charge is imposed on cars entering the city center during business hours. Drivers buy passes, which are then debited electronically as they drive by monitoring stations. Compliance is monitored with automatic cameras that photograph license plates.

The current daily cost of driving in London ranges from £8 to £10 (about $13 to $16). And drivers who don't pay and are caught pay a fine of £120 (about $195) for each transgression.

Not surprisingly, studies have shown that after the implementation of congestion pricing, traffic does indeed decrease. In the 1990s, London had some of the worst traffic in Europe. The introduction of its congestion charge in 2003 immediately reduced traffic in the London city center by about 15%, with overall traffic falling by 21% between 2002 and 2006. And there was increased use of substitutes, such as public transportation, bicycles, motorbikes, and ride-sharing.

In the United States, the U.S. Department of Transportation has implemented pilot programs to study congestion pricing. The programs were so successful that congestion pricing has become policy in some states. Other states, taking suggestions from traffic experts, are trying variable congestion prices, raising prices during peak commuting hours. So even though congestion pricing has been controversial, it appears to be gaining acceptance.

Cities can reduce traffic congestion by raising the price of driving.

MODULE 4 Review

Solutions appear at the back of the book.

Check Your Understanding

1. Explain whether each of the following events represents (i) a *change in demand* (a *shift of* the demand curve) or (ii) a *change in the quantity demanded* (a *movement along* the demand curve).

   a. A store owner finds that customers are willing to pay more for umbrellas on rainy days.

   b. When XYZ Telecom, a long-distance telephone service provider, offered reduced rates on weekends, its volume of weekend calling increased sharply.

   c. People buy more long-stem roses the week of Valentine's Day, even though the prices are higher than at other times during the year.

   d. A sharp rise in the price of gasoline leads many commuters to join carpools in order to reduce their gasoline purchases.

Multiple-Choice Questions

1. Which of the following would increase demand for a normal good? A decrease in
   a. price.
   b. income.
   c. the price of a substitute.
   d. consumer taste for a good.
   e. the price of a complement.

2. A decrease in the price of butter would most likely decrease the demand for
   a. margarine.
   b. bagels.
   c. jelly.
   d. milk.
   e. syrup.

3. If an increase in income leads to a decrease in demand, the good is
   a. a complement.
   b. a substitute.
   c. inferior.
   d. abnormal.
   e. normal.

Critical-Thinking Question

Draw a graph showing the demand for apples. On your graph, illustrate what happens to the demand for apples if a new report from the Surgeon General finds that an apple a day really *does* keep the doctor away.

4. Which of the following will occur if consumers expect the price of a good to fall in the coming months?
   a. The quantity demanded will rise today.
   b. The quantity demanded will remain the same today.
   c. Demand will increase today.
   d. Demand will decrease today.
   e. No change will occur today.

5. Which of the following will increase the demand for disposable diapers?
   a. a new "baby boom"
   b. concern over the environmental effect of landfills
   c. a decrease in the price of cloth diapers
   d. a move toward earlier potty training of children
   e. a decrease in the price of disposable diapers

PITFALLS

DEMAND VERSUS QUANTITY DEMANDED

(?) Consider how the term *demand* is used in the following sentence. Why is the sentence incorrect?

If the price of the good goes up then people will buy less and this will lead to a fall in demand which shifts the demand curve to the left.

(>) THIS STATEMENT MISTAKES A CHANGE IN QUANTITY DEMANDED FOR A CHANGE IN DEMAND. WHEN DOING ECONOMIC ANALYSIS, IT IS IMPORTANT TO MAKE THE DISTINCTION BETWEEN CHANGES IN *DEMAND*, WHICH MEAN SHIFTS OF THE DEMAND CURVE, AND CHANGES IN *QUANTITY DEMANDED*. When economists say "an increase in demand," they mean a rightward shift of the demand curve, and when they say "a decrease in demand," they mean a leftward shift of the demand curve—that is, when they're being careful. In ordinary speech, most people, including professional economists, use the word *demand* casually. For example, an economist might say "the demand for air travel has doubled over the past fifteen years, partly because of falling airfares" when he or she really means that the *quantity demanded* has doubled. The key point to remember is that a change in price causes a *movement along the demand curve*, and not a shift of the demand curve.

To learn more, see Figure 4-3 for an illustration of a movement along the demand curve versus a shift of the demand curve. For an explanation of the difference, see pages 35–36.

Supply and Equilibrium

WHAT YOU WILL LEARN

1 What the supply curve is

2 The difference between movements along the supply curve and changes in supply

3 The factors that shift the supply curve

4 How supply and demand curves determine a market's equilibrium price and equilibrium quantity

5 In the case of a shortage or surplus, how price moves the market back to equilibrium

The Supply Curve

Some parts of the world are especially well suited to growing cotton, and the United States is one of those. But even in the United States, some land is better suited to growing cotton than other land. Whether American farmers restrict their cotton-growing to only the most ideal locations or expand it to less suitable land depends on the price they expect to get for their cotton. Moreover, there are many other areas in the world where cotton could be grown—such as Pakistan, Brazil, Turkey, and China. Whether farmers there actually grow cotton depends, again, on the price.

So just as the quantity of cotton that consumers want to buy depends on the price they have to pay, the quantity that producers are willing to produce and sell—the **quantity supplied**—depends on the price they are offered.

The Supply Schedule and the Supply Curve

The table in Figure 5-1 shows how the quantity of cotton made available varies with the price—that is, it shows a hypothetical **supply schedule** for cotton.

A supply schedule works the same way as the demand schedule shown in Figure 4-1 (page 34): in this case, the table shows the number of pounds of cotton farmers are willing to sell at different prices. At a price of $0.50 per pound, farmers are willing to sell only 8 billion pounds of cotton per year. At $0.75 per pound, they're willing to sell 9.1 billion pounds. At $1, they're willing to sell 10 billion pounds, and so on.

In the same way that a demand schedule can be represented graphically by a demand curve, a supply schedule can be represented by a **supply curve**, as shown in Figure 5-1. Each point on the curve represents an entry from the table.

Suppose that the price of cotton rises from $1 to $1.25; we can see that the quantity of cotton farmers are willing to sell rises from 10 billion to 10.7 billion pounds. This

The **quantity supplied** is the actual amount of a good or service people are willing to sell at some specific price.

A **supply schedule** shows how much of a good or service would be supplied at different prices.

A **supply curve** shows the relationship between quantity supplied and price.

5-1   The Supply Schedule and the Supply Curve

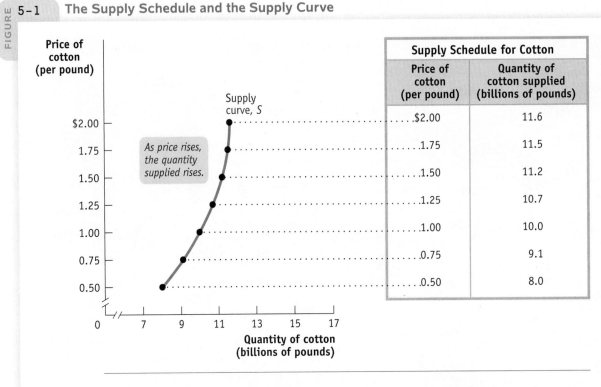

Supply Schedule for Cotton	
Price of cotton (per pound)	Quantity of cotton supplied (billions of pounds)
$2.00	11.6
1.75	11.5
1.50	11.2
1.25	10.7
1.00	10.0
0.75	9.1
0.50	8.0

The supply schedule for cotton is plotted to yield the corresponding supply curve, which shows how much of a good producers are willing to sell at any given price. The supply curve and the sup- ply schedule reflect the fact that supply curves are usually upward sloping: the quantity supplied rises when the price rises.

is the normal situation for a supply curve, reflecting the general proposition that a higher price leads to a higher quantity supplied. Some economists refer to this relationship as the **law of supply.**

Shifts of the Supply Curve

Until recently, cotton remained relatively cheap for several decades. One reason is that the amount of land cultivated for cotton expanded by more than 35% from 1945 to 2007. However, the major factor accounting for cotton's relative cheapness was advances in the production technology, with output per acre more than quadrupling from 1945 to 2007. Figure 5-2 illustrates these events in terms of the supply schedule and the supply curve for cotton.

The table in Figure 5-2 shows two supply schedules. The schedule before improved cotton-growing technology was adopted is the same one as in Figure 5-1. The second schedule shows the supply of cotton *after* the improved technology was adopted. Just as a change in demand schedules leads to a shift of the demand curve, a change in supply schedules leads to a shift of the supply curve—a **change in supply.** This is shown in Figure 5-2 by the shift of the supply curve before the adoption of new cotton-growing technology, S_1, to its new position after the adoption of new cotton-growing technology, S_2. Notice that S_2 lies to the right of S_1, a reflection of the fact that quantity supplied rises at any given price.

As in the analysis of demand, it's crucial to draw a distinction between such shifts of the supply curve and **movements along the supply curve**—changes in the quantity supplied arising from a change in price. We can see this difference in Figure 5-3. The movement from point *A* to point *B* is a movement along the supply curve: the quantity supplied rises along S_1 due to a rise in price. Here, a rise in price from $1 to

The **law of supply** is the general proposition that, all else constant, a higher price leads to higher quantity supplied, and a lower price leads to lower quantity supplied.

A **change in supply** is a shift of the supply curve, which changes the quantity supplied at any given price.

A **movement along the supply curve** is a change in the quantity supplied of a good arising from a change in the good's price.

FIGURE 5-2   An Increase in Supply

Price of cotton (per pound)

S_1 S_2

Supply curve before new technology

Supply curve after new technology

0   7   9   11   13   15   17

Quantity of cotton (billions of pounds)

	Supply Schedules for Cotton	
Price of cotton (per pound)	Quantity of cotton supplied (billions of pounds)	
	Before new technology	After new technology
$2.00	11.6	13.9
1.75	11.5	13.8
1.50	11.2	13.4
1.25	10.7	12.8
1.00	10.0	12.0
0.75	9.1	10.9
0.50	8.0	9.6

The adoption of improved cotton-growing technology generated an increase in supply—a rise in the quantity supplied at any given price. This event is represented by the two supply schedules—one showing supply before the new technology was adopted, the other showing supply after the new technology was adopted—and their corresponding supply curves. The increase in supply shifts the supply curve to the right.

$1.50 leads to a rise in the quantity supplied from 10 billion to 11.2 billion pounds of cotton. But the quantity supplied can also rise when the price is unchanged if there is an increase in supply—a rightward shift of the supply curve. This is shown by the rightward shift of the supply curve from S_1 to S_2. Holding the price constant at $1, the quantity supplied rises from 10 billion pounds at point A on S_1 to 12 billion pounds at point C on S_2.

FIGURE 5-3   Movement Along the Supply Curve versus Shift of the Supply Curve

The increase in quantity supplied when going from point A to point B reflects a movement along the supply curve: it is the result of a rise in the price of the good. The increase in quantity supplied when going from point A to point C reflects a shift of the supply curve: it is the result of an increase in the quantity supplied at any given price.

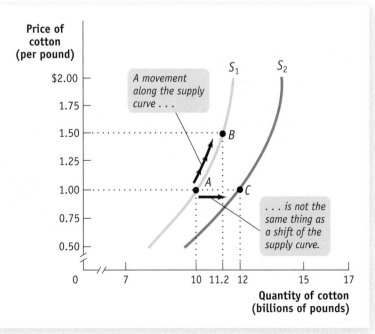

Price of cotton (per pound)

A movement along the supply curve . . .

S_1 S_2

. . . is not the same thing as a shift of the supply curve.

0   7   10 11.2 12   15   17

Quantity of cotton (billions of pounds)

An **input** is a good or service that
is used to produce another good or
service.

Understanding Shifts of the Supply Curve

Figure 5-4 illustrates the two basic ways in which supply curves can shift. When economists talk about an "increase in supply," they mean a *rightward* shift of the supply curve: at any given price, producers supply a larger quantity of the good than before. This is shown in Figure 5-4 by the rightward shift of the original supply curve S_1 to S_2. And when economists talk about a "decrease in supply," they mean a *leftward* shift of the supply curve: at any given price, producers supply a smaller quantity of the good than before. This is represented by the leftward shift of S_1 to S_3.

Economists believe that shifts of the supply curve for a good or service are mainly the result of five factors (though, as in the case of demand, there are other possible causes):

- Changes in input prices
- Changes in the prices of related goods or services
- Changes in technology
- Changes in expectations
- Changes in the number of producers

CHANGES IN INPUT PRICES To produce output, you need inputs. For example, to make vanilla ice cream, you need vanilla beans, cream, sugar, and so on. An **input** is any good or service that is used to produce another good or service. Inputs, like outputs, have prices. And an increase in the price of an input makes the production of the final good more costly for those who produce and sell it. So producers are less willing to supply the final good at any given price, and the supply curve shifts to the left. For example, fuel is a major cost for airlines. When oil prices surged in 2007–2008, airlines began cutting back on their flight schedules and some went out of business. Similarly, a fall in the price of an input makes the production of the final good less costly for sellers. They are more willing to supply the good at any given price, and the supply curve shifts to the right.

CHANGES IN THE PRICES OF RELATED GOODS OR SERVICES A single producer often produces a mix of goods rather than a single product. For example, an oil refinery produces gasoline from crude oil, but it also produces heating oil and other products

FIGURE 5-4   **Shifts of the Supply Curve**

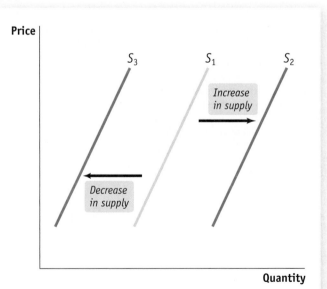

Any event that increases supply shifts the supply curve to the right, reflecting a rise in the quantity supplied at any given price. Any event that decreases supply shifts the supply curve to the left, reflecting a fall in the quantity supplied at any given price.

from the same raw material. When a producer sells several products, the quantity of any one good it is willing to supply at any given price depends on the prices of its other co-produced goods.

This effect can run in either direction. An oil refiner will supply less gasoline at any given price when the market price of heating oil rises, shifting the supply curve for gasoline to the left. But it will supply more gasoline at any given price when the market price of heating oil falls, shifting the supply curve for gasoline to the right. This means that gasoline and other co-produced oil products are *substitutes in production* for refiners.

In contrast, due to the nature of the production process, other goods can be *complements in production*. For example, producers of crude oil—oil-well drillers—often find that oil wells also produce natural gas as a by-product of oil extraction. The higher the price at which a driller can sell its natural gas, the more oil wells it will drill and the more oil it will supply at any given price for oil. As a result, natural gas is a complement in production for crude oil.

CHANGES IN TECHNOLOGY When economists talk about "technology," they don't necessarily mean high tech—they mean all the methods people can use to turn inputs into useful goods and services. In that sense, the whole complex sequence of activities that turn cotton from Pakistan into the pair of jeans hanging in your closet is technology.

Improvements in technology enable producers to sell more of their product at the same price. When a better technology becomes available, reducing the cost of production, supply increases, and the supply curve shifts to the right. Improved technology enabled farmers to more than quadruple cotton output per acre planted over the past several decades. Improved technology is also the main reason that, until recently, cotton remained relatively cheap even as worldwide demand grew.

CHANGES IN EXPECTATIONS Just as changes in expectations can shift the demand curve, they can also shift the supply curve. When suppliers have some choice about when they put their good up for sale, changes in the expected future price of the good can lead a supplier to supply less or more of the good today.

For example, consider the fact that gasoline and other oil products are often stored for significant periods of time at oil refineries before being sold to consumers. In fact, storage is usually part of producers' business strategy. Knowing that the demand for gasoline peaks in the summer, oil refiners usually store some of their gasoline produced during the spring for summer sale. Similarly, knowing that the demand for heating oil peaks in the winter, they usually store some of their heating oil produced during the fall for winter sale. In each case, there's a decision to be made between selling the product now versus storing it for later sale. Which choice a producer makes depends on a comparison of the current price versus the expected future price. This example illustrates how changes in expectations can alter supply: an increase in the anticipated future price of a good or service reduces supply today, a leftward shift of the supply curve. But a fall in the anticipated future price increases supply today, a rightward shift of the supply curve.

CHANGES IN THE NUMBER OF PRODUCERS Just as changes in the number of consumers affect the demand curve, changes in the number of producers affect the supply curve. Let's examine the **individual supply curve,** which shows the relationship between quantity supplied and price for an individual producer. For example, suppose

An **individual supply curve** illustrates the relationship between quantity supplied and price for an individual producer.

that Mr. Silva is a Brazilian cotton farmer and that panel (a) of Figure 5-5 shows how many pounds of cotton he will supply per year at any given price. Then S_{Silva} is his individual supply curve.

The *market supply curve* shows how the combined total quantity supplied by all individual producers in the market depends on the market price of that good. Just as the market demand curve is the horizontal sum of the individual demand curves of all consumers, the market supply curve is the horizontal sum of the individual supply curves of all producers.

Assume for a moment that there are only two producers of cotton, Mr. Silva and Mr. Liu, a Chinese cotton farmer. Mr. Liu's individual supply curve is shown in panel (b). Panel (c) shows the market supply curve. At any given price, the quantity supplied to the market is the sum of the quantities supplied by Mr. Silva and Mr. Liu. For example, at a price of $2 per pound, Mr. Silva supplies 3,000 pounds of cotton per year and Mr. Liu supplies 2,000 pounds per year, making the quantity supplied to the market 5,000 pounds.

FIGURE 5-5   The Individual Supply Curve and the Market Supply Curve

Panel (a) shows the individual supply curve for Mr. Silva, S_{Silva}, the quantity of cotton he will sell at any given price. Panel (b) shows the individual supply curve for Mr. Liu, S_{Liu}. The market supply curve, which shows the quantity of cotton supplied by all producers at any given price, is shown in panel (c). The market supply curve is the horizontal sum of the individual supply curves of all producers.

Clearly, the quantity supplied to the market at any given price is larger with Mr. Liu present than it would be if Mr. Silva were the only supplier. The quantity supplied at a given price would be even larger if we added a third producer, then a fourth, and so on. So an increase in the number of producers leads to an increase in supply and a rightward shift of the supply curve.

For a review of the factors that shift supply, see Table 5-1.

TABLE 5-1

Factors That Shift Supply

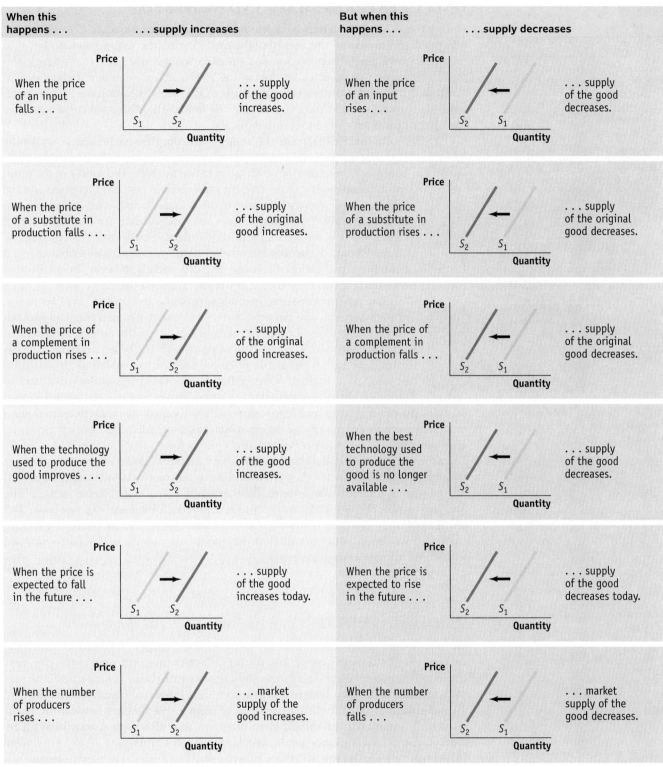

When this happens . . .	. . . supply increases	But when this happens . . .	. . . supply decreases
When the price of an input falls . . .	. . . supply of the good increases.	When the price of an input rises . . .	. . . supply of the good decreases.
When the price of a substitute in production falls . . .	. . . supply of the original good increases.	When the price of a substitute in production rises . . .	. . . supply of the original good decreases.
When the price of a complement in production rises . . .	. . . supply of the original good increases.	When the price of a complement in production falls . . .	. . . supply of the original good decreases.
When the technology used to produce the good improves . . .	. . . supply of the good increases.	When the best technology used to produce the good is no longer available . . .	. . . supply of the good decreases.
When the price is expected to fall in the future . . .	. . . supply of the good increases today.	When the price is expected to rise in the future . . .	. . . supply of the good decreases today.
When the number of producers rises . . .	. . . market supply of the good increases.	When the number of producers falls . . .	. . . market supply of the good decreases.

ECONOMICS ▶ IN ACTION

WORLD VIEW

ONLY CREATURES SMALL AND PAMPERED

During the 1970s, British television featured a popular show titled *All Creatures Great and Small*. It chronicled the real life of James Herriot, a country veterinarian who tended to cows, pigs, sheep, horses, and the occasional house pet, often under arduous conditions, in rural England during the 1930s. The show made it clear that in those days the local vet was a critical member of farming communities, saving valuable farm animals and helping farmers survive financially. And it was also clear that Mr. Herriot considered his life's work well spent.

Higher spending on pets means fewer veterinarians are available to tend to farm animals.

But that was then and this is now. According to a recent article in the *New York Times*, the United States has experienced a severe decline in the number of farm veterinarians over the past two decades. The source of the problem is competition. As the number of household pets has increased and the incomes of pet owners have grown, the demand for pet veterinarians has increased sharply. As a result, vets are being drawn away from the business of caring for farm animals into the more lucrative business of caring for pets. As one vet stated, she began her career caring for farm animals but changed her mind after "doing a C-section on a cow and it's 50 bucks. Do a C-section on a Chihuahua and you get $300. It's the money. I hate to say that."

How can we translate this into supply and demand curves? Farm veterinary services and pet veterinary services are like gasoline and fuel oil: they're related goods that are substitutes in production. A veterinarian typically specializes in one type of practice or the other, and that decision often depends on the going price for the service. America's growing pet population, combined with the increased willingness of doting owners to spend on their companions' care, has driven up the price of pet veterinary services. As a result, fewer and fewer veterinarians have gone into farm animal practice. So the supply curve of farm veterinarians has shifted leftward—fewer farm veterinarians are offering their services at any given price.

In the end, farmers understand that it is all a matter of dollars and cents; they get fewer veterinarians because they are unwilling to pay more. As one farmer, who had recently lost an expensive cow due to the unavailability of a veterinarian, stated, "The fact that there's nothing you can do, you accept it as a business expense now. You didn't used to. If you have livestock, sooner or later you're going to have deadstock." (Although we should note that this farmer could have chosen to pay more for a vet who would have then saved his cow.)

Supply, Demand, and Equilibrium

We have now covered the first three key elements in the supply and demand model: the demand curve, the supply curve, and the set of factors that shift each curve. The next step is to put these elements together to show how they can be used to predict the actual price at which the good is bought and sold, as well as the actual quantity transacted.

In competitive markets this interaction of supply and demand tends to move toward what economists call *equilibrium*. Imagine a busy afternoon at your local supermarket; there are long lines at the checkout counters. Then one of the previously closed registers opens. The first thing that happens is a rush to the newly opened register. But soon enough things settle down and shoppers have rearranged themselves so that the line at the newly opened register is about as long as all the others. This situation—all the checkout lines are now the same length, and none of the shoppers can be better off by doing something different—is what economists call **equilibrium.**

The concept of equilibrium helps us understand the price at which a good or service is bought and sold as well as the quantity transacted of the good or service. A

An economic situation is in **equilibrium** when no individual would be better off doing something different.

iStockphoto/Thinkstock

competitive market is in equilibrium when the price has moved to a level at which the quantity of a good demanded equals the quantity of that good supplied. At that price, no individual seller could make herself better off by offering to sell either more or less of the good and no individual buyer could make himself better off by offering to buy more or less of the good. Think of shoppers at the supermarket who cannot make themselves better off (cannot save time) by changing lines. Similarly, at the market equilibrium, the price has moved to a level that exactly matches the quantity demanded by consumers to the quantity supplied by sellers.

The price that matches the quantity supplied and the quantity demanded is the **equilibrium price;** the quantity bought and sold at that price is the **equilibrium quantity.** The equilibrium price is also known as the **market-clearing price:** it is the price that "clears the market" by ensuring that every buyer willing to pay that price finds a seller willing to sell at that price, and vice versa. So how do we find the equilibrium price and quantity?

Finding the Equilibrium Price and Quantity

The easiest way to determine the equilibrium price and quantity in a market is by putting the supply curve and the demand curve on the same diagram. Since the supply curve shows the quantity supplied at any given price and the demand curve shows the quantity demanded at any given price, the price at which the two curves cross is the equilibrium price: the price at which quantity supplied equals quantity demanded.

Figure 5-6 combines the demand curve from Figure 4-1 (page 34) and the supply curve from Figure 5-1. They *intersect* at point *E*, which is the equilibrium of this market; $1 is the equilibrium price and 10 billion pounds is the equilibrium quantity.

Let's confirm that point *E* fits our definition of equilibrium. At a price of $1 per pound, cotton farmers are willing to sell 10 billion pounds a year and cotton consumers want to buy 10 billion pounds a year. So at the price of $1 a pound, the quantity of cotton supplied equals the quantity demanded. Notice that at any other price the market would not clear: every willing buyer would not be able to find a willing seller, or vice versa. More specifically, if the price were more than $1, the quantity supplied would exceed the quantity demanded; if the price were less than $1, the quantity demanded would exceed the quantity supplied.

A competitive market is in equilibrium when price has moved to a level at which the quantity demanded of a good equals the quantity supplied of that good. The price at which this takes place is the **equilibrium price,** also referred to as the **market-clearing price.** The quantity of the good bought and sold at that price is the **equilibrium quantity.**

FIGURE 5-6 **Market Equilibrium**

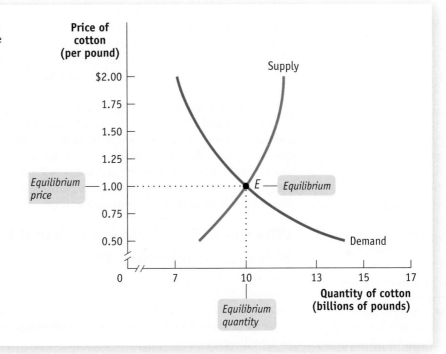

Market equilibrium occurs at point *E*, where the supply curve and the demand curve intersect. In equilibrium, the quantity demanded is equal to the quantity supplied. In this market, the equilibrium price is $1 per pound and the equilibrium quantity is 10 billion pounds per year.

The model of supply and demand, then, predicts that given the demand and supply curves shown in Figure 5-6, 10 billion pounds of cotton would change hands at a price of $1 per pound. But how can we be sure that the market will arrive at the equilibrium price? We begin by answering three simple questions:

1. Why do all sales and purchases in a market take place at the same price?

2. Why does the market price fall if it is above the equilibrium price?

3. Why does the market price rise if it is below the equilibrium price?

Why Do All Sales and Purchases in a Market Take Place at the Same Price?

There are some markets where the same good can sell for many different prices, depending on who is selling or who is buying. For example, have you ever bought a souvenir in a "tourist trap" and then seen the same item on sale somewhere else (perhaps even in the shop next door) for a lower price? Because tourists don't know which shops offer the best deals and don't have time for comparison shopping, sellers in tourist areas can charge different prices for the same good.

But in any market where the buyers and sellers have both been around for some time, sales and purchases tend to converge at a generally uniform price, so we can safely talk about *the* market price. It's easy to see why. Suppose a seller offered a potential buyer a price noticeably above what the buyer knew other people to be paying. The buyer would clearly be better off shopping elsewhere—unless the seller were prepared to offer a better deal. Conversely, a seller would not be willing to sell for significantly less than the amount he knew most buyers were paying; he would be better off waiting to get a more reasonable customer. So in any well-established, ongoing market, all sellers receive and all buyers pay approximately the same price. This is what we call the *market price*.

Why Does the Market Price Fall if It Is Above the Equilibrium Price?

Suppose the supply and demand curves are as shown in Figure 5-6 but the market price is above the equilibrium level of $1—say, $1.50. This situation is illustrated in Figure 5-7. Why can't the price stay there?

As the figure shows, at a price of $1.50 there would be more pounds of cotton available than consumers wanted to buy: 11.2 billion pounds versus 8.1 billion pounds. The difference of 3.1 billion pounds is the **surplus**—also known as the *excess supply*—of cotton at $1.50.

This surplus means that some cotton farmers are frustrated: at the current price, they cannot find consumers who want to buy their cotton. The surplus offers an incentive for those frustrated would-be sellers to offer a lower price in order to poach business from other producers and entice more consumers to buy. The result of this price cutting will be to push the prevailing price down until it reaches the equilibrium price. So the price of a good will fall whenever there is a surplus—that is, whenever the market price is above its equilibrium level.

Why Does the Market Price Rise if It Is Below the Equilibrium Price?

Now suppose the price is below its equilibrium level—say, at $0.75 per pound, as shown in Figure 5-8. In this case, the quantity demanded, 11.5 billion pounds, exceeds the quantity supplied, 9.1 billion pounds, implying that there are would-be buyers who cannot find cotton: there is a **shortage,** also known as an *excess demand*, of 2.4 billion pounds.

There is a **surplus** of a good or service when the quantity supplied exceeds the quantity demanded. Surpluses occur when the price is above its equilibrium level.

There is a **shortage** of a good or service when the quantity demanded exceeds the quantity supplied. Shortages occur when the price is below its equilibrium level.

5-7 Price Above Its Equilibrium Level Creates a Surplus

The market price of $1.50 is above the equilibrium price of $1. This creates a surplus: at a price of $1.50, producers would like to sell 11.2 billion pounds but consumers want to buy only 8.1 billion pounds, so there is a surplus of 3.1 billion pounds. This surplus will push the price down until it reaches the equilibrium price of $1.

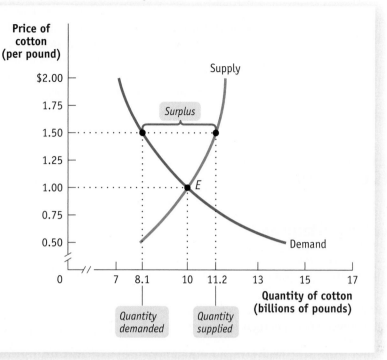

When there is a shortage, there are frustrated would-be buyers—people who want to purchase cotton but cannot find willing sellers at the current price. In this situation, either buyers will offer more than the prevailing price or sellers will realize that they can charge higher prices. Either way, the result is to drive up the prevailing price. This bidding up of prices happens whenever there are shortages—and there will be shortages whenever the price is below its equilibrium level. So the market price will always rise if it is below the equilibrium level.

5-8 Price Below Its Equilibrium Level Creates a Shortage

The market price of $0.75 is below the equilibrium price of $1. This creates a shortage: consumers want to buy 11.5 billion pounds, but only 9.1 billion pounds are for sale, so there is a shortage of 2.4 billion pounds. This shortage will push the price up until it reaches the equilibrium price of $1.

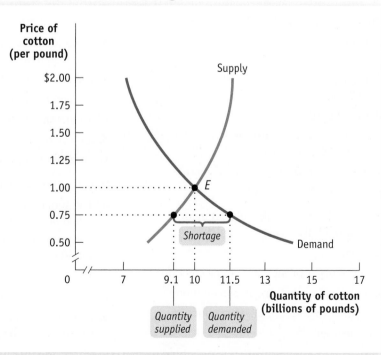

Using Equilibrium to Describe Markets

We have now seen that a market tends to have a single price, the equilibrium price. If the market price is above the equilibrium level, the ensuing surplus leads buyers and sellers to take actions that lower the price. And if the market price is below the equilibrium level, the ensuing shortage leads buyers and sellers to take actions that raise the price. So the market price always *moves toward* the equilibrium price, the price at which there is neither surplus nor shortage.

MODULE 5 Review

Solutions appear at the back of the book.

Check Your Understanding

1. Explain whether each of the following events represents (i) a *change in* supply or (ii) a *movement along* the supply curve.

   a. During a real estate boom that causes house prices to rise, more homeowners put their houses up for sale.

   b. Many strawberry farmers open temporary roadside stands during harvest season, even though prices are usually low at that time.

   c. Immediately after the school year begins, fewer young people are available to work. Fast-food chains must raise wages, which represent the price of labor, to attract workers.

   d. Many construction workers temporarily move to areas that have suffered hurricane damage, lured by higher wages.

   e. Since new technologies have made it possible to build larger cruise ships (which are cheaper to run per passenger), Caribbean cruise lines have offered more cabins, at lower prices, than before.

2. In the following three situations, the market is initially in equilibrium. After each event described below, does a surplus or shortage exist at the original equilibrium price? What will happen to the equilibrium price as a result?

   a. In 2013 there was a bumper crop of wine grapes.

   b. After a hurricane, Florida hoteliers often find that many people cancel their upcoming vacations, leaving them with empty hotel rooms.

   c. After a heavy snowfall, many people want to buy second-hand snowblowers at the local tool shop.

Multiple-Choice Questions

1. Which of the following will decrease the supply of good "X"?

   a. There is a technological advance that affects the production of *all* goods.

   b. The price of good "X" falls.

   c. The price of good "Y" (which consumers regard as a substitute for good "X") decreases.

   d. The wages of workers producing good "X" increase.

   e. The demand for good "X" decreases.

2. An increase in the demand for steak will lead to an increase in which of the following?

   a. the supply of steak

   b. the supply of hamburger (a substitute in production)

   c. the supply of chicken (a substitute in consumption)

   d. the supply of leather (a complement in production)

   e. the demand for leather

3. A technological advance in textbook production will lead to which of the following?

   a. a decrease in textbook supply

   b. an increase in textbook demand

   c. an increase in textbook supply

   d. a movement along the supply curve for textbooks

   e. an increase in textbook prices

4. Which of the following is true at equilibrium?

   a. The supply schedule is identical to the demand schedule at every price.

   b. The quantity demanded is the same as the quantity supplied.

   c. The quantity is zero.

   d. Every consumer who enjoys the good can consume it.

   e. Producers could not make any more of the product regardless of the price.

5. The market price of a good will tend to rise if

 a. demand decreases.

 b. supply increases.

 c. it is above the equilibrium price.

 d. it is below the equilibrium price.

 e. demand shifts to the left.

Critical-Thinking Question

Draw a graph showing the market for oranges in equilibrium. Show on your graph how a hurricane that destroys large numbers of orange groves in Florida will affect supply and demand, if at all.

PITFALLS

SUPPLY VERSUS QUANTITY SUPPLIED

? Where does the writer of this statement go wrong?

Economists generally agree that when demand decreases, the price falls. But a fall in price leads to a decrease in supply that, in turn, causes the price to rise again.

> THE WRITER CONFUSES A SHIFT OF THE SUPPLY CURVE (A DECREASE IN SUPPLY) AND A MOVEMENT ALONG THE SUPPLY CURVE (A CHANGE IN THE QUANTITY SUPPLIED). While economists agree that a decrease in demand leads to a fall in price, the fall in price leads only to a *movement along the supply curve*, not a shift of the supply curve. So that part of the statement is false. Always be careful to distinguish between a shift of the supply curve and a movement along the supply curve. A corrected statement would read:

Economists generally agree that when there is a decrease in demand, the price falls. And when the price falls, this leads to a decrease in the quantity supplied. It's as simple as that!

To learn more, see Figure 5-3, which illustrates a movement along the supply curve versus a shift of the supply curve. For an explanation of the difference, see pages 44–45.

Changes in Equilibrium

AP Photo/Khalid Tanveer

WHAT YOU WILL LEARN

1 **How equilibrium price and quantity are affected when there is a change in either supply or demand**

2 **How equilibrium price and quantity are affected when there is a simultaneous change in both supply and demand**

Changes in Supply and Demand

The 2010 floods in Pakistan came as a surprise, but the subsequent increase in the price of cotton was no surprise at all. Suddenly there was a fall in supply: the quantity of cotton available at any given price fell. Predictably, a fall in supply raises the equilibrium price.

The flooding in Pakistan is an example of an event that shifted the supply curve for a good without having much effect on the demand curve. There are many such events. There are also events that shift the demand curve without shifting the supply curve. For example, a medical report that chocolate is good for you increases the demand for chocolate but does not affect the supply. Events often shift either the supply curve or the demand curve, but not both; it is therefore useful to ask what happens in each case.

We have seen that when a curve shifts, the equilibrium price and quantity change. We will now concentrate on exactly how the shift of a curve alters the equilibrium price and quantity.

What Happens When the Demand Curve Shifts

Cotton and polyester are substitutes: if the price of polyester rises, the demand for cotton will increase, and if the price of polyester falls, the demand for cotton will decrease. But how does the price of polyester affect the *market equilibrium* for cotton?

Figure 6-1 shows the effect of a rise in the price of polyester on the market for cotton. The rise in the price of polyester increases the demand for cotton. Point E_1 shows the equilibrium corresponding to the original demand curve, with P_1 the equilibrium price and Q_1 the equilibrium quantity bought and sold.

An increase in demand is indicated by a *rightward* shift of the demand curve from D_1 to D_2. At the original market price P_1, this market is no longer in equilibrium: a shortage occurs because the quantity demanded exceeds the quantity supplied. So the

FIGURE 6-1 Equilibrium and Shifts of the Demand Curve

The original equilibrium in the market for cotton is at E_1, at the intersection of the supply curve and the original demand curve, D_1. A rise in the price of polyester, a substitute, shifts the demand curve for cotton products rightward to D_2. A shortage exists at the original price, P_1, causing both the price and quantity supplied to rise, a movement along the supply curve. A new equilibrium is reached at E_2, with a higher equilibrium price, P_2, and a higher equilibrium quantity, Q_2. When demand for a good or service increases, the equilibrium price and the equilibrium quantity of the good or service both rise.

price of cotton rises and generates an increase in the quantity supplied, an upward *movement along the supply curve.* A new equilibrium is established at point E_2, with a higher equilibrium price, P_2, and higher equilibrium quantity, Q_2. This sequence of events reflects a general principle: *When demand for a good or service increases, the equilibrium price and the equilibrium quantity of the good or service both rise.*

What would happen in the reverse case, a fall in the price of polyester? A fall in the price of polyester reduces the demand for cotton, shifting the demand curve to the *left.* At the original price, a surplus occurs as quantity supplied exceeds quantity demanded. The price falls and leads to a decrease in the quantity supplied, resulting in a lower equilibrium price and a lower equilibrium quantity. This illustrates another general principle: *When demand for a good or service decreases, the equilibrium price and the equilibrium quantity of the good or service both fall.*

To summarize how a market responds to a change in demand: *An increase in demand leads to a rise in both the equilibrium price and the equilibrium quantity. A decrease in demand leads to a fall in both the equilibrium price and the equilibrium quantity.*

What Happens When the Supply Curve Shifts

In the real world, it is a bit easier to predict changes in supply than changes in demand. Physical factors that affect supply, like the availability of inputs, are easier to get a handle on than the fickle tastes that affect demand. Still, with supply as with demand, what we can best predict are the *effects* of shifts of the supply curve.

As we mentioned in this chapter's opening story, devastating floods in Pakistan sharply reduced the supply of cotton in 2010. Figure 6-2 shows how this shift affected the market equilibrium. The original equilibrium is at E_1, the point of intersection of the original supply curve, S_1, and the demand curve, with an equilibrium price P_1 and equilibrium quantity Q_1. As a result of the bad weather, supply falls and S_1 shifts *leftward* to S_2. At the original price P_1, a shortage of cotton now exists and the market is no longer in equilibrium. The shortage causes a rise in price and a fall in quantity demanded, an upward movement along the demand curve. The new equilibrium is at E_2, with an equilibrium price P_2 and an equilibrium quantity Q_2. In the new equilibrium,

A fall in the price of polyester reduces the demand for cotton, shifting the demand curve to the left.

iStockphoto/Thinkstock

6-2   Equilibrium and Shifts of the Supply Curve

The original equilibrium in the market for cotton is at E_1. Bad weather in cotton-growing areas causes a fall in the supply of cotton and shifts the supply curve leftward from S_1 to S_2. A new equilibrium is established at E_2, with a higher equilibrium price, P_2, and a lower equilibrium quantity, Q_2.

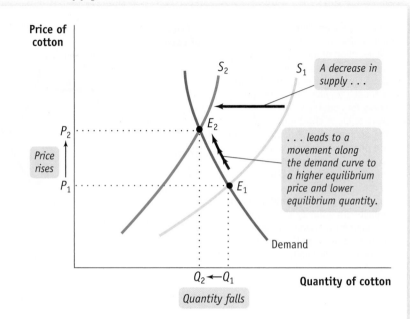

E_2, the price is higher and the equilibrium quantity lower than before. This can be stated as a general principle: *When supply of a good or service decreases, the equilibrium price of the good or service rises and the equilibrium quantity of the good or service falls.*

What happens to the market when supply increases? An increase in supply leads to a *rightward* shift of the supply curve. At the original price, a surplus now exists; as a result, the equilibrium price falls and the quantity demanded rises. This describes what happened to the market for cotton as new technology increased cotton yields. We can formulate a general principle: *When supply of a good or service increases, the equilibrium price of the good or service falls and the equilibrium quantity of the good or service rises.*

To summarize how a market responds to a change in supply: *An increase in supply leads to a fall in the equilibrium price and a rise in the equilibrium quantity. A decrease in supply leads to a rise in the equilibrium price and a fall in the equilibrium quantity.*

Simultaneous Shifts of Supply and Demand Curves

Finally, it sometimes happens that events shift *both* the demand and supply curves at the same time. This is not unusual; in real life, supply curves and demand curves for many goods and services shift quite often because the economic environment continually changes. Figure 6-3 illustrates two examples of simultaneous shifts. In both panels there is an increase in demand—that is, a rightward shift of the demand curve, from D_1 to D_2—say, for example, representing an increase in the demand for cotton due to changing tastes. Notice that the rightward shift in panel (a) is larger than the one in panel (b): we can suppose that panel (a) represents a year in which many more people than usual choose to buy jeans and cotton T-shirts and panel (b) represents a normal year. Both panels also show a decrease in supply—that is, a leftward shift of the supply curve from S_1 to S_2. Also notice that the leftward shift in panel (b) is relatively larger than the one in panel (a): we can suppose that panel (b) represents the effect of particularly bad weather in Pakistan and panel (a) represents the effect of a much less severe weather event.

In both cases, the equilibrium price rises from P_1 to P_2, as the equilibrium moves from E_1 to E_2. But what happens to the equilibrium quantity, the quantity of cotton bought and sold? In panel (a) the increase in demand is large relative to the decrease in supply, and the equilibrium quantity rises as a result. In panel (b), the decrease in

FIGURE 6-3   **Simultaneous Shifts of the Demand and Supply Curves**

(a) One Possible Outcome: Price Rises, Quantity Rises

(b) Another Possible Outcome: Price Rises, Quantity Falls

In panel (a) there is a simultaneous rightward shift of the demand curve and leftward shift of the supply curve. Here the increase in demand is relatively larger than the decrease in supply, so the equilibrium price and equilibrium quantity both rise. In panel (b) there is also a simultaneous rightward shift of the demand curve and leftward shift of the supply curve. Here the decrease in supply is relatively larger than the increase in demand, so the equilibrium price rises and the equilibrium quantity falls.

supply is large relative to the increase in demand, and the equilibrium quantity falls as a result. That is, when demand increases and supply decreases, the actual quantity bought and sold can go either way, depending on *how much* the demand and supply curves have shifted.

In general, when supply and demand shift in opposite directions, we can't predict what the ultimate effect will be on the quantity bought and sold. What we can say is that a curve that shifts a disproportionately greater distance than the other curve will have a disproportionately greater effect on the quantity bought and sold. That said, we can make the following prediction about the outcome when the supply and demand curves shift in opposite directions:

- When demand increases and supply decreases, the equilibrium price rises but the change in the equilibrium quantity is ambiguous.

- When demand decreases and supply increases, the equilibrium price falls but the change in the equilibrium quantity is ambiguous.

But suppose that the demand and supply curves shift in the same direction. Before 2010, this was the case in the global market for cotton, where both supply and demand had increased over the past decade. Can we safely make any predictions about the changes in price and quantity? In this situation, the change in quantity bought and sold can be predicted, but the change in price is ambiguous. The two possible outcomes when the supply and demand curves shift in the same direction (which you should check for yourself) are as follows:

- When both demand and supply increase, the equilibrium quantity rises but the change in equilibrium price is ambiguous.

- When both demand and supply decrease, the equilibrium quantity falls but the change in equilibrium price is ambiguous.

ECONOMICS ▶ IN ACTION

WORLD VIEW

THE RICE RUN OF 2008

In April 2008, the price of rice exported from Thailand—a global benchmark for the price of rice traded in international markets—reached $950 per ton, up from $360 per ton at the beginning of 2008. Within hours, prices for rice at major rice-trading exchanges around the world were breaking record levels. The factors that lay behind the surge in rice prices were both demand-related and supply-related: growing incomes in China and India, traditionally large consumers of rice; drought in Australia; and pest infestation in Vietnam. But it was hoarding by farmers, panic buying by consumers, and an export ban by India, one of the largest exporters of rice, that explained the breathtaking speed of the rise in price.

In much of Asia, governments are major buyers of rice. They buy rice from their rice farmers, who are paid a government-set price, and then sell it to the poor at subsidized prices (prices lower than the market equilibrium price). In the past, the government-set price was better than anything farmers could get in the private market.

Now, even farmers in rural areas of Asia have access to the Internet and can see the price quotes on global rice exchanges. And as rice prices rose in response to changes in demand and supply, farmers grew dissatisfied with the government price and instead hoarded their rice in the belief that they would eventually get higher prices. This was a self-fulfilling belief, as the hoarding shifted the supply curve leftward and raised the price of rice even further.

At the same time, India, one of the largest growers of rice, banned Indian exports of rice in order to protect its domestic consumers, causing yet another leftward shift of the supply curve and pushing the price of rice even higher.

As shown in Figure 6-4, the effects even spilled over to the United States, which had not suffered any fall in its rice production. American rice consumers grew alarmed when large retailers limited some bulk rice purchases in response to the turmoil in the global rice market.

Fearful of paying even higher prices in the future, panic buying set in. As one woman who was in the process of buying 30 pounds of rice said, "We don't even eat that much rice. But I read about it in the newspaper and decided to buy some." In San Francisco, some Asian markets reported runs on rice. And, predictably, this led to even higher prices as panic buying shifted the demand curve rightward, further feeding the buying frenzy. As one market owner said, "People are afraid. We tell them, 'There's no shortage yet' but it was crazy in here."

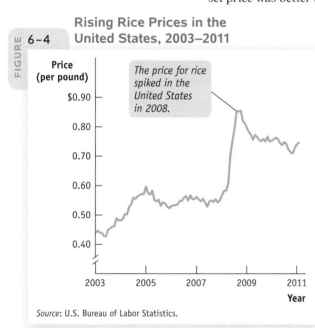

FIGURE 6-4

Rising Rice Prices in the United States, 2003–2011

Price (per pound)

The price for rice spiked in the United States in 2008.

Source: U.S. Bureau of Labor Statistics.

MODULE

6 Review

Solutions appear at the back of the book.

Check Your Understanding

1. For each of the following examples, explain how the indicated change affects supply or demand for the good in question and how the shift you describe affects equilibrium price and quantity.

   a. As the price of gasoline fell in the United States during the 1990s, more people bought large cars.

   b. As technological innovation has lowered the cost of recycling used paper, fresh paper made from recycled stock is used more frequently.

   c. When a local cable company offers cheaper pay-per-view films, local movie theaters have more unfilled seats.

2. Periodically, a computer chip maker like Intel introduces a new chip that is faster than the previous one. In response, demand for computers using the earlier chip decreases as customers put off purchases in anticipation of machines containing the new chip. Simultaneously, computer makers increase their production of computers containing the earlier chip in order to clear out their stocks of those chips.

Draw two diagrams of the market for computers containing the earlier chip: (a) one in which the equilibrium quantity falls in response to these events and (b) one in which the equilibrium quantity rises. What happens to the equilibrium price in each diagram?

Multiple-Choice Questions

1. Which of the following describes what will happen in the market for tomatoes if a salmonella outbreak is attributed to tainted tomatoes?

   a. Supply will increase and price will increase.

   b. Supply will increase and price will decrease.

   c. Demand will decrease and price will increase.

   d. Demand will decrease and price will decrease.

   e. Supply and demand will both increase.

2. Which of the following will lead to an increase in the equilibrium price of product "X"? A(n)

   a. increase in consumer incomes if product "X" is an inferior good

   b. increase in the price of machinery used to produce product "X"

   c. technological advance in the production of good "X"

   d. decrease in the price of good "Y" (a substitute for good "X")

   e. expectation by consumers that the price of good "X" is going to fall

3. The equilibrium price will rise, but equilibrium quantity may increase, decrease, or stay the same if

   a. demand increases and supply decreases.

   b. demand increases and supply increases.

   c. demand decreases and supply increases.

   d. demand decreases and supply decreases.

   e. demand increases and supply does not change.

4. An increase in the number of buyers and a technological advance will cause

   a. demand to increase and supply to increase.

   b. demand to increase and supply to decrease.

   c. demand to decrease and supply to increase.

   d. demand to decrease and supply to decrease.

   e. no change in demand and an increase in supply.

5. Which of the following is certainly true if demand and supply increase at the same time?

   a. The equilibrium price will increase.

   b. The equilibrium price will decrease.

   c. The equilibrium quantity will increase.

   d. The equilibrium quantity will decrease.

   e. The equilibrium quantity may increase, decrease, or stay the same.

Critical-Thinking Question

Draw a graph showing the market for cotton in equilibrium. On your graph, show the effect of an increase in the supply of cotton on equilibrium price and equilibrium quantity in the market for cotton.

Price Controls and Quantity Controls

Why Governments Control Prices and Quantities

You learned in Module 6 that a market moves to equilibrium—that is, the market price moves to the level at which the quantity supplied equals the quantity demanded. But this equilibrium price does not necessarily please either buyers or sellers. Buyers would always prefer to pay less and sellers would always like to get more money for what they sell.

As a result, there is often a strong political demand for governments to intervene in markets. And powerful interests can make a compelling case that a market intervention favoring them is "fair." When a government intervenes to regulate prices, we say that it imposes **price controls.** Price controls typically take the form of either an upper limit, a **price ceiling,** or a lower limit, a **price floor.**

When a government intervenes to regulate quantities, we say that it imposes a **quantity control,** or **quota.** Typically the government limits quantity in a market by issuing **licenses** so that only people with a license can legally supply the good. New York's taxi medallion is an example of such a license.

Unfortunately, it's not that easy to tell a market what to do. As we will now see, when a government tries to legislate prices or quantities there are certain predictable and unpleasant side effects.

Price Ceilings

Aside from rent control, a law that prevents landlords from raising rents except when specifically given permission, there are not many price ceilings in the United States today. But at times they have been widespread.

WHAT YOU WILL LEARN

1. The meaning of price controls and quantity controls, two ways government intervenes in markets

2. How price controls can create problems and make a market inefficient

3. Who benefits and who loses from price controls, and why they are used despite their well-known problems

4. How quantity controls can create problems and make a market inefficient

Price controls are legal restrictions on how high or low a market price may go.

Price controls can take two forms: a **price ceiling,** a maximum price sellers are allowed to charge for a good or service, or a **price floor,** a minimum price buyers are required to pay for a good or service.

A **quantity control,** or **quota,** is an upper limit on the quantity of some good that can be bought or sold.

A **license** gives its owner the right to supply a good or service.

Price ceilings are typically imposed during crises—wars, harvest failures, natural disasters—because these events often lead to sudden price increases that hurt many people but produce big gains for a lucky few. The U.S. government imposed ceilings on many prices during World War II: the war sharply increased demand for raw materials, such as aluminum and steel, and price controls prevented those with access to these raw materials from earning huge profits.

Price controls on oil were imposed in 1973, when an embargo by Arab oil-exporting countries seemed likely to generate huge profits for U.S. oil companies. Price controls were instituted again in 2012 by New York and New Jersey authorities in the aftermath of Hurricane Sandy as gas shortages led to rampant price-gouging.

Rent control in New York is, believe it or not, a legacy of World War II: it was imposed because wartime production created an economic boom, which increased demand for apartments at a time when the labor and raw materials that might have been used to build them were being used to win the war instead. Although most price controls were removed soon after the war ended, New York's rent limits were retained and gradually extended to buildings not previously covered, leading to some very strange situations.

How a Price Ceiling Causes Inefficiency

To see what can go wrong when a government imposes a price ceiling on an efficient market, consider Figure 7-1, which shows a simplified model of the market for apartments in New York. For the sake of simplicity, we imagine that all apartments are exactly the same and so would rent for the same price in an unregulated market.

The table in the figure shows the demand and supply schedules; the demand and supply curves are shown on the left. We show the quantity of apartments on the horizontal axis and the monthly rent per apartment on the vertical axis. You can see that in an unregulated market the equilibrium would be at point E: 2 million apartments would be rented for $1,000 each per month.

FIGURE 7-1   The Market for Apartments in the Absence of Government Controls

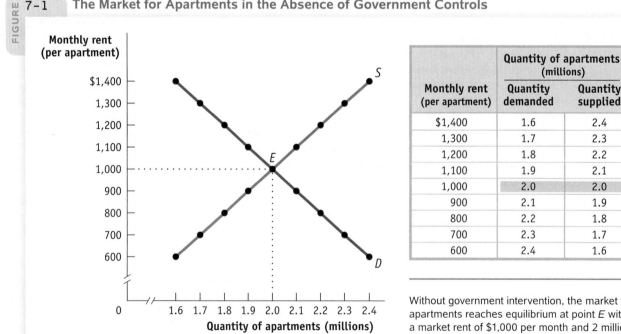

Monthly rent (per apartment)	Quantity of apartments (millions)	
	Quantity demanded	Quantity supplied
$1,400	1.6	2.4
1,300	1.7	2.3
1,200	1.8	2.2
1,100	1.9	2.1
1,000	2.0	2.0
900	2.1	1.9
800	2.2	1.8
700	2.3	1.7
600	2.4	1.6

Without government intervention, the market for apartments reaches equilibrium at point E with a market rent of $1,000 per month and 2 million apartments rented.

Now suppose that the government imposes a price ceiling, limiting rents to a price below the equilibrium price—say, no more than $800.

Figure 7-2 shows the effect of the price ceiling, represented by the line at $800. At the enforced rental rate of $800, landlords have less incentive to offer apartments, so they won't be willing to supply as many as they would at the equilibrium rate of $1,000. They will choose point A on the supply curve, offering only 1.8 million apartments for rent, 200,000 fewer than in the unregulated market.

At the same time, more people will want to rent apartments at a price of $800 than at the equilibrium price of $1,000; as shown at point B on the demand curve, at a monthly rent of $800 the quantity of apartments demanded rises to 2.2 million, 200,000 more than in the unregulated market and 400,000 more than are actually available at the price of $800. So there is now a persistent shortage of rental housing: at that price, 400,000 more people want to rent than are able to find apartments.

Do price ceilings always cause shortages? No. If a price ceiling is set above the equilibrium price, it won't have any effect. Suppose that the equilibrium rental rate on apartments is $1,000 per month and the city government sets a ceiling of $1,200. Who cares? In this case, the price ceiling won't be binding—it won't actually constrain market behavior—and it will have no effect.

Price ceilings do create inefficiency in at least four distinct ways and can be seriously harmful as a result.

INEFFICIENT ALLOCATION TO CONSUMERS Rent control doesn't just lead to too few apartments being available. It can also lead to misallocation of the apartments that are available: people who badly need a place to live may not be able to find an apartment, while some apartments may be occupied by people with much less urgent needs.

In the case shown in Figure 7-2, 2.2 million people would like to rent an apartment at $800 per month, but only 1.8 million apartments are available. Of those 2.2 million who are seeking an apartment, some want an apartment badly and are willing to pay a high price to get one. Others have a less urgent need and are only willing to pay a low price, perhaps because they have alternative housing.

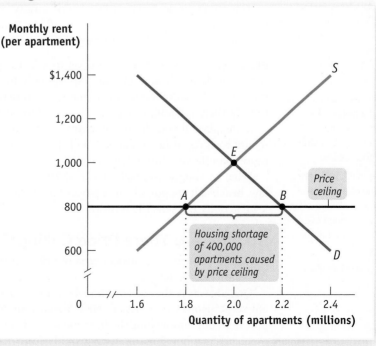

FIGURE 7-2   The Effects of a Price Ceiling

The black horizontal line represents the government-imposed price ceiling on rents of $800 per month. This price ceiling reduces the quantity of apartments supplied to 1.8 million, point A, and increases the quantity demanded to 2.2 million, point B. This creates a persistent shortage of 400,000 units: 400,000 people who want apartments at the legal rent of $800 but cannot get them.

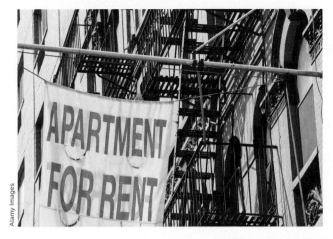

Rent control often leads to the misal-location of available apartments.

Price ceilings often lead to inefficiency in the form of **inefficient allocation to consumers:** people who want the good badly and are willing to pay a high price don't get it, and those who care relatively little about the good and are only willing to pay a relatively low price do get it.

Price ceilings typically lead to inefficiency in the form of **wasted resources:** people expend money, effort, and time to cope with the shortages caused by the price ceiling.

Price ceilings often lead to inefficiency in that the goods being offered are of **inefficiently low quality:** sellers offer low quality goods at a low price even though buyers would prefer a higher quality at a higher price.

A **black market** is a market in which goods or services are bought and sold illegally—either because it is illegal to sell them at all or because the prices charged are legally prohibited by a price ceiling.

An efficient allocation of apartments would reflect these differences: people who really want an apartment will get one and people who aren't all that eager to find an apartment won't. In an inefficient distribution of apartments, the opposite will happen: some people who are not especially eager to find an apartment will get one and others who are very eager to find an apartment won't.

Because people usually get apartments through luck or personal connections under rent control, it generally results in an **inefficient allocation to consumers** of the few apartments available.

WASTED RESOURCES Another reason a price ceiling causes inefficiency is that it leads to **wasted resources:** people expend money, effort, and time to cope with the shortages caused by the price ceiling. Back in 1979, U.S. price controls on gasoline led to shortages that forced millions of Americans to spend hours each week waiting in lines at gas stations. The opportunity cost of the time spent in gas lines—the wages not earned, the leisure time not enjoyed—constituted wasted resources from the point of view of consumers and of the economy as a whole.

INEFFICIENTLY LOW QUALITY Yet another way a price ceiling causes inefficiency is by causing goods to be of inefficiently low quality. **Inefficiently low quality** means that sellers offer low-quality goods at a low price even though buyers would rather have higher quality and are willing to pay a higher price for it.

Again, consider rent control. Landlords have no incentive to provide better conditions because they cannot raise rents to cover their repair costs but are able to find tenants easily. In many cases, tenants would be willing to pay much more for improved conditions than it would cost for the landlord to provide them—for example, the upgrade of an antiquated electrical system that cannot safely run air conditioners or computers. But any additional payment for such improvements would be legally considered a rent increase, which is prohibited. Indeed, rent-controlled apartments are notoriously badly maintained, rarely painted, subject to frequent electrical and plumbing problems, and sometimes even hazardous to inhabit.

This whole situation is a missed opportunity—some tenants would be happy to pay for better conditions, and landlords would be happy to provide them for payment. But such an exchange would occur only if the market were allowed to operate freely.

BLACK MARKETS And that leads us to a last aspect of price ceilings: the incentive they provide for illegal activities, specifically the emergence of **black markets.** One type of black market activity is illegal subletting by tenants. But it does not stop there. Clearly, there is a temptation for a landlord to say to a potential tenant, "Look, you can have the place if you slip me an extra few hundred in cash each month"—and for the tenant to agree, if he or she is one of those people who would be willing to pay much more than the maximum legal rent.

What's wrong with black markets? In general, it's a bad thing if people break *any* law, because it encourages disrespect for the law in general. Worse yet, in this case illegal activity worsens the position of those who try to be honest.

So Why Are There Price Ceilings?

Given the unpleasant consequences of price ceilings, why do governments still sometimes impose them?

One answer is that although price ceilings may have adverse effects, they do benefit some people. In practice, New York's rent-control rules—which are more complex than our simple model—hurt most residents but give a small minority of renters much cheaper housing than they would get in an unregulated market. And those who benefit from the controls may be better organized and more vocal than those who are harmed by them.

Also, when price ceilings have been in effect for a long time, buyers may not have a realistic idea of what would happen without them. In our previous example, the rental rate in an unregulated market (Figure 7-1) would be only 25% higher than in the regulated market (Figure 7-2): $1,000 instead of $800. But how would renters know that? Indeed, they might have heard about black market transactions at much higher prices and would not realize that these black market prices are much higher than the price that would prevail in a fully unregulated market.

A last answer is that government officials often do not understand supply and demand analysis! It is a great mistake to suppose that economic policies in the real world are always sensible or well informed.

Price Floors

Sometimes governments intervene to push market prices up instead of down. *Price floors* have been widely legislated for agricultural products, such as wheat and milk, as a way to support the incomes of farmers. Historically, there were also price floors on such services as trucking and air travel, although these were phased out by the U.S. government in the 1970s. If you have ever worked in a fast-food restaurant, you are likely to have encountered a price floor: governments in the United States and many other countries maintain a lower limit on the hourly wage rate of a worker's labor—that is, a floor on the price of labor—called the **minimum wage.**

Just like price ceilings, price floors are intended to help some people but generate predictable and undesirable side effects. Figure 7-3 shows hypothetical supply and demand curves for butter. Left to itself, the market would move to equilibrium at point *E*, with 10 million pounds of butter bought and sold at a price of $1 per pound.

The **minimum wage** is a legal floor on the wage rate, which is the market price of labor.

7-3 The Market for Butter in the Absence of Government Controls

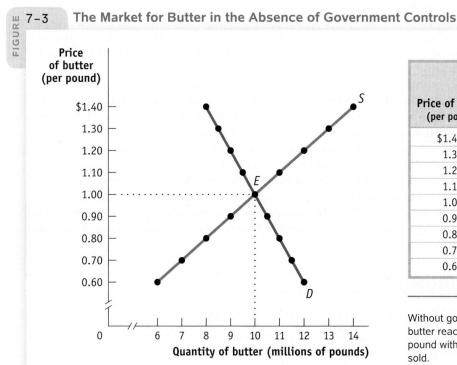

Price of butter (per pound)	Quantity of butter (millions of pounds)	
	Quantity demanded	Quantity supplied
$1.40	8.0	14.0
1.30	8.5	13.0
1.20	9.0	12.0
1.10	9.5	11.0
1.00	10.0	10.0
0.90	10.5	9.0
0.80	11.0	8.0
0.70	11.5	7.0
0.60	12.0	6.0

Without government intervention, the market for butter reaches equilibrium at a price of $1 per pound with 10 million pounds of butter bought and sold.

7-4   **The Effects of a Price Floor**

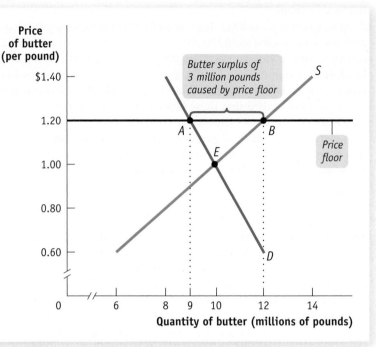

The black horizontal line represents the government-imposed price floor of $1.20 per pound of butter. The quantity of butter demanded falls to 9 million pounds, and the quantity supplied rises to 12 million pounds, generating a persistent surplus of 3 million pounds of butter.

Now suppose that the government, in order to help dairy farmers, imposes a price floor on butter of $1.20 per pound. Its effects are shown in Figure 7-4, where the line at $1.20 represents the price floor. At a price of $1.20 per pound, producers would want to supply 12 million pounds (point *B* on the supply curve) but consumers would want to buy only 9 million pounds (point *A* on the demand curve). So the price floor leads to a persistent surplus of 3 million pounds of butter.

Does a price floor always lead to an unwanted surplus? No. Just as in the case of a price ceiling, the floor may not be binding—that is, it may be irrelevant. If the equilibrium price of butter is $1 per pound but the floor is set at only $0.80, the floor has no effect.

But suppose that a price floor *is* binding: what happens to the unwanted surplus? The answer depends on government policy. In the case of agricultural price floors, governments buy up unwanted surplus. As a result, the U.S. government has at times found itself warehousing thousands of tons of butter, cheese, and other farm products. The government then has to find a way to dispose of these unwanted goods.

When the government is not prepared to purchase the unwanted surplus, a price floor means that would-be sellers cannot find buyers. This is what happens when there is a price floor on the wage rate paid for an hour of labor, the *minimum wage:* when the minimum wage is above the equilibrium wage rate, some people who are willing to work—that is, sell labor—cannot find buyers—that is, employers—willing to give them jobs.

ECONOMICS ▶ IN ACTION

PRICE FLOORS AND SCHOOL LUNCHES

When you were in grade school, did your school offer free or very cheap lunches? If so, you were probably a beneficiary of price floors.

Where did all the cheap food come from? During the 1930s, when the U.S. economy was going through the Great Depression, a prolonged economic slump, prices were low and farmers were suffering severely. In an effort to help rural Americans, the U.S.

government imposed price floors on a number of agricultural products. The system of agricultural price floors—officially called price support programs—continues to this day. Among the products subject to price support are sugar and various dairy products; at times grains, beef, and pork have also had a minimum price.

The big problem with any attempt to impose a price floor is that it creates a surplus. To some extent the U.S. Department of Agriculture has tried to head off surpluses by taking steps to reduce supply; for example, by paying farmers *not* to grow crops. As a last resort, however, the U.S. government has been willing to buy up the surplus, taking the excess supply off the market.

But then what? The government can't just sell the agricultural products: that would depress market prices, forcing the government to buy the stuff right back. So it has to give it away in ways that don't depress market prices. One way to do this is by giving surplus food, free, to school lunch programs. These gifts are known as "bonus foods." Along with financial aid, bonus foods allow many school districts to provide free or very cheap lunches to their students. Is this a story with a happy ending?

Not really. Nutritionists, concerned about growing child obesity in the United States, place part of the blame on those bonus foods. Schools get whatever the government has too much of—and that has tended to include a lot of dairy products, beef, and corn, and not much in the way of fresh vegetables or fruit.

As a result, school lunches that make extensive use of bonus foods tend to be very high in fat and calories. So this is a case in which there is such a thing as a free lunch—but this lunch may be bad for your health.

How a Price Floor Causes Inefficiency

The persistent surplus that results from a price floor creates missed opportunities—inefficiencies—that resemble those created by the shortage that results from a price ceiling.

INEFFICIENTLY LOW QUANTITY Because a price floor raises the price of a good to consumers, it reduces the quantity of that good demanded; because sellers can't sell more units of a good than buyers are willing to buy, a price floor reduces the quantity of a good bought and sold below the market equilibrium quantity. Notice that this is the *same* effect as a price ceiling. You might be tempted to think that a price floor and a price ceiling have opposite effects, but both have the effect of reducing the quantity of a good bought and sold.

INEFFICIENT ALLOCATION OF SALES AMONG SELLERS Like a price ceiling, a price floor can lead to *inefficient allocation*—but in this case **inefficient allocation of sales among sellers** rather than inefficient allocation to consumers.

An episode from the Belgian movie *Rosetta*, a realistic fictional story, illustrates the problem of inefficient allocation of selling opportunities quite well. Like many European countries, Belgium has a high minimum wage, and jobs for young people are scarce. At one point Rosetta, a young woman who is very eager to work, loses her job at a fast-food stand because the owner of the stand replaces her with his son—a very reluctant worker. Rosetta would be willing to work for less money, and with the money he would save, the owner could give his son an allowance and let him do something else. But to hire Rosetta for less than the minimum wage would be illegal.

WASTED RESOURCES Also like a price ceiling, a price floor generates inefficiency by *wasting resources*. The most graphic examples involve government purchases of the unwanted surpluses of agricultural products caused by price floors. When the surplus production is simply destroyed, and when the stored produce goes, as officials euphemistically put it, "out of condition" and must be thrown away, it is pure waste.

Price floors also lead to wasted time and effort. Consider the minimum wage. Would-be workers who spend many hours searching for jobs, or waiting in line in the

Price floors lead to inefficient allocation of sales among sellers: those who would be willing to sell the good at the lowest price are not always those who manage to sell it.

hope of getting jobs, play the same role in the case of price floors as hapless individuals searching for apartments in the case of price ceilings.

INEFFICIENTLY HIGH QUALITY Again like price ceilings, price floors lead to inefficiency in the quality of goods produced.

We've seen that when there is a price ceiling, suppliers produce goods that are of inefficiently low quality: buyers prefer higher-quality products and are willing to pay for them, but sellers refuse to improve the quality of their products because the price ceiling prevents their being compensated for doing so. This same logic applies to price floors, but in reverse: suppliers offer goods of **inefficiently high quality.**

How can this be? Isn't high quality a good thing? Yes, but only if it is worth the cost. Suppose that suppliers spend a lot to make goods of very high quality but that this quality isn't worth much to consumers, who would rather receive the money spent on that quality in the form of a lower price. This represents a missed opportunity: suppliers and buyers could make a mutually beneficial deal in which buyers got goods of lower quality for a much lower price.

A good example of the inefficiency of excessive quality comes from the days when transatlantic airfares were set artificially high by international treaty. Forbidden to compete for customers by offering lower ticket prices, airlines instead offered expensive services, like lavish in-flight meals that went largely uneaten.

ILLEGAL ACTIVITY Finally, like price ceilings, price floors provide incentives for illegal activity. For example, in countries where the minimum wage is far above the equilibrium wage rate, workers desperate for jobs sometimes agree to work off the books for employers who conceal their employment from the government—or bribe the government inspectors. This practice, known in Europe as "black labor," is especially common in southern European countries such as Italy and Spain.

Since airline deregulation in the 1970s, American passengers have seen ticket prices decrease along with the quality of in-flight service.

So Why Are There Price Floors?

So why do governments impose price floors when they have so many negative side effects? The reasons are similar to those for imposing price ceilings. Government officials often disregard warnings about the consequences of price floors either because they believe that the relevant market is poorly described by the supply and demand model or, more often, because they do not understand the model. Above all, just as price ceilings are often imposed because they benefit some influential buyers of a good, price floors are often imposed because they benefit some influential sellers.

Quantity Controls

In the 1930s, New York City instituted a system of licensing for taxicabs: only taxis with a medallion were allowed to pick up passengers. This licensing system, a form of *quantity control* also known as a *quota*, was intended to ensure quality. In the last 60 years the number of medallions has increased by about 16%, to a total of 13,237 medallions, while at the same time the population of New York City has increased by about 60%. The result has been a very high price for a medallion—the price of a medallion in 2012 was about $700,000!

To understand why a New York taxi medallion is worth so much money, we consider a simplified version of the market for taxi rides, shown in Figure 7-5. Just as we assumed in the analysis of rent control that all apartments were the same, we now suppose that all taxi rides are the same—ignoring the real-world complication that some taxi rides are longer, and so more expensive, than others. The table in the figure shows supply and demand schedules. The equilibrium—indicated by point *E* in the

Price floors often lead to inefficiency in that goods of **inefficiently high quality** are offered: sellers offer high-quality goods at a high price, even though buyers would prefer a lower quality at a lower price.

7-5 The Market for Taxi Rides in the Absence of Government Controls

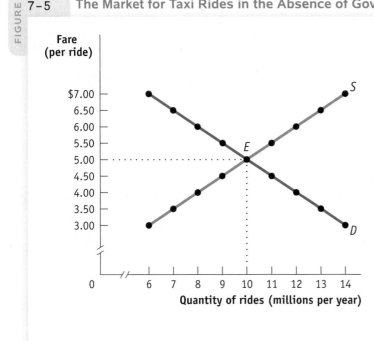

Fare (per ride)	Quantity of rides (millions per year)	
	Quantity demanded	Quantity supplied
$7.00	6	14
6.50	7	13
6.00	8	12
5.50	9	11
5.00	10	10
4.50	11	9
4.00	12	8
3.50	13	7
3.00	14	6

Without government intervention, the market reaches equilibrium with 10 million rides taken per year at a fare of $5 per ride.

figure and by the shaded entries in the table—is a fare of $5 per ride, with 10 million rides taken per year.

The New York medallion system limits the number of taxis, but each taxi driver can offer as many rides as he or she can manage. (Now you know why New York taxi drivers are so aggressive!) To simplify our analysis, however, we will assume that a medallion system limits the number of taxi rides that can legally be given to 8 million per year.

Until now, we have derived the demand curve by answering questions of the form: "How many taxi rides will passengers want to take if the price is $5 per ride?" But it is possible to reverse the question and ask instead: "At what price will consumers want to buy 10 million rides per year?" The price at which consumers want to buy a given quantity—in this case, 10 million rides at $5 per ride—is the **demand price** of that quantity. You can see from the demand schedule in Figure 7-5 that the demand price of 6 million rides is $7 per ride, the demand price of 7 million rides is $6.50 per ride, and so on.

Similarly, the supply curve represents the answer to questions of the form: "How many taxi rides would taxi drivers supply at a price of $5 each?" But we can also reverse this question to ask: "At what price will producers be willing to supply 10 million rides per year?" The price at which producers will supply a given quantity—in this case, 10 million rides at $5 per ride—is the **supply price** of that quantity. We can see from the supply schedule in Figure 7-5 that the supply price of 6 million rides is $3 per ride, the supply price of 7 million rides is $3.50 per ride, and so on.

Now we are ready to analyze a quota. We have assumed that the city government limits the quantity of taxi rides to 8 million per year. Medallions, each of which carries the right to provide a certain number of taxi rides per year, are made available to selected people in such a way that a total of 8 million rides will be provided. Medallion-holders may then either drive their own taxis or rent their medallions to others for a fee.

The **demand price** of a given quantity is the price at which consumers will demand that quantity.

The **supply price** of a given quantity is the price at which producers will supply that quantity.

Figure 7-6 shows the resulting market for taxi rides, with the black vertical line at 8 million rides per year representing the quota. Because the quantity of rides is limited to 8 million, consumers must be at point A on the demand curve, corresponding to the shaded entry in the demand schedule: the demand price of 8 million rides is $6 per ride. Meanwhile, taxi drivers must be at point B on the supply curve, corresponding to the shaded entry in the supply schedule: the supply price of 8 million rides is $4 per ride.

FIGURE 7-6   Effect of a Quota on the Market for Taxi Rides

Fare (per ride)	Quantity of rides (millions per year)	
	Quantity demanded	Quantity supplied
$7.00	6	14
6.50	7	13
6.00	8	12
5.50	9	11
5.00	10	10
4.50	11	9
4.00	12	8
3.50	13	7
3.00	14	6

The table shows the demand price and the supply price corresponding to each quantity: the price at which that quantity would be demanded and supplied, respectively. The city government imposes a quota of 8 million rides by selling enough medallions for only 8 million rides, represented by the black vertical line. The price paid by consumers rises to $6 per ride, the demand price of 8 million rides, shown by point A.

The supply price of 8 million rides is only $4 per ride, shown by point B. The difference between these two prices is the quota rent per ride, the earnings that accrue to the owner of a medallion. The quota rent drives a wedge between the demand price and the supply price. Because the quota discourages mutually beneficial transactions, it creates a deadweight loss equal to the shaded triangle.

But how can the price received by taxi drivers be $4 when the price paid by taxi riders is $6? The answer is that in addition to the market in taxi rides, there is also a market in medallions. Medallion-holders may not always want to drive their taxis: they may be ill or on vacation. Those who do not want to drive their own taxis will sell the right to use the medallion to someone else. Since the holder of the medallion is willing to offer a ride for $4 but the consumer is willing to buy a ride for $6, the medallion can be rented for $2 per ride. Whoever holds the medallion can earn $2 per ride so the rental price will be bid up to $2. As for the medallion-holder, she makes $2 whether she rents the medallion or uses it herself.

It is no coincidence that $2 is exactly the difference between $6, the demand price of 8 million rides, and $4, the supply price of 8 million rides. In every case in which the supply of a good is legally restricted, there is a **wedge** between the demand price of the quantity transacted and the supply price of the quantity transacted. This wedge, illustrated by the double-headed arrow in Figure 7-6, has a special name: the **quota rent**. It is the earnings that accrue to the medallion-holder from ownership of a valuable commodity, the medallion.

A quantity control, or quota, drives a **wedge** between the demand price and the supply price of a good; that is, the price paid by buyers ends up being higher than that received by sellers. The difference between the demand and supply price at the quota amount is the **quota rent**, the earnings that accrue to the license-holder from ownership of the right to sell the good. It is equal to the market price of the license when the licenses are traded.

So Figure 7-6 also illustrates the quota rent in the market for New York taxi rides. The quota limits the quantity of rides to 8 million per year, a quantity at which the demand price of $6 exceeds the supply price of $4. The wedge between these two prices, $2, is the quota rent that results from the restrictions placed on the quantity of taxi rides in this market.

So regardless of whether the medallion owner uses the medallion himself or herself, or rents it to others, it is a valuable asset. And this is represented in the going price for a New York City taxi medallion. Notice, by the way, that quotas—like price ceilings and price floors—don't always have a real effect. If the quota were set at 12 million rides— that is, above the equilibrium quantity in an unregulated market—it would have no effect because it would not be binding.

In addition to the market for taxi rides, there is also a market in taxi medallions.

The Costs of Quantity Controls

Like price controls, quantity controls can have some predictable and undesirable side effects. The first is the by-now-familiar problem of inefficiency due to missed opportunities: quantity controls prevent mutually beneficial transactions from oc- curring, transactions that would benefit both buyers and sellers. Looking back at Figure 7-6, you can see that starting at the quota of 8 million rides, New Yorkers would be willing to pay at least $5.50 per ride for an additional 1 million rides and that taxi drivers would be willing to provide those rides as long as they got at least $4.50 per ride. These are rides that would have taken place if there had been no quota.

The same is true for the next 1 million rides: New Yorkers would be willing to pay at least $5 per ride when the quantity of rides is increased from 9 to 10 million, and taxi drivers would be willing to provide those rides as long as they got at least $5 per ride. Again, these rides would have occurred without the quota.

Only when the market has reached the unregulated market equilibrium quantity of 10 million rides are there no "missed-opportunity rides"—the quota of 8 million rides has caused 2 million "missed-opportunity rides." A buyer would be willing to buy the good at a price that the seller would be willing to accept, but such a transaction does not occur because it is forbidden by the quota.

Economists have a special term for the lost gains from missed opportunities such as these: **deadweight loss.** Generally, when the demand price exceeds the supply price, there is a deadweight loss. Figure 7-6 illustrates the deadweight loss with a shaded triangle between the demand and supply curves. This triangle represents the missed gains from taxi rides prevented by the quota, a loss that is experienced by both disappointed would-be riders and frustrated would-be drivers.

Because there are transactions that people would like to make but are not allowed to, quantity controls generate an incentive to evade them or even to break the law. New York's taxi industry again provides clear examples. Taxi regulation applies only to those drivers who are hailed by passengers on the street. A car service that makes prearranged pickups does not need a medallion. As a result, such hired cars provide much of the service that might otherwise be provided by taxis, as in other cities.

In addition, there are substantial numbers of unlicensed cabs that simply defy the law by picking up passengers without a medallion. Because these cabs are illegal, their drivers are completely unregulated, and they generate a disproportionately large share of traffic accidents in New York City.

Deadweight loss is the lost gains as- sociated with transactions that do not occur due to market intervention.

ECONOMICS ▶ IN ACTION

THE CLAMS OF THE JERSEY SHORE

One industry that New Jersey *really* dominates is clam fishing. The Garden State typically supplies about 70% of the country's surf clams, whose tongues are used in fried-clam dinners, and about 90% of the quahogs, which are used to make clam chowder.

In the 1980s, however, excessive fishing threatened to wipe out New Jersey's clam beds. To save the resource, the U.S. government introduced a clam quota, which sets an overall limit on the number of bushels of clams that may be caught and allocates licenses to owners of fishing boats based on their historical catches.

Notice, by the way, that this is an example of a quota that is probably justified by broader economic and environmental considerations—unlike the New York taxicab quota, which has long since lost any economic rationale. Still, whatever its rationale, the New Jersey clam quota works the same way as any other quota.

Clam quotas were introduced in New Jersey to help save a threatened natural resource.

MODULE
7 Review

Solutions appear at the back of the book.

Check Your Understanding

1. On game days, homeowners near Middletown University's stadium used to rent parking spaces in their driveways to fans at a going rate of $11. A new town ordinance now sets a maximum parking fee of $7. Use the accompanying supply and demand diagram to explain how each of the following can result from the price ceiling.

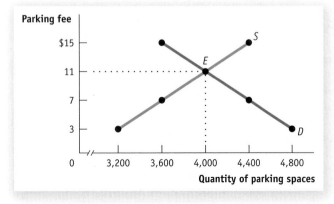

   a. Some homeowners now think it's not worth the hassle to rent out spaces.
   b. Some fans who used to carpool to the game now drive alone.
   c. Some fans can't find parking and leave without seeing the game.

   Explain how each of the following adverse effects arises from the price ceiling.

   d. Some fans now arrive several hours early to find parking.
   e. Friends of homeowners near the stadium regularly attend games, even if they aren't big fans. But some serious fans have given up because of the parking situation.
   f. Some homeowners rent spaces for more than $7 but pretend that the buyers are nonpaying friends or family.

2. The state legislature mandates a price floor for gasoline of P_F per gallon. Assess the following statements and illustrate your answer using the figure provided.

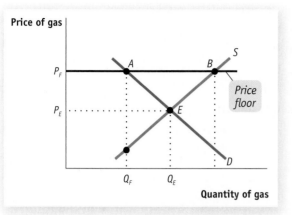

Price of gas

Quantity of gas

a. Proponents of the law claim it will increase the income of gas station owners. Opponents claim it will hurt gas station owners because they will lose customers.

b. Proponents claim consumers will be better off because gas stations will provide better service.

Opponents claim consumers will be generally worse off because they prefer to buy gas at cheaper prices.

c. Proponents claim that they are helping gas station owners without hurting anyone else. Opponents claim that consumers are hurt and will end up doing things like buying gas in a nearby state or on the black market.

3. Suppose that the supply and demand for taxi rides is given by Figure 7-5 and a quota is set at 6 million rides. Replicate the graph from Figure 7-5, and explain where to find each of the following on your graph:

a. the price of a ride

b. the quota rent

c. the deadweight loss resulting from the quota

Suppose the quota on taxi rides is increased to 9 million.

d. Draw another graph to illustrate what happens to the quota rent and the deadweight loss in this scenario. Explain your findings.

Multiple-Choice Questions

1. Refer to the graph provided to determine whether a price ceiling set at $3 will result in:

   a. a shortage of 100 units.

   b. a surplus of 100 units.

   c. a shortage of 200 units.

   d. a surplus of 200 units.

   e. a surplus of 50 units.

2. Effective price ceilings are inefficient because they

   a. create surplus.

   b. are harmful to all consumers.

   c. increase quality.

   d. create black markets.

   e. allow some consumers to pay a lower price for the good.

3. Refer to the graph provided. If the government establishes a minimum wage at $10, how many workers will benefit from the higher wage?

   a. 30

   b. 50

   c. 60

   d. 80

   e. 110

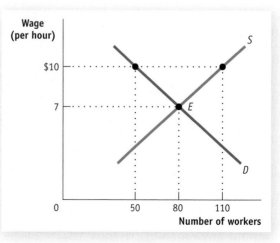

4. Based on the information in the graph provided, if the government established a quota of 1,000 in this market the demand price would be _____ and the supply price would be _____.

   a. $6, $6

   b. $4, $4

   c. $8, $8

   d. $8, $6

   e. $8, $4

5. Quotas lead to which of the following?

   I. inefficiency due to missed opportunities

   II. incentives to evade or break the law

   III. a surplus in the market

   a. I

   b. II

   c. III

   d. I and II

   e. I, II, and III

Critical-Thinking Questions

Draw separate graphs to illustrate each of the following and explain each graph.

1. How a price ceiling results in a shortage of the good.

2. How a price floor results in a surplus of the good.

3. How a quantity restriction or quota results in quota rent to the holder of the license.

PITFALLS

CEILINGS, FLOORS, AND QUANTITIES

? A price ceiling pushes the price of a good *down*. A price floor pushes the price of a good *up*. So it looks like we can assume that the effects of a price floor are the opposite of the effects of a price ceiling. Put another way, if a price ceiling reduces the quantity of a good bought and sold, doesn't a price floor increase the quantity?

> NO, IT DOESN'T, BECAUSE BOTH FLOORS AND CEILINGS REDUCE THE QUANTITY BOUGHT AND SOLD. Why? When the quantity of a good supplied isn't equal to the quantity demanded, the actual quantity sold is determined by the "short side" of the market—whichever quantity is less. If sellers don't want to sell as much as buyers want to buy, it's the sellers who determine the actual quantity sold, because buyers can't force unwilling sellers to sell. If buyers don't want to buy as much as sellers want to sell, it's the buyers who determine the actual quantity sold, because sellers can't force unwilling buyers to buy.

To learn more, see pages 63–70, including Figures 7-2 and 7-4.

International Trade

Glow Images/Superstock

Until now, we have analyzed the economy as if it were self-sufficient, as if the economy produces all the goods and services it consumes, and vice versa. This is, of course, true for the world economy as a whole. But it's not true for any individual country.

The model of supply and demand that was developed in preceding modules implicitly assumed self-sufficiency. In other words, if the quantity of a good produced in the country is equal to the quantity of the good consumed, then there are no imports or exports.

Assuming self-sufficiency would have been far more accurate 50 years ago, when the United States exported only a small fraction of what it produced and imported only a small fraction of what it consumed.

Since then, however, both U.S. imports and exports have grown dramatically. Moreover, compared to the United States, other countries engage in far more foreign trade relative to the size of their economies. To have a full picture of how national economies work, we must understand the economics of international trade.

International Trade and Globalization

The United States buys auto parts—and many other goods and services—from other countries. At the same time, it sells many goods and services to other countries. Goods and services purchased from abroad are **imports;** goods and services sold abroad are **exports.**

Imports and exports have taken on an increasingly important role in the U.S. economy. Over the last 50 years, both imports into and exports from the United States have grown faster than the U.S. economy as a whole. Panel (a) of Figure 8-1 shows how the values of U.S. imports and exports have grown as a percentage of gross domestic product (GDP). Panel (b) shows imports and exports as a percentage of GDP

Goods and services purchased from other countries are **imports;** goods and services sold to other countries are **exports.**

FIGURE

8-1   **The Growing Importance of International Trade**

Panel (a) illustrates the fact that over the past 52 years, the United States has exported a steadily growing share of its GDP to other countries and imported a growing share of what it consumes. Panel (b) demonstrates that international trade is significantly more important to many other countries than it is to the United States, with the exception of Japan.

Source: Bureau of Economic Analysis [panel (a)] and World Trade Organization [panel (b)].

for a number of countries. It shows that foreign trade is significantly more important for many other countries than it is for the United States. (Japan is one exception.)

Foreign trade isn't the only way countries interact economically. In the modern world, investors from one country often invest funds in another nation; many companies are multinational, with subsidiaries operating in several countries; and a growing number of individuals work in a country different from the one in which they were born. The growth of all these forms of economic linkages among countries is often called **globalization.**

In the rest of this module, we'll focus on international trade. Later on, in Section 13, we'll address other interactions that occur between countries.

Supply, Demand, and International Trade

In Module 3 we learned about comparative advantage, where by definition *a country has a comparative advantage in producing a good or service if the opportunity cost of producing the good or service is lower for that country than for other countries.* In this simple model, we used the production possibility frontier *(PPF)* to show how a country could specialize in one good, trade some of this good for another good, and end up consuming more of both goods. Although the production possibility frontier model allows us to demonstrate gains from trade, to analyze the effects of international trade at a more detailed level and to understand trade policy, it helps to return to the supply and demand model. We'll start by looking at the effects of imports on domestic producers and consumers, then turn to the effects of exports.

The Effects of Imports

Figure 8-2 shows the U.S. market for auto seats. It introduces a few new concepts: the *domestic demand curve,* the *domestic supply curve,* and the domestic or *autarky price.* Economists use the term **autarky** to refer to a situation in which a country does not

Globalization is the phenomenon of growing economic linkages among countries.

Autarky is a situation in which a country does not trade with other countries.

trade with other countries. In Figure 8-2, the autarky price is P_A, and at this price, the quantity consumed domestically is equal to the quantity produced domestically.

The **domestic demand curve** shows how the quantity of a good demanded by residents of a country depends on the price of that good. Why "domestic"? Because people living in other countries may demand the good, too. Once we introduce international trade, we need to distinguish between purchases of a good by domestic consumers and purchases by foreign consumers. So the domestic demand curve reflects only the demand of residents of our own country. Similarly, the **domestic supply curve** shows how the quantity of a good supplied by producers inside our own country depends on the price of that good. Once we introduce international trade, we need to distinguish between the supply of domestic producers and foreign supply—supply brought in from abroad.

In autarky, with no international trade in auto seats, the equilibrium in this market would be determined by the intersection of the domestic demand and domestic supply curves, point A. The equilibrium price of auto seats would be P_A, and the equilibrium quantity of auto seats produced and consumed would be Q_A.

Now let's imagine opening up this market to imports. To do this, we must make an assumption about the supply of imports. The simplest assumption, which we will adopt here, is that unlimited quantities of auto seats can be purchased from abroad at a fixed price, known as the **world price** of auto seats. Figure 8-2 shows a situation in which the world price of an auto seat, P_W, is lower than the price of an auto seat that would prevail in the domestic market in autarky, P_A.

Given that the world price is below the domestic price of an auto seat, it is profitable for importers to buy auto seats abroad and resell them domestically. The imported auto seats increase the supply of auto seats in the domestic market, driving down the domestic market price. Auto seats will continue to be imported until the domestic price falls to a level equal to the world price.

The result is shown in Figure 8-2. Because of imports, the domestic price of an auto seat falls from P_A to P_W. The quantity of auto seats demanded by domestic consumers rises from Q_A to Q_D, and the quantity supplied by domestic producers falls from Q_A to

The **domestic demand curve** shows how the quantity of a good demanded by domestic consumers depends on the price of that good.

The **domestic supply curve** shows how the quantity of a good supplied by domestic producers depends on the price of that good.

The **world price** of a good is the price at which that good can be bought or sold abroad.

The opportunity cost of producing auto parts is higher in the United States than in Mexico.

FIGURE 8-2   The Domestic Market with Imports

Here the world price of auto seats, P_W, is below the autarky price, P_A. When the economy is opened to international trade, imports enter the domestic market, and the domestic price falls from the autarky price, P_A, to the world price, P_W. As the price falls, the domestic quantity demanded rises from Q_A to Q_D and the domestic quantity supplied falls from Q_A to Q_S. The difference between domestic quantity demanded and domestic quantity supplied at P_W, the quantity $Q_D - Q_S$, is filled by imports.

Thinkstock

Opening up a market to imports and exports leads to a net gain in total surplus, but creates losers as well as winners.

Q_S. The difference between the domestic quantity demanded and the domestic quantity supplied, $Q_D - Q_S$, is filled by imports.

Having the ability to buy more of a good at a lower price is a gain to consumers, while the decrease in quantity supplied results in a loss to producers. As we'll see shortly, the fact that international trade typically creates losers as well as winners is crucial for understanding the politics of trade policy.

We turn next to the case in which a country exports a good.

The Effects of Exports

Figure 8-3 shows the effects on a country when it exports a good, in this case airplanes. For this example, we assume that unlimited quantities of airplanes can be sold abroad at a given world price, P_W, which is higher than the price that would prevail in the domestic market in autarky, P_A.

The higher world price makes it profitable for exporters to buy airplanes domestically and sell them overseas. The purchases of domestic airplanes drive the domestic price up until it is equal to the world price. As a result, the quantity demanded by domestic consumers falls from Q_A to Q_D and the quantity supplied by domestic producers rises from Q_A to Q_S. This difference between domestic production and domestic consumption, $Q_S - Q_D$, is exported.

Having the ability to sell more of a good at a higher price is a gain to producers, while the decrease in quantity demanded results in a loss to consumers. So, just like imports, exports create losers as well as winners.

FIGURE 8-3   **The Domestic Market with Exports**

Here the world price, P_W, is greater than the autarky price, P_A. When the economy is opened to international trade, some of the domestic supply is now exported. The domestic price rises from the autarky price, P_A, to the world price, P_W. As the price rises, the domestic quantity demanded falls from Q_A to Q_D and the domestic quantity supplied rises from Q_A to Q_S. The portion of domestic production that is not consumed domestically, $Q_S - Q_D$, is exported.

International Trade and Wages

So far we have focused on the effects of international trade on producers and consumers in a particular industry. However, producers and consumers are not the only parts of society affected by trade—so are the owners of factors of production. In particular, the owners of labor, land, and capital employed in producing goods that are exported, or goods that compete with imported goods, can be deeply affected by trade.

Moreover, the effects of trade aren't limited to just those industries that export or compete with imports because *factors of production can often move between industries.* So now we turn our attention to the long-run effects of international trade on income distribution—how a country's total income is allocated among its various factors of production.

To begin our analysis, consider the position of Maria, an accountant at Midwest Auto Parts, Inc. If the economy is opened up to imports of auto parts from Mexico, the domestic auto parts industry will contract, and it will hire fewer accountants. But accounting is a profession with employment opportunities in many industries, and Maria might well find a better job in the aircraft industry, which expands as a result of international trade. So it may not be appropriate to think of her as a producer of auto parts who is hurt by competition from imported parts. Rather, we should think of her as an accountant who is affected by auto part imports only to the extent that these imports change the wages of accountants in the economy as a whole.

The wage rate of accountants is a *factor price*—the price employers have to pay for the services of a factor of production. One key question about international trade is how it affects factor prices—not just narrowly defined factors of production like accountants, but broadly defined factors such as capital, unskilled labor, and college-educated labor.

The prices of factors of production, like the prices of goods and services, are determined by supply and demand. If international trade increases the demand for a factor of production, that factor's price will rise; if international trade reduces the demand for a factor of production, that factor's price will fall.

Now think of a country's industries as consisting of two kinds: **exporting industries,** which produce goods and services that are sold abroad, and **import-competing industries,** which produce goods and services that are also imported from abroad. Compared with autarky, international trade leads to higher production in exporting industries and lower production in import-competing industries. This indirectly increases the demand for the factors used by exporting industries and decreases the demand for factors used by import-competing industries.

The United States has a comparative advantage in producing high-technology goods, like airplanes and computer chips, that require skilled labor whereas newly industrialized countries like China have a comparative advantage in producing unskilled, labor-intensive products, such as clothing and consumer electronics. In the United States the result is an increase in the demand for the skilled labor used by the exporting industries and a decrease in the demand for the less skilled labor used by the import-competing industries.

This suggests that the effect of international trade on U.S. factor markets is to raise the wage rate of highly educated American workers and reduce the wage rate of unskilled American workers.

This effect has been a source of much concern in recent years. Wage inequality—the gap between the wages of high-paid and low-paid workers—has increased substantially over the last 30 years. Some economists believe that growing international trade is an important factor in that trend. But keep in mind another phenomenon: trade reduces the income inequality *between* countries as poor countries improve their standard of living by exporting to rich countries.

The effects of trade on wages in the United States have generated considerable controversy in recent years. Most economists who have studied the issue agree that growing imports of labor-intensive products from newly industrializing economies, and the export of high-technology goods in return, have helped cause a widening wage gap between highly educated and less educated workers in this country. However, most economists believe that it is only one of several forces explaining the growth in American wage inequality.

Exporting industries produce goods and services that are sold abroad.

Import-competing industries produce goods and services that are also imported.

Trade benefits highly educated American workers when exporting industries demand more skilled labor and wages increase.

ECONOMICS ▶ IN ACTION

SKILL AND COMPARATIVE ADVANTAGE

In 1953 U.S. workers were clearly better equipped with machinery than their counterparts in other countries. Most economists at the time thought that America's comparative advantage lay in capital-intensive goods. However, data showed that goods the United States exported were slightly less capital-intensive than goods the country imported.

The explanation for this finding depends on the definition of *capital*. U.S. exports aren't intensive in *physical* capital—machines and buildings. Instead, they are *skill-intensive*—that is, they are intensive in *human* capital. U.S. exporting industries use a substantially higher ratio of highly educated workers to other workers than is found in U.S. industries that compete against imports. For example, one of America's biggest export sectors is aircraft; the aircraft industry employs large numbers of engineers and other people with graduate degrees relative to the number of manual laborers. Conversely, we import a lot of clothing, which is often produced by workers with little formal education.

In general, countries with highly educated workforces tend to export skill-intensive goods, while countries with less educated workforces tend to export goods whose production requires little skilled labor.

Figure 8-4 illustrates this point by comparing the goods the United States imports from Germany, a country with a highly educated labor force, with the goods the United States imports from Bangladesh, where about half of the adult population is still illiterate. In each country industries are ranked, first, according to how skill-intensive they are. Next, for each industry, we calculate its share of U.S. imports. This allows us to plot, for each country, various industries according to their skill intensity and their share of U.S. imports.

In Figure 8-4, the horizontal axis shows a measure of the skill intensity of different industries, and the vertical axes show the share of U.S. imports in each industry coming from Germany (on the left) and Bangladesh (on the right). As you can see, each country's share of U.S. imports reflects its skill level. The curve representing Germany slopes upward: the more skill-intensive a German industry is, the higher its share of U.S. imports. In contrast, the curve representing Bangladesh slopes downward: the less skill-intensive a Bangladeshi industry is, the higher its share of U.S. imports.

FIGURE 8-4   Education, Skill Intensity, and Trade

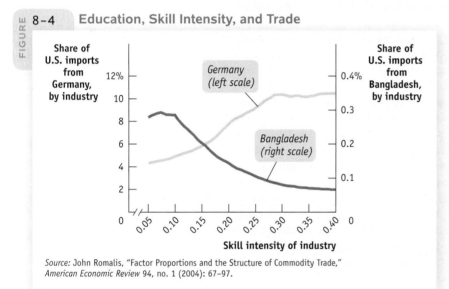

Source: John Romalis, "Factor Proportions and the Structure of Commodity Trade," *American Economic Review* 94, no. 1 (2004): 67–97.

The Effects of Trade Protection

Ever since the principle of comparative advantage was laid out in the early nineteenth century, most economists have advocated **free trade.** That is, they have argued that government policy should not attempt either to reduce or to increase the levels of exports and imports that occur naturally as a result of supply and demand.

Despite the free-trade arguments of economists, however, many governments use taxes and other restrictions to limit imports. Less frequently, governments offer subsidies to encourage exports. Policies that limit imports, usually with the goal of

An economy has **free trade** when the government does not attempt either to reduce or to increase the levels of exports and imports that occur naturally as a result of supply and demand.

protecting domestic producers in import-competing industries from foreign competition, are known as **trade protection** or simply as **protection.**

Let's look at the two most common protectionist policies, tariffs and import quotas.

Policies that limit imports are known as trade protection or simply as protection.

A tariff is a tax levied on imports.

The Effects of a Tariff

A **tariff** is a form of excise tax, one that is levied only on sales of imported goods. For example, the U.S. government could declare that anyone bringing in auto seats must pay a tariff of $100 per unit. In the distant past, tariffs were an important source of government revenue because they were relatively easy to collect. But in the modern world, tariffs are usually intended to discourage imports and protect import-competing domestic producers rather than to serve as a source of government revenue.

The tariff raises both the price received by domestic producers and the price paid by domestic consumers. Suppose, for example, that our country imports auto seats, and an auto seat costs $200 on the world market. As we saw earlier, under free trade the domestic price would also be $200. But if a tariff of $100 per unit is imposed, the domestic price will rise to $300, because it won't be profitable to import auto seats unless the price in the domestic market is high enough to compensate importers for the cost of paying the tariff.

Figure 8-5 illustrates the effects of a tariff on imports of auto seats. As before, we assume that P_W is the world price of an auto seat. Before the tariff is imposed, imports have driven the domestic price down to P_W, so that pre-tariff domestic production is Q_S, pre-tariff domestic consumption is Q_D, and pre-tariff imports are $Q_D - Q_S$.

Now suppose that the government imposes a tariff on each auto seat imported. As a consequence, it is no longer profitable to import auto seats unless the domestic price received by the importer is greater than or equal to the world price *plus* the tariff. So the domestic price rises to P_T, which is equal to the world price, P_W, plus the tariff. Domestic production rises to Q_{ST}, domestic consumption falls to Q_{DT}, and imports fall to $Q_{DT} - Q_{ST}$.

A tariff, then, raises domestic prices, leading to increased domestic production and reduced domestic consumption compared to the situation under free trade.

FIGURE 8-5   The Effect of a Tariff

A tariff raises the domestic price of the good from P_W to P_T. The domestic quantity demanded shrinks from Q_D to Q_{DT}, and the domestic quantity supplied increases from Q_S to Q_{ST}. As a result, imports—which had been $Q_D - Q_S$ before the tariff was imposed—shrink to $Q_{DT} - Q_{ST}$ after the tariff is imposed.

An **import quota** is a legal limit on the quantity of a good that can be imported.

The Effects of an Import Quota

An **import quota,** another form of trade protection, is a legal limit on the quantity of a good that can be imported. For example, a U.S. import quota on Mexican auto seats might limit the quantity imported each year to 500,000 units. Import quotas are usually administered through licenses: a number of licenses are issued, each giving the license-holder the right to import a limited quantity of the good each year.

An import quota has the same effect as a tariff, with one difference: the money that would otherwise have been government revenue becomes *quota rents,* or earnings that accrue to license-holders.

Look again at Figure 8-5. An import quota that limits imports to $Q_{DT} - Q_{ST}$ will raise the domestic price of auto parts by the same amount as the tariff we considered previously. That is, it will raise the domestic price from P_W to P_T. This difference between P_T and P_W now goes to the license-holder.

Who receives import licenses and so collects the quota rents? In the case of U.S. import protection, the answer may surprise you: the most important import licenses—mainly for clothing, to a lesser extent for sugar—are granted to foreign governments.

Because the quota rents for most U.S. import quotas go to foreigners, the cost to the nation of such quotas is larger than that of a comparable tariff (a tariff that leads to the same level of imports).

Challenges to Globalization

We have seen that international trade produces mutual benefits to the countries that engage in it. The forward march of globalization over the past century is generally considered a major political and economic success. Economists and policy makers alike have viewed growing world trade, in particular, as a good thing.

We would be remiss, however, if we failed to acknowledge that many people are having second thoughts about globalization. To a large extent, these second thoughts reflect two concerns shared by many economists: worries about the effects of globalization on inequality and worries that new developments, in particular the growth in *offshore outsourcing,* are increasing economic insecurity.

GLOBALIZATION AND INEQUALITY We've already mentioned the implications of international trade for factor prices, such as wages: when wealthy countries like the United States export skill-intensive products like aircraft while importing labor-intensive products like clothing, they can expect to see the wage gap between more educated and less educated domestic workers widen.

Thirty years ago, this wasn't a significant concern, because most of the goods wealthy countries imported from poorer countries were raw materials or goods where comparative advantage depended on climate. Today, however, many manufactured goods are imported from relatively poor countries, with a potentially much larger effect on the distribution of income.

Economists and policy makers view growing world trade as a positive, but not everyone agrees.

Trade with China, in particular, raises concerns among labor groups trying to maintain wage levels in rich countries. Although China has experienced spectacular economic growth since the economic reforms that began in the late 1970s, it remains a poor, low-wage country: wages in Chinese manufacturing are estimated to be only about 6% of U.S. wages.

Meanwhile, imports from China have soared. In 1983 less than 1% of U.S. imports came from China; by 2012, the figure was 18%. There's not much question that these surging imports from China put at least some downward pressure on the wages of less educated American workers.

OUTSOURCING Chinese exports to the United States overwhelmingly consist of labor-intensive manufactured goods. However, some U.S. workers have recently found themselves facing another form of international competition. *Outsourcing,* in which a company hires another company to perform some task, such as running the corporate computer system, is a long-standing business practice. Until recently, however, outsourcing was normally done locally, with a company hiring another company in the same city or country.

Now, modern telecommunications make it possible to engage in **offshore outsourcing,** in which businesses hire people in another country to perform various tasks. The classic example is a call center: the person answering the phone when you call a company's 1-800 help line may well be in India, which has taken the lead in attracting offshore outsourcing. Offshore outsourcing has also spread to fields such as software design and even health care: the radiologist examining your X-rays, like the person giving you computer help, may be on another continent.

Although offshore outsourcing has come as a shock to some U.S. workers, such as programmers whose jobs have been outsourced to India, it's still relatively small compared with more traditional trade. Some economists have warned, however, that millions or even tens of millions of workers who have never thought they could face foreign competition for their jobs may face unpleasant surprises in the not-too-distant future.

Do these challenges to globalization undermine the argument that international trade is a good thing? The great majority of economists would argue that the gains from reducing trade protection still exceed the losses. However, it has become more important than before to make sure that the gains from international trade are widely spread. And the politics of international trade is becoming increasingly difficult as the extent of trade has grown.

Offshore outsourcing takes place when businesses hire people in another country to perform various tasks.

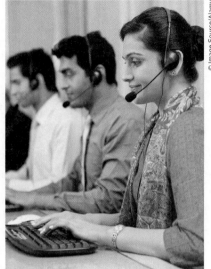
© Image Source/Alamy

Offshore outsourcing is relatively small compared with more traditional trade.

8) Review

MODULE

Solutions appear at the back of the book.

Check Your Understanding

1. Suppose that the United States now imports tomatoes from Mexico and exports chicken to Mexico. How would you expect the following groups to be affected, relative to an initial state where there is autarky in each industry?

   a. Mexican and U.S. consumers of tomatoes

   b. Mexican and U.S. producers of tomatoes

   c. Mexican and U.S. tomato workers

   d. Mexican and U.S. consumers of poultry

   e. Mexican and U.S. producers of poultry

   f. Mexican and U.S. poultry workers

2. Suppose the world price of butter is $0.50 per pound and the domestic price in autarky is $1.00 per pound. Use a diagram similar to Figure 8-5 to show the following.

   a. If there is free trade, domestic butter producers want the government to impose a tariff of no less than $0.50 per pound.

   b. What happens if a tariff greater than $0.50 per pound is imposed?

3. Suppose the government imposes an import quota rather than a tariff on butter. What quota limit would generate the same quantity of imports as a tariff of $0.50 per pound?

Multiple-Choice Questions

1. When a country imports a good,

   a. the domestic quantity supplied equals zero.

   b. the domestic quantity demanded equals zero.

   c. the domestic quantity demanded equals the quantity of imports.

   d. the domestic quantity demanded is greater than the domestic quantity supplied.

   e. the domestic quantity demanded is less than the domestic quantity supplied.

2. When a country exports a good,

   a. the domestic quantity supplied equals zero.

   b. the domestic quantity demanded equals zero.

   c. the domestic quantity supplied equals the quantity of exports.

   d. the domestic quantity demanded is greater than the domestic quantity supplied.

   e. the domestic quantity demanded is less than the domestic quantity supplied.

3. When a country becomes an exporter of a good,

   a. domestic quantity supplied increases.

   b. domestic quantity demanded increases.

   c. the world price is less than the autarky price.

   d. the domestic supply curve shifts to the right.

   e. the domestic demand curve shifts to the left.

4. When a country opens up to trade and begins to export a particular good, the domestic quantity supplied of the good will _____ and the wages of the workers who produce the good will _____.

   a. increase; increase

   b. increase; decrease

   c. decrease; decrease

   d. decrease; increase

   e. remain unchanged : remain unchanged

5. If the world price is higher than the domestic autarky price, then when the economy opens up to trade the country will become an _____ of the good and the price in the domestic market will _____.

   a. exporter; decrease

   b. importer; decrease

   c. importer; increase

   d. exporter; increase

   e. exporter; remain unchanged

Critical-Thinking Questions

Assume that in autarky the equilibrium price of a good in the domestic market is $10, the world price of the same good is $8, and the country opens up to trade. Then answer the following questions.

1. How will the domestic quantity supplied and demanded be affected?

2. Will the country be an importer or an exporter of the good?

3. Draw a graph to support your answers.

BUSINESS :
CASE :
Li & Fung: From Guangzhou to You

It's a very good bet that as you read this, you're wearing something manufactured in Asia. And if you are, it's also a good bet that the Hong Kong company Li & Fung was involved in getting your garment designed, produced, and shipped to your local store. From Levi's to The Limited to Walmart, Li & Fung is a critical conduit from factories around the world to the shopping mall nearest you.

The company was founded in 1906 in Guangzhou, China. According to Victor Fung, the company's chairman, his grandfather's "value added" was that he spoke English, allowing him to serve as an interpreter in business deals between Chinese and foreigners. When Mao's Communist Party seized control in mainland China, the company moved to Hong Kong. There, as Hong Kong's market economy took off during the 1960s and 1970s, Li & Fung grew as an export broker, bringing together Hong Kong manufacturers and foreign buyers.

The real transformation of the company came, however, as Asian economies grew and changed. Hong Kong's rapid growth led to rising wages, making Li & Fung increasingly uncompetitive in garments, its main business. So the company reinvented itself: rather than being a simple broker, it became a "supply chain manager." Not only would it allocate production of a good to a manufacturer, it would also break production down, allocate production of the inputs, and then allocate final assembly of the good among its 12,000+ suppliers around the globe. Sometimes production would be done in sophisticated economies like those of Hong Kong or even Japan, where wages are high but so is quality and productivity; sometimes it would be done in less advanced locations like mainland China or Thailand, where labor is less productive but cheaper.

For example, suppose you own a U.S. retail chain and want to sell garment-washed blue jeans. Rather than simply arrange for production of the jeans, Li & Fung will work with you on their design, providing you with the latest production and style information, like what materials and colors are hot. After the design has been finalized, Li & Fung will arrange for the creation of a prototype, find the most cost-effective way to manufacture it, and then place an order on your behalf. Through Li & Fung, the yarn might be made in Korea and dyed in Taiwan, and the jeans sewn in Thailand or mainland China. And because production is taking place in so many locations, Li & Fung provides transport logistics as well as quality control.

Li & Fung has been enormously successful. In late 2013, the company had a market value of approximately $12.5 billion, with offices and distribution centers in more than 40 countries. Year after year, it continues to post sizeable profits.

Questions for Thought

1. Why do you think it was profitable for Li & Fung to go beyond brokering exports to becoming a supply chain manager, breaking down the production process and sourcing the inputs from various suppliers across many countries?

2. What principle do you think underlies Li & Fung's decisions on how to allocate production of a good's inputs and its final assembly among various countries?

3. Why do you think a retailer prefers to have Li & Fung arrange international production of its jeans rather than purchase them directly from a jeans manufacturer in mainland China?

4. What is the source of Li & Fung's success? Is it based on human capital, on ownership of a natural resource, or on ownership of capital?

SECTION 2 REVIEW

Summary

Demand

1. The **supply and demand model** illustrates how a **competitive market,** one with many buyers and sellers of the same product, works.

2. The **demand schedule** shows the **quantity demanded** at each price and is represented graphically by a **demand curve.** The **law of demand** says that demand curves slope downward, meaning that as price decreases, the quantity demanded increases.

3. A **movement along the demand curve** occurs when the price changes and causes a change in the quantity demanded. When economists talk of **changes in demand,** they mean shifts of the demand curve—a change in the quantity demanded at any given price. An increase in demand causes a rightward shift of the demand curve. A decrease in demand causes a leftward shift.

4. There are five main factors that shift the demand curve:
   - A change in the prices of related goods, such as **substitutes** or **complements**
   - A change in income: when income rises, the demand for **normal goods** increases and the demand for **inferior goods** decreases
   - A change in tastes
   - A change in expectations
   - A change in the number of consumers

Supply and Equilibrium

5. The **supply schedule** shows the **quantity supplied** at each price and is represented graphically by a **supply curve.** Supply curves usually slope upward.

6. A **movement along the supply curve** occurs when the price changes and causes a change in the quantity supplied. When economists talk of **changes in supply,** they mean shifts of the supply curve—a change in the quantity supplied at any given price. An increase in supply causes a rightward shift of the supply curve. A decrease in supply causes a leftward shift.

7. There are five main factors that shift the supply curve:
   - A change in **input** prices
   - A change in the prices of related goods and services
   - A change in technology
   - A change in expectations
   - A change in the number of producers

8. The supply and demand model is based on the principle that the price in a market moves to its **equilibrium price,** or **market-clearing price,** the price at which the quantity demanded is equal to the quantity supplied. This quantity is the **equilibrium quantity.** When the price is above its market-clearing level, there is a **surplus** that pushes the price down. When the price is below its market-clearing level, there is a **shortage** that pushes the price up.

Changes in Equilibrium

9. An increase in demand increases both the equilibrium price and the equilibrium quantity; a decrease in demand has the opposite effect. An increase in supply reduces the equilibrium price and increases the equilibrium quantity; a decrease in supply has the opposite effect.

10. Shifts of the demand curve and the supply curve can happen simultaneously. When they shift in opposite directions, the change in price is predictable but the change in quantity is not. When they shift in the same direction, the change in quantity is predictable but the change in price is not. In general, the curve that shifts the greater distance has a greater effect on the changes in price and quantity.

Price Controls and Quantity Controls

11. Even when a market is efficient, governments often intervene to pursue greater fairness or to please a powerful interest group. Interventions can take the form of **price controls** or **quantity controls,** both of which generate predictable and undesirable side effects, consisting of various forms of inefficiency and illegal activity.

12. A **price ceiling,** a maximum market price below the equilibrium price, benefits successful buyers but creates persistent shortages. Because the price is maintained below the equilibrium price, the quantity demanded is increased and the quantity supplied is decreased compared to the equilibrium quantity. This leads to predictable problems including **inefficient allocation to consumers, wasted resources,** and **inefficiently low quality.** It also encourages illegal activity as people turn to **black markets** to get the good. Because of these problems, price ceilings have generally lost favor as an economic policy tool. But some governments continue to impose them either because they don't understand the effects or because the price ceilings benefit some influential group.

13. A **price floor,** a minimum market price above the equilibrium price, benefits successful sellers but creates a persistent surplus: because the price is maintained above the equilibrium price, the quantity demanded is decreased and the quantity supplied is increased compared to the equilibrium quantity. This leads to

predictable problems: inefficiencies in the form of **inefficient allocation of sales among sellers,** wasted resources, and **inefficiently high quality.** It also encourages illegal activity and black markets. The most well known kind of price floor is the **minimum wage,** but price floors are also commonly applied to agricultural products.

14. Quantity controls, or **quotas,** limit the quantity of a good that can be bought or sold. The government issues **licenses** to individuals, the right to sell a given quantity of the good. The owner of a license earns a **quota rent,** earnings that accrue from ownership of the right to sell the good. It is equal to the difference between the **demand price** at the quota amount, what consumers are willing to pay for that amount, and the **supply price** at the quota amount, what suppliers are willing to accept for that amount. Economists say that a quota drives a **wedge** between the demand price and the supply price; this wedge is equal to the quota rent. By limiting mutually beneficial transactions, quantity controls generate inefficiency. Like price controls, quantity controls lead to **deadweight loss** and encourage illegal activity.

International Trade

15. International trade is of growing importance to the United States and of even greater importance to most other countries. International trade, like trade among individuals, arises from comparative advantage: the opportunity cost of producing an additional unit of a good is lower in some countries than in others. Goods and services purchased abroad are **imports;** those sold abroad are **exports.** Foreign trade, like other economic linkages between countries, has been growing rapidly, a phenomenon called **globalization.**

16. **Autarky** refers to a situation in which a country does not trade with other countries. The **domestic demand curve** and the **domestic supply curve** determine the price of a good in autarky. When international trade occurs, the domestic price is driven to equality with the **world price,** the price at which the good is bought and sold abroad.

17. If the world price is below the autarky price, a good is imported. This leads to an increase in domestic consumption and a decrease in domestic production. If the world price is above the autarky price, a good is exported. This leads to an increase in domestic production and a decrease in domestic consumption.

18. International trade leads to expansion in **exporting industries** and contraction in **import-competing industries.** This raises the domestic demand for factors of production used in the exporting industries and reduces the demand for factors of production used in the import-competing industries.

19. Most economists advocate **free trade,** but in practice many governments engage in **trade protection.** The two most common forms of **protection** are tariffs and quotas. On rare occasions, export industries are subsidized.

20. A **tariff** is a tax levied on imports. It raises the domestic price above the world price, hurting consumers, benefiting domestic producers, and generating government revenue. An **import quota** is a legal limit on the quantity of a good that can be imported. It has the same effects as a tariff, except that the revenue goes not to the government but to those who receive import licenses.

21. In the past few years, many concerns have been raised about the effects of globalization. One issue is the increase in income inequality due to the surge in imports from relatively poor countries over the past 20 years. Another is the increase in **offshore outsourcing,** as many jobs once considered safe from foreign competition have been moved abroad.

Key Terms

Competitive market, p. 32
Supply and demand model, p. 32
Demand schedule, p. 33
Quantity demanded, p. 33
Demand curve, p. 33
Law of demand, p. 34
Change in demand, p. 35
Movement along the demand curve, p. 35
Substitutes, p. 37
Complements, p. 37
Normal good, p. 38

Inferior good, p. 38
Individual demand curve, p. 39
Quantity supplied, p. 43
Supply schedule, p. 43
Supply curve, p. 43
Law of supply, p. 44
Change in supply, p. 44
Movement along the supply curve, p. 44
Input, p. 46
Individual supply curve, p. 47
Equilibrium, p. 50
Equilibrium price, p. 51

Market-clearing price, p. 51
Equilibrium quantity, p. 51
Surplus, p. 52
Shortage, p. 52
Price controls, p. 63
Price ceiling, p. 63
Price floor, p. 63
Quantity control or quota, p. 63
License, p. 63
Inefficient allocation to consumers, p. 66
Wasted resources, p. 66

Inefficiently low quality, p. 66
Black markets, p. 66
Minimum wage, p. 67
Inefficient allocation of sales among sellers, p. 67
Inefficiently high quality, p. 70
Demand price, p. 71
Supply price, p. 71
Wedge, p. 72
Quota rent, p. 72
Deadweight loss, p. 73
Imports, p. 77
Exports, p. 77

Problems

1. A survey indicated that chocolate ice cream is America's favorite ice-cream flavor. For each of the following, indicate the possible effects on the demand and/or supply, equilibrium price, and equilibrium quantity of chocolate ice cream.

   a. A severe drought in the Midwest causes dairy farmers to reduce the number of milk-producing cows in their herds by a third. These dairy farmers supply cream that is used to manufacture chocolate ice cream.

   b. A new report by the American Medical Association reveals that chocolate does, in fact, have significant health benefits.

   c. The discovery of cheaper synthetic vanilla flavoring lowers the price of vanilla ice cream.

   d. New technology for mixing and freezing ice cream lowers manufacturers' costs of producing chocolate ice cream.

2. In a supply and demand diagram, draw the change in demand for hamburgers in your hometown due to the following events. In each case show the effect on equilibrium price and quantity.

   a. The price of tacos increases.

   b. All hamburger sellers raise the price of their french fries.

   c. Income falls in town. Assume that hamburgers are a normal good for most people.

   d. Income falls in town. Assume that hamburgers are an inferior good for most people.

   e. Hot dog stands cut the price of hot dogs.

3. The market for many goods changes in predictable ways according to the time of year, in response to events such as holidays, vacation times, seasonal changes in production, and so on. Using supply and demand, explain the change in price in each of the following cases. Note that supply and demand may shift simultaneously.

   a. Lobster prices usually fall during the summer peak harvest season, despite the fact that people like to eat lobster during the summer months more than during any other time of year.

   b. The price of a Christmas tree is lower after Christmas than before and fewer trees are sold.

   c. The price of a round-trip ticket to Paris on Air France falls by more than $200 after the end of school vacation in September. This happens despite the fact that generally worsening weather increases the cost of operating flights to Paris, and Air France therefore reduces the number of flights to Paris at any given price.

4. Show in a diagram the effect on the demand curve, the supply curve, the equilibrium price, and the equilibrium quantity of each of the following events on the designated market.

   a. the market for newspapers in your town

   Case 1: The salaries of journalists go up.

   Case 2: There is a big news event in your town, which is reported in the newspapers, and residents want to learn more about it.

   b. the market for St. Louis Rams cotton T-shirts

   Case 1: The Rams win the championship.

   Case 2: The price of cotton increases.

   c. the market for bagels

   Case 1: People realize how fattening bagels are.

   Case 2: People have less time to make themselves a cooked breakfast.

5. Find the flaws in reasoning in the following statements, paying particular attention to the distinction between changes in and movements along the supply and demand curves. Draw a diagram to illustrate what actually happens in each situation.

   a. "A technological innovation that lowers the cost of producing a good might seem at first to result in a reduction in the price of the good to consumers. But a fall in price will increase demand for the good, and higher demand will send the price up again. It is not certain, therefore, that an innovation will really reduce price in the end."

   b. "A study shows that eating a clove of garlic a day can help prevent heart disease, causing many consumers to demand more garlic. This increase in demand results in a rise in the price of garlic. Consumers, seeing that the price of garlic has gone up, reduce their demand for garlic. This causes the demand for garlic to decrease and the price of garlic to fall. Therefore, the ultimate effect of the study on the price of garlic is uncertain."

6. In *Rolling Stone* magazine, several fans and rock stars, including Pearl Jam, were bemoaning the high price of concert tickets. One superstar argued, "It just isn't worth $75 to see me play. No one should have to pay that much to go to a concert." Assume this star sold out arenas around the country at an average ticket price of $75.

   a. How would you evaluate the argument that ticket prices are too high?

   b. Suppose that due to this star's protests, ticket prices were lowered to $50. In what sense is this price too low? Draw a diagram using supply and demand curves to support your argument.

   c. Suppose Pearl Jam really wanted to bring down ticket prices. Since the band controls the supply of its services, what do you recommend they do? Explain using a supply and demand diagram.

d. Suppose the band's next CD was a total dud. Do you think they would still have to worry about ticket prices being too high? Why or why not? Draw a supply and demand diagram to support your argument.

e. Suppose the group announced their next tour was going to be their last. What effect would this likely have on the demand for and price of tickets? Illustrate with a supply and demand diagram.

7. After several years of decline, the market for handmade acoustic guitars is making a comeback. These guitars, which are normal goods, are usually made in small workshops employing relatively few highly skilled luthiers. Assess the impact on the equilibrium price and quantity of handmade acoustic guitars as a result of each of the following events. In your answers, indicate which curve(s) shift(s) and in which direction.

a. Environmentalists succeed in having the use of Brazilian rosewood banned in the United States, forcing luthiers to seek out alternative, more costly woods.

b. A foreign producer reengineers the guitar-making process and floods the market with identical guitars.

c. Music featuring handmade acoustic guitars makes a comeback as audiences tire of heavy metal and grunge music.

d. The country goes into a deep recession and the income of the average American falls sharply.

8. Will Shakespeare is a struggling playwright in sixteenth-century London. As the price he receives for writing a play increases, he is willing to write more plays. For the following situations, use a diagram to illustrate how each event affects the equilibrium price and quantity in the market for Shakespeare's plays.

a. The playwright Christopher Marlowe, Shakespeare's chief rival, is killed in a bar brawl.

b. The bubonic plague, a deadly infectious disease, breaks out in London.

c. To celebrate the defeat of the Spanish Armada, Queen Elizabeth declares several weeks of festivities, which involves commissioning new plays.

9. The small town of Middling experiences a sudden doubling of the birth rate. After three years, the birth rate returns to normal. Use a diagram to illustrate the effect of these events on the following:

a. the market for an hour of babysitting services in Middling today

b. the market for an hour of babysitting services 14 years into the future, after the birth rate has returned to normal, by which time children born today are old enough to work as babysitters

c. the market for an hour of babysitting services 30 years into the future, when children born today are likely to be having children of their own

10. Use a diagram to illustrate how each of the following events affects the equilibrium price and quantity of pizza.

a. The price of mozzarella cheese rises.

b. The health hazards of hamburgers are widely publicized.

c. The price of tomato sauce falls.

d. The incomes of consumers rise and pizza is an inferior good.

e. Consumers expect the price of pizza to fall next week.

11. Although he was a prolific artist, Pablo Picasso painted only 1,000 canvases during his "Blue Period." Picasso is now dead, and all of his Blue Period works are currently on display in museums and private galleries throughout Europe and the United States.

a. Draw a supply curve for Picasso Blue Period works. Why is this supply curve different from ones you have seen?

b. Given the supply curve from part a, the price of a Picasso Blue Period work will be entirely dependent on what factor(s)? Draw a diagram showing how the equilibrium price of such a work is determined.

c. Suppose that rich art collectors decide that it is essential to acquire Picasso Blue Period art for their collections. Show the impact of this on the market for these paintings.

12. Suppose it is decided that rent control in New York City will be abolished and that market rents will now prevail. Assume that all rental units are identical and are therefore offered at the same rent. To address the plight of residents who may be unable to pay the market rent, an income supplement will be paid to all low-income households equal to the difference between the old controlled rent and the new market rent.

a. Use a diagram to show the effect on the rental market of the elimination of rent control. What will happen to the quality and quantity of rental housing supplied?

b. Now use a second diagram to show the additional effect of the income-supplement policy on the market, namely the resulting increase in demand. What effect does it have on the market rent and quantity of rental housing supplied in comparison to your answers to part a?

c. Are tenants better or worse off as a result of these policies? Are landlords better or worse off?

d. From a political standpoint, why do you think cities have been more likely to resort to rent control rather than a policy of income supplements to help low-income people pay for housing?

13. In the late eighteenth century, the price of bread in New York City was controlled, set at a predetermined price above the market price.

a. Draw a diagram showing the effect of the policy. Did the policy act as a price ceiling or a price floor?

b. What kinds of inefficiencies were likely to have arisen when the controlled price of bread was above the market price? Explain in detail.

One year during this period, a poor wheat harvest caused a leftward shift in the supply of bread and therefore an increase in its market price. New York bakers found that the controlled price of bread in New York was below the market price.

c. Draw a diagram showing the effect of the price control on the market for bread during this one-year period. Did the policy act as a price ceiling or a price floor?

d. What kinds of inefficiencies do you think occurred during this period? Explain in detail.

14. Suppose the U.S. government decides that the incomes of dairy farmers should be maintained at a level that allows the traditional family dairy farm to survive. It therefore implements a price floor of $1 per pint by buying surplus milk until the market price is $1 per pint. Use the accompanying diagram to answer the following questions.

a. How much surplus milk will be produced as a result of this policy?

b. What will be the cost to the government of this policy?

c. Since milk is an important source of protein and calcium, the government decides to provide the surplus milk it purchases to elementary schools at a price of only $0.60 per pint. Assume that schools will buy any amount of milk available at this low price. But parents now reduce their purchases of milk at any price by 50 million pints per year because they know their children are getting milk at school. How much will the dairy program now cost the government?

d. Give two examples of inefficiencies arising from wasted resources that are likely to result from this policy. What is the missed opportunity in each case?

15. European governments tend to make greater use of price controls than the U.S. government. For example, the French government sets minimum starting yearly wages for new hires who have completed *le bac*, certification roughly equivalent to a high school diploma. The demand schedule for new hires with *le bac* and the supply schedule for similarly credentialed new job seekers are given in the accompanying table. The price here—given in euros, the currency used in France—is the same as the yearly wage.

Wage (per year)	Quantity demanded (new job offers per year)	Quantity supplied (new job seekers per year)
€45,000	200,000	325,000
40,000	220,000	320,000
35,000	250,000	310,000
30,000	290,000	290,000
25,000	370,000	200,000

a. In the absence of government interference, what is the equilibrium wage and number of graduates hired per year? Illustrate with a diagram. Will there be anyone seeking a job at the equilibrium wage who is unable to find one—that is, will there be anyone who is involuntarily unemployed?

b. Suppose the French government sets a minimum yearly wage of 35,000 euros. Is there any involuntary unemployment at this wage? If so, how much? Illustrate with a diagram. What if the minimum wage is set at 40,000 euros? Also illustrate with a diagram.

c. Given your answer to part b and the information in the table, what do you think is the relationship between the level of involuntary unemployment and the level of the minimum wage? Who benefits from such a policy? Who loses? What is the missed opportunity here?

16. Until recently, the standard number of hours worked per week for a full-time job in France was 39 hours, similar to that in the United States. But in response to social unrest over high levels of involuntary unemployment, the French government instituted a 35-hour workweek—a worker could not work more than 35 hours per week even if both the worker and employer wanted it. The motivation behind this policy was that if current employees worked fewer hours, employers would be forced to hire more new workers. Assume that it is costly for employers to train new workers. French employers were greatly opposed to this policy and threatened to move their operations to neighboring countries that did not have such employment restrictions. Can you explain their attitude? Give an example of both an inefficiency and an illegal activity that are likely to arise from this policy.

17. For the last 70 years, the U.S. government has used price supports to provide income assistance to U.S. farmers. At times the government has used price floors, which it maintains by buying up the surplus farm products. At other times, it has used target prices, giving the farmer an amount equal to the difference between the market price and the target price for each unit sold. Use the accompanying diagram to answer the following questions.

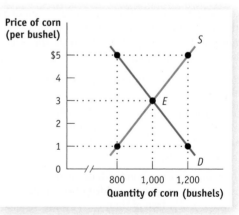

a. If the government sets a price floor of $5 per bushel, how many bushels of corn are produced? How many are purchased by consumers? by the government? How much does the program cost the government? How much revenue do corn farmers receive?

b. Suppose the government sets a target price of $5 per bushel for any quantity supplied up to 1,000 bushels. How many bushels of corn are purchased by consumers and at what price? by the government? How much does the program cost the government? How much revenue do corn farmers receive?

c. Which of these programs (in parts a and b) costs corn consumers more? Which program costs the government more? Explain.

d. What are the inefficiencies that arise in each of these cases (parts a and b)?

18. The waters off the north Atlantic coast were once teeming with fish. Now, due to overfishing by the commercial fishing industry, the stocks of fish are seriously depleted. In 1991, the National Marine Fishery Service of the U.S. government implemented a quota to allow fish stocks to recover. The quota limited the amount of swordfish caught per year by all U.S.-licensed fishing boats to 7 million pounds. As soon as the U.S. fishing fleet had met the quota, the swordfish catch was closed down for the rest of the year. The accompanying table gives the hypothetical demand and supply schedules for swordfish caught in the United States per year.

Price of swordfish (per pound)	Quantity of swordfish (millions of pounds per year)	
	Quantity demanded	Quantity supplied
$20	6	15
18	7	13
16	8	11
14	9	9
12	10	7

a. Use a diagram to show the effect of the quota on the market for swordfish in 1991.

b. How do you think fishermen will change how they fish in response to this policy?

19. The accompanying table indicates the U.S. domestic demand schedule and domestic supply schedule for commercial jet airplanes. Suppose that the world price of a commercial jet airplane is $100 million.

Price of jet (millions)	Quantity of jets demanded	Quantity of jets supplied
$120	100	1,000
110	150	900
100	200	800
90	250	700
80	300	600
70	350	500
60	400	400
50	450	300
40	500	200

a. In autarky, how many commercial jet airplanes does the United States produce, and at what price are they bought and sold?

b. With trade, what will the price for commercial jet airplanes be? Will the United States import or export airplanes? How many?

20. The accompanying table shows the U.S. domestic demand schedule and domestic supply schedule for oranges. Suppose that the world price of oranges is $0.30 per orange.

Price of orange	Quantity of oranges demanded (thousands)	Quantity of oranges supplied (thousands)
$1.00	2	11
0.90	4	10
0.80	6	9
0.70	8	8
0.60	10	7
0.50	12	6
0.40	14	5
0.30	16	4
0.20	18	3

a. Draw the U.S. domestic supply curve and domestic demand curve.

b. With free trade, how many oranges will the United States import or export?

Suppose that the U.S. government imposes a tariff on oranges of $0.20 per orange.

c. How many oranges will the United States import or export after introduction of the tariff?

21. The U.S. domestic demand schedule and domestic supply schedule for oranges was given in Problem 20. Suppose that the world price of oranges is $0.30. The United States introduces an import quota of 3,000 oranges and assigns the quota rents to foreign orange exporters.

a. Draw the domestic demand and supply curves.

b. What will the domestic price of oranges be after introduction of the quota?

c. What is the value of the quota rents that foreign exporters of oranges receive?

22. As the United States has opened up to trade, it has lost many of its low-skill manufacturing jobs, but it has gained jobs in high-skill industries, such as the software industry. Explain whether the United States as a whole has been made better off by trade.

Macroeconomic Measurement

THE NEW #2 WORLD VIEW

"China Passes Japan as Second-Largest Economy." That was the headline in the *New York Times* on August 15, 2010. Citing economic data suggesting that Japan's economy was weakening while China's was roaring ahead, the article predicted—correctly, as it turned out—that 2010 would mark the first year in which the surging Chinese economy finally overtook Japan's, taking second place to the United States on the world economic stage.

"The milestone," wrote the *Times*, "though anticipated for some time, is the most striking evidence yet that China's ascendance is for real and that the rest of the world will have to reckon with a new economic superpower."

But wait a minute—what does it mean to say that China's economy is larger than Japan's? The two economies are, after all, producing very different mixes of goods. Despite its rapid advance, China is still a fairly poor country whose greatest strength is in relatively low-tech production. Japan, by contrast, is very much a high-tech nation, and it dominates world output of some sophisticated goods, like electronic sensors for automobiles. That's why the 2011 earthquake in northeastern Japan, which put many factories out of action, temporarily caused major production disruptions for auto factories around the world.

How can you compare the sizes of two economies when they aren't producing the same things?

The answer is that comparisons of national economies are based on the *value* of their production. When news reports declared that China's economy had overtaken Japan's, they meant that China's *gross domestic product*, or *GDP*—a measure of the overall value of goods and services produced—had surpassed Japan's GDP.

GDP is one of the most important measures used to track the macroeconomy—that is, to quantify movements in the overall level of output and prices. Measures like GDP and the rates of unemployment and inflation play an important role in formulating economic policy, since policy makers need to know what's going on, and anecdotes are no substitute for hard data. The data are also important for business decisions (for an example, see the business case at the end of this section, on page 124).

In this section we start with a general description of some of the field's major concerns. Then we explain how macroeconomists measure key aspects of the economy. We will explore ways to measure the economy's total output and total income using the circular-flow diagram. We then formally define GDP and explain how to calculate it. We also learn about the value of real GDP and how it is calculated.

MODULE 9 Introduction to Macroeconomics

American Stock/Getty Images

WHAT YOU WILL LEARN

1 What a business cycle is and why diminishing the severity of business cycles is a goal for policy makers

2 How long-run economic growth determines a country's standard of living

3 The meaning of inflation and deflation and why price stability is preferred

4 The importance of open-economy macroeconomics and how economies interact through trade deficits and trade surpluses

Today many people enjoy walking through New York's beautiful Central Park. But in 1932 there were many people living there in squalor in one of the many "Hoovervilles"—the shantytowns that had sprung up across America as a result of a catastrophic economic slump that started in 1929. Millions of people were out of work and unable to feed, clothe, and house themselves and their families. Beginning in 1933, the U.S. economy would stage a partial recovery. But joblessness stayed high throughout the 1930s—a period that came to be known as the Great Depression.

These shantytowns were named after Herbert Hoover, who had been elected president in 1928. When the Depression struck, people blamed Hoover who, along with his economic advisers, didn't seem to understand the crisis and had no idea what to do about it.

At the time of the Great Depression, *microeconomics,* which is concerned with the consumption and production decisions of individual consumers and producers and with the allocation of scarce resources among industries, was already a well-developed branch of economics. *Macroeconomics,* which focuses on the behavior of the economy as a whole, was still in its infancy.

But macroeconomics came into its own during the Depression. Economists realized that they needed to understand the nature of the catastrophe that had overtaken the United States and much of the rest of the world in order to learn how to avoid such events in the future. To this day, the effort to understand economic slumps and find ways to prevent them is at the core of macroeconomics.

In this module we will begin to explore the key features of macroeconomic analysis. We will look at some of the field's major concerns, including

- Business cycles
- Economic growth
- Price stability
- Trade imbalances

96

The Business Cycle

Figure 9-1 shows a stylized representation of the way the economy evolves over time. The vertical axis shows either employment or an indicator of how much the economy is producing, such as *real gross domestic product (real GDP)*, a measure of the economy's overall output that we'll learn about in the next module

A broad-based downturn, in which output and employment fall in many industries, is called a **recession** (sometimes referred to as a *contraction*). Recessions, as officially declared by the National Bureau of Economic Research, or NBER, are indicated by the shaded areas in Figure 9-1. When the economy isn't in a recession, when most economic numbers are following their normal upward trend, the economy is said to be in an **expansion** (sometimes referred to as a *recovery*). The alternation between recessions and expansions is known as the **business cycle.** The point in time at which the economy shifts from expansion to recession is known as a **business-cycle peak;** the point at which the economy shifts from recession to expansion is known as a **business-cycle trough.**

Recessions, or contractions, are periods of economic downturn when output and employment are falling.

Expansions, or recoveries, are periods of economic upturn when output and employment are rising.

The **business cycle** is the short-run alternation between recessions and expansions.

The point at which the economy turns from expansion to recession is a **business-cycle peak.**

The point at which the economy turns from recession to expansion is a **business-cycle trough.**

FIGURE 9-1 The Business Cycle

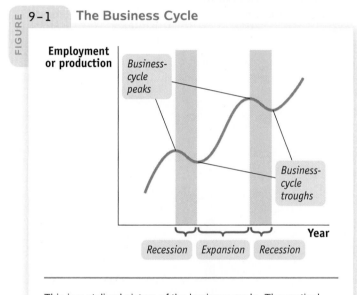

This is a stylized picture of the business cycle. The vertical axis measures either employment or total output in the economy. Periods when these two variables turn down are *recessions;* periods when they turn up are *expansions*. The point at which the economy turns down is a *business-cycle peak;* the point at which it turns up again is a *business-cycle trough*.

The business cycle is an enduring feature of the economy. Table 9-1 shows the official list of business-cycle peaks and troughs. As you can see, there have been recessions and expansions for at least the past 155 years. Whenever there is a prolonged expansion, as there was in the 1960s and again in the 1990s, books and articles come out proclaiming the end of the business cycle. Such proclamations have always proved wrong: the cycle always comes back. But why does it matter?

TABLE 9-1

The History of the Business Cycle

Business-Cycle Peak	Business-Cycle Trough
no prior data available	December 1854
June 1857	December 1858
October 1860	June 1861
April 1865	December 1867
June 1869	December 1870
October 1873	March 1879
March 1882	May 1885
March 1887	April 1888
July 1890	May 1891
January 1893	June 1894
December 1895	June 1897
June 1899	December 1900
September 1902	August 1904
May 1907	June 1908
January 1910	January 1912
January 1913	December 1914
August 1918	March 1919
January 1920	July 1921
May 1923	July 1924
October 1926	November 1927
August 1929	March 1933
May 1937	June 1938
February 1945	October 1945
November 1948	October 1949
July 1953	May 1954
August 1957	April 1958
April 1960	February 1961
December 1969	November 1970
November 1973	March 1975
January 1980	July 1980
July 1981	November 1982
July 1990	March 1991
March 2001	November 2001
December 2007	June 2009

Source: National Bureau of Economic Research.

The Pain of Recession

Not many people complain about the business cycle when the economy is expanding. Recessions, however, create a great deal of pain.

The most important effect of a recession is its impact on the ability of workers to find and hold jobs. The most widely used indicator of conditions in the labor market

"I can't move in with my parents. They moved in with my grandparents."

is the *unemployment rate*. We'll explain how that rate is calculated in the next section, but for now it's enough to say that a high unemployment rate tells us that jobs are scarce and a low unemployment rate tells us that jobs are easy to find. Figure 9-2 shows the unemployment rate from 1988 to 2013. As you can see, the U.S. unemployment rate surged during and after each recession but eventually fell during periods of expansion. The rising unemployment rate in 2008 was a sign that a new recession might be under way, which was later confirmed by the NBER to have begun in December 2007.

Because recessions cause many people to lose their jobs and also make it hard to find new ones, recessions hurt the standard of living of many families. Recessions are usually associated with a rise in the number of people living below the poverty line, an increase in the number of people who lose their houses because they can't afford the mortgage payments, and a fall in the percentage of Americans with health insurance coverage.

You should not think, however, that workers are the only group that suffers during a recession. Recessions are also bad for firms: like employment and wages, profits suffer during recessions, with many small businesses failing.

All in all, then, recessions are bad for almost everyone. Can anything be done to reduce their frequency and severity?

FIGURE 9-2   The U.S. Unemployment Rate, 1988–2013

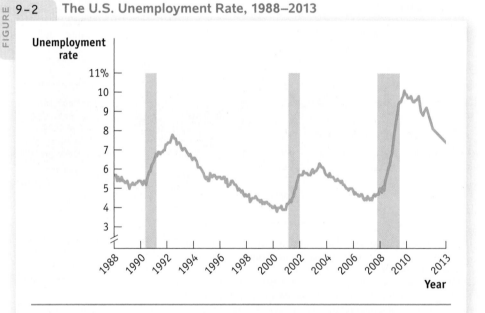

The unemployment rate, a measure of joblessness, rises sharply during recessions and usually falls during expansions. The shaded areas indicate periods of recession.
Source: Bureau of Labor Statistics.

ECONOMICS ▶ IN ACTION   WORLD VIEW

DEFINING RECESSIONS AND EXPANSIONS

How exactly are recessions and expansions defined? The answer is that there is no exact definition!

In many countries, economists adopt the rule that a recession is a period of at least two consecutive quarters (a quarter is three months) during which the total output of the economy shrinks. The two-consecutive-quarters requirement is designed to avoid classifying brief hiccups in the economy's performance, with no lasting significance, as recessions.

Sometimes, however, this definition seems too strict. For example, an economy that has three months of sharply declining output, then three months of slightly positive growth, then another three months of rapid decline, should surely be considered to have endured a nine-month recession.

In the United States, we try to avoid such misclassifications by assigning the task of determining when a recession begins and ends to an independent panel of experts at the National Bureau of Economic Research (NBER). This panel looks at a variety of economic indicators, with the main focus on employment and production, and then makes a judgment call.

Sometimes this judgment is controversial. In fact, there is lingering controversy over the 2001 recession. According to the NBER, that recession began in March 2001 and ended in November 2001 when output began rising. Some critics argue, however, that the recession really began several months earlier, when industrial production began falling. Other critics argue that the recession didn't really end in 2001 because employment continued to fall and the job market remained weak for another year and a half.

Taming the Business Cycle

Modern macroeconomics largely came into being as a response to the worst recession in history—the 43-month downturn that began in 1929 and continued into 1933, ushering in the Great Depression. The havoc wreaked by the 1929–1933 recession spurred economists to search both for understanding and for solutions: they wanted to know how such things could happen and how to prevent them.

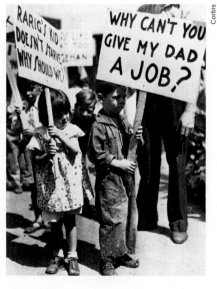

The work of the British economist John Maynard Keynes, published during the Great Depression, suggested that a depressed economy results from inadequate spending, and that using *monetary policy* (changing the quantity of money to alter interest rates, which in turn affect overall spending) and *fiscal policy* (changing taxes and government spending to affect overall spending) can mitigate the effect of recessions. To this day, governments turn to these policies, known as *Keynesian Economics,* when recession strikes. Later work, notably that of another great macroeconomist, Milton Friedman, led to a consensus that it's important to rein in booms as well as to fight slumps.

Modern macroeconomics came into being as a response to the Great Depression of 1929–1933.

So modern policy makers try to "smooth out" the business cycle. They haven't been completely successful, as a look at Table 9-1 makes clear. It's widely believed, however, that policy guided by macroeconomic analysis has helped make the economy more stable.

Although the business cycle is one of the main concerns of macroeconomics and historically played a crucial role in fostering the development of the field, macroeconomists are also concerned with other issues, such as the question of long-run growth.

ECONOMICS ▶ IN ACTION

COMPARING RECESSIONS

The alternation of recessions and expansions seems to be an enduring feature of economic life. However, not all business cycles are created equal. In particular, some recessions have been much worse than others.

9-3   Two Recessions

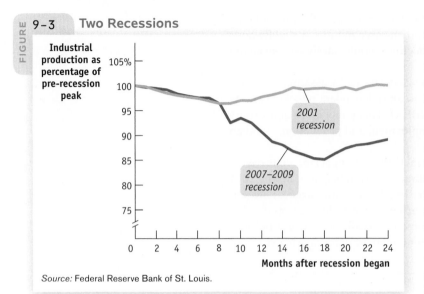

Source: Federal Reserve Bank of St. Louis.

Let's compare the two most recent recessions: the 2001 recession and the Great Recession of 2007–2009. These recessions differed in duration: the first lasted only eight months, the second more than twice as long. Even more important, however, they differed greatly in depth.

In Figure 9-3 we compare the depth of the recessions by looking at what happened to industrial production over the months after the recession began. In each case, production is measured as a percentage of its level at the recession's start. Thus the line for the 2007–2009 recession shows that industrial production eventually fell to about 85% of its initial level.

Clearly, the 2007–2009 recession hit the economy vastly harder than the 2001 recession. Indeed, by comparison to many recessions, the 2001 slump was very mild.

Of course, this was no consolation to the millions of American workers who lost their jobs, even in that mild recession.

Long-Run Economic Growth

In 1955, Americans were delighted with the nation's prosperity. The economy was expanding, consumer goods that had been rationed during World War II were available for everyone to buy, and most Americans believed, rightly, that they were better off than the citizens of any other nation, past or present.

Yet by today's standards, Americans were quite poor in 1955. Figure 9-4 shows the percentage of American homes equipped with a variety of appliances in 1905, 1955, and 2005: in 1955 only 37% of American homes contained washing machines

9-4   The Fruits of Long-Run Growth in America

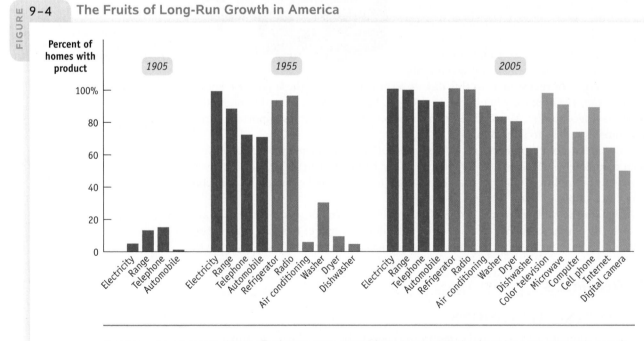

Americans have become able to afford many more material goods over time thanks to long-run economic growth.

Source: W. Michael Cox and Richard Alm, "How Are We Doing?" *The American* (July/August 2008). http://www.american.com/archive/2008/july-august-magazine-contents/how-are-we-doing

and hardly anyone had air conditioning. And if we turn the clock back another half-century, to 1905, we find that life for many Americans was startlingly primitive by today's standards.

Why are the vast majority of Americans today able to afford conveniences that many Americans lacked in 1955? The answer is **long-run economic growth,** the sustained rise in the quantity of goods and services the economy produces. Figure 9-5 shows the growth since 1900 in real GDP per capita, a measure of total output per person in the economy. The severe recession of 1929–1933 stands out, but business cycles between World War II and 2007 are almost invisible, dwarfed by the strong upward trend.

Long-run economic growth is the sustained upward trend in the economy's output over time.

FIGURE 9-5 Growth, the Long View

Over the long run, growth in real GDP per capita has dwarfed the ups and downs of the business cycle. Except for the recession that began the Great Depression, recessions are almost invisible until 2007.

Sources: Angus Maddison, *Statistics on World Population, GDP, and Per Capita GDP, 1–2008AD,* http://www.ggdc.net/MADDISON/oriindex.htm; Bureau of Economic Analysis.

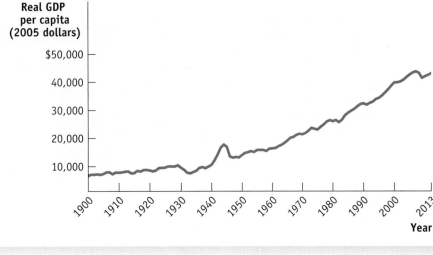

Part of the long-run increase in output is accounted for by the fact that we have a growing population and workforce. But the economy's overall production has increased by much more than the population. On average, in 2013 the U.S. economy produced about $43,000 worth of goods and services per person, about twice as much as in 1971, about three times as much as in 1951, and almost eight times as much as in 1900.

Long-run economic growth is fundamental to many of the most pressing economic questions today. Responses to key policy questions, like the country's ability to bear the future costs of government programs such as Social Security and Medicare, depend in part on how fast the U.S. economy grows over the next few decades. More broadly, the public's sense that the country is making progress depends crucially on success in achieving long-run growth.

When growth slows, as it did in the 1970s, it can help feed a national mood of pessimism. In particular, *long-run growth per capita*—a sustained upward trend in output per person—is the key to higher wages and a rising standard of living. A major concern of macroeconomics is trying to understand the forces behind long-run growth.

Long-run growth is an even more urgent concern in poorer, less developed countries which would like to achieve a higher standard of living. In these cases, the central concern of economic policy is how to accelerate long-run growth.

Long-run growth is the key to higher living standards in the poorer, less developed countries of the world.

Inflation and Deflation

In January 1980 the average production worker in the United States was paid $6.57 an hour. By December 2013, the average hourly earnings for such a worker had risen to $19.40 an hour. Three cheers for economic progress!

But wait. American workers were paid much more in 2013, but they also faced a much higher cost of living. In early 1980, a dozen eggs cost only about $0.88; by December 2013, that was up to $2.00. The price of a loaf of white bread went from about $0.50 to $1.39. And the price of a gallon of gasoline rose from just $1.11 to $3.33.

Figure 9-6 compares the percentage increase in hourly earnings between 1980 and 2013 with the increases in the prices of some standard items: the average worker's paycheck went further in terms of some goods, but less far in terms of others. Overall, the rise in the cost of living wiped out many, if not all, of the wage gains of the typical worker from 1980 to 2013. In other words, once changes in prices are taken into account, the living standard of the typical U.S. worker has stagnated from 1980 to the present.

FIGURE **9-6   Rising Prices**

Between 1980 and 2013, American workers' hourly earnings rose by 195%. But the prices of just about all the goods bought by workers also rose, some by more, some by less. Overall, the rising cost of living offset much of the rise in the average U.S. worker's wage.

Source: Bureau of Labor Statistics.

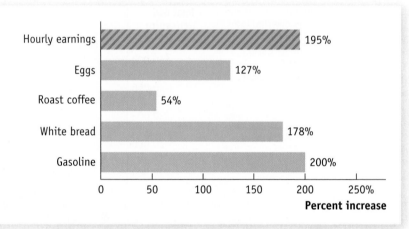

The point is that between 1980 and 2013 the economy experienced substantial **inflation:** a rise in the overall level of prices. Understanding the causes of inflation and its opposite, **deflation**—a fall in the overall level of prices—is another main concern of macroeconomics because both inflation and deflation can pose problems for the economy. Here are two examples:

- Inflation discourages people from holding onto cash, because cash loses value over time if the overall price level is rising. That is, the amount of goods and services you can buy with a given amount of cash falls. In extreme cases, people stop holding cash altogether and turn to barter.

- Deflation can cause the reverse problem. If the price level is falling, cash gains value over time. In other words, the amount of goods and services you can buy with a given amount of cash increases. So holding on to it can become more attractive than investing in new factories and other productive assets. This can deepen a recession.

We'll describe other costs of inflation and deflation in a later section. For now, let's just note that, in general, economists regard **price stability**—in which the overall level of prices is changing, if at all, only slowly—as a desirable goal. Price stability is a goal that seemed far out of reach for much of the post–World War II period but was achieved to most macroeconomists' satisfaction in the 1990s.

A rising overall level of prices is inflation.

A falling overall level of prices is deflation.

The economy has price stability when the overall level of prices changes slowly or not at all.

An open economy is an economy that trades goods and services with other countries.

International Imbalances

The United States is an **open economy** that trades goods and services with other countries. There have been times when that trade was more or less balanced—when the United States sold about as much to the rest of the world as it bought. But this isn't one of those times.

In 2012, the United States ran a big **trade deficit**—that is, the value of the goods and services U.S. residents bought from the rest of the world was a lot larger than the value of the goods and services American producers sold to customers abroad.

Meanwhile, some other countries were in the opposite position, selling much more to foreigners than they bought. Figure 9-7 shows the exports and imports of goods and services for several important economies in 2012. As you can see, the United States imported much more than it exported, but Germany, China, and Saudi Arabia did the reverse: they each ran a **trade surplus.**

A country runs a trade surplus when the value of the goods and services it buys from the rest of the world is smaller than the value of the goods and services it sells abroad. Was America's trade deficit a sign that something was wrong with our economy—that we weren't able to make things that people in other countries wanted to buy?

A country runs a **trade deficit** when the value of goods and services bought from foreigners is more than the value of goods and services it sells to them. It runs a **trade surplus** when the value of goods and services bought from foreigners is less than the value of the goods and services it sells to them.

No, not really. Trade deficits and their opposite, trade surpluses, are macroeconomic phenomena. They're the result of situations in which the whole is very different from the sum of its parts. You might think that countries with highly productive workers or widely desired products and services to sell run trade surpluses while countries with unproductive workers or poor-quality products and services run deficits. But the reality is that there's no simple relationship between the success of an economy and whether it runs trade surpluses or deficits.

Microeconomic analysis tells us why countries trade but not why they run trade surpluses or deficits. Earlier we learned that international trade is the result of comparative advantage: countries export goods they're relatively good at producing and import goods they're not as good at producing. That's why the United States exports wheat and imports coffee. One important question the concept of comparative advantage doesn't answer, however, is why the value of a country's imports is sometimes much larger than the value of its exports, or vice versa.

There isn't an obvious relationship between the success of an economy and whether it runs trade surpluses or deficits.

So what does determine whether a country runs a trade surplus or a trade deficit? Later on we'll learn the surprising answer: the determinants of the overall balance between exports and imports lie in decisions about savings and investment spending—spending on goods like machinery and factories that are in turn used to produce goods and services for consumers. Countries with high investment spending relative to savings run trade deficits; countries with low investment spending relative to savings run trade surpluses.

FIGURE

9-7   **Unbalanced Trade**

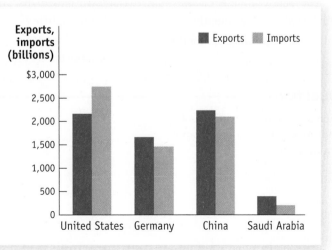

In 2012, the goods and services the United States bought from other countries were worth considerably more than the goods and services sold abroad. Germany, China, and Saudi Arabia were in the reverse position. Trade deficits and trade surpluses reflect macroeconomic forces, especially differences in savings and investment spending.

Source: World Trade Organization.

9 Review

Solutions appear at the back of the book.

Check Your Understanding

1. Why do we talk about business cycles for the economy as a whole, rather than just talking about the ups and downs of particular industries?

2. Many poor countries have high rates of population growth. What does this imply about the long-run growth rates of overall output that they must achieve in order to generate a higher standard of living per person?

3. Which of these sound like inflation, which sound like deflation, and which are ambiguous?

   a. Gasoline prices are up 10%, food prices are down 20%, and the prices of most services are up 1%–2%.

   b. Gas prices have doubled, food prices are up 50%, and prices of most services seem to be up 5% or 10%.

   c. Gas prices haven't changed, food prices are way down, and services have gotten cheaper, too.

Multiple-Choice Questions

1. During the recession phase of a business cycle, which of the following is likely to increase?

   a. the unemployment rate

   b. the price level

   c. economic growth rates

   d. the production of goods and services

   e. wages

2. Based on the data below, which of the following is true about the period from 1990–2009?

Business-Cycle Peak	Business-Cycle Trough
July 1990	March 1991
March 2001	November 2001
December 2007	June 2009

   a. The economy spent more years in recession than expansion.

   b. Each of the recessions during this period lasted for less than a year.

   c. The longest expansion in this period lasted for 10 years.

   d. The shortest recession lasted for three months.

   e. Each recession lasted the same number of months.

3. A sustained increase in aggregate output over several decades represents

   a. an expansion.

   b. a recovery.

   c. a recession.

   d. a depression.

   e. economic growth.

4. Which of the following is the most likely result of inflation?

   a. falling employment

   b. a dollar buys more than it did before

   c. people are discouraged from holding cash

   d. price stability

   e. low aggregate output per capita

5. If the value of goods and services bought from other countries is more than the value of goods and services sold to other countries, this is called

   a. a trade deficit.

   b. a trade surplus.

   c. an expansion.

   d. a recession.

   e. a business cycle.

Critical-Thinking Question

Argentina used to be as rich as Canada; now it's much poorer. Does this mean that Argentina is poorer than it was in the past? Explain your answer.

The Circular-Flow Diagram and the National Accounts

SFC/Shutterstock

The National Accounts

Almost all countries calculate a set of numbers known as the *national income and product accounts.* In fact, the accuracy of a country's accounts is a remarkably reliable indicator of its state of economic development—in general, the more reliable the accounts, the more economically advanced the country. When international economic agencies seek to help a less developed country, typically the first order of business is to send a team of experts to audit and improve the country's accounts.

In the United States, these numbers are calculated by the Bureau of Economic Analysis (BEA), a division of the U.S. government's Department of Commerce. The **national income and product accounts,** often referred to simply as the **national accounts,** keep track of the spending of consumers, sales of producers, business investment spending, government purchases, and a variety of other flows of money among different sectors of the economy. Let's see how they work.

The Circular-Flow Diagram

To understand the principles behind the national accounts, it helps to look at a graphic called a **circular-flow diagram.** Some of you have already encountered a version of this diagram in your study of microeconomics.

The circular-flow diagram is a simplified representation of the economy that shows the flows of money, goods and services, and factors of production through the economy. It allows us to visualize the key concepts behind the national accounts. The underlying principle is that the flow of money into each market or sector is equal to the flow of money coming out of that market or sector.

National income and product accounts, or national accounts, keep track of spending and the flows of money between different sectors of the economy.

The circular-flow diagram illustrates the flows of money, goods and services, and factors of production in an economy.

The Simple Circular-Flow Diagram

The U.S. economy is incredibly complex, with more than a hundred million workers employed by millions of companies, producing millions of different goods and services. Yet you can learn some very important things about the economy by considering Figure 10-1. This simple diagram represents the transactions that take place by two kinds of flows around a circle: flows of physical things such as goods, services, labor, or raw materials in one direction, and flows of money that pay for these things in the opposite direction. In this case, the physical flows are shown in yellow, the money flows in green.

FIGURE 10-1   The Simple Circular-Flow Diagram

This diagram represents the flows of money and of goods and services in the economy. In the markets for goods and services, households purchase goods and services from firms, generating a flow of money to the firms and a flow of goods and services to the households. The money flows back to households as firms purchase factors of production from the households in factor markets.

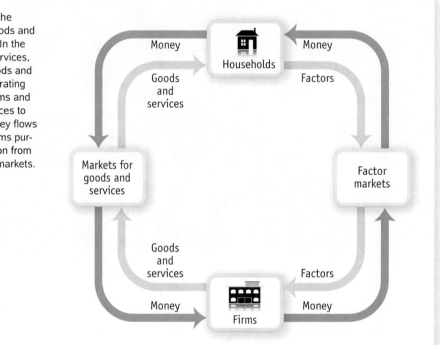

The simplest circular-flow diagram illustrates an economy that contains only two kinds of "inhabitants": households and firms. A **household** consists of either an individual or a group of people who share their income. A **firm** is an organization that produces goods and services for sale—and that employs members of households.

As you can see in Figure 10-1, there are two kinds of markets in this simple economy. On one side (here the left side) there are markets for goods and services (also known as **product markets**) in which households buy the goods and services they want from firms. This produces a flow of goods and services to the households and a return flow of money to firms.

On the other side (at right) there are **factor markets** in which firms buy the resources they need to produce goods and services. The best known factor market is the *labor market*, in which workers are paid for their time. Besides labor, we can think of households as owning and selling the other factors of production to firms.

This simple circular-flow diagram omits a number of real-world complications in the interest of simplicity. It does not offer a complete picture of participants in the economy and the flows that take place among them. But, it is a useful aid to thinking about the economy. And, we will use the simple diagram as the starting point for developing a more realistic (and therefore more detailed and complicated) circular-flow diagram.

A household is a person or group of people who share income.

A firm is an organization that produces goods and services for sale.

Product markets are where goods and services are bought and sold.

Factor markets are where resources, especially capital and labor, are bought and sold.

The Expanded Circular-Flow Diagram

Figure 10-2 is a revised and expanded circular-flow diagram. This diagram shows only the flows of money in the economy, but is expanded to include extra elements that were ignored in the interest of simplicity in the simple circular-flow diagram. The underlying principle that the inflow of money into each market or sector must equal the outflow of money coming from that market or sector still applies in this diagram.

In Figure 10-2, the circular flow of money between households and firms illustrated in Figure 10-1 remains. In the product markets, households engage in **consumer spending,** buying goods and services from domestic firms and from firms in the rest

Consumer spending is household spending on goods and services.

FIGURE **10-2** **An Expanded Circular-Flow Diagram: The Flows of Money Through the Economy**

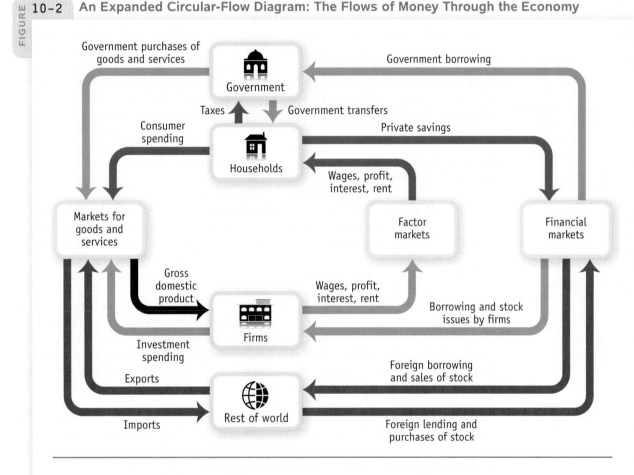

A circular flow of funds connects the four sectors of the economy—households, firms, government, and the rest of the world—via three types of markets: the factor markets, the markets for goods and services, and the *financial markets*.

- Funds flow from firms to households in the form of wages, profit, interest, and rent through the factor markets. After paying taxes to the government and receiving *government transfers,* households allocate the remaining income—*disposable income*—to private savings and consumer spending.

- Via the financial markets, *private savings* and funds from the rest of the world are channeled into investment spending by firms, government borrowing, foreign borrowing and lending, and foreign transactions of stocks.

- In turn, funds flow from the government and households to firms to pay for purchases of goods and services.

- Finally, exports to the rest of the world generate a flow of funds into the economy and imports lead to a flow of funds out of the economy.

If we add up consumer spending on goods and services, investment spending by firms, government purchases of goods and services, and exports, then subtract the value of imports, the total flow of funds represented by this calculation is total spending on final goods and services produced in the United States. Equivalently, it's the value of all the final goods and services produced in the United States—that is, the *gross domestic product* of the economy.

A **stock** is a share in the ownership of a company held by a shareholder.

A **bond** is a loan in the form of an IOU that pays interest.

Government transfers are payments that the government makes to individuals without expecting a good or service in return.

Disposable income, equal to income plus government transfers minus taxes, is the total amount of household income available to spend on consumption and to save.

Private savings, equal to disposable income minus consumer spending, is disposable income that is not spent on consumption.

The banking, stock, and bond markets, which channel private savings and foreign lending into investment spending, government borrowing, and foreign borrowing, are known as the **financial markets**.

Government borrowing is the amount of funds borrowed by the government in the financial markets.

Government purchases of goods and services are total expenditures on goods and services by federal, state, and local governments.

of the world. Households also own factors of production—land, labor, and capital. They sell the use of these factors of production to firms, receiving rent, wages, and interest payments in return. Firms buy, and pay households for, the use of those factors of production in factor markets, represented to the right of center in the diagram. Most households derive the bulk of their income from wages earned by selling labor.

Some households derive additional income from their indirect ownership of the physical capital used by firms, mainly in the form of **stocks**—shares in the ownership of a company—and **bonds**—loans to firms in the form of an IOU that pays interest. In other words, the income households receive from the factor markets includes profit distributed to company shareholders and the interest payments on any bonds that they hold. Households also receive rent from firms in exchange for the use of land or structures that the households own. So in factor markets, households receive income in the form of wages, profit, interest, and rent via factor markets.

Households spend most of the income received from factors of production on goods and services. However, in Figure 10-2 we see two reasons why the markets for goods and services don't in fact absorb *all* of a household's income. First, households don't get to keep all the income they receive via the factor markets. They must pay part of their income to the government in the form of taxes, such as income taxes and sales taxes. In addition, some households receive **government transfers**—payments that the government makes to individuals without expecting a good or service in return. Unemployment insurance payments are one example of a government transfer. The total income households have left after paying taxes and receiving government transfers is **disposable income.**

Because the markets for goods and services do not absorb all household income, many households set aside a portion of their income for **private savings.** These private savings go into **financial markets** where individuals, banks, and other institutions buy and sell stocks and bonds as well as make loans. As Figure 10-2 shows, the financial markets (on the far right of the circular flow diagram) also receive funds from the rest of the world and provide funds to the government, to firms, and to the rest of the world.

Before going further, we can use the box representing households to illustrate an important general characteristic of the circular-flow diagram: *the total sum of flows of money out of a given box is equal to the total sum of flows of money into that box. It's simply a matter of accounting: what goes in must come out.* So, for example, the total flow of money out of households—the sum of taxes paid, consumer spending, and private savings—must equal the total flow of money into households—the sum of wages, profit, interest, rent, and government transfers.

Now let's look at the other inhabitants in the circular-flow diagram, including the government and the rest of the world. The government returns a portion of the money it collects from taxes to households in the form of government transfers. However, it uses much of its tax revenue, plus additional funds borrowed in the financial markets through **government borrowing,** to buy goods and services. **Government purchases of goods and services,** the total of purchases made by federal, state, and local governments, includes everything from military spending on ammunition to your local public school's spending on chalk, erasers, and teacher salaries.

Shutterstock

Thinkstock

The rest of the world participates in the U.S. economy in three ways. First, some of the goods and services produced in the United States are sold to residents of other countries. For example, more than half of America's annual wheat and cotton crops are sold abroad. Goods and services sold to other countries are known as *exports*. Export sales lead to a flow of funds from the rest of the world into the United States to pay for them.

Second, some of the goods and services purchased by residents of the United States are produced abroad. For example, many consumer goods are now made in China. Goods and services purchased from residents of other countries are known as *imports*. Import purchases lead to a flow of funds out of the United States to pay for them.

Third, foreigners can participate in U.S. financial markets. Foreign lending—lending by foreigners to borrowers in the United States and purchases by foreigners of shares of stock in American companies—generates a flow of funds into the United States from the rest of the world. Conversely, foreign borrowing—borrowing by foreigners from U.S. lenders and purchases by Americans of stock in foreign companies—leads to a flow of funds out of the United States to the rest of the world.

Note that like households, firms also buy goods and services in our economy. An automobile company that is building a new factory will buy investment goods—machinery like stamping presses and welding robots—from companies that manufacture these items. It will also accumulate an inventory of finished cars in preparation for shipment to dealers. **Inventories,** then, are goods and raw materials that firms hold to facilitate their operations. The national accounts count this **investment spending**—spending on new productive physical capital, such as machinery and buildings, and on changes in *inventories*—as part of total spending on goods and services.

> **Inventories** are stocks of goods and raw materials held to facilitate business operations.
>
> **Investment spending** is spending on new productive physical capital, such as machinery and structures, and on changes in inventories.

You might ask why changes in inventories are included in investment spending—finished cars aren't, after all, used to produce more cars. Changes in inventories of finished goods are counted as investment spending because, like machinery, they change the ability of a firm to make future sales. So spending on additions to inventories is a form of investment spending by a firm. Conversely, a drawing-down of inventories is counted as a fall in investment spending because it leads to lower future sales.

Richard Peterson/Shutterstock

It's also important to understand that investment spending includes spending on the construction of any structure, regardless of whether it is an assembly plant or a new house. Why include the construction of homes? Because, like a plant, a new house produces a future stream of output—housing services for its occupants.

Suppose we add up consumer spending on goods and services, investment spending, government purchases of goods and services, and the value of exports, then subtract the value of imports. This gives us a measure of the overall market value of the goods and services the economy produces. That measure has a name: it's a country's *gross domestic product*, which is the topic of the next module.

ΕCONOMICS ▶ *IN ACTION*

CREATING THE NATIONAL ACCOUNTS

The national accounts, like modern macroeconomics, owe their creation to the Great Depression. As the economy plunged into depression, government officials found their ability to respond crippled not only by the lack of adequate economic theories but also by the lack of adequate information. All they had were scattered statistics: railroad freight car loadings, stock prices, and incomplete indexes of industrial production. They could only guess at what was happening to the economy as a whole.

> **National income accounting** is a tool of economic analysis and policy making used around the world.

In response to this perceived lack of information, the Department of Commerce commissioned Simon Kuznets, a young Russian-born economist, to develop a set of national income accounts. (Kuznets later won the Nobel Prize in economics for his work.) The first version of these accounts was presented to Congress in 1937 and in a research report titled *National Income, 1929–35*.

Thinkstock

Kuznets's initial estimates fell short of the full modern set of accounts because they focused on income, not production. The push to complete the national accounts came during World War II, when policy makers were in need of comprehensive measures of the economy's performance. The federal government began issuing estimates of gross domestic product and gross national product in 1942.

In January 2000, in the *Survey of Current Business,* the Department of Commerce ran an article titled "GDP: One of the Great Inventions of the 20th Century." This may seem a bit over the top, but national income accounting, invented in the United States, has since become a tool of economic analysis and policy making around the world.

MODULE 10 Review

Solutions appear at the back of the book.

Check Your Understanding

1. How does a circular-flow diagram of the economy explain the connection between the following sectors, in terms of the flows that occur between the sectors?

   a. households and firms

   b. households and government

   c. households and the rest of the world

2. Define the four different types of income received by households from firms via the factor markets. What is this income used for?

Multiple-Choice Questions

1. The government uses the _____ to keep track of the flows of money between different sectors of the economy.

   a. national income and product accounts

   b. circular-flow diagram

   c. production possibilities frontier

   d. financial market

   e. factor market

2. Markets in which labor and capital are bought and sold are called _____ markets.

   a. consumer

   b. factor

   c. product

   d. investment

   e. money

3. A circular-flow diagram assumes the factors of production are owned by

   a. firms.

   b. the government.

   c. foreigners.

   d. firms and the government.

   e. households.

4. In a circular-flow diagram, funds that flow between households and the government are

   a. taxes and government spending.

   b. wages, taxes, and transfers.

   c. taxes and transfers.

   d. taxes, transfers, and profit.

   e. taxes, transfers, and government spending.

5. The bank, stock, and money markets are collectively known as the _____ market.

   a. investment

   b. savings

   c. money

   d. financial

   e. factor

Critical-Thinking Question

Explain the difference between the market for goods and services, the factor market, and the financial market.

Gross Domestic Product (GDP)

WHAT YOU WILL LEARN

1. An exact definition for gross domestic product, or GDP

2. Three different ways to calculate GDP

In the previous module we used the circular-flow diagram to show that adding up consumer spending, investment spending, government spending, and the value of exports minus the value of imports would give us a measure of a country's gross domestic product.

In this module we will formally define *gross domestic product,* or *GDP,* and then look at how it is calculated.

Gross Domestic Product Defined

A consumer's purchase of a new car from a dealer is one example of a sale of **final goods and services:** goods and services sold to the final, or end, user. But an automobile manufacturer's purchase of steel from a steel foundry or glass from a glassmaker is an example of a sale of **intermediate goods and services:** goods and services that are inputs into the production of final goods and services. In the case of intermediate goods and services, the purchaser—another firm—is *not* the final user.

Gross domestic product, or **GDP,** is the total value of all *final goods and services* produced in an economy during a given period, usually a year. In 2013 the GDP of the United States was $16,803 billion, or about $53,086 per person.

Calculating GDP

Government statisticians use three methods to calculate GDP:

1. Survey and add up the total value of the production of final goods and services.

2. Add up **aggregate spending** on domestically produced final goods and services in the economy—the sum of consumer spending, investment spending, government purchases of goods and services, and exports minus imports.

3. Sum the total factor income earned by households from firms in the economy.

Final goods and services are goods and services sold to the final, or end, user.

Intermediate goods and services are goods and services bought from one firm by another firm to be used as inputs into the production of final goods and services.

Gross domestic product, or **GDP,** is the total value of all final goods and services produced in the economy during a given year.

Aggregate spending—the total spending on domestically produced final goods and services in the economy—is the sum of consumer spending (C), investment spending (I), government purchases of goods and services (G), and exports minus imports ($X - IM$).

The **value added** of a producer is the value of its sales minus the value of its purchases of inputs.

Steel is an intermediate good because it is sold to other product manufacturers like automakers or refrigerator makers, and rarely to final buyers, such as consumers.

To illustrate how the methods of calculating GDP work, we will consider a hypothetical economy, shown in Figure 11-1. This economy consists of three firms—American Motors, Inc., which produces one car per year; American Steel, Inc., which produces the steel that goes into the car; and American Ore, Inc., which mines the iron ore that goes into the steel. GDP in this economy is $21,500, the value of the one car per year the economy produces. Let's look at how the three different methods of calculating GDP yield the same result.

MEASURING GDP AS THE VALUE OF PRODUCTION OF FINAL GOODS AND SERVICES
The first method for calculating GDP is to add up the value of all the final goods and services produced in the economy—a calculation that excludes the value of intermediate goods and services. Why are intermediate goods and services excluded? After all, don't they represent a very large and valuable portion of the economy?

To understand why only final goods and services are included in GDP, look at the simplified economy described in Figure 11-1. Should we measure the GDP of this economy by adding up the total sales of the iron ore producer, the steel producer, and the auto producer?

If we did, we would in effect be counting the value of the steel twice—once when it is sold by the steel plant to the auto plant and again when the steel auto body is sold to a consumer as a finished car. And we would be counting the value of the iron ore *three* times— once when it is mined and sold to the steel company, a second time when it is made into steel and sold to the auto producer, and a third time when the steel is made into a car and sold to the consumer. So counting the full value of each producer's sales would cause us to count the same items several times and artificially inflate the calculation of GDP.

In Figure 11-1, the total value of all sales, intermediate and final, is $34,700: $21,500 from the sale of the car, plus $9,000 from the sale of the steel, plus $4,200 from the sale of the iron ore. Yet we know that GDP—the total value of all final goods and services in a given year—is only $21,500.

To avoid double-counting, we count only each producer's **value added** in the calculation of GDP: the difference between the value of its sales and the value of the inputs it purchases from other businesses. That is, at each stage of the production process we subtract the cost of inputs—the intermediate goods—at that stage. In this case, the

FIGURE 11-1   Calculating GDP

In this hypothetical economy consisting of three firms, GDP can be calculated in three different ways: 1) measuring GDP as the value of production of final goods and services, by summing each firm's value added; 2) measuring GDP as aggregate spending on domestically produced final goods and services; and 3) measuring GDP as factor income earned by households from firms in the economy.

2. Aggregate spending on domestically produced final goods and services = $21,500

	American Ore, Inc.	American Steel, Inc.	American Motors, Inc.	Total factor income
Value of sales	$4,200 (ore)	$9,000 (steel)	$21,500 (car)	
Intermediate goods	0	4,200 (iron ore)	9,000 (steel)	
Wages	2,000	3,700	10,000	$15,700
Interest payments	1,000	600	1,000	2,600
Rent	200	300	500	1,000
Profit	1,000	200	1,000	2,200
Total expenditure by firm	4,200	9,000	21,500	
Value added per firm **=** **Value of sales – Cost of intermediate goods**	4,200	4,800	12,500	

3. Total payments to factors = $21,500

1. Value of production of final goods and services, sum of value added = $21,500

value added of the auto producer is the dollar value of the cars it manufactures *minus* the cost of the steel it buys, or $12,500. The value added of the steel producer is the dollar value of the steel it produces *minus* the cost of the ore it buys, or $4,800.

Only the ore producer, who we have assumed doesn't buy any inputs, has value added equal to its total sales, $4,200. The sum of the three producers' value added is $21,500, equal to GDP.

MEASURING GDP AS SPENDING ON DOMESTICALLY PRODUCED FINAL GOODS AND SERVICES Another way to calculate GDP is by adding up aggregate spending on domestically produced final goods and services. That is, GDP can be measured by the flow of funds into firms. Like the method that estimates GDP as the value of domestic production of final goods and services, this measurement must be carried out in a way that avoids double-counting.

In terms of our steel and auto example, we don't want to count both consumer spending on a car (represented in Figure 11-1 by the sales price of the car) and the auto producer's spending on steel (represented in Figure 11-1 by the price of a car's worth of steel). If we counted both, we would be counting the steel embodied in the car twice.

We solve this problem by counting only the value of sales to *final buyers*, such as consumers, firms that purchase investment goods, the government, or foreign buyers. In other words, in order to avoid the double-counting of spending, we omit sales of inputs from one business to another when estimating GDP using spending data. You can see from Figure 11-1 that aggregate spending on final goods and services—the finished car—is $21,500.

As we've already pointed out, the national accounts *do* include investment spending by firms as a part of final spending. That is, an auto company's purchase of steel to make a car isn't considered a part of final spending, but the company's purchase of new machinery for its factory *is* considered a part of final spending. What's the difference? Steel is an input that is used up in production; machinery will last for a number of years. Since purchases of capital goods that will last for a considerable time aren't closely tied to current production, the national accounts consider such purchases a form of final sales.

What types of spending make up GDP? Look again at Figure 10-2 of the circular-flow diagram (page 107), and you will see that one source of sales revenue for firms is consumer spending. Let's denote consumer spending with the symbol C. Figure 10-2 shows three other components of sales: sales of investment goods to other businesses, or investment spending, which we will denote by I; government purchases of goods and services, which we will denote by G; and sales to foreigners—that is, exports—which we will denote by X.

In reality, not all of this final spending goes toward domestically produced goods and services. We must take account of spending on imports, which we will denote by IM. Income spent on imports is income not spent on domestic goods and services—it is income that has "leaked" across national borders. So to calculate domestic production using spending data, we must subtract spending on imports. Putting this all together gives us the following equation, which breaks GDP down by the four sources of aggregate spending:

(11-1) $GDP = C + I + G + X - IM$

where C = consumer spending, I = investment spending, G = government purchases of goods and services, X = sales to foreigners, or exports, and IM = spending on imports. Note that the value of $X - IM$—the difference between the value of exports and the value of imports—is known as **net exports.** We'll be seeing a lot of Equation 11-1 in later modules!

MEASURING GDP AS FACTOR INCOME EARNED FROM FIRMS IN THE ECONOMY A final way to calculate GDP is to add up all the income earned by factors of production in the economy—the wages earned by labor; the interest earned by those who lend their savings to firms and the government; the rent earned by those who lease their land or structures to firms; and the profit earned by the shareholders, the owners of the firms' physical capital. This is a valid measure

Net exports are the difference between the value of exports and the value of imports ($X - IM$).

because the money firms earn by selling goods and services must go somewhere; whatever isn't paid as wages, interest, or rent is profit. And part of profit is paid out to shareholders as *dividends*.

Figure 11-1 shows how this calculation works for our simplified economy. The shaded column at the far right shows the total wages, interest, and rent paid by all these firms as well as their total profit. Summing up all of these yields a total factor income of $21,500—again, equal to GDP.

We won't emphasize the income method as much as the other two methods of calculating GDP. It's important to keep in mind, however, that all the money spent on domestically produced goods and services generates factor income to households—that is, there really is a circular flow.

The Components of GDP

Now that we know how GDP is calculated in principle, let's see what it looks like in practice.

Figure 11-2 shows the first two methods of calculating GDP side by side. The height of each bar above the horizontal axis represents the GDP of the U.S. economy in 2013: $16,803 billion. Each bar is divided to show the breakdown of that total in terms of where the value was added and how the money was spent.

In the left bar in Figure 11-2, we see the breakdown of GDP by value added according to sector, the first method of calculating GDP. Of the $16,803 billion, $12,688 billion consisted of value added by businesses. Another $2,036 billion consisted of value added by government, in the form of military, education, and other government services. Finally, $2,079 billion of value added was added by households and institutions. For example, the value added by households includes the value of work performed in homes by professional gardeners, maids, and cooks.

FIGURE 11-2   U.S. GDP in 2013: Two Methods of Calculating GDP

The two bars show two equivalent ways of calculating GDP. The height of each bar above the horizontal axis represents $16,803 billion, U.S. GDP in 2013. The left bar shows the breakdown of GDP according to the value added of each sector of the economy. The right bar shows the breakdown of GDP according to the four types of aggregate spending: $C + I + G + X - IM$. The right bar has a total length of $16,803 billion + $494 billion = $17,297 billion. The $494 billion, shown as the area extending below the horizontal axis, is the amount of total spending absorbed by net imports (negative net exports) in 2013.

Source: Bureau of Economic Analysis.

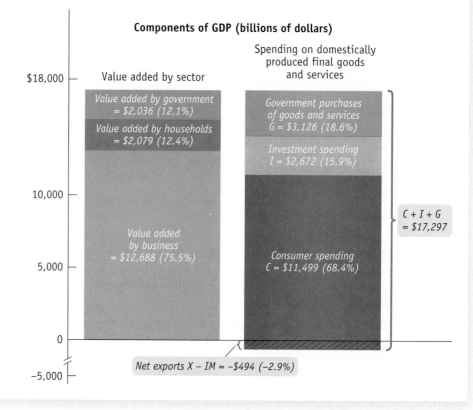

Components of GDP (billions of dollars)

Value added by sector

Spending on domestically produced final goods and services

Value added by government = $2,036 (12.1%)
Value added by households = $2,079 (12.4%)
Value added by business = $12,688 (75.5%)

Government purchases of goods and services G = $3,126 (18.6%)
Investment spending I = $2,672 (15.9%)
Consumer spending C = $11,499 (68.4%)

$C + I + G$ = $17,297

Net exports $X - IM$ = −$494 (−2.9%)

The right bar in Figure 11-2 corresponds to the second method of calculating GDP, showing the breakdown by the four types of aggregate spending. The total length of the right bar is longer than the total length of the left bar, a difference of $494 billion (which, as you can see, extends below the horizontal axis). That's because the total length of the right bar represents total spending in the economy, spending on both domestically produced and foreign-produced—imported—final goods and services.

Within the bar at right, consumer spending (*C*), which is 68.4% of GDP, dominates the picture. But some of that spending was absorbed by foreign-produced goods and services. In 2013, the value of net exports, the difference between the value of exports and the value of imports (*X – IM* in Equation 11-1), was negative—the United States was a net importer of foreign goods and services. The 2013 value of *X – IM* was –$494 billion, or –2.9% of GDP. Thus, a portion of the right bar extends below the horizontal axis by $494 billion to represent the amount of total spending that was absorbed by net imports and so did not lead to higher U.S. GDP. Investment spending (*I*) constituted 15.9% of GDP; government purchases of goods and services (*G*) constituted 18.6% of GDP.

GDP: What's In and What's Out?

It's easy to confuse what is included and what isn't included in GDP. So let's stop here and make sure the distinction is clear.

Be sure not to confuse investment spending with spending on inputs. Investment spending—spending on productive physical capital, the construction of structures (residential as well as commercial), and changes to inventories—is included in GDP. But spending on inputs is not. Why the difference?

Recall the distinction between resources that are *used up* and those that are *not used up* in production. An input, like steel, is used up in production. A metal-stamping machine, an investment good, is not. It will last for many years and will be used repeatedly to make many cars. Since spending on productive physical capital—investment goods—and the construction of structures is not directly tied to current output, economists consider such spending to be spending on final goods. Spending on changes to inventories is considered a part of investment spending so it is also included in GDP. Why? Because, like a machine, additional inventory is an investment in future sales. And when a good is released for sale from inventories, its value is subtracted from the value of inventories and so from GDP.

Used goods are not included in GDP because, as with inputs, to include them would be to double-count: counting them once when sold as new and again when sold as used.

Also, financial assets such as stocks and bonds are not included in GDP because they don't represent either the production or the sale of final goods and services. Rather, a bond represents a promise to repay with interest, and a stock represents a proof of ownership. And for obvious reasons, foreign-produced goods and services are not included in calculations of gross *domestic* product.

Here is a summary of what's included and not included in GDP:

Included

- Domestically produced final goods and services, including capital goods, new construction of structures, and changes to inventories

Not Included

- Intermediate goods and services
- Inputs
- Used goods
- Financial assets such as stocks and bonds
- Foreign-produced goods and services

The United States is a net importer of goods and services, such as computers from China, which is, by far, the biggest exporter to the United States.

Liu Zheng/Color China Photo/AP Images

ECONOMICS ▶ IN ACTION

OUR IMPUTED LIVES

The value of the services that family members provide to each other is not counted as part of GDP.

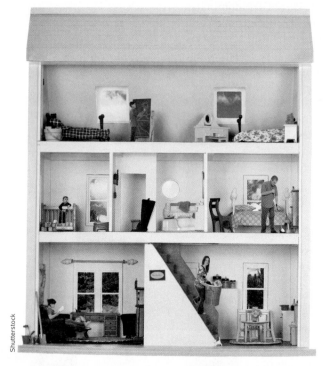

Shutterstock

An old line says that when a person marries the household cook, GDP falls. And it's true: when someone provides services for pay, those services are counted as a part of GDP. But the services family members provide to each other are not. Some economists have produced alternative measures that try to "impute" the value of household work—that is, assign an estimate of what the market value of that work would have been if it had been paid for. But the standard measure of GDP doesn't contain that imputation.

GDP estimates do, however, include an imputation for the value of "owner-occupied housing." That is, if you buy the home you were formerly renting, GDP does not go down. It's true that because you no longer pay rent to your landlord, the landlord no longer sells a service to you—namely, use of the house or apartment. But the statisticians make an estimate of what you would have paid if you rented whatever you live in, whether it's an apartment or a house. For the purposes of the statistics, it's as if you were renting your dwelling from yourself.

If you think about it, this makes a lot of sense. In a homeowning country like the United States, the pleasure we derive from our houses is an important part of the standard of living. So to be accurate, estimates of GDP must take into account the value of housing that is occupied by owners as well as the value of rental housing.

MODULE

11 Review

Solutions appear at the back of the book.

Check Your Understanding

1. Explain why the three methods of calculating GDP produce the same estimate of GDP.

2. What does the investment spending category of GDP measure?

3. Consider Figure 11-1. Explain why it would be incorrect to calculate total value added as $30,500, the sum of the sales price of a car and a car's worth of steel.

Multiple-Choice Questions

1. GDP is equal to

   a. the total value of all goods and services produced in an economy during a given period.

   b. the sum of the spending by consumers and firms.

   c. the total value of the intermediate and final goods produced during a given period.

   d. the profit earned by the firms producing new goods and services.

   e. the income earned by the factors of production.

2. Which of the following is included in GDP?

   a. changes to inventories

   b. intermediate goods

   c. used goods

   d. financial assets such as stocks and bonds

   e. foreign-produced goods

3. Value added is best defined as

   a. the profit earned by firms.

b. the value of a firm's sales.

c. the value of a firm's sales minus the value of purchased intermediate goods and services.

d. the increase in aggregate income during a given period.

e. the value of investment spending in the economy during a given period.

4. Which of the following is *not* included in GDP?

   a. capital goods such as machinery

   b. imports

c. the value of domestically produced services

d. government purchases of goods and services

e. the construction of structures

5. Which of the following components make up the largest percentage of GDP measured by aggregate spending?

   a. consumer spending

   b. investment spending

   c. government purchases of goods and services

   d. exports

   e. imports

Critical-Thinking Questions

1. Explain why the government cannot simply add up the total value of new goods and services produced in the economy during a given time period to come up with an estimate of GDP.

2. How does the concept of value added help the government obtain a more accurate measure of GDP?

12 Interpreting Real Gross Domestic Product

Corbis/Superstock

Andersen Ross/Getty Images

WHAT YOU WILL LEARN

1 **The difference between real GDP and nominal GDP**

2 **Why real GDP is the appropriate measure of real economic activity**

What GDP Tells Us

We now know what gross domestic product (GDP) is and how it's calculated. But what does the measurement of GDP tell us?

The most important use of GDP is as a measure of the size of the economy, providing us a scale against which to compare the economic performance of other years or other countries. For example, in 2013, U.S. GDP was $16,803 billion, China's GDP was $9,272 billion, and the combined GDP of the 28 countries that make up the European Union was $17,267 billion. This comparison tells us that China, although it has the world's second-largest national economy, carries considerably less economic weight than does the United States. When taken in aggregate, Europe's economy is larger than the U.S. economy.

Still, one must be careful when using GDP numbers, especially when making comparisons over time. That's because part of the increase in the value of GDP over time represents *increases in the prices* of goods and services rather than an increase in output. For example, U.S. GDP was $7,085 billion in 1994 and had approximately doubled to $14,990 billion by 2011. But U.S. production didn't actually double over that period. To measure actual changes in aggregate output, we need a modified version of GDP that is adjusted for price changes, known as *real GDP*. We'll see how real GDP is calculated next.

Real GDP: A Measure of Aggregate Output

In the section-opening story, we described how China passed Japan as the world's second-largest economy in 2010. At the time, Japan's economy was weakening: during the second quarter of 2010, output declined by an annual rate of 6.3%. Oddly, however, GDP was up. In fact, Japan's GDP measured in yen, its national currency, rose by an annual rate of 4.8% during the quarter. How was that possible? The answer is that Japan was experiencing inflation at the time. As a result, the yen value of Japan's GDP rose although output actually fell.

The moral of this story is that the commonly cited GDP number is an interesting and useful statistic, one that provides a good way to compare the size of different economies, but *it's not a good measure of the economy's growth over time*. GDP can grow because the economy grows, but it can also grow simply because of inflation. Even if an economy's output doesn't change, GDP will go up if the prices of the goods and services the economy produces increase. Likewise, GDP can fall either because the economy is producing less or because prices have fallen.

To measure the economy's growth with accuracy, we need a measure of **aggregate output:** the total quantity of final goods and services the economy produces. The measure that is used for this purpose is known as *real GDP*. By tracking real GDP over time, we avoid the problem of changes in prices distorting the value of changes in production over time. Let's look first at how real GDP is calculated and then at what it means.

Aggregate output is the total quantity of final goods and services produced within an economy.

Real GDP is the total value of all final goods and services produced in the economy during a given year, calculated using the prices of a selected base year.

Nominal GDP is the total value of all final goods and services produced in the economy during a given year, calculated with the prices current in the year in which the output is produced.

Calculating Real GDP

To understand how real GDP is calculated, imagine an economy in which only two goods, apples and oranges, are produced and in which both goods are sold only to final consumers. The outputs and prices of the two fruits for two consecutive years are shown in Table 12-1.

The first thing we can say about these data is that the value of sales increased from year 1 to year 2. In the first year, the total value of sales was (2,000 billion × $0.25) + (1,000 billion × $0.50) = $1,000 billion; in the second, it was (2,200 billion × $0.30) + (1,200 billion × $0.70) = $1,500 billion, which is 50% larger. But it is also clear from the table that this increase in the dollar value of GDP overstates the real growth in the economy. Although the quantities of both apples and oranges increased, the prices of both apples and oranges also rose. So part of the 50% increase in the dollar value of GDP simply reflects higher prices, not higher production of output.

TABLE 12-1

Calculating GDP and Real GDP in a Simple Economy

	Year 1	Year 2
Quantity of apples (billions)	2,000	2,200
Price of an apple	$0.25	$0.30
Quantity of oranges (billions)	1,000	1,200
Price of an orange	$0.50	$0.70
GDP (billions of dollars)	$1,000	$1,500
Real GDP (billions of year 1 dollars)	$1,000	$1,150

To estimate the true increase in aggregate output produced, we have to ask the following question: How much would GDP have gone up if prices had *not* changed? To answer this question, we need to find the value of output in year 2 expressed in year 1 prices. In year 1, the price of apples was $0.25 each and the price of oranges $0.50 each. So year 2 output *at year 1 prices* is (2,200 billion × $0.25) + (1,200 billion × $0.50) = $1,150 billion. And output in year 1 at year 1 prices was $1,000 billion. So in this example, GDP measured in year 1 prices rose 15%—from $1,000 billion to $1,150 billion.

Now we can define **real GDP:** it is the total value of final goods and services produced in the economy during a year, calculated as if prices had stayed constant at the level of some given base year. A real GDP number always comes with information about what the base year is. A GDP number that has not been adjusted for changes in prices is calculated using the prices in the year in which the output is produced. Economists call this measure **nominal GDP,** GDP at current prices. If we had used nominal GDP to measure the true change in output from year 1 to year 2 in our apples and oranges example, we would have overstated the true growth in output: we would have claimed it to be 50%, when in fact it was only 15%. By comparing output in the two years using a common

Chained dollars is the method of calculating changes in real GDP using the average between the growth rate calculated using an early base year and the growth rate calculated using a late base year.

TABLE 12-2

Nominal versus Real GDP in 2001, 2005, and 2012

	Nominal GDP (billions of current dollars)	Real GDP (billions of 2005 dollars)
2001	$10,286	$11,347
2005	12,683	12,638
2012	15,829	13,648

Source: Bureau of Economic Analysis.

set of prices—the year 1 prices in this example—we are able to focus solely on changes in the quantity of output by eliminating the influence of changes in prices.

Table 12-2 shows a real-life version of our apples and oranges example. The second column shows nominal GDP in 2001, 2005, and 2012. The third column shows real GDP for each year in 2005 dollars (that is, using the value of the dollar in the year 2005). For 2005 the nominal GDP and the real GDP are the same. But real GDP in 2001 expressed in 2005 dollars was higher than nominal GDP in 2001, reflecting the fact that prices were in general higher in 2005 than in 2001. Real GDP in 2012 expressed in 2005 dollars, however, was less than nominal GDP in 2012 because prices in 2005 were lower than in 2012.

You might have noticed that there is an alternative way to calculate real GDP using the data in Table 12-1. Why not measure it using the prices of year 2 rather than year 1 as the base-year prices? This procedure seems equally valid. According to that calculation, real GDP in year 1 at year 2 prices is (2,000 billion × $0.30) + (1,000 billion × $0.70) = $1,300 billion; real GDP in year 2 at year 2 prices is $1,500 billion, the same as nominal GDP in year 2. So using year 2 prices as the base year, the growth rate of real GDP is equal to ($1,500 billion − $1,300 billion)/$1,300 billion = 0.154, or 15.4%. This is slightly higher than the figure we got from the previous calculation, in which year 1 prices were the base-year prices. In that calculation, we found that real GDP increased by 15%. Neither answer, 15.4% versus 15%, is more "correct" than the other.

In reality, the government economists who put together the U.S. national accounts have adopted a method to measure the change in real GDP known as chain linking, which uses the average between the GDP growth rate calculated using an early base year and the GDP growth rate calculated using a late base year. As a result, U.S. statistics on real GDP are always expressed in **chained dollars.**

ECONOMICS ▶ IN ACTION   WORLD VIEW

FIGURE 12-1 **Real Versus Nominal GDP in Venezuela**

Source: Banco Central de Venezuela.

MIRACLE IN VENEZUELA?

The South American nation of Venezuela has a distinction that may surprise you: in recent years, it has had one of the world's fastest-growing nominal GDPs. Between 2000 and 2011, Venezuelan nominal GDP grew by an average of 29% each year—much faster than nominal GDP in the United States or even in booming economies like China.

So is Venezuela experiencing an economic miracle? No, it's just suffering from unusually high inflation. Figure 12-1 shows Venezuela's nominal and real GDP from 2000 to 2011, with real GDP measured in 1997 prices. Real GDP did grow over the period, but at an annual rate of only 3%. That's about twice the U.S. growth rate over the same period, but it is far short of China's 10% growth.

What Real GDP Doesn't Measure

GDP is a measure of a country's aggregate output. Other things equal, a country with a larger population will have higher GDP simply because there are more people working. So if we want to compare GDP across countries but want to eliminate the effect of differences in population size, we use the measure **GDP per capita**—GDP divided by the size of the population, equivalent to the average GDP per person. Correspondingly, **real GDP per capita** is the average real GDP per person.

Real GDP per capita can be a useful measure in some circumstances, such as in a comparison of labor productivity between two countries. However, despite the fact that it is a rough measure of the average real output per person, real GDP per capita has well-known limitations as a measure of a country's living standards.

Every once in a while economists are accused of believing that growth in real GDP per capita is the only thing that matters—that is, thinking that increasing real GDP per capita is a goal in itself. In fact, economists rarely make that mistake; the idea that economists care only about real GDP per capita is a sort of urban legend. Let's take a moment to be clear about why a country's real GDP per capita is not a sufficient measure of human welfare in that country and why growth in real GDP per capita is not an appropriate policy goal in itself.

Real GDP does not include many of the things that contribute to happiness, such as leisure time, volunteerism, housework, and natural beauty. And real GDP increases with expenditures on some things that make people unhappy, including disease, divorce, crime, and natural disasters.

Real GDP per capita is a measure of an economy's average aggregate output per person—and so of what it *can* do. A country with a high real GDP can afford to be healthy, to be well educated, and in general to have a good quality of life. But there is not a one-to-one match between real GDP and the quality of life. Real GDP doesn't address how a country uses that output to affect living standards, it doesn't include some sources of well-being, and it does include some things that are detriments to well-being.

> **GDP per capita** is GDP divided by the size of the population; it is equivalent to the average GDP per person.
>
> **Real GDP per capita** is the average real GDP per person.

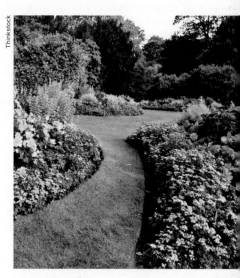

Real GDP doesn't include many of the things that contribute to quality of life and happiness.

ECONOMICS ▶ IN ACTION

GDP AND THE MEANING OF LIFE

"I've been rich and I've been poor," the actress Mae West famously declared. "Believe me, rich is better." But is the same true for countries?

This figure shows two pieces of information for a number of countries: how rich they are, as measured by GDP per capita, and how people assess their well-being. Well-being was measured by a Gallup world survey that asked people to rate their lives at the current time and their expectations for the next five years. The graph shows the percentage of people who rated their well-being as "thriving."

The figure seems to tell us three things:

1. *Rich is better.* Richer countries on average have higher well-being than poor countries.

2. *Money matters less as you grow richer.* The gain in life satisfaction as you go from GDP per capita of $20,000 to $30,000 is greater than the gain as you go from $40,000 to $50,000.

3. *Money isn't everything.* Israelis, though rich by world standards, are poorer than Americans—but they seem more satisfied with their lives. Japan is richer than most other nations, but by and large, quite miserable.

These results are consistent with the observation that high GDP per capita makes it easier to achieve a good life but that countries aren't equally successful in taking advantage of that possibility.

FIGURE 12-2   Percentage of Population for Select Countries That Rate Their Well-Being as Thriving

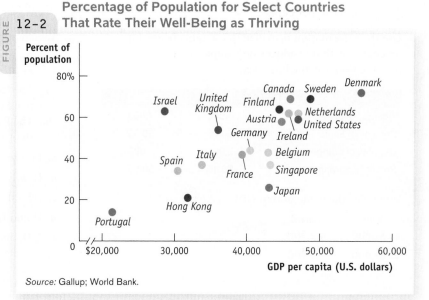

Source: Gallup; World Bank.

MODULE 12 Review

Solutions appear at the back of the book.

Check Your Understanding

1. Assume there are only two goods in the economy, french fries and onion rings. In 2012, 1,000,000 servings of french fries were sold for $0.40 each and 800,000 servings of onion rings were sold for $0.60 each. From 2012 to 2013, the price of french fries rose to $0.50 and the servings sold fell to 900,000; the price of onion rings fell to $0.51 and the servings sold rose to 840,000.

    a. Calculate nominal GDP in 2012 and 2013. Calculate real GDP in 2013 using 2012 prices.

    b. Why would an assessment of growth using nominal GDP be misguided?

2. From 1990 to 2000 the price of housing rose dramatically. What are the implications of this in deciding whether to use 1990 or 2000 as the base year in calculating 2010 real GDP?

Multiple-Choice Questions

1. Which of the following is true of real GDP?

    I. It is adjusted for changes in prices.
    II. It is always equal to nominal GDP.
    III. It increases whenever aggregate output increases.

    a. I only

    b. II only

    c. III only

    d. I and III

    e. I, II, and III

2. The best measure for comparing a country's aggregate output over time is

    a. nominal GDP.

    b. real GDP.

    c. nominal GDP per capita.

    d. real GDP per capita.

    e. average GDP per capita.

3. Use the information provided in the table below for an economy that produces only apples and oranges. Assume year 1 is the base year.

	Year 1	Year 2
Quantity of apples	3,000	4,000
Price of an apple	$0.20	$0.30
Quantity of oranges	2,000	3,000
Price of an orange	$0.40	$0.50

What was the value of real GDP in each year?

	Year 1	Year 2
a.	$1,400	$2,700
b.	$1,900	$2,700
c.	$1,400	$2,000
d.	$1,900	$2,000
e.	$1,400	$1,900

4. Real GDP per capita is an imperfect measure of the quality of life in part because it

    a. includes the value of leisure time.

    b. excludes expenditures on education.

    c. includes expenditures on natural disasters.

    d. excludes expenditures on entertainment.

    e. includes the value of housework.

5. Refer to the 2011 data in the following table.

	Nominal GDP in billions of dollars
United States	$14,990
China	7,318
European Union	17,570

Which of the following must be true?

    I. Residents of China were worse off than residents of the United States or the European Union.
    II. The European Union had a higher nominal GDP per capita than the United States.
    III. The European Union had a larger economy than the United States.

    a. I only

    b. II only

    c. III only

    d. II and III

    e. I, II, and III

Critical-Thinking Questions

Use the information in the accompanying table to answer the following questions.

1. Calculate the percent increase in nominal GDP between 2008 and 2013 for each country.

2. What happened to the price level in each country between 2008 and 2013?

3. Calculate real GDP in each country in 2013, using 2008 as the base year.

4. Calculate the percent increase in real GDP between 2008 and 2013 for each country.

5. Compare the two countries' real GDP per capita in 2013 using 2008 as the base year.

	Year	Nominal GDP	Price Level	Population
Country A	2008	$2,000	$100	10
	2013	4,000	100	20
Country B	2008	$2,000	$100	10
	2013	6,000	200	15

BUSINESS CASE : Getting a Jump on GDP

OSOMEDIA/AgeFotostock/SuperStock

GDP matters. Investors and business leaders are always eager to get the latest numbers. When the Bureau of Economic Analysis releases its first estimate of each quarter's GDP, normally on the 27th or 28th day of the month after the quarter ends, it's invariably a big news story.

In fact, many companies and other players in the economy are so eager to know what's happening to GDP that they don't want to wait for the official estimate. So a number of organizations produce numbers that can be used to predict what the official GDP number will say. Let's talk about two of those organizations, the economic consulting firm Macroeconomic Advisers and the nonprofit Institute of Supply Management.

Macroeconomic Advisers takes a direct approach: it produces its own estimates of GDP based on raw data from the U.S. government. But whereas the Bureau of Economic Analysis estimates GDP only on a quarterly basis, Macroeconomic Advisers produces monthly estimates. This means that clients can, for example, look at the estimates for January and February and make a pretty good guess at what first-quarter GDP, which also includes March, will turn out to be. The monthly estimates are derived by looking at a number of monthly measures that track purchases, such as car and truck sales, new housing construction, and exports.

The Institute for Supply Management (ISM) takes a very different approach. It relies on monthly surveys of purchasing managers—that is, executives in charge of buying supplies—who are basically asked whether their companies are increasing or reducing production. (We say "basically" because the ISM asks a longer list of questions.)

Responses to the surveys are released in the form of indexes showing the percentage of companies that are expanding. Obviously, these indexes don't directly tell you what is happening to GDP. But historically, the ISM indexes have been strongly correlated with the rate of growth of GDP, and this historical relationship can be used to translate ISM data into "early warning" GDP estimates.

So if you just can't wait for those quarterly GDP numbers, you're not alone. The private sector has responded to demand, and you can get your data fix every month.

Questions for Thought

1. Why do businesses care about GDP to such an extent that they want early estimates?

2. How do the methods of Macroeconomic Advisers and the Institute of Supply Management fit into the three different ways to calculate GDP?

3. If private firms are producing GDP estimates, why do we need the Bureau of Economic Analysis?

SECTION 3 REVIEW

Summary

Introduction to Macroeconomics

1. One key concern of macroeconomics is the **business cycle,** the short-run alternation between **recessions,** periods of falling employment and output, and **expansions,** periods of rising employment and output.

2. The point at which expansion turns to recession is a **business-cycle peak.** The point at which recession turns to expansion is a **business-cycle trough.**

3. Another key area of macroeconomic study is **long-run economic growth,** the sustained upward trend in the economy's output over time. Long-run economic growth is the force behind long-term increases in living standards and is important for financing some economic programs. It is especially important for poorer countries.

4. When the prices of most goods and services are rising, so that the overall level of prices is going up, the economy experiences **inflation.** When the overall level of prices is going down, the economy experiences **deflation.**

5. In the short run, inflation and deflation are closely related to the business cycle. In the long run, prices tend to reflect changes in the overall quantity of money. Because both inflation and deflation can cause problems, economists and policy makers generally aim for **price stability.**

6. Although comparative advantage explains why **open economies** export some things and import others, macroeconomic analysis is needed to explain why countries run **trade surpluses** or **trade deficits.** The determinants of the overall balance between exports and imports lie in decisions about savings and investment spending.

The Circular-Flow Diagram and the National Accounts

7. Economists keep track of the flows of money between sectors with the **national income and product accounts,** or **national accounts.** To understand the principles behind the national accounts, it helps to look at a **circular-flow diagram,** a simplified representation of the economy showing the flows of money, goods and services, and factors of production through the economy.

8. Households earn income via the factor markets from wages, interest on **bonds,** profit accruing to owners of **stocks,** and rent on land. In addition, they receive **government transfers** from the government. **Disposable income,** total household income minus taxes plus government transfers, is allocated to **consumer spending** (C) and **private savings.**

9. Via the **financial markets,** private savings and foreign lending are channeled to **investment spending** (I), government borrowing, and foreign borrowing.

10. **Government purchases of goods and services** (G) are paid for by tax revenues and any **government borrowing.**

11. Exports (X) generate an inflow of funds into the country from the rest of the world, but imports (IM) lead to an outflow of funds to the rest of the world. Foreigners can also buy stocks and bonds in the U.S. financial markets.

Gross Domestic Product (GDP)

12. **Gross domestic product,** or **GDP,** measures the value of all **final goods and services** produced in the economy. It does not include the value of **intermediate goods and services,** but it does include **inventories** and **net exports** (X − IM).

13. GDP can be calculated in three ways: add up the **value added** by all producers; add up all spending on domestically produced final goods and services, leading to the equation GDP = C + I + G + X − IM, also known as **aggregate spending;** or add up all the income paid by domestic firms to factors of production.

14. The three methods of calculating GDP are equivalent, because in the economy as a whole, total income paid by domestic firms to factors of production must equal total spending on domestically produced final goods and services.

Interpreting Real Gross Domestic Product

15. **Real GDP** is the value of the final goods and services produced calculated using the prices of a selected base year. Except in the base year, real GDP is usually not the same as **nominal GDP,** the value of **aggregate output** calculated using current prices.

16. Analysis of the growth rate of aggregate output must use real GDP because doing so eliminates any change in the value of aggregate output due solely to price changes. U.S. statistics on real GDP are always expressed in **chained dollars.**

17. **Real GDP per capita** is a measure of average aggregate output per person but is not in itself an appropriate policy goal.

Key Terms

Problems

1. How do economists in the United States determine when a recession begins and when it ends? How do other countries determine whether or not a recession is occurring?

2. The U.S. Department of Labor reports statistics on employment and earnings that are used as key indicators by many economists to gauge the health of the economy. Figure 9-2 in the text plots historical data on the unemployment rate each month. Noticeably, the numbers were high during the recessions in the early 1990s, in 2001, and in 2007–2009.

   a. Locate the latest data on the national unemployment rate. (*Hint:* Go to the website of the Bureau of Labor Statistics, www.bls.gov, and locate the latest release of the Employment Situation.)

   b. Compare the current numbers with the recessions in the early 1990s, in 2001, and in 2007–2009 as well as with the periods of relatively high economic growth just before the recessions. Are the current numbers indicative of a recessionary trend?

3. The accompanying figure shows the annual rate of growth in employment for the United Kingdom and Japan from 1991 to 2010. (The annual growth rate is the percent change in each year's employment over the previous year.) Comment on the business cycles of these two economies. Are their business cycles similar or dissimilar?

4. a. What three measures of the economy tend to move together during the business cycle? Which way do they move during an upturn? During a downturn?

   b. Who in the economy is hurt during a recession? How?

   c. How did Milton Friedman alter the consensus that had developed in the aftermath of the Great Depression on how the economy should be managed? What is the current goal of policy makers in managing the economy?

5. Why do we consider a business-cycle expansion different from long-run economic growth? Why do we care about the size of the long-run growth rate of real GDP versus the size of the growth rate of the population?

6. College tuition has risen significantly in the last few decades. From the 1979–1980 academic year to the 2009–2010 academic year, total tuition, room, and board paid by full-time undergraduate students went from $2,327 to $15,041 at public institutions and from $5,013 to $35,061 at private institutions. This is an average annual tuition increase of 6.4% at public institutions and 6.7% at private institutions. Over the same time, average personal income after taxes rose from $7,956 to $35,088 per year, which is an average annual rate of growth of personal income of 5.0%. Have these tuition increases made it more difficult for the average student to afford college tuition?

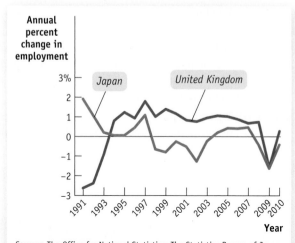

Sources: The Office for National Statistics; The Statistics Bureau of Japan.

7. Each year, *The Economist* publishes data on the price of the Big Mac in different countries and exchange rates. The accompanying table shows some data used for the index from 2007 and 2011. Use this information to answer the following questions.

Country	2007		2011	
	Price of Big Mac (in local currrency)	Price of Big Mac (in U.S. dollars)	Price of Big Mac (in local currency)	Price of Big Mac (in U.S. dollars)
Argentina	peso8.25	$2.65	peso20.0	$4.84
Canada	C$3.63	$3.08	C$4.73	$5.00
Euro area	€2.94	$3.82	€3.44	$4.93
Japan	¥280	$2.31	¥320	$4.08
United States	$3.22	$3.22	$4.07	$4.07

   a. Where was it cheapest to buy a Big Mac in U.S. dollars in 2007?

   b. Where was it cheapest to buy a Big Mac in U.S. dollars in 2011?

   c. Using the increase in the local currency price of the Big Mac in each country to measure the percent change in the overall price level from 2007 to 2011, which nation experienced the most inflation? Did any of the nations experience deflation?

8. The accompanying figure illustrates the trade deficit of the United States since 1992. The United States has been consistently and, on the whole, increasingly importing more goods than it has been exporting. One of the countries it runs a trade deficit with is China. Which of the following statements are valid possible explanations of this fact? Explain.

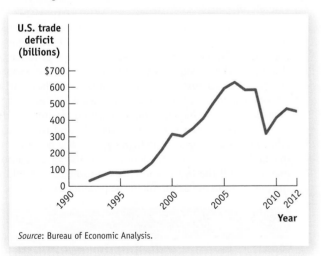

Source: Bureau of Economic Analysis.

   a. Many products, such as televisions, that were formerly manufactured in the United States are now manufactured in China.

   b. The wages of the average Chinese worker are far lower than the wages of the average American worker.

   c. Investment spending in the United States is high relative to its level of savings.

9. Following is a simplified circular-flow diagram for the economy of Micronia. (Note that there is no investment in Micronia.)

   a. What is the value of GDP in Micronia?

   b. What is the value of net exports?

   c. What is the value of disposable income?

   d. Does the total flow of money out of households—the sum of taxes paid and consumer spending—equal the total flow of money into households?

   e. How does the government of Micronia finance its purchases of goods and services?

10. A more complex circular-flow diagram for the economy of Macronia is shown at right. (Note that Macronia has investment and financial markets.)

a. What is the value of GDP in Macronia?

b. What is the value of net exports?

c. What is the value of disposable income?

d. Does the total flow of money out of households—the sum of taxes paid, consumer spending, and private savings—equal the total flow of money into households?

e. How does the government finance its spending?

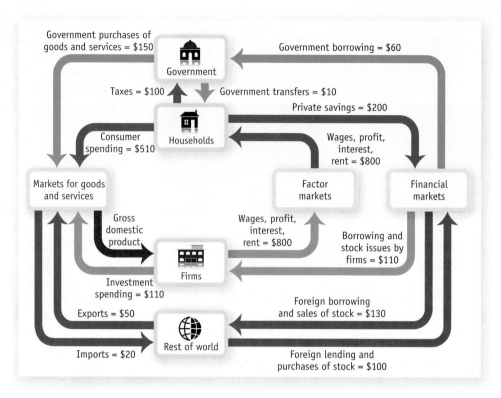

11. The components of GDP in the accompanying table were produced by the Bureau of Economic Analysis.

Category	Components of GDP in 2012 (billions of dollars)
Consumer spending	
Durable goods	$1,218.80
Nondurable goods	2,563.00
Services	7,337.68
Private investment spending	
Fixed investment spending	1,998.98
Nonresidential	1,616.58
Structures	458.48
Equipment and software	1,158.13
Residential	382.38
Change in private inventories	60.63
Net exports	
Exports	2,179.70
Imports	2,746.35
Government purchases of goods and services and investment spending	
Federal	1,214.23
National defense	809.10
Nondefense	405.10
State and local	1,849.40

a. Calculate 2012 consumer spending.

b. Calculate 2012 private investment spending.

c. Calculate 2012 net exports.

d. Calculate 2012 government purchases of goods and services and investment spending.

e. Calculate 2012 gross domestic product.

f. Calculate consumer spending on services as a percentage of total consumer spending.

g. Calculate 2012 exports as a percentage of imports.

h. Calculate 2012 government purchases on national defense as a percentage of federal government purchases of goods and services.

12. The small economy of Pizzania produces three goods (bread, cheese, and pizza), each produced by a separate company. The bread and cheese companies produce all the inputs they need to make bread and cheese, respectively. The pizza company uses the bread and cheese from the other companies to make its pizzas. All three companies employ labor to help produce their goods, and the difference between the value of goods sold and the sum of labor and input costs is the firm's profit. The accompanying table summarizes the activities of the three companies when all the bread and cheese produced are sold to the pizza company as inputs in the production of pizzas.

	Bread company	Cheese company	Pizza company
Cost of inputs	$0	$0	$50 (bread) 35 (cheese)
Wages	15	20	75
Value of output	50	35	200

a. Calculate GDP as the value added in production.

b. Calculate GDP as spending on final goods and services.

c. Calculate GDP as factor income.

13. In the economy of Pizzania (from Problem 13), bread and cheese produced are sold both to the pizza company for inputs in the production of pizzas and to consumers as final goods. The accompanying table summarizes the activities of the three companies.

	Bread company	Cheese company	Pizza company
Cost of inputs	$0	$0	$50 (bread) 35 (cheese)
Wages	25	30	75
Value of output	100	60	200

a. Calculate GDP as the value added in production.

b. Calculate GDP as spending on final goods and services.

c. Calculate GDP as factor income.

14. Which of the following transactions will be included in GDP for the United States?

a. Coca-Cola builds a new bottling plant in the United States.

b. Delta sells one of its existing airplanes to Korean Air.

c. Ms. Moneybags buys an existing share of Disney stock.

d. A California winery produces a bottle of Chardonnay and sells it to a customer in Montreal, Canada.

e. An American buys a bottle of French perfume in Paris.

f. A book publisher produces too many copies of a new book; the books don't sell this year, so the publisher adds the surplus books to inventories.

15. The economy of Britannica produces three goods: computers, DVDs, and pizza. The accompanying table shows the prices and output of the three goods for the years 2010, 2011, and 2012.

	Computers		DVDs		Pizzas	
Year	Price	Quantity	Price	Quantity	Price	Quantity
2010	$900	10	$10	100	$15	2
2011	1,000	10.5	12	105	16	2
2012	1,050	12	14	110	17	3

a. What is the percent change in production of each of the goods from 2010 to 2011 and from 2011 to 2012?

b. What is the percent change in prices of each of the goods from 2010 to 2011 and from 2011 to 2012?

c. Calculate nominal GDP in Britannica for each of the three years. What is the percent change in nominal GDP from 2010 to 2011 and from 2011 to 2012?

d. Calculate real GDP in Britannica using 2010 prices for each of the three years. What is the percent change in real GDP from 2010 to 2011 and from 2011 to 2012?

16. The accompanying table shows data on nominal GDP (in billions of dollars), real GDP (in billions of 2005 dollars), and population (in thousands) of the United States in 1960, 1970, 1980, 1990, 2000, and 2010. The U.S. price level rose consistently over the period 1960–2010.

Year	Nominal GDP (billions of dollars)	Real GDP (billions of 2005 dollars)	Population (thousands)
1960	$526.4	$2,828.5	180,760
1970	1,038.5	4,266.3	205,089
1980	2,788.1	5,834.0	227,726
1990	5,800.5	8,027.1	250,181
2000	9,951.5	11,216.4	282,418
2010	14,526.5	13,088.0	310,106

a. Why is real GDP greater than nominal GDP for all years until 2000 and lower for 2010?

b. Calculate the percent change in real GDP from 1960 to 1970, 1970 to 1980, 1980 to 1990, 1990 to 2000, and 2000 to 2010. Which period had the highest growth rate?

c. Calculate real GDP per capita for each of the years in the table.

d. Calculate the percent change in real GDP per capita from 1960 to 1970, 1970 to 1980, 1980 to 1990, 1990 to 2000, and 2000 to 2010. Which period had the highest growth rate?

e. How do the percent change in real GDP and the percent change in real GDP per capita compare? Which is larger? Do we expect them to have this relationship?

Unemployment and Inflation

A VERY BRITISH DILEMMA

WORLD VIEW

The Bank of England is a venerable institution—so venerable that it makes the Federal Reserve, its American counterpart, look like a youthful upstart. The Old Lady of Threadneedle Street, as the Bank is sometimes known, has been managing Great Britain's money supply for three centuries—pumping up the money supply when the economy needs a boost, putting on the brakes when inflation looms.

But in early 2011, it wasn't at all clear what the Bank should do. British inflation was rising: consumer prices were 4.4 percent higher than they had been a year earlier, a rate of increase far above the Bank's comfort level. At the same time, the British economy was still suffering the aftereffects of a severe recession, and unemployment, especially among young people, was disturbingly high. So should the Bank have focused on fighting inflation, or should it have kept trying to bring down unemployment?

Opinion was sharply divided. The Bank faced "a genuine problem of credibility," declared Patrick Minford, a professor at Cardiff University, who urged the Bank to fight inflation by raising interest rates. The rise in inflation

reflected temporary factors and would soon reverse course, countered Adam Posen, a member of the Bank's Policy Committee, who argued that any tightening would risk putting Britain into a prolonged slump.

Whoever was right, the dispute highlighted the key concerns of macroeconomic policy. Unemployment and inflation are the two great evils of macroeconomics. So the two principal goals of macroeconomic policy are low unemployment and price stability, usually defined as a low but positive rate of inflation.

Unfortunately, those goals sometimes appear to be in conflict with each other: economists often warn that policies intended to fight unemployment run the risk of increasing inflation; conversely, policies intended to bring down inflation can raise unemployment.

We look at the nature of the trade-off between low unemployment and price stability in Section 12. In this section we will provide an overview of the basic facts about unemployment and inflation: how they're measured, how they affect consumers and firms, and how they change over time.

Frances Roberts/Alamy

The Unemployment Rate

One of the most important issues in both the 2008 and 2012 presidential elections was the high unemployment rate. Figure 13-1 shows the U.S. unemployment rate from 1948 to 2013. As you can see, the labor market hit a difficult patch starting in mid-2008, with the unemployment rate rising from 4.8% in February 2008 to 10.1% in October 2009. What did the rise in the unemployment rate during the Great Recesssion mean, and why was it such a big factor in people's lives? To understand why policy makers pay so much attention to employment and unemployment, we need to understand how both are defined and measured.

Defining and Measuring Unemployment

It's easy to define employment: you're **employed** if and only if you have a job.

Unemployment, however, is a more subtle concept. Just because a person isn't working doesn't mean that we consider that person unemployed. For example, in November 2013 there were 42 million retired workers in the United States receiving Social Security checks. Most of them were probably happy that they were no longer working, so we wouldn't consider someone who has settled into a comfortable, well-earned retirement to be unemployed. There were also 14 million disabled U.S. workers receiving benefits because they were unable to work. Again, although they weren't working, we wouldn't normally consider them to be unemployed.

The U.S. Census Bureau, the federal agency that collects data on unemployment, considers the unemployed to be those who are "jobless, looking for jobs, and available for work." Retired people don't count because they aren't looking for jobs; the disabled don't count because they aren't available for work. More specifically, an individual is considered unemployed if he or she doesn't currently have a job and has been actively seeking a job during the past four weeks. So the **unemployed** are people who are actively looking for work but aren't currently employed.

Employed people are currently holding a job in the economy, either full time or part time.

Unemployed people are actively looking for work but aren't currently employed.

FIGURE **13-1** The U.S. Unemployment Rate, 1948–2013

The unemployment rate has fluctuated widely over time. It always rises during recessions, which are shown by the shaded bars. It usually, but not always, falls during periods of economic expansion.

Source: Bureau of Labor Statistics; National Bureau of Economic Research.

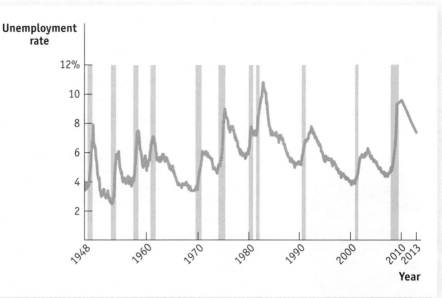

A country's **labor force** is the sum of the employed and the unemployed—that is, the people who are currently working and the people who are currently looking for work. The **labor force participation rate,** defined as the share of the working-age population that is in the labor force, is calculated as follows:

$$\textbf{(13-1)} \quad \text{Labor force participation rate} = \frac{\text{Labor force}}{\text{Population age 16 and older}} \times 100$$

The **unemployment rate,** defined as the percentage of the total number of people in the labor force who are unemployed, is calculated as follows:

$$\textbf{(13-2)} \quad \text{Unemployment rate} = \frac{\text{Number of unemployed workers}}{\text{Labor force}} \times 100$$

To estimate the numbers that go into calculating the unemployment rate, the U.S. Census Bureau carries out a monthly survey called the Current Population Survey, which involves interviewing a random sample of 60,000 American families. People are asked whether they are currently employed. If they are not employed, they are asked whether they have been looking for a job during the past four weeks. The results are then scaled up, using estimates of the total population, to estimate the total number of employed and unemployed Americans.

The Significance of the Unemployment Rate

In general, the unemployment rate is a good indicator of how easy or difficult it is to find a job given the current state of the economy. When the unemployment rate is low, nearly everyone who wants a job can find one. In 2000, when the unemployment rate averaged 4%, jobs were so abundant that employers spoke of a "mirror test" for getting a job: if you were breathing (therefore, your breath would fog a mirror), you could find work. By contrast, in 2009, the unemployment rate in 17 states rose to over 10% (over 15% in Michigan). Even in 2013, with the unemployment rate averaging 7.4%, it was difficult to find work. More than three times as many Americans were looking for work as there were job openings.

Although the unemployment rate is a good indicator of current labor market conditions, it is not a perfect measure. It has been known to overstate or understate the true level of unemployment.

The **labor force** is equal to the sum of the employed and the unemployed.

The **labor force participation rate** is the percentage of the population aged 16 or older that is in the labor force.

The **unemployment rate** is the percentage of the total number of people in the labor force who are unemployed.

Only those without a job and actively seeking work are considered to be unemployed.

Discouraged workers are nonworking people who are capable of working but have given up looking for a job due to the state of the job market.

Marginally attached workers would like to be employed and have looked for a job in the recent past but are not currently looking for work.

The **underemployed** are people who work part time because they cannot find full-time jobs.

People who would like to work but have given up searching for a job are not counted as unemployed.

HOW THE UNEMPLOYMENT RATE CAN OVERSTATE THE TRUE LEVEL OF UNEMPLOYMENT If you are searching for work, it's normal to take at least a few weeks to find a suitable job. Yet a worker who is quite confident of finding a job, but has not yet accepted a position, is counted as unemployed. As a consequence, the unemployment rate never falls to zero, even in boom times when jobs are plentiful. Even in the buoyant labor market of 2000, when it was easy to find work, the unemployment rate was still 4%. Later, we'll discuss in greater depth the reasons that measured unemployment persists even when jobs are abundant.

HOW THE UNEMPLOYMENT RATE CAN UNDERSTATE THE TRUE LEVEL OF UNEMPLOYMENT Frequently, people who would like to work but aren't working still don't get counted as unemployed. In particular, an individual who has given up looking for a job for the time being because there are no jobs available isn't counted as unemployed because he or she has not been searching for a job during the previous four weeks.

Individuals who want to work but aren't currently searching because they see little prospect of finding a job given the state of the job market are known as **discouraged workers.** Because it does not count discouraged workers, the measured unemployment rate may understate the percentage of people who want to work but are unable to find jobs.

Discouraged workers are part of a larger group known as **marginally attached workers.** These are people who say they would like to have a job and have looked for work in the recent past but are not currently looking for work. They are also not included when calculating the unemployment rate.

Finally, another category of workers who are frustrated in their ability to find work but aren't counted as unemployed are the **underemployed:** workers who would like to find full-time jobs but are currently working part time "for economic reasons"—that is, they can't find a full-time job. Again, they aren't counted in the unemployment rate.

The Bureau of Labor Statistics is the federal agency that calculates the official unemployment rate. It also calculates broader "measures of labor underutilization" that include the three categories of frustrated workers. Figure 13-2 shows what happens to the measured unemployment rate once marginally attached workers (including discouraged workers) and the underemployed are counted.

The broadest measure of unemployment and underemployment, known as *U6*, is the sum of these three measures plus the unemployed; it is substantially higher than the rate usually quoted by the news media. But U6 and the unemployment rate move very much in parallel, so changes in the unemployment rate remain a good guide to what's happening in the overall labor market.

FIGURE 13-2   Alternative Measures of Unemployment, 1994–2013

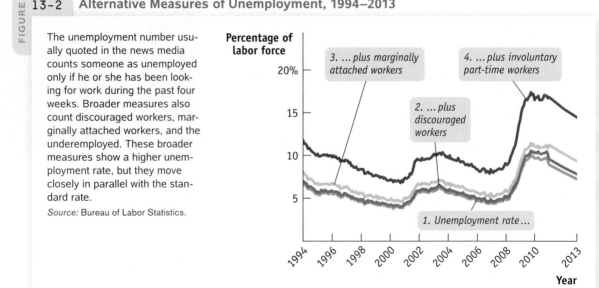

The unemployment number usually quoted in the news media counts someone as unemployed only if he or she has been looking for work during the past four weeks. Broader measures also count discouraged workers, marginally attached workers, and the underemployed. These broader measures show a higher unemployment rate, but they move closely in parallel with the standard rate.

Source: Bureau of Labor Statistics.

Finally, it's important to realize that the unemployment rate varies greatly among demographic groups. Other things equal, jobs are generally easier to find for more experienced workers and for workers during their "prime" working years, from ages 25 to 54. For younger workers, as well as workers nearing retirement age, jobs are typically harder to find, other things equal.

Figure 13-3 shows unemployment rates for different groups in December 2007, when the overall unemployment rate of 5.0% was low by historical standards. As you can see, in December 2007 the unemployment rate for African-American workers was much higher than the national average; the unemployment rate for White teenagers (ages 16–19) was more than three times the national average; and the unemployment rate for African-American teenagers, at 33.1%, was over six times the national average. (Bear in mind that a teenager isn't considered unemployed, even if he or she isn't working, unless that teenager is looking for work but can't find it.) So even at a time when the overall unemployment rate was relatively low, jobs were hard to find for some groups.

So although the unemployment rate is not an exact, literal measure of the percentage of people unable to find jobs, it is a good indicator of overall labor market conditions. The ups and downs of the unemployment rate closely reflect economic changes that have a significant impact on people's lives. Let's turn now to the causes of these fluctuations.

Growth and Unemployment

Compared to Figure 13-1, Figure 13-4 shows the U.S. unemployment rate over a somewhat shorter period, the 35 years from 1978 to 2013. The shaded bars represent periods of recession. As you can see, during every recession, without exception, the unemployment rate rose. The severe recession of 2007–2009, like the earlier one of 1981–1982, led to a huge rise in unemployment.

FIGURE 13-3   Unemployment Rates of Different Groups, 2007

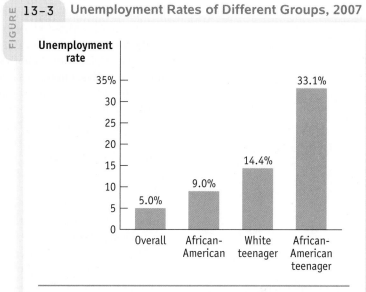

Unemployment rates vary greatly among different demographic groups. For example, although the overall unemployment rate in December 2007 was 5.0%, the unemployment rate among African-American teenagers was 33.1%. As a result, even during periods of low overall unemployment, unemployment remains a serious problem for some groups.

Source: Bureau of Labor Statistics.

FIGURE 13-4   Unemployment and Recessions, 1978–2013

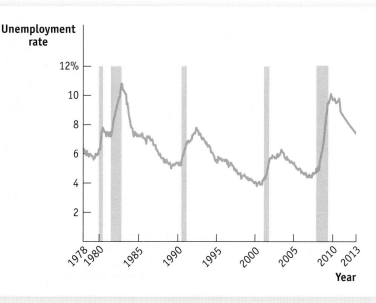

This figure shows a close-up of the unemployment rate for the past three decades, with the shaded bars indicating recessions. It's clear that unemployment always rises during recessions and *usually* falls during expansions. But in both the early 1990s and the early 2000s, unemployment continued to rise for some time after the recession was officially declared over.

Source: Bureau of Labor Statistics.

Correspondingly, during periods of economic expansion the unemployment rate usually falls. The long economic expansion of the 1990s eventually brought the unemployment rate below 4%, and the expansion of the mid-2000s brought the rate down to 4.7%. However, it's important to recognize that *economic expansions aren't always periods of falling unemployment.* Look at the periods immediately following two recent recessions, those of 1990–1991 and 2001 in Figure 13-4. In each case the unemployment rate continued to rise for more than a year after the recession was officially over. The explanation in both cases is that although the economy was growing, it was not growing fast enough to reduce the unemployment rate.

Figure 13-5 is a scatter diagram showing U.S. data for the period from 1949 to 2012. The horizontal axis measures the annual rate of growth in real GDP—the percent by which each year's real GDP changed compared to the previous year's real GDP. (Notice that there were ten years in which growth was negative—that is, real GDP shrank.) The vertical axis measures the *change* in the unemployment rate over the previous year in percentage points. Each dot represents the observed growth rate of real GDP and change in the unemployment rate for a given year. For example, in 2000 the average unemployment rate fell to 4.0% from 4.2% in 1999; this is shown as a value of −0.2 along the vertical axis for the year 2000. Over the same period, real GDP grew by 4.1%; this is the value shown along the horizontal axis for the year 2000.

The downward trend of the scatter points in Figure 13-5 shows that there is a generally strong negative relationship between growth in the economy and the rate of unemployment. Years of high growth in real GDP were also years in which the unemployment rate fell, and years of low or negative growth in real GDP were years in which the unemployment rate rose.

The green vertical line in Figure 13-5 at the value of 3.19% indicates the average growth rate of real GDP over the period from 1949 to 2012. Points lying to the right of the vertical line are years of above-average growth. In these years, the value on the

FIGURE 13-5   Growth and Changes in Unemployment, 1949–2012

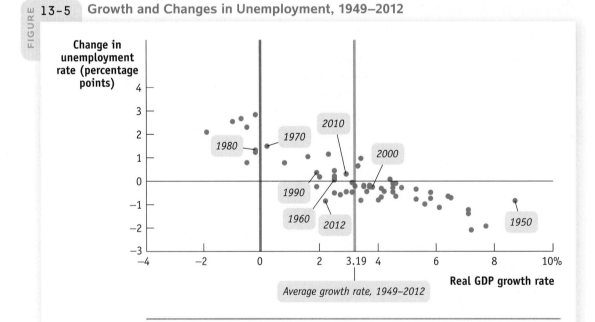

Each dot shows the growth rate of the economy and the change in the unemployment rate for a specific year between 1949 and 2012. For example, in 2000 the economy grew 4.1% and the unemployment rate fell 0.2 percentage point, from 4.2% to 4.0%. In general, the unemployment rate fell when growth was above its average rate of 3.19% a year and rose when growth was below average. Unemployment always rose when real GDP fell.

Sources: Bureau of Labor Statistics; Bureau of Economic Analysis.

vertical axis is usually negative, meaning that the unemployment rate fell. That is, years of above-average growth were usually years in which the unemployment rate was falling. Conversely, points lying to the left of the vertical line were years of below-average growth. In these years, the value on the purple vertical line is usually positive, meaning that the unemployment rate rose. That is, years of below-average growth were usually years in which the unemployment rate was rising.

A period in which GDP is growing at a below-average rate and unemployment is rising is called a **jobless recovery** or a "growth recession." Since 1990, there have been three recessions, in 1990–1991, 2001, and 2007–2009, all of which have been followed by jobless recoveries.

But true recessions, periods when real GDP falls, are especially painful for workers. As illustrated by the points to the left of the purple vertical line in Figure 13-5 (representing years in which the real GDP growth rate is negative), falling real GDP is always associated with a rising rate of unemployment, causing a great deal of hardship to families.

> A **jobless recovery** is a period in which the GDP growth rate is positive but the unemployment rate is still rising.

ECONOMICS ▶ *IN ACTION*

FAILURE TO LAUNCH

In March 2010, when the U.S. job situation was near its worst, the *Harvard Law Record* published a brief note titled "Unemployed law student will work for $160K plus benefits." In a self-mocking tone, the author admitted to having graduated from Harvard Law School the previous year but not landing a job offer. "What mark on our résumé is so bad that it outweighs the crimson H?" the note asked.

The answer, of course, is that it wasn't about the résumé—it was about the economy. Times of high unemployment are especially hard on new graduates, who often find it hard to get any kind of full-time job.

How bad was it in March 2010, around the time that note was written? Researchers at the San Francisco Fed analyzed the employment experience of college graduates, ages 21–23, and their findings are in Figure 13-6.

Although the overall unemployment rate for college graduates 25 and older, even at its peak, was only about 5%, unemployment among recent graduates aged 21–23 peaked in 2010 at 10.7%. And many of those who *were* employed had been able to get only part-time jobs. In December 2007, at the beginning of the 2007–2009 recession, 83% of college graduates under the age of 24 who weren't still in school were employed full time. By December 2009, that number was down to just 72%. Quite simply, many college graduates were having a hard time getting their working lives started.

The situation is improving, but slowly: by the end of 2010, 74% of recent graduates had full-time jobs and by the end of 2012 this figure was up to 81%. The rest were either unemployed or employed part time. However, even for those college graduates with jobs, 40% had landed jobs that required no college degree in 2012, up from 30% before the recession began in 2007. The U.S. labor market has a long way to go before being able to offer college graduates—and young people in general—the kinds of opportunities they deserve.

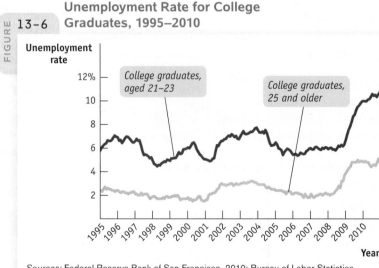

FIGURE 13-6

Unemployment Rate for College Graduates, 1995–2010

Sources: Federal Reserve Bank of San Francisco, 2010; Bureau of Labor Statistics.

MODULE

13 Review

Solutions appear at the back of the book.

Check Your Understanding

1. Suppose that employment websites enable job-seekers to find suitable jobs more quickly. What effect will this have on the unemployment rate over time? Also suppose that these websites encourage job-seekers who had given up their searches to begin looking again. What effect will this have on the unemployment rate?

2. In which of the following cases would the worker be counted as unemployed? Explain.

   a. Rosa, an older worker, has been laid off and gave up looking for work months ago.

   b. Anthony, a schoolteacher, is not working during his three-month summer break.

   c. Grace, an investment banker, has been laid off and is currently searching for another position.

   d. Sergio, a classically trained musician, can only find work playing for local parties.

   e. Natasha, a graduate student, went back to school because jobs were scarce.

3. Which of the following are consistent with the observed relationship between growth in real GDP and changes in the unemployment rate? Which are not?

   a. A rise in the unemployment rate accompanies a fall in real GDP.

   b. An exceptionally strong business recovery is associated with a greater percentage of the labor force being employed.

   c. Negative real GDP growth is associated with a fall in the unemployment rate.

Multiple-Choice Questions

1. To be considered unemployed, a person must

   I. not be working.
   II. be actively seeking a job.
   III. be available for work.

   a. I only

   b. II only

   c. III only

   d. II and III

   e. I, II, and III

Use the information for a hypothetical economy presented in the following table to answer questions 2, 3, and 4.

Population age 16 and older	200,000
Labor force	100,000
Number of people working part time	20,000
Number of people working full time	70,000

2. What is the labor force participation rate?

   a. 70%

   b. 50%

   c. 20%

   d. 10%

   e. 5%

3. How many people are unemployed?

   a. 10,000

   b. 20,000

   c. 30,000

   d. 100,000

   e. 110,000

4. What is the unemployment rate?

   a. 70%

   b. 50%

   c. 20%

   d. 10%

   e. 5%

5. The unemployment problem in an economy may be understated by the unemployment rate due to

   a. people lying about seeking a job.

   b. discouraged workers.

   c. job candidates with one offer but waiting for more.

   d. overemployed workers.

   e. none of the above.

Critical-Thinking Questions

What is the labor market classification for each of the following individuals? Be as specific as possible, and explain your answer.

1. Julie has a graduate degree in mechanical engineering. She works full-time mowing lawns.

2. Jeff was laid off from his previous job. He would very much like to work at any job, but, after looking for work for a year, has stopped looking for work.

3. Ian is working 25 hours per week at a bookstore, and has no desire to work full time.

4. Raj has decided to take a year off from work to stay home with his daughter.

Lightspring/Shutterstock

WHAT YOU WILL LEARN

1 The three different types of unemployment and their causes

2 The factors that determine the natural rate of unemployment

Fast economic growth tends to reduce the unemployment rate. So how low can the unemployment rate go? You might be tempted to say zero, but that isn't feasible. Over the past half-century, the national unemployment rate has never dropped below 2.9%.

How can there be so much unemployment even when many businesses are having a hard time finding workers? To answer this question, we need to examine the nature of labor markets and why they normally lead to substantial measured unemployment even when jobs are plentiful. Our starting point is the observation that even in the best of times, jobs are constantly being created and destroyed.

Job Creation and Job Destruction

Even during good times, most Americans know someone who has lost his or her job. The U.S. unemployment rate in July 2007 was only 4.7%, relatively low by historical standards, yet in that month there were 4.5 million "job separations"—terminations of employment that occurred because a worker was either fired or quit voluntarily.

There are many reasons for such job loss. One is structural change in the economy: industries rise and fall as new technologies emerge and consumers' tastes change. For example, employment in high-tech industries such as telecommunications surged in the late 1990s but slumped severely after 2000. However, structural change also brings the creation of new jobs: since 2000, the number of jobs in the American health care sector has surged as new medical technologies have emerged and the aging of the population has increased the demand for medical care.

Poor management or bad luck at a company also leads to job loss for employees. For example, in 2005 General Motors announced plans to eliminate 30,000 jobs after several years of lagging sales, even as Japanese companies such as Toyota announced plans to open new plants in North America to meet growing demand for their cars.

140

Continual job creation and destruction are a feature of modern economies, making a naturally occurring amount of unemployment inevitable. Within this naturally occurring amount, there are two types of unemployment—*frictional* and *structural*.

Frictional Unemployment

Workers who lose a job involuntarily due to job destruction often choose not to take the first new job offered. For example, suppose a skilled programmer, laid off because her software company's product line was unsuccessful, sees a help-wanted ad for clerical work online. She might respond to the ad and get the job—but that would be foolish. Instead, she should take the time to look for a job that takes advantage of her skills and pays accordingly. In addition, individual workers are constantly leaving jobs voluntarily, typically for personal reasons—family moves, dissatisfaction, and better job prospects elsewhere.

Economists say that workers who spend time looking for employment are engaged in **job search.** If all workers and all jobs were alike, job search wouldn't be necessary; if information about jobs and workers were perfect, job search would be very quick. In practice, however, it's normal for a worker who loses a job, or a young worker seeking a first job, to spend at least a few weeks searching.

Frictional unemployment is unemployment due to the time workers spend in job search. A certain amount of frictional unemployment is inevitable due to the constant process of economic change. Even in 2007, a year of low unemployment, there were 62 million "job separations," in which workers left or lost their jobs. Total employment grew because these separations were more than offset by more than 63 million hires. Inevitably, some of the workers who left or lost their jobs spent at least some time unemployed, as did some of the workers newly entering the labor force.

Figure 14-1 shows the 2007 average monthly flows of workers among three states: employed, unemployed, and not in the labor force. What the figure suggests is how much churning is constantly taking place in the labor market. An inevitable consequence of that churning is a significant number of workers who haven't yet found their next job—that is, frictional unemployment.

A limited amount of frictional unemployment is relatively harmless and may even be a good thing. The economy is more productive if workers take the time to find jobs that are well matched to their skills and workers who are unemployed for a brief

Workers who spend time looking for employment are engaged in **job search.**

Frictional unemployment is unemployment due to the time workers spend in job search.

"At this point, I'm just happy to still have a job"

FIGURE **14-1** **Labor Market Flows in an Average Month in 2007**

Even in 2007, a low-unemployment year, large numbers of workers moved into and out of both employment and unemployment each month. On average, each month in 2007, 1.781 million unemployed became employed, and 1.929 million employed became unemployed.

Source: Bureau of Labor Statistics.

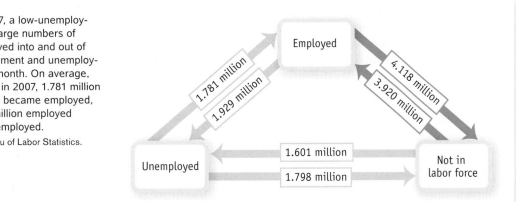

FIGURE 14-2

Distribution of the Unemployed by Duration of Unemployment, 2007

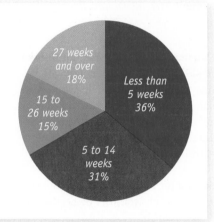

In years when the unemployment rate is low, most unemployed workers are unemployed for only a short period. In 2007, a year of low unemployment, 36% of the unemployed had been unemployed for less than 5 weeks and 67% for less than 15 weeks. The short duration of unemployment for most workers suggests that most unemployment in 2007 was frictional.

Source: Bureau of Labor Statistics.

period while searching for the right job don't experience great hardship. In fact, when there is a low unemployment rate, periods of unemployment tend to be quite short, suggesting that much of the unemployment is frictional.

Figure 14-2 shows the composition of unemployment for all of 2007, when the unemployment rate was only 4.6%. Thirty-six percent of the unemployed had been unemployed for less than 5 weeks, and only 33% had been unemployed for 15 or more weeks. Only about one in six unemployed workers were considered to be "long-term unemployed"—unemployed for 27 or more weeks.

In periods of higher unemployment, however, workers tend to be jobless for longer periods of time, suggesting that a smaller share of unemployment is frictional. By 2010, the fraction of unemployed workers considered "long-term unemployed" had jumped to 43%.

Structural Unemployment

Frictional unemployment exists even when the number of people seeking jobs is equal to the number of jobs being offered—that is, the existence of frictional unemployment doesn't mean that there is a surplus of labor. Sometimes, however, there is a *persistent surplus* of job-seekers in a particular labor market, even when the economy is performing well. There may be more workers with a particular skill than there are jobs available using that skill, or there may be more workers in a particular geographic region than there are jobs available in that region. **Structural unemployment** is unemployment that results when there are more people seeking jobs in a labor market than there are jobs available at the current wage rate.

The supply and demand model tells us that the price of a good, service, or factor of production tends to move toward an equilibrium level that matches the quantity supplied with the quantity demanded. This is equally true, in general, of labor markets.

Figure 14-3 shows a typical market for labor. The labor demand curve indicates that when the price of labor—the wage rate—increases, employers demand less labor. The labor supply curve indicates that when the price of labor increases, more workers are willing to supply labor at the prevailing wage rate. These two forces coincide to lead to an equilibrium wage rate for any given type of labor in a particular location. That equilibrium wage rate is shown as W_E.

Even at the equilibrium wage rate, W_E, there will still be some frictional unemployment. That's because there will always be some workers engaged in job search even when the number of jobs available is equal to the number of workers seeking jobs. But there wouldn't be any structural unemployment in this labor market. *Structural unemployment occurs when the wage rate is, for some reason, persistently above W_E.* Several factors can lead to a wage rate in excess of W_E, the most important being minimum wages, labor unions, *efficiency wages,* the side effects of government policies, and mismatches between employees and employers.

MINIMUM WAGES A *minimum wage* is a government-mandated floor on the price of labor. In the United States, the national minimum wage in 2013 was $7.25 an hour. For many American workers, the minimum wage is irrelevant; the market equilibrium wage for these workers is well above this price floor. But for less-skilled workers, the minimum wage may be binding—it affects the wages that people are actually paid and can lead to structural unemployment. In countries that have higher minimum wages, the range of workers for whom the minimum wage is binding is larger.

In **structural unemployment,** more people are seeking jobs in a particular labor market than there are jobs available at the current wage rate.

FIGURE **14-3** The Effect of a Minimum Wage on the Labor Market

When the government sets a minimum wage, W_F, that exceeds the market equilibrium wage rate, W_E, the number of workers, Q_S, who would like to work at that minimum wage is greater than the number of workers, Q_D, demanded at that wage rate. This surplus of labor is considered structural unemployment.

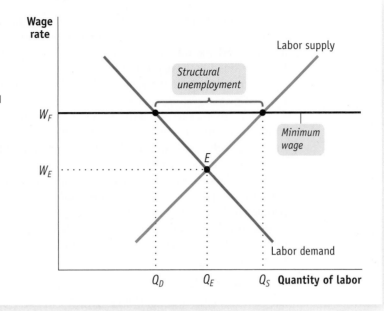

Figure 14-3 shows the effect of a binding minimum wage. In this market, there is a legal floor on wages, W_F, which is above the equilibrium wage rate, W_E. This leads to a persistent surplus in the labor market: the quantity of labor supplied, Q_S, is larger than the quantity demanded, Q_D. In other words, more people want to work than can find jobs at the minimum wage, leading to structural unemployment.

Given that minimum wages—that is, binding minimum wages—generally lead to structural unemployment, you might wonder why governments impose them. The rationale is to help ensure that people who work can earn enough income to afford at least a minimally comfortable lifestyle. However, this may come at a cost, because it may eliminate employment opportunities for some workers who would have willingly worked for lower wages. As illustrated in Figure 14-3, not only are there more sellers of labor than there are buyers, but there are also fewer people working at a minimum wage (Q_D) than there would have been with no minimum wage at all (Q_E).

Although economists broadly agree that a high minimum wage has the employment-reducing effects shown in Figure 14-3, there is some question about whether this is a good description of how the

Minimum-wage workers advocating for a *living wage*, one that is high enough to maintain a normal standard of living.

minimum wage actually works in the United States. The minimum wage in the United States is quite low compared with that in other wealthy countries. For three decades, from the 1970s to the mid-2000s, the U.S. minimum wage was so low that it was not binding for the vast majority of workers.

In addition, some researchers have produced evidence that increases in the minimum wage actually lead to higher employment when, as was the case in the United States at one time, the minimum wage is low compared to average wages. They argue that firms employing low-skilled workers sometimes restrict their hiring in order to keep wages low and that, as a result, the minimum wage can sometimes be increased without any loss of jobs. Most economists, however, agree that a sufficiently high minimum wage *does* lead to structural unemployment.

LABOR UNIONS The actions of *labor unions* can have effects similar to those of minimum wages, leading to structural unemployment. By bargaining collectively for all of a firm's workers, unions can win higher wages from employers than workers would have obtained by bargaining individually. This process, known as *collective bargaining*, is intended to tip the scales of bargaining power more toward workers and away from employers.

Labor unions exercise bargaining power by threatening firms with a *labor strike*, a collective refusal to work. The threat of a strike can have serious consequences for firms. In such cases, workers acting collectively can exercise more power than they could if they acted individually.

When workers have greater bargaining power, they tend to demand and push the wage that workers receive above the equilibrium wage. Consequently, there are more people willing to work at the wage being paid than there are jobs available, leading to structural unemployment. In the United States, however, because of a low level of unionization, the amount of unemployment generated by union demands is likely to be very small.

EFFICIENCY WAGES Actions by firms may also contribute to structural unemployment. Firms may choose to pay **efficiency wages**—wages that employers set above the equilibrium wage rate as an incentive for their workers to deliver better performance.

Employers may feel the need for such incentives for several reasons. For example, employers often have difficulty observing directly how hard an employee works. They can, however, elicit more work effort by paying above-market wages: employees receiving these higher wages are more likely to work harder to ensure that they aren't fired, which would cause them to lose their higher wages.

When many firms pay efficiency wages, the result is a pool of workers who want jobs but can't find them. So the use of efficiency wages by firms leads to structural unemployment.

SIDE EFFECTS OF GOVERNMENT POLICIES In addition, government policies designed to help workers who lose their jobs can lead to structural unemployment as an unintended side effect. Most economically advanced countries provide benefits to laid-off workers as a way to tide them over until they find a new job. In the United States, these benefits typically replace only a small fraction of a worker's income and expire after 26 weeks. This was extended in some cases to 99 weeks during the period of high unemployment that began in 2009. Although the extension expired at the end of 2013, at the time of this writing, Congress was considering whether to once again extend the benefits.

In other countries, particularly in Europe, benefits are more generous and last longer. The drawback to this generosity is that it reduces the incentive to quickly find a new job, and by keeping more people searching for longer, the benefits increase structural and frictional unemployment. Generous unemployment benefits in some European countries are widely believed to be one of the main causes of "Eurosclerosis," the persistent high unemployment that afflicts a number of European economies.

MISMATCHES BETWEEN EMPLOYEES AND EMPLOYERS It takes time for workers and firms to adjust to shifts in the economy. The result can be a mismatch between what employees have to offer and what employers are looking for. A skills mismatch is one form; for example, in the aftermath of the housing bust of 2009, there were more construction workers looking for jobs than jobs available. Another form is geographic, as in Michigan, which has had a long-standing surplus of workers since its auto industry went into decline.

Until the mismatch is resolved through a fall in wages for surplus workers that is big enough to induce retraining or relocation, there will be structural unemployment.

Efficiency wages are wages that employers set above the equilibrium wage rate as an incentive for better employee performance.

The Natural Rate of Unemployment

Because some frictional unemployment is inevitable and because many economies also suffer from structural unemployment, a certain amount of unemployment is normal, or "natural. " Actual unemployment fluctuates around this normal level.

The **natural rate of unemployment** is the normal unemployment rate around which the actual unemployment rate fluctuates. It is the rate of unemployment that arises from the effects of frictional plus structural unemployment. **Cyclical unemployment** is the deviation of the actual rate of unemployment from the natural rate; that is, it is the difference between the actual and natural rates of unemployment. As the name suggests, cyclical unemployment is the share of unemployment that arises from the business cycle. Later we'll see that government policy cannot keep the unemployment rate persistently below the natural rate without leading to accelerating inflation.

> The **natural rate of unemployment** is the unemployment rate that arises from the effects of frictional plus structural unemployment.
>
> **Cyclical unemployment** is the deviation of the actual rate of unemployment from the natural rate.

We can summarize the relationships between the various types of unemployment as follows:

(14-1) Natural unemployment =
  Frictional unemployment + Structural unemployment

(14-2) Actual unemployment =
  Natural unemployment + Cyclical unemployment

Perhaps because of its name, people often imagine that the natural rate of unemployment is a constant that doesn't change over time and can't be affected by policy. Neither proposition is true. Let's take a moment to stress two facts: the natural rate of unemployment changes over time, and it can be affected by economic policies.

Changes in the Natural Rate of Unemployment

Private-sector economists and government agencies need estimates of the natural rate of unemployment to make forecasts and conduct policy analyses. Almost all these estimates show that the U.S. natural rate rises and falls over time. For example, the Congressional Budget Office, the independent agency that conducts budget and economic analyses for Congress, believes that the U.S. natural rate of unemployment was 5.3% in 1950, rose to 6.3% by the end of the 1970s, but has fallen to 5.5% today. European countries have experienced even larger swings in their natural rates of unemployment.

What causes the natural rate of unemployment to change? The most important factors are

- Changes in the characteristics of the labor force
- Changes in labor market institutions
- Changes in government policies.

CHANGES IN LABOR FORCE CHARACTERISTICS In December 2013 the overall rate of unemployment in the United States was 6.7%. Young workers, however, had much higher unemployment rates: 20.2% for teenagers and 11.1% for workers aged 20 to 24. Workers aged 25 to 54 had an unemployment rate of only 5.8%.

In general, unemployment rates tend to be lower for experienced than for inexperienced workers. Because experienced workers tend to stay in a given job longer, they have lower frictional unemployment. Also, because older workers are more likely than young workers to be family breadwinners, they have a stronger incentive to find and keep jobs.

One reason the natural rate of unemployment rose during the 1970s was a large rise in the number of new workers—children

Luna Vandoorne/Shutterstock

14-4   The Changing Makeup of the U.S. Labor Force, 1948–2013

In the 1970s the percentage of the labor force consisting of women rose rapidly, as did the percentage under age 25. These changes reflected the entry of large numbers of women into the paid labor force for the first time and the fact that baby boomers were reaching working age. The natural rate of unemployment may have risen because many of these workers were relatively inexperienced. Today, the labor force is much more experienced, which is one possible reason the natural rate has fallen since the 1970s.

Source: Bureau of Labor Statistics.

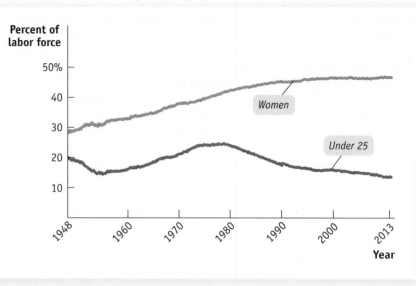

of the post–World War II baby boom entered the labor force, as did a rising percentage of married women.

As Figure 14-4 shows, both the percentage of the labor force less than 25 years old and the percentage of women in the labor force surged in the 1970s. By the end of the 1990s, however, the share of women in the labor force had leveled off and the percentage of workers under 25 had fallen sharply. As a result, the labor force as a whole is more experienced today than it was in the 1970s, one likely reason that the natural rate of unemployment is lower today than in the 1970s.

CHANGES IN LABOR MARKET INSTITUTIONS As we pointed out earlier, unions that negotiate wages above the equilibrium level can be a source of structural unemployment. Some economists believe that strong labor unions are one reason for the high natural rate of unemployment in Europe. In the United States, a sharp fall in union membership after 1980 may have been one reason the natural rate of unemployment fell between the 1970s and the 1990s.

Other institutional changes may also have been at work. For example, some labor economists believe that temporary employment agencies, which have proliferated in recent years, have reduced frictional unemployment by helping match workers to jobs. And, of course, job-search websites such as Monster.com may have reduced frictional unemployment.

Technological change, coupled with labor market institutions, can also affect the natural rate of unemployment. Technological change probably leads to an increase in the demand for skilled workers who are familiar with the relevant technology and a reduction in the demand for unskilled workers. Economic theory predicts that wages should increase for skilled workers and decrease for unskilled workers.

But if wages for unskilled workers cannot go down—say, due to a binding minimum wage—increased structural unemployment, and therefore a higher natural rate of unemployment, will result.

CHANGES IN GOVERNMENT POLICIES A high minimum wage can cause structural unemployment and generous unemployment benefits can increase both structural and frictional unemployment. So government policies intended to help workers can have the undesirable side effect of raising the natural rate of unemployment.

Some government policies, however, may reduce the natural rate. Two examples are job training and employment subsidies. Job-training programs are supposed to provide unemployed workers with skills that widen the range of jobs they can perform. Employment subsidies are payments either to workers or to employers that provide a financial incentive to accept or offer jobs.

ECONOMICS ▶ IN ACTION

NATURAL UNEMPLOYMENT AROUND THE OECD

The Organization for Economic Co-operation and Development (OECD) is an association of relatively wealthy countries, in Europe and North America but also including Japan, Korea, New Zealand, and Australia. Among other activities, the OECD collects data on unemployment rates for member nations. Figure 14-5 shows average unemployment, which is a rough estimate of the natural rate of unemployment, for select OECD members, from 2000–2012. The purple bar in the middle shows the average across all the OECD countries.

FIGURE 14-5 Average Unemployment Rates for Select OECD Members, 2000–2012

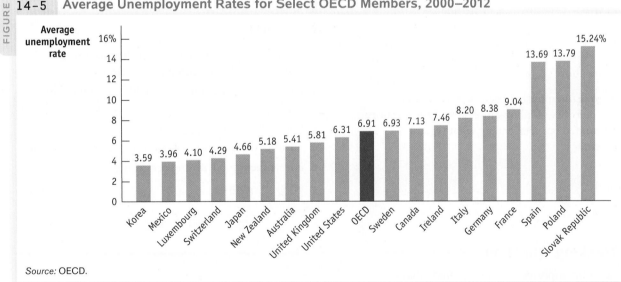

Source: OECD.

The U.S. natural rate of unemployment appears to be somewhat below average; those of many European countries (including the major economies of Germany, Italy, and France) are above average. Many economists think that persistently high European unemployment rates are the result of government policies, such as high minimum wages and generous unemployment benefits, which discourage employers from offering jobs and discourage workers from accepting jobs, leading to high rates of structural unemployment.

MODULE

14 Review

Solutions appear at the back of the book.

Check Your Understanding

1. Explain the following.

   a. Frictional unemployment always exists.

   b. Frictional unemployment accounts for a larger share of total unemployment when the unemployment rate is low.

2. Why does collective bargaining have the same general effect on unemployment as a minimum wage? Illustrate your answer with a diagram.

3. Suppose the United States dramatically increases benefits for unemployed workers. Explain what will happen to the natural rate of unemployment.

Multiple-Choice Questions

1. A person who moved to a new state and took two months to find a new job experienced which type of unemployment?

   a. frictional

   b. structural

   c. cyclical

   d. natural

   e. none of the above

2. What type of unemployment is created by a recession?

   a. frictional

   b. structural

   c. cyclical

   d. natural

   e. none of the above

3. A person who is unemployed because of a mismatch between the quantity of labor supplied and the quantity of labor demanded is experiencing what type of unemployment?

   a. frictional

   b. structural

   c. cyclical

   d. natural

   e. none of the above

4. Which of the following is true of the natural rate of unemployment?

   I. It includes frictional unemployment.
   II. It includes structural unemployment.
   III. It is equal to 0%.

   a. I only

   b. II only

   c. III only

   d. I and II

   e. I, II, and III

5. Which of the following can affect the natural rate of unemployment in an economy over time?

   a. labor force characteristics such as age and work experience

   b. the existence of labor unions

   c. advances in technologies that help workers find jobs

   d. government job training programs

   e. all of the above

Critical-Thinking Question

If the number of unemployed people who find jobs is greater than the number of employed people who lose their jobs in a given month then the unemployment rate will decrease. Is this statement true or false? Explain.

The Costs of Inflation

AP Photo/Paul Sakuma

The Inflation Rate

Why do policy makers get anxious when they see the inflation rate moving upward? Why is inflation something to worry about? The answer to both questions is that inflation can impose costs on the economy—but not in the way most people think. In this module we will look at these costs, including the related problems of deflation and disinflation.

The Level of Prices Doesn't Matter . . .

The most common complaint about *inflation*, an increase in the price level, is that it makes everyone poorer—after all, a given amount of money buys less. But inflation does *not* make everyone poorer. To see why, it's helpful to imagine what would happen if the United States did something other countries have done from time to time—replaced the dollar with a new currency.

An example of this kind of currency conversion happened in 2002, when France, like a number of other European countries, replaced its national currency, the franc, with the new Pan-European currency, the euro. People turned in their franc coins and notes, and received euro coins and notes in exchange, at a rate of precisely 6.55957 francs per euro. At the same time, all contracts were restated in euros at the same rate of exchange. For example, if a French citizen had a home mortgage debt of 500,000 francs, this became a debt of 500,000/6.55957 = 76,224.51 euros. If a worker's contract specified that he or she should be paid 100 francs per hour, it became a contract specifying a wage of 100/6.55957 = 15.2449 euros per hour, and so on.

You could imagine doing the same thing here, replacing the dollar with a "new dollar" at a rate of exchange of, say, 7 to 1. If you owed $140,000 on your home, that would become a debt of 20,000 new dollars. If you had a wage rate of $14 an hour, it

The **real wage** is the wage rate divided by the price level.

Real income is income divided by the price level.

The **inflation rate** is the percent change per year in a price index—typically the consumer price index.

would become 2 new dollars an hour, and so on. This would bring the overall U.S. price level back to about what it was when John F. Kennedy was president.

So would everyone be richer as a result because prices would be only one-seventh as high? Of course not. Prices would be lower, but so would wages and incomes in general. If you cut a worker's wage to one-seventh of its previous value, but also cut all prices to one-seventh of their previous level, the worker's **real wage**—the wage rate divided by the price level—doesn't change. In fact, bringing the overall price level back to what it was during the Kennedy administration would have no effect on overall purchasing power, because doing so would reduce income exactly as much as it reduced prices.

Conversely, the rise in prices that has actually taken place since the early 1960s hasn't made America poorer, because it has also raised incomes by the same amount: **real income**—income divided by the price level—hasn't been affected by the rise in overall prices.

The moral of this story is that the *level* of prices doesn't matter: the United States would be no richer than it is now if the overall level of prices were still as low as it was in 1961; conversely, the rise in prices over the past 50 years hasn't made us poorer.

. . . But the Rate of Change of Prices Does

The conclusion that the level of prices doesn't matter might seem to imply that the inflation rate doesn't matter either. But that's not true.

To see why, it's crucial to distinguish between the *level of prices* and the *inflation rate*. In the next module, we will discuss precisely how the level of prices in the economy is measured using price indexes such as the consumer price index. For now, let's look at the **inflation rate,** the percent increase in the overall level of prices per year. The inflation rate is calculated as follows:

$$\text{Inflation rate} = \frac{\text{Price level in year 2} - \text{Price level in year 1}}{\text{Price level in year 1}} \times 100$$

Figure 15-1 highlights the difference between the price level and the inflation rate in the United States since 1960, with the price level measured along the left vertical axis

15-1   The Price Level versus the Inflation Rate, 1960–2013

With the exception of 2009, over the past half-century the consumer price index has continuously increased. But the *inflation rate*—the rate at which consumer prices are rising—has had both ups and downs. And in 2009, the inflation rate briefly turned negative, a phenomenon called *deflation*.

Source: Bureau of Labor Statistics.

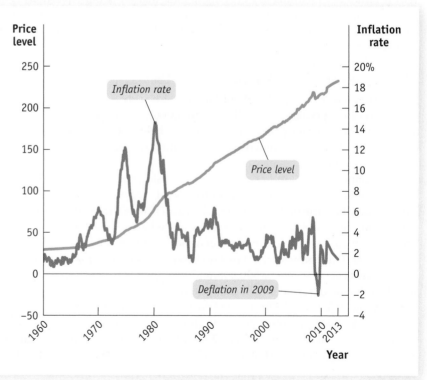

and the inflation rate measured along the right vertical axis. In the 2000s, the overall level of prices in the United States was much higher than it was in 1960—but that, as we've learned, didn't matter. The inflation rate in the 2000s, however, was much lower than in the 1970s—and that almost certainly made the economy richer than it would have been if high inflation had continued.

The Economic Costs of High Inflation

Economists believe that high rates of inflation impose significant economic costs. The most important of these costs are *shoe-leather costs, menu costs,* and *unit-of-account costs.*

SHOE-LEATHER COSTS People hold money—cash in their wallets and bank deposits on which they can write checks—for convenience in making transactions. A high inflation rate, however, discourages people from holding money, because the purchasing power of the cash in your wallet and the funds in your bank account steadily erodes as the overall level of prices rises. This leads people to search for ways to reduce the amount of money they hold, often at considerable economic cost.

During the most famous of all inflations, the German *hyperinflation* of 1921–1923, merchants employed runners to take their cash to the bank many times a day to convert it into something that would hold its value, such as a stable foreign currency. In an effort to avoid having the purchasing power of their money eroded, people used up valuable resources—the time and labor of the runners—that could have been used productively elsewhere. During the German hyperinflation, so many banking transactions were taking place that the number of employees at German banks nearly quadrupled—from around 100,000 in 1913 to 375,000 in 1923.

In addition, Brazil experienced hyperinflation during the early 1990s; during that episode, the Brazilian banking sector grew so large that it accounted for 15% of GDP, more than twice the size of the financial sector in the United States measured as a share of GDP. The large increase in the Brazilian banking sector that was needed to cope with the consequences of inflation represented a loss of real resources to its society.

Increased costs of transactions caused by inflation are known as **shoe-leather costs,** an allusion to the wear and tear caused by the extra running around that takes place when people are trying to avoid holding money. Shoe-leather costs are substantial in economies with very high inflation rates, as anyone who has lived in such an economy—say, one suffering inflation of 100% or more per year—can attest. Most estimates suggest, however, that the shoe-leather costs of inflation at the rates seen in the United States—which in peacetime has never had inflation above 15%—are quite small.

> **Shoe-leather costs** are the increased costs of transactions caused by inflation.

ECONOMICS ▶ *IN ACTION*   W☮RLD VIEW

ISRAEL'S EXPERIENCE WITH INFLATION

It's hard to see the costs of inflation clearly because serious inflation is often associated with other problems that disrupt the economy and life in general, notably war or political instability (or both). In the mid-1980s, however, Israel experienced a "clean" inflation: there was no war, the government was stable, and there was order in the streets. Yet a series of policy errors led to very high inflation, with prices often rising more than 10% a month.

As it happens, one of the authors spent a month visiting Tel Aviv University at the height of the inflation, so we can give a first-hand account of the effects.

First, the shoe-leather costs of inflation were substantial. At the time, Israelis spent a lot of time in lines at the bank, moving

An inflation rate of 500% came with very high costs for Israeli citizens.

Ricki Rosen/Corbis Saba

Menu costs are the real costs of changing listed prices.

money in and out of accounts that provided high enough interest rates to offset inflation. People walked around with very little cash in their wallets; they had to go to the bank whenever they needed to make even a moderately large cash payment. Banks responded by opening a lot of branches, a costly business expense.

Second, although menu costs weren't that visible to a visitor, what you could see were the efforts businesses made to minimize them. For example, restaurant menus often didn't list prices. Instead, they listed numbers that you had to multiply by another number, written on a chalkboard and changed every day, to figure out the price of a dish.

Finally, it was hard to make decisions because prices changed so much and so often. It was a common experience to walk out of a store because prices were 25% higher than at one's usual shopping destination, only to discover that prices had just been increased 25% there, too.

MENU COSTS In a modern economy, most of the things we buy have a listed price. There's a price listed under each item on a supermarket shelf, a price printed on the front page of your newspaper, a price listed for each dish on a restaurant's menu. Changing a listed price has a real cost, called a **menu cost.** For example, to change a price in a supermarket may require a clerk to change the price listed under the item on the shelf and a worker to change the price associated with the item's UPC code in the store's computer. In the face of inflation, of course, firms are forced to change prices more often than they would if the price level were more or less stable. This means higher costs for the economy as a whole.

In times of very high inflation rates, menu costs can be substantial. During the Brazilian inflation of the early 1990s, for instance, supermarket workers reportedly spent half of their time replacing old price stickers with new ones. When the inflation rate is high, merchants may decide to stop listing prices in terms of the local currency and use either an artificial unit—in effect, measuring prices relative to one another—or a more stable currency, such as the U.S. dollar. This is exactly what the Israeli real estate market began doing in the mid-1980s: prices were quoted in U.S. dollars,

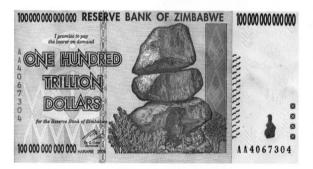

even though payment was made in Israeli shekels. And this is what happened in Zimbabwe, in 2008, as official estimates of the inflation rate reached 1,694,000%. By 2009, the government suspended the Zimbabwean dollar altogether.

Menu costs are also present in low-inflation economies, but they are not severe. In low-inflation economies, businesses might update their prices only sporadically—not daily or even more frequently, as is the case in high-inflation or hyperinflation economies. Also, with technological advances, menu costs are becoming less important, since prices can be changed electronically and fewer merchants attach price stickers to merchandise.

UNIT-OF-ACCOUNT COSTS In the Middle Ages, contracts were often specified "in kind": a tenant might, for example, be obliged to provide his landlord with a certain number of cattle each year (the phrase *in kind* actually comes from an ancient word for *cattle*). This may have made sense at the time, but it would be an awkward way to conduct modern business. Instead, we state contracts in monetary terms: a renter owes a certain number of dollars per month, a company that issues a bond promises to pay the bondholder the dollar value of the bond when it comes due, and so on. We also tend to make our economic calculations in dollars: a family planning its budget, or a small business owner trying to figure out how well the business is doing, makes estimates of the amount of money coming in and going out.

This role of the dollar as a basis for contracts and calculation is called the *unit-of-account* role of money. It's an important aspect of the modern economy. Yet it's a role that can be degraded by inflation, which causes the purchasing power of a dollar to change over time—a dollar next year is worth less than a dollar this year. The effect, many economists argue, is to reduce the quality of economic decisions: the economy as a whole makes less efficient use of its resources because of the uncertainty caused by changes in the unit of account, the dollar. The **unit-of-account costs** of inflation are the costs arising from the way inflation makes money a less reliable unit of measurement.

Unit-of-account costs may be particularly important in the tax system, because inflation can distort the measures of income on which taxes are collected. Here's an example: Assume that the inflation rate is 10%, so that the overall level of prices rises 10% each year. Suppose that a business buys an asset, such as a piece of land, for $100,000 and then resells it a year later at a price of $110,000. In a fundamental sense, the business didn't make a profit on the deal: in real terms, it got no more for the land than it paid for it, because the $110,000 would purchase no more goods than the $100,000 would have a year earlier. But U.S. tax law would say that the business made a capital gain of $10,000, and it would have to pay taxes on that phantom gain.

"Of course I know the value of a dollar . . . that's why I'm asking if I can borrow your credit card"

During the 1970s, when the United States had a relatively high inflation rate, the distorting effects of inflation on the tax system were a serious problem. Some businesses were discouraged from productive investment spending because they found themselves paying taxes on phantom gains. Meanwhile, some unproductive investments became attractive because they led to phantom losses that reduced tax bills. When the inflation rate fell in the 1980s—and tax rates were reduced—these problems became much less important.

Winners and Losers from Inflation

As we've just learned, a high inflation rate imposes overall costs on the economy. In addition, inflation can produce winners and losers within the economy. The main reason inflation sometimes helps some people while hurting others is that economic transactions, such as loans, often involve contracts that extend over a period of time and these contracts are normally specified in nominal—that is, in dollar—terms.

In the case of a loan, the borrower receives a certain amount of funds at the beginning, and the loan contract specifies how much he or she must repay at some future date. But what that dollar repayment is worth in real terms—that is, in terms of purchasing power—depends greatly on the rate of inflation over the intervening years of the loan.

The *interest rate* on a loan is the percentage of the loan amount that the borrower must pay to the lender, typically on an annual basis, in addition to the repayment of the loan amount itself. Economists summarize the effect of inflation on borrowers and lenders by distinguishing between *nominal* interest rates and *real* interest rates.

The **nominal interest rate** is the interest rate that is actually paid for a loan, unadjusted for the effects of inflation. For example, the interest rates advertised on student loans and every interest rate you see listed by a bank is a nominal rate. The **real interest rate** is the nominal interest rate adjusted for inflation. This adjustment is achieved by simply subtracting the inflation rate from the nominal interest rate. For example, if a loan carries a nominal interest rate of 8%, but the inflation rate is 5%, the real interest rate is 8% − 5% = 3%.

When a borrower and a lender enter into a loan contract, the contract normally specifies a nominal interest rate. But each party has an expectation about the future

Unit-of-account costs arise from the way inflation makes money a less reliable unit of measurement.

The **nominal interest rate** is the interest rate actually paid for a loan.

The **real interest rate** is the nominal interest rate minus the rate of inflation.

When inflation is higher than expected, borrowers gain at the expense of lenders; but when inflation is lower than expected, lenders come out ahead.

rate of inflation and therefore an expectation about the real interest rate on the loan. If the actual inflation rate is *higher* than expected, borrowers gain at the expense of lenders: borrowers will repay their loans with funds that have a lower real value than had been expected—they can purchase fewer goods and services than expected due to the surprisingly high inflation rate. Conversely, if the inflation rate is *lower* than expected, lenders will gain at the expense of borrowers: borrowers must repay their loans with funds that have a higher real value than had been expected.

Historically, the fact that inflation creates winners and losers has sometimes been a major source of political controversy. In 1896 William Jennings Bryan electrified the Democratic presidential convention with a speech in which he declared, "You shall not crucify mankind on a cross of gold." What he was actually demanding was an inflationary policy. At the time, the U.S. dollar had a fixed value in terms of gold. Bryan wanted the U.S. government to abandon the gold standard and print more money, which would have raised the level of prices and, he believed, helped the nation's farmers who were deeply in debt.

In modern America, home mortgages (loans for the purchase of homes) are the most important source of gains and losses from inflation. Americans who took out mortgages in the early 1970s quickly found their real payments reduced by higher-than-expected inflation: by 1983, the purchasing power of a dollar was only 45% of what it had been in 1973. Those who took out mortgages in the early 1990s were not so lucky, because the inflation rate fell to lower-than-expected levels in the following years: in 2003 the purchasing power of a dollar was 78% of what it had been in 1993.

Because gains for some and losses for others result from inflation that is either higher or lower than expected, yet another problem arises: uncertainty about the future inflation rate discourages people from entering into any form of long-term contract. This is an additional cost of high inflation, because high rates of inflation are usually unpredictable, too. In countries with high and uncertain inflation, long-term loans are rare. This, in turn, makes it difficult for people to commit to long-term investments.

One last point: unexpected **deflation**—a surprise fall in the price level—creates winners and losers, too. Between 1929 and 1933, as the U.S. economy plunged into the Great Depression, the price level fell by 35%. This meant that debtors, including many farmers and homeowners, saw a sharp rise in the real value of their debts, which led to widespread bankruptcy and helped create a banking crisis, as lenders found their customers unable to pay back their loans.

Inflation Is Easy; Disinflation Is Hard

A falling overall level of prices is **deflation**.

Disinflation is the process of bringing the inflation rate down.

There is not much evidence that a rise in the inflation rate from, say, 2% to 5% would do a great deal of harm to the economy. Still, policy makers generally move forcefully to bring inflation back down when it creeps above 2% or 3%. Why? Because experience shows that bringing the inflation rate down—a process called **disinflation**—is very difficult and costly once a higher rate of inflation has become well established in the economy.

Figure 15-2 shows what happened during two major episodes of disinflation in the United States, in the mid-1970s and in the early 1980s. The horizontal axis shows the unemployment rate. The vertical axis shows "core" inflation over the previous year, a measure that excludes volatile food and energy prices and is widely considered a better measure of underlying inflation than overall consumer prices. Each marker represents the inflation rate and the unemployment rate for one month. In each episode, unemployment and inflation followed a sort of clockwise spiral, with high inflation gradually falling in the face of an extended period of very high unemployment.

FIGURE

15-2   The Cost of Disinflation

There were two major periods of disinflation in modern U.S. history, in the mid-1970s and the early 1980s. This figure shows the track of the unemployment rate and the "core" inflation rate, which excludes food and energy, during these two episodes. In each case bringing inflation down required a temporary but very large increase in the unemployment rate, demonstrating the high cost of disinflation.

Source: Bureau of Labor Statistics.

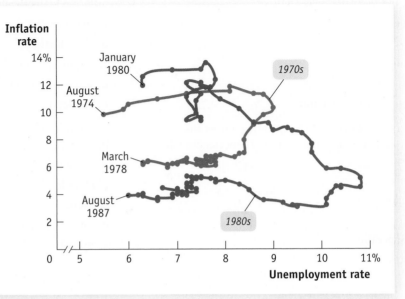

Many economists believe that these periods of high unemployment are necessary, because they are the only way to reduce inflation that has become deeply embedded in the economy. The best way to avoid having to put the economy through a wringer to reduce inflation, however, is to avoid having a serious inflation problem in the first place. So, policy makers respond forcefully to signs that inflation may be accelerating as a form of preventive medicine for the economy.

MODULE

15) Review

Solutions appear at the back of the book.

Check Your Understanding

1. The widespread use of technology has revolutionized the banking industry, making it much easier for customers to access and manage their assets. Does this mean that the shoe-leather costs of inflation are higher or lower than they used to be? Explain.

2. Most Americans have grown accustomed to a modest inflation rate of around 2–3%. Who would gain and who would lose if inflation came to a complete stop for several years? Explain.

Multiple-Choice Questions

1. Which of the following is true regarding prices in an economy?

   I. An increase in the price level is called inflation.
   II. The level of prices doesn't matter.
   III. The rate of change in prices matters.

   a. I only
   b. II only
   c. III only
   d. II and III only
   e. I, II, and III

2. If your nominal wage doubles at the same time as prices double, your real wage will

   a. increase.

   b. decrease

   c. not change.

   d. double.

   e. be impossible to determine.

3. If inflation causes people to frequently convert their dollars into other assets, the economy experiences what type of cost?

   a. price level

   b. shoe-leather

   c. menu

   d. unit-of-account

   e. monetary

4. Because dollars are used as the basis for contracts, inflation leads to which type of cost?

   a. price level

   b. shoe-leather

   c. menu

   d. unit-of-account

   e. monetary

5. Changing the listed price when inflation leads to a price increase is an example of which type of cost?

   a. price level

   b. shoe-leather

   c. menu

   d. unit-of-account

   e. monetary

Critical-Thinking Questions

You borrow $1,000 for one year at 5% interest to buy a couch. Although you did not anticipate any inflation, there is unexpected inflation of 5% over the life of your loan.

1. What was the real interest rate on your loan?

2. Explain how you gained from the inflation.

3. Who lost as a result of the situation described? Explain.

Oleg Doroshin/Shutterstock

Measuring Inflation

The Aggregate Price Level

In the fall of 2012, Americans were facing sticker shock at the gas pump: the price of a gallon of regular gasoline had risen from about $3.40 that spring, to $3.90—an increase of 15%. For consumers, that meant paying $5.00 more for every 10 gallons of gas purchased. Food prices were also up, rising about 3% per year for each of the last five years. Some prices, though, were falling: housing prices had dropped dramatically since 2008, and most electronics were getting cheaper. Yet practically everyone felt that the overall cost of living seemed to be rising. But how fast?

Clearly there is a need for a single number summarizing what happens to consumer prices. Just as macroeconomists find it useful to have a single number to represent the overall level of output, they also find it useful to have a single number to represent the overall level of prices: the **aggregate price level.** Yet a huge variety of goods and services are produced and consumed in the economy. How can we summarize the prices of all these goods and services with a single number? The answer lies in the concept of a *price index*—a concept best introduced with an example.

Market Baskets and Price Indexes

Suppose that a frost in Florida destroys most of the citrus harvest. As a result, the price of oranges rises from $0.20 each to $0.40 each, the price of grapefruit rises from $0.60 to $1.00, and the price of lemons rises from $0.25 to $0.45. How much has the price of citrus fruit increased?

One way to answer that question is to state three numbers—the changes in prices for oranges, grapefruit, and lemons. But this is a very cumbersome method. Rather than having to recite three numbers in an effort to track changes in the prices of

The **aggregate price level** is a measure of the overall level of prices in the economy.

© PhotoAlto/Alamy

citrus fruit, we would prefer to have some kind of overall measure of the *average* price change.

To measure average price changes for consumer goods and services, economists track changes in the cost of a typical consumer's *consumption bundle*—the typical basket of goods and services purchased before the price changes. A hypothetical consumption bundle, used to measure changes in the overall price level, is known as a **market basket.** For our market basket in this example we will suppose that, before the frost, a typical consumer bought 200 oranges, 50 grapefruit, and 100 lemons over the course of a year.

Table 16-1 shows the pre-frost and post-frost costs of this market basket. Before the frost, it cost $95; after the frost, the same basket of goods cost $175. Since $175/$95 = 1.842, the post-frost basket costs 1.842 times the cost of the pre-frost basket, a cost increase of 84.2%. In this example, the average price of citrus fruit has increased 84.2% since the base year as a result of the frost, where the base year is the initial year used in the measurement of the price change.

TABLE 16-1

Calculating the Cost of a Market Basket

	Pre-frost	Post-frost
Price of orange	$0.20	$0.40
Price of grapefruit	0.60	1.00
Price of lemon	0.25	0.45
Cost of market basket (200 oranges, 50 grapefruit, 100 lemons)	(200 × $0.20) + (50 × $0.60) + (100 × $0.25) = $95.00	(200 × $0.40) + (50 × $1.00) + (100 × $0.45) = $175.00

Economists use the same method to measure changes in the overall price level: they track changes in the cost of buying a given market basket. Working with a market basket and a base year, we obtain what is known as a **price index,** a measure of the overall price level. It is always cited along with the year for which the aggregate price level is being measured and the base year. A price index can be calculated using the following formula:

$$\textbf{(16-1)} \ \text{Price index in a given year} = \frac{\text{Cost of market basket in a given year}}{\text{Cost of market basket in base year}} \times 100$$

In our example, the citrus fruit market basket cost $95 in the base year, the year before the frost. So by applying Equation 16-1, we define the price index for citrus fruit as (cost of market basket in the current year/$95) × 100, yielding an index of 100 for the period before the frost and 184.2 after the frost.

You should note that applying Equation 16-1 to calculate the price index for the base year always results in a price index of (cost of market basket in base year/cost of market basket in base year) × 100 = 100. Choosing a price index formula that always normalizes the index value to 100 in the base year avoids the need to keep track of the cost of the market basket, for example, $95, in such and such a year.

The price index makes it clear that the average price of citrus has risen 84.2% as a consequence of the frost. Because of its simplicity and intuitive appeal, the method we've just described is used to calculate a variety of price indexes to track average price changes among a variety of different groups of goods and services. Examples include the *consumer price index* and the *producer price index*, which we'll discuss shortly.

A **market basket** is a hypothetical set of consumer purchases of goods and services.

A **price index** measures the cost of purchasing a given market basket in a given year. The index value is normalized so that it is equal to 100 in the selected base year.

Price indexes are also the basis for measuring inflation. The price level mentioned in the inflation rate formula in the previous module is simply a price index value, and the inflation rate is determined as the annual percent change in an official price index. The inflation rate from year 1 to year 2 is thus calculated using the following formula, with year 1 and year 2 being consecutive years.

> The **consumer price index**, or **CPI**, measures the cost of the market basket of a typical urban American family.

(16-2) Inflation rate = $\dfrac{\text{Price index in year 2} - \text{Price index in year 1}}{\text{Price index in year 1}} \times 100$

Typically, a news report that cites "the inflation rate" is referring to the annual percent change in the consumer price index.

The Consumer Price Index

The most widely used measure of the overall price level in the United States is the **consumer price index** (often referred to simply as the **CPI**), which is intended to show how the cost of all purchases by a typical urban family has changed over time. It is calculated by surveying market prices for a market basket that is constructed to represent the consumption of a typical family of four living in a typical American city. The base period for the index is currently 1982–1984, that is, the index is calculated so that the average of consumer prices in 1982–1984 is 100.

The market basket used to calculate the CPI is far more complex than the three-fruit market basket we just described. In fact, to calculate the CPI, the Bureau of Labor Statistics sends its employees out to survey supermarkets, gas stations, hardware stores, and so on—some 23,000 retail outlets in 87 cities. Every month it tabulates about 80,000 prices, on everything from romaine lettuce to movie rentals. Figure 16-1 shows the weight of major categories in the consumer price index as of December 2012. For example, motor fuel, mainly gasoline, accounted for 5% of the CPI in December 2012.

Every few years the Bureau of Labor Statistics updates the market basket used to calculate the CPI to reflect changes in the monthly purchases of the typical urban family of four. For example, food and beverages are now a smaller percentage of the basket, having gone from 21% in 1978 to 15% in 2012. In addition, as technology has changed over time, new goods are added to the basket, such as smart phones and tablets like the iPad.

Figure 16-2 shows how the CPI has changed since measurement began in 1913. Since 1940, the CPI has risen steadily, although the annual percent increases in recent years have been much smaller than those of the 1970s and early 1980s. A logarithmic scale is used so that equal percent changes in the CPI appear the same.

Nearly every country in the world calculates a consumer price index. As you might expect, the market baskets that make up these indexes differ quite a lot

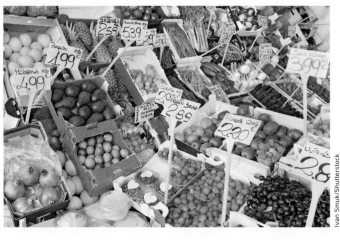

The CPI measures the changes in price level for a representative basket of goods and services purchased by a typical household.

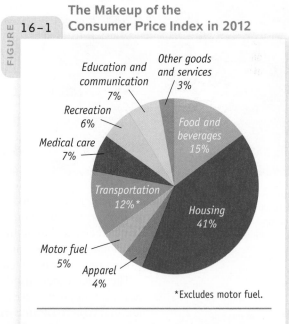

FIGURE 16-1

The Makeup of the Consumer Price Index in 2012

- Education and communication 7%
- Other goods and services 3%
- Recreation 6%
- Food and beverages 15%
- Medical care 7%
- Transportation 12% *
- Housing 41%
- Motor fuel 5%
- Apparel 4%

*Excludes motor fuel.

This chart shows the percentage shares of major types of spending in the CPI as of December 2012. Housing, food, transportation, and motor fuel made up about 73% of the CPI market basket.
Source: Bureau of Labor Statistics.

FIGURE 16-2   The CPI, 1913–2013

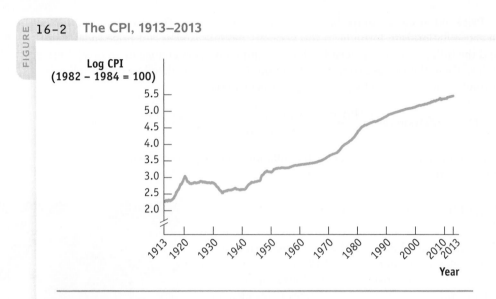

Since 1940, the CPI has risen steadily. But the annual percent increases in recent years have been much smaller than those of the 1970s and early 1980s. (The vertical axis is measured on a logarithmic scale so that equal percent changes in the CPI have the same slope.)

Source: Bureau of Labor Statistics.

Because consumption patterns vary, market baskets vary dramatically between rich and poor counties and then from country to country.

The **producer price index,** or **PPI,** measures changes in the prices of goods and services purchased by producers.

The **GDP deflator** for a given year is 100 times the ratio of nominal GDP to real GDP in that year.

from country to country. In poor countries, where people must spend a high proportion of their income just to feed themselves, food makes up a large share of the price index. Among high-income countries, differences in consumption patterns lead to differences in the price indexes: the Japanese price index puts a larger weight on raw fish and a smaller weight on beef than ours does, and the French price index puts a larger weight on wine.

Other Price Measures

There are two other price measures that are also widely used to track economy-wide price changes. One is the **producer price index** (or **PPI,** which used to be known as the *wholesale price index*). As its name suggests, the producer price index measures the cost of a typical basket of goods and services—containing raw commodities such as steel, electricity, coal, and so on—purchased by producers. Because commodity producers are relatively quick to raise prices when they perceive a change in overall demand for their goods, the PPI often responds to inflationary or deflationary pressures more quickly than the CPI. As a result, the PPI is often regarded as an "early warning signal" of changes in the inflation rate.

The other widely used price measure is the *GDP deflator;* it isn't exactly a price index, although it serves the same purpose. Recall how we distinguished between nominal GDP (GDP in current prices) and real GDP (GDP calculated using the prices of a base year). The **GDP deflator** for a given year is equal to 100 times the ratio of nominal GDP for that year to real GDP for that year expressed in prices of a selected base year. Since real GDP is currently expressed in 2005 dollars, the GDP deflator for 2005 is equal to 100. If nominal GDP doubles but real GDP does not change, the GDP deflator indicates that the aggregate price level doubled.

Perhaps the most important point about the different inflation rates generated by these three measures of prices is that they usually move closely together (although the producer price index tends to fluctuate more than either of the other two measures). Figure 16-3 shows the annual percent changes in the three indexes since 1930. By all three measures, the U.S. economy experienced deflation during the early years of the Great Depression, inflation during World War II, accelerating inflation during the 1970s, and a return to relative price stability in the 1990s.

FIGURE 16-3   **The CPI, the PPI, and the GDP Deflator**

As the figure shows, the three different measures of inflation, the PPI (orange), the CPI (green), and the GDP deflator (purple), usually move closely together. Each reveals a drastic acceleration of inflation during the 1970s and a return to relative price stability in the 1990s.

Sources: Bureau of Labor Statistics; Bureau of Economic Analysis.

Notice, by the way, the dramatic ups and downs in producer prices from 2000 through 2012 shown in Figure 16-3. This roller-coaster ride in prices reflects large changes in energy and food prices, which play a much bigger role in the PPI than they do in either the CPI or the GDP deflator.

ECONOMICS ▶ IN ACTION

INDEXING TO THE CPI

Although GDP is a very important number for shaping economic policy, official statistics on GDP don't have a direct effect on people's lives. The CPI, by contrast, has a direct and immediate impact on millions of Americans. The reason is that many payments are tied, or "indexed," to the CPI—the amount paid rises or falls when the CPI rises or falls.

The practice of indexing payments to consumer prices goes back to the dawn of the United States as a nation. In 1780 the Massachusetts State Legislature recognized that the pay of its soldiers fighting the British needed to be increased because of inflation that occurred during the Revolutionary War. The legislature adopted a formula that made a soldier's pay proportional to the cost of a market basket consisting of 5 bushels of corn, 68⁴⁄₇ pounds of beef, 10 pounds of sheep's wool, and 16 pounds of sole leather.

Today, over 56 million people, most of them old or disabled, receive checks from Social Security, a national retirement program that accounts for almost a quarter of current total federal spending—more than the defense budget. The amount of an individual's check is determined by a formula that reflects his or her previous payments into the system as well as other factors.

In addition, all Social Security payments are adjusted each year to offset any increase in consumer prices over the previous year. The CPI is used to calculate the official estimate of the inflation rate used to adjust these payments yearly. So every percentage point added to the official estimate of the rate of inflation adds 1% to the checks received by tens of millions of individuals.

Other government payments are also indexed to the CPI. In addition, income tax brackets, the bands of income levels that determine a taxpayer's income tax rate, are indexed to the CPI. (An individual in a higher income bracket pays a higher income tax rate in a progressive tax system like ours.) Indexing also extends to the private sector, where many private contracts, including some wage settlements, contain cost-of-living allowances (called COLAs) that adjust payments in proportion to changes in the CPI.

Because the CPI plays such an important and direct role in people's lives, it's a politically sensitive number. The Bureau of Labor Statistics, which calculates the CPI, takes great care in collecting and interpreting price and consumption data. It uses a complex method in which households are surveyed to determine what they buy and where they shop, and a carefully selected sample of stores are surveyed to get representative prices.

The Bureau of Labor Statistics calculates the CPI by collecting and interpreting price and consumption data.

MODULE 16 Review

Solutions appear at the back of the book.

Check Your Understanding

1. Consider Table 16-1 but suppose that the market basket is composed of 100 oranges, 50 grapefruit, and 200 lemons. How does this change the pre-frost and post-frost consumer price indexes? Explain. Generalize your answer to explain how the construction of the market basket affects the CPI.

2. For each of the following events, explain how the use of a 10-year-old market basket would bias measurements of price changes over the past decade.

   a. A typical family owns more cars than it would have a decade ago. Over that time, the average price of a car has increased more than the average prices of other goods.

   b. Virtually no households had Internet access a decade ago. Now many households have it, and the price has been falling.

3. The consumer price index in the United States (base period 1982–1984) was 224.9 in 2011 and 229.6 in 2012. Calculate the inflation rate from 2011 to 2012.

Multiple-Choice Questions

1. If the cost of a market basket of goods increases from $100 in year 1 to $108 in year 2, what is the consumer price index in year 2 if year 1 is the base year?

   a. 8

   b. 10

   c. 100

   d. 108

   e. 110

2. If the consumer price index increases from 80 to 120 from one year to the next, the inflation rate over that time period was

   a. 20%.

   b. 40%.

   c. 50%.

   d. 80%.

   e. 120%.

3. Which of the following is true of the CPI?

   I. It is the most common measure of the price level.

   II. It measures the price of a typical market basket of goods.

   III. It currently uses a base period of 1982–1984.

   a. I only

   b. II only

   c. III only

   d. I and II only

   e. I, II, and III

4. The value of a price index in the base year is

   a. 0.

   b. 100.

   c. 200.

   d. the inflation rate.

   e. the average cost of a market basket of goods.

5. If your wage doubles at the same time as the consumer price index goes from 100 to 300, your real wage

   a. doubles.

   b. falls.

   c. increases.

   d. stays the same.

   e. cannot be determined.

Critical-Thinking Question

The accompanying table contains the values of two price indexes for the years 2010, 2011, and 2012: the GDP deflator and the CPI. For each price index, calculate the inflation rate from 2010 to 2011 and from 2011 to 2012.

Year	GDP deflator	CPI
2010	111.0	218.1
2011	113.4	224.9
2012	115.4	229.6

BUSINESS CASE: A Monster Slump

NetPhotos/Alamy

The 1990s were famously an era of business hype, a decade when numerous online companies were created, then sold their stock at incredibly high prices, and, in the end, went bust. Some of the dot-coms, however, turned out to have workable business models and have endured. Among them is Monster.com, a job-search company that, along with its competitors, has helped replace traditional help-wanted ads in newspapers with online listings.

Monster Worldwide (the company's current name) and its competitors sell services to both employers seeking workers and workers seeking jobs. The employers place job listings, to which workers can respond; in addition to responding to these listings, job-seekers can pay for premium services such as résumé-writing and priority listing of their résumés.

The growing importance of online job listings was brought home in 2007 when The Conference Board, a business group that has long tracked the economy by producing an index of help-wanted ads, added an index of online help-wanted ads. As the figure shows, a plunge in online help-wanted ads heralded the surge in unemployment in 2008–2009; when online ads began to recover, unemployment stabilized and began a slow decline.

In the late 1990s, when the U.S. economy was experiencing unusually low unemployment, some economists suggested that Monster Worldwide and other online job services might be partly responsible, by making it easier for workers to get new jobs without a prolonged intervening period of unemployment. The evidence for this effect is, however, inconclusive.

You might have thought that the 2007–2009 recession, in which many laid-off workers were desperately seeking new jobs, would have been good for Monster Worldwide. And the company did, in fact, receive a lot more business from workers wanting to post their résumés. But the company makes much more money from employer job listings, and these were sharply lower during the slump, hurting their bottom line.

By late 2010, the economy seemed to be on the road to recovery, and so was Monster Worldwide, with one caveat: by 2010, online job listings, which were cutting-edge a decade earlier, were losing ground to Twitter and social-networking sites like LinkedIn—a trend that continues.

A Plunge in Online Help-Wanted Ads Heralds a Surge in Unemployment, 2008–2009

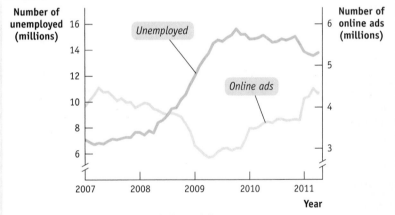

Sources: The Conference Board; Bureau of Labor Statistics.

Questions for Thought

1. How is the existence of services such as Monster.com likely to affect frictional and structural unemployment?

2. In light of our discussion of the determinants of the unemployment rate, how could improved matching of job-seekers and employers through online job listings help?

3. What does the fact that Monster Worldwide did badly during the 2008–2009 surge in unemployment suggest about the nature of that surge?

SECTION **4** REVIEW

Summary

Defining Unemployment

1. **Employed** people currently hold a part-time or full-time job; **unemployed** people do not hold a job but are actively looking for work. Their sum is equal to the **labor force,** and the **labor force participation rate** is the percentage of the population age 16 or older that is in the labor force.

2. The **unemployment rate,** the percentage of the labor force that is unemployed and actively looking for work, can overstate or understate the true level of unemployment. It can overstate because it counts as unemployed those who are continuing to search for a job despite having been offered one (that is, workers who are frictionally unemployed). It can understate because it ignores frustrated workers, such as **discouraged workers, marginally attached workers,** and the **underemployed.** In addition, the unemployment rate varies greatly among different groups in the population; it is typically higher for younger workers and for workers near retirement age than for workers in their prime working years.

3. The unemployment rate is affected by the business cycle. The unemployment rate generally falls when the growth rate of real GDP is above average and generally rises when the growth rate of real GDP is below average. In a **jobless recovery** the GDP growth rate is positive but the unemployment rate is still rising.

Categories of Unemployment

4. Job creation and destruction, as well as voluntary job separations, lead to **job search** and **frictional unemployment.** In addition, a variety of factors such as minimum wages, unions, **efficiency wages,** and government policies designed to help laid-off workers result in a situation in which there is a surplus of labor at the market wage rate, creating **structural unemployment.** As a result, the **natural rate of unemployment,** the sum of frictional and structural unemployment, is well above zero, even when jobs are plentiful.

5. The actual unemployment rate is equal to the natural rate of unemployment, the share of unemployment that is independent of the business cycle, plus **cyclical unemployment,** the share of unemployment that depends on fluctuations in the business cycle.

6. The natural rate of unemployment changes over time, largely in response to changes in labor force characteristics, labor market institutions, and government policies.

The Costs of Inflation

7. Inflation does not, as many assume, make everyone poorer by raising the level of prices. That's because if wages and incomes are adjusted to take into account a rising price level, **real wages** and **real income** remain unchanged. However, a high inflation rate imposes overall costs on the economy: **shoe-leather costs, menu costs,** and **unit-of-account costs.**

8. Inflation can produce winners and losers within the economy, because long-term contracts are generally written in dollar terms. Loans typically specify a **nominal interest rate,** which differs from the **real interest rate** due to inflation. A higher-than-expected inflation rate is good for borrowers and bad for lenders. A lower-than-expected inflation rate is good for lenders and bad for borrowers.

9. It is very costly to create **disinflation,** so policy makers try to prevent inflation from becoming excessive in the first place.

Measuring Inflation

10. To measure the **aggregate price level,** economists calculate the cost of purchasing a **market basket.** A **price index** is the ratio of the current cost of that market basket to the cost in a selected base year, multiplied by 100.

11. The **inflation rate** is the yearly percent change in a price index, typically based on the **consumer price index,** or **CPI,** the most common measure of the aggregate price level. A similar index for goods and services purchased by firms is the **producer price index, or PPI.** Finally, economists also use the **GDP deflator,** which measures the price level by calculating the ratio of nominal to real GDP times 100.

Key Terms

Employed, p. 132
Unemployed, p. 132
Labor force, p. 133
Labor force participation rate, p. 133
Unemployment rate, p. 133
Discouraged workers, p. 134
Marginally attached workers, p. 134
Underemployed, p. 134
Jobless recovery, p. 137
Job search, p. 141
Frictional unemployment, p. 141

Problems

1. Each month, usually on the first Friday of the month, the Bureau of Labor Statistics releases the Employment Situation Summary for the previous month. Go to www.bls.gov and find the latest report. (On the Bureau of Labor Statistics home page, at the top of the page, select the "Subject" tab, find "Unemployment," and select "National Unemployment Rate." You will find the Employment Situation Summary on the middle of the page under "CPS News Releases" by selecting "Employment Situation.") How does the unemployment rate compare to the rate one month earlier? How does the unemployment rate compare to the rate one year earlier?

2. In general, how do changes in the unemployment rate vary with changes in real GDP? After several quarters of a severe recession, explain why we might observe a decrease in the official unemployment rate. Explain why we could see an increase in the official unemployment rate after several quarters of a strong expansion.

3. In each of the following situations, what type of unemployment is Melanie facing?

a. After completing a complex programming project, Melanie is laid off. Her prospects for a new job requiring similar skills are good, and she has signed up with a programmer placement service. She has passed up offers for low-paying jobs.

b. When Melanie and her co-workers refused to accept pay cuts, her employer outsourced their programming tasks to workers in another country. This phenomenon is occurring throughout the programming industry.

c. Due to the current slump, Melanie has been laid off from her programming job. Her employer promises to rehire her when business picks up.

4. Part of the information released in the Employment Situation Summary concerns how long individuals have been unemployed. Go to www.bls.gov to find the latest report. Use the same technique as in Problem 1 to find the Employment Situation Summary. Near the end of the Employment Situation, click on Table A-12, titled "Unemployed persons by duration of unemployment." Use the seasonally adjusted numbers to answer the following questions.

a. How many workers were unemployed less than 5 weeks? What percentage of all unemployed workers do these workers represent? How do these numbers compare to the previous month's data?

b. How many workers were unemployed for 27 or more weeks? What percentage of all unemployed workers do

these workers represent? How do these numbers compare to the previous month's data?

c. How long has the average worker been unemployed (average duration, in weeks)? How does this compare to the average for the previous month's data?

d. Comparing the latest month for which there are data with the previous month, has the problem of long-term unemployment improved or deteriorated?

5. There is only one labor market in Profunctia. All workers have the same skills, and all firms hire workers with these skills. Use the accompanying diagram, which shows the supply of and demand for labor, to answer the following questions. Illustrate each answer with a diagram.

a. What is the equilibrium wage rate in Profunctia? At this wage rate, what are the level of employment, the size of the labor force, and the unemployment rate?

b. If the government of Profunctia sets a minimum wage equal to $12, what will be the level of employment, the size of the labor force, and the unemployment rate?

c. If unions bargain with the firms in Profunctia and set a wage rate equal to $14, what will be the level of employment, the size of the labor force, and the unemployment rate?

d. If the concern for retaining workers and encouraging high-quality work leads firms to set a wage rate equal to $16, what will be the level of employment, the size of the labor force, and the unemployment rate?

6. A country's labor force is the sum of the number of employed and unemployed workers. The accompanying table provides data on the size of the labor force and the number of unemployed workers for different regions of the United States.

Region	Labor force (thousands)		Unemployed (thousands)	
	Dec 2011	Dec 2012	Dec 2011	Dec 2012
Northeast	28,241.8	28,492.7	2,245.5	2,310.5
South	56,378.0	56,732.4	4,713.8	4,064.8
Midwest	34,352.0	34,260.3	2,710.8	2,439.6
West	35,964.7	35,876.0	3,534.2	3,102.1

Source: Bureau of Labor Statistics.

a. Calculate the number of workers employed in each of the regions in December 2011 and December 2012. Use your answers to calculate the change in the total number of workers employed between December 2011 and December 2012.

b. For each region, calculate the growth in the labor force from December 2011 and December 2012.

c. Compute unemployment rates in the different regions of the country in December 2011 and December 2012.

d. What can you infer about the fall in unemployment rates over this period? Was it caused by a net gain in the number of jobs or by a large fall in the number of people seeking jobs?

7. In which of the following cases is it more likely for efficiency wages to exist? Why?

a. Jane and her boss work as a team selling ice cream.

b. Jane sells ice cream without any direct supervision by her boss.

c. Jane speaks Korean and sells ice cream in a neighborhood in which Korean is the primary language. It is difficult to find another worker who speaks Korean.

8. How will the following changes affect the natural rate of unemployment?

a. The government reduces the time during which an unemployed worker can receive unemployment benefits.

b. More teenagers focus on their studies and do not look for jobs until after college.

c. Greater access to the Internet leads both potential employers and potential employees to use the Internet to list and find jobs.

d. Union membership declines.

9. With its tradition of a job for life for most citizens, Japan once had a much lower unemployment rate than that of the United States; from 1960 to 1995, the unemployment rate in Japan exceeded 3% only once. However, since the crash of its stock market in 1989 and slow economic growth in the 1990s, the job-for-life system has broken down and unemployment rose to more than 5% in 2003.

a. Explain the likely effect of the breakdown of the job-for-life system in Japan on the Japanese natural rate of unemployment.

b. As the accompanying diagram shows, the rate of growth of real GDP picked up in Japan after 2001 and before the global economic crisis of 2007–2009. Explain the likely effect of this increase in real GDP growth on the unemployment rate. Was the likely cause of the change in the unemployment rate during this period a change in the natural rate of unemployment or a change in the cyclical unemployment rate?

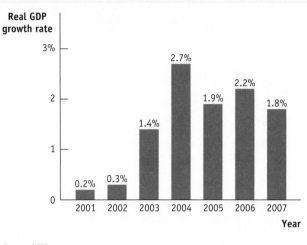

Source: OECD.

10. In the following examples, is inflation creating winners and losers at no net cost to the economy or is inflation imposing a net cost on the economy? If a net cost is being imposed, which type of cost is involved?

a. When inflation is expected to be high, workers get paid more frequently and make more trips to the bank.

b. Lanwei is reimbursed by her company for her work-related travel expenses. Sometimes, however, the company takes a long time to reimburse her. So when inflation is high, she is less willing to travel for her job.

c. Hector Homeowner has a mortgage with a fixed nominal 6% interest rate that he took out five years ago. Over the years, the inflation rate has crept up unexpectedly to its present level of 7%.

d. In response to unexpectedly high inflation, the manager of Cozy Cottages of Cape Cod must reprint and resend expensive color brochures correcting the price of rentals this season.

11. The accompanying diagram shows the interest rate on one-year loans and inflation during 1995–2010 in the economy of Albernia. When would one-year loans have been especially attractive and why?

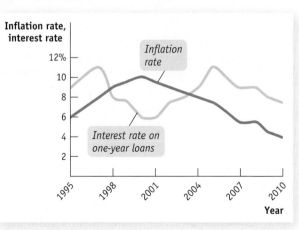

12. The accompanying table provides the inflation rate in the year 2000 and the average inflation rate over the period 2001–2010 for seven different countries.

Country	Inflation rate in 2000	Average inflation rate in 2001–2010
Brazil	7.06%	6.70%
China	0.4	2.16
France	1.83	1.86
Indonesia	3.77	8.55
Japan	−0.78	−0.25
Turkey	55.03	18.51
United States	3.37	2.40

Source: IMF.

a. Given the expected relationship between average inflation and menu costs, rank the countries in descending order of menu costs using average inflation over the period 2001–2010.

b. Rank the countries in order of inflation rates that most favored borrowers with ten-year loans that were taken out in 2000. Assume that the loans were agreed upon with the expectation that the inflation rate for 2001 to 2010 would be the same as the inflation rate in 2000.

c. Did borrowers who took out ten-year loans in Japan gain or lose overall versus lenders? Explain.

13. The accompanying diagram shows the inflation rate in the United Kingdom from 1980 to 2010.

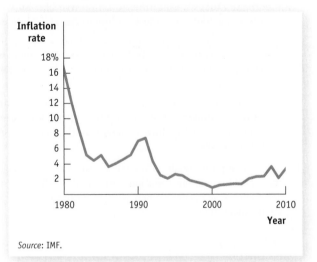

Source: IMF.

a. Between 1980 and 1985, policy makers in the United Kingdom worked to lower the inflation rate. What

would you predict happened to unemployment between 1980 and 1985?

b. Policy makers in the United Kingdom react forcefully when the inflation rate rises above a target rate of 2%. Why would it be harmful if inflation rose from 3.4% (the level in 2010) to, say, a level of 5%?

14. Eastland College is concerned about the rising price of textbooks that students must purchase. To better identify the increase in the price of textbooks, the dean asks you, the Economics Department's star student, to create an index of textbook prices. The average student purchases three English, two math, and four economics textbooks per year. The prices of these books are given in the accompanying table.

	2010	2011	2012
English textbook	$50	$55	$57
Math textbook	70	72	74
Economics textbook	80	90	100

a. What is the percent change in the price of an English textbook from 2010 to 2012?

b. What is the percent change in the price of a math textbook from 2010 to 2012?

c. What is the percent change in the price of an economics textbook from 2010 to 2012?

d. Using 2010 as a base year, create a price index for these books for all years.

e. What is the percent change in the price index from 2010 to 2012?

15. The consumer price index, or CPI, measures the cost of living for a typical urban household by multiplying the price for each category of expenditure (housing, food, and so on) times a measure of the importance of that expenditure in the average consumer's market basket and summing over all categories. However, using data from the consumer price index, we can see that changes in the cost of living for different types of consumers can vary a great deal. Let's compare the cost of living for a hypothetical retired person and a hypothetical college student. Let's assume that the market basket of a retired person is allocated in the following way: 10% on housing, 15% on food, 5% on transportation, 60% on medical care, 0% on education, and 10% on recreation. The college student's market basket is allocated as follows: 5% on housing, 15% on food, 20% on transportation, 0% on medical care, 40% on education, and 20% on recreation. The accompanying table shows the December 2012 CPI for each of the relevant categories.

	CPI December 2012
Housing	235.2
Food	224.0
Transportation	211.9
Medical care	418.7
Education	134.7
Recreation	114.4

Calculate the overall CPI for the retired person and for the college student by multiplying the CPI for each of the categories by the relative importance of that category to the individual and then summing each of the categories. The CPI for all items in December 2012 was 229.6. How do your calculations for a CPI for the retired person and the college student compare to the overall CPI?

16. Each month the Bureau of Labor Statistics releases the Consumer Price Index Summary for the previous month. Go to the Bureau of Labor Statistics home page at www.bls.gov. Place the cursor over the "Data Tools" tab and then click on "Top Picks." On that page, scroll down to "Price Indexes" and select the "CPI for all urban consumers," for base year 1982–84, to retrieve the data. What was the CPI last month? How did it change from the previous month? How does the CPI compare to the same month one year ago?

17. The accompanying table provides the annual real GDP (in billions of 2005 dollars) and nominal GDP (in billions of dollars) for the United States.

	2008	2009	2010	2011	2012
Real GDP (billions of 2005 dollars)	13,161.9	12,757.9	13,063.0	13,299.1	13,588.8
Nominal GDP (billions of dollars)	14,291.5	13,973.7	14,498.9	15,075.7	15,676.0

a. Calculate the GDP deflator for each year.

b. Use the GDP deflator to calculate the inflation rate for all years except 2008.

18. The cost of a college education in the United States is rising at a rate faster than inflation. The following table shows the average cost of a college education in the United States during the academic year that began in 2009 and the academic year that began in 2010 for public and private colleges. Assume the costs listed in the table are the only costs experienced by the various college students in a single year.

a. Calculate the cost of living for an average college student in each category for 2009 and 2010.

b. Calculate an inflation rate for each type of college student between 2009 and 2010.

	Cost of college education during academic year beginning 2009 (averages in 2009 dollars)				
	Tuition and fees	Room and board	Books and supplies	Transportation	Other expenses
Two-year public college: commuter	$2,544	$7,202	$1,098	$1,445	$1,996
Four-year public college: in-state, on-campus	7,020	8,193	1,122	1,079	1,974
Four-year public college: out-of-state, on-campus	18,548	8,193	1,122	1,079	1,974
Four-year private college: on-campus	26,273	9,363	1,116	849	1,427
	Cost of college education during academic year beginning 2010 (averages in 2010 dollars)				
	Tuition and fees	Room and board	Books and supplies	Transportation	Other expenses
Two-year public college: commuter	$2,713	$7,259	$1,133	$1,491	$2,041
Four-year public college: in-state, on-campus	7,605	8,535	1,137	1,073	1,989
Four-year public college: out-of-state, on-campus	19,595	8,535	1,137	1,073	1,989
Four-year private college: on-campus	27,293	9,700	1,181	862	1,440

Long-Run Economic Growth

TALL TALES

WORLD VIEW

China is growing—and so are the Chinese. According to official statistics, children in China are almost 2½ inches taller now than they were 30 years ago. The average Chinese citizen is still a lot shorter than the average American, but at the current rate of growth the difference may be largely gone in a couple of generations.

If that does happen, China will be following in Japan's footsteps. Older Americans tend to think of the Japanese as short, but today young Japanese men are more than 5 inches taller on average than they were in 1900, which makes them almost as tall as their American counterparts.

There's no mystery about why the Japanese grew taller—it's because they grew richer. In the early twentieth century, Japan was a relatively poor country in which many families couldn't afford to give their children adequate nutrition. As a result, their children grew up to be short adults. However, since World War II, Japan has become an economic power-house in which food is ample and young adults are much taller than before.

The same phenomenon is now happening in China. Although it continues to be a relatively poor country, China has made great economic strides over the past 30 years. Its recent history is probably the world's most dramatic example of economic growth—a sustained increase in output per capita. Yet despite its impressive performance, China is currently playing catch-up with economically advanced countries like the United States and Japan. It's still relatively poor because these other nations began their own processes of economic growth many decades ago—and in the case of the United States and European countries, more than a century ago.

Many economists have argued that long-run economic growth—why it happens and how to achieve it—is the single most important issue in macroeconomics. In this section, we present some facts about long-run growth, look at the factors that economists believe determine the pace at which long-run growth takes place, examine how government policies can help or hinder growth, and address questions about the environmental sustainability of long-run growth.

Comparing Economies Across Time and Space

Before we analyze the sources of long-run economic growth, it's useful to have a sense of just how much the U.S. economy has grown over time and how large the gaps are between wealthy countries like the United States and countries that have yet to achieve comparable growth. So let's take a look at the numbers.

Real GDP per Capita

The key statistic used to track economic growth is *real GDP per capita*—real GDP divided by the population size. We focus on GDP because, as we learned, GDP measures the total value of an economy's production of final goods and services as well as the income earned in that economy in a given year. We use *real* GDP because we want to separate changes in the quantity of goods and services from the effects of a rising price level. We focus on real GDP *per capita* because we want to isolate the effect of changes in the population. For example, other things equal, an increase in the population lowers the standard of living for the average person—there are now more people to share a given amount of real GDP. An increase in real GDP that only matches an increase in population leaves the average standard of living unchanged.

Although we also learned that growth in real GDP per capita should not be a policy goal in and of itself, it does serve as a very useful summary measure of a country's economic progress over time. Figure 17-1 shows real GDP per capita for the United States, India, and China, measured in 1990 dollars, from 1900 to 2010. The vertical axis is drawn on a logarithmic scale so that equal percent changes in real GDP per capita across countries are the same size in the graph.

FIGURE 17-1   Economic Growth in the United States, India, and China over the Past Century

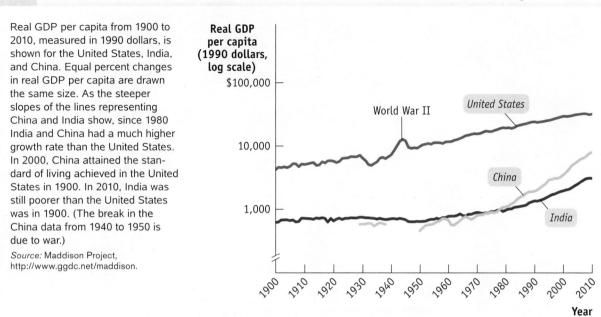

Real GDP per capita from 1900 to 2010, measured in 1990 dollars, is shown for the United States, India, and China. Equal percent changes in real GDP per capita are drawn the same size. As the steeper slopes of the lines representing China and India show, since 1980 India and China had a much higher growth rate than the United States. In 2000, China attained the standard of living achieved in the United States in 1900. In 2010, India was still poorer than the United States was in 1900. (The break in the China data from 1940 to 1950 is due to war.)

Source: Maddison Project, http://www.ggdc.net/maddison.

To give a sense of how much the U.S. economy grew during the last century, Table 17-1 shows real GDP per capita at selected years, expressed two ways: as a percentage of the 1900 level and as a percentage of the 2010 level. In 1920, the U.S. economy already produced 136% as much per person as it did in 1900. In 2010, it produced 745% as much per person as it did in 1900, a more than sevenfold increase. Alternatively, in 1900 the U.S. economy produced only 13% as much per person as it did in 2010.

The income of the typical family normally grows more or less in proportion to per capita income. For example, a 1% increase in real GDP per capita corresponds, roughly, to a 1% increase in the income of the median or typical family—a family at the center of the income distribution. In 2010, the median American household had an income of about $50,000. Since Table 17-1 tells us that real GDP per capita in 1900 was only 13% of its 2010 level, a typical family in 1900 probably had a purchasing power only 13% as large as the purchasing power of a typical family in 2010. That's around $6,100 in today's dollars, representing a standard of living that we would now consider severe poverty. Today's typical American family, if transported back to the United States of 1900, would feel quite a lot of deprivation.

Yet about 50% of the world's people live in countries with a lower standard of living than the United States had a century ago. That's the message about China and India in Figure 17-1: despite dramatic economic growth in China over the last three decades and the less dramatic acceleration of economic growth in India, China has only recently exceeded the standard of living that the United States enjoyed in the early twentieth century, while India is still poorer than the United States was at that time. And much of the world today is poorer than China or India.

You can get a sense of how poor much of the world remains by looking at Figure 17-2, a map of the world in which countries are classified according to their 2010 levels of GDP per capita, in U.S. dollars. As you can see, large parts of the world have very low incomes. Generally speaking, the countries of Europe and North America, as well as a few in the Pacific, have high incomes. The rest of the world, containing most of its population, is dominated by countries with GDP less than $3,976 per capita—and often much less.

TABLE 17-1

U.S. Real GDP per Capita

Year	Percentage of 1900 real GDP per capita	Percentage of 2010 real GDP per capita
1900	100%	13%
1920	136	18
1940	171	23
1980	454	61
2000	701	94
2010	745	100

Source: Maddison Project, http://www.ggdc.net/maddison.

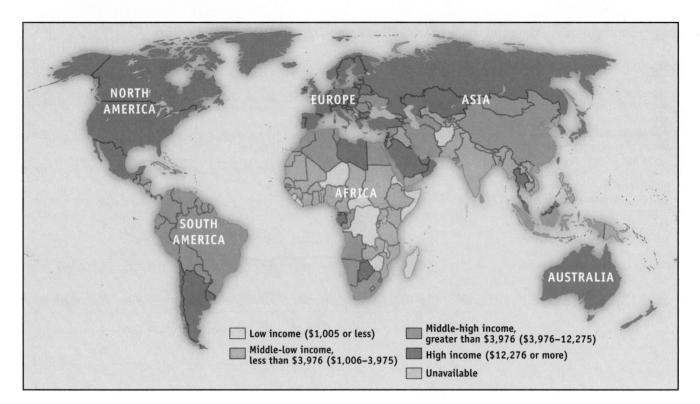

Low income ($1,005 or less)

Middle-low income, less than $3,976 ($1,006–3,975)

Middle-high income, greater than $3,976 ($3,976–12,275)

High income ($12,276 or more)

Unavailable

FIGURE 17-2 **Per Capita Income Around the World, 2010** Although the countries of Europe and North America—along with a few in the Pacific—have high incomes, much of the world is still very poor. Today, about 50% of the world's population lives in countries with a lower standard of living than the United States had a century ago.
Source: International Monetary Fund.

According to the Rule of 70, the time it takes a variable that grows gradually over time to double is approximately 70 divided by that variable's annual growth rate.

Growth Rates

How did the United States manage to produce over seven times as much per person in 2010 than in 1900? The answer is a little bit at a time. Long-run economic growth is normally a gradual process in which real GDP per capita grows at most a few percent per year. From 1900 to 2010, real GDP per capita in the United States increased an average of 1.9% each year.

To have a sense of the relationship between the annual growth rate of real GDP per capita and the long-run change in real GDP per capita, it's helpful to keep in mind the **Rule of 70,** a mathematical formula that tells us how long it takes real GDP per capita, or any other variable that grows gradually over time, to double. The approximate answer is:

(17-1) Number of years for variable to double $= \dfrac{70}{\text{Annual growth rate of variable}}$

(Note that the Rule of 70 can only be applied to a positive growth rate.) So if real GDP per capita grows at 1% per year, it will take 70 years to double. If it grows at 2% per year, it will take only 35 years to double.

In fact, U.S. real GDP per capita rose on average 1.9% per year over the last century. Applying the Rule of 70 to this information implies that it should have taken 37 years for real GDP per capita to double; it would have taken 111 years—three periods of 37 years each—for U.S. real GDP per capita to double three times. That is, the Rule of 70 implies that over the course of 111 years, U.S. real GDP per capita should have increased by a factor of 2 × 2 × 2 = 8. And this does turn out to be a pretty good approximation of reality. Between 1899 and 2010—a period of 111 years—real GDP per capita rose just about eightfold.

Figure 17-3 shows the average annual rate of growth of real GDP per capita for selected countries from 1980 to 2010. Some countries were notable success stories: for example, China, though still quite a poor country, has made spectacular progress. India, although not matching China's performance, has also achieved impressive growth, as discussed in the following Economics in Action.

FIGURE

17-3   **Comparing Recent Growth Rates**

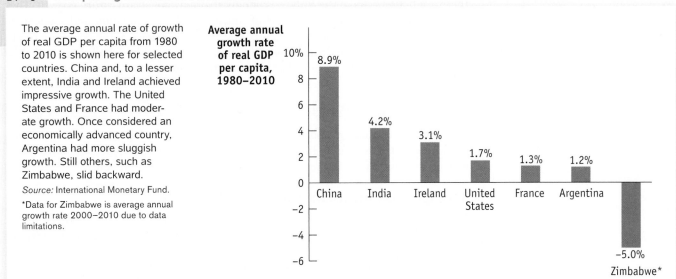

The average annual rate of growth of real GDP per capita from 1980 to 2010 is shown here for selected countries. China and, to a lesser extent, India and Ireland achieved impressive growth. The United States and France had moderate growth. Once considered an economically advanced country, Argentina had more sluggish growth. Still others, such as Zimbabwe, slid backward.

Source: International Monetary Fund.

*Data for Zimbabwe is average annual growth rate 2000–2010 due to data limitations.

Some countries, though, have had very disappointing growth. Argentina was once considered a wealthy nation. In the early years of the twentieth century, it was in the same league as the United States and Canada. But since then it has lagged far behind more dynamic economies. And still others, like Zimbabwe, have slid backward.

What explains these differences in growth rates? To answer that question, we need to examine the sources of long-run economic growth.

ECONOMICS ▶ IN ACTION   WORLD VIEW

INDIA TAKES OFF

India achieved independence from Great Britain in 1947, becoming the world's most populous democracy—a status it has maintained to this day. For more than three decades after independence, however, this happy political story was partly overshadowed by economic disappointment. Despite ambitious economic development plans, India's performance was consistently sluggish. In 1980, India's real GDP per capita was only about 50% higher than it had been in 1947; the gap between Indian living standards and those in wealthy countries like the United States had been growing rather than shrinking.

Since then, however, India has done much better. As Figure 17-3 shows, real GDP per capita has grown at an average rate of 4.2% a year, more than tripling between 1980 and 2010. India now has a large and rapidly growing middle class. And yes, the well-fed children of that middle class are much taller than their parents.

What went right in India after 1980? Many economists point to policy reforms. For decades after independence, India had a tightly controlled, highly regulated economy. Today, things are very different: a series of reforms opened the economy to international trade and freed up domestic competition. Some economists, however, argue that this can't be the main story because the big policy reforms weren't adopted until 1991, yet growth accelerated around 1980.

Regardless of the explanation, India's economic rise has transformed it into a major new economic power—and allowed hundreds of millions of people to have a much better life, better than their grandparents could have dreamed.

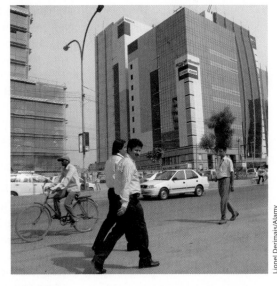

India's high rate of economic growth has raised living standards and led to the emergence of a rapidly growing middle class.

The big question now is whether this growth can continue. Skeptics argue that there are bottlenecks in the Indian economy that may constrain future growth. They point to the still low education level of much of India's population and inadequate infrastructure—that is, the poor quality and limited capacity of the country's roads, railroads, power supplies, and so on. But India's economy has defied the skeptics for several decades and the hope is that it can continue doing so.

What Are the Sources of Long-Run Growth?

Long-run economic growth depends almost entirely on one ingredient: rising *productivity*. However, a number of factors affect the growth of productivity. Let's look first at why productivity is the key ingredient and then examine what affects it.

The Crucial Importance of Productivity

Sustained economic growth occurs only when the amount of output produced by the average worker increases steadily. The term **labor productivity,** or **productivity** for short, is used to refer either to output per worker or, in some cases, to output per hour. (The number of hours worked by an average worker differs to some extent across countries, although this isn't an important factor in the difference between living standards in, say, India and the United States.)

In this book we'll focus on output per worker. For the economy as a whole, productivity—output per worker—is simply real GDP divided by the number of people working.

You might wonder why we say that higher productivity is the only source of long-run growth. Can't an economy also increase its real GDP per capita by putting more of the population to work? The answer is, yes, but . . . . For short periods of time, an economy can experience a burst of growth in output per capita by putting a higher percentage of the population to work.

That happened in the United States during World War II, when millions of women who previously worked only in the home entered the paid workforce. The percentage of adult civilians employed outside the home rose from 50% in 1941 to 58% in 1944, and you can see the resulting bump in real GDP per capita during those years in Figure 17-1.

Over the longer run, however, the rate of employment growth is never very different from the rate of population growth. Over the course of the twentieth century, for example, the population of the United States rose at an average rate of 1.3% per year and employment rose 1.5% per year. Real GDP per capita rose 1.9% per year; of that, 1.7%—that is, almost 90% of the total—was the result of rising productivity. In general, overall real GDP can grow because of population growth, but any large increase in real GDP *per capita* must be the result of increased output *per worker*. That is, it must be due to higher productivity.

So increased productivity is the key to long-run economic growth. But what leads to higher productivity?

Explaining Growth in Productivity

There are three main reasons why the average U.S. worker today produces far more than his or her counterpart a century ago. First, the modern worker has far more *physical capital*, such as machinery and office space, to work with. Second, the modern worker is much better educated and so possesses much more *human capital*. Finally, modern firms have the advantage of a century's accumulation of technical advancements reflecting a great deal of *technological progress*.

Let's look at each of these factors in turn.

INCREASE IN PHYSICAL CAPITAL Economists define **physical capital** as manufactured resources such as buildings and machines. Physical capital makes workers more productive. For example, a worker operating a backhoe can dig a lot more feet of trench per day than one equipped only with a shovel.

Labor productivity, often referred to simply as **productivity,** is output per worker.

Physical capital consists of human-made resources such as buildings and machines.

The average U.S. private-sector worker today is backed up by more than $150,000 worth of physical capital—far more than a U.S. worker had 100 years ago and far more than the average worker in most other countries has today.

INCREASE IN HUMAN CAPITAL It's not enough for a worker to have good equipment—he or she must also know what to do with it. **Human capital** refers to the improvement in labor created by the education and knowledge embodied in the workforce.

The human capital of the United States has increased dramatically over the past century. A century ago, although most Americans were able to read and write, very few had an extensive education. In 1910, only 13.5% of Americans over 25 had graduated from high school and only 3% had four-year-college degrees. By 2010, the percentages were 87% and 30%, respectively. It would be impossible to run today's economy with a population as poorly educated as that of a century ago.

Analyses based on *growth accounting,* described in the next module, suggest that education—and its effect on productivity—is an even more important determinant of growth than increases in physical capital.

TECHNOLOGICAL PROGRESS Probably the most important driver of productivity growth is **technological progress,** which is broadly defined as an advance in the technical means of the production of goods and services. We'll see shortly how economists measure the impact of technology on growth.

Workers today are able to produce more than those in the past, even with the same amount of physical and human capital, because technology has advanced over time. It's important to realize that economically important technological progress need not be flashy or rely on cutting-edge science. Historians have noted that past economic growth has been driven not only by major inventions, such as the railroad or the semiconductor chip, but also by thousands of modest innovations, such as the flat-bottomed paper bag, patented in 1870, which made packing groceries and many other goods much easier, and the Post-it® note, introduced in 1981, which has had surprisingly large benefits for office productivity. Experts attribute much of the productivity surge that took place in the United States late in the twentieth century to new technology adopted by retail companies like Walmart rather than to high-technology companies.

> **Human capital** is the improvement in labor created by the education and knowledge embodied in the workforce.
>
> **Technological progress** is an advance in the technical means of the production of goods and services.

HUNT & GATHER   POINT & CLICK

The Evolution Of Man

Marty Bucella/Cartoonstock

17 Review

Solutions appear at the back of the book.

Check Your Understanding

1. Why do economists focus on real GDP per capita as a measure of economic progress rather than on some other measure, such as nominal GDP per capita or real GDP?

2. Apply the Rule of 70 to the data in Figure 17-3 to determine how long it will take each of the countries listed there to double its real GDP per capita. Would India's real GDP per capita exceed that of the United States in the future if growth rates remained the same? Why or why not?

3. Although China and India currently have growth rates much higher than the U.S. growth rate, the typical Chinese or Indian household is far poorer than the typical American household. Explain why.

Multiple-Choice Questions

1. Which of the following is true regarding growth rates for countries around the world compared to the United States?

    I. Fifty percent of the world's people live in countries with a lower standard of living than the U.S. in 1900.
    II. The U.S. growth rate is six times the growth rate in the rest of the world.
    III. China has only just attained the same standard of living the U.S. had in 1900.

    a. I only
    b. II only
    c. III only
    d. I and III only
    e. I, II, and III

2. Which of the following is the key statistic used to track economic growth?

    a. GDP
    b. real GDP
    c. real GDP per capita
    d. median real GDP
    e. median real GDP per capita

3. According to the Rule of 70, if a country's real GDP per capita grows at a rate of 2% per year, it will take how many years for real GDP per capita to double?

    a. 3.5
    b. 20
    c. 35
    d. 70
    e. It will never double at that rate.

Critical-Thinking Question

Increases in real GDP per capita result mostly from changes in what variable? Define that variable. What other factor could also lead to increased real GDP per capita? Why is this other factor not as significant?

4. If a country's real GDP per capita doubles in 10 years, what was its average annual rate of growth of real GDP per capita?

    a. 3.5%
    b. 7%
    c. 10%
    d. 70%
    e. 700%

5. Long-run economic growth depends almost entirely on

    a. technological change.
    b. rising productivity.
    c. increased labor force participation.
    d. rising real GDP per capita.
    e. population growth.

PITFALLS

CHANGE IN LEVEL VERSUS RATE OF CHANGE

? What's the difference between a *change in the level of real GDP* and a *change in the growth rate*?

> WHEN YOU HEAR THAT REAL GDP "GREW," IT MEANS THAT THE *LEVEL* OF REAL GDP INCREASED. WHEN YOU HEAR STATEMENTS ABOUT ECONOMIC GROWTH OVER A PERIOD OF YEARS, YOU ARE ALMOST ALWAYS HEARING ABOUT *CHANGES IN THE GROWTH RATE*. Consider this example. We might say that U.S. real GDP grew during 2010 by $385 billion. If we knew the level of U.S. real GDP in 2009, we could also represent the amount of 2010 growth in terms of a rate of change. So, if U.S. real GDP in 2009 was $12,703 billion, then U.S. real GDP in 2010 was $12,703 billion + $385 billion = $13,088 billion. We could calculate the rate of change, or the growth rate, of U.S. real GDP during 2010 as: ($13,088 billion − $12,703 billion)/$12,703 billion) × 100 = ($385 billion/$12,703 billion) × 100 = 3.03%.

When talking about growth or growth rates, economists often use phrases that appear to mix the two concepts. Admittedly, this can be confusing. For example, when economists say that "U.S. growth fell during the 1970s," they are really saying that the U.S. growth rate of real GDP was lower in the 1970s in comparison to the 1960s. When they say that "growth accelerated during the early 1990s," what they mean is that the growth rate increased year after year in the early 1990s—for example, going from 3% to 3.5% to 4%.

To learn more, see pages 174 and 175.

Productivity and Growth

Kim Steele/Getty Images

MODULE **18**

WHAT YOU WILL LEARN

1 How changes in productivity are illustrated using an aggregate production function

2 About challenges to growth posed by limited natural resources and efforts to make growth sustainable

The Aggregate Production Function

Productivity is higher, other things equal, when workers are equipped with more physical capital, more human capital, better technology, or any combination of the three. But can we put numbers to these effects? To do this, economists make use of the **aggregate production function,** which shows how productivity depends on the quantities of physical capital per worker and human capital per worker as well as the state of technology. In general, all three factors tend to rise over time, as workers are equipped with more machinery, receive more education, and benefit from technological advances.

In analyzing historical economic growth, economists have discovered a crucial fact about the estimated aggregate production function: it exhibits **diminishing returns to physical capital.** That is, when the amount of human capital per worker and the state of technology are held fixed, each successive increase in the amount of physical capital per worker leads to a smaller increase in productivity. Figure 18-1 and the accompanying table give a hypothetical example of how the level of physical capital per worker might affect the level of real GDP per worker, holding human capital per worker and the state of technology fixed. In this example, we measure the quantity of physical capital in dollars.

To see why the relationship between physical capital per worker and productivity exhibits diminishing returns, think about how having farm equipment affects the productivity of farmworkers. A little bit of equipment makes a big difference: a worker equipped with a tractor can do much more than a worker without one. And a worker using more expensive equipment will, other things equal, be more productive: a worker with a $40,000 tractor will normally be able to cultivate more farmland in a given amount of time than a worker with a $20,000 tractor because the more expensive machine will be more powerful, perform more tasks, or both.

The **aggregate production function** is a hypothetical function that shows how productivity (real GDP per worker) depends on the quantities of physical capital per worker and human capital per worker as well as the state of technology.

An aggregate production function exhibits **diminishing returns to physical capital** when, holding the amount of human capital per worker and the state of technology fixed, each successive increase in the amount of physical capital per worker leads to a smaller increase in productivity.

18-1   Physical Capital and Productivity

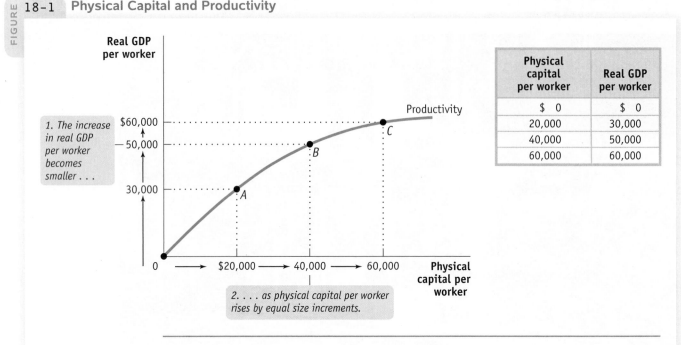

Physical capital per worker	Real GDP per worker
$ 0	$ 0
20,000	30,000
40,000	50,000
60,000	60,000

1. The increase in real GDP per worker becomes smaller . . .

2. . . . as physical capital per worker rises by equal size increments.

The aggregate production function shows how, in this case holding human capital per worker and technology fixed, productivity increases as physical capital per worker rises. Other things equal, a greater quantity of physical capital per worker leads to higher real GDP per worker but is subject to diminishing returns: each successive addition to physical capital per worker produces a smaller increase in productivity. Starting at the origin, 0, a $20,000 increase in physical capital per worker leads to an increase in real GDP per worker of $30,000, indicated by point *A*. Starting from point *A*, another $20,000 increase in physical capital per worker leads to an increase in real GDP per worker but only of $20,000, indicated by point *B*. Finally, a third $20,000 increase in physical capital per worker leads to only a $10,000 increase in real GDP per worker, indicated by point *C*.

But will a worker with a $40,000 tractor, holding human capital and technology constant, be twice as productive as a worker with a $20,000 tractor? Probably not: there's a huge difference between not having a tractor at all and having even an inexpensive tractor; there's much less difference between having an inexpensive tractor and having a better tractor. And we can be sure that a worker with a $200,000 tractor won't be 10 times as productive: a tractor can be improved only so much. Because the same is true of other kinds of equipment, the aggregate production function shows diminishing returns to physical capital.

Diminishing returns to physical capital imply a relationship between physical capital per worker and output per worker like the one shown in Figure 18-1. As the productivity curve for physical capital and the accompanying table illustrate, more physical capital per worker leads to more output per worker. But each $20,000 increment in physical capital per worker adds less to productivity.

As you can see from the table, there is a big payoff for the first $20,000 of physical capital: real GDP per worker rises by $30,000. The second $20,000 of physical capital also raises productivity, but not by as much: real GDP per worker goes up by only $20,000. The third $20,000 of physical capital raises real GDP per worker by only $10,000.

By comparing points along the curve you can also see that as physical capital per worker rises, output per worker also rises—but at a diminishing rate. Going from the origin at 0 to point *A*, a $20,000 increase in physical capital per worker, leads to an increase of $30,000 in real GDP per worker. Going from point *A* to point *B*, a second $20,000 increase in physical capital per worker, leads to an increase of only $20,000 in real GDP per worker. And from point *B* to point *C*, a $20,000 increase in physical capital per worker increased real GDP per worker by only $10,000.

It's important to realize that diminishing returns to physical capital is an "other things equal" phenomenon: additional amounts of physical capital are less productive *when the amount of human capital per worker and the technology are held fixed*. Diminishing returns may disappear if we increase the amount of human capital per worker, or improve the technology, or both at the same time the amount of physical capital per worker is increased.

For example, a worker with a $40,000 tractor who has also been trained in the most advanced cultivation techniques may in fact be more than twice as productive as a worker with only a $20,000 tractor and no additional human capital. But diminishing returns to any one input—regardless of whether it is physical capital, human capital, or number of workers—is a pervasive characteristic of production.

Growth Accounting

In practice, all the factors contributing to higher productivity rise during the course of economic growth: both physical capital and human capital per worker increase, and technology advances as well. To disentangle the effects of these factors, economists use **growth accounting,** which estimates the contribution of each major factor in the aggregate production function to economic growth. For example, suppose the following are true:

- The amount of physical capital per worker grows 3% a year.

- Each 1% rise in physical capital per worker, holding human capital and technology constant, raises output per worker by one-third of 1%, or 0.33%.

In that case, we would estimate that growing physical capital per worker is responsible for 3% × 0.33 = 1 percentage point of productivity growth per year. A similar but more complex procedure is used to estimate the effects of growing human capital. The procedure is more complex because there aren't simple dollar measures of the quantity of human capital.

Growth accounting allows us to calculate the effects of greater physical and human capital on economic growth. But how can we estimate the effects of technological progress? We do so by estimating what is left over after the effects of physical and human capital have been taken into account. For example, let's imagine that there was no increase in human capital per worker so that we can focus on changes in physical capital and in technology.

In Figure 18-2, the lower curve shows the same hypothetical relationship between physical capital per worker and output per worker shown in Figure 18-1. Let's assume that this was the relationship given the technology available in 1942. The upper curve also shows a relationship between physical capital per worker and productivity, but this time given the technology available in 2012. (We've chosen a 70-year stretch to allow us to use the Rule of 70.) The 2012 curve is shifted up compared to the 1942 curve because technologies developed over the previous 70 years made it possible to produce more output for a given amount of physical capital per worker than was possible with the technology available in 1942. (Note that the two curves are measured in constant dollars.)

Let's assume that between 1942 and 2012 the amount of physical capital per worker rose from $20,000 to $60,000. If this increase in physical capital per worker had taken place without any technological progress, the economy would have moved from *A* to *C:* output per worker would have risen, but only from $30,000 to $60,000, or 1% per year (using the Rule of 70 tells us that a 1% growth rate over 70 years doubles output). In fact, however, the economy moved from *A* to *D:* output rose from $30,000 to $120,000, or 2% per year. There was an increase in both physical capital per worker and technological progress, which shifted the aggregate production function.

In this case, 50% of the annual 2% increase in productivity—that is, 1% in annual productivity growth—is due to higher **total factor productivity,** the amount of output that can be produced with a given amount of factor inputs. So when total factor

Growth accounting estimates the contribution of each major factor in the aggregate production function to economic growth.

Total factor productivity is the amount of output that can be achieved with a given amount of factor inputs.

Technological progress is central to economic growth.

FIGURE **18-2   Technological Progress and Productivity Growth**

Technological progress raises productivity at any given level of physical capital per worker, and therefore shifts the aggregate production function upward. Here we hold human capital per worker fixed. We assume that the lower curve (the same curve as in Figure 18-1) reflects technology in 1942 and the upper curve reflects technology in 2012. Holding technology and human capital fixed, tripling physical capital per worker from $20,000 to $60,000 leads to a doubling of real GDP per worker, from $30,000 to $60,000. This is shown by the movement from point *A* to point *C*, reflecting an approximately 1% per year rise in real GDP per worker. In reality, technological progress raised productivity at any given level of physical capital—shown here by the upward shift of the curve—and the actual rise in real GDP per worker is shown by the movement from point *A* to point *D*. Real GDP per worker grew 2% per year, leading to a quadrupling during the period. The extra 1% in growth of real GDP per worker is due to higher total factor productivity.

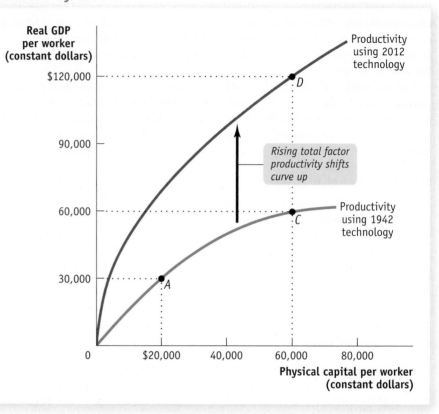

productivity increases, the economy can produce more output with the same quantity of physical capital, human capital, and labor.

Most estimates find that increases in total factor productivity are central to a country's economic growth. We believe that observed increases in total factor productivity in fact measure the economic effects of technological progress. All of this implies that technological change is crucial to economic growth. The Bureau of Labor Statistics estimates the growth rate of both labor productivity and total factor productivity for nonfarm business in the United States. According to the Bureau's estimates, during the past 70 years, only about half of the productivity in the economy is explained by increases in physical and human capital per worker; the rest is explained by rising total factor productivity—that is, by technological progress.

ECONOMICS ▶ IN ACTION

THE INFORMATION TECHNOLOGY PARADOX

From the early 1970s through the mid-1990s, the United States went through a slump in total factor productivity growth. Figure 18-3 shows Bureau of Labor Statistics estimates of annual total factor productivity growth, averaged for each 10-year period from 1948 to 2010. As you can see, there was a large fall in the total factor productivity growth rate beginning in the early 1970s. Because higher total factor productivity plays such a key role in long-run growth, the economy's overall growth was also disappointing, leading to a widespread sense that economic progress had ground to a halt.

Many economists were puzzled by the slowdown in total factor productivity growth after 1973, since in other ways the era seemed to be one of rapid technological progress. Modern information technology really began with the development of the first microprocessor—a computer on a chip—in 1971. In the 25 years that followed, a series of inventions that seemed revolutionary became standard equipment in the business world: computers, the Internet, cell phones, and e-mail.

Yet the rate of growth of total factor productivity remained stagnant. In a famous remark, MIT economics professor and Nobel laureate Robert Solow, a pioneer in the analysis of economic growth, declared that the information technology revolution could be seen everywhere except in the economic statistics. Why didn't information technology show large rewards?

Paul David, a Stanford University economic historian, offered a theory and a prediction. He pointed out that 100 years earlier another miracle technology—electric power—had spread through the economy, again with surprisingly little impact on productivity growth at first. The reason, he suggested, was that a new technology doesn't yield its full potential if you use it in old ways.

For example, a traditional factory around 1900 was a multistory building, with the machinery tightly crowded together and designed to be powered by a steam engine in the basement. This design had problems: it was very difficult to move people and materials around. Yet owners who electrified their factories initially maintained the multistory, tightly packed layout. Only with the switch to spread-out, one-story factories that took advantage of the flexibility of electric power—most famously Henry Ford's auto assembly line—did productivity take off.

David suggested that the same phenomenon was happening with information technology. Productivity, he predicted, would take off when people really changed their way of doing business to take advantage of the new technology—such as replacing letters and phone calls with e-mail. Sure enough, productivity growth accelerated dramatically in the second half of the 1990s as companies discovered how to effectively use information technology. (The business case at the end of the section details Walmart's innovative practices.)

FIGURE 18-3 **The U.S. Productivity Growth Slowdown and Recovery**

Source: Bureau of Labor Statistics.

What About Natural Resources?

In our discussion so far, we haven't mentioned natural resources, which certainly have an effect on productivity. Other things equal, countries that are abundant in valuable natural resources, such as highly fertile land or rich mineral deposits, have higher real GDP per capita than less fortunate countries. The most obvious modern example is the Middle East, where enormous oil deposits have made a few sparsely populated countries very rich. For example, Kuwait has about the same level of real GDP per capita as Germany, but Kuwait's wealth is based on oil, not manufacturing, the source of Germany's high output per worker.

But other things are often not equal. In the modern world, natural resources are a much less important determinant of productivity than human or physical capital for the great majority of countries. For example, some nations with very high real GDP per capita, such as Japan, have very few natural resources. Some resource-rich nations, such as Nigeria (which has sizable oil deposits), are very poor.

Historically, natural resources played a much more prominent role in determining productivity. In the nineteenth century, the countries with the highest real GDP per capita were those abundant in rich farmland and mineral deposits: the United States, Canada, Argentina, and Australia. As a consequence, natural resources figured prominently in the development of economic thought.

In a famous book published in 1798, *An Essay on the Principle of Population*, the English economist Thomas Malthus made the fixed quantity of land in the world the basis of a pessimistic prediction about future productivity. As population grew, he pointed out, the amount of land per worker would decline. And this, other things equal, would cause productivity to fall.

Sustainable long-run economic growth is long-run growth that can continue in the face of the limited supply of natural resources and the impact of growth on the environment.

His view, in fact, was that improvements in technology or increases in physical capital would lead only to temporary improvements in productivity because they would always be offset by the pressure of rising population and more workers on the supply of land. In the long run, he concluded, the great majority of people were condemned to living on the edge of starvation. Only then would death rates be high enough and birth rates low enough to prevent rapid population growth from outstripping productivity growth.

It hasn't turned out that way, although many historians believe that Malthus's prediction of falling or stagnant productivity was valid for much of human history. Population pressure probably did prevent large productivity increases until the eighteenth century. But in the time since Malthus wrote his book, any negative effects on productivity from population growth have been far outweighed by other, positive factors—advances in technology, increases in human and physical capital, and the opening up of enormous amounts of cultivatable land in the New World.

Is World Growth Sustainable?

Some skeptics have expressed doubt about whether **sustainable long-run economic growth** is possible—whether it can continue in the face of the limited supply of natural resources and the impact of growth on the environment.

In 1972 a group of scientists made a big splash with a book titled *The Limits to Growth*, which argued that long-run economic growth wasn't sustainable due to limited supplies of nonrenewable resources such as oil and natural gas.

These concerns at first seemed to be validated by a sharp rise in resource prices in the 1970s, then came to seem foolish when resource prices fell sharply in the 1980s.

After 2005, however, resource prices rose sharply again, leading to renewed concern about resource limitations to growth. Figure 18-4 shows the real price of oil—the price of oil adjusted for inflation in the rest of the economy. The rise, fall, and rise of concern about resource-based limits to growth have more or less followed the rise, fall, and rise of oil prices shown in the figure.

Differing views about the impact of limited natural resources on long-run economic growth turn on the answers to the following three questions:

1. HOW LARGE ARE THE SUPPLIES OF KEY NATURAL RESOURCES? It's mainly up to geologists to answer this question. And the response changes as new technologies, such as hydraulic fracking, are developed, allowing access to previously inaccessible oil and natural gas resources. Unfortunately, there's wide disagreement among the experts, especially about the prospects for future oil production.

Some analysts believe that there is enough untapped oil in the ground that world oil production can continue to rise for several decades. Others, including a number of oil company executives, believe that the growing difficulty of finding new oil fields will cause oil production to plateau—that is, stop growing and eventually begin a gradual decline—in the fairly near future. Some analysts believe that we have already reached that plateau.

FIGURE 18-4 The Real Price of Oil, 1950–2012

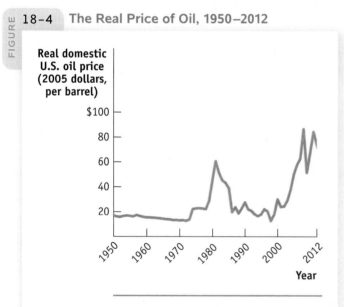

The real price of natural resources, like oil, rose dramatically in the 1970s and then fell just as dramatically in the 1980s. Since 2005, however, the real prices of natural resources have soared.

Sources: Energy Information Administration; Bureau of Labor Statistics.

2. HOW EFFECTIVE WILL TECHNOLOGY BE AT FINDING ALTERNATIVES TO NATURAL RESOURCES? This question will have to be answered by engineers. There's no question that there are many alternatives to the natural resources currently being depleted, some of which are already being exploited. For example, oil extracted from

Canadian tar sands is making a significant contribution to world oil supplies, and the amount of electricity generated by wind and solar power continues to grow.

3. CAN LONG-RUN ECONOMIC GROWTH CONTINUE IN THE FACE OF RESOURCE SCARCITY? This is mainly a question for economists. And most, though not all, economists are optimistic: they believe that modern economies can find ways to work around limits in the supply of natural resources. One reason for this optimism is the fact that resource scarcity leads to high resource prices. These high prices in turn provide strong incentives to conserve the scarce resource and to find alternatives.

For example, after the sharp oil price increases of the 1970s, American consumers turned to smaller, more fuel-efficient cars, and U.S. industry also greatly intensified its efforts to reduce energy bills. The result is shown in Figure 18-5, which compares U.S. real GDP per capita and oil consumption before and after the 1970s energy crisis. In the United States before 1973, there seemed to be a more or less one-to-one relationship between economic growth and oil consumption.

FIGURE 18-5 U.S. Oil Consumption and Growth over Time

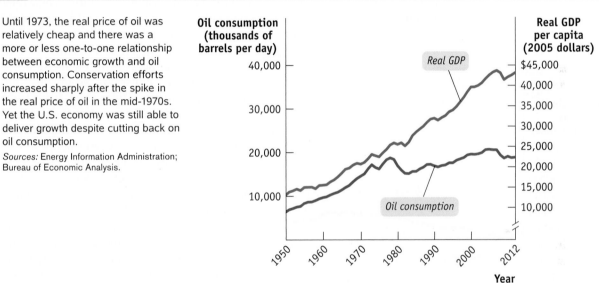

Until 1973, the real price of oil was relatively cheap and there was a more or less one-to-one relationship between economic growth and oil consumption. Conservation efforts increased sharply after the spike in the real price of oil in the mid-1970s. Yet the U.S. economy was still able to deliver growth despite cutting back on oil consumption.

Sources: Energy Information Administration; Bureau of Economic Analysis.

However, after 1973 the U.S. economy continued to deliver growth in real GDP per capita even as it substantially reduced the use of oil. This move toward conservation paused after 1990, as low real oil prices encouraged consumers to shift back to gas-guzzling larger cars and SUVs. But a sharp rise in oil prices since 2005 encouraged renewed shifts toward oil conservation.

Given such responses to prices, economists generally tend to see resource scarcity as a problem that modern economies handle fairly well, and so not as a fundamental limit to long-run economic growth. Environmental issues, however, pose a more difficult problem because dealing with them requires effective political action.

One response to resource scarcity.

Economic Growth and the Environment

Economic growth, other things equal, tends to increase the human impact on the environment. For example, China's spectacular economic growth has also brought a spectacular increase in air pollution in that nation's cities. But again, other things aren't necessarily equal: countries can and do take action to protect their environments.

In fact, air and water quality in today's advanced countries is generally much better than it was a few decades ago. London's famous "fog"—actually a form of air pollution, which killed more than 4,000 people during a two-week episode in 1952—is gone, thanks to regulations that virtually eliminated the use of coal heat. The equally famous smog of Los Angeles, although not extinguished, is far less severe than it was in the 1960s and early 1970s, again thanks to pollution regulations.

Despite these past environmental success stories, there is widespread concern today about the environmental impacts of continuing economic growth, reflecting a change in the scale of the problem. Environmental success stories have mainly involved dealing with *local* impacts of economic growth, such as the effect of widespread car ownership on air quality in the Los Angeles basin. Today, however, we are faced with *global* environmental issues—the adverse impacts on the environment of the Earth as a whole by worldwide economic growth.

The biggest of these issues involves the impact of fossil-fuel consumption on the world's climate. Burning coal and oil releases carbon dioxide into the atmosphere. There is broad scientific consensus that rising levels of carbon dioxide and other gases are causing a greenhouse effect on the Earth, trapping more of the sun's energy and raising the planet's overall average temperature. And rising temperatures may impose high human and economic costs: rising sea levels may flood coastal areas; changing climate may disrupt agriculture, especially in poor countries; and so on.

The problem of climate change is clearly linked to economic growth. Figure 18-6 shows carbon dioxide emissions from the United States, Europe, and China since 1980. Historically, the wealthy nations have been responsible for the bulk of these emissions because they have consumed far more energy per person than poorer countries. As China and other emerging economies have grown, however, they have begun to consume much more energy and emit much more carbon dioxide.

Is it possible to continue long-run economic growth while curbing the emissions of greenhouse gases? The answer, according to most economists who have studied the issue, is yes. It should be possible to reduce greenhouse gas emissions in a wide variety of ways, ranging from the use of non-fossil-fuel energy sources such as wind, solar, and nuclear power, to preventive measures such as capturing the carbon dioxide from power plants and storing it, to simpler things like designing buildings so that they're easier to keep warm in winter and cool in summer. Such measures would impose costs on the economy, but the best available estimates suggest that even a large reduction in greenhouse gas emissions over the next few decades would only modestly dent the long-term rise in real GDP per capita.

The big question is how to make all of this happen. Unlike resource scarcity, environmental problems don't automatically provide incentives for changed behavior. Pollution is an example of a *negative externality*, a cost that individuals or firms impose on others without having to offer compensation. In the absence of government intervention, individuals and firms have no incentive to reduce negative externalities, which is why it took regulation to reduce air pollution in America's cities.

FIGURE 18-6   Climate Change and Growth

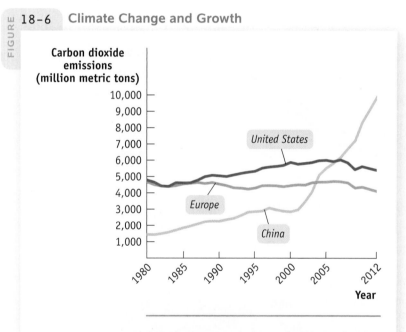

Greenhouse gas emissions are positively related to growth. As shown here by the United States and Europe, wealthy countries have historically been responsible for the great bulk of greenhouse gas emissions because of their richer and faster-growing economies. As China and other emerging economies have grown, they have begun to emit much more carbon dioxide.

Source: Energy Information Administration.

So there is a broad consensus among economists—although there are some dissenters—that government action is needed to deal with climate change. There is also broad consensus that this action should take the form of market-based incentives, either in the form of a carbon tax—a tax per unit of carbon emitted—or a cap and trade system in which the total amount of emissions is capped, and producers must buy licenses to emit greenhouse gases. There is, however, considerable dispute about how to proceed.

There are also several aspects of the climate change problem that make it much more difficult to deal with than, say, smog in Los Angeles. One is the problem of taking the long view. The impact of greenhouse gas emissions on the climate is very gradual: carbon dioxide put into the atmosphere today won't have its full effect on the climate for several generations. As a result, there is the political problem of persuading voters to accept pain today in return for gains that will benefit future generations.

There is also a difficult problem of international burden sharing. As Figure 18-6 shows, rich economies have historically been responsible for most greenhouse gas emissions, but newly emerging economies like China are responsible for most of the recent growth. Inevitably, rich countries are reluctant to pay the price of reducing emissions only to have their efforts frustrated by rapidly growing emissions from new players. At the same time, countries like China, which are still relatively poor, consider it unfair that they should be expected to bear the burden of protecting an environment threatened by the past actions of rich nations.

The general moral of this story is that it is possible to reconcile long-run economic growth with protecting the environment. The main question is one of getting political consensus around the necessary policies.

Emissions from coal-fired municipal heating systems contribute to the heavy smog that has become a problem in many Chinese cities.

18 Review

Solutions appear at the back of the book.

Check Your Understanding

1. Explain the effect of each of the following on the growth rate of productivity.
   a. The amounts of physical and human capital per worker are unchanged, but there is significant technological progress.
   b. The amount of physical capital per worker grows, but the level of human capital per worker and technology are unchanged.

2. The economy of Erehwon has grown 3% per year over the past 30 years. The labor force has grown at 1% per year, and the quantity of physical capital has grown at 4% per year. The average education level hasn't changed. Estimates by economists say that each 1% increase in physical capital per worker, other things equal, raises productivity by 0.3%.
   a. How fast has productivity in Erehwon grown?
   b. How fast has physical capital per worker grown?

   c. How much has growing physical capital per worker contributed to productivity growth? What percentage of total productivity growth is that?
   d. How much has technological progress contributed to productivity growth? What percentage of total productivity growth is that?

3. Multinomics, Inc., is a large company with many offices around the country. It has just adopted a new computer system that will affect virtually every function performed within the company. Why might a period of time pass before employees' productivity is improved by the new computer system? Why might there be a temporary decrease in employees' productivity?

4. What is the link between greenhouse gas emissions and growth? What is the expected effect on growth from emissions reduction? Why is international burden sharing of greenhouse gas emissions reduction a contentious problem?

Multiple-Choice Questions

1. Which of the following is a source of increased productivity growth?

    I. increased physical capital
    II. increased human capital
    III. technological progress

    a. I only

    b. II only

    c. III only

    d. I and II only

    e. I, II, and III

2. Which of the following is an example of physical capital?

    a. machinery

    b. healthcare

    c. education

    d. money

    e. all of the above

3. Which of the following is true of sustainable long-run economic growth?

    a. Long-run growth can continue in the face of the limited supply of natural resources.

    b. It was predicted by Thomas Malthus.

    c. Modern economies handle resource scarcity problems poorly.

    d. It is less likely when we find alternatives to natural resources.

    e. All of the above are true.

Critical-Thinking Questions

Assume that between 1942 and 2012:

- The amount of physical capital per worker grows at 2% per year.
- Each 1% rise in physical capital per worker (holding human capital and technology constant) raises output per worker by ½ of a percent, or 0.5%.
- There is no growth in human capital.
- Real GDP per capita rises from $30,000 to $60,000.

1. Growing physical capital per worker is responsible for how much productivity growth per year? Show your calculation.

2. By how much did total factor productivity grow over the time period? Explain.

4. Which of the following statements is true of environmental quality?

    a. It is typically not affected by government policy.

    b. Other things equal, it tends to improve with economic growth.

    c. There is broad scientific consensus that rising levels of carbon dioxide and other gases are raising the planet's overall temperature.

    d. Most economists believe it is not possible to reduce greenhouse gas emissions while economic growth continues.

    e. Most environmental success stories involve dealing with global, rather than local, impacts.

5. When economists talk about *diminishing returns to physical capital,* they mean that

    a. an increase in physical capital per worker will cause a reduction in real GDP per worker.

    b. an increase in physical capital per worker will lead to smaller and smaller increases in real GDP per worker.

    c. over time physical capital wears out.

    d. increasing physical capital per worker has no effect on real GDP per worker.

    e. increasing physical capital is not a source of economic growth.

PITFALLS

IT MAY BE DIMINISHED . . . BUT IT'S STILL POSITIVE

? If there are diminishing returns to physical capital per worker, does it mean that GDP per worker is falling?

> NO, IT DOES NOT. AN INCREASE IN PHYSICAL CAPITAL PER WORKER WILL NEVER REDUCE PRODUCTIVITY. BUT DUE TO DIMINISHING RETURNS, AT SOME POINT INCREASING THE AMOUNT OF PHYSICAL CAPITAL PER WORKER WILL NO LONGER PRODUCE AN ECONOMIC PAYOFF: AT THAT POINT, THE INCREASE IN OUTPUT WILL BE SO SMALL THAT IT WON'T BE WORTH THE COST OF THE ADDITIONAL PHYSICAL CAPITAL. To answer the question, keep in mind what diminishing returns to physical capital per worker means and what it doesn't mean. As we've seen, it is an "other things equal" statement: holding the amount of human capital per worker and the technology fixed, each successive increase in the amount of physical capital per worker results in a smaller increase in real GDP per worker. But this doesn't mean that real GDP per worker eventually falls as more and more physical capital is added. It's just that the increase in real GDP per worker gets smaller and smaller, while remaining at or above zero.

To learn more, see pages 179–181.

Long-Run Growth Policy

FocusJapan/Alamy

Why Growth Rates Differ

In 1820, Mexico had somewhat higher real GDP per capita than Japan. Today, Japan has higher real GDP per capita than most European nations and Mexico is a poor country, though by no means among the poorest. The difference? Over the long run—since 1820—real GDP per capita grew at 1.9% per year in Japan but at only 1.3% per year in Mexico.

As this example illustrates, even small differences in growth rates have large consequences over the long run. So why do growth rates differ across countries and across periods of time?

Explaining Differences in Growth Rates

As one might expect, economies with rapid growth tend to add physical capital, increase their human capital, or experience rapid technological progress. Striking economic success stories, like Japan in the 1950s and 1960s or China today, tend to be countries that do all three:

1. Rapidly add to their physical capital through high savings and investment spending

2. Upgrade their educational level

3. Make fast technological progress.

Evidence also points to the importance of government policies, property rights, political stability, and good governance in fostering the sources of growth.

SAVINGS AND INVESTMENT SPENDING One reason for differences in growth rates between countries is that some countries are increasing their stock of physical capital much more rapidly than others, through high rates of investment spending. In the 1960s, Japan was the fastest-growing major economy; it also spent a much higher share of its GDP on investment goods than did other major economies.

Today, China is the fastest-growing major economy, and it similarly spends a very large share of its GDP on investment goods. In 2010, investment spending was 38% of China's GDP, compared with only 16% in the United States.

Where does the money for high investment spending come from? From savings. Investment spending must be paid for either out of savings from domestic households or by savings from foreign households—that is, an inflow of foreign capital.

Foreign capital has played an important role in the long-run economic growth of some countries, including the United States, which relied heavily on foreign funds during its early industrialization. For the most part, however, countries that invest a large share of their GDP are able to do so because they have high domestic savings. In fact, China in 2012 saved an even higher percentage of its GDP than it invested at home. The extra savings were invested abroad, largely in the United States.

EDUCATION Just as countries differ substantially in the rate at which they add to their physical capital, there have been large differences in the rate at which countries add to their human capital through education.

A case in point is the comparison between Argentina and China. In both countries the average educational level has risen steadily over time, but it has risen much faster in China. Figure 19-1 shows the average years of education of adults in China, which we have highlighted as a spectacular example of long-run growth, and in Argentina, a country whose growth has been disappointing. Compared to China, sixty years ago, Argentina had a much more educated population, while many Chinese were still illiterate.

As of 2010, the average educational level in China was still slightly below that in Argentina—but that's mainly because there are still many elderly adults who never received basic education. In terms of secondary and tertiary education, China has outstripped once-rich Argentina.

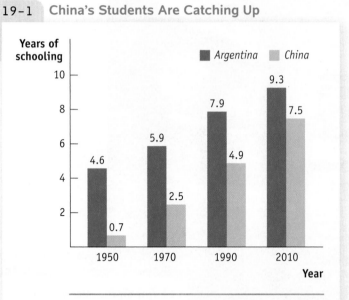

FIGURE 19-1   China's Students Are Catching Up

Years of schooling

In both China and Argentina, the average educational level—measured by the number of years the average adult aged 25 or older has spent in school—has risen over time. Although China is still lagging behind Argentina, it is catching up—and China's success at adding human capital is one key to its spectacular long-run growth.

Source: Robert Barro and Jong-Wha Lee, "A New Data Set of Educational Attainment in the World, 1950–2010," NBER Working Paper No. 15902 (April 2010).

Thomas Edison (shown here), is known as the inventor of R&D because he was first to form an organization devoted solely to creating new products and processes for business.

RESEARCH AND DEVELOPMENT The advance of technology is a key force behind economic growth. What drives technological progress?

Scientific advances make new technologies possible. To take the most spectacular example in today's world, the semiconductor chip—which is the basis for all modern information technology—could not have been developed without the theory of quantum mechanics in physics.

But science alone is not enough: scientific knowledge must be translated into useful products and processes. And that often requires devoting a lot of resources to **research and development,** or **R&D,** spending to create new technologies and apply them to practical use.

Although some research and development is conducted by governments, much R&D is paid for by the private sector. The United States became the world's leading economy in large part because American businesses were among the first to make systematic research and development a part of their operations.

The Role of Government in Promoting Economic Growth

Governments can play an important role in promoting—or blocking—all three sources of long-term economic growth: physical capital, human capital, and technological progress. They can either affect growth directly through subsidies to factors that enhance growth, or by creating an environment that either fosters or hinders growth.

Government policies can increase the economy's growth rate through four main channels.

1. GOVERNMENT SUBSIDIES TO INFRASTRUCTURE Governments play an important direct role in building **infrastructure:** roads, power lines, ports, information networks, and other large-scale physical capital projects that provide a foundation for economic activity. Although some infrastructure is provided by private companies, much of it is either provided by the government or requires a great deal of government regulation and support.

Ireland offers an example of the importance of government-provided infrastructure. After the government invested in an excellent telecommunications infrastructure in the 1980s, Ireland became a favored location for high-technology companies from abroad and its economy took off in the 1990s.

Poor infrastructure, such as a power grid that frequently fails and cuts off electricity, is a major obstacle to economic growth in many countries. To provide good infrastructure, an economy must not only be able to afford it, but it must also have the political discipline to maintain it.

Perhaps the most crucial infrastructure is something we, in an advanced country, rarely think about: basic public health measures in the form of a clean water supply and disease control. Poor health infrastructure is a major obstacle to economic growth in poor countries, especially those in Africa.

2. GOVERNMENT SUBSIDIES TO EDUCATION In contrast to physical capital, which is mainly created by private investment spending, much of an economy's human capital is the result of government spending on education. Government pays for the great bulk of primary and secondary education. And it pays for a significant share of higher education: 75% of students attend public colleges and universities, and government significantly subsidizes research performed at private colleges and universities. As a result, differences in the rate at which countries add to their human capital largely reflect government policy. As we saw in Figure 19-1, educational levels in China are increasing much more rapidly than in Argentina. This isn't because China is richer than Argentina; until recently, China was, on average, poorer than Argentina. Instead, it reflects the fact that the Chinese government has made education a high priority.

Economic growth depends on an educated and skilled workforce.

3. GOVERNMENT SUBSIDIES TO R&D Technological progress is largely the result of private initiative. But in the more advanced countries, important R&D is done by government agencies as well. In the upcoming Economics in Action, we describe Brazil's agricultural boom, which was made possible by government researchers who made discoveries that expanded the amount of arable land in Brazil, as well as developing new varieties of crops that flourish in Brazil's climate.

4. MAINTAINING A WELL-FUNCTIONING FINANCIAL SYSTEM Governments play an important indirect role in making high rates of private investment spending possible. Both the amount of savings and the ability of an economy to direct savings into productive investment spending depend on the economy's institutions, especially its financial system. In particular, a well-regulated and well-functioning financial system is very important for economic growth because in most countries it is the principal way in which savings are channeled into investment spending.

If a country's citizens trust their banks, they will place their savings in bank deposits, which the banks will then lend to their business customers. But if people don't trust their banks, they will hoard gold or foreign currency, keeping their savings in safe deposit boxes or under the mattress, where it cannot be turned into productive investment spending. A well-functioning financial system requires appropriate government regulation to assure depositors that their funds are protected from loss.

Governments can also create an environment that fosters economic growth by providing the following.

PROTECTION OF PROPERTY RIGHTS *Property rights* are the rights of owners of valuable items to dispose of those items as they choose. A subset, *intellectual property rights*, are the rights of an innovator to accrue the rewards of her innovation.

The state of property rights generally, and intellectual property rights in particular, are important factors in explaining differences in growth rates across economies. Why? Because no one would bother to spend the effort and resources required to innovate if someone else could appropriate that innovation and capture the rewards. So, for innovation to flourish, intellectual property rights must receive protection.

Sometimes this is accomplished by the nature of the innovation: it may be too difficult or expensive to copy. But, generally, the government has to protect intellectual property rights. A *patent* is a government-created temporary monopoly given to an innovator for the use or sale of his or her innovation. It's a temporary rather than permanent monopoly because while it's in society's interests to give an innovator an incentive to invent, it's also in society's interests to eventually encourage competition.

POLITICAL STABILITY AND GOOD GOVERNANCE There's not much point in investing in a business if rioting mobs are likely to destroy it, or saving your money if someone with political connections can steal it. Political stability and good governance (including the protection of property rights) are essential ingredients in fostering economic growth in the long run.

Long-run economic growth in successful economies, like that of the United States, has been possible because there are good laws, institutions that enforce those laws, and a stable political system that maintains those institutions. The law must state that your property is really yours so that someone else can't take it away. The courts and the police must be honest so that they can't be bribed to ignore the law. And the political system must be stable so that laws don't change capriciously.

Americans take these preconditions for granted, but they are by no means guaranteed. Aside from the disruption caused by war or revolution, many countries find that their economic growth suffers due to corruption among the government officials who should be enforcing the law.

For example, until 1991 the Indian government imposed many bureaucratic restrictions on businesses, which often had to bribe government officials to get approval for even routine activities—a tax on business, in effect. Economists have argued that a reduction in this burden of corruption is one reason Indian growth has been much faster in recent years.

Even when the government isn't corrupt, excessive government intervention can be a brake on economic growth. If large parts of the economy are supported by government subsidies, protected from imports, subject to unnecessary monopolization, or otherwise insulated from competition, productivity tends to suffer because of a lack of incentives.

ECONOMICS ▶ IN ACTION

WORLD VIEW

THE BRAZILIAN BREADBASKET

A wry Brazilian joke says that "Brazil is the country of the future—and always will be." The world's fifth most populous country has often been considered as a possible major economic power yet has never fulfilled that promise.

In recent years, however, Brazil's economy has made a better showing, especially in agriculture. This success depends on exploiting a natural resource, the tropical savanna land known as the *cerrado*. Until a quarter-century ago, the land was considered unsuitable for farming. A combination of three factors changed that: technological progress due to research and development, improved economic policies, and greater physical capital.

The Brazilian Enterprise for Agricultural and Livestock Research, a government-run agency, developed the crucial technologies. It showed that adding lime and phosphorus made *cerrado* land productive, and it developed breeds of cattle and varieties of soybeans suited for the climate.

Also, until the 1980s, Brazilian international trade policies discouraged exports, as did an overvalued exchange rate that made the country's goods more expensive to foreigners. After economic reform, investing in Brazilian agriculture became much more profitable and companies began putting in place the farm machinery, buildings, and other forms of physical capital needed to exploit the land.

Fandrade/Getty Images

In Brazil, government-funded R&D has resulted in crucial agricultural technologies that turn unusable land into profitable farmland.

What still limits Brazil's growth? Infrastructure. According to a report in the *New York Times,* Brazilian farmers are "concerned about the lack of reliable highways, railways and barge routes, which adds to the cost of doing business." Recognizing this, the Brazilian government is investing in infrastructure, and Brazilian agriculture is continuing to expand.

Success, Disappointment, and Failure

As we've seen, rates of long-run economic growth differ quite a lot around the world. Now let's look at three regions of the world that have had quite different experiences with economic growth over the last few decades.

Figure 19-2 shows trends since 1960 in real GDP per capita for three countries: Argentina, Nigeria, and South Korea. We have chosen these countries because each is a particularly striking example of what has happened in its region.

South Korea's amazing rise is part of a broad "economic miracle" in East Asia. Argentina's slow progress, interrupted by repeated setbacks, is more or less typical of the disappointing growth that has characterized much of Latin America. And Nigeria's unhappy story until very recently—with little growth in real GDP until after 2000—was, unfortunately, an experience shared by many African countries.

FIGURE **19-2**   **Success and Disappointment**

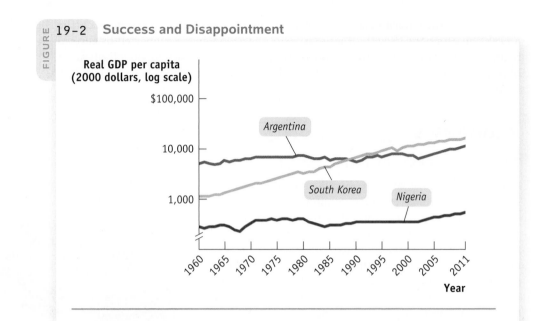

Real GDP per capita is shown for Argentina, South Korea, and Nigeria, using a logarithmic scale. South Korea and some other East Asian countries have been highly successful at achieving economic growth. Argentina, like much of Latin America, has had several setbacks, slowing its growth. Nigeria's standard of living barely budged higher over the decades, an experience shared by many African countries. Neither Argentina nor Nigeria exhibited much growth over the period either, although both have had significantly higher growth in recent years.

Source: World Bank.

East Asia's Miracle

In 1960 South Korea was a very poor country. In fact, in 1960 its real GDP per capita was lower than that of India today. But, as you can see from Figure 19-2, beginning in the early 1960s South Korea began an extremely rapid economic ascent: real GDP per capita grew about 7% per year for more than 30 years. Today South Korea, though still somewhat poorer than Europe or the United States, looks very much like an economically advanced country.

South Korea's economic growth is unprecedented in history: it took the country only 35 years to achieve growth that required centuries elsewhere. Yet South Korea is only part of a broader phenomenon, often referred to as the East Asian economic miracle. High growth rates first appeared in South Korea, Taiwan, Hong Kong, and Singapore but then spread across the region, most notably to China. Since 1975, the whole region has increased real GDP per capita by 6% per year, more than three times America's historical rate of growth.

How have the Asian countries achieved such high growth rates? The answer is that all of the sources of productivity growth have been firing on all cylinders. Very high savings rates, the percentage of GDP that is saved nationally in any given year, have allowed the countries to significantly increase the amount of physical capital per worker. Very good basic education has permitted a rapid improvement in human capital. And these countries have experienced substantial technological progress.

Why didn't any economy achieve this kind of growth in the past? Most economic analysts think that East Asia's growth spurt was possible because of its *relative* backwardness. That is, by the time that East Asian economies began to move into the modern world, they could benefit from adopting the technological advances that had been generated in technologically advanced countries such as the United States.

In 1900, the United States could not have moved quickly to a modern level of productivity because much of the technology that powers the modern economy, from jet planes to computers, hadn't been invented yet. In 1970, South Korea probably still had lower labor productivity than the United States had in 1900, but it could rapidly upgrade its productivity by adopting technology that had been developed in the United States, Europe, and Japan over the previous century. This was aided by a huge investment in human capital through widespread schooling.

The East Asian experience demonstrates that economic growth can be especially fast in countries that are playing catch-up to other countries with higher GDP per capita. On this basis, many economists have suggested a general principle known as the **convergence hypothesis.** It says that differences in real GDP per capita among countries tend to narrow over time because countries that start with lower real GDP per capita tend to have higher growth rates. We'll look at the evidence on the convergence hypothesis in the Economics in Action at the end of this module.

Even before we get to that evidence, however, we can say right away that starting with a relatively low level of real GDP per capita is no guarantee of rapid growth, as the examples of Latin America and Africa demonstrate.

According to the **convergence hypothesis**, international differences in real GDP per capita tend to narrow over time.

Latin America's Disappointment

In 1900, Latin America was not considered an economically backward region. Natural resources, including both minerals and cultivatable land, were abundant. Some countries, notably Argentina, attracted millions of immigrants from Europe in search of a better life. Measures of real GDP per capita in Argentina, Uruguay, and southern Brazil were comparable to those in economically advanced countries.

Since about 1920, however, growth in Latin America has been disappointing. As Figure 19-2 shows in the case of Argentina, growth has been disappointing for many decades, until 2000 when it finally began to increase. The fact that South Korea is now much richer than Argentina would have seemed inconceivable a few generations ago.

Why did Latin America stagnate? Comparisons with East Asian success stories suggest several factors.

- The rates of savings and investment spending in Latin America have been much lower than in East Asia, partly as a result of irresponsible government policy that has eroded savings through high inflation, bank failures, and other disruptions.

- Education—especially broad basic education—has been underemphasized: even Latin American nations rich in natural resources often failed to channel that wealth into their educational systems.

- Political instability, leading to irresponsible economic policies, has taken a toll.

In the 1980s, many economists came to believe that Latin America was suffering from excessive government intervention in markets. They recommended opening the economies to imports, selling off government-owned companies, and, in general, freeing up individual initiative. The hope was that this would produce an East Asian–type economic surge.

So far, however, only one Latin American nation, Chile, has achieved sustained rapid growth. It now seems that pulling off an economic miracle is harder than it looks. Although, in recent years Brazil and Argentina have seen their growth rates increase significantly as they exported large amounts of commodities to the advanced countries and rapidly developing China.

Africa's Troubles and Promise

Africa south of the Sahara is home to about 910 million people, more than 2½ times the population of the United States. On average, they are very poor, nowhere close to U.S. living standards 100 or even 200 years ago. And economic progress has been

Slow and uneven economic growth in sub-Saharan Africa has led to extreme and ongoing poverty for many of its people.

both slow and uneven, as the example of Nigeria, the most populous nation in the region, suggests.

In fact, real GDP per capita in sub-Saharan Africa actually fell 13% from 1980 to 1994, although it has recovered since then. The consequence of this poor growth performance has been intense and continuing poverty.

This is a very disheartening story. What explains it?

Several factors are probably crucial. Perhaps first and foremost is the problem of political instability. In the years since 1975, large parts of Africa have experienced savage civil wars (often with outside powers backing rival sides) that have killed millions of people and made productive investment spending impossible. The threat of war and general anarchy has also inhibited other important preconditions for growth, such as education and provision of necessary infrastructure.

Property rights are also a major problem. The lack of legal safeguards means that property owners are often subject to extortion because of government corruption, making them averse to owning property or improving it. This is especially damaging in a very poor country.

But not all economists see political instability and government corruption as the leading causes of underdevelopment in Africa; some believe the opposite. They argue that Africa is politically unstable because Africa is poor. And Africa's poverty, they go on to claim, stems from its extremely unfavorable geographic conditions—much of the continent is landlocked, hot, infested with tropical diseases, and cursed with poor soil.

They also highlight the importance of health problems in Africa. In poor countries, worker productivity is often severely hampered by malnutrition and disease. In particular, tropical diseases such as malaria can only be controlled with an effective public health infrastructure, something that is lacking in much of Africa.

Although the example of African countries represents a warning that long-run economic growth cannot be taken for granted, there are some signs of hope. As we noted in Figure 19-2, Nigeria's per capita GDP, after decades of stagnation, turned upward after 2000, achieving a 5.5% real GDP per capita growth rate in 2010. The same is true for sub-Saharan African economies as a whole.

In 2012, real GDP per capita growth rates averaged around 5.5% across sub-Saharan African countries and were projected to be nearly 6% in 2014. Rising prices for their exports are part of the reason for recent success, but there is growing optimism among development experts that a period of relative peace and better government is ushering in a new era for Africa's economies.

ECONOMICS ▶ IN ACTION   WORLD VIEW

ARE ECONOMIES CONVERGING?

In the 1950s, much of Europe seemed quaint and backward to American visitors, and Japan seemed very poor. Today, a visitor to Paris or Tokyo sees a city that looks about as rich as New York. Although real GDP per capita is still somewhat higher in the United States, the differences in the standards of living among the United States, Europe, and Japan are relatively small.

Many economists have argued that this convergence in living standards is normal; the convergence hypothesis says that relatively poor countries should have higher rates of growth of real GDP per capita than relatively rich countries. And if we look at today's relatively well-off countries, the convergence hypothesis seems to be true.

FIGURE

19-3   **Do Economies Converge?**

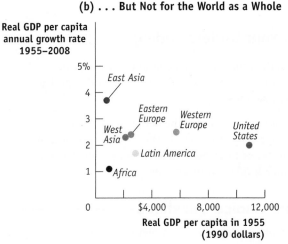

Source: Angus Maddison, *Statistics on World Population, GDP, and Per Capita GDP, 1–2008AD,* http://www.ggdc.net/maddison.

Panel (a) of Figure 19-3 shows data for a number of today's wealthy economies measured in 1990 dollars. On the horizontal axis is real GDP per capita in 1955; on the vertical axis is the average annual growth rate of real GDP per capita from 1955 to 2008. There is a clear negative relationship as can be seen from the line fitted through the points. The United States was the richest country in this group in 1955 and had the slowest rate of growth. Japan and Spain were the poorest countries in 1955 and had the fastest rates of growth. These data suggest that the convergence hypothesis is true.

But economists who looked at similar data realized that these results depend on the countries selected. If you look at successful economies that have a high standard of living today, you find that real GDP per capita has largely converged in the last half-century. But looking across the world as a whole, including countries that remain poor, there is little evidence of convergence. Panel (b) of Figure 19-3 illustrates this point using data for regions rather than individual countries (other than the United States). In 1955, East Asia and Africa were both very poor regions. Over the next 53 years, the East Asian regional economy grew quickly, as the convergence hypothesis would have predicted, but the African regional economy grew very slowly. Likewise, Western Europe had substantially higher real GDP per capita than Latin America. But, contrary to the convergence hypothesis, the Western European regional economy grew more quickly, widening the gap between the regions.

So is the convergence hypothesis all wrong? No: economists still believe that countries with relatively low real GDP per capita tend to have higher rates of growth than countries with relatively high real GDP per capita, *other things equal.* But other things—education, infrastructure, rule of law, and so on—are often not equal. Statistical studies find that when you adjust for differences in these other factors, poorer countries do tend to have higher growth rates. This result is known as *conditional convergence.*

Because other factors differ, however, there is no clear tendency toward convergence in the world economy as a whole. Western Europe, North America, and parts of Asia are becoming more similar in real GDP per capita, but the gap between these regions and the rest of the world is growing.

MODULE
19 Review

Solutions appear at the back of the book.

Check Your Understanding

1. Explain the link between a country's growth rate, its investment spending as a percent of GDP, and its domestic savings.

2. Which of the following is the better predictor of a future high long-run growth rate: a high standard of living today or high levels of savings and investment spending? Explain your answer.

3. Some economists think the best way to help African countries is for wealthier countries to provide more funds for basic infrastructure. Others think this policy will have no long-run effect unless African countries have the financial and political means to maintain this infrastructure. What policies would you suggest?

Multiple-Choice Questions

1. What explains the different growth rates economies experience?

    I. savings and investment spending
    II. research and development
    III. government policies

    a. I only
    b. II only
    c. III only
    d. I and II only
    e. I, II, and III

2. Which of the following can lead to increases in physical capital in an economy?

    a. increased investment spending
    b. increased savings by domestic households
    c. increased savings from foreign households
    d. an inflow of foreign capital
    e. all of the above

3. The following statement describes which area of the world? "This area has experienced growth rates unprecedented in history and now looks like an economically advanced country."

    a. North America
    b. Latin America
    c. Europe
    d. East Asia
    e. Africa

4. Which of the following is cited as an important factor preventing long-run economic growth in Africa?

    a. political instability
    b. lack of property rights
    c. unfavorable geographic conditions
    d. poor health
    e. all of the above

5. The convergence hypothesis

    a. states that differences in real GDP per capita among countries widen over time.
    b. states that low levels of real GDP per capita are associated with higher growth rates.
    c. states that low levels of real GDP per capita are associated with lower growth rates.
    d. contradicts the Rule of 70.
    e. has been proven by evidence from around the world.

Critical-Thinking Question

Some economists think the high rates of growth of productivity achieved by many East Asian economies cannot be sustained. Why might they be right? What would have to happen for them to be wrong?

BUSINESS
CASE : Big Box Boom

After 20 years of being sluggish, U.S. productivity growth accelerated sharply in the late 1990s; that is, productivity began to grow at a much faster rate than previously. What caused that acceleration? Was it the rise of the Internet?

Not according to analysts at McKinsey and Co., the famous business consulting firm. They found that a major source of productivity improvement after 1995 was a surge in output per worker in retailing—stores were selling much more merchandise per worker.

Other analysts agree. The accompanying figure shows the result of an analysis of total factor productivity growth in France, Germany, and the United States between 1995 and 2004, the decade of the U.S. productivity surge. As you can see, the United States did considerably better than either European nation. The key to the surge was very fast growth in the productivity of the distribution sector, that is, in wholesale and retail trade.

Why did productivity surge in retailing in the United States? "The reason can be explained in just two syllables: Walmart," wrote McKinsey.

Walmart is famed in the business world for its successful focus on the unglamorous but crucial area of *logistics*: getting stuff where it was needed, when it was needed. Walmart was one of the first companies to use computers to track inventory, to use bar-code scanners, to establish direct electronic links with suppliers, and so on. These practices gave it a huge advantage over competitors, leading to high profits and rapid expansion. Other firms, observing Walmart's success, have emulated its business practices, spreading productivity gains through the economy as a whole.

There are two lessons from the "Walmart effect," as McKinsey calls it. One is that how you apply a technology makes all the difference: everyone in the retail business knew about computers, but Walmart figured out what to do with them. The other is that a lot of economic growth comes from everyday improvements rather than flashy new technologies.

U.S. and European Productivity Growth, 1995–2004

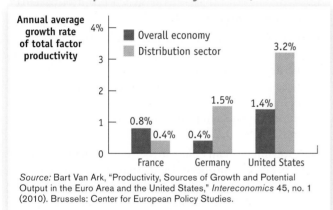

Source: Bart Van Ark, "Productivity, Sources of Growth and Potential Output in the Euro Area and the United States," *Intereconomics* 45, no. 1 (2010). Brussels: Center for European Policy Studies.

Questions for Thought

1. In this section we described several sources of productivity growth. Which of these sources corresponds to the "Walmart effect"?

2. How does the Walmart story relate to the "information technology paradox"?

SECTION 5 REVIEW

Summary

Sources of Long-Run Economic Growth

1. Growth is measured as changes in real GDP per capita in order to eliminate the effects of changes in the price level and changes in population size.

2. Levels of real GDP per capita vary greatly around the world: more than half of the world's population lives in countries that are still poorer than the United States was in 1900. Over the course of the twentieth century, real GDP per capita in the United States increased more than fivefold.

3. Growth rates of real GDP per capita also vary widely. According to the **Rule of 70,** the number of years it takes for real GDP per capita to double is equal to 70 divided by the annual growth rate of real GDP per capita.

4. The key to long-run economic growth is rising **labor productivity,** or just **productivity,** which is output per worker. Increases in productivity arise from increases in **physical capital** per worker and **human capital** per worker as well as **technological progress.**

Productivity and Growth

5. The **aggregate production function** shows how real GDP per worker depends on these three factors. Other things equal, there are **diminishing returns to physical capital:** holding human capital per worker and technology fixed, each successive addition to physical capital per worker yields a smaller increase in productivity than the one before. Equivalently, more physical capital per worker results in a lower, but still positive, increase in productivity.

6. **Growth accounting,** which estimates the contribution of each factor to a country's economic growth, has shown that rising **total factor productivity,** the amount of output produced from a given amount of factor inputs, is key to long-run growth. It is usually interpreted as the effect of technological progress.

7. In contrast to earlier times, natural resources are a less significant source of productivity growth in most countries today.

8. Economists generally believe that environmental issues pose a greater challenge to **sustainable long-run economic growth** than does natural resource scarcity.

9. The emission of greenhouse gases is clearly linked to growth, and limiting them will require some reduction in growth. However, the best available estimates suggest that a large reduction in emissions would require only a modest reduction in the growth rate.

10. There is broad consensus that government action to address climate change and greenhouse gases should be in the form of market-based incentives, like a carbon tax or a cap and trade system. It will also require rich and poor countries to come to some agreement on how the cost of emissions reductions will be shared.

Long-Run Growth Policy

11. The large differences in countries' growth rates are largely due to differences in their rates of accumulation of physical and human capital as well as differences in technological progress. Although inflows of foreign savings from abroad help, a prime factor is differences in domestic savings and investment spending rates, since most countries that have high investment spending in physical capital finance it by high domestic savings.

12. Technological progress is largely a result of **research and development,** or **R&D.**

13. Governments can help or hinder growth. Government policies that directly foster growth are subsidies to **infrastructure,** particularly public health infrastructure, subsidies to education, subsidies to R&D, and maintenance of a well-functioning financial system that channels savings into investment spending, education, and R&D.

14. Governments can enhance the environment for growth by protecting property rights (particularly intellectual property rights through patents), by being politically stable, and by providing good governance. Poor governance includes corruption and excessive government intervention.

15. The world economy contains examples of success and failure in the effort to achieve long-run economic growth. East Asian economies have done many things right and achieved very high growth rates. The low growth rates of Latin American and African economies over many years led economists to believe that the **convergence hypothesis,** the claim that differences in real GDP per capita across countries narrow over time, fits the data only when factors that affect growth, such as education, infrastructure, and favorable government policies and institutions, are held equal across countries. In recent years, there has been an uptick in growth among some Latin American and sub-Saharan African countries, largely due to a boom in commodity exports.

Key Terms

Rule of 70, p. 174
Labor productivity, p. 176
Productivity, p. 176
Physical capital, p. 176
Human capital, p. 177

Technological progress, p. 177
Aggregate production
  function, p. 179
Diminishing returns to physical
  capital, p. 179

Growth accounting, p. 181
Total factor productivity, p. 181
Sustainable long-run
  economic growth, p. 184

Research and development
  (R&D), p. 191
Infrastructure, p. 191
Convergence hypothesis,
  p. 195

Problems

1. The accompanying table shows data from the Penn World Table, Version 7.1, for real GDP per capita in 2005 U.S. dollars for Argentina, Ghana, South Korea, and the United States for 1960, 1970, 1980, 1990, 2000, and 2010.

	Argentina			Ghana			South Korea			United States		
	Real GDP per capita (2005 dollars)	Percentage of		Real GDP per capita (2005 dollars)	Percentage of		Real GDP per capita (2005 dollars)	Percentage of		Real GDP per capita (2005 dollars)	Percentage of	
Year		1960 real GDP per capita	2010 real GDP per capita		1960 real GDP per capita	2010 real GDP per capita		1960 real GDP per capita	2010 real GDP per capita		1960 real GDP per capita	2010 real GDP per capita
1960	$6,043	?	?	$1,286	?	?	$1,656	?	?	$15,398	?	?
1970	7,617	?	?	1,525	?	?	2,808	?	?	20,436	?	?
1980	8,496	?	?	1,295	?	?	5,179	?	?	24,952	?	?
1990	6,928	?	?	1,273	?	?	11,643	?	?	31,389	?	?
2000	8,909	?	?	1,478	?	?	18,729	?	?	36,669	?	?
2010	12,340	?	?	2,094	?	?	26,609	?	?	41,365	?	?

a. Complete the table by expressing each year's real GDP per capita as a percentage of its 1960 and 2010 levels.

b. How does the growth in living standards from 1960 to 2010 compare across these four nations? What might account for these differences?

2. The accompanying table shows the average annual growth rate in real GDP per capita for Argentina, Ghana, and South Korea using data from the Penn World Table, Version 7.1, for the past few decades.

	Average annual growth rate of real GDP per capita		
Years	Argentina	Ghana	South Korea
1960–1970	3.01%	2.08%	4.82%
1970–1980	1.21	0.68	6.35
1980–1990	−1.61	−0.47	7.19
1990–2000	2.41	1.49	5.51
2000–2010	2.97	3.66	4.00

a. For each decade and for each country, use the Rule of 70 where possible to calculate how long it would take for that country's real GDP per capita to double.

b. Suppose that the average annual growth rate that each country achieved over the period 2000–2010 continues indefinitely into the future. Starting from 2010, use the Rule of 70 to calculate the year in which a country will have doubled its real GDP per capita.

3. The accompanying table provides approximate statistics on per capita income levels and growth rates for regions defined by income levels. According to the Rule of 70, starting in 2010 the high-income countries are projected to double their per capita GDP in approximately 78 years, in 2088. Throughout this question, assume constant growth rates for each of the regions that are equal to their average value between 2000 and 2010.

Region	GDP per capita (2010)	Average annual growth rate of real GDP per capita (2000–2010)
High-income countries	$38,293	0.9%
Middle-income countries	3,980	4.8
Low-income countries	507	3.0

Source: World Bank.

a. Calculate the ratio of per capita GDP in 2010 of the following:
   i. Middle-income to high-income countries
   ii. Low-income to high-income countries
   iii. Low-income to middle-income countries

b. Calculate the number of years it will take the low-income and middle-income countries to double their per capita GDP.

c. Calculate the per capita GDP of each of the regions in 2088. (*Hint:* How many times does their per capita GDP double in 78 years, the number of years from 2010 to 2088?)

d. Repeat part a with the projected per capita GDP in 2088.

e. Compare your answers to parts a and d. Comment on the change in economic inequality between the regions.

4. You are hired as an economic consultant to the countries of Albernia and Brittania. Each country's current relationship between physical capital per worker and output per worker is given by the curve labeled "Productivity₁" in the accompanying diagram. Albernia is at point A and Brittania is at point B.

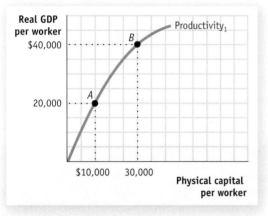

a. In the relationship depicted by the curve Productivity₁, what factors are held fixed? Do these countries experience diminishing returns to physical capital per worker?

b. Assuming that the amount of human capital per worker and the technology are held fixed in each country, can you recommend a policy to generate a doubling of real GDP per capita in Albernia?

c. How would your policy recommendation change if the amount of human capital per worker could be changed? Assume that an increase in human capital doubles the output per worker when physical capital per worker equals $10,000. Draw a curve on the diagram that represents this policy for Albernia.

5. The country of Androde is currently using Method 1 for its production function. By chance, scientists stumble onto a technological breakthrough that will enhance Androde's productivity. This technological breakthrough is reflected in another production function, Method 2. The accompanying table shows combinations of physical capital per worker and output per worker for both methods, assuming that human capital per worker is fixed.

Method 1		Method 2	
Physical capital per worker	Real GDP per worker	Physical capital per worker	Real GDP per worker
0	0.00	0	0.00
50	35.36	50	70.71
100	50.00	100	100.00
150	61.24	150	122.47
200	70.71	200	141.42
250	79.06	250	158.11
300	86.60	300	173.21
350	93.54	350	187.08
400	100.00	400	200.00
450	106.07	450	212.13
500	111.80	500	223.61

a. Using the data in the accompanying table, draw the two production functions in one diagram. Androde's current amount of physical capital per worker is 100. In your figure, label that point A.

b. Starting from point A, over a period of 70 years, the amount of physical capital per worker in Androde rises to 400. Assuming Androde still uses Method 1, in your diagram, label the resulting point of production B. Using the Rule of 70, calculate by how many percent per year output per worker has grown.

c. Now assume that, starting from point A, over the same period of 70 years, the amount of physical capital per worker in Androde rises to 400, but that during that time period, Androde switches to Method 2. In your diagram, label the resulting point of production C. Using the Rule of 70, calculate by how many percent per year output per worker has grown now.

d. As the economy of Androde moves from point A to point C, what share of the annual productivity growth is due to higher total factor productivity?

6. The Bureau of Labor Statistics regularly releases the "Productivity and Costs" report for the previous month. Go to www.bls.gov and find the latest report. (On the Bureau of Labor Statistics home page, from the tab "Subject Areas," look under the head titled "Productivity," and select the link to "Labor Productivity & Costs"; then, from the heading "LPC News Releases," find the most recent "Productivity and Costs" report.) What was the percent change in nonfarm business sector labor productivity for the previous quarter? How does the percent change in that quarter's productivity compare to data from the previous quarter?

7. What roles do physical capital, human capital, technology, and natural resources play in influencing long-run economic growth of aggregate output per capita?

8. How have U.S. policies and institutions influenced the country's long-run economic growth?

9. Over the next 100 years, real GDP per capita in Groland is expected to grow at an average annual rate of 2.0%. In Sloland, however, growth is expected to be somewhat slower, at an average annual growth rate of 1.5%. If both countries have a real GDP per capita today of $20,000, how will their real GDP per capita differ in 100 years? [*Hint:* A country that has a real GDP today of x and grows at y% per year will achieve a real GDP of $\$x \times (1 + (y/100))^z$ in z years. We assume that $0 \le y < 10$.]

10. The accompanying table shows data from the Penn World Table, Version 7.1, for real GDP per capita (2005 U.S. dollars) in France, Japan, the United Kingdom, and the United States in 1950 and 2010. Complete the table. Have these countries converged economically?

	1950		2010	
Country	Real GDP per capita (2005 dollars)	Percentage of U.S. real GDP per capita	Real GDP per capita (2005 dollars)	Percentage of U.S. real GDP per capita
France	$7,084	?	$31,299	?
Japan	2,787	?	31,447	?
United Kingdom	8,988	?	34,268	?
United States	13,069	?	41,365	?

11. The accompanying table shows data from the Penn World Table, Version 7.1, for real GDP per capita (2005 U.S. dollars) for Argentina, Ghana, South Korea, and the United States in 1960 and 2010. Complete the table. Have these countries converged economically?

	1960		2010	
Country	Real GDP per capita (2005 dollars)	Percentage of U.S. real GDP per capita	Real GDP per capita (2005 dollars)	Percentage of U.S. real GDP per capita
Argentina	$6,043	?	$12,340	?
Ghana	1,286	?	2,094	?
South Korea	1,656	?	26,609	?
United States	15,398	?	41,365	?

12. Why would you expect real GDP per capita in California and Pennsylvania to exhibit convergence but not in California and Baja California, a state of Mexico that borders the United States? What changes would allow California and Baja California to converge?

13. According to the *World Factbook,* published by the U.S. Central Intelligence Agency, the proven oil reserves existing in the world in 2012 consisted of 1,532 billion barrels. In that year, the U.S. Energy Information Administration reported that the world oil production was 88.97 million barrels a day.

   a. At this rate, for how many years will the proven oil reserves last? Discuss the Malthusian view in the context of the number you just calculated.

   b. In order to do the calculations in part a, what did you assume about the total quantity of oil reserves over time? About oil prices over time? Are these assumptions consistent with the Malthusian view on resource limits?

   c. Discuss how market forces may affect the amount of time the proven oil reserves will last, assuming that no new oil reserves are discovered and that the demand curve for oil remains unchanged.

14. The accompanying table shows the annual growth rate for the years 2000–2009 in per capita emissions of carbon dioxide (CO_2) and the annual growth rate in real GDP per capita for selected countries.

	2000–2009 average annual growth rate of:	
Country	Real GDP per capita	CO_2 emissions per capita
Argentina	2.81%	1.01%
Bangladesh	4.17	5.47
Canada	0.68	−1.46
China	9.85	11.11
Germany	0.59	−1.23
Ireland	1.05	−2.10
Japan	0.29	−1.03
South Korea	3.48	1.68
Mexico	0.18	0.44
Nigeria	6.07	−2.46
Russia	5.22	0.52
South Africa	2.39	0.80
United Kingdom	0.88	−1.35
United States	0.58	−1.78

Sources: Energy Information Administration; International Monetary Fund.

   a. Rank the countries in terms of their growth in CO_2 emissions, from highest to lowest. What five countries have the highest growth rate in emissions? What five countries have the lowest growth rate in emissions?

   b. Now rank the countries in terms of their growth in real GDP per capita, from highest to lowest. What five countries have the highest growth rate? What five countries have the lowest growth rate?

   c. Would you infer from your results that CO_2 emissions are linked to growth in output per capita?

   d. Do high growth rates necessarily lead to high CO_2 emissions?

SECTION 6

Savings, Investment Spending, and the Financial System

FUNDS FOR FACEBOOK

"Facebook Is Hunting For More Money"— so read a headline in *Business Week,* which reported that the social networking site was seeking to secure a $100 million credit line. Why would a wildly successful business like Facebook need to borrow money?

Everyone knows Facebook. Founded in 2004, it has gone on to become arguably the biggest business success story of the twenty-first century—so far. Currently, Facebook has more than a billion users worldwide. How did Facebook grow so big, so fast?

In large part, of course, the answer is that the company had a good idea. Personalized web pages providing information to friends turned out to be something many people really wanted. Equally important, since advertisers wanted access to the readers of those pages, Facebook could make a lot of money selling advertising space.

But having a good idea isn't enough to build a business. Entrepreneurs need funds: you have to spend money to make money. Although businesses like Facebook seem to exist solely in the virtual world of cyberspace, free of the worldly burdens of brick-and-mortar establishments, the truth is that running such businesses requires a lot of very real and expensive hardware. Like Google, Yahoo!, and other Internet giants, Facebook maintains huge "server farms," arrays of linked computers that track and process all the information needed to provide the user experience.

So where did Facebook get the money to equip these server farms? Some of it came from investors who acquired shares in the business, but much of it was borrowed. As Facebook grew bigger, so did the amount it borrowed.

The ability of Facebook to raise large sums of money to finance its growth is, in its own way, as remarkable as the company's product. In effect, some young guy with a bright idea is able to lay his hands on hundreds of millions of dollars to build his business. It's an amazing story.

Yet this sort of thing is common in modern economies. The long-run growth we analyzed in the previous section depends crucially on a set of markets and institutions, collectively known as the *financial system,* that channels the funds of savers into productive investment spending. Without this system, businesses like Facebook would not be able to purchase the physical capital that is an important source of productivity growth. And savers would be forced to accept a lower return on their funds.

Historically, financial systems channeled funds into investment spending projects such as railroads and factories. Today, financial systems channel funds into new sources of growth such as green technology, social media, and investments in human capital. Without a well-functioning financial system, a country will suffer stunted economic growth.

In this section, we begin by focusing on the economy as a whole. We examine the relationship between savings and investment spending. Next, we look at the financial system to see how savings is transformed into investment spending, as well as the role that time plays in financial decision making. We'll also look at how the financial system works to increase the welfare of savers with funds to invest as well as those with investment spending projects to finance.

205

Savings and Investment Spending

© Michael Belardo/Alamy

Matching Up Savings and Investment Spending

We learned in the previous section that two of the essential ingredients in economic growth are increases in the economy's levels of *human capital* and *physical capital*. Human capital is largely provided by governments through public education. But physical capital, with the exception of infrastructure, is mainly created through private investment spending—that is, spending by firms rather than by the government.

Who pays for private investment spending? In some cases it's the people or corporations that actually do the spending—for example, a family that owns a business might use its own savings to buy new equipment, or a corporation might reinvest some of its profits to build a new factory. In the modern economy, however, individuals and firms that create physical capital often do it with other people's money—money that they borrow or raise by selling stock.

To understand how investment spending is financed, we need to look first at how savings and investment spending are related for the economy as a whole.

The Savings–Investment Spending Identity

According to the **savings–investment spending identity,** savings and investment spending are always equal for the economy as a whole.

The most basic point to understand about savings and investment spending is that they are always equal. This is not a theory; it's a fact of accounting called the **savings–investment spending identity.**

To see why the savings–investment spending identity must be true, let's look again at the national income accounting that we learned about earlier. Recall that GDP is equal to total spending on domestically produced final goods and services, and that we can write the following equation:

(20-1) $GDP = C + I + G + X - IM$

where C is spending by consumers, I is investment spending, G is government purchases of goods and services, X is the value of exports to other countries, and IM is spending on imports from other countries.

THE SAVINGS–INVESTMENT SPENDING IDENTITY IN A CLOSED ECONOMY In a closed economy, there are no exports or imports. So $X = 0$ and $IM = 0$, which makes Equation 20-1 simpler. As we learned, the overall income of this simplified economy would, by definition, equal total spending. Why?

Recall that one person's spending is another person's income: the only way people can earn income is by selling something to someone else, and every dollar spent in the economy creates income for somebody. This is represented by Equation 20-2: on the left, GDP represents total income earned in the economy, and on the right, $C + I + G$ represents total spending in the economy:

(20-2) $GDP = C + I + G$
Total income = Total spending

Now, what can be done with income? It can either be spent on consumption—consumer spending (C) plus government purchases of goods and service (G)—or saved (S). So it must be true that:

(20-3) $GDP = C + G + S$
Total income = Consumption spending + Savings

where S is savings. Meanwhile, as Equation 20-2 tells us, total spending consists of either consumption spending ($C + G$) or investment spending (I):

(20-4) $GDP = C + G + I$
Total income = Consumption spending + Investment spending

Putting Equations 20-3 and 20-4 together, we get:

(20-5) $C + G + S = C + G + I$
Consumption spending + Savings = Consumption Spending + Investment spending

Subtract consumption spending ($C + G$) from both sides, and we get:

(20-6) $S = I$
Savings = Investment spending

As we said, then, it's a basic accounting fact that savings equals investment spending for the economy as a whole.

Now, let's take a closer look at savings. Households are not the only parties that can save in an economy. In any given year, the government can save, too, if it collects more tax revenue than it spends. When this occurs, the difference is called a **budget surplus** and is equivalent to savings by the government.

If, alternatively, government spending exceeds tax revenue, there is a **budget deficit**—a negative budget surplus. In this case, we often say that the government is "dis-saving": by spending more than its tax revenues, the government is engaged in the opposite of savings.

We'll define the term **budget balance** to refer to both cases, with the understanding that the budget balance can be positive (a budget surplus) or negative (a budget deficit). The budget balance is defined as:

(20-7) $S_{Government} = T - G - TR$

Where T is the value of tax revenues and TR is the value of government transfers. The budget balance is equivalent to savings by government—if it's positive, the government

The **budget surplus** is the difference between tax revenue and government spending when tax revenue exceeds government spending.

The **budget deficit** is the difference between tax revenue and government spending when government spending exceeds tax revenue.

The **budget balance** is the difference between tax revenue and government spending.

National savings, the sum of private savings and the budget balance, is the total amount of savings generated within the economy.

Net capital inflow is the total inflow of funds into a country minus the total outflow of funds out of a country.

is saving; if it's negative, the government is dissaving. **National savings,** which we just called savings for short, is equal to the sum of the budget balance and private savings, where private savings is disposable income (income after taxes) minus consumption. It is given by:

$$(20\text{-}8) \quad S_{National} = S_{Government} + S_{Private}$$

So Equations 20-6 and 20-8 tell us that, in a closed economy, the savings–investment spending identity has the following form:

$$(20\text{-}9) \qquad S_{National} = I$$
$$\text{National savings} = \text{Investment spending}$$

THE SAVINGS–INVESTMENT SPENDING IDENTITY IN AN OPEN ECONOMY An open economy is an economy in which goods and money can flow into and out of the country. This changes the savings–investment spending identity because savings need not be spent on investment spending projects in the same country in which the savings are generated. That's because the savings of people who live in any one country can be used to finance investment spending that takes place in other countries.

So any given country can receive *inflows* of funds—foreign savings that finance investment spending in that country. Any given country can also generate *outflows* of funds—domestic savings that finance investment spending in another country.

The net effect of international inflows and outflows of funds on the total savings available for investment spending in any given country is known as the **net capital inflow** into that country, equal to the total inflow of foreign funds minus the total outflow of domestic funds to other countries. Like the budget balance, a net capital inflow can be negative—that is, more capital can flow out of a country than flows into it.

In recent years, the United States has experienced a consistent positive net capital inflow from foreigners, who view our economy as an attractive place to put their savings. In 2012, for example, net capital inflows into the United States were $432 billion.

In recent years, the United States has experienced a consistent positive net capital inflow.

It's important to note that, from a national perspective, a dollar generated by national savings and a dollar generated by capital inflow are not equivalent. Yes, they can both finance the same dollar's worth of investment spending. But any dollar borrowed from a saver must eventually be repaid with interest.

A dollar that comes from national savings is repaid with interest to someone domestically—either a private party or the government. But a dollar that comes as capital inflow must be repaid with interest to a foreigner. So a dollar of investment spending financed by a capital inflow comes at a higher *national* cost—the interest that must eventually be paid to a foreigner—than a dollar of investment spending financed by national savings.

The fact that a net capital inflow represents funds borrowed from foreigners is an important aspect of the savings–investment spending identity in an open economy. Consider an individual who spends more than his or her income; that person must borrow the difference from others.

Similarly, a country that spends more on imports than it earns from exports must borrow the difference from foreigners. And that difference, the amount of funds borrowed from foreigners, is the country's net capital inflow. This means that the net capital inflow into a country is equal to the difference between imports and exports:

$$(20\text{-}10) \qquad NCI = IM - X$$
$$\text{Net capital inflow} = \text{Imports} - \text{Exports}$$

Re-arranging Equation 20-1 we get:

$$(20\text{-}11) \quad I = (GDP - C - G) + (IM - X)$$

Media Bakery

Using Equations 20-3 and 20-9 we know that $GDP - C - G$ is equal to national savings, so that:

(20-12) $I = S_{National} + (IM - X) = S_{National} + NCI$
Investment spending = National savings + Net capital inflow

So the application of the savings–investment spending identity to an economy that is open to inflows or outflows of capital means that investment spending is equal to savings, where savings is equal to national savings *plus* net capital inflow. That is, in an economy with a positive net capital inflow, some investment spending is funded by the savings of foreigners. And in an economy with a negative net capital inflow (that is, more capital is flowing out than flowing in), some portion of national savings is funding investment spending in other countries.

In the United States in 2012, investment spending totaled $2,475 billion. Private savings totaled $3,015 billion, offset by a government budget deficit of $1,087 billion and supplemented by a net capital inflow of $432 billion. Notice that these numbers don't quite add up; because data collection isn't perfect, there is a "statistical discrepancy" of $115 billion. But we know that this is an error in the data, not in the theory, because the savings–investment spending identity must hold in reality.

It's also worth noting that 2012 was not a normal year. As we have pointed out previously, in 2008 the U.S. economy (along with the economies of many other nations) was struck by a severe financial crisis. This crisis led both to a plunge in investment spending and to large government budget deficits, effects that have continued. By using data from 2007, the last year before the crisis, we get a much better picture of what savings and investment look like in more normal times.

Figure 20-1 shows what the savings–investment spending identity looked like in 2007 for two of the world's largest economies at the time, those of the United States and Japan. To make the two economies easier to compare, we've measured savings and investment spending as percentages of GDP.

20-1   **The Savings–Investment Spending Identity in Open Economies: The United States and Japan, 2007**

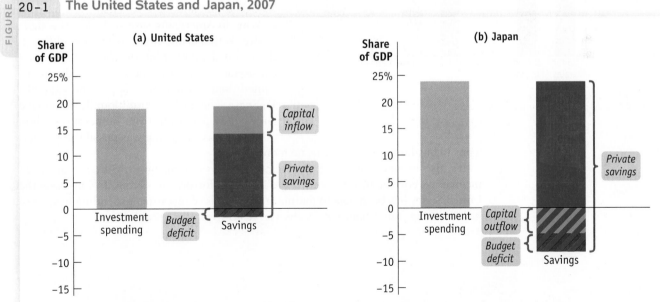

U.S. investment spending in 2007 (equal to 18.8% of GDP) was financed by a combination of private savings (15.7% of GDP) and a capital inflow (5.2% of GDP), which was partially offset by a government budget deficit (–1.6% of GDP). Japanese investment spending in 2007 was higher as a percentage of GDP (23.8%). It was financed by a higher level of private savings as a percentage of GDP (32.1%), which was offset by both a capital outflow (–4.9% of GDP) and a relatively high government budget deficit (–3.4% of GDP).

Source: Bureau of Economic Analysis; OECD.

In each panel the orange bars on the left show total investment spending and the multicolored bars on the right show the components of savings. U.S. investment spending was 18.8% of GDP, financed by a combination of private savings (15.7% of GDP) and positive net capital inflow or capital inflow (5.2% of GDP) and partly offset by a government budget deficit (–1.6% of GDP). (These numbers sum to more than 18.8% due to statistical discrepancy.)

Japanese investment spending was higher as a percentage of GDP, at 23.8%. It was financed by a higher level of private savings as a percentage of GDP (32.1%) and was offset by both a negative net capital inflow or capital outflow (–4.9% of GDP) and a budget deficit (–3.4% of GDP).

The economy's savings finance its investment spending. But how are these funds that are available for investment spending allocated among various projects? That is, what determines which projects get financed (such as Facebook's server farms) and which don't? We'll see shortly that funds get allocated to investment spending projects using a familiar method: by the market, via supply and demand.

ECONOMICS ▶ IN ACTION

WORLD VIEW

AMERICA'S LOW SAVINGS

Figure 20-2 shows national savings as a percentage of GDP for seven wealthy economies in 2007. (Again, we focus on 2007 as the last pre-crisis year). The United States had the lowest savings rate, although the United Kingdom's savings were only slightly higher.

In this respect, 2007 wasn't unusual. The United States has had consistently low national savings compared with other wealthy countries since the 1980s. The main source of these international differences in national savings lies in low U.S. private savings rather than in large U.S. government budget deficits.

Why do Americans save so little? The short answer is that economists aren't sure, although there are a number of theories. One is that consumers have easier access to credit in the United States than elsewhere. For example, Japanese lenders have traditionally demanded large down payments from home-buyers; but, until the housing bust, it was possible for Americans to buy homes with little or no money down.

It's also argued that the U.S. Social Security system, by providing guaranteed income in retirement, may reduce the incentive for private saving. In any case, the United States has been able to maintain high levels of investment spending in spite of its low savings rate because it receives large positive net capital inflows.

FIGURE 20-2

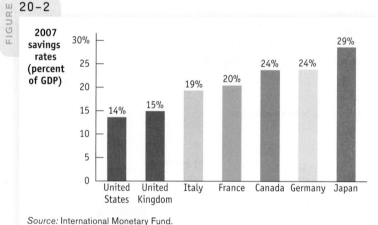

2007 savings rates (percent of GDP)

Source: International Monetary Fund.
Note: IMF data differ slightly from other data sources.

20 Review

Check Your Understanding

1. Explain whether each of the following statements is true or false for an open economy.

   a. If the budget balance has a value of zero, then private savings must be equal to investment spending.

   b. If net capital inflow is positive, then national savings must be less than investment spending.

2. Given the values in the table, find the values for investment spending, national savings, tax revenues, net capital inflow, and private savings.

	Billions of dollars
GDP	$15,851
Consumption	11,254
Government spending	3,049
Exports	2,185
Imports	2,718
Budget balance	−1,227

Multiple-Choice Questions

1. The difference between tax revenue and government spending is equal to
   a. the budget balance.
   b. national savings.
   c. net exports.
   d. the trade balance.
   e. investment spending.

2. If government savings is positive, then
   a. tax revenues exceed government spending.
   b. net exports must be positive.
   c. national savings must be greater than investment spending.
   d. there is a trade surplus.
   e. the budget balance is negative.

3. In an open economy
   a. national savings is equal to investment spending.
   b. national savings is equal to net capital inflow.
   c. net capital inflow is equal to investment spending.
   d. there is a budget deficit.
   e. investment spending is equal to national savings plus net capital inflow.

4. If national savings is less than investment spending, then
   a. net capital inflow is positive.
   b. net capital inflow is negative.
   c. there is a budget deficit.
   d. there is a budget surplus.
   e. there is a trade surplus.

5. The federal government is said to be "dissaving" when
   a. there is a budget deficit.
   b. there is a budget surplus.
   c. there is no budget surplus or deficit.
   d. savings does not equal investment spending.
   e. national savings equals private savings.

Critical-Thinking Question

Identify and describe the relationship between national savings, investment spending, and net capital inflow in an open economy.

PITFALLS

INVESTMENT VS. INVESTMENT SPENDING

? What is the difference between investment and investment spending?

> WHEN ECONOMISTS USE THE TERM *INVESTMENT SPENDING*, THEY ALMOST ALWAYS MEAN "SPENDING ON NEW PHYSICAL CAPITAL." This can be confusing, because in ordinary life we often say that someone who buys stocks or purchases an existing building is "investing." The important point to keep in mind is that only spending that adds to the economy's stock of physical capital is "investment spending." In contrast, the act of purchasing an asset such as a share of stock, a bond, or existing real estate is "making an investment."

To learn more, see pages 206–207.

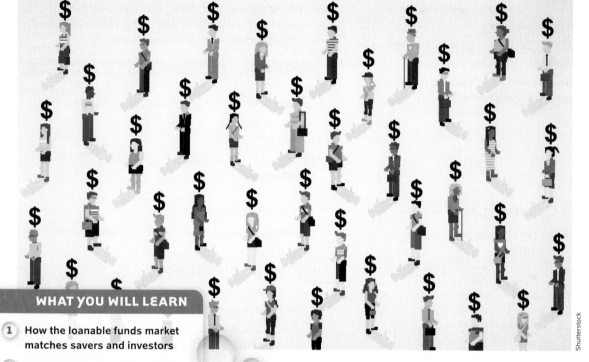

Shutterstock

The Role of the Loanable Funds Market

For the economy as a whole, savings always equals investment spending. In a closed economy, savings is equal to national savings. In an open economy, savings is equal to national savings plus capital inflow. At any given time, however, savers, the people with funds to lend, are usually not the same as borrowers, the people who want to borrow to finance their investment spending. How are savers and borrowers brought together?

Savers and borrowers are matched up with one another in much the same way producers and consumers are matched up: through markets governed by supply and demand. In Figure 10-2, the expanded circular-flow diagram on page 107, we noted that the *financial markets* channel the savings of households to businesses that want to borrow in order to purchase capital equipment. It's now time to take a look at how those financial markets work.

Although there are a large number of different financial markets in the financial system, such as the bond market and the stock market, economists often work with a simplified model in which they assume that there is just one market. The market brings together those who want to lend money (savers) and those who want to borrow (firms with investment spending projects). This hypothetical market is known as the **loanable funds market.**

The price that is determined in the loanable funds market is the interest rate, denoted by *r*. As we've learned, loans typically specify a nominal interest rate. So although we call *r* "the interest rate," it is with the understanding that *r* is a nominal interest rate—an interest rate that is unadjusted for inflation.

In the interest of simplicity we are also going to assume that there is only one type of loan. This, despite the fact that in reality there are many different kinds of interest

The **loanable funds market** is a hypothetical market that illustrates the market outcome of the demand for funds generated by borrowers and the supply of funds provided by lenders.

rates because there are many different kinds of loans—short-term loans, long-term loans, loans made to corporate borrowers, loans made to governments, and so on.

Now we're ready to analyze how savings and investment get matched up.

The Demand for Loanable Funds

Figure 21-1 illustrates a hypothetical demand curve for loanable funds, D, which slopes downward. On the horizontal axis we show the quantity of loanable funds demanded. On the vertical axis we show the interest rate, which is the "price" of borrowing. But why does the demand curve for loanable funds slope downward?

To answer this question, consider what a firm is doing when it engages in investment spending—say, by buying new equipment. Investment spending means laying out money right now, expecting that this outlay will lead to higher profits at some point in the future. In fact, however, the promise of a dollar five or ten years from now is worth less than an actual dollar right now.

So an investment is worth making only if it generates a future return that is *greater* than the monetary cost of making the investment today. How much greater? To answer that, we need to take into account the *present value* of the future return the firm expects to get.

We will look at the concept of present value in more detail in the next module. For now, keep in mind that in present value calculations, we use the interest rate to determine how the value of a dollar in the future compares to the value of a dollar today. But the fact is that future dollars are worth less than a dollar today, and they are worth even less when the interest rate is higher.

The intuition behind present value calculations is simple. The interest rate measures the opportunity cost of investment spending that results in a future return: instead of spending money on an investment spending project, a company could simply put the money into the bank and earn interest on it. And the higher the interest rate, the more attractive it is to simply put money into the bank instead of investing it in an investment spending project. In other words, the higher the interest rate, the higher the opportunity cost of investment spending. And, the higher the opportunity cost of investment spending, the lower the number of investment spending projects firms want to carry out, and therefore the lower the quantity of loanable funds demanded. It is this insight that explains why the demand curve for loanable funds is downward sloping.

When firms invest in projects, they spend money today in return for an expected payoff in the future.

FIGURE

21-1 The Demand for Loanable Funds

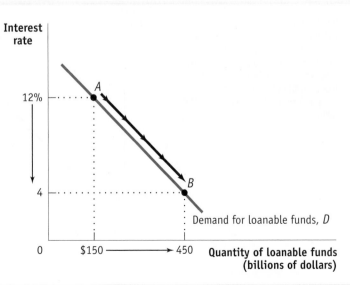

The demand curve for loanable funds slopes downward: the lower the interest rate, the greater the quantity of loanable funds demanded. Here, reducing the interest rate from 12% to 4% increases the quantity of loanable funds demanded from $150 billion to $450 billion.

When businesses engage in investment spending, they spend money right now in return for an expected payoff in the future. So, to evaluate whether a particular investment spending project is worth undertaking, a business must compare the present value of the future payoff with the current cost of that project. If the present value of the future payoff is greater than the current cost, a project is profitable and worth investing in. If the interest rate falls, then the present value of any given project rises, so more projects pass that test. If the interest rate rises, then the present value of any given project falls, so fewer projects pass that test.

So total investment spending, and therefore the demand for loanable funds to finance that spending, is negatively related to the interest rate. Thus, the demand curve for loanable funds slopes downward. You can see this in Figure 21-1. When the interest rate falls from 12% to 4%, the quantity of loanable funds demanded rises from $150 billion (point *A*) to $450 billion (point *B*).

The Supply of Loanable Funds

Figure 21-2 shows a hypothetical supply curve for loanable funds, *S*. Again, the interest rate plays the same role that the price plays in ordinary supply and demand analysis. But why is this curve upward sloping?

The answer is that loanable funds are supplied by savers, and savers incur an opportunity cost when they lend to a business: the funds could instead be spent on consumption—say, a nice vacation. Whether a given saver becomes a lender by making funds available to borrowers depends on the interest rate received in return. By saving your money today and earning interest on it, you are rewarded with higher consumption in the future when the loan you made is repaid with interest.

So it is a good assumption that more people will forgo current consumption and make a loan to a borrower when the interest rate is higher. As a result, our hypothetical supply curve of loanable funds slopes upward. In Figure 21-2, lenders will supply $150 billion to the loanable funds market at an interest rate of 4% (point *X*); if the interest rate rises to 12%, the quantity of loanable funds supplied will rise to $450 billion (point *Y*).

Savers supply loanable funds to businesses and incur an opportunity cost in doing so.

Hemera/Thinkstock

FIGURE 21-2   The Supply of Loanable Funds

The supply curve for loanable funds slopes upward: the higher the interest rate, the greater the quantity of loanable funds supplied. Here, increasing the interest rate from 4% to 12% increases the quantity of loanable funds supplied from $150 billion to $450 billion.

The Equilibrium Interest Rate

The interest rate at which the quantity of loanable funds supplied equals the quantity of loanable funds demanded is the *equilibrium interest rate*. As you can see in Figure 21-3, the equilibrium interest rate, r^*, and the total quantity of lending, Q^*, are determined by the intersection of the supply and demand curves, at point E. Here, the equilibrium interest rate is 8%, at which $300 billion is lent and borrowed. In this equilibrium, only investment spending projects that are profitable if the interest rate is 8% or higher are funded.

Projects that are profitable only when the interest rate falls below 8% are not funded. Correspondingly, only lenders who are willing to accept an interest rate of 8% or less will have their offers to lend funds accepted; lenders who demand an interest rate higher than 8% do not have their offers to lend accepted.

Figure 21-3 shows how the market for loanable funds matches up desired savings with desired investment spending: in equilibrium, the quantity of funds that savers want to lend is equal to the quantity of funds that firms want to borrow. The figure also shows that this match-up is efficient, in two senses. First, the right investments get made: the investment spending projects that are actually financed have higher payoffs (in terms of present value) than those that do not get financed. Second, the right people do the saving and lending: the savers who actually lend funds are willing to lend for lower interest rates than those who do not.

The insight that the loanable funds market leads to an efficient use of savings, although drawn from a highly simplified model, has important implications for real life: it is the reason that a well-functioning financial system increases an economy's long-run economic growth rate.

Let's look at how the market for loanable funds responds to shifts of demand and supply. As in the standard model of supply and demand, where the equilibrium price changes in response to shifts of the demand or supply curves, here the equilibrium interest rate changes when there are shifts of the demand curve for loanable funds, the supply curve for loanable funds, or both.

FIGURE 21-3   Equilibrium in the Loanable Funds Market

At the equilibrium interest rate, the quantity of loanable funds supplied equals the quantity of loanable funds demanded. Here, the equilibrium interest rate is 8%, with $300 billion of funds lent and borrowed. Lenders who demand an interest rate of 8% or lower have their offers of loans accepted; those who demand a higher interest rate do not. Projects that are profitable at an interest rate of 8% or higher are funded; those that are profitable only when the interest rate falls below 8% are not.

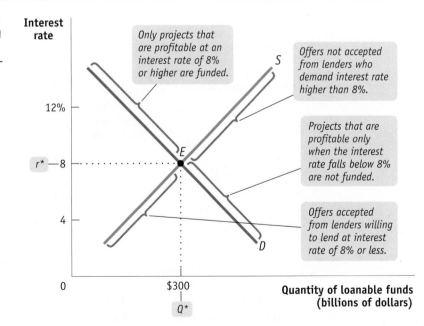

Shifts of the Demand for Loanable Funds

Let's start by looking at the causes and effects of changes in demand.

The factors that can cause the demand curve for loanable funds to shift include the following:

1. *Changes in perceived business opportunities.* A change in beliefs about the payoff of investment spending can increase or reduce the amount of desired spending at any given interest rate. If there is great excitement over the business possibilities created by new technology, as there was when the Internet came into wide use in the 1990s, businesses will rush to buy computer equipment, put fiber-optic cables in the ground, and so on, shifting the demand for loanable funds to the right. But if there is disillusionment with technology-related investment, as there was in 2001 when many dot-com businesses failed, the demand for loanable funds will shift back to the left.

2. *Changes in government borrowing.* A government runs a budget deficit when, in a given year, it spends more than it receives. Running budget deficits can be a major source of demand for loanable funds, with the result that changes in the government budget deficit can shift the demand curve for loanable funds. For example, between 2000 and 2003, as the U.S. federal government went from a budget surplus to a budget deficit, the government went from being a net saver that provided loanable funds to the market to being a net borrower, borrowing funds from the market. In 2000, net federal borrowing was *minus* $189 billion, as the federal government was paying off some of its pre-existing debt. But by 2003, net federal borrowing was *plus* $416 billion because the government had to borrow large sums to pay its bills. This change had the effect, other things equal, of shifting the demand curve for loanable funds to the right.

Figure 21-4 shows the effects of an increase in the demand for loanable funds. S is the supply of loanable funds, and D_1 is the initial demand curve. The initial equilibrium interest rate is r_1. An increase in the demand for loanable funds means that the quantity of funds demanded rises at any given interest rate, so the demand curve shifts rightward to D_2. As a result, the equilibrium interest rate rises to r_2.

FIGURE   21-4   An Increase in the Demand for Loanable Funds

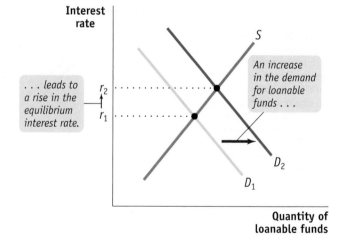

If the quantity of funds demanded by borrowers rises at any given interest rate, the demand for loanable funds shifts rightward from D_1 to D_2. As a result, the equilibrium interest rate rises from r_1 to r_2.

The fact that an increase in the demand for loanable funds leads, other things equal, to a rise in the interest rate has one especially important implication: it tells us that increasing or persistent government budget deficits are cause for concern because an increase in the government's deficit shifts the demand curve for loanable funds to the right, which leads to a higher interest rate. If the interest rate rises, businesses will cut back on their investment spending.

So, other things equal, a rise in the government budget deficit tends to reduce overall investment spending. Economists call the negative effect of government budget deficits on investment spending **crowding out.** Concerns about crowding out are one key reason to worry about increasing or persistent budget deficits.

However, it's important to add a qualification here: crowding out may not occur if the economy is depressed. When the economy is operating far below full employment, government spending can lead to higher incomes; and these higher incomes lead to increased savings at any given interest rate. Higher savings allows the government to borrow without raising interest rates. Many economists believe, for example, that the large budget deficits that the U.S. government ran from 2008 to 2013, in the face of a depressed economy, caused little if any crowding out.

> **Crowding out** occurs when a government budget deficit drives up the interest rate and leads to reduced investment spending.

Shifts of the Supply of Loanable Funds

Like the demand for loanable funds, the supply of loanable funds can shift. Among the factors that can cause the supply of loanable funds to shift are the following:

1. *Changes in private savings behavior.* A number of factors can cause the level of private savings to change at any given interest rate. For example, rising home prices in the United States will make many homeowners feel richer, leading them to spend more and save less. This will have the effect of shifting the supply curve of loanable funds to the left.

2. *Changes in net capital inflows.* Capital flows into and out of a country can change as investors' perceptions of that country change. For example, Greece experienced large net capital inflows after the creation of the euro, Europe's common currency, in 1999, because investors believed that Greece's adoption of the euro as its currency had made it a safe place to put their funds. But, in the years that followed, worries about the Greek government's solvency (and the discovery that it had been understating its debt) led to a collapse in investor confidence, and the net inflow of funds dried up. The effect of shrinking capital inflows was to shift the supply curve in the Greek loanable funds market to the left.

Figure 21-5 shows the effects of an increase in the supply of loanable funds. D is the demand for loanable funds, and S_1 is the initial supply curve. The initial equilibrium interest rate is r_1. An increase in the supply of loanable funds means that the quantity of funds supplied rises at any given interest rate, so the supply curve shifts rightward to S_2. As a result, the equilibrium interest rate falls to r_2.

FIGURE 21-5   An Increase in the Supply of Loanable Funds

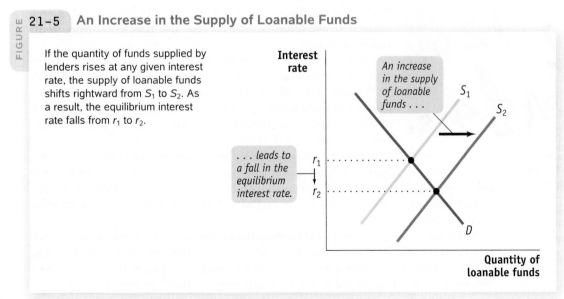

If the quantity of funds supplied by lenders rises at any given interest rate, the supply of loanable funds shifts rightward from S_1 to S_2. As a result, the equilibrium interest rate falls from r_1 to r_2.

Inflation and Interest Rates

Anything that shifts either the supply of loanable funds curve or the demand for loanable funds curve changes the interest rate. Historically, major changes in interest rates have been driven by many factors, including changes in government policy and technological innovations that created new investment opportunities.

However, arguably the most important factor affecting interest rates over time—the reason, for example, that interest rates today are much lower than they were in the late 1970s and early 1980s—is changing expectations about future inflation, which shift both the supply and the demand for loanable funds.

To understand the effect of expected future inflation on interest rates, let's look at an example: in the 1970s and 1980s higher than expected U.S. inflation reduced the real value of homeowners' mortgages, which was good for the homeowners but bad for the banks. Economists summarize the effect of inflation on borrowers and lenders by distinguishing between the *nominal interest rate* and the *real interest rate*, where the difference is:

$$\text{Real interest rate} = \text{Nominal interest rate} - \text{Inflation rate}$$

The true cost of borrowing is the real interest rate, not the nominal interest rate.

To see why, suppose a firm borrows $10,000 for one year at a 10% nominal interest rate. At the end of the year, it must repay $11,000—the amount borrowed plus the interest. But suppose that over the course of the year the average level of prices increases by 10%, so that the real interest rate is zero. Then the $11,000 repayment has the same purchasing power as the original $10,000 loan. In real terms, the borrower has received a zero-interest loan.

Similarly, the true payoff to lending is the real interest rate, not the nominal rate. Suppose that a bank makes a $10,000 loan for one year at a 10% nominal interest rate. At the end of the year, the bank receives an $11,000 repayment. But if the average level of prices rises by 10% per year, the purchasing power of the money the bank gets back is no more than that of the money it lent out. In real terms, the bank has made a zero-interest loan.

Now we can add an important detail to our analysis of the loanable funds market. Figures 21-4 and 21-5 are drawn with the vertical axis measuring the *nominal interest rate for a given expected future inflation rate.* Why do we use the nominal interest rate rather than the real interest rate? Because in the real world neither borrowers nor lenders know what the future inflation rate will be when they make a deal.

Actual loan contracts therefore specify a nominal interest rate rather than a real interest rate. Because we are holding the expected future inflation rate fixed in Figures 21-4 and 21-5, however, changes in the nominal interest rate also lead to changes in the real interest rate.

The expectations of borrowers and lenders about future inflation rates are normally based on recent experience. In the late 1970s, after a decade of high inflation, borrowers and lenders expected future inflation to be high. By the late 1990s, after a decade of fairly low inflation, borrowers and lenders expected future inflation to be low.

Changing expectations about future inflation is the most important factor affecting interest rates over time.

These changing expectations about future inflation had a strong effect on the nominal interest rate, largely explaining why nominal interest rates were much lower in the early years of the twenty-first century than they were in the early 1980s. Let's look at how changes in the expected future rate of inflation are reflected in the loanable funds model.

In Figure 21-6, the curves S_0 and D_0 show the supply and demand for loanable funds given that the expected future rate of inflation is 0%. In that case, equilibrium is at E_0 and the equilibrium nominal interest rate is 4%. Because expected future inflation is 0%, the equilibrium expected real interest rate over the life of the loan is also 4%.

FIGURE 21-6   The Fisher Effect

D_0 and S_0 are the demand and supply curves for loanable funds when the expected future inflation rate is 0%. At an expected inflation rate of 0%, the equilibrium nominal interest rate is 4%. An increase in expected future inflation pushes both the demand and supply curves upward by 1 percentage point for every percentage point increase in expected future inflation. D_{10} and S_{10} are the demand and supply curves for loanable funds when the expected future inflation rate is 10%. The 10 percentage point increase in expected future inflation raises the equilibrium nominal interest rate to 14%. The expected real interest rate remains at 4%, and the equilibrium quantity of loanable funds also remains unchanged.

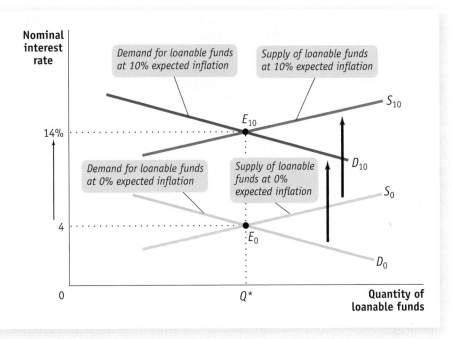

Now suppose that the expected future inflation rate rises to 10%. The demand curve for loanable funds shifts upward to D_{10}: borrowers are now willing to borrow as much at a nominal interest rate of 14% as they were previously willing to borrow at 4%. That's because with a 10% inflation rate, a 14% nominal interest rate corresponds to a 4% real interest rate.

Similarly, the supply curve of loanable funds shifts upward to S_{10}: lenders require a nominal interest rate of 14% to persuade them to lend as much as they would previously have lent at 4%. The new equilibrium is at E_{10}: the result of an expected future inflation rate of 10% is that the equilibrium nominal interest rate rises from 4% to 14%.

This situation can be summarized as a general principle, known as the **Fisher effect,** which states that *the expected real interest rate is unaffected by changes in expected future inflation.* According to the Fisher effect, an increase in expected future inflation drives up the nominal interest rate, where each additional percentage point of expected future inflation drives up the nominal interest rate by 1 percentage point.

The central point is that both lenders and borrowers base their decisions on the expected real interest rate. As a result, a change in the expected rate of inflation does not affect the equilibrium quantity of loanable funds or the expected real interest rate; all it affects is the equilibrium nominal interest rate.

ECONOMICS ▶ IN ACTION

FIFTY YEARS OF FLUCTUATIONS IN U.S. INTEREST RATES

There have been some large movements in U.S. interest rates over the past half-century. These movements clearly show how both changes in expected future inflation and changes in the expected return on investment spending move interest rates.

Panel (a) of Figure 21-7 illustrates the first effect. It shows the average interest rate on bonds issued by the U.S. government—specifically, bonds for which the government promises to repay the full amount after 10 years—from 1960 to 2012, along with the rate of consumer price inflation over the same period. As you can see, the big story about interest rates is the way they soared in the 1970s, before coming back down in the 1980s.

According to the **Fisher effect,** an increase in expected future inflation drives up the nominal interest rate, leaving the expected real interest rate unchanged.

FIGURE **21-7   Changes in U.S. Interest Rates Over Time**

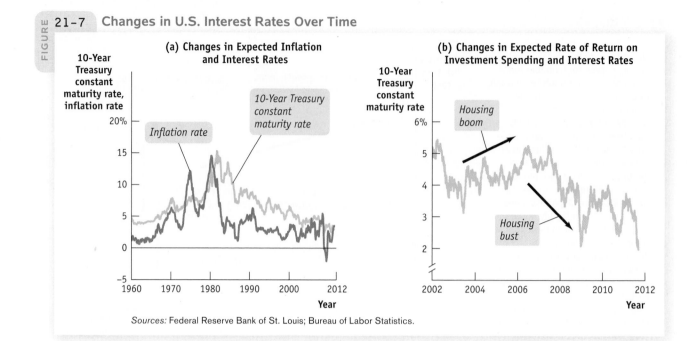

Sources: Federal Reserve Bank of St. Louis; Bureau of Labor Statistics.

It's not hard to see why that happened: inflation shot up during the 1970s, leading to widespread expectations that high inflation would continue. And as we've seen, expected inflation raises the equilibrium interest rate. As inflation came down in the 1980s, so did expectations of future inflation, and this brought interest rates down as well.

Panel (b) illustrates the second effect: changes in the expected return on investment spending and interest rates, with a "close-up" of interest rates from 2002 to 2012. Notice the rise in interest rates during the middle years of the last decade, followed by a sharp drop. We know from other evidence (such as surveys of investor opinion) that expected inflation didn't change much over those years.

What happened, instead, was the boom and bust in housing: interest rates rose as demand for housing soared, pushing the demand curve for loanable funds to the right, then fell as the housing boom collapsed, shifting the demand curve for loanable funds back to the left. Throughout this whole process, total savings was equal to total investment spending, and the rise and fall of the interest rate played a key role in matching lenders with borrowers.

MODULE

21 Review

Solutions appear at the back of the book.

Check Your Understanding

1. Use a diagram of the loanable funds market to illustrate the effect of the following events on the equilibrium interest rate and investment spending.

   a. An economy is opened to international movements of capital, and a net capital inflow occurs.

   b. Retired people generally save less than working people at any interest rate. The proportion of retired people in the population goes up.

2. Explain what is wrong with the following statement: "Savings and investment spending may not be equal in

the economy as a whole because when the interest rate rises, households will want to save more money than businesses will want to invest."

3. Suppose that expected inflation rises from 3% to 6%.

   a. How will the real interest rate be affected by this change?

   b. How will the nominal interest rate be affected by this change?

   c. What will happen to the equilibrium quantity of loanable funds?

Multiple-Choice Questions

1. If the interest rate falls, then the present value of any given project _____ and total investment spending will _____.
   a. rises : remain unchanged
   b. rises : decrease
   c. falls : decrease
   d. falls : increase
   e. rises : increase

2. The real interest rate equals the
   a. nominal interest rate plus the inflation rate.
   b. nominal interest rate minus the inflation rate.
   c. nominal interest rate divided by the inflation rate.
   d. nominal interest rate times the inflation rate.
   e. federal funds rate.

3. Which of the following will increase the demand for loanable funds?
   a. a federal government budget surplus
   b. an increase in perceived business opportunities
   c. a decrease in the interest rate
   d. positive capital inflows
   e. decreased private saving rates

4. Which of the following will increase the supply of loanable funds?
   a. an increase in perceived business opportunities
   b. decreased government borrowing
   c. an increased private saving rate
   d. an increase in the expected inflation rate
   e. a decrease in capital inflows

5. Both lenders and borrowers base their decisions on
   a. expected real interest rates.
   b. expected nominal interest rates.
   c. real interest rates.
   d. nominal interest rates.
   e. nominal interest rates minus real interest rates.

Critical-Thinking Questions

Does each of the following affect either the supply or the demand for loanable funds, and if so, does the affected curve increase (shift to the right) or decrease (shift to the left)?

1. There is an increase in capital inflows into the economy.

2. Businesses are pessimistic about future business conditions.

3. The government increases borrowing.

4. The private savings rate decreases.

Shutterstock

WHAT YOU WILL LEARN

1. Why a dollar today is worth more than a dollar a year from now

2. How the concept of present value can help individuals and firms make decisions when costs or benefits occur in the future

In the previous module we learned that *present value* helps to explain why the demand curve for loanable funds slopes downward. In this module, we'll look more closely at present value, and consider how it is put to use by individuals and firms when making financial decisions.

The Concept of Present Value

Individuals and firms are often faced with financial decisions that will have consequences long into the future. For example, when you decided to attend college, you committed yourself to years of study, which you expect will pay off for the rest of your life. So the decision to attend college is a decision to embark on a long-term project.

The basic rule in deciding whether or not to undertake a project is that you should compare the benefits of that project with its costs, implicit as well as explicit. But making these comparisons can sometimes be difficult because the benefits and costs of a project may not arrive at the same time.

This is true of the saving and investment decisions made by individuals: these decisions also have benefits and costs that do not arrive at the same time. For example, if you save more today the benefit is that you will earn interest and have more accumulated wealth at a later date. The cost is that you have less income available for consumption today.

Likewise, when a firm decides to invest in new physical capital today, it is anticipating benefits like increased output, productivity, and profit that will come later, possibly much later. But how, specifically, is time an issue in economic decision making?

Borrowing, Lending, and Interest

In general, having a dollar today is worth more than having a dollar a year from now. To see why, let's consider two examples.

First, suppose that you get a new job that comes with a $1,000 bonus, which will be paid at the end of the first year. But you would like to spend the extra money now—say, on new clothes for work. Can you do that?

The answer is yes—you can borrow money today and use the bonus to repay the debt a year from now. But if that is your plan, you cannot borrow the full $1,000 today. You must borrow *less* than that because a year from now you will have to repay the amount borrowed *plus interest*.

Now consider a different scenario. Suppose that you are paid a bonus of $1,000 today, and you decide that you don't want to spend the money until a year from now. What do you do with it? You may decide to put it in the bank; in effect, you would be lending the $1,000 to the bank, which in turn lends it out to its customers who wish to borrow. At the end of a year, you will get *more* than $1,000 back—you will receive the $1,000 plus the interest earned.

All of this means that having $1,000 today is worth more than having $1,000 a year from now. As any borrower and lender know, this is what allows a lender to charge a borrower interest on a loan: borrowers are willing to pay interest in order to have money today rather than waiting until they acquire that money later on.

Most interest rates are stated as the percentage of the borrowed amount that must be paid to the lender for each year of the loan. Whether money is actually borrowed for 1 month or 10 years, and regardless of the amount, the same principle applies: money in your pocket today is worth more than money in your pocket tomorrow. To keep things simple in the discussions that follow, we'll restrict ourselves to examples of 1-year loans of $1.

Because the value of money depends on when it is paid or received, you can't evaluate a project by simply adding up the costs and benefits when those costs and benefits arrive at different times. You must take time into account when evaluating the project because $1 that is paid to you today is worth more than $1 that is paid to you a year from now. Similarly, $1 that you must pay today is more burdensome than $1 that you must pay next year.

Fortunately, there is a simple way to adjust for these complications so that we can correctly compare the value of dollars received and paid out at different times.

Next we'll see how the interest rate can be used to convert future benefits and costs into what economists call *present values*. By using present values when evaluating a project, you can evaluate a project *as if* all relevant costs and benefits were occurring today rather than at different times. This allows people to "factor out" the complications created by time. We'll start by defining the concept of present value.

Having a dollar today is worth more than having a dollar a year from now.

Defining Present Value

The key to the concept of present value is to understand that the interest rate can be used to compare the value of a dollar realized today with the value of a dollar realized later. Why the interest rate? Because the interest rate correctly measures the cost of delaying the receipt of a dollar of benefit and, correspondingly, the benefit of delaying the payment of a dollar of cost.

Let's illustrate this with some examples.

Suppose that you are evaluating whether or not to take a job in which your employer promises to pay you a bonus at the end of the first year. What is the value to you today of $1 of bonus money to be paid one year in the future? A slightly different way of asking the same

iStockphoto/Thinkstock

The **present value** of $1 realized one year from now is equal to $1/(1 + r): the amount of money you must lend out today in order to have $1 in one year. It is the value to you today of $1 realized one year from now.

question: what amount would you be willing to accept today as a substitute for receiving $1 one year from now?

To answer this question, begin by observing that you need *less* than $1 today in order to be assured of having $1 one year from now. Why? Because any money that you have today can be lent out at interest—say, by depositing it in a bank account so that the bank can then lend it out to its borrowers. This turns any amount you have today into a greater sum at the end of the year.

Let's work this out mathematically. We'll use the symbol r to represent the interest rate, expressed in decimal terms—that is, if the interest rate is 10%, then $r = 0.10$. If you lend out $X, at the end of a year you will receive your $X back, plus the interest on your $X, which is $X \times r$. Thus, at the end of the year you will receive:

(22-1) Amount received one year from now as a result of lending $X today:
$$\$X + \$X \times r = \$X \times (1 + r)$$

The next step is to find out how much you would have to lend out today to have $1 a year from now. To do that, we just need to set Equation 22-1 equal to $1 and solve for $X. That is, we solve the following equation for $X:

(22-2) Condition satisfied when $1 is received one year from now as a result of lending $X today:
$$\$X \times (1 + r) = \$1$$

Rearranging Equation 22-2 to solve for $X, the amount you need today in order to receive $1 one year from now is:

(22-3) Amount lent today in order to receive $1 one year from now:
$$\$X = \$1/(1 + r)$$

This means that you would be willing to accept today the amount $X defined by Equation 22-3 for every $1 to be paid to you one year from now. The reason is that if you were to lend out $X today, you would be assured of receiving $1 one year from now. Returning to our original question, this also means that if someone promises to pay you a sum of money one year in the future, you are willing to accept $X today in place of every $1 to be paid one year from now.

Now let's solve Equation 22-3 for the value of $X. To do this we simply need to use the actual value of r (a value determined by the financial markets). Let's assume that the actual value of r is 10%, which means that $r = 0.10$. In that case:

(22-4) Value of $X when $r = 0.10$: $\$X = \$1/(1 + 0.10) = \$1/1.10 = \$0.91$

So you would be willing to accept $0.91 today in exchange for every $1 to be paid to you one year from now. Economists refer to $X as the **present value** of $1. Note that the present value of any given amount will change as the interest rate changes.

The present value of a given amount will change as the interest rate changes.

To see that this technique works for evaluating future costs as well as evaluating future benefits, consider the following example. Suppose you enter into an agreement that obliges you to pay $1 one year from now—say, to pay off a car loan from your parents when you graduate in a year. How much money would you need today to ensure that you have $1 in a year? The answer is $X, the present value of $1, which in our example is $0.91.

The reason $0.91 is the right answer is that if you lend it out for one year at an interest rate of 10%, you will receive $1 in return at the end. So if, for example, you must pay back $5,000 one year from now, then you need to deposit $5,000 × 0.91 = $4,550 into a bank account today earning an interest rate of 10% in order to have $5,000 one year from now. (There is a slight discrepancy due to rounding.) In other words, today you need to have the present value of $5,000, which equals $4,550, in order to be assured of paying off your debt in a year.

These examples show us that the present value concept provides a way to calculate the value today of $1 that is realized in a year—regardless of whether that $1 is realized as a benefit (the bonus) or a cost (the car loan payback). To evaluate a project today that has benefits, costs, or both to be realized in a year, we just use the relevant interest rate to convert those future dollars into their present values. In that way we have "factored out" the complication that time creates for decision making.

Below we will use the present value concept to evaluate a project. But before we do that, it is worthwhile to note that the present value method can be used for projects in which the $1 is realized more than a year later—say, two, three, or even more years. Let's consider a project that will pay $1 *two* years from today. What is the value to you today of $1 received two years into the future? We can find the answer to that question by expanding our formula for present value.

Let's call $V the amount of money that would need to be lent today at an interest rate of r in order to have $1 in two years. So if an individual or firm lends $V today, it will receive $V \times (1 + r)$ in one year. And if it *relends* that sum for another year, it will receive $V \times (1 + r) \times (1 + r) = $V \times (1 + r)^2$ at the end of the second year. At the end of two years, $V will be worth $V \times (1 + r)^2$. In other words:

(22-5) Amount received in one year from lending $V = $V \times (1 + r)$

Amount received in two years from lending $V = $V \times (1 + r) \times (1 + r) = $V \times (1 + r)^2$ and so on. For example, if $r = 0.10$, then $V \times (1.10)^2 = $V \times 1.21$.

Now we are ready to answer the question of what $1 realized two years in the future is worth today. In order for the amount lent today, $V, to be worth $1 two years from now, it must satisfy this formula:

(22-6) Condition satisfied when $1 is received two years from now as a result of lending $V today:
$$\$V \times (1 + r)^2 = \$1$$

Rearranging Equation 22-6, we can solve for $V:

(22-7) Amount lent today in order to receive $1 two years from now:
$$\$V = \$1/(1 + r)^2$$

Given $r = 0.10$ and using Equation 22-7, we arrive at $V = $1/1.21 = $0.83. So, when the interest rate is 10%, $1 realized two years from today is worth $0.83 today because by lending out $0.83 today the individual or firm can be assured of having $1 in two years. And that means that the present value of $1 realized two years into the future is $0.83.

(22-8) Present value of $1 realized two years from now:
$$\$V = \$1/(1.10)^2 = \$1/1.21 = \$0.83$$

From this example we can see how the present value concept can be expanded to a number of years even greater than two. If we ask what the present value is of $1 realized any number of years, represented by N, into the future, the answer is given by a generalization of the present value formula: it is equal to $\$1/(1 + r)^N$.

Using Present Value

Suppose an individual or firm has to choose one of three hypothetical projects to undertake. Project A costs nothing and has an immediate payoff of $100. Project B requires a payment of $10 today in order to receive $115 a year from now. Project C offers an immediate payoff of $119 but requires a payment of $20 a year from now. We'll assume that the annual interest rate is 10%—that is, $r = 0.10$.

The problem in evaluating these three projects is that their costs and benefits are realized at different times. That is, of course, where the concept of present value becomes extremely helpful: by using present value to convert any dollars realized in the future into today's value, we factor out the issue of time. Appropriate comparisons can be made using the **net present value** of a project—the present value of current and future benefits minus the present value of current and future costs. The best project to undertake is the one with the highest net present value.

The **net present value** of a project is the present value of current and future benefits minus the present value of current and future costs.

TABLE 22-1

The Net Present Value of Three Hypothetical Projects

Project	Dollars realized today	Dollars realized one year from today	Present value formula	Net present value given $r = 0.10$
A	$100	—	$100	$100.00
B	–$10	$115	–$10 + $115/(1 + r)	$94.55
C	$119	–$20	119 – $20/(1 + r)	$100.82

Table 22-1 shows how to calculate net present value for each of the three projects. The second and third columns show how many dollars are realized and when they are realized; costs are indicated by a minus sign. The fourth column shows the equations used to convert the flows of dollars into their present value, and the fifth column shows the actual amounts of the total net present value for each of the three projects.

For instance, to calculate the net present value of project B, we need to calculate the present value of $115 received in one year. The present value of $1 received in one year would be $1/(1 + r)$. So the present value of $115 is equal to $115 \times \$1/(1 + r)$; that is, $\$115/(1 + r)$. The net present value of project B is the present value of today's and future benefits minus the present value of today's and future costs: $-\$10 + \$115/(1 + r)$.

From the fifth column, we can immediately see which is the preferred project—it is project C. That's because it has the highest net present value, $100.82, which is higher than the net present value of project A ($100) and much higher than the net present value of project B ($94.55).

This example shows how important the concept of present value is. If we had failed to use the present value calculations and instead simply added up the dollars generated by each of the three projects, we could have easily been misled into believing that project B was the best project and project C was the worst.

ΕCONOMICS ▶ IN ACTION

HOW BIG IS THAT JACKPOT, ANYWAY?

For a clear example of present value at work, consider the case of lottery jackpots.

On March 30, 2012, Mega Millions set a record for the largest jackpot ever in North America, with a payout of $656 million. Well, sort of. That $656 million was available only if the winner chose to take his or her winnings in the form of an "annuity," consisting of an annual payment for the next 26 years. If the winner wanted cash up front, the jackpot was only $474 million and change.

Why was Mega Millions so stingy about quick payoffs? It was all a matter of present value. If the winner had been willing to take the annuity, the lottery would have invested the jackpot money, buying U.S. government bonds (in effect lending the money to the federal government). The money would have been invested in such a way that the investments would pay just enough to cover the annuity. This worked, of course, because at the interest rates prevailing at the time, the present value of a $656 million annuity spread over 26 years was just about $474 million. To put it another way, the opportunity cost to the lottery of that annuity in present value terms was $474 million.

So why didn't they just call it a $474 million jackpot? Well, $656 million sounds more impressive! But receiving $656 million over 26 years is essentially the same as receiving $474 million today.

22 Review

MODULE

Check Your Understanding

1. Consider the three hypothetical projects shown in Table 22-1. This time, however, suppose that the interest rate is only 2%.

   a. Calculate the net present values of the three projects. Which one is now preferred?

   b. Explain why the preferred choice with a 2% interest rate differs from one with a 10% interest rate.

Multiple-Choice Questions

1. Suppose, for simplicity, that a bank uses a single interest rate for loans and deposits, there is no inflation, and all unspent money is deposited in the bank. The interest rate measures which of the following?

   I. the cost of using a dollar today rather than a year from now

   II. the benefit of delaying the use of a dollar from today until a year from now

   III. the price of borrowing money calculated as a percentage of the amount borrowed

   a. I only

   b. II only

   c. III only

   d. I and II only

   e. I, II, and III

2. If the interest rate is zero, then the present value of a dollar received at the end of the year is

   a. more than $1.

   b. equal to $1.

   c. less than $1.

   d. zero.

   e. infinite.

3. If the interest rate is 10%, the present value of $1 paid to an individual or firm one year from now is

   a. $0.

   b. $0.89.

   c. $0.91.

   d. $1.

   e. more than $1.

4. If the interest rate is 5%, the amount received one year from now as a result of lending $100 today is

   a. $90.

   b. $95.

   c. $100.

   d. $105.

   e. $110.

5. What is the present value of $100 realized two years from now if the interest rate is 10%?

   a. $80

   b. $83

   c. $90

   d. $100

   e. $110

Critical-Thinking Questions

1. What is the amount an individual or firm will receive in three years if it lends $1,000 at 5% interest?

2. What is the present value of $1,000 received in three years if the interest rate is 5%?

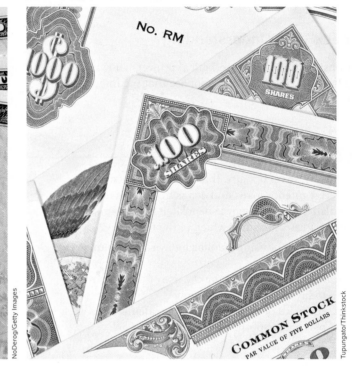

NoDerog/Getty Images

Tupungato/Thinkstock

WHAT YOU WILL LEARN

1 **The purpose of the four main types of financial assets: stocks, bonds, loans, and bank deposits**

2 **How financial intermediaries help investors achieve diversification**

3 **How financial fluctuations occur in the financial system**

Understanding the Financial System

A well-functioning financial system brings together the funds of investors with those looking to fund investment spending projects (making the rise of Facebook, as we saw in the section-opener, possible). Financial markets have been around for centuries. In fact, capital inflows financed the early economic development of the United States, through investment spending in mining, railroads, and canals. Let's begin by understanding exactly what is traded in financial markets.

Financial markets are where households invest their current savings and their accumulated savings, or **wealth,** by purchasing *financial assets*.

A **financial asset** is a paper claim that entitles the buyer to future income from the seller. For example, when a saver lends funds to a company, the loan is a financial asset sold by the company that entitles the lender (the buyer of the financial asset) to future income from the company.

A household can also invest its current savings or wealth by purchasing a **physical asset,** a tangible object that can be used to generate future income such as a preexisting house or preexisting piece of equipment. It gives the owner the right to dispose of the object as he or she wishes (for example, rent it or sell it).

If you get a loan from your local bank—say, to buy a new car—you and the bank are creating a financial asset: your loan. A *loan* is one important kind of financial asset in the real world, one that is owned by the lender—in this case, your local bank. In creating that loan, you and the bank are also creating a **liability,** a requirement to pay income in the future. So although your loan is a financial asset from the bank's point of view, it is a liability from your point of view: a requirement that you repay the loan, including any interest.

In addition to loans, there are three other important kinds of financial assets: stocks, bonds, and *bank deposits*. Because a financial asset is a claim to future in-

A household's **wealth** is the value of its accumulated savings.

A **financial asset** is a paper claim that entitles the buyer to future income from the seller.

A **physical asset** is a tangible object that can be used to generate future income.

A **liability** is a requirement to pay income in the future.

come that someone has to pay, it is also someone else's liability. We'll explain in detail shortly who bears the liability for each type of financial asset.

The four types of financial assets—loans, stocks, bonds, and bank deposits—exist because the economy has developed a set of specialized markets, like the stock market and the bond market, and specialized institutions, like banks, that facilitate the flow of funds from lenders to borrowers.

Earlier, in the context of the circular-flow diagram, we defined the financial markets and institutions that make up the financial system. A well-functioning financial system encourages greater savings and investment spending and ensures that both are undertaken efficiently. To understand how these processes occur, we need to know what tasks the financial system needs to accomplish. Then we can see how the job gets done.

Three Tasks of a Financial System

Our earlier analysis of the loanable funds market ignored three important problems facing borrowers and lenders: *transaction costs, risk,* and the desire for *liquidity.* The three tasks of a financial system are to reduce these problems in a cost-effective way. Doing so enhances the efficiency of financial markets, making it more likely that lenders and borrowers will make mutually beneficial trades that make society as a whole richer.

TASK 1: REDUCING TRANSACTION COSTS The expenses involved in actually putting together and executing a deal are known as **transaction costs.** For example, arranging a loan requires spending time and money negotiating the terms of the deal, verifying the borrower's ability to pay, drawing up and executing legal documents, and so on.

Suppose a large business decided that it wanted to raise $1 billion for investment spending. No individual would be willing to lend that much. And negotiating individual loans from thousands of different people, each willing to lend a modest amount, would impose very large total costs because each individual transaction would incur a cost, with the result that the entire deal would probably be unprofitable.

Fortunately, there is another option: when large businesses want to borrow money, they either go to a bank or sell bonds in the bond market. Obtaining a loan from a bank avoids large transaction costs because it involves only a single borrower and a single lender. We'll explain more about how bonds work shortly. For now, it is enough to know that the principal reason there is a bond market is that it allows companies to borrow large sums of money without incurring large transaction costs.

TASK 2: REDUCING RISK Another problem that real-world borrowers and lenders face is **financial risk,** or simply, *risk,* uncertainty about future outcomes that involve the potential for financial losses or gains. For example, owning and driving a car entails the financial risk of a costly accident.

Most people experience the loss in welfare from losing a given amount of money more intensely than they experience the increase in welfare from gaining the same amount of money. A person who is more sensitive to a loss than to a gain of an equal dollar amount is called *risk-averse.* Most people are risk-averse, although to differing degrees. For example, people who are wealthy are typically less risk-averse than those who are not so well-off.

A well-functioning financial system helps people reduce their exposure to risk, which risk-averse people prefer to do. Suppose the owner of a business expects to make a greater profit if she buys additional capital equipment, but she isn't completely sure that this will indeed happen. She could pay for the equipment by using her savings or selling her house. But if the profit is significantly less than expected, she will have lost her savings, or her house, or both.

So, being risk-averse, this business owner wants to share the risk of purchasing new capital equipment with someone, even if that requires sharing some of the profit

Transaction costs are the expenses of negotiating and executing a deal.

Financial risk is uncertainty about future outcomes that involve financial losses or gains.

An individual can engage in **diversification** by investing in several different assets so that the possible losses are independent events.

An asset is **liquid** if it can be quickly converted into cash with relatively little loss of value.

An asset is **illiquid** if it cannot be quickly converted into cash with relatively little loss of value.

if all goes well. How can she do this? By selling shares of her company to other people and using the money she receives from selling shares, rather than money from the sale of her other assets, to finance the equipment purchase.

By selling shares in her company, she reduces her personal losses if the profit is less than expected: she won't have lost her other assets. But if things go well, the shareholders earn a share of the profit as a return on their investment.

By selling a share of her business, the owner has also achieved *diversification:* she has been able to invest in a way that lowers her total risk. She has maintained her investment in her bank account, a financial asset; in ownership of her house, a physical asset; and in ownership of the unsold portion of her business, a financial asset. These investments are likely to carry some risk of their own; for example, her bank may fail or her house may burn down (though in the United States it is likely that she is partly protected against these risks by insurance).

But even in the absence of insurance, she is better off having maintained investments in these different assets because their different risks are *unrelated,* or *independent, events.* This means that her house is no more likely to burn down if her business does poorly and that her bank is no more likely to fail if her house burns down. To put it another way, if one asset performs poorly, it is very likely that her other assets will be unaffected and, as a result, her total risk of loss has been reduced. But if she had invested all her wealth in her business, she would have faced the prospect of losing everything if the business had performed poorly. By engaging in **diversification**— investing in several assets with unrelated, or independent, risks—our business owner has lowered her total risk of loss.

The desire to reduce total risk by engaging in diversification is why we have stocks and a stock market.

TASK 3: PROVIDING LIQUIDITY Financial systems also exist to provide investors with *liquidity,* a concern that—like risk—arises because the future is uncertain. Suppose that, having made a loan, a lender suddenly finds himself in need of cash—say, to meet a medical emergency. Unfortunately, if that loan was made to a business that used it to buy new equipment, the business cannot repay the loan on short notice to satisfy the lender's need to recover his money. Knowing in advance that there is a danger of needing to get his money back before the term of the loan is up, our lender might be reluctant to lock up his money by lending it to a business.

An asset is **liquid** if it can be quickly converted into cash with relatively little loss of value, **illiquid** if it cannot. As we'll see, stocks and bonds are a partial answer to the problem of liquidity. Banks provide an additional way for individuals to hold liquid assets and still finance illiquid investment spending projects.

Now that we've learned the three ways the financial system helps lenders and borrowers make mutually beneficial deals—by reducing transaction costs and risk, and by providing liquidity—we'll look at how it goes about achieving these tasks.

A loan is a financial asset to the issuer but a liability to the person taking it out.

Media Bakery

Types of Financial Assets

In the modern economy there are four main types of financial assets: *loans, bonds, stocks,* and *bank deposits.* In addition, financial innovation has allowed the creation of a wide range of *loan-backed securities.* Each serves a somewhat different purpose. We'll examine loans, bonds, stocks, and loan-backed securities now. Then we'll turn to the role played by bank deposits.

LOANS A lending agreement made between an individual lender and an individual borrower is a *loan.* Individuals are likely to encounter loans in the form of a student loan or a bank loan to finance the purchase of a car or a house. Small businesses usually use bank loans to buy new equipment.

On the positive side, loans are typically tailored to the needs of the borrower. Before a small business can get a loan, it usually has to discuss its business plans, its profits, and so on with the lender. This results in a loan that meets the borrower's needs and ability to pay.

On the negative side, making a loan to an individual person or a business involves a lot of transaction costs, such as the cost of negotiating the terms of the loan, investigating the borrower's credit history and ability to repay, and so on. To minimize these costs, large borrowers such as major corporations and governments often take a more streamlined approach: they sell (or issue) bonds.

BONDS An IOU issued by a borrower is called a *bond*. Normally, the seller of the bond promises to pay a fixed sum of interest each year and to repay the principal—the value stated on the face of the bond—to the owner of the bond on a particular date. So a bond is a financial asset from its owner's point of view and a liability from its issuer's point of view.

A bond issuer sells a number of bonds with a given interest rate and maturity date to anyone willing to buy them, a process that avoids costly negotiation of the terms of a loan with many individual lenders.

> A **default** occurs when a borrower fails to make payments as specified by the loan or bond contract.
>
> A **loan-backed security** is an asset created by pooling individual loans and selling shares in that pool.

Bond purchasers can acquire information free of charge on the quality of the bond issuer, such as the bond issuer's credit history, from bond-rating agencies rather than having to incur the expense of investigating it themselves. A particular concern for investors is the possibility of **default,** the risk that the bond issuer will fail to make payments as specified by the bond contract. Once a bond's risk of default has been rated, it can be sold on the bond market as a more or less standardized product—one with clearly defined terms and quality. In general, bonds with a higher default risk must pay a higher interest rate to attract investors.

Another important advantage of bonds is that they are easy to resell. This provides liquidity to bond purchasers. Indeed, a bond will often pass through many hands before it finally comes due. Loans, in contrast, are much more difficult to resell because, unlike bonds, they are not standardized: they differ in size, quality, terms, and so on, making them a lot less liquid than bonds.

LOAN-BACKED SECURITIES **Loan-backed securities,** assets created by pooling individual loans and selling shares in that pool (a process called *securitization*), have become extremely popular over the past two decades. While mortgage-backed securities, in which thousands of individual home mortgages are pooled and then shares are sold to investors, are the best-known example, securitization has also been widely applied to student loans, credit card loans, and auto loans. These loan-backed securities are traded on financial markets like bonds; they are preferred by investors because they provide more diversification and liquidity than individual loans.

However, with so many loans packaged together, it can be difficult to assess the true quality of the asset. That difficulty came to haunt investors during the financial crisis of 2008, when the bursting of the housing bubble led to widespread defaults on mortgages and large losses for holders of "supposedly safe" mortgage-backed securities, creating pain that spread throughout the entire financial system.

STOCKS A *stock* is a share in the ownership of a company. A share of stock is a financial asset from its owner's point of view and a liability from the company's point of view. Not all companies sell shares of their stock; "privately held" companies are owned by an individual or a few partners, who get to keep all of the company's profit.

Most large companies, however, do sell stock. For example, Microsoft has over 8 billion shares outstanding; if you buy one of those shares, you are entitled to one-eight-billionth of the company's profit, as well as 1 of 8 billion votes on company decisions.

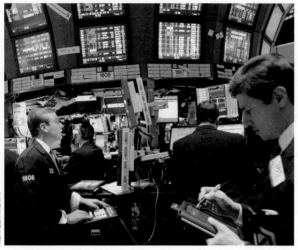

Mark Lennihan/AP

Selling stock reduces risk for business owners and benefits investors who buy the stock.

Why does Microsoft, historically a very profitable company, allow you to buy a share in its ownership? Why don't Bill Gates and Paul Allen, the two founders of Microsoft, keep complete ownership for themselves and just sell bonds for their investment spending needs? The reason is risk: few individuals are risk-tolerant enough to face the risk involved in being the sole owner of a large company.

But stocks do more than reduce the risk that business owners face. The existence of stocks improves society's welfare and improves the welfare of investors who buy stocks. Shareowners are able to enjoy the higher returns over time that stocks generally offer in comparison to bonds. Over the past century, stocks have typically yielded about 7% after adjusting for inflation; bonds have yielded only about 2%. But as investment companies warn you, "past performance is no guarantee of future performance."

And there is a downside: owning the stock of a given company is riskier than owning a bond issued by the same company. Why? Loosely speaking, a bond is a promise while a stock is a hope: by law, a company must pay what it owes its lenders before it distributes any profit to its shareholders. And if the company should fail (that is, be unable to pay its interest obligations and declare bankruptcy), its physical and financial assets go to its bondholders—its lenders—while its shareholders generally receive nothing. So although a stock generally provides a higher return to an investor than a bond, it also carries higher risk.

But the financial system has devised ways to help investors as well as business owners simultaneously manage risk and enjoy somewhat higher returns through the services of institutions known as *financial intermediaries*.

Financial Intermediaries

A **financial intermediary** is an institution that transforms funds gathered from many individuals into financial assets. The most important types of financial intermediaries are *mutual funds, pension funds, life insurance companies,* and *banks.* About three-quarters of the financial assets Americans own are held through these intermediaries rather than directly.

MUTUAL FUNDS Owning shares of a company entails accepting risk in return for a higher potential reward. But it should come as no surprise that stock investors can lower their total risk by engaging in diversification.

By owning a *diversified portfolio* of stocks—a group of stocks in which risks are unrelated to, or offset, one another—rather than concentrating investment in the shares of a single company or a group of related companies, investors can reduce their risk. In addition, financial advisers, aware that most people are risk-averse, almost always advise their clients to diversify not only their stock portfolio but also their entire wealth by holding other assets in addition to stock—assets such as bonds, real estate, and cash. (And, for good measure, to have plenty of insurance in case of accidental losses!)

However, for individuals who don't have a large amount of money to invest—say $1 million or more—building a diversified stock portfolio can incur high transaction costs (particularly fees paid to stockbrokers) because they are buying a few shares of a lot of companies. Fortunately for such investors, mutual funds help solve the problem of achieving diversification without high transaction costs.

A **mutual fund** is a financial intermediary that creates a stock portfolio by buying and holding shares in companies and then selling shares of the stock portfolio to individual investors. By buying these shares, investors with a relatively small amount of money to invest can indirectly hold a diversified portfolio, achieving a better return for any given level of risk than they could otherwise achieve.

A **financial intermediary** is an institution that transforms the funds it gathers from many individuals into financial assets.

A **mutual fund** is a financial intermediary that creates a stock portfolio and then resells shares of this portfolio to individual investors.

Many mutual funds also perform market research on the companies they invest in. This is important because there are thousands of stock-issuing U.S. companies (not to mention foreign companies), each differing in terms of its likely profitability, dividend payments, and so on. It would be extremely time-consuming and costly for an individual investor to do adequate research on even a small number of companies. Mutual funds save transaction costs by doing this research for their customers.

The mutual fund industry represents a huge portion of the modern U.S. economy, not just of the U.S. financial system. In total, U.S. mutual funds had assets of $14.8 trillion at the end of 2013.

We should mention, by the way, that mutual funds charge fees for their services. These fees are quite small for mutual funds that simply hold a diversified portfolio of stocks, without trying to pick winners. But the fees charged by mutual funds that claim to have special expertise in investing your money can be quite high.

PENSION FUNDS AND LIFE INSURANCE COMPANIES In addition to mutual funds, many Americans have holdings in **pension funds,** nonprofit institutions that collect the savings of their members and invest those funds in a wide variety of assets, providing their members with income when they retire. Although pension funds are subject to some special rules and receive special treatment for tax purposes, they function much like mutual funds. They invest in a diverse array of financial assets, allowing their members to achieve more cost-effective diversification and market research than they would be able to achieve on their own.

Americans also have substantial holdings in the policies of **life insurance companies,** which guarantee a payment to the policyholder's beneficiaries (typically, the family) when the policyholder dies. By enabling policyholders to cushion their beneficiaries from financial hardship arising from their death, life insurance companies also improve welfare by reducing risk.

BANKS Recall that, other things equal, people want assets that can be readily converted into cash. Bonds and stocks are much more liquid than physical assets or loans, yet the transaction cost of selling bonds or stocks to meet a sudden expense can be large. Furthermore, for many small and moderate-sized companies, the cost of issuing bonds and stocks is too large given the modest amount of money they seek to raise. A *bank* is an institution that helps resolve the conflict between lenders' needs for liquidity and the financing needs of borrowers who don't want to use the stock or bond markets.

An increase in bank deposits in South Korea in the late 1960s allowed businesses to launch an investment spending boom that contributed to the country's spectacular economic growth.

A bank works by first accepting funds from *depositors:* when you put your money in a bank, you are essentially becoming a lender by lending the bank your money. In return, you receive credit for a **bank deposit**—a claim on the bank, which is obliged to give you your cash if and when you demand it.

So a bank deposit is a financial asset owned by the depositor and a liability of the bank that holds it.

A bank, however, keeps only a fraction of its customers' deposits in the form of ready cash. Most of its deposits are lent out to businesses, buyers of new homes, and other borrowers. These loans come with a long-term commitment by the bank to the borrower: as long as the borrower makes his or her payments on time, the loan cannot be recalled by the bank and converted into cash. So a bank enables those who wish to borrow for long lengths of time to use the funds of those who wish to lend but simultaneously want to maintain the ability to get their cash back on demand. More formally, a **bank** is a financial intermediary that provides liquid financial assets in the form of deposits to lenders and uses their funds to finance the illiquid investment spending needs of borrowers.

A **pension fund** is a type of mutual fund that holds assets in order to provide retirement income to its members.

A **life insurance company** sells policies that guarantee a payment to a policyholder's beneficiaries when the policyholder dies.

A **bank deposit** is a claim on a bank that obliges the bank to give the depositor his or her cash when demanded.

A **bank** is a financial intermediary that provides liquid assets in the form of bank deposits to lenders and uses those funds to finance the illiquid investment spending needs of borrowers.

In essence, a bank is engaging in a kind of mismatch: lending for long periods of time while subject to the condition that its depositors could demand their funds back at any time. How can it manage that?

The bank counts on the fact that, on average, only a small fraction of its depositors will want their cash at the same time. On any given day, some people will make withdrawals and others will make new deposits; these will roughly cancel each other out. So the bank needs to keep only a limited amount of cash on hand to satisfy its depositors.

In addition, if a bank becomes financially incapable of paying its depositors, individual bank deposits are guaranteed to depositors up to $250,000 by the Federal Deposit Insurance Corporation, or FDIC, a federal agency. This reduces the risk to a depositor of holding a bank deposit, in turn reducing the incentive to withdraw funds if concerns about the financial state of the bank should arise. So, under normal conditions, banks need hold only a fraction of their depositors' cash.

By reconciling the needs of savers for liquid assets with the needs of borrowers for long-term financing, banks play a key economic role.

Financial Fluctuations and Macroeconomic Policy

We've learned that the financial system is an essential part of the economy; without stock markets, bond markets, and banks, long-run economic growth would be hard to achieve. Yet the news isn't entirely good: the financial system sometimes doesn't function well and instead is a source of instability in the short run because of asset price fluctuations. We saw this in 2008 as the economy faced a severe slump resulting from a sharp reduction in home values (a situation that we examine in detail in the upcoming Economics in Action).

How should economists and policy makers deal with the fact that asset prices fluctuate a lot and that these fluctuations can have important economic effects? This question has become one of the major problems for macroeconomic policy. On one side, policy makers are reluctant to assume that the market is wrong—that asset prices are either too high or too low. It's hard to make the general case that government officials are better judges of appropriate prices than private investors who are putting their own money on the line.

On the other side, the past 15 years were marked by not one but two huge asset bubbles, each of which created major macroeconomic problems when it burst. In the late 1990s the prices of technology stocks, including but not limited to dot-com Internet firms, soared to hard-to-justify heights. When the bubble burst, these stocks lost, on average, two-thirds of their value in a short time, helping to cause the 2001 recession and a period of high unemployment. A few years later there was a major bubble in housing prices. The collapse of this bubble in 2008 triggered a severe financial crisis followed by a deep recession.

These events have led to a fierce debate among economists over whether policy makers should try to pop asset bubbles before they get too big.

ECONOMICS ▶ *IN ACTION*

THE GREAT AMERICAN HOUSING BUBBLE

Between 2000 and 2006, there was a huge increase in the price of houses in America. By the summer of 2006, home prices were well over twice as high as they had been in January 2000 in a number of major U.S. metropolitan areas, including Los Angeles, San Diego, San Francisco, Washington, Miami, Las Vegas, and New York. By 2004, as the increase in home prices accelerated, a number of economists (including the authors of this textbook) argued that this price increase was excessive—that it was a bubble, a rise in asset prices driven by unrealistic expectations about future prices.

It was certainly true that home prices rose much more than the cost of renting a comparable place to live. Panel (a) of Figure 23-1 compares a widely used index of U.S. housing prices with the U.S. government's index of the cost of renting, both shown as index numbers with January 2000 = 100. Home prices shot up, even though rental rates grew only gradually.

FIGURE 23-1   The Great American Housing Bubble

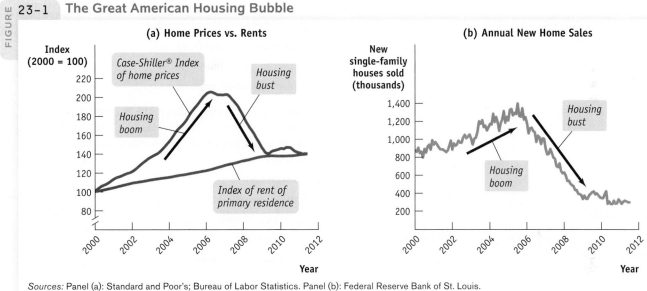

Sources: Panel (a): Standard and Poor's; Bureau of Labor Statistics. Panel (b): Federal Reserve Bank of St. Louis.

Yet there were also a number of economists who argued that the rise in housing prices was completely justified. They pointed, in particular, to interest rates that were unusually low in the years of rapid price increases, and they argued that low interest rates combined with other factors, such as growing population, explained the surge in prices. Alan Greenspan, then chairman of the Federal Reserve, conceded in 2005 that there might be some "froth" in the markets but denied that there was any national bubble.

Unfortunately, it turned out that the skeptics were right. Greenspan himself would later concede that there had, in fact, been a huge national bubble. In 2006, as home prices began to level off, it became apparent that many buyers had held unrealistic expectations about future prices. As home prices began to fall, expectations of future increases in home prices were revised downward, precipitating a sudden and dramatic collapse in prices. And with home prices falling, the demand for housing fell drastically, as illustrated by panel (b) of Figure 23-1.

The implosion in housing, in turn, created numerous economic difficulties, including severe stress on the banking system.

MODULE

23 Review

Solutions appear at the back of the book.

Check Your Understanding

1. Rank the following assets from the lowest level to the highest level of (i) transaction costs, (ii) risk, (iii) liquidity. Ties are acceptable for items that have indistinguishable rankings.

   a. a bank deposit with a guaranteed interest rate

   b. a share of a highly diversified mutual fund, which can be quickly sold

   c. a share of the family business, which can be sold only if you find a buyer and all other family members agree to the sale

2. What relationship would you expect to find between the level of development of a country's financial system and its level of economic development? Explain in terms of the country's levels of savings and investment spending.

Multiple-Choice Questions

1. Decreasing which of the following is a task of the financial system?

   I. transaction costs
   II. risk
   III. liquidity

   a. I only

   b. II only

   c. III only

   d. I and II only

   e. I, II, and III

2. A financial asset that pays a fixed sum of interest each year and then repays the principal on a given date is called a

   a. bond.

   b. stock.

   c. mutual fund.

   d. loan.

   e. loan-backed security.

3. Which of the following assets is the most diversified?

   a. stock in a company

   b. a bond issued by a company

   c. shares in a mutual fund

   d. a loan to a company

   e. a physical asset, such as a house

4. A nonprofit institution collects the savings of its members and invests those funds in a wide variety of assets in order to provide its members with income after retirement. This describes a

   a. mutual fund.

   b. bank.

   c. savings and loan.

   d. pension fund.

   e. life insurance company.

5. A financial intermediary that provides liquid financial assets in the form of deposits to lenders and uses their funds to finance the illiquid investment spending needs of borrowers is called a

   a. mutual fund.

   b. bank.

   c. corporation.

   d. pension fund.

   e. life insurance company.

Critical-Thinking Question

List and describe the four most important types of financial intermediaries.

SECTION **6** REVIEW

Summary

Savings and Investment Spending

1. Investment in physical capital is necessary for long-run economic growth. So in order for an economy to grow, it must channel savings into investment spending.

2. According to the **savings–investment spending identity,** savings and investment spending are always equal for the economy as a whole.

3. The government is a source of savings when it runs a positive **budget balance,** also known as a **budget surplus;** it is a source of dissavings when it runs a negative budget balance, also known as a **budget deficit.**

4. In a closed economy, savings is equal to **national savings,** the sum of private savings plus the budget balance. In an open economy, savings is equal to national savings plus **net capital inflow** of foreign savings. When a negative net capital inflow occurs, some portion of national savings is funding investment spending in other countries.

The Market for Loanable Funds

5. The hypothetical **loanable funds market** shows how loans from savers are allocated among borrowers with investment spending projects. By showing how gains from trade between lenders and borrowers are maximized, the loanable funds market shows why a well-functioning financial system leads to greater long-run economic growth.

6. Increasing or persistent government budget deficits can lead to **crowding out:** higher interest rates and reduced investment spending. This tells us that the demand curve for loanable funds is downward sloping. Changes in perceived business opportunities and in government borrowing shift the demand curve for loanable funds; changes in private savings and capital inflows shift the supply curve.

7. Because neither borrowers nor lenders can know the future inflation rate, loans specify a nominal interest rate rather than a real interest rate. For a given expected future inflation rate, shifts of the demand and supply curves of loanable funds result in changes in the underlying real interest rate, leading to changes in the nominal interest rate. According to the **Fisher effect,** an increase in expected future inflation raises the nominal interest rate one-to-one so that the expected real interest rate remains unchanged.

The Time Value of Money

8. The **present value** of a sum of money measures its value today.

9. The **net present value** of a project is the present value of current and future benefits minus the present value of current and future costs.

The Financial System

10. Households invest their current savings or **wealth**—their accumulated savings—by purchasing assets. Assets come in the form of either a **financial asset,** a paper claim that entitles the buyer to future income from the seller, or a **physical asset,** a tangible object that can generate future income.

11. A financial asset is also a **liability** from the point of view of its seller. There are four main types of financial assets: **loans,** bonds, stocks, and **bank deposits.** Each of them serves a different purpose in addressing the three fundamental tasks of a financial system: reducing **transaction costs**—the cost of making a deal; reducing **financial risk**—uncertainty about future outcomes that involves financial gains and losses; and providing **liquid** assets—assets that can be quickly converted into cash without much loss of value (in contrast to **illiquid** assets, which are not easily converted).

12. Although many small and moderate-sized borrowers use bank loans to fund investment spending, larger companies typically issue bonds. Bonds with a higher risk of **default** must typically pay a higher interest rate.

13. Business owners reduce their risk by selling stock. Although stocks usually generate a higher return than bonds, investors typically wish to reduce their risk by engaging in **diversification,** owning a wide range of assets whose returns are based on unrelated, or independent, events. Most people are risk-averse, more sensitive to a loss than to an equal-sized gain.

14. **Loan-backed securities,** a recent innovation, are assets created by pooling individual loans and selling shares of that pool to investors. Because they are more diversified and more liquid than individual loans, bonds are preferred by investors. It can be difficult, however, to assess a bond's quality.

15. **Financial intermediaries**—institutions such as **mutual funds, pension funds, life insurance companies,** and **banks**—are critical components of the financial system. Mutual funds and pension funds allow small investors to diversify, and life insurance companies reduce risk.

16. A bank allows individuals to hold liquid bank deposits that are then used to finance illiquid loans. Banks can perform this mismatch because on average only a small fraction of depositors withdraw their funds at any one time. A well-functioning banking sector is a key ingredient of long-run economic growth.

Key Terms

Savings–investment spending
  identity, p. 206
Budget surplus, p. 207
Budget deficit, p. 207
Budget balance, p. 207
National savings, p. 208
Net capital inflow, p. 208
Loanable funds market, p. 212

Crowding out, p. 217
Fisher effect, p. 219
Present value, p. 224
Net present value, p. 225
Wealth, p. 228
Financial asset, p. 228
Physical asset, p. 228
Liability, p. 228

Transaction costs, p. 229
Financial risk, p. 229
Diversification, p. 230
Liquid, p. 230
Illiquid, p. 230
Default, p. 231
Loan-backed securities, p. 231
Financial intermediary, p. 232

Mutual fund, p. 232
Pension fund, p. 233
Life insurance company,
  p. 233
Bank deposit, p. 233
Bank, p. 233

Problems

1. Given the following information about the closed economy of Brittania, what is the level of investment spending and private savings, and what is the budget balance? What is the relationship among the three? Is national savings equal to investment spending? There are no government transfers.

   GDP = $1,000 million T = $50 million
   C = $850 million G = $100 million

2. Explain how a well-functioning financial system increases savings and investment spending, holding the budget balance and any capital flows fixed.

3. Boris Borrower and Lynn Lender agree that Lynn will lend Boris $10,000 and that Boris will repay the $10,000 with interest in one year. They agree to a nominal interest rate of 8%, reflecting a real interest rate of 3% on the loan and a commonly shared expected inflation rate of 5% over the next year.

   a. If the inflation rate is actually 4% over the next year, how does that lower-than-expected inflation rate affect Boris and Lynn? Who is better off?

   b. If the actual inflation rate is 7% over the next year, how does that affect Boris and Lynn? Who is better off?

4. Explain why equilibrium in the loanable funds market maximizes efficiency.

5. Use the market for loanable funds shown in the accompanying diagram to explain what happens to private savings, private investment spending, and the interest rate if each of the following events occur. Assume that there are no capital inflows or outflows.

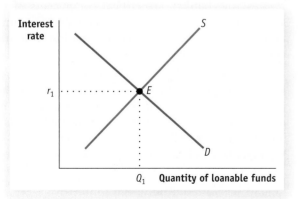

a. The government reduces the size of its deficit to zero.

b. At any given interest rate, consumers decide to save more. Assume the budget balance is zero.

c. At any given interest rate, businesses become very optimistic about the future profitability of investment spending. Assume the budget balance is zero.

6. In 2010, Congress estimated that the cost of increasing the U.S. presence in Afghanistan by 30,000 troops was approximately $36 billion. The U.S. government was running a budget deficit at the time, so assume that the surge in troop levels was financed by government borrowing, which increases the demand for loanable funds without affecting supply. This question considers the likely effect of this government expenditure on the interest rate.

   a. Draw typical demand (D_1) and supply (S_1) curves for loanable funds without the cost of the surge in troop levels accounted for. Label the vertical axis "Interest rate" and the horizontal axis "Quantity of loanable funds." Label the equilibrium point (E_1) and the equilibrium interest rate (r_1).

   b. Now draw a new diagram with the cost of the surge in troop levels included in the analysis. Shift the demand curve in the appropriate direction. Label the new equilibrium point (E_2) and the new equilibrium interest rate (r_2).

   c. How does the equilibrium interest rate change in response to government expenditure on the troop surge? Explain.

7. How would you respond to a friend who claims that the government should eliminate all purchases that are financed by borrowing because such borrowing crowds out private investment spending?

8. Using the accompanying diagram, explain what will happen to the market for loanable funds when there is a fall of 2 percentage points in the expected future inflation rate. How will the change in the expected future inflation rate affect the equilibrium quantity of loanable funds?

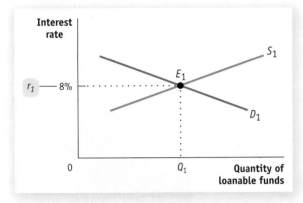

9. You have won the state lottery. There are two ways in which you can receive your prize. You can either have $1 million in cash now, or you can have $1.2 million that is paid out as follows: $300,000 now, $300,000 in one year's time, $300,000 in two years' time, and $300,000 in three years' time. The interest rate is 20%. How would you prefer to receive your prize?

10. The drug company Pfizer is considering whether to invest in the development of a new cancer drug. Development will require an initial investment of $10 million now; beginning one year from now, the drug will generate annual profits of $4 million for three years.

    a. If the interest rate is 12%, should Pfizer invest in the development of the new drug? Why or why not?

    b. If the interest rate is 8%, should Pfizer invest in the development of the new drug? Why or why not?

11. What are the important types of financial intermediaries in the U.S. economy? What are the primary assets of these intermediaries, and how do they facilitate investment spending and saving?

12. Sallie Mae is a quasi-governmental agency that packages individual student loans into pools of loans and sells shares of these pools to investors as Sallie Mae bonds.

    a. What is this process called? What effect will it have on investors compared to situations in which they could only buy and sell individual student loans?

    b. What effect do you think Sallie Mae's actions will have on the ability of students to get loans?

    c. Suppose that a very severe recession hits and, as a consequence, many graduating students cannot get jobs and default on their student loans. What effect will this have on Sallie Mae bonds? Why is it likely that investors now believe Sallie Mae bonds to be riskier than expected? What will be the effect on the availability of student loans?

13. For each of the following, is it an example of investment spending, investing in financial assets, or investing in physical assets?

    a. Rupert Moneybucks buys 100 shares of existing Coca-Cola stock.

    b. Rhonda Moviestar spends $10 million to buy a mansion built in the 1970s.

    c. Ronald Basketballstar spends $10 million to build a new mansion with a view of the Pacific Ocean.

    d. Rawlings builds a new plant to make catcher's mitts.

    e. Russia buys $100 million in U.S. government bonds.

Income and Expenditure

FROM BOOM TO BUST

Ft. Myers, Florida, was a boom town from 2003 to 2005. Jobs were plentiful: the unemployment rate in the Ft. Myers–Cape Coral metropolitan area was less than 3%. Shopping malls were humming, and new stores were opening everywhere.

But then the boom went bust. Jobs became scarce, and by the middle of 2010, the unemployment rate was above 13%. Stores had few customers, and many were closing. One new business was flourishing, however. As the local economy plunged, real estate agents began offering "foreclosure tours": visits to homes that had been seized by banks after the owners were unable to make mortgage payments—and were available at bargain prices.

What happened? Ft. Myers boomed because of a surge in home construction, fueled in part by speculators who bought houses not to live in, but to resell at much higher prices. Home construction gave jobs to construction workers, electricians, roofers, real estate agents, and others. These workers, in turn, spent money locally, creating jobs for waiters, gardeners, pool cleaners, sales people, and more. These workers, in turn, also spent money locally, creating further expansion, and so on.

The boom turned into a bust when home construction suddenly came to a virtual halt. It turned out that specula-tion had been feeding on itself: people were buying houses as investments, then selling them to others who were also buying houses as investments, and prices had risen to levels far beyond what people who actually wanted to live in houses were willing to pay.

The local economy then collapsed, as the process that had created the earlier boom operated in reverse. The jobs created by home construction went away, leading to a fall in local spending, leading to a loss of other local jobs, leading to further declines in spending, and so on.

The boom and bust in Ft. Myers illustrates, on a small scale, the way booms and busts happen for the economy as a whole. The business cycle is often driven by ups or downs in investment spending—either residential investment spending (that is, home construction) or nonresidential investment spending (such as the construction of office buildings, factories, and shopping malls). Changes in investment spending, in turn, indirectly lead to changes in consumer spending, which magnify—or, as economists usually say, *multiply*—the effect of the investment spending changes on the economy as a whole.

In this section we'll study how this process works, showing how *multiplier* analysis helps us understand the business cycle.

Thinkstock

WHAT YOU WILL LEARN

1 The significance of the marginal propensity to consume

2 The nature of the multiplier, which shows how initial changes in spending lead to further changes in spending

The Multiplier: An Informal Introduction

The story of the boom and bust in Ft. Myers that opens this section involves a sort of chain reaction in which an initial rise or fall in aggregate spending leads to changes in income, which lead to further changes in aggregate spending, and so on. Let's examine that chain reaction more closely, this time thinking through the effects of changes in aggregate spending in the economy as a whole.

For the sake of this analysis, we'll make four simplifying assumptions that we'll revisit later.

1. We assume that *producers are willing to supply additional output at a fixed price.* That is, if consumers or businesses buying investment goods decide to spend an additional $1 billion, that will translate into the production of $1 billion worth of additional goods and services without driving up the overall level of prices. As a result, *changes in aggregate spending translate into changes in aggregate output,* as measured by real GDP. As we'll learn, this assumption isn't too unrealistic in the short run, but it needs to be changed when we think about the long-run effects of changes in demand.

2. We take the interest rate as given.

3. We assume that there is no government spending and no taxes.

4. We assume that exports and imports are zero.

Given these simplifying assumptions, consider what happens if there is a change in investment spending. Specifically, imagine that for some reason home builders decide to spend an extra $100 billion on home construction over the next year.

The direct effect of this increase in investment spending will be to increase income and the value of aggregate output by the same amount. That's because each dollar spent on home construction translates into a dollar's worth of income for construction workers, suppliers of building materials, electricians, and so on. If the process stopped there, the increase in housing investment spending would raise overall income by exactly $100 billion.

But the process doesn't stop there. The increase in aggregate output leads to an increase in disposable income that flows to households in the form of profits and wages. The increase in households' disposable income leads to a rise in consumer spending, which, in turn, induces firms to increase output yet again. This generates another rise in disposable income, which leads to another round of consumer spending increases, and so on. So there are multiple rounds of increases in aggregate output.

How large is the total effect on aggregate output if we sum the effect from all these rounds of spending increases? To answer this question, we need to introduce the concept of the **marginal propensity to consume,** or **MPC:** the increase in consumer spending when disposable income rises by $1. When consumer spending changes because of a rise or fall in disposable income, *MPC* is the change in consumer spending divided by the change in disposable income:

(24-1) $MPC = \dfrac{\Delta \text{ Consumer spending}}{\Delta \text{ Disposable income}}$

where the symbol Δ (delta) means "change in." For example, if consumer spending goes up by $6 billion when disposable income goes up by $10 billion, *MPC* is $6 billion/ $10 billion = 0.6.

Because consumers normally spend part but not all of an additional dollar of disposable income, *MPC* is a number between 0 and 1. The additional disposable income that consumers don't spend is saved; the **marginal propensity to save,** or **MPS,** is the fraction of an additional dollar of disposable income that is saved. *MPS* is equal to $1 - MPC$.

Because we assumed that there are no taxes and no international trade, each $1 increase in aggregate spending raises both real GDP and disposable income by $1. So the $100 billion increase in investment spending initially raises real GDP by $100 billion. This leads to a second-round increase in consumer spending, which raises real GDP by a further $MPC \times$ $100 billion. It is followed by a third-round increase in consumer spending of $MPC \times MPC \times$ $100 billion, and so on. After an infinite number of rounds, the total effect on real GDP is:

Increase in investment spending $=$ $100 billion

+ Second-round increase in consumer spending $= MPC \times$ $100 billion

+ Third-round increase in consumer spending $= MPC^2 \times$ $100 billion

+ Fourth-round increase in consumer spending $= MPC^3 \times$ $100 billion

•   •
•   •
•   •

Total increase in real GDP $= (1 + MPC + MPC^2 + MPC^3 + \ldots) \times$ $100 billion

So the $100 billion increase in investment spending sets off a chain reaction in the economy. The net result of this chain reaction is that a $100 billion increase in investment spending leads to a change in real GDP that is a *multiple* of the size of that initial change in spending.

How large is this multiple? It's a mathematical fact that an infinite series of the form $1 + x + x^2 + x^3 + \ldots$, where x is between 0 and 1, is equal to $1/(1 - x)$. So the total effect of a $100 billion increase in investment spending, *I,* taking into account all the subsequent increases in consumer spending (and assuming no taxes and no international trade), is given by:

(24-2) Total increase in real GDP from a $100 billion rise in *I*

$$= \frac{1}{1 - MPC} \times \$100 \text{ billion}$$

> The **marginal propensity to consume,** or *MPC,* is the increase in consumer spending when disposable income rises by $1.
>
> The **marginal propensity to save,** or *MPS,* is the increase in household savings when disposable income rises by $1.

TABLE 24-1

Rounds of Increases of Real GDP
When *MPC* = 0.6

	Increase in real GDP (billions)	Total increase in real GDP (billions)
First round	$100	$100
Second round	60	160
Third round	36	196
Fourth round	21.6	217.6
...	...	...
Final round	0	250

Let's consider a numerical example in which *MPC* = 0.6: each $1 in additional disposable income causes a $0.60 rise in consumer spending. In that case, a $100 billion increase in investment spending raises real GDP by $100 billion in the first round. The second-round increase in consumer spending raises real GDP by another 0.6 × $100 billion, or $60 billion. The third-round increase in consumer spending raises real GDP by another 0.6 × $60 billion, or $36 billion.

Table 24-1 shows the successive stages of increases, where "..." means the process goes on an infinite number of times. In the end, real GDP rises by $250 billion as a consequence of the initial $100 billion rise in investment spending:

$$\frac{1}{1 - 0.6} \times \$100 \text{ billion} = 2.5 \times \$100 \text{ billion} = \$250 \text{ billion}$$

Notice that even though there are an infinite number of rounds of expansion of real GDP, the total rise in real GDP is limited to $250 billion. The reason is that at each stage some of the rise in disposable income "leaks out" because it is saved. How much of an additional dollar of disposable income is saved depends on *MPS*, the marginal propensity to save.

We've described the effects of a change in investment spending, but the same analysis can be applied to any other change in aggregate spending. The important thing is to distinguish between the initial change in aggregate spending, before real GDP rises, and the additional change in aggregate spending caused by the change in real GDP as the chain reaction unfolds.

Thinkstock

For example, suppose that a boom in housing prices makes consumers feel richer and that, as a result, they become willing to spend more at any given level of disposable income. This will lead to an initial rise in consumer spending, before real GDP rises. But it will also lead to second and later rounds of higher consumer spending as real GDP rises.

An initial rise or fall in aggregate spending at a given level of real GDP is called an **autonomous change in aggregate spending.** It's autonomous—which means "self-governing"—because it's the cause, not the result, of the chain reaction we've just described.

Spending by one person or firm has a domino effect that leads to progressively more spending in the economy.

Formally, the **multiplier** is the ratio of the total change in real GDP caused by an autonomous change in aggregate spending to the size of that autonomous change. If we let Δ*AAS* stand for autonomous change in aggregate spending and Δ*Y* stand for the change in real GDP, then the multiplier is equal to Δ*Y*/Δ*AAS*. And we've already seen how to find the value of the multiplier. Assuming no taxes and no trade, the change in real GDP caused by an autonomous change in spending is:

$$(24\text{-}3) \quad \Delta Y = \frac{1}{1 - MPC} \times \Delta AAS$$

So the multiplier is:

$$(24\text{-}4) \quad \text{Multiplier} = \frac{\Delta Y}{\Delta AAS} = \frac{1}{1 - MPC}$$

Notice that the size of the multiplier depends on *MPC*. If the marginal propensity to consume is high, so is the multiplier. This is true because the size of *MPC* determines how large each round of expansion is compared with the previous round. To put it another way, the higher *MPC* is, the less disposable income "leaks out" into savings at each round of expansion.

An **autonomous change in aggregate spending** is an initial change in the desired level of spending by firms, households, or government at a given level of real GDP.

The **multiplier** is the ratio of the total change in real GDP caused by an autonomous change in aggregate spending to the size of that autonomous change.

In later modules we'll use the concept of the multiplier to analyze the effects of fiscal and monetary policies. We'll also see that the formula for the multiplier changes when we introduce various complications, including taxes and foreign trade. First we need to look more deeply at what determines consumer spending.

ECONOMICS ▶ *IN ACTION*

THE MULTIPLIER AND THE GREAT DEPRESSION

The concept of the multiplier was originally devised by economists trying to understand the greatest economic disaster in history, the collapse of output and employment from 1929 to 1933, which began the Great Depression. Most economists believe that the slump from 1929 to 1933 was driven by a collapse in investment spending. But as the economy shrank, consumer spending also fell sharply, multiplying the effect on real GDP.

TABLE 24-2

Investment Spending, Consumer Spending, and
Real GDP in the Great Depression (billions of 2005 dollars)

	1929	1933	Change
Investment spending	$101.4	$18.9	–$82.5
Consumer spending	736.3	600.8	–135.5
Real GDP	976.1	715.8	–260.3

Source: Bureau of Economic Analysis.

Table 24-2 shows what happened to investment spending, consumer spending, and GDP during those four terrible years. What we see is that investment spending imploded, falling by more than 80%. But consumer spending also fell drastically and actually accounted for more of the fall in real GDP. (The total fall in real GDP was larger than the combined fall in consumer and investment spending, mainly because of technical accounting issues.)

The numbers in Table 24-2 suggest that at the time of the Great Depression, the multiplier was around 3. Most current estimates put the size of the multiplier considerably lower—but there's a reason for that change. In 1929, government in the United States was very small by modern standards: taxes were low and major government programs like Social Security and Medicare had not yet come into being. In the modern U.S. economy, taxes are much higher, and so is government spending. Why does this matter? Because taxes and some government programs act as *automatic stabilizers*, reducing the size of the multiplier.

24 Review

Solutions appear at the back of the book.

Check Your Understanding

1. Explain why a decline in investment spending caused by a change in business expectations leads to a fall in consumer spending.

2. What is the multiplier if the marginal propensity to consume is 0.5? What is it if *MPC* is 0.8?

3. As a percentage of GDP, savings accounts for a larger share of the economy in the country of Scania compared to the country of Amerigo. Which country is likely to have the larger multiplier? Explain.

Multiple-Choice Questions

1. A $100 million increase in investment spending will cause real GDP to

   a. decrease by $100 million.

   b. increase by $100 million.

   c. decrease by less than $100 million.

   d. increase by less than $100 million.

   e. increase by more than $100 million.

2. The marginal propensity to consume measures the

   a. increase in consumer spending when disposable income rises by $1.

   b. increase in consumer spending when investment spending rises by $1.

   c. increase in consumer spending when taxes rise by $1.

   d. increase in disposable income when consumer spending rises by $1.

   e. increase in disposable income when investment spending rises by $1.

3. Assuming no taxes and no trade, the multiplier is equal to:

   a. MPC

   b. $\dfrac{1}{1 - MPC}$

   c. $\dfrac{1}{1 + MPC}$

   d. $\dfrac{1}{MPC}$

   e. $1 - MPC$

4. If the marginal propensity to consume is 0.5, then a $100 million increase in investment spending will increase real GDP by

   a. $100 million.

   b. $200 million.

   c. $50 million.

   d. $150 million.

   e. $300 million.

5. When income is $1,000, the level of consumption spending is equal to $850. When income rises to $1,200, the level of consumption spending is equal to $1,000. In this case the value of the marginal propensity to consume is

   a. 0.85.

   b. 0.83.

   c. 0.75.

   d. 0.50.

   e. 0.80.

Critical-Thinking Question

Explain how an autonomous change in aggregate spending affects real GDP, making reference to the multiplier concept.

Consumption and Investment Spending

Consumer Spending

Should you splurge on a restaurant meal or save money by eating at home? Should you buy a new car and, if so, how expensive a model? Should you redo that bathroom or live with it for another year? In the real world, households are constantly confronted with such choices—not just about the consumption mix, but also about how much to spend in total. These choices, in turn, have a powerful effect on the economy: consumer spending normally accounts for two-thirds of total spending on final goods and services. In particular, the decision about how much of an additional dollar in income to spend—the marginal propensity to consume—determines the size of the multiplier, which determines the ultimate effect on the economy of autonomous changes in spending.

But what determines how much consumers spend?

Current Disposable Income and Consumer Spending

The most important factor affecting a family's consumer spending is its current disposable income—income after taxes are paid and government transfers are received. It's obvious from daily life that people with high disposable incomes on average drive more expensive cars, live in more expensive houses, and spend more on meals and clothing than people with lower disposable incomes. And the relationship between current disposable income and spending is clear in the data.

The Bureau of Labor Statistics (BLS) collects annual data on family income and spending. Families are grouped by levels of before-tax income, and after-tax income for each group is also reported. Since the income figures include transfers from the government, what the BLS calls a household's after-tax income is equivalent to its current disposable income.

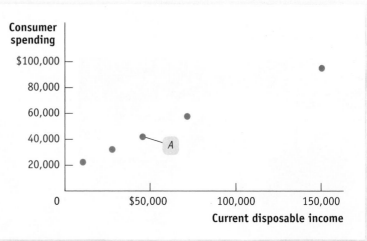

FIGURE

25-1 Current Disposable Income and Consumer Spending for American Households in 2012

For each income group of households, average current disposable income in 2012 is plotted versus average consumer spending in 2012. For example, the middle income group, with an annual income of $36,134 to $59,514, is represented by point *A*, indicating a household average current disposable income of $46,777 and average household consumer spending of $43,004. The data clearly show a positive relationship between current disposable income and consumer spending: families with higher current disposable income have higher consumer spending.

Source: Bureau of Labor Statistics.

Figure 25-1 is a scatter diagram showing the relationship between household current disposable income and household consumer spending for American households by income group in 2012. For example, point *A* shows that in 2012 the middle fifth of the population had an average current disposable income of $46,777 and average spending of $43,004. The pattern of the dots slopes upward from left to right, making it clear that households with higher current disposable income had higher consumer spending.

It's very useful to represent the relationship between an individual household's current disposable income and its consumer spending with an equation. The **consumption function** is an equation showing how an individual household's consumer spending varies with the household's current disposable income. The simplest version of a consumption function is a linear equation:

(25-1) $c = a + MPC \times yd$

where lowercase letters indicate variables measured for an individual household.

In this equation, c is individual household consumer spending and yd is individual household current disposable income. Recall that *MPC*, the marginal propensity to consume, is the amount by which consumer spending rises if current disposable income rises by $1. Finally, a is a constant term—individual household *autonomous consumer spending*, the amount of spending a household would do if it had zero disposable income. We assume that a is greater than zero because a household with zero disposable income is able to fund some consumption by borrowing or using its savings.

Notice, by the way, that we're using y for income. That's standard practice in macroeconomics, even though *income* isn't actually spelled "yncome." The reason is that I is reserved for investment spending.

Recall that we expressed *MPC* as the ratio of a change in consumer spending to the change in current disposable income. We've rewritten it for an individual household as Equation 25-2:

(25-2) $MPC = \Delta c / \Delta yd$

Multiplying both sides of Equation 25-2 by Δyd, we get:

(25-3) $MPC \times \Delta yd = \Delta c$

Equation 25-3 tells us that when yd goes up by $1, c goes up by $MPC \times \$1$.

Panorama
Productions Inc./Alamy

People with high disposable incomes tend to spend more than those with lower disposable incomes.

The **consumption function** is an equation showing how an individual household's consumer spending varies with the household's current disposable income.

FIGURE **25-2**   The Consumption Function

The consumption function relates a household's current disposable income to its consumer spending. The vertical intercept, *a*, is individual household autonomous consumer spending: the amount of a household's consumer spending if its current disposable income is zero. The slope of the consumption function line, *cf*, is the marginal propensity to consume, or *MPC*: of every additional $1 of current disposable income, *MPC* × $1 is spent.

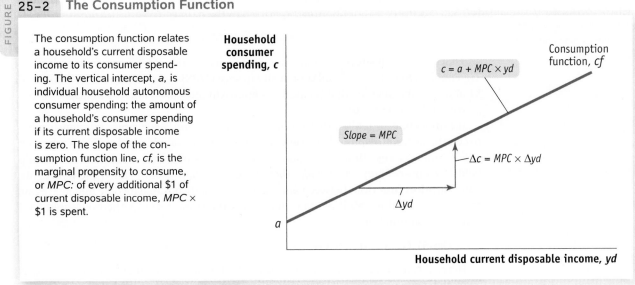

Figure 25-2 shows what Equation 25-1 looks like graphically, plotting *yd* on the horizontal axis and *c* on the vertical axis. Individual household autonomous consumer spending, *a*, is the value of *c* when *yd* is zero—it is the vertical *intercept* of the consumption function, *cf*. *MPC* is the *slope* of the line, measured by rise over run. If current disposable income rises by Δ*yd*, household consumer spending, *c*, rises by Δ*c*. Since *MPC* is defined as Δ*c*/Δ*yd*, the slope of the consumption function is:

(25-4) Slope of consumption function

   = Rise over run

   = Δ*c*/Δ*yd*

   = *MPC*

In reality, actual data never fit Equation 25-1 perfectly, but the fit can be pretty good. Figure 25-3 shows the data from Figure 25-1 again, together with a line drawn to fit the data as closely as possible. According to the data on households' consumer

FIGURE **25-3**   A Consumption Function Fitted to Data

The data from Figure 25-1 are reproduced here, along with a line drawn to fit the data as closely as possible. For American households in 2012, the best estimate of the average household's autonomous consumer spending, *a*, is $18,478 and the best estimate of *MPC* is approximately 0.520.

Source: Bureau of Labor Statistics.

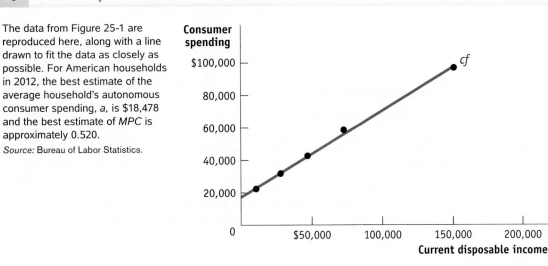

The **aggregate consumption function** is the relationship for the economy as a whole between aggregate current disposable income and aggregate consumer spending.

spending and current disposable income, the best estimate of a is \$18,478 and of MPC is 0.520. So the consumption function fitted to the data is:

$$c = \$18{,}478 + 0.520 \times yd$$

That is, the data suggest a marginal propensity to consume of approximately 0.52. This implies that the marginal propensity to save (MPS)—the amount of an additional \$1 of disposable income that is saved—is approximately 0.48, and the multiplier is approximately $1/0.48 = 2.08$.

It's important to realize that Figure 25-3 shows a *microeconomic* relationship between the current disposable income of individual households and their spending on goods and services. However, macroeconomists assume that a similar relationship holds *for the economy as a whole*: that there is a relationship, called the **aggregate consumption function,** between aggregate current disposable income and aggregate consumer spending. We'll assume that it has the same form as the household-level consumption function:

(25-5) $C = A + MPC \times YD$

Here, C is aggregate consumer spending (called just "consumer spending"); YD is aggregate current disposable income (called, for simplicity, just "disposable income"); and A is aggregate autonomous consumer spending, the amount of consumer spending when YD equals zero. This is the relationship represented in Figure 25-4 by CF, analogous to cf in Figure 25-3.

FIGURE **25-4**   Shifts of the Aggregate Consumption Function

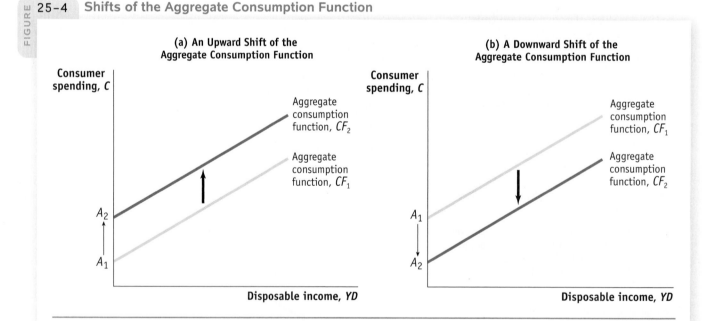

(a) An Upward Shift of the Aggregate Consumption Function

(b) A Downward Shift of the Aggregate Consumption Function

Panel (a) illustrates the effect of an increase in expected aggregate future disposable income. Consumers will spend more at every given level of aggregate current disposable income, YD. As a result, the initial aggregate consumption function CF_1, with aggregate autonomous consumer spending A_1, shifts up to a new position at CF_2 and aggregate autonomous consumer spending A_2. An increase in aggregate wealth will also shift the aggregate consumption function up. Panel (b), in contrast, illustrates the effect of a reduction in expected aggregate future disposable income. Consumers will spend less at every given level of aggregate current disposable income, YD. Consequently, the initial aggregate consumption function CF_1, with aggregate autonomous consumer spending A_1, shifts down to a new position at CF_2 and aggregate autonomous consumer spending A_2. A reduction in aggregate wealth will have the same effect.

Shifts of the Aggregate Consumption Function

The aggregate consumption function shows the relationship between disposable income and consumer spending for the economy as a whole, other things equal. When things other than disposable income change, the aggregate consumption function shifts. There are two principal causes of shifts of the aggregate consumption function: changes in expected future disposable income and changes in aggregate wealth.

CHANGES IN EXPECTED FUTURE DISPOSABLE INCOME Suppose you land a really good, well-paying job on graduating from college in May—but the job, and the paychecks, won't start until September. So your disposable income hasn't risen yet. Even so, it's likely that you will start spending more on final goods and services right away— maybe buying nicer work clothes than you originally planned—because you know that higher income is coming.

Conversely, suppose you have a good job but learn that the company is planning to downsize your division, raising the possibility that you may lose your job and have to take a lower-paying one somewhere else. Even though your disposable income hasn't gone down yet, you might well cut back on spending even while still employed, to save for a rainy day.

Both of these examples show how expectations about future disposable income can affect consumer spending. The two panels of Figure 25-4, which plot disposable income against consumer spending, show how changes in expected future disposable income affect the aggregate consumption function. In both panels, CF_1 is the initial aggregate consumption function. Panel (a) shows the effect of good news: information that leads consumers to expect higher disposable income in the future than they did before. Consumers will now spend more at any given level of current disposable income, YD, corresponding to an increase in A, aggregate autonomous consumer spending, from A_1 to A_2. The effect is to shift the aggregate consumption function up, from CF_1 to CF_2.

Panel (b) shows the effect of bad news: information that leads consumers to expect lower disposable income in the future than they did before. Consumers will now spend less at any given level of current disposable income, YD, corresponding to a fall in A from A_1 to A_2. The effect is to shift the aggregate consumption function down, from CF_1 to CF_2.

CHANGES IN AGGREGATE WEALTH Imagine two individuals, Maria and Mark, both of whom expect to earn $30,000 this year. Suppose, however, that they have different histories. Maria has been working steadily for the past 10 years, owns her own home, and has $200,000 in the bank. Mark is the same age as Maria, but he has been in and out of work, hasn't managed to buy a house, and has very little in savings. In this case, Maria has something that Mark doesn't have: wealth. Even though they have the same disposable income, other things equal, you'd expect Maria to spend more on consumption than Mark. That is, *wealth* has an effect on consumer spending.

The effect of wealth on spending is emphasized by an influential economic model of how consumers make choices about spending versus saving called the *life-cycle hypothesis*. According to this hypothesis, consumers plan their spending over a lifetime, not just in response to their current disposable income. As a result, people try to smooth their consumption over their lifetimes—they save some of their current disposable income during their years of peak earnings (typically occurring during a worker's 40s and 50s) and during their retirement live off the wealth they accumulated while working.

We won't go into the details of the life-cycle hypothesis but will simply point out that it implies an important role for wealth in determining consumer spending. For example, a middle-aged couple

Consumers tend to avoid high-priced brand-name goods and seek out less expensive alternatives when aggregate wealth declines.

Joseph Sibilsky/Alamy

who have accumulated a lot of wealth—who have paid off the mortgage on their house and already own plenty of stocks and bonds—will, other things equal, spend more on goods and services than a couple who have the same current disposable income but still need to save for their retirement.

Because wealth affects household consumer spending, changes in wealth across the economy can shift the aggregate consumption function. A rise in aggregate wealth—say, because of a booming stock market—increases the vertical intercept A, aggregate autonomous consumer spending. This, in turn, shifts the aggregate consumption function up in the same way as does an expected increase in future disposable income. A decline in aggregate wealth—say, because of a fall in housing prices—reduces A and shifts the aggregate consumption function down.

Investment Spending

Although consumer spending is much larger than investment spending, booms and busts in investment spending tend to drive the business cycle. In fact, most recessions originate as a fall in investment spending. Figure 25-5 illustrates this point; it shows the annual percent change of investment spending and consumer spending in the United States, measured in real terms, during six recessions from 1973 to 2009. As you can see, swings in investment spending are much more dramatic than those in consumer spending. In addition, due to the multiplier process, economists believe that declines in consumer spending are usually the result of a process that begins with a slump in investment spending. Soon we'll examine in more detail how a slump in investment spending generates a fall in consumer spending through the multiplier process.

FIGURE 25-5   Fluctuations in Investment Spending and Consumer Spending

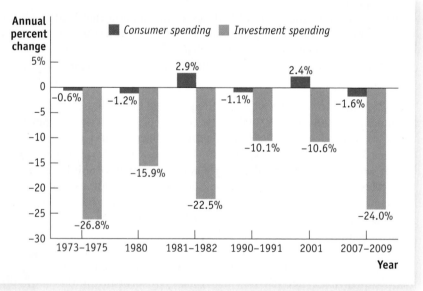

The bars illustrate the annual percent change in investment spending and consumer spending during six recent recessions. As the lengths of the bars show, swings in investment spending were much larger in percentage terms than those in consumer spending. This pattern has led economists to believe that recessions typically originate as a slump in investment spending.

Source: Bureau of Economic Analysis.

Before we do that, however, let's analyze the factors that determine investment spending, which are somewhat different from those that determine consumer spending. The most important ones are the interest rate and expected future real GDP.

It's also important to note that the level of investment spending businesses *actually* carry out is sometimes not the same level as **planned investment spending,** the investment spending that firms *intend* to undertake during a given period. Planned investment spending depends on three principal factors: the interest rate, the expected future level of real GDP, and the current level of production capacity. First, we'll analyze the effect of the interest rate.

Planned investment spending is the investment spending that businesses intend to undertake during a given period.

The Interest Rate and Investment Spending

Interest rates have their clearest effect on one particular form of investment spending: spending on residential construction—that is, on the construction of homes. The reason is straightforward: home builders only build houses they think they can sell, and houses are more affordable—and so more likely to sell—when the interest rate is low.

Consider a potential home-buying family that needs to borrow $150,000 to buy a house. At an interest rate of 7.5%, a 30-year home mortgage will mean payments of $1,048 per month. At an interest rate of 5.5%, those payments would be only $851 per month, making houses significantly more affordable. As described in the upcoming Economics in Action, lower interest rates helped set off the great housing boom described in the section-opening story.

Interest rates also affect other forms of investment spending. Firms with investment spending projects will only go ahead with a project if they expect a rate of return higher than the cost of the funds they would have to borrow to finance that project. As the interest rate rises, fewer projects will pass that test, and as a result investment spending will be lower.

Interest rates directly impact whether or not construction companies decide to invest in the building of new homes.

You might think that the trade-off a firm faces is different if it can fund its investment project with its past profits rather than through borrowing. Past profits used to finance investment spending are called *retained earnings*. But even if a firm pays for investment spending out of retained earnings, the trade-off it must make in deciding whether or not to fund a project remains the same because it must take into account the opportunity cost of its funds. For example, instead of purchasing new equipment, the firm could lend out the funds and earn interest. The forgone interest earned is the opportunity cost of using retained earnings to fund an investment project.

So the trade-off the firm faces when comparing a project's rate of return to the market interest rate has not changed when it uses retained earnings rather than borrowed funds, which means that regardless of whether a firm funds investment spending through borrowing or retained earnings, a rise in the market interest rate makes any given investment project less profitable. Conversely, a fall in the interest rate makes some investment projects that were unprofitable before profitable at the now lower interest rate. So some projects that had been unfunded before will be funded now.

So planned investment spending—spending on investment projects that firms voluntarily decide whether or not to undertake—is negatively related to the interest rate. Other things equal, a higher interest rate leads to a lower level of planned investment spending.

Expected Future Real GDP, Production Capacity, and Investment Spending

Suppose a firm has enough capacity to continue to produce the amount it is currently selling but doesn't expect its sales to grow in the future. Then it will engage in investment spending only to replace existing equipment and structures that wear out or are rendered obsolete by new technologies. But if, instead, the firm expects its sales to grow rapidly in the future, it will find its existing production capacity insufficient for its future production needs. So the firm will undertake investment spending to meet those needs. This implies that, other things equal, firms will undertake more investment spending when they expect their sales to grow.

Now suppose that the firm currently has considerably more capacity than necessary to meet current production needs. Even if it expects sales to grow, it won't have to undertake investment spending for a while—not until the growth in sales catches up with its excess capacity. This illustrates the fact that, other things equal, the current

According to the **accelerator princi-ple,** a higher growth rate of real GDP leads to higher planned investment spending, but a lower growth rate of real GDP leads to lower planned investment spending.

Inventories are stocks of goods held to satisfy future sales.

Inventory investment is the value of the change in total inventories held in the economy during a given period.

Unplanned inventory investment occurs when actual sales are more or less than businesses expected, leading to unplanned changes in inventories.

Actual investment spending is the sum of planned investment spending and unplanned inventory investment.

level of productive capacity has a negative effect on investment spending: other things equal, the higher the current capacity, the lower the investment spending.

If we put together the effects on investment spending of growth in expected future sales and the size of current production capacity, we can see one situation in which we can be reasonably sure that firms will undertake high levels of investment spending: when they expect sales to grow rapidly. In that case, even excess production capacity will soon be used up, leading firms to resume investment spending.

What is an indicator of high expected growth of future sales? It's a high expected future growth rate of real GDP. A higher expected future growth rate of real GDP results in a higher level of planned investment spending, but a lower expected future growth rate of real GDP leads to lower planned investment spending. This relationship is summarized in a proposition known as the **accelerator principle.**

As we explain in the upcoming Economics in Action, when expectations of future real GDP growth turned negative, planned investment spending—and, in particular, residential investment spending—plunged, accelerating the economy's slide into recession. Generally, the effects of the accelerator principle play an important role in *investment spending slumps,* periods of low investment spending.

Inventories and Unplanned Investment Spending

Most firms maintain **inventories,** stocks of goods held to satisfy future sales. Firms hold inventories so they can quickly satisfy buyers—a consumer can purchase an item off the shelf rather than waiting for it to be manufactured. In addition, businesses often hold inventories of their inputs to be sure they have a steady supply of necessary materials and spare parts. At the end of 2012, the overall value of inventories in the U.S. economy was estimated at $1.5 trillion, just over 10% of GDP.

A firm that increases its inventories is engaging in a form of investment spending. Suppose, for example, that the U.S. auto industry produces 800,000 cars per month but sells only 700,000. The remaining 100,000 cars are added to the inventory at auto company warehouses or car dealerships, ready to be sold in the future.

Inventory investment is the value of the change in total inventories held in the economy during a given period. Unlike other forms of investment spending, inventory investment can actually be negative. If, for example, the auto industry reduces its inventory over the course of a month, we say that it has engaged in negative inventory investment.

Firms undertake high levels of investment spending when they expect the economy to grow rapidly. If an economic slump is expected, they do the opposite.

Johner Images/Alamy

To understand inventory investment, think about a manager stocking the canned goods section of a supermarket. The manager tries to keep the store fully stocked so that shoppers can almost always find what they're looking for. But the manager does not want the shelves too heavily stocked because shelf space is limited and products can spoil.

Similar considerations apply to many firms and typically lead them to manage their inventories carefully. However, sales fluctuate. And because firms cannot always accurately predict sales, they often find themselves holding more or less inventories than they had intended. These unintended swings in inventories due to unforeseen changes in sales are called **unplanned inventory investment.** They represent investment spending, positive or negative, that occurred but was unplanned.

So in any given period, **actual investment spending** is equal to planned investment spending plus unplanned inventory investment. If we let $I_{Unplanned}$ represent unplanned inventory investment, $I_{Planned}$ represent planned investment spending, and *I* represent actual investment spending, then the relationship among all three can be represented as:

(25-6) $I = I_{Unplanned} + I_{Planned}$

To see how unplanned inventory investment can occur, let's continue to focus on the auto industry and make the following assumptions. First, let's assume that the industry must determine each month's production volume in advance, before it knows the volume of actual sales. Second, let's assume that it anticipates selling 800,000 cars next month and that it plans neither to add to nor subtract from existing inventories. In that case, it will produce 800,000 cars to match anticipated sales.

Now imagine that next month's actual sales are less than expected, only 700,000 cars. As a result, the value of 100,000 cars will be added to investment spending as unplanned inventory investment.

The auto industry will, of course, eventually adjust to this slowdown in sales and the resulting unplanned inventory investment. It is likely that it will cut next month's production volume in order to reduce inventories. In fact, economists who study macroeconomic variables in an attempt to determine the future path of the economy pay careful attention to changes in inventory levels. Rising inventories typically indicate positive unplanned inventory investment and a slowing economy, as sales are less than had been forecast. Falling inventories typically indicate negative unplanned inventory investment and a growing economy, as sales are greater than forecast.

ECONOMICS ▶ IN ACTION

INTEREST RATES AND THE U.S. HOUSING BOOM

The housing boom in the Ft. Myers metropolitan area, described at the beginning of this section, was part of a broader housing boom in the country as a whole. There is little question that this housing boom was caused, in the first instance, by low interest rates.

Figure 25-6 shows the interest rate on 30-year home mortgages—the traditional way to borrow money for a home purchase—and the number of housing starts, the number of homes for which construction is started per month, from 1997 to early 2013, in the United States. Panel (a), which shows the mortgage rate, gives you an idea of how much interest rates fell. In the second half of the 1990s, mortgage rates

FIGURE 25-6   Interest Rates and the U.S. Housing Boom

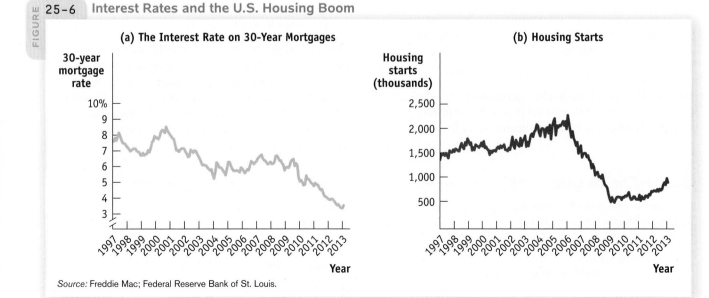

Source: Freddie Mac; Federal Reserve Bank of St. Louis.

generally fluctuated between 7% and 8%; by 2003, they were down to between 5% and 6%. These lower rates were largely the result of Federal Reserve policy: the Fed cut rates in response to the 2001 recession and continued cutting them into 2003 out of concern that the economy's recovery was too weak to generate sustained job growth.

The low interest rates led to a large increase in residential investment spending, reflected in a surge of housing starts, shown in panel (b). This rise in investment spending drove an overall economic expansion, both through its direct effects and through the multiplier process.

Unfortunately, the housing boom eventually turned into too much of a good thing. By 2006, it was clear that the U.S. housing market was experiencing a bubble: people were buying housing based on unrealistic expectations about future price increases. When the bubble burst, housing—and the U.S. economy—took a fall. The fall was so severe that even when the Fed cut rates to near zero, and mortgage rates consequently dropped to below 5% beginning in 2009, housing starts merely stabilized. It wasn't until 2012 that housing starts began to increase again.

MODULE

25 Review

Solutions appear at the back of the book.

Check Your Understanding

1. Suppose the economy consists of three people: Angelina, Felicia, and Marina. The table shows how their consumer spending varies as their current disposable income rises by $10,000.

Current disposable income	Consumer spending		
	Angelina	Felicia	Marina
$0	$8,000	$6,500	$7,250
10,000	12,000	14,500	14,250

   a. Derive each individual's consumption function, where *MPC* is calculated for a $10,000 change in current disposable income.

   b. Derive the aggregate consumption function.

2. Suppose that problems in the capital markets make consumers unable either to borrow or to put money aside for future use. What implication does this have for the effects of expected future disposable income on consumer spending?

3. For each event, explain whether planned investment spending or unplanned inventory investment will change and in what direction.

   a. an unexpected increase in consumer spending

   b. a sharp rise in the cost of business borrowing

   c. a sharp increase in the economy's growth rate of real GDP

   d. an unanticipated fall in sales

4. When consumer spending is sluggish an *inventory overhang*—a high level of unplanned inventory investment throughout the economy—can make it difficult for the economy to recover quickly. Explain why an inventory overhang might, like the existence of too much production capacity, depress current economic activity.

Multiple-Choice Questions

1. Changes in which of the following lead to a shift of the aggregate consumption function?

   I. expected future disposable income

   II. aggregate wealth

   III. current disposable income

   a. I only

   b. II only

   c. III only

   d. I and II only

   e. I, II, and III

2. The slope of a family's consumption function is equal to
   a. the real interest rate.
   b. the inflation rate.
   c. the marginal propensity to consume.
   d. the rate of increase in household current disposable income.
   e. the tax rate.

3. Given the consumption function $c = \$16,000 + 0.5\,yd$, if individual household current disposable income is $20,000, individual household consumer spending will equal
   a. $36,000.
   b. $26,000.
   c. $20,000.
   d. $16,000.
   e. $6,000.

4. The level of planned investment spending is negatively related to the
   a. rate of return on investment.
   b. level of consumer spending.
   c. level of actual investment spending.
   d. interest rate.
   e. all of the above.

5. Actual investment spending in any period is equal to
   a. planned investment spending + unplanned inventory investment.
   b. planned investment spending – unplanned inventory investment.
   c. planned investment spending + inventory decreases.
   d. unplanned inventory investment + inventory increases.
   e. unplanned inventory investment – inventory increases.

Critical-Thinking Question

List the three most important factors affecting planned investment spending. Explain how each is related to actual investment spending.

MODULE 26 The Income–Expenditure Model

moodboard/Alamy

WHAT YOU WILL LEARN

1. **How planned aggregate spending determines income–expenditure equilibrium**

2. **How the inventory adjustment process moves the economy to a new equilibrium after a change in planned aggregate spending**

Using the Income–Expenditure Model

Earlier in this section, we described how autonomous changes in spending—such as a fall in investment spending when a housing bubble bursts—lead to a multistage process through the actions of the multiplier that magnifies the effect of these changes on real GDP. In this module, we will examine this multistage process more closely. We'll see that the multiple rounds of changes in real GDP are accomplished through changes in the amount of output produced by firms—changes that they make in response to changes in their inventories. We'll come to understand why inventories play a central role in macroeconomic models of the economy in the short run as well as why economists pay particular attention to the behavior of firms' inventories when trying to understand the likely future state of the economy.

Before we begin, let's quickly recap the assumptions underlying the multiplier process.

1. *Changes in overall spending lead to changes in aggregate output.* We assume that producers are willing to supply additional output at a fixed price level. As a result, changes in spending translate into changes in output rather than moves of the overall price level up or down. A fixed aggregate price level also implies that there is no difference between nominal GDP and real GDP. So we can use the two terms interchangeably in this module.

2. *The interest rate is fixed.* As we'll see, the model we examine here can still be used to study the effects of a change in the interest rate.

3. *Taxes, government transfers, and government purchases are all zero.*

4. *Exports and imports are both zero.*

258

Planned Aggregate Spending and Real GDP

In an economy with no government and no foreign trade, there are only two sources of aggregate spending: consumer spending, C, and investment spending, I. And since we assume that there are no taxes or transfers, aggregate disposable income is equal to GDP (which, since the aggregate price level is fixed, is the same as real GDP): the total value of final sales of goods and services ultimately accrues to households as income. So in this highly simplified economy, there are two basic equations of national income accounting:

(26-1) $GDP = C + I$

(26-2) $YD = GDP$

As we learned in the previous module, the aggregate consumption function shows the relationship between disposable income and consumer spending. Let's continue to assume that the aggregate consumption function is of the same form as in Equation 25-5:

(26-3) $C = A + MPC \times YD$

In our simplified model, we will also assume planned investment spending, $I_{Planned}$, is fixed.

We need one more concept before putting the model together: **planned aggregate spending,** the total amount of planned spending in the economy. Unlike firms, households don't take unintended actions like unplanned inventory investment. So planned aggregate spending is equal to the sum of consumer spending and planned investment spending. We denote planned aggregate spending by $AE_{Planned}$, so:

(26-4) $AE_{Planned} = C + I_{Planned}$

The level of planned aggregate spending in a given year depends on the level of real GDP in that year. To see why, let's look at a specific example, shown in Table 26-1. We assume that the aggregate consumption function is:

(26-5) $C = 300 + 0.6 \times YD$

Real GDP, YD, C, $I_{Planned}$, and $AE_{Planned}$ are all measured in billions of dollars, and we assume that the level of planned investment, $I_{Planned}$, is fixed at $500 billion per year. The first column shows possible levels of real GDP. The second column shows disposable income, YD, which in our simplified model is equal to real GDP. The third column shows consumer spending, C, equal to $300 billion plus 0.6 times disposable income, YD. The fourth column shows planned investment spending, $I_{Planned}$, which we have assumed is $500 billion regardless of the level of real GDP.

Finally, the last column shows planned aggregate spending, $AE_{Planned}$, the sum of aggregate consumer spending, C, and planned investment spending, $I_{Planned}$. (To economize on notation, we'll assume that it is understood from now on that all the variables in Table 26-1 are measured in billions of dollars per year.) As you can see, a higher level of real GDP leads to a higher level of disposable income: every 500 increase in real GDP raises YD by 500, which in turn raises C by $500 \times 0.6 = 300$ and $AE_{Planned}$ by 300.

Figure 26-1 illustrates the information in Table 26-1 graphically. Real GDP is measured on the horizontal axis. CF is the aggregate consumption function; it shows how consumer spending depends on real GDP. $AE_{Planned}$, the planned aggregate spending line, corresponds to the aggregate consumption function shifted up by 500 (the amount of $I_{Planned}$). It shows how planned aggregate spending depends on real GDP. Both lines have a slope of 0.6, equal to MPC, the marginal propensity to consume.

But this isn't the end of the story. Table 26-1 reveals that real GDP equals planned aggregate spending, $AE_{Planned}$, only when the level of real GDP is at 2,000. Real GDP does not equal $AE_{Planned}$ at any other level. Is that possible? Didn't we learn from the circular-flow diagram that total spending on final goods and services in the economy

TABLE 26-1

Real GDP	YD	C	$I_{Planned}$	$AE_{Planned}$
(billions of dollars)				
$0	$0	$300	$500	$800
500	500	600	500	1,100
1,000	1,000	900	500	1,400
1,500	1,500	1,200	500	1,700
2,000	2,000	1,500	500	2,000
2,500	2,500	1,800	500	2,300
3,000	3,000	2,100	500	2,600
3,500	3,500	2,400	500	2,900

Planned aggregate spending is the total amount of planned spending in the economy.

FIGURE 26-1   The Aggregate Consumption Function and Planned Aggregate Spending

The lower line, *CF*, is the aggregate consumption function constructed from the data in Table 26-1. The upper line, *AE*_{Planned}, is the planned aggregate spending line, also constructed from the data in Table 26-1. It is equivalent to the aggregate consumption function shifted up by $500 billion, the amount of planned investment spending, *I*_{Planned}.

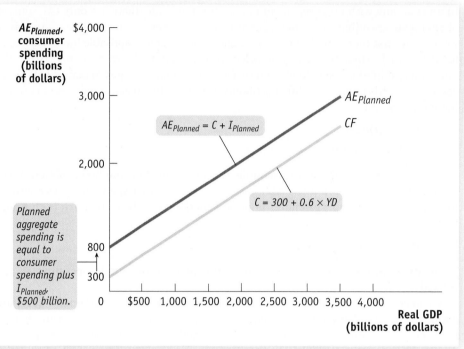

is equal to the total value of output of final goods and services? The answer is that for *brief* periods of time, planned aggregate spending can differ from real GDP because of the role of *unplanned* aggregate spending—$I_{Unplanned}$, unplanned inventory investment. But as we'll see, the economy moves over time to a situation in which there is no unplanned inventory investment, a situation called *income–expenditure equilibrium*. And when the economy is in income–expenditure equilibrium, planned aggregate spending on final goods and services equals aggregate output.

Income–Expenditure Equilibrium

For all but one value of real GDP shown in Table 26-1, real GDP is either more or less than $AE_{Planned}$, the sum of consumer spending and *planned* investment spending. For example, when real GDP is 1,000, consumer spending, C, is 900 and planned investment spending is 500, making planned aggregate spending 1,400. This is 400 *more* than the corresponding level of real GDP. Now consider what happens when real GDP is 2,500; consumer spending, C, is 1,800 and planned investment spending is 500, making planned aggregate spending only 2,300, 200 *less* than real GDP.

As we've just explained, planned aggregate spending can be different from real GDP only if there is unplanned inventory investment, $I_{Unplanned}$, in the economy. Let's examine Table 26-2, which includes the numbers for real GDP and for planned aggregate spending from Table 26-1. It also includes the levels of unplanned inventory investment, $I_{Unplanned}$, that each combination of real GDP and planned aggregate spending implies. For example, if real GDP is 2,500, planned aggregate spending is only 2,300. This 200 excess of real GDP over $AE_{Planned}$ must consist of positive unplanned inventory investment. This can happen only if firms have overestimated sales and produced too much, leading to unintended additions to inventories. More generally, any level of real GDP in excess of 2,000 corresponds to a situation in which firms are producing more than consumers and other firms want to purchase, creating an unintended increase in inventories.

Conversely, a level of real GDP below 2,000 implies that planned aggregate spending is *greater* than real GDP. For example, when real GDP is 1,000, planned aggregate

TABLE 26-2

Real GDP	AE_{Planned}	I_{Unplanned}
(billions of dollars)		
$0	$800	−$800
500	1,100	−600
1,000	1,400	−400
1,500	1,700	−200
2,000	2,000	0
2,500	2,300	200
3,000	2,600	400
3,500	2,900	600

spending is much larger, at 1,400. The 400 excess of $AE_{Planned}$ over real GDP corresponds to negative unplanned inventory investment equal to −400. More generally, any level of real GDP below 2,000 implies that firms have underestimated sales, leading to a negative level of unplanned inventory investment in the economy.

By putting together Equations 26-6, 26-1, and 26-4, we can summarize the general relationships among real GDP, planned aggregate spending, and unplanned inventory investment as follows:

$$(26-6) \quad GDP = C + I$$
$$= C + I_{Planned} + I_{Unplanned}$$
$$= AE_{Planned} + I_{Unplanned}$$

So whenever real GDP exceeds $AE_{Planned}$, $I_{Unplanned}$ is positive; whenever real GDP is less than $AE_{Planned}$, $I_{Unplanned}$ is negative.

But firms will act to correct their mistakes. We've assumed that they don't change their prices, but they *can* adjust their output. Specifically, they will reduce production if they have experienced an unintended rise in inventories or increase production if they have experienced an unintended fall in inventories. And these responses will eventually eliminate the unanticipated changes in inventories and move the economy to a point at which real GDP is equal to planned aggregate spending.

Staying with our example, if real GDP is 1,000, negative unplanned inventory investment will lead firms to increase production, leading to a rise in real GDP. In fact, this will happen whenever real GDP is less than 2,000—that is, whenever real GDP is less than planned aggregate spending. Conversely, if real GDP is 2,500, positive unplanned inventory investment will lead firms to reduce production, leading to a fall in real GDP. This will happen whenever real GDP is greater than planned aggregate spending.

Firms can adjust output and inventory to correct for sales projections that were too high or low, helping to move the economy back to equilibrium.

The only situation in which firms won't have an incentive to change output in the next period is when aggregate output, measured by real GDP, is equal to planned aggregate spending in the current period, an outcome known as **income–expenditure equilibrium.** In Table 26-2, income–expenditure equilibrium is achieved when real GDP is 2,000, the only level of real GDP at which unplanned inventory investment is zero. From now on, we'll denote the real GDP level at which income–expenditure equilibrium occurs as Y^* and call it the **income–expenditure equilibrium GDP.**

Figure 26-2 illustrates the concept of income–expenditure equilibrium graphically. Real GDP is on the horizontal axis and planned aggregate spending, $AE_{Planned}$, is on the vertical axis. There are two lines in the figure. The solid line is the planned aggregate spending line. It shows how $AE_{Planned}$, equal to $C + I_{Planned}$, depends on real GDP; it has a slope of 0.6, equal to the marginal propensity to consume, MPC, and a vertical intercept equal to $A + I_{Planned}$ (300 + 500 = 800).

The dashed line, which goes through the origin with a slope of 1 (often called a 45-degree line), shows all the possible points at which planned aggregate spending is equal to real GDP. This line allows us to easily spot the point of income–expenditure equilibrium, which must lie on both the 45-degree line and the planned aggregate spending line. So the point of income–expenditure equilibrium is at E, where the two lines cross. And the income–expenditure equilibrium GDP, Y^*, is 2,000—the same outcome we derived in Table 26-2.

The economy is in **income–expenditure equilibrium** when aggregate output, measured by real GDP, is equal to planned aggregate spending.

Income–expenditure equilibrium GDP is the level of real GDP at which real GDP equals planned aggregate spending.

26-2   Income–Expenditure Equilibrium

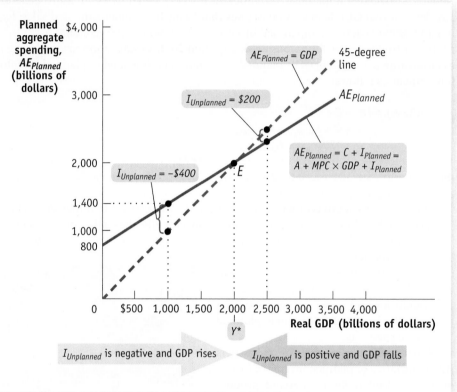

Income–expenditure equilibrium occurs at E, the point where the planned aggregate spending line, $AE_{Planned}$, crosses the 45-degree line. At E, the economy produces real GDP of $2,000 billion per year, the only point at which real GDP equals planned aggregate spending, $AE_{Planned}$, and unplanned inventory investment, $I_{Unplanned}$, is zero. This is the level of income–expenditure equilibrium GDP, Y^*. At any level of real GDP less than Y^*, $AE_{Planned}$ exceeds real GDP. As a result, unplanned inventory investment, $I_{Unplanned}$, is negative and firms respond by increasing production. At any level of real GDP greater than Y^*, real GDP exceeds $AE_{Planned}$. Unplanned inventory investment, $I_{Unplanned}$, is positive and firms respond by reducing production.

Now consider what happens if the economy isn't in income–expenditure equilibrium. We can see from Figure 26-2 that whenever real GDP is less than Y^*, the planned aggregate spending line lies above the 45-degree line and $AE_{Planned}$ exceeds real GDP. In this situation, $I_{Unplanned}$ is negative: as shown in the figure, at a real GDP of 1,000, $I_{Unplanned}$ is −400. As a consequence, real GDP will rise. In contrast, whenever real GDP is greater than Y^*, the planned aggregate expenditure line lies below the 45-degree line. Here, $I_{Unplanned}$ is positive: as shown, at a real GDP of 2,500, $I_{Unplanned}$ is 200. The unanticipated accumulation of inventory leads to a fall in real GDP.

The type of diagram shown in Figure 26-2, which identifies income–expenditure equilibrium as the point at which the planned aggregate spending line crosses the 45-degree line, has a special place in the history of economic thought. Known as the **Keynesian cross,** it was developed by Paul Samuelson, one of the greatest economists of the twentieth century (as well as a Nobel Prize winner), to explain the ideas of John Maynard Keynes, the founder of macroeconomics as we know it.

The Multiplier Process and Inventory Adjustment

We've just learned about a very important feature of the macroeconomy: when planned spending by households and firms does not equal the current aggregate output by firms, this difference shows up in changes in inventories. The response of firms to those inventory changes moves real GDP over time to the point at which real GDP and planned aggregate spending are equal. That's why, as we mentioned earlier, changes in inventories are considered a leading indicator of future economic activity.

Now that we understand how real GDP moves to achieve income–expenditure equilibrium for a given level of planned aggregate spending, let's turn to understanding what happens when there is *a shift of the planned aggregate spending line.* How does the economy move from the initial point of income–expenditure equilibrium to a new point of income–expenditure equilibrium? And what are the possible sources of changes in planned aggregate spending?

The **Keynesian cross** diagram identifies income–expenditure equilibrium as the point where the planned aggregate spending line crosses the 45-degree line.

In our simple model there are only two possible sources of a shift of the planned aggregate spending line: a change in planned investment spending, $I_{Planned}$, or a shift of the aggregate consumption function, CF. For example, a change in $I_{Planned}$ can occur because of a change in the interest rate. (Remember, we're assuming that the interest rate is fixed by factors that are outside the model. But we can still ask what happens when the interest rate changes.) A shift of the aggregate consumption function (that is, a change in its vertical intercept, A) can occur because of a change in aggregate wealth—say, due to a rise in house prices.

When the planned aggregate spending line shifts—when there is a change in the level of planned aggregate spending at any given level of real GDP—there is an autonomous change in planned aggregate spending. Recall that an autonomous change in planned aggregate spending is a change in the desired level of spending by firms, households, and government at any given level of real GDP (although we've assumed away the government for the time being). How does an autonomous change in planned aggregate spending affect real GDP in income–expenditure equilibrium?

Table 26-3 and Figure 26-3 start from the same numerical example we used in Table 26-2 and Figure 26-2. They also show the effect of an autonomous increase in planned aggregate spending of 400—what happens when planned aggregate spending is 400 higher at each level of real GDP. Look first at Table 26-3. Before the autonomous increase in planned aggregate spending, the level of real GDP at which planned aggregate spending is equal to real GDP, Y^*, is 2,000. After the autonomous change, Y^* has risen to 3,000.

The same result is visible in Figure 26-3. The initial income–expenditure equilibrium is at E_1, where Y_1^* is 2,000. The autonomous rise in planned aggregate spending shifts the planned aggregate spending line up, leading to a new income–expenditure equilibrium at E_2, where Y_2^* is 3,000.

TABLE 26-3

Real GDP	$AE_{Planned}$ before autonomous change	$AE_{Planned}$ after autonomous change
	(billions of dollars)	
$0	$800	$1,200
500	1,100	1,500
1,000	1,400	1,800
1,500	1,700	2,100
2,000	2,000	2,400
2,500	2,300	2,700
3,000	2,600	3,000
3,500	2,900	3,300
4,000	3,200	3,600

FIGURE 26-3   The Multiplier

This figure illustrates the change in Y^* caused by an autonomous increase in planned aggregate spending. The economy is initially at equilibrium point E_1 with an income–expenditure equilibrium GDP, Y_1^*, equal to 2,000. An autonomous increase in $AE_{Planned}$ of 400 shifts the planned aggregate spending line upward by 400. The economy is no longer in income–expenditure equilibrium: real GDP is equal to 2,000 but $AE_{Planned}$ is now 2,400, represented by point X. The vertical distance between the two planned aggregate spending lines, equal to 400, represents $I_{Unplanned} = -400$—the negative inventory investment that the economy now experiences. Firms respond by increasing production, and the economy eventually reaches a new income–expenditure equilibrium at E_2 with a higher level of income–expenditure equilibrium GDP, Y_2^*, equal to 3,000.

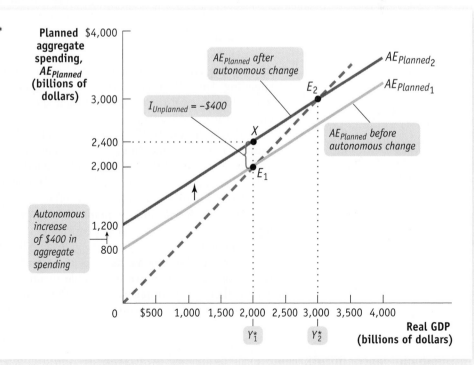

The fact that the rise in income–expenditure equilibrium GDP, from 2,000 to 3,000, is much larger than the autonomous increase in aggregate spending, which is only 400, has a familiar explanation: the multiplier process. In the specific example we have just described, an autonomous increase in planned aggregate spending of 400 leads to an increase in Y^* from 2,000 to 3,000, a rise of 1,000. So the multiplier in this example is $1,000/400 = 2.5$.

We can examine in detail what underlies the multistage multiplier process by looking more closely at Figure 26-3. First, starting from E_1, the autonomous increase in planned aggregate spending leads to a gap between planned aggregate spending and real GDP. This is represented by the vertical distance between X, at 2,400, and E_1, at 2,000. This gap illustrates an unplanned fall in inventory investment: $I_{Unplanned} = -400$. Firms respond by increasing production, leading to a rise in real GDP from Y_1^*. The rise in real GDP translates into an increase in disposable income, YD.

That's the first stage in the chain reaction. But it doesn't stop there—the increase in YD leads to a rise in consumer spending, C, which sets off a second-round rise in real GDP. This in turn leads to a further rise in disposable income and consumer spending, and so on. And we could play this process in reverse: an autonomous fall in aggregate spending will lead to a chain reaction of reductions in real GDP and consumer spending.

We can summarize these results in an equation, where $\Delta AAE_{Planned}$ represents the autonomous change in $AE_{Planned}$, and $\Delta Y^* = Y_2^* - Y_1^*$, the subsequent change in income–expenditure equilibrium GDP:

$$\textbf{(26-7)} \quad \Delta Y^* = \text{Multiplier} \times \Delta AAE_{Planned} = \frac{1}{1 - MPC} \times \Delta AAE_{Planned}$$

Recalling that the multiplier, $1/(1 - MPC)$, is greater than 1, Equation 26-7 tells us that the change in income–expenditure equilibrium GDP, ΔY^*, is several times as large as the autonomous change in planned aggregate spending, $\Delta AAE_{Planned}$. It also helps us recall an important point: because the marginal propensity to consume is less than 1, each increase in disposable income and each corresponding increase in consumer spending is smaller than in the previous round. That's because at each round some of the increase in disposable income leaks out into savings. As a result, although real GDP grows at each round, the increase in real GDP diminishes from each round to the next. At some point the increase in real GDP is negligible, and the economy converges to a new income–expenditure equilibrium GDP at Y_2^*.

THE PARADOX OF THRIFT Let's now consider what happens when there is a slump in consumer spending or investment spending, or both. This causes a fall in income–expenditure equilibrium GDP that is several times larger than the original fall in spending. The fall in real GDP leaves consumers and producers worse off than they would have been if they hadn't cut their spending. Economists refer to this phenomenon as the *paradox of thrift*.

In the paradox of thrift, households and firms cut their spending in anticipation of future tough economic times. These actions depress the economy, leaving households and firms worse off than if they hadn't acted virtuously to prepare for tough times. It is called a paradox because what's usually "good" (saving for hard times) is "bad" (because it can make everyone worse off).

We've seen that declines in planned investment spending are usually the major factor causing recessions, because historically they have been the most common source of autonomous reductions in aggregate spending. Likewise, we know that consumption spending can change as a result of an increase or decrease in the aggregate wealth or expected future disposable income of individuals. But regardless of the source, there are multiplier effects in the economy that magnify the size of the initial change in aggregate spending.

ECONOMICS ▶ IN ACTION

INVENTORIES AND THE END OF A RECESSION

A very clear example of the role of inventories in the multiplier process took place in late 2001, as that year's recession came to an end.

The driving force behind the recession was a slump in business investment spending. It took several years before investment spending bounced back in the form of a housing boom. Still, the economy did start to recover in late 2001, largely because of an increase in consumer spending—especially on durable goods such as automobiles.

FIGURE 26-4 Inventories and the End of a Recession

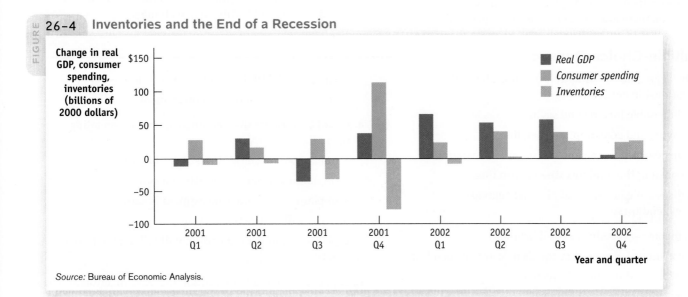

Source: Bureau of Economic Analysis.

Initially, this increase in consumer spending caught manufacturers by surprise. Figure 26-4 shows changes in real GDP, real consumer spending, and real inventories in each quarter of 2001 and 2002. Notice the surge in consumer spending in the fourth quarter of 2001. It didn't lead to a lot of GDP growth because it was offset by a plunge in inventories. But in the first quarter of 2002 producers greatly increased their production, leading to a jump in real GDP.

26 Review

Solutions appear at the back of the book.

Check Your Understanding

1. Although economists believe that recessions typically begin as slumps in investment spending, they also believe that consumer spending eventually slumps during a recession. Explain why.

2. **a.** Use a diagram like Figure 26-3 to show what happens when there is an autonomous fall in planned aggregate spending. Describe how the economy adjusts to a new income–expenditure equilibrium.

   b. Suppose Y^* is originally $500 billion, the autonomous reduction in planned aggregate spending is $300 million ($0.3 billion), and $MPC = 0.5$. Calculate Y^* after such a change.

Multiple-Choice Questions

1. The aggregate consumption function shows the relationship between
   a. disposable income and saving.
   b. saving and consumption spending.
   c. disposable income and consumption spending.
   d. consumption and investment spending.
   e. disposable income and planned aggregate expenditure.

2. In income–expenditure equilibrium
   a. consumption spending equals investment spending.
   b. unplanned inventory investment is zero.
   c. inventory investment is zero.
   d. investment spending is zero.
   e. consumption spending equals real GDP.

3. Planned aggregate spending
   a. always equals real GDP.
   b. never equals real GDP.
   c. equals real GDP if unplanned inventory investment is zero.
   d. equals real GDP if inventory investment is zero.
   e. equals consumption plus investment spending.

4. If real GDP is less than planned aggregate spending then
   a. unplanned inventory investment is positive.
   b. unplanned inventory investment is negative.
   c. unplanned inventory investment is zero.
   d. firms will reduce production.
   e. planned aggregate spending will fall to match real GDP.

5. Suppose there is a $200 million increase in autonomous planned aggregate spending. This will cause the planned aggregate spending line to shift upwards by _____ and real GDP will increase by _____.
   a. $200 million; $200 million
   b. $200 million; less than $200 million
   c. $200 million; more than $200 million
   d. more than $200 million; more than $200 million
   e. more than $200 million; $200 million

Critical-Thinking Question

What is the value of unplanned inventory investment in income–expenditure equilibrium? Why?

BUSINESS CASE : Making It Through in Muskegon

Muskegon, Michigan, is no Ft. Myers. Unlike the Florida city whose boom and bust we described in this section's opening story, Muskegon didn't have a housing boom in the mid-2000s. And it didn't have that much of a housing bust, either.

Since real estate wasn't a big part of the local economy, the housing bubble burst couldn't do much to drag that economy down. So you might think that Muskegon-area businesses were somewhat insulated from the resulting national downturn.

However, Muskegon businesses were nonetheless hit hard by the recession. For example, Eagle Alloy—a manufacturing company that sells its products to a wide variety of industries, but not especially to the housing or construction sectors—saw its sales drop by 50%. And it wasn't only manufacturers selling to a national market that were hit.

As factories in the Muskegon–Norton Shores metropolitan area laid off workers, and the local unemployment rate increased from around 6% in 2001 to over 15% during 2010, local businesses that depended on these workers' paychecks were hurt as well; employment in retail businesses fell about 8% over the course of the recession.

This story does, however, have a somewhat happy ending.

As the U.S. economy as a whole began to recover, so did Eagle Alloy and other Muskegon-area manufacturing companies. During the recession, Eagle cut its workforce from 430 to 200, but following the recession, the workforce was back to more than 400, and the company was planning to hire another 150 workers. Eagle Alloy's president, Mark Fazakerley, was predicting a 25% increase in sales.

In the broader Muskegon–Norton Shores metropolitan area, by mid-2013, the local unemployment rate had fallen back down to under 9%. And as manufacturing for the national market revived, businesses with local sales also bounced back; the redevelopment of Muskegon's downtown, which stalled during the recession, had resumed.

Questions for Thought

1. Why did a national slump that began with housing affect companies like Eagle Alloy that didn't sell much to the construction industry?

2. Why did the troubles of Muskegon manufacturers spread to other industries, like retailing?

3. How does this story about Muskegon help explain how a slump in housing—a relatively small part of the U.S. economy—could produce such a deep national recession?

SECTION 7 REVIEW

Summary

The Multiplier

1. An **autonomous change in aggregate spending** leads to a chain reaction in which the total change in real GDP is equal to the **multiplier** times the initial change in aggregate spending.

2. The size of the multiplier, $1/(1 - MPC)$, depends on the **marginal propensity to consume, MPC,** the fraction of an additional dollar of disposable income spent on consumption.

3. The larger the *MPC*, the larger the multiplier and the larger the change in real GDP for any given autonomous change in aggregate spending. The **marginal propensity to save, MPS,** is equal to $1 - MPC$.

Consumption and Investment Spending

4. The **consumption function** shows how an individual household's consumer spending is determined by its current disposable income. The **aggregate consumption function** shows the relationship for the entire economy. According to the life-cycle hypothesis, households try to smooth their consumption over their lifetimes. As a result, the aggregate consumption function shifts in response to changes in expected future disposable income and changes in aggregate wealth.

5. **Planned investment spending** depends negatively on the interest rate and on existing production capacity; it depends positively on expected future real GDP. The **accelerator principle** says that investment spending is greatly influenced by the expected growth rate of real GDP.

6. Firms hold **inventories** of goods so that they can satisfy consumer demand quickly. **Inventory investment** is positive when firms add to their inventories, nega-

tive when they reduce them. Often, however, changes in inventories are not a deliberate decision but the result of mistakes in forecasts about sales. The result is **unplanned inventory investment,** which can be either positive or negative. **Actual investment spending** is the sum of planned investment spending and unplanned inventory investment.

The Income–Expenditure Model

7. In **income–expenditure equilibrium, planned aggregate spending,** which in a simplified model with no government and no foreign trade is the sum of consumer spending and planned investment spending, is equal to real GDP.

8. At the **income–expenditure equilibrium GDP,** or Y^*, unplanned inventory investment is zero. When planned aggregate spending is larger than Y^*, unplanned inventory investment is negative; there is an unanticipated reduction in inventories and firms increase production. When planned aggregate spending is less than Y^*, unplanned inventory investment is positive; there is an unanticipated increase in inventories and firms reduce production.

9. The **Keynesian cross** shows how the economy self-adjusts to income–expenditure equilibrium through inventory adjustments.

10. After an autonomous change in planned aggregate spending, the inventory adjustment process moves the economy to a new income–expenditure equilibrium. The change in income–expenditure equilibrium GDP arising from an autonomous change in spending is equal to $(1/(1 - MPC)) \times \Delta AAE_{Planned}$.

Key Terms

Problems

1. Due to an increase in consumer wealth, there is a $40 billion autonomous increase in consumer spending in the economies of Westlandia and Eastlandia. Assuming that the aggregate price level is constant, the interest rate is fixed in both countries, and there are no taxes and no foreign trade, complete the accompanying tables to show the various rounds of increased spending that will occur in both economies if the marginal propensity to consume is 0.5 in Westlandia and 0.75 in Eastlandia. What do your results indicate about the relationship between the size of the marginal propensity to consume and the multiplier?

Westlandia		
Rounds	Incremental change in GDP	Total change in GDP
1	$\Delta C =$ $40 billion	?
2	$MPC \times \Delta C =$?	?
3	$MPC \times MPC \times \Delta C =$?	?
4	$MPC \times MPC \times MPC \times \Delta C =$?	?
...	...	...
Total change in GDP	$(1/(1 - MPC)) \times \Delta C =$	?

Eastlandia		
Rounds	Incremental change in GDP	Total change in GDP
1	$\Delta C =$ $40 billion	?
2	$MPC \times \Delta C =$?	?
3	$MPC \times MPC \times \Delta C =$?	?
4	$MPC \times MPC \times MPC \times \Delta C =$?	?
...	...	...
Total change in GDP	$(1/(1 - MPC)) \times \Delta C =$	?

2. Assuming that the aggregate price level is constant, the interest rate is fixed, and there are no taxes and no foreign trade, what will be the change in GDP if the following events occur?

   a. There is an autonomous increase in consumer spending of $25 billion; the marginal propensity to consume is 2/3.

   b. Firms reduce investment spending by $40 billion; the marginal propensity to consume is 0.8.

   c. The government increases its purchases of military equipment by $60 billion; the marginal propensity to consume is 0.6.

3. Economists observed the only five residents of a very small economy and estimated each one's consumer spending at various levels of current disposable income. The accompanying table shows each resident's consumer spending at three income levels.

Individual consumer spending by	Individual current disposable income		
	$0	$20,000	$40,000
Andre	1,000	$15,000	29,000
Barbara	2,500	12,500	22,500
Casey	2,000	20,000	38,000
Declan	5,000	17,000	29,000
Elena	4,000	19,000	34,000

a. What is each resident's consumption function? What is the marginal propensity to consume for each resident?

b. What is the economy's aggregate consumption function? What is the marginal propensity to consume for the economy?

4. From 2008 to 2013, Eastlandia experienced large fluctuations in both aggregate consumer spending and disposable income, but wealth, the interest rate, and expected future disposable income did not change. The accompanying table shows the level of aggregate consumer spending and disposable income in millions of dollars for each of these years. Use this information to answer the following questions.

Year	Disposable income (millions of dollars)	Consumer spending (millions of dollars)
2008	$100	$180
2009	350	380
2010	300	340
2011	400	420
2012	375	400
2013	500	500

a. Plot the aggregate consumption function for Eastlandia.

b. What is the marginal propensity to consume? What is the marginal propensity to save?

c. What is the aggregate consumption function?

5. The Bureau of Economic Analysis reported that, in real terms, overall consumer spending increased by $18.2 billion during January 2013.

   a. If the marginal propensity to consume is 0.52, by how much will real GDP change in response?

   b. If there are no other changes to autonomous spending other than the increase in consumer spending in part a, and unplanned inventory investment, $I_{Unplanned}$, decreased by $10 billion, what is the change in real GDP?

   c. GDP at the end of December 2012 was $15,851 billion. If GDP were to increase by the amount calculated in part b, what would be the percent increase in GDP?

6. During the early 2000s, the Case–Shiller U.S. Home Price Index, a measure of average home prices, rose continuously until it peaked in March 2006. From March 2006 to May 2009, the index lost 32% of its value. Meanwhile, the stock market experienced similar ups and downs. From March 2003 to October 2007, the Standard and Poor's 500 (S&P 500) stock index, a broad measure of stock market prices, almost doubled, from 800.73 to a high of 1,565.15. From that time until March 2009, the index fell by almost 60%, to a low of 676.53. How do you think the movements in home prices both influenced the growth in real GDP during the first half of the decade and added to the concern about maintaining consumer spending after the collapse in the housing market that began in 2006? To what extent did the movements in the stock market hurt or help consumer spending?

7. How will planned investment spending change as the following events occur?

  a. The interest rate falls as a result of Federal Reserve policy.

  b. The U.S. Environmental Protection Agency decrees that corporations must upgrade or replace their machinery in order to reduce their emissions of sulfur dioxide.

  c. Baby boomers begin to retire in large numbers and reduce their savings, resulting in higher interest rates.

8. Explain how each of the following actions will affect the level of planned investment spending and unplanned inventory investment. Assume the economy is initially in income–expenditure equilibrium.

  a. The Federal Reserve raises the interest rate.

  b. There is a rise in the expected growth rate of real GDP.

  c. A sizable inflow of foreign funds into the country lowers the interest rate.

9. a. The accompanying table shows GDP, disposable income (YD), consumer spending (C), and planned investment spending ($I_{Planned}$) in an economy. Assume there is no government or foreign sector in this economy. Complete the table by calculating planned aggregate spending ($AE_{Planned}$) and unplanned inventory investment ($I_{Unplanned}$).

GDP	YD	C	$I_{Planned}$	$AE_{Planned}$	$I_{Unplanned}$
(billions of dollars)					
$0	$0	$100	$300	?	?
400	400	400	300	?	?
800	800	700	300	?	?
1,200	1,200	1,000	300	?	?
1,600	1,600	1,300	300	?	?
2,000	2,000	1,600	300	?	?
2,400	2,400	1,900	300	?	?
2,800	2,800	2,200	300	?	?
3,200	3,200	2,500	300	?	?

  b. What is the aggregate consumption function?

  c. What is Y^*, income–expenditure equilibrium GDP?

  d. What is the value of the multiplier?

  e. If planned investment spending falls to $200 billion, what will be the new Y^*?

  f. If autonomous consumer spending rises to $200 billion, what will be the new Y^*?

10. In an economy with no government and no foreign sectors, autonomous consumer spending is $250 billion, planned investment spending is $350 billion, and the marginal propensity to consume is 2/3.

  a. Plot the aggregate consumption function and planned aggregate spending.

  b. What is unplanned inventory investment when real GDP equals $600 billion?

  c. What is Y^*, income–expenditure equilibrium GDP?

  d. What is the value of the multiplier?

  e. If planned investment spending rises to $450 billion, what will be the new Y^*?

11. An economy has a marginal propensity to consume of 0.5, and Y^*, income–expenditure equilibrium GDP, equals $500 billion. Given an autonomous increase in planned investment of $10 billion, show the rounds of increased spending that take place by completing the accompanying table. The first and second rows are filled in for you. In the first row, the increase of planned investment spending of $10 billion raises real GDP and YD by $10 billion, leading to an increase in consumer spending of $5 billion ($MPC \times$ change in disposable income) in row 2, raising real GDP and YD by a further $5 billion.

	Change in $I_{Planned}$ or C	Change in real GDP	Change in YD
Rounds	(billions of dollars)		
1	$\Delta I_{Planned} = \$10.00$	$10.00	$10.00
2	$\Delta C = \$5.00$	$5.00	$5.00
3	$\Delta C = ?$	?	?
4	$\Delta C = ?$	?	?
5	$\Delta C = ?$	?	?
6	$\Delta C = ?$	?	?
7	$\Delta C = ?$	?	?
8	$\Delta C = ?$	?	?
9	$\Delta C = ?$	?	?
10	$\Delta C = ?$	?	?

  a. What is the total change in real GDP after the 10 rounds? What is the value of the multiplier? What would you expect the total change in Y^* to be based on the multiplier formula? How do your answers to the first and third questions compare?

  b. Redo the table starting from round 2, assuming the marginal propensity to consume is 0.75. What is the total change in real GDP after 10 rounds? What is the value of the multiplier? As the marginal propensity to consume increases, what happens to the value of the multiplier?

12. Although the United States is one of the richest nations in the world, it is also the world's largest debtor nation. We often hear that the problem is the nation's low savings rate. Suppose policy makers attempt to rectify this by encouraging greater savings in the economy. What effect will their successful attempts have on real GDP?

13. The U.S. economy slowed significantly in early 2008, and policy makers were extremely concerned about growth. To boost the economy, Congress passed several relief packages that combined would deliver about $700 billion in government spending. Assume, for the sake of argument, that this spending was in the form of payments made directly to consumers. The objective was to boost the economy by increasing the disposable income of American consumers.

a. Calculate the initial change in aggregate consumer spending as a consequence of this policy measure if the marginal propensity to consume (MPC) in the United States is 0.5. Then calculate the resulting change in real GDP arising from the $700 billion in payments.

b. Illustrate the effect on real GDP with the use of a graph depicting the income–expenditure equilibrium. Label the vertical axis "Planned aggregate spending, $AE_{Planned}$" and the horizontal axis "Real GDP." Draw two planned aggregate expenditure curves ($AE_{Planned1}$ and $AE_{Planned2}$) and a 45-degree line to show the effect of the autonomous policy change on the equilibrium.

Aggregate Demand and Aggregate Supply

SHOCKS TO THE SYSTEM

Sometimes it's not easy being at the helm of the Federal Reserve—the institution that sets U.S. *monetary policy,* along with regulating the financial sector. The Federal Reserve's job is to help the economy avoid the twin evils of high inflation and high unemployment. It does this, loosely speaking, either by pumping cash into the economy to fight unemployment or by pulling cash out of the economy to fight inflation.

When the U.S. economy went into a recession in 2001, the Fed, under the leadership of then chairman Alan Greenspan, rushed cash into the system. It was an easy choice: unemployment was rising, and inflation was low and falling. In fact, for much of 2002 the Fed was actually worried about the possibility of *deflation.*

For much of 2008, however, the Fed chairman at the time, Ben Bernanke, faced a much more difficult problem. In fact, he faced the problem people in his position dread most: a combination of unacceptably high inflation and rising unemployment, often referred to as *stagflation.* Stagflation was the scourge of the 1970s: the two deep recessions of 1973–1975 and 1979–1982 were both accompanied by soaring inflation. And in the first half of 2008, the threat of stagflation seemed to be back.

Why did the economic difficulties of early 2008 look so different from those of 2001? Because they had a different cause. The lesson of stagflation in the 1970s was that recessions can have different causes and that the appropriate policy response depends on the cause.

Many recessions, from the great slump of 1929–1933 to the much milder recession of 2001, have been caused by a fall in investment and consumer spending. In these recessions high inflation isn't a threat. In fact, the 1929–1933 slump was accompanied by a sharp fall in the aggregate price level. And because inflation isn't a problem in such recessions, policy makers know what they must do: pump cash in, to fight rising unemployment.

The recessions of the 1970s, however, were largely caused by events in the Middle East that led to sharp cuts in world oil production and soaring prices for oil and other fuels. Not coincidentally, soaring oil prices also contributed to the economic difficulties of early 2008. In both periods, high energy prices led to a combination of unemployment and high inflation. They also created a dilemma: should the Fed fight the slump by pumping cash *into* the economy, or should it fight inflation by pulling cash *out* of the economy?

It's worth noting, by the way, that in 2011 the Fed faced some of the same problems it faced in 2008, as rising oil and food prices led to rising inflation despite high unemployment. In 2011, however, the Fed was fairly sure that demand was the main problem.

In the previous section we developed the *income–expenditure model,* which focuses on the determinants of aggregate spending. This model is extremely useful for understanding events like the recession of 2001 and the recovery that followed. However, the income–expenditure model takes the price level as given, and is therefore much less helpful for understanding the problems policy makers faced in 2008.

In this section, we'll develop a model that shows us how to distinguish between different types of short-run economic fluctuations—*demand shocks,* like those of the Great Depression and the 2001 recession, and *supply shocks,* like those of the 1970s and 2008.

To develop this model, we'll proceed in three steps.

1. We start by developing the concept of *aggregate demand.*

2. Next we turn to the parallel concept of *aggregate supply.*

3. Then we put the two together in the *AD–AS model.*

WHAT YOU WILL LEARN

1 How the aggregate demand curve illustrates the relationship between the aggregate price level and the quantity of aggregate output demanded in the economy

2 How the wealth effect and interest rate effect explain the aggregate demand curve's negative slope

3 How the aggregate demand curve can be derived from the income–expenditure model

4 What factors can shift the aggregate demand curve

The **aggregate demand curve** shows the relationship between the aggregate price level and the quantity of aggregate output demanded by households, businesses, the government, and the rest of the world.

The Aggregate Demand Curve

The Great Depression, the great majority of economists agree, was the result of a massive negative demand shock. What does that mean? When economists talk about a fall in the demand for a particular good or service, they're referring to a leftward shift of the demand curve. Similarly, when economists talk about a negative demand shock to the economy as a whole, they're referring to a leftward shift of the **aggregate demand curve,** a curve that shows the relationship between the aggregate price level and the quantity of aggregate output demanded by households, firms, the government, and the rest of the world.

Figure 27-1 shows what the aggregate demand curve may have looked like in 1933, at the end of the 1929–1933 recession. The horizontal axis shows the total quantity of domestic goods and services demanded, measured in 2005 dollars. We use real GDP to measure aggregate output and will often use the two terms interchangeably. The vertical axis shows the aggregate price level, measured by the GDP deflator. With these variables on the axes, we can draw a curve, *AD*, showing how much aggregate output would have been demanded at any given aggregate price level. Since *AD* is meant to illustrate aggregate demand in 1933, one point on the curve corresponds to actual data for 1933, when the aggregate price level was 7.9 and the total quantity of domestic final goods and services purchased was $716 billion in 2005 dollars.

As drawn in Figure 27-1, the aggregate demand curve is downward sloping, indicating a negative relationship between the aggregate price level and the quantity of aggregate output demanded. A higher aggregate price level, other things equal, reduces the quantity of aggregate output demanded; a lower aggregate price level, other things equal, increases the quantity of aggregate output demanded. According to Figure 27-1, if the price level in 1933 had been 4.2 instead of 7.9, the total quantity of domestic

27-1 The Aggregate Demand Curve

The aggregate demand curve shows the relationship between the aggregate price level and the quantity of aggregate output demanded. The curve is downward sloping due to the wealth effect of a change in the aggregate price level and the interest rate effect of a change in the aggregate price level. Corresponding to the actual 1933 data, here the total quantity of goods and services demanded at an aggregate price level of 7.9 is $716 billion in 2005 dollars. According to our hypothetical curve, however, if the aggregate price level had been only 4.2, the quantity of aggregate output demanded would have risen to $1,000 billion.

final goods and services demanded would have been $1,000 billion in 2005 dollars instead of $716 billion.

The first key question about the aggregate demand curve is: why should the curve be downward sloping?

Why Is the Aggregate Demand Curve Downward Sloping?

In Figure 27-1, the curve *AD* is downward sloping. Why? Recall the basic equation of national income accounting:

(27-1) $GDP = C + I + G + X - IM$

where C is consumer spending, I is investment spending, G is government purchases of goods and services, X is exports to other countries, and IM is imports. If we measure these variables in constant dollars—that is, in prices of a base year—then $C + I + G + X - IM$ is the quantity of domestically produced final goods and services demanded during a given period. G is decided by the government, but the other variables are private-sector decisions. To understand why the aggregate demand curve slopes downward, we need to understand why a rise in the aggregate price level reduces C, I, and $X - IM$.

You might think that the downward slope of the aggregate demand curve is a natural consequence of the *law of demand*. That is, since the demand curve for any one good is downward sloping, isn't it natural that the demand curve for aggregate output is also downward sloping? This turns out, however, to be a misleading parallel. The demand curve for any individual good shows how the quantity demanded depends on the price of that good, *holding the prices of other goods and services constant*. The main reason the quantity of a good demanded falls when the price of that good rises—that is, the quantity of a good demanded falls as we move up the demand curve—is that people switch their consumption to other goods and services.

But when we consider movements up or down the aggregate demand curve, we're considering *a simultaneous change in the prices of all final goods and services*. Furthermore, changes in the composition of goods and services in consumer spending aren't relevant to the aggregate demand curve: if consumers decide to buy fewer clothes

A rise or fall in the aggregate price level will have an impact on the purchasing power of our savings accounts.

but more cars, this doesn't necessarily change the total quantity of final goods and services they demand.

Why, then, does a rise in the aggregate price level lead to a fall in the quantity of all domestically produced final goods and services demanded? There are two main reasons: the *wealth effect* and the *interest rate effect* of a change in the aggregate price level.

THE WEALTH EFFECT An increase in the aggregate price level, other things equal, reduces the purchasing power of many assets. Consider, for example, someone who has $5,000 in a bank account. If the aggregate price level were to rise by 25%, what used to cost $5,000 would now cost $6,250, and would no longer be affordable. And what used to cost $4,000 would now cost $5,000, so that the $5,000 in the bank account would now buy only as much as $4,000 would have bought previously. With the loss in purchasing power, the owner of that bank account would probably scale back his or her consumption plans. Millions of other people would respond the same way, leading to a fall in spending on final goods and services, because a rise in the aggregate price level reduces the purchasing power of everyone's bank account.

Correspondingly, a fall in the aggregate price level increases the purchasing power of consumers' assets and leads to more consumer demand. The **wealth effect of a change in the aggregate price level** is the effect on consumer spending caused by the effect of a change in the aggregate price level on the purchasing power of consumers' assets. Because of the wealth effect, consumer spending, *C*, falls when the aggregate price level rises, leading to a downward-sloping aggregate demand curve.

THE INTEREST RATE EFFECT Economists use the term *money* in its narrowest sense to refer to cash and bank deposits on which people can write checks. People and firms hold money because it reduces the cost and inconvenience of making transactions. An increase in the aggregate price level, other things equal, reduces the purchasing power of a given amount of money holdings. To purchase the same basket of goods and services as before, people and firms now need to hold more money. So, in response to an increase in the aggregate price level, the public tries to increase its money holdings, either by borrowing more or by selling assets such as bonds. This reduces the funds available for lending to other borrowers and drives interest rates up.

We have already learned that a rise in the interest rate reduces investment spending because it makes the cost of borrowing higher. It also reduces consumer spending because households save more of their disposable income. So a rise in the aggregate price level depresses investment spending, *I*, and consumer spending, *C*, through its effect on the purchasing power of money holdings, an effect known as the **interest rate effect of a change in the aggregate price level.** This also leads to a downward-sloping aggregate demand curve.

We'll have a lot more to say about interest rates in upcoming sections. For now, the important point to remember is that the aggregate demand curve is downward sloping due to both the wealth effect and the interest rate effect of a change in the aggregate price level.

The Aggregate Demand Curve and the Income–Expenditure Model

In the preceding section we introduced the *income–expenditure model*, which shows how the economy arrives at *income–expenditure equilibrium*. Now we've introduced the aggregate demand curve, which relates the overall demand for goods and services to the overall price level. How do these concepts fit together?

Recall that one of the assumptions of the income–expenditure model is that the aggregate price level is fixed. We now drop that assumption. We can still use the income–

The **wealth effect of a change in the aggregate price level** is the effect on consumer spending caused by the effect of a change in the aggregate price level on the purchasing power of consumers' assets.

The **interest rate effect of a change in the aggregate price level** is the effect on consumer spending and investment spending caused by the effect of a change in the aggregate price level on the purchasing power of consumers' and firms' money holdings.

expenditure model, however, to ask what aggregate spending would be *at any given aggregate price level*, which is precisely what the aggregate demand curve shows. So the *AD* curve is actually derived from the income–expenditure model. Economists sometimes say that the income–expenditure model is "embedded" in the *AD–AS* model.

Figure 27-2 shows, once again, how income–expenditure equilibrium is determined. Real GDP is on the horizontal axis; real planned aggregate spending is on the vertical axis. Other things equal, planned aggregate spending, equal to consumer spending plus planned investment spending, rises with real GDP. This is illustrated by the upward-sloping lines $AE_{Planned_1}$ and $AE_{Planned_2}$. Income–expenditure equilibrium, as you will recall, is at the point where the line representing planned aggregate spending crosses the 45-degree line. For example, if $AE_{Planned_1}$ is the relationship between real GDP and planned aggregate spending, then income–expenditure equilibrium is at point E_1, corresponding to a level of real GDP equal to Y_1.

FIGURE 27-2   How Changes in the Aggregate Price Level Affect Income–Expenditure Equilibrium

Income–expenditure equilibrium occurs at the point where the curve $AE_{Planned}$, which shows real aggregate planned spending, crosses the 45-degree line. A fall in the aggregate price level causes the $AE_{Planned}$ curve to shift from $AE_{Planned_1}$ to $AE_{Planned_2}$, leading to a rise in income–expenditure equilibrium GDP from Y_1 to Y_2.

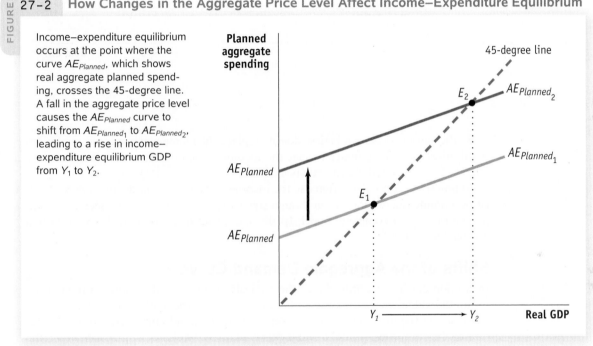

We've just seen, however, that changes in the aggregate price level change the level of planned aggregate spending *at any given level of real GDP*. This means that when the aggregate price level changes, the $AE_{Planned}$ curve shifts. For example, suppose that the aggregate price level falls. As a result of both the wealth effect and the interest rate effect, the fall in the aggregate price level will lead to higher planned aggregate spending at any given level of real GDP. So the $AE_{Planned}$ curve will shift up, as illustrated in Figure 27-2 by the shift from $AE_{Planned_1}$ to $AE_{Planned_2}$. The increase in planned aggregate spending leads to a multiplier process that moves the income–expenditure equilibrium from point E_1 to point E_2, raising real GDP from Y_1 to Y_2.

Figure 27-3 shows how this result can be used to derive the aggregate demand curve. In this figure, we show a fall in the aggregate price level from P_1 to P_2. We saw in Figure 27-2 that a fall in the aggregate price level would lead to an upward shift of the $AE_{Planned}$ curve and hence a rise in real GDP. You can see this same result in Figure 27-3 as a movement along the *AD* curve: as the aggregate price level falls, real GDP rises from Y_1 to Y_2.

27-3   The Income–Expenditure Model and the Aggregate Demand Curve

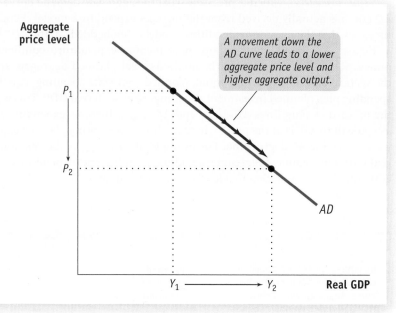

In Figure 27-2 we saw how a fall in the aggregate price level shifts the planned aggregate spending curve up, leading to a rise in real GDP. Here we show that same result as a movement along the aggregate demand curve. If the aggregate price level falls from P_1 to P_2, real GDP rises from Y_1 to Y_2. The AD curve is therefore downward sloping.

A movement down the AD curve leads to a lower aggregate price level and higher aggregate output.

So the aggregate demand curve doesn't replace the income–expenditure model. Instead, it's a way to summarize what the income–expenditure model says about the effects of changes in the aggregate price level.

In practice, economists often use the income–expenditure model to analyze short-run economic fluctuations, even though strictly speaking it should be seen as a component of a more complete model. In the short run, in particular, this is usually a reasonable shortcut.

Shifts of the Aggregate Demand Curve

In Section 2, where we introduced the analysis of supply and demand in the market for an individual good, we stressed the importance of the distinction between *movements along* the demand curve and *shifts of* the demand curve. The same distinction applies to the aggregate demand curve. Figure 27-1 shows a *movement along* the aggregate demand curve, a change in the aggregate quantity of goods and services demanded as the aggregate price level changes.

But there can also be *shifts of* the aggregate demand curve, changes in the quantity of goods and services demanded at any given price level, as shown in Figure 27-4. When we talk about an increase in aggregate demand, we mean a shift of the aggregate demand curve to the right, as shown in panel (a) by the shift from AD_1 to AD_2. A rightward shift occurs when the quantity of aggregate output demanded increases at any given aggregate price level. A decrease in aggregate demand means that the AD curve shifts to the left, as in panel (b). A leftward shift implies that the quantity of aggregate output demanded falls at any given aggregate price level.

A number of factors can shift the aggregate demand curve. Among the most important factors are changes in expectations, changes in wealth, and the size of the existing stock of physical capital. In addition, both fiscal and monetary policy can shift the aggregate demand curve. All five factors set the multiplier process in motion. By causing an initial rise or fall in real GDP, they change disposable income, which leads to additional changes in aggregate spending, which lead to further changes in real GDP, and so on. For an overview of factors that shift the aggregate demand curve, see upcoming Table 27-1.

FIGURE **27-4**   Shifts of the Aggregate Demand Curve

(a) Rightward Shift

Aggregate price level

Increase in aggregate demand

AD_1 AD_2

Real GDP

(b) Leftward Shift

Aggregate price level

Decrease in aggregate demand

AD_2 AD_1

Real GDP

Panel (a) shows the effect of events that increase the quantity of aggregate output demanded at any given aggregate price level, such as improvements in business and consumer expectations or increased government spending. Such changes shift the aggregate demand curve to the right, from AD_1 to AD_2. Panel (b) shows the effect of events that decrease the quantity of aggregate output demanded at any given aggregate price level, such as a fall in wealth caused by a stock market decline. This shifts the aggregate demand curve leftward from AD_1 to AD_2.

CHANGES IN EXPECTATIONS As explained in the previous section, both consumer spending and planned investment spending depend in part on people's expectations about the future. Consumers base their spending not only on the income they have now but also on the income they expect to have in the future. Firms base their planned investment spending not only on current conditions but also on the sales they expect to make in the future. As a result, changes in expectations can push consumer spending and planned investment spending up or down. If consumers and firms become more optimistic, aggregate spending rises; if they become more pessimistic, aggregate spending falls. In fact, short-run economic forecasters pay careful attention to surveys of consumer and business sentiment. In particular, forecasters watch the Consumer Confidence Index, a monthly measure calculated by the Conference Board.

CHANGES IN WEALTH Consumer spending depends in part on the value of household assets. When the real value of these assets rises, the purchasing power they embody also rises, leading to an increase in aggregate spending. For example, in the 1990s there was a significant rise in the stock market that increased aggregate demand. And when the real value of household assets falls—for example, because of a stock market crash—the purchasing power they embody is reduced and aggregate demand also falls. The stock market crash of 1929 was a significant factor leading to the Great Depression. Similarly, a sharp decline in real estate values was a major factor depressing consumer spending during the 2007–2009 recession.

SIZE OF THE EXISTING STOCK OF PHYSICAL CAPITAL Firms engage in planned investment spending to add to their stock of physical capital. Their incentive to spend depends in part on how much physical capital they already have: the more they have,

TABLE 27-1

Factors That Shift Aggregate Demand

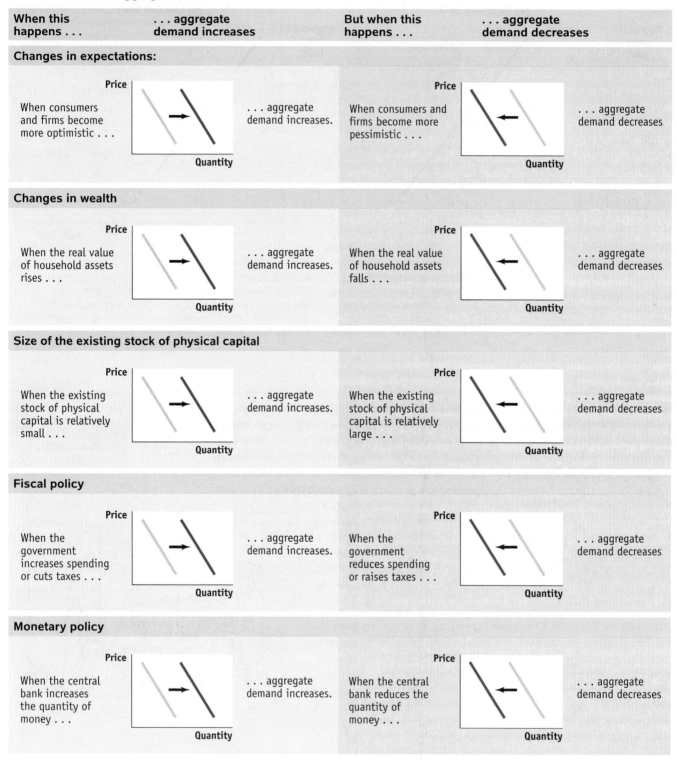

When this happens . . .	. . . aggregate demand increases	But when this happens . . .	. . . aggregate demand decreases
Changes in expectations:			
When consumers and firms become more optimistic . . .	. . . aggregate demand increases.	When consumers and firms become more pessimistic . . .	. . . aggregate demand decreases.
Changes in wealth			
When the real value of household assets rises . . .	. . . aggregate demand increases.	When the real value of household assets falls . . .	. . . aggregate demand decreases.
Size of the existing stock of physical capital			
When the existing stock of physical capital is relatively small . . .	. . . aggregate demand increases.	When the existing stock of physical capital is relatively large . . .	. . . aggregate demand decreases.
Fiscal policy			
When the government increases spending or cuts taxes . . .	. . . aggregate demand increases.	When the government reduces spending or raises taxes . . .	. . . aggregate demand decreases.
Monetary policy			
When the central bank increases the quantity of money . . .	. . . aggregate demand increases.	When the central bank reduces the quantity of money . . .	. . . aggregate demand decreases.

the less they will feel a need to add more, other things equal. The same applies to other types of investment spending—for example, if a large number of houses have been built in recent years, this will depress the demand for new houses and as a result also tend to reduce residential investment spending.

In fact, that's part of the reason for the deep slump in residential investment spending that began in 2006. The housing boom of the previous few years had created an oversupply of houses: by spring 2009, the inventory of unsold houses on the market was equal to more than 14 months of sales, and prices of new homes had fallen more than 25% from their peak. This gave the construction industry little incentive to build even more homes.

FISCAL POLICY One of the key insights of macroeconomics is that the government can have a powerful influence on aggregate demand and that, in some circumstances, this influence can be used to improve economic performance.

One of the ways government can influence the aggregate demand curve is through fiscal policy, which, as we learned earlier, is the use of either government spending—government purchases of final goods and services and government transfers—or tax policy to stabilize the economy. In practice, governments often respond to recessions by increasing spending, cutting taxes, or both. They often respond to inflation by reducing spending or increasing taxes.

The effect of government purchases of final goods and services, *G*, on the aggregate demand curve is *direct* because government purchases are themselves a component of aggregate demand. So an increase in government purchases shifts the aggregate demand curve to the right and a decrease shifts it to the left. History's most dramatic example of how increased government purchases affect aggregate demand was the effect of wartime government spending during World War II. Because of the war, U.S. federal purchases surged 400%. This increase in purchases is usually credited with ending the Great Depression. Similarly, in 2009, the United States began spending more than $100 billion on infrastructure projects such as improving highways, bridges, public transportation, and more, to stimulate overall spending in the face of a slumping economy.

In contrast, changes in either tax rates or government transfers influence the economy *indirectly* through their effect on disposable income. A lower tax rate means that consumers get to keep more of what they earn, increasing their disposable income. An increase in government transfers also increases consumers' disposable income. In either case, this increases consumer spending and shifts the aggregate demand curve to the right. A higher tax rate or a reduction in transfers reduces the amount of disposable income received by consumers. This reduces consumer spending and shifts the aggregate demand curve to the left.

MONETARY POLICY Another way the government can influence the aggregate demand curve is through monetary policy. In the section-opening story we talked about the problems faced by the Federal Reserve, which controls monetary policy—the use of changes in the quantity of money or the interest rate to stabilize the economy. We've just discussed how a rise in the aggregate price level, by reducing the purchasing power of money holdings, causes a rise in the interest rate. That, in turn, reduces both investment spending and consumer spending.

But what happens if the quantity of money in the hands of households and firms changes? In modern economies, the quantity of money in circulation is largely determined by the decisions of a *central bank* created by the government. As we'll learn in upcoming sections, the Federal Reserve, the U.S. central bank, is a special institution that is neither exactly part of the government nor exactly a private institution.

When the central bank increases the quantity of money in circulation, households and firms have more money, which they are willing to lend out. The effect is to drive the interest rate down at any given aggregate price level, leading to higher investment spending and higher consumer spending. That is, increasing the quantity of money shifts the aggregate demand curve to the right. Reducing the quantity of money has the opposite effect: households and firms have less money holdings than before, leading them to borrow more and lend less. This raises the interest rate, reduces investment spending and consumer spending, and shifts the aggregate demand curve to the left.

ECONOMICS ▶ *IN ACTION*

MOVING ALONG THE AGGREGATE DEMAND CURVE, 1979–1980

When looking at data, it's often hard to distinguish between changes in spending that represent *movements along* the aggregate demand curve and *shifts of* the aggregate demand curve. One telling exception, however, is what happened right after the oil crisis of 1979 (which we mention in the section-opening story). Faced with a sharp increase in the aggregate price level—the rate of consumer price inflation reached 14.8% in March of 1980—the Federal Reserve stuck to a policy of increasing the quantity of money slowly. The aggregate price level was rising steeply, but the quantity of money circulating in the economy was growing slowly. The net result was that the purchasing power of the quantity of money in circulation fell.

This led to an increase in the demand for borrowing and a surge in interest rates. The *prime rate*, which is the interest rate banks charge their best customers, climbed above 20%. High interest rates, in turn, caused both consumer spending and investment spending to fall: in 1980 purchases of durable consumer goods like cars fell by 5.3% and real investment spending fell by 8.9%.

In other words, in 1979–1980 the economy responded just as we'd expect if it were moving upward along the aggregate demand curve from right to left: due to the wealth effect and the interest rate effect of a change in the aggregate price level, the quantity of aggregate output demanded fell as the aggregate price level rose. This does not explain, of course, why the aggregate price level rose. But as we'll see in the next module, the answer to that question lies in the behavior of the *short-run aggregate supply curve*.

	Yesterday	6 mos. ago	Year ago
·$0.38			
$0.06			
$0.33	Prime rate	5.50	4.50	4.00
	Discount rate	3.50	2.50	2.00
		2.50	1.50	1.00
	–mo.) 2.89	1.74	1.12
	x mort. 5.72	5.82	5.58
	rt. 4.47	4.09	3.60
	0.55	0.48	0.48
	2.615	1.470	0.915

The interest rate effect of a rise in the aggregate price level leads to a drop in consumer and investment spending.

Rob Friedman/Getty Images

MODULE
27 Review

Solutions appear at the back of the book.

Check Your Understanding

1. Determine the effect on aggregate demand of each of the following events. Explain whether it represents a movement along the aggregate demand curve (up or down) or a shift of the curve (leftward or rightward).

   a. a rise in the interest rate caused by a change in monetary policy

   b. a fall in the real value of money in the economy due to a higher aggregate price level

   c. news of a worse-than-expected job market next year

   d. a fall in tax rates

   e. a rise in the real value of assets in the economy due to a lower aggregate price level

   f. a rise in the real value of assets in the economy due to a surge in real estate values

Multiple-Choice Questions

1. Which of the following explains the slope of the aggregate demand curve?

   I. the wealth effect of a change in the aggregate price level

   II. the interest rate effect of a change in the aggregate price level

   III. the product-substitution effect of a change in the aggregate price level

   a. I only

   b. II only

   c. III only

   d. I and II only

   e. I, II, and III

2. Which of the following will shift the aggregate demand curve to the right?

   a. a decrease in wealth

   b. pessimistic consumer expectations

   c. a decrease in the existing stock of capital

   d. contractionary fiscal policy

   e. a decrease in the quantity of money

3. The Consumer Confidence Index is used to measure which of the following?

   a. the level of consumer spending

   b. the rate of return on investments

   c. consumer expectations

   d. planned investment spending

   e. the level of current disposable income

Critical-Thinking Question

Identify the two effects that cause the aggregate demand curve to have a downward slope. Explain each.

4. Decreases in the stock market decrease aggregate demand by decreasing which of the following?

   a. consumer wealth

   b. the price level

   c. the stock of existing physical capital

   d. interest rates

   e. tax revenues

5. Which of the following government policies will shift the aggregate demand curve to the left?

   a. a decrease in the quantity of money

   b. an increase in government purchases of goods and services

   c. a decrease in taxes

   d. a decrease in interest rates

   e. an increase in government transfers

PITFALLS

CHANGES IN WEALTH: A MOVEMENT ALONG VERSUS A SHIFT OF THE AGGREGATE DEMAND CURVE

? Does a change in wealth move the economy along the *AD* curve or does it shift the *AD* curve?

> THE ANSWER IS THAT IT DOES BOTH, DEPENDING ON THE SOURCE OF THE CHANGE IN WEALTH. A movement along the *AD* curve occurs when a change in the aggregate price level changes the purchasing power of consumers' existing wealth (the real value of their assets). For example, a fall in the aggregate price level increases the purchasing power of consumers' assets and leads to a movement down the *AD* curve. In contrast, a change in wealth *independent of a change in the aggregate price level* shifts the *AD* curve. For example, a rise in the stock market or a rise in real estate values leads to an increase in the real value of consumers' assets at any given aggregate price level. In this case, the aggregate demand curve shifts to the right as consumers increase their spending due to the increase in wealth.

To learn more, see pages 276–279.

Tristan Savatier/Getty Images

The Aggregate Supply Curve

Between 1929 and 1933, there was a sharp fall in aggregate demand—a reduction in the quantity of goods and services demanded at any given price level. Consequences of the economy-wide decline in demand included:

- A fall in the prices of most goods and services. By 1933, the GDP deflator (one of the price indexes) was 26% below its 1929 level, and other indexes were down by similar amounts.

- A decline in the output of most goods and services: by 1933, real GDP was 27% below its 1929 level.

- And closely tied to the fall in real GDP was a surge in the unemployment rate from 3% to 25%.

The association between the plunge in real GDP and the plunge in prices wasn't an accident. Between 1929 and 1933, the U.S. economy was moving down its **aggregate supply curve,** which shows the relationship between the economy's aggregate price level (the overall price level of final goods and services in the economy) and the total quantity of final goods and services, or aggregate output, producers are willing to supply. (As you will recall, we use real GDP to measure aggregate output. So we'll often use the two terms interchangeably.) More specifically, between 1929 and 1933 the U.S. economy moved down its *short-run aggregate supply curve*.

The Short-Run Aggregate Supply Curve

The period from 1929 to 1933 demonstrated that there is a positive relationship in the short run between the aggregate price level and the quantity of aggregate output supplied. That is, a rise in the aggregate price level is associated with a rise in the

The **aggregate supply curve** shows the relationship between the aggregate price level and the quantity of aggregate output supplied in the economy.

quantity of aggregate output supplied, other things equal; a fall in the aggregate price level is associated with a fall in the quantity of aggregate output supplied, other things equal. To understand why this positive relationship exists, consider the most basic question facing a producer: is producing a unit of output profitable or not? Let's define profit per unit:

(28-1) Profit per unit of output =
        Price per unit of output − Production cost per unit of output

Thus, the answer to the question depends on whether the price the producer receives for a unit of output is greater or less than the cost of producing that unit of output. At any given point in time, many of the costs producers face are fixed per unit of output and can't be changed for an extended period of time. Typically, the largest source of inflexible production cost is the wages paid to workers. *Wages* here refers to all forms of worker compensation, such as employer-paid health care and retirement benefits in addition to earnings.

Wages are typically an inflexible production cost because the dollar amount of any given wage paid, called the **nominal wage,** is often determined by contracts that were signed some time ago. And even when there are no formal contracts, there are often informal agreements between management and workers, making companies reluctant to change wages in response to economic conditions. For example, companies usually will not reduce wages during poor economic times—unless the downturn has been particularly long and severe—for fear of generating worker resentment. Correspondingly, they typically won't raise wages during better economic times—until they are at risk of losing workers to competitors—because they don't want to encourage workers to routinely demand higher wages.

As a result of both formal and informal agreements, then, the economy is characterized by **sticky wages:** nominal wages that are slow to fall even in the face of high unemployment and slow to rise even in the face of labor shortages. It's important to note, however, that nominal wages cannot be sticky forever: ultimately, formal contracts and informal agreements will be renegotiated to take into account changed economic circumstances.

To understand how the fact that many costs are fixed in nominal terms gives rise to an upward-sloping short-run aggregate supply curve, it's helpful to know that prices are set somewhat differently in different kinds of markets. In *perfectly competitive markets,* producers take prices as given; in *imperfectly competitive markets,* producers have some ability to choose the prices they charge. In both kinds of markets, there is a short-run positive relationship between prices and output, but for slightly different reasons.

Let's start with the behavior of producers in perfectly competitive markets; remember, they take the price as given. Imagine that, for some reason, the aggregate price level falls, which means that the price received by the typical producer of a final good or service falls. Because many production costs are fixed in the short run, production cost per unit of output doesn't fall by the same proportion as the fall in the price of output. So the profit per unit of output declines, leading perfectly competitive producers to reduce the quantity supplied in the short run.

On the other hand, suppose that for some reason the aggregate price level rises. As a result, the typical producer receives a higher price for its final good or service. Again, many production costs are fixed in the short run, so production cost per unit of output doesn't rise by the same proportion as the rise in the price of a unit. And since the typical perfectly competitive producer takes the price as given, profit per unit of output rises and output increases.

Now consider an imperfectly competitive producer that is able to set its own price. If there is a rise in the demand for this producer's product, it will be able to sell more

The **nominal wage** is the dollar amount of the wage paid.

Sticky wages are nominal wages that are slow to fall even in the face of high unemployment and slow to rise even in the face of labor shortages.

Nominal wages are sticky in the short run but not forever.

The **short-run aggregate supply curve** shows the relationship between the aggregate price level and the quantity of aggregate output supplied that exists in the short run, the time period when many production costs can be taken as fixed.

at any given price. Given stronger demand for its products, it will probably choose to increase its prices as well as its output, as a way of increasing profit per unit of output. In fact, industry analysts often talk about variations in an industry's "pricing power": when demand is strong, firms with pricing power are able to raise prices—and they do.

Conversely, if there is a fall in demand, firms will normally try to limit the fall in their sales by cutting prices.

Both the responses of firms in perfectly competitive industries and those of firms in imperfectly competitive industries lead to an upward-sloping relationship between aggregate output and the aggregate price level. The positive relationship between the aggregate price level and the quantity of aggregate output producers are willing to supply during the time period when many production costs, particularly nominal wages, can be taken as fixed is illustrated by the **short-run aggregate supply curve.** The positive relationship between the aggregate price level and aggregate output in the short run gives the short-run aggregate supply curve its upward slope.

Figure 28-1 shows a hypothetical short-run aggregate supply curve, *SRAS*, which matches actual U.S. data for 1929 and 1933. On the horizontal axis is aggregate output (or, equivalently, real GDP)—the total quantity of final goods and services supplied in the economy—measured in 2005 dollars. On the vertical axis is the aggregate price level as measured by the GDP deflator, with the value for the year 2005 equal to 100. In 1929, the aggregate price level was 10.6 and real GDP was $976 billion. In 1933, the aggregate price level was 7.9 and real GDP was only $716 billion. The movement down the *SRAS* curve corresponds to the deflation and fall in aggregate output experienced over those years.

FIGURE 28-1   The Short-Run Aggregate Supply Curve

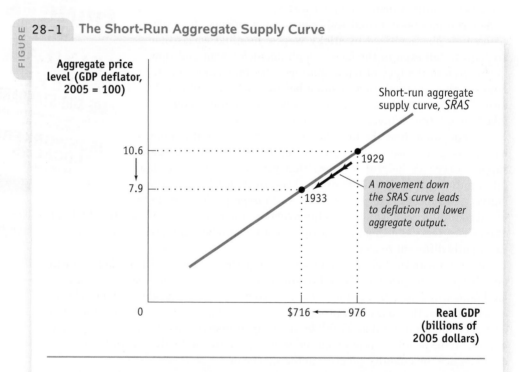

The short-run aggregate supply curve shows the relationship between the aggregate price level and the quantity of aggregate output supplied in the short run, the period in which many production costs such as nominal wages are fixed. It is upward sloping because a higher aggregate price level leads to higher profit per unit of output and higher aggregate output given fixed nominal wages. Here we show numbers corresponding to the Great Depression, from 1929 to 1933: when deflation occurred and the aggregate price level fell from 10.6 (in 1929) to 7.9 (in 1933), firms responded by reducing the quantity of aggregate output supplied from $976 billion to $716 billion measured in 2005 dollars.

Shifts of the Short-Run Aggregate Supply Curve

Figure 28-1 shows a *movement along* the short-run aggregate supply curve, as the aggregate price level and aggregate output fell from 1929 to 1933. But there can also be *shifts of* the short-run aggregate supply curve, as shown in Figure 28-2. Panel (a) shows a *decrease in short-run aggregate supply*—a leftward shift of the short-run aggregate supply curve. Aggregate supply decreases when producers reduce the quantity of aggregate output they are willing to supply at any given aggregate price level. Panel (b) shows an *increase in short-run aggregate supply*—a rightward shift of the short-run aggregate supply curve. Aggregate supply increases when producers increase the quantity of aggregate output they are willing to supply at any given aggregate price level.

To understand why the short-run aggregate supply curve can shift, it's important to recall that producers make output decisions based on their profit per unit of output. The short-run aggregate supply curve illustrates the relationship between the aggregate price level and aggregate output: because some production costs are fixed in the short run, a change in the aggregate price level leads to a change in producers' profit per unit of output and, in turn, leads to a change in aggregate output. But other factors besides the aggregate price level can affect profit per unit and, in turn, aggregate output. It is changes in these other factors that will shift the short-run aggregate supply curve.

To develop some intuition, suppose that something happens that raises production costs—say, an increase in the price of oil. At any given price of output, a producer now earns a smaller profit per unit of output. As a result, producers reduce the quantity supplied at any given aggregate price level, and the short-run aggregate supply curve shifts to the left. If, in contrast, something happens that lowers production costs—say, a fall in the nominal wage—a producer now earns a higher profit per unit of output at any given price of output. This leads producers to increase the quantity of aggregate output supplied at any given aggregate price level, and the short-run aggregate supply curve shifts to the right.

FIGURE 28-2   Shifts of the Short-Run Aggregate Supply Curve

Panel (a) shows a decrease in short-run aggregate supply: the short-run aggregate supply curve shifts leftward from SRAS₁ to SRAS₂, and the quantity of aggregate output supplied at any given aggregate price level falls. Panel

(b) shows an increase in short-run aggregate supply: the short-run aggregate supply curve shifts rightward from SRAS₁ to SRAS₂, and the quantity of aggregate output supplied at any given aggregate price level rises.

Now we'll discuss some of the important factors that affect producers' profit per unit and so can lead to shifts of the short-run aggregate supply curve.

CHANGES IN COMMODITY PRICES A surge in the price of oil caused problems for the U.S. economy in the 1970s, early in 2008, and again in 2011. Oil is a commodity, a standardized input bought and sold in bulk quantities. An increase in the price of a commodity—oil—raised production costs across the economy and reduced the quantity of aggregate output supplied at any given aggregate price level, shifting the short-run aggregate supply curve to the left. Conversely, a decline in commodity prices reduces production costs, leading to an increase in the quantity supplied at any given aggregate price level and a rightward shift of the short-run aggregate supply curve.

Because commodities like oil are not final goods, their prices are not included in the aggregate price level.

Why isn't the influence of commodity prices already captured by the short-run aggregate supply curve? Because commodities—unlike, say, soft drinks—are not a final good, their prices are not included in the calculation of the aggregate price level. Further, commodities represent a significant cost of production to most suppliers, just like nominal wages do. So changes in commodity prices have large impacts on production costs. And in contrast to noncommodities, the prices of commodities can sometimes change drastically due to industry-specific shocks to supply—such as wars in the Middle East or rising Chinese demand that leaves less oil for the United States.

CHANGES IN NOMINAL WAGES At any given point in time, the dollar wages of many workers are fixed because they are set by contracts or informal agreements made in the past. Nominal wages can change, however, once enough time has passed for contracts and informal agreements to be renegotiated.

Suppose, for example, that there is an economy-wide rise in the cost of health care insurance premiums paid by employers as part of employees' wages. From the employers' perspective, this is equivalent to a rise in nominal wages because it is an increase in employer-paid compensation. So this rise in nominal wages increases production costs and shifts the short-run aggregate supply curve to the left. Conversely, suppose there is an economy-wide fall in the cost of such premiums. This is equivalent to a fall in nominal wages from the point of view of employers; it reduces production costs and shifts the short-run aggregate supply curve to the right.

An important historical fact is that during the 1970s the surge in the price of oil had the indirect effect of also raising nominal wages. This "knock-on" effect occurred because many wage contracts included *cost-of-living allowances* that automatically raised the nominal wage when consumer prices increased. Through this channel, the surge in the price of oil—which led to an increase in overall consumer prices—ultimately caused a rise in nominal wages. So the economy, in the end, experienced two leftward shifts of the aggregate supply curve: the first generated by the initial surge in the price of oil, the second generated by the induced increase in nominal wages. The negative effect on the economy of rising oil prices was greatly magnified through the cost-of-living allowances in wage contracts. Today, cost-of-living allowances in wage contracts are rare.

CHANGES IN PRODUCTIVITY An increase in productivity means that a worker can produce more units of output with the same quantity of inputs. For example, the introduction of bar-code scanners in retail stores greatly increased the ability of a single worker to stock, inventory, and resupply store shelves. As a result, the cost to a store of "producing" a dollar

Technologies like bar-code scanners allow firms to quickly track merchandise, increasing productivity and profits.

of sales fell and profit rose. And, correspondingly, the quantity supplied increased. (Think of Walmart and the increase in the number of its stores as an increase in aggregate supply.)

So a rise in productivity, whatever the source, increases producers' profits and shifts the short-run aggregate supply curve to the right. Conversely, a fall in productivity—say, due to new regulations that require workers to spend more time filling out forms—reduces the number of units of output a worker can produce with the same quantity of inputs. Consequently, the cost per unit of output rises, profit falls, and quantity supplied falls. This shifts the short-run aggregate supply curve to the left.

For a summary of the factors that shift the short-run aggregate supply curve, see Table 28-1.

TABLE 28-1

Factors That Shift Aggregate Supply

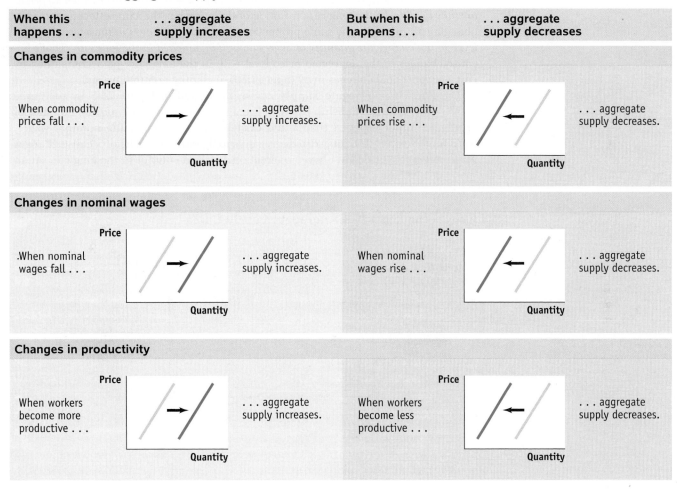

When this happens . . .	. . . aggregate supply increases	But when this happens . . .	. . . aggregate supply decreases
Changes in commodity prices			
When commodity prices fall . . .	. . . aggregate supply increases.	When commodity prices rise . . .	. . . aggregate supply decreases.
Changes in nominal wages			
When nominal wages fall . . .	. . . aggregate supply increases.	When nominal wages rise . . .	. . . aggregate supply decreases.
Changes in productivity			
When workers become more productive . . .	. . . aggregate supply increases.	When workers become less productive . . .	. . . aggregate supply decreases.

The Long-Run Aggregate Supply Curve

We've seen that in the short run a fall in the aggregate price level leads to a decline in the quantity of aggregate output supplied because nominal wages are sticky in the short run. But, as we mentioned earlier, contracts and informal agreements are renegotiated in the long run. So in the long run, nominal wages—like the aggregate price level—are flexible, not sticky. This fact greatly alters the long-run relationship between the aggregate price level and aggregate supply. In fact, in the long run the aggregate price level has *no* effect on the quantity of aggregate output supplied.

The **long-run aggregate supply curve** shows the relationship between the aggregate price level and the quantity of aggregate output supplied that would exist if all prices, including nominal wages, were fully flexible.

To see why, let's conduct a thought experiment. Imagine that you could wave a magic wand and cut *all prices* in the economy in half at the same time. By "all prices" we mean the prices of all inputs, including nominal wages, as well as the prices of final goods and services. What would happen to aggregate output, given that the aggregate price level has been halved and all input prices, including nominal wages, have been halved?

The answer is: nothing. Consider Equation 28-1 again: each producer would receive a lower price for its product, but costs would fall by the same proportion. As a result, every unit of output profitable to produce before the change in prices would still be profitable to produce after the change in prices. So a halving of *all* prices in the economy has no effect on the economy's aggregate output. In other words, changes in the aggregate price level now have no effect on the quantity of aggregate output supplied.

In reality, of course, no one can change all prices by the same proportion at the same time. But now, we'll consider the *long run, the period of time over which all prices are fully flexible.* In the long run, inflation or deflation has the same effect as someone changing all prices by the same proportion. *As a result, changes in the aggregate price level do not change the quantity of aggregate output supplied in the long run.* That's because changes in the aggregate price level will, in the long run, be accompanied by equal proportional changes in *all* input prices, including nominal wages.

The **long-run aggregate supply curve,** illustrated in Figure 28-3 by the curve *LRAS*, shows the relationship between the aggregate price level and the quantity of aggregate output supplied that would exist if all prices, including nominal wages, were fully flexible. The long-run aggregate supply curve is vertical because changes in the aggregate price level have *no* effect on aggregate output in the long run. At an

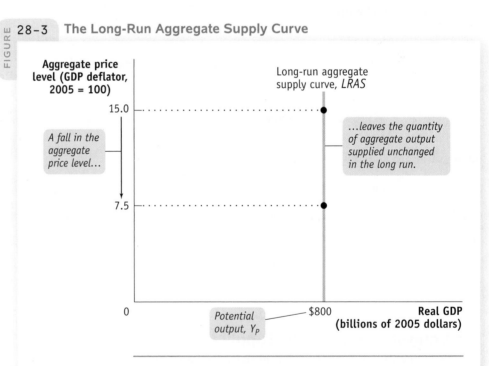

FIGURE 28-3   The Long-Run Aggregate Supply Curve

The long-run aggregate supply curve shows the quantity of aggregate output supplied when all prices, including nominal wages, are flexible. It is vertical at potential output, Y_P, because in the long run a change in the aggregate price level has no effect on the quantity of aggregate output supplied.

aggregate price level of 15.0, the quantity of aggregate output supplied is $800 billion in 2005 dollars. If the aggregate price level falls by 50% to 7.5, the quantity of aggregate output supplied is unchanged in the long run at $800 billion in 2005 dollars.

It's important to understand not only that the *LRAS* curve is vertical but also that its position along the horizontal axis represents a significant measure. The horizontal intercept in Figure 28-3, where *LRAS* touches the horizontal axis ($800 billion in 2005 dollars), is the economy's **potential output,** Y_P: the level of real GDP the economy would produce if all prices, including nominal wages, were fully flexible.

In reality, the actual level of real GDP is almost always either above or below potential output. We'll see why later in this section, when we discuss the *AD–AS* model. Still, an economy's potential output is an important number because it defines the trend around which actual aggregate output fluctuates from year to year.

In the United States, the Congressional Budget Office, or CBO, estimates annual potential output for the purpose of federal budget analysis. In Figure 28-4, the CBO's estimates of U.S. potential output from 1990 to 2012 are represented by the orange line and the actual values of U.S. real GDP over the same period are represented by the blue line. Years shaded purple on the horizontal axis correspond to periods in which actual aggregate output fell short of potential output, years shaded green to periods in which actual aggregate output exceeded potential output.

As you can see, U.S. potential output has risen steadily over time—implying a series of rightward shifts of the *LRAS* curve. What has caused these rightward shifts? The answer lies in the factors related to long-run growth that we discussed in Section

> **Potential output** is the level of real GDP the economy would produce if all prices, including nominal wages, were fully flexible.

FIGURE 28-4 **Actual and Potential Output from 1990 to 2012**

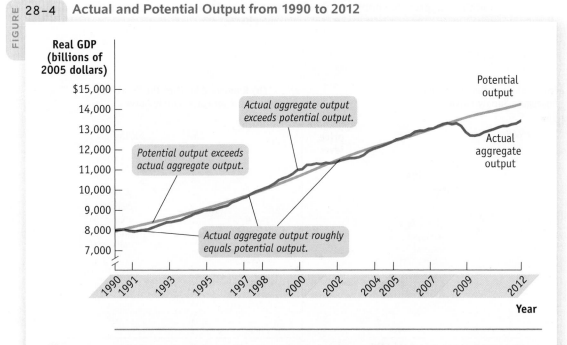

This figure shows the performance of actual and potential output in the United States from 1990 to 2012. The orange line shows estimates of U.S. potential output, produced by the Congressional Budget Office, and the blue line shows actual aggregate output. The purple-shaded years are periods in which actual aggregate output fell below potential output, and the green-shaded years are periods in which actual aggregate output exceeded potential output. As shown, significant shortfalls occurred in the recessions of the early 1990s and after 2000. Actual aggregate output was significantly above potential output in the boom of the late 1990s, and a huge shortfall occurred after the recession of 2007–2009.

Sources: Congressional Budget Office; Bureau of Economic Analysis.

5, such as increases in physical capital and human capital as well as technological progress.

Over the long run, as the size of the labor force and the productivity of labor both rise, the level of real GDP that the economy is capable of producing also rises. Indeed, one way to think about long-run economic growth is that it is the growth in the economy's potential output. We generally think of the long-run aggregate supply curve as shifting to the right over time as an economy experiences long-run growth.

From the Short Run to the Long Run

As you can see in Figure 28-4, the economy normally produces more or less than potential output: actual aggregate output was below potential output in the early 1990s, above potential output in the late 1990s, below potential output for most of the 2000s, and significantly below potential output after the recession of 2007–2009. So the economy is normally on its short-run aggregate supply curve—but not on its long-run aggregate supply curve. So why is the long-run curve relevant? Does the economy ever move from the short run to the long run? And if so, how?

The first step to answering these questions is to understand that the economy is always in one of only two states with respect to the short-run and long-run aggregate supply curves. It can be on both curves simultaneously by being at a point where the curves cross (as in the few years in Figure 28-4 in which actual aggregate output and potential output roughly coincided). Or it can be on the short-run aggregate supply curve but not the long-run aggregate supply curve (as in the years in which actual aggregate output and potential output *did not* coincide).

But that is not the end of the story. If the economy is on the short-run but not the long-run aggregate supply curve, the short-run aggregate supply curve will shift over

FIGURE **28-5**   **From the Short Run to the Long Run**

In panel (a), the initial short-run aggregate supply curve is $SRAS_1$. At the aggregate price level, P_1, the quantity of aggregate output supplied, Y_1, exceeds potential output, Y_P. Eventually, low unemployment will cause nominal wages to rise, leading to a leftward shift of the short-run aggregate supply curve from $SRAS_1$ to $SRAS_2$. In panel

(b), the reverse happens: at the aggregate price level, P_1, the quantity of aggregate output supplied is less than potential output. High unemployment eventually leads to a fall in nominal wages over time and a rightward shift of the short-run aggregate supply curve.

time until the economy is at a point where both curves cross—a point where actual aggregate output is equal to potential output.

Figure 28-5 shows how this process works. In both panels *LRAS* is the long-run aggregate supply curve, *SRAS*$_1$ is the initial short-run aggregate supply curve, and the aggregate price level is at P_1. In panel (a) the economy starts at the initial production point, A_1, which corresponds to a quantity of aggregate output supplied, Y_1, that is higher than potential output, Y_P. Producing an aggregate output level (such as Y_1) that is higher than potential output (Y_P) is possible only because nominal wages haven't yet fully adjusted upward. Until this upward adjustment in nominal wages occurs, producers are earning high profits and producing a high level of output. But a level of aggregate output higher than potential output means a low level of unemployment. Because jobs are abundant and workers are scarce, nominal wages will rise over time, gradually shifting the short-run aggregate supply curve leftward. Eventually it will be in a new position, such as *SRAS*$_2$.

In panel (b), the initial production point, A_1, corresponds to an aggregate output level, Y_1, that is lower than potential output, Y_P. Producing an aggregate output level (such as Y_1) that is lower than potential output (Y_P) is possible only because nominal wages haven't yet fully adjusted downward. Until this downward adjustment occurs, producers are earning low (or negative) profits and producing a low level of output. An aggregate output level lower than potential output means high unemployment. Because workers are abundant and jobs are scarce, nominal wages will fall over time, shifting the short-run aggregate supply curve gradually to the right. Eventually it will be in a new position, such as *SRAS*$_2$.

We'll soon see that these shifts of the short-run aggregate supply curve will return the economy to potential output in the long run.

ECONOMICS ▶ *IN ACTION*

PRICES AND OUTPUT DURING THE GREAT DEPRESSION

Figure 28-6 shows the actual track of the aggregate price level, as measured by the GDP deflator and real GDP, from 1929 to 1942. As you can see, aggregate output and the aggregate price level fell together from 1929 to 1933 and rose together from 1933 to 1937. This is what we'd expect to see if the economy was moving down the short-run aggregate supply curve from 1929 to 1933 and moving up it (with a brief reversal in 1937–1938) thereafter.

But even in 1942 the aggregate price level was still lower than it was in 1929; yet real GDP was much higher. What happened?

The answer is that the short-run aggregate supply curve shifted to the right over time. This shift partly reflected rising productivity—a rightward shift of the underlying long-run aggregate supply curve. But since the U.S. economy was producing below potential output and had high unemployment during this period, the rightward shift of the short-run aggregate supply curve also reflected the adjustment process shown in panel (b) of Figure 28-5. So the change in aggregate output from 1929 to 1942 reflected both movements along and shifts of the short-run aggregate supply curve.

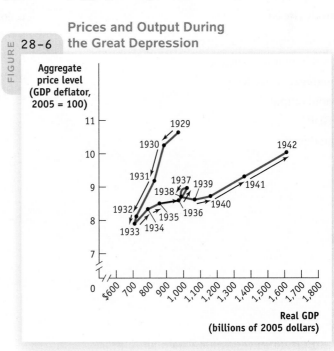

FIGURE 28-6   Prices and Output During the Great Depression

MODULE

28 Review

Solutions appear at the back of the book.

Check Your Understanding

1. Determine the effect on short-run aggregate supply of each of the following events. Explain whether it represents a movement along the *SRAS* curve or a shift of the *SRAS* curve.

   a. A rise in the consumer price index (CPI) leads producers to increase output.

   b. A fall in the price of oil leads producers to increase output.

   c. A rise in legally mandated retirement benefits paid to workers leads producers to reduce output.

2. Suppose the economy is initially at potential output and the quantity of aggregate output supplied increases. What information would you need to determine whether this was due to a movement along the *SRAS* curve or a shift of the *LRAS* curve?

Multiple-Choice Questions

1. A change in which of the following variables will cause a shift of the *SRAS* curve?

   a. profit per unit at any given price level

   b. commodity prices

   c. nominal wages

   d. productivity

   e. all of the above

2. The long-run aggregate supply curve is

   a. vertical.

   b. horizontal.

   c. fixed.

   d. negatively sloped.

   e. positively sloped.

3. The long-run aggregate supply curve shows

   a. the level of nominal wages.

   b. the aggregate price level.

   c. potential output.

   d. real GDP.

   e. productivity.

4. A decrease in which of the following will cause the short-run aggregate supply curve to shift to the left?

   a. commodity prices

   b. the cost of health care insurance premiums paid by employers

   c. nominal wages

   d. productivity

   e. the use of cost-of-living allowances in labor contracts

5. That employers are reluctant to decrease nominal wages during economic downturns and raise nominal wages during economic expansions leads nominal wages to be described as

   a. long-run.

   b. unyielding.

   c. flexible.

   d. real.

   e. sticky.

Critical-Thinking Questions

The short-run aggregate supply curve is upward sloping as a result of the price and output decisions made by firms in the short run.

1. Explain why perfectly competitive firms increase output when there is an increase in the aggregate price level.

2. Explain why imperfectly competitive firms increase both price and output when there is an increase in demand.

PITFALLS

WHAT THE LONG RUN REALLY MEANS

? You've seen the term *long run* used in two different contexts. In an earlier section, we discussed *long-run economic growth*. In this section, we introduced the *long-run aggregate supply curve*. What is the difference between the two?

> THERE IS NO DIFFERENCE! *Long-run economic growth* is growth that takes place over decades, while the *long-run aggregate supply curve* shows the economy's potential output at a particular point in time: that is, the level of aggregate output that the economy would produce if all prices, including nominal wages, were fully flexible. Because the economy always tends to return to potential output in the long run, actual aggregate output *fluctuates around* potential output. As a result, the economy's rate of growth over long periods of time is very close to the rate of growth of potential output. So this means that the "long run" of long-run growth and the "long run" of the long-run aggregate supply curve are really the same thing.

To learn more about both concepts, see pages 290–293.

Dorset Media Service/Alamy

In the *AD–AS* model, the aggregate supply curve and the aggregate demand curve are used together to analyze economic fluctuations.

The economy is in short-run macroeconomic equilibrium when the quantity of aggregate output supplied is equal to the quantity demanded.

The short-run equilibrium aggregate price level is the aggregate price level in the short-run macroeconomic equilibrium.

Short-run equilibrium aggregate output is the quantity of aggregate output produced in the short-run macroeconomic equilibrium.

Putting the Aggregate Supply Curve and the Aggregate Demand Curve Together

From 1929 to 1933, the U.S. economy moved down the short-run aggregate supply curve as the aggregate price level fell. In contrast, from 1979 to 1980, the U.S. economy moved up the aggregate demand curve as the aggregate price level rose. In each case, the cause of the movement along the curve was a shift of the other curve. In 1929–1933, it was a leftward shift of the aggregate demand curve—a major fall in consumer spending. In 1979–1980, it was a leftward shift of the short-run aggregate supply curve—a dramatic fall in short-run aggregate supply caused by the oil *price shock*.

So to understand the behavior of the economy, we must put the aggregate supply curve and the aggregate demand curve together. The result is the *AD–AS* **model,** the basic model we use to understand economic fluctuations.

Short-Run Macroeconomic Equilibrium

We'll begin our analysis by focusing on the short run. Figure 29-1 shows the aggregate demand curve and the short-run aggregate supply curve on the same diagram. The point at which the *AD* and *SRAS* curves intersect, E_{SR}, is the **short-run macroeconomic equilibrium:** the point at which the quantity of aggregate output supplied is equal to the quantity demanded by domestic households, businesses, the government, and the rest of the world. The aggregate price level at E_{SR}, P_E, is the **short-run equilibrium aggregate price level.** The level of aggregate output at E_{SR}, Y_E, is the **short-run equilibrium aggregate output.**

We have seen that a shortage of any individual good causes its market price to rise and a surplus of the good causes its market price to fall. These forces ensure that the market reaches equilibrium. The same logic applies to short-run macroeconomic

FIGURE **29-1** The *AD–AS* Model

The *AD–AS* model combines the aggregate demand curve and the short-run aggregate supply curve. Their point of intersection, E_{SR}, is the point of short-run macroeconomic equilibrium where the quantity of aggregate output demanded is equal to the quantity of aggregate output supplied. P_E is the short-run equilibrium aggregate price level, and Y_E is the short-run equilibrium level of aggregate output.

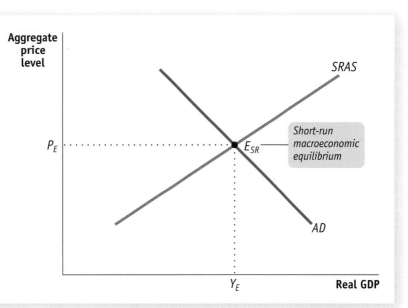

equilibrium. If the aggregate price level is above its equilibrium level, the quantity of aggregate output supplied exceeds the quantity of aggregate output demanded. This leads to a fall in the aggregate price level and pushes it toward its equilibrium level.

If the aggregate price level is below its equilibrium level, the quantity of aggregate output supplied is less than the quantity of aggregate output demanded. This leads to a rise in the aggregate price level, again pushing it toward its equilibrium level. In the discussion that follows, we'll assume that the economy is always in short-run macroeconomic equilibrium.

We'll also make another important simplification based on the observation that in reality there is a long-term upward trend in both aggregate output and the aggregate price level. We'll assume that a fall in either variable really means a fall compared to the long-run trend. For example, if the aggregate price level normally rises 4% per year, a year in which the aggregate price level rises only 3% would count, for our purposes, as a 1% decline.

In fact, since the Great Depression there have been very few years in which the aggregate price level of any major nation actually declined—Japan's period of deflation from 1995 to 2005 is one of the few exceptions. However, there have been many cases in which the aggregate price level fell relative to the long-run trend.

The short-run equilibrium aggregate output and the short-run equilibrium aggregate price level can change because of shifts of either the *AD* curve or the *SRAS* curve. Let's look at each case in turn.

Shifts of Aggregate Demand: Short-Run Effects

An event that shifts the aggregate demand curve, such as a change in expectations or wealth, the effect of the size of the existing stock of physical capital, or the use of fiscal or monetary policy, is known as a **demand shock.** The Great Depression was caused by a negative demand shock—the collapse of wealth and of business and consumer confidence that followed the stock market crash of 1929 and

An event that shifts the aggregate demand curve is a **demand shock.**

The Great Depression was caused by a negative demand shock and ended by a positive demand shock.

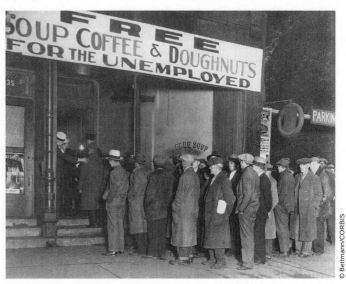

the banking crises of 1930–1931. The Depression was ended by a positive demand shock—the huge increase in government purchases during World War II. In 2008, the U.S. economy experienced another significant negative demand shock as the housing market turned from boom to bust, leading consumers and firms to scale back their spending.

Figure 29-2 shows the short-run effects of negative and positive demand shocks. A negative demand shock shifts the aggregate demand curve, *AD*, to the left, from *AD*$_1$ to *AD*$_2$, as shown in panel (a). The economy moves down along the *SRAS* curve from E_1 to E_2, leading to lower short-run equilibrium aggregate output and a lower short-run equilibrium aggregate price level. A positive demand shock shifts the aggregate demand curve, *AD*, to the right, as shown in panel (b). Here, the economy moves up along the *SRAS* curve, from E_1 to E_2. This leads to higher short-run equilibrium aggregate output and a higher short-run equilibrium aggregate price level. Demand shocks cause aggregate output and the aggregate price level to move in the same direction.

FIGURE **29-2**   Demand Shocks

A demand shock shifts the aggregate demand curve, moving the aggregate price level and aggregate output in the same direction. In panel (a), a negative demand shock shifts the aggregate demand curve leftward from *AD*$_1$ to *AD*$_2$, reducing the aggregate price level from P_1 to P_2 and

aggregate output from Y_1 to Y_2. In panel (b), a positive demand shock shifts the aggregate demand curve rightward, increasing the aggregate price level from P_1 to P_2 and aggregate output from Y_1 to Y_2.

Shifts of the *SRAS* Curve

An event that shifts the short-run aggregate supply curve, such as a change in commodity prices, nominal wages, or productivity, is known as a **supply shock.** A *negative* supply shock raises production costs and reduces the quantity producers are willing to supply at any given aggregate price level, leading to a leftward shift of the short-run aggregate supply curve. The U.S. economy experienced severe negative supply shocks following disruptions to world oil supplies in 1973 and 1979.

In contrast, a *positive* supply shock reduces production costs and increases the quantity supplied at any given aggregate price level, leading to a rightward shift of the short-run aggregate supply curve. The United States experienced a positive supply

An event that shifts the short-run aggregate supply curve is a **supply shock.**

shock between 1995 and 2000, when the increasing use of the Internet and other information technologies caused productivity growth to surge.

The effects of a negative supply shock are shown in panel (a) of Figure 29-3. The
initial equilibrium is at E_1, with aggregate price level P_1 and aggregate output Y_1. The
disruption in the oil supply causes the short-run aggregate supply curve to shift to the
left, from $SRAS_1$ to $SRAS_2$. As a consequence, aggregate output falls and the aggregate
price level rises, an upward movement along the *AD* curve. At the new equilibrium, E_2,
the short-run equilibrium aggregate price level, P_2, is higher, and the short-run equilibrium aggregate output level, Y_2, is lower than before.

The combination of inflation and falling aggregate output shown in panel (a) has a
special name: **stagflation,** for "stagnation plus inflation." When an economy experiences stagflation, it's very unpleasant: falling aggregate output leads to rising unemployment, and people feel that their purchasing power is squeezed by rising prices.
Stagflation in the 1970s led to a mood of national pessimism. It also, as we'll see
shortly, poses a dilemma for policy makers.

A positive supply shock, shown in panel (b), has exactly the opposite effects. A
rightward shift of the *SRAS* curve, from $SRAS_1$ to $SRAS_2$, results in a rise in aggregate
output and a fall in the aggregate price level, a downward movement along the *AD*
curve. The favorable supply shocks of the late 1990s led to a combination of full employment and declining inflation. That is, the aggregate price level fell compared with
the long-run trend. This combination produced, for a time, a great wave of national
optimism.

The distinctive feature of supply shocks, both negative and positive, is that, unlike
demand shocks, they cause the aggregate price level and aggregate output to move in
opposite directions.

Producers are vulnerable to supply
shocks caused by dramatic changes
in oil prices.

Stagflation is the combination of
inflation and stagnating (or falling)
aggregate output.

FIGURE 29-3   Supply Shocks

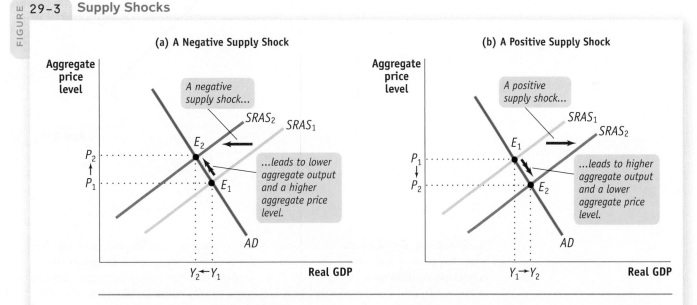

A supply shock shifts the short-run aggregate supply
curve, moving the aggregate price level and aggregate
output in opposite directions. Panel (a) shows a negative supply shock, which shifts the short-run aggregate
supply curve leftward and causes stagflation—lower
aggregate output and a higher aggregate price level. Here
the short-run aggregate supply curve shifts from $SRAS_1$
to $SRAS_2$, and the economy moves from E_1 to E_2. The

aggregate price level rises from P_1 to P_2, and aggregate
output falls from Y_1 to Y_2. Panel (b) shows a positive supply shock, which shifts the short-run aggregate supply
curve rightward, generating higher aggregate output and a
lower aggregate price level. The short-run aggregate supply curve shifts from $SRAS_1$ to $SRAS_2$, and the economy
moves from E_1 to E_2. The aggregate price level falls from
P_1 to P_2, and aggregate output rises from Y_1 to Y_2.

The economy is in **long-run macroeconomic equilibrium** when the point of short-run macroeconomic equilibrium is on the long-run aggregate supply curve.

There's another important contrast between supply shocks and demand shocks. As we've seen, monetary policy and fiscal policy enable the government to shift the aggregate demand curve, meaning that governments are in a position to create the kinds of shocks shown in Figure 29-2. It's much harder for governments to shift the aggregate supply curve. Are there good policy reasons to shift the aggregate demand curve? We'll turn to that question soon. First, however, let's look at the difference between short-run macroeconomic equilibrium and long-run macroeconomic equilibrium.

Long-Run Macroeconomic Equilibrium

Figure 29-4 combines the aggregate demand curve with both the short-run and long-run aggregate supply curves. The aggregate demand curve, AD, crosses the short-run aggregate supply curve, $SRAS$, at E_{LR}. Here we assume that enough time has elapsed that the economy is also on the long-run aggregate supply curve, $LRAS$. As a result, E_{LR} is at the intersection of all three curves—$SRAS$, $LRAS$, and AD. So short-run equilibrium aggregate output is equal to potential output, Y_P. Such a situation, in which the point of short-run macroeconomic equilibrium is on the long-run aggregate supply curve, is known as **long-run macroeconomic equilibrium.**

FIGURE 29-4   Long-Run Macroeconomic Equilibrium

Here the point of short-run macroeconomic equilibrium also lies on the long-run aggregate supply curve, *LRAS*. As a result, short-run equilibrium aggregate output is equal to potential output, Y_P. The economy is in long-run macroeconomic equilibrium at E_{LR}.

To see the significance of long-run macroeconomic equilibrium, let's consider what happens if a demand shock moves the economy away from long-run macroeconomic equilibrium. In Figure 29-5, we assume that the initial aggregate demand curve is AD_1 and the initial short-run aggregate supply curve is $SRAS_1$. So the initial macroeconomic equilibrium is at E_1, which lies on the long-run aggregate supply curve, $LRAS$. The economy, then, starts from a point of short-run and long-run macroeconomic equilibrium, and short-run equilibrium aggregate output equals potential output at Y_1.

Now suppose that for some reason—such as a sudden worsening of business and consumer expectations—aggregate demand falls and the aggregate demand curve shifts leftward to AD_2. This results in a lower equilibrium aggregate price level at P_2 and a lower equilibrium aggregate output level at Y_2 as the economy settles in the

29-5 Short-Run versus Long-Run Effects of a Negative Demand Shock

In the long run the economy is self-correcting: demand shocks have only a short-run effect on aggregate output. Starting at E_1, a negative demand shock shifts AD_1 leftward to AD_2. In the short run the economy moves to E_2 and a recessionary gap arises: the aggregate price level declines from P_1 to P_2, aggregate output declines from Y_1 to Y_2, and unemployment rises. But in the long run nominal wages fall in response to high unemployment at Y_2, and $SRAS_1$ shifts rightward to $SRAS_2$. Aggregate output rises from Y_2 to Y_1, and the aggregate price level declines again, from P_2 to P_3. Long-run macroeconomic equilibrium is eventually restored at E_3.

short run at E_2. The short-run effect of such a fall in aggregate demand is what the U.S. economy experienced in 1929–1933: a falling aggregate price level and falling aggregate output.

Aggregate output in this new short-run equilibrium, E_2, is below potential output. When this happens, the economy faces a **recessionary gap.** A recessionary gap inflicts a great deal of pain because it corresponds to high unemployment. The large recessionary gap that had opened up in the United States by 1933 caused intense social and political turmoil. And the devastating recessionary gap that opened up in Germany at the same time played an important role in Hitler's rise to power.

But this isn't the end of the story. In the face of high unemployment, nominal wages eventually fall, as do any other sticky prices, ultimately leading producers to increase output. As a result, a recessionary gap causes the short-run aggregate supply curve to gradually shift to the right. This process continues until $SRAS_1$ reaches its new position at $SRAS_2$, bringing the economy to equilibrium at E_3, where AD_2, $SRAS_2$, and *LRAS* all intersect. At E_3, the economy is back in long-run macroeconomic equilibrium; it is back at potential output Y_1 but at a lower aggregate price level, P_3, reflecting a long-run fall in the aggregate price level. The economy is *self-correcting* in the long run.

What if, instead, there was an increase in aggregate demand? The results are shown in Figure 29-6, where we again assume that the initial aggregate demand curve is AD_1 and the initial short-run aggregate supply curve is $SRAS_1$, so that the initial macroeconomic equilibrium, at E_1, lies on the long-run aggregate supply curve, *LRAS*. Initially, then, the economy is in long-run macroeconomic equilibrium.

Now suppose that aggregate demand rises, and the *AD* curve shifts rightward to AD_2. This results in a higher aggregate price level, at P_2, and a higher aggregate output level, at Y_2, as the economy settles in the short run at E_2. Aggregate output in this new

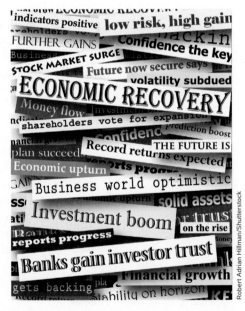

The economy is self-correcting in the long run.

There is a **recessionary gap** when aggregate output is below potential output.

29-6   Short-Run versus Long-Run Effects of a Positive Demand Shock

Starting at E_1, a positive demand shock shifts AD_1 rightward to AD_2, and the economy moves to E_2 in the short run. This results in an inflationary gap as aggregate output rises from Y_1 to Y_2, the aggregate price level rises from P_1 to P_2, and unemployment falls to a low level. In the long run, $SRAS_1$ shifts leftward to $SRAS_2$ as nominal wages rise in response to low unemployment at Y_2. Aggregate output falls back to Y_1, the aggregate price level rises again to P_3, and the economy self-corrects as it returns to long-run macroeconomic equilibrium at E_3.

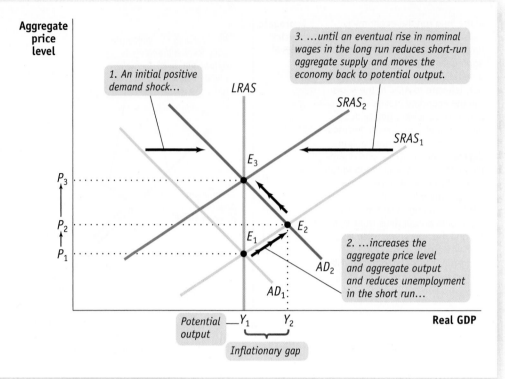

short-run equilibrium is above potential output, and unemployment is low in order to produce this higher level of aggregate output. When this happens, the economy experiences an **inflationary gap.** As in the case of a recessionary gap, this isn't the end of the story.

In the face of low unemployment, nominal wages will rise, as will other sticky prices. An inflationary gap causes the short-run aggregate supply curve to shift gradually to the left as producers reduce output in the face of rising nominal wages. This process continues until $SRAS_1$ reaches its new position at $SRAS_2$, bringing the economy into equilibrium at E_3, where AD_2, $SRAS_2$, and $LRAS$ all intersect. At E_3, the economy is back in long-run macroeconomic equilibrium. It is back at potential output, but at a higher price level, P_3, reflecting a long-run rise in the aggregate price level. Again, the economy is self-correcting in the long run.

To summarize the analysis of how the economy responds to recessionary and inflationary gaps, we can focus on the **output gap,** the percentage difference between actual aggregate output and potential output. The output gap is calculated as follows:

There is an *inflationary gap* when aggregate output is above potential output.

The *output gap* is the percentage difference between actual aggregate output and potential output.

The economy is *self-correcting* when shocks to aggregate demand affect aggregate output in the short run, but not in the long run.

$$\textbf{(29-1)} \quad \text{Output gap} = \frac{\text{Actual aggregate output} - \text{Potential output}}{\text{Potential output}} \times 100$$

Our analysis says that the output gap always tends toward zero.

If there is a recessionary gap, so that the output gap is negative, nominal wages eventually fall, moving the economy back to potential output and bringing the output gap back to zero. If there is an inflationary gap, so that the output gap is positive, nominal wages eventually rise, also moving the economy back to potential output and again bringing the output gap back to zero. So in the long run the economy is **self-correcting:** shocks to aggregate demand affect aggregate output in the short run but not in the long run.

ECONOMICS ▶ *IN ACTION*

SUPPLY SHOCKS VERSUS DEMAND SHOCKS IN PRACTICE

How often do supply shocks and demand shocks, respectively, cause recessions? The verdict of most, though not all, macroeconomists is that recessions are mainly caused by demand shocks. But when a negative supply shock does happen, the resulting recession tends to be particularly severe.

Let's get specific. Officially there have been twelve recessions in the United States since World War II. However, two of these, in 1979–1980 and 1981–1982, are often treated as a single "double-dip" recession, bringing the total number down to eleven. Of these eleven recessions, only two—the recession of 1973–1975 and the double-dip recession of 1979–1982—showed the distinctive combination of falling aggregate output and a surge in the price level that we call stagflation.

In each case, the cause of the supply shock was political turmoil in the Middle East—the Arab–Israeli war of 1973 and the Iranian revolution of 1979—that disrupted world oil supplies and sent oil prices skyrocketing. In fact, economists sometimes refer to the two slumps as "OPEC I" and "OPEC II," after the Organization of Petroleum Exporting Countries, the world oil cartel. A third recession that began in 2007 and lasted until 2009 was at least partially exacerbated, if not at least partially caused, by a spike in oil prices.

So eight of eleven postwar recessions were purely the result of demand shocks, not supply shocks. The few supply-shock recessions, however, were the worst as measured by the unemployment rate. Figure 29-7 shows the U.S. unemployment rate from 1948 through 2011, with the dates of the 1973 Arab–Israeli war and the 1979 Iranian revolution highlighted. Some of the highest unemployment rates since World War II came after these big negative supply shocks.

There's a reason the aftermath of a supply shock tends to be particularly severe for the economy: macroeconomic policy has a much harder time dealing with supply shocks than with demand shocks. Indeed, the reason the Federal Reserve was having a hard time in 2008, as described in the section-opening story, was the fact that in early 2008 the U.S. economy was in a recession partially caused by a supply shock (although it was also facing a demand shock). We'll see in a moment why supply shocks present such a problem.

FIGURE 29-7

Negative Supply Shocks Are Relatively Rare but Nasty

Source: Bureau of Labor Statistics.

Macroeconomic Policy

We've just seen that the economy is self-correcting in the long run: it will eventually trend back to potential output.

Most macroeconomists believe, however, that the process of self-correction typically takes a decade or more. In particular, if aggregate output is below potential output, the economy can suffer an extended period of depressed aggregate output and high unemployment before it returns to normal.

This belief is the background to one of the most famous quotations in economics: John Maynard Keynes's declaration, "In the long run we are all dead." Economists usually interpret Keynes as having recommended that governments not wait for the

Stabilization policy is the use of government policy to reduce the severity of recessions and rein in excessively strong expansions.

economy to correct itself. Instead, it is argued by many economists, but not all, that the government should use fiscal policy to get the economy back to potential output in the aftermath of a shift of the aggregate demand curve.

This is the rationale for active **stabilization policy,** which is the use of government policy to reduce the severity of recessions and rein in excessively strong expansions.

Can stabilization policy improve the economy's performance? As we saw in Figure 28-4, the answer certainly appears to be yes. Under active stabilization policy, the U.S. economy returned to potential output in 1996 after an approximately five-year recessionary gap. Likewise, in 2001, it also returned to potential output after an approximately four-year inflationary gap. These periods are much shorter than the decade or more that economists believe it would take for the economy to self-correct in the absence of active stabilization policy. However, the ability to improve the economy's performance is not always guaranteed. It depends on the kinds of shocks the economy faces.

Policy in the Face of Demand Shocks

Imagine that the economy experiences a negative demand shock, like the one shown by the shift from AD_1 to AD_2 in Figure 29-5. As we know, fiscal policy shifts the aggregate demand curve. If policy makers react quickly to the fall in aggregate demand, they can use monetary or fiscal policy to shift the aggregate demand curve back to the right. And if policy were able to perfectly anticipate shifts of the aggregate demand curve and counteract them, it could short-circuit the whole process shown in Figure 29-5. Instead of going through a period of low aggregate output and falling prices, the government could manage the economy so that it would stay at E_1.

Why might a policy that short-circuits the adjustment shown in Figure 29-5 and maintains the economy at its original equilibrium be desirable? For two reasons: First, the temporary fall in aggregate output that would happen without policy intervention is a bad thing, particularly because such a decline is associated with high unemployment. Second, *price stability* is generally regarded as a desirable goal. So preventing deflation—a fall in the aggregate price level—is a good thing.

Does this mean that policy makers should always act to offset declines in aggregate demand? Not necessarily. Some policy measures to increase aggregate demand, especially those that increase budget deficits, may have long-term costs in terms of lower long-run growth.

Furthermore, in the real world policy makers aren't perfectly informed, and the effects of their policies aren't perfectly predictable. This creates the danger that stabilization policy will do more harm than good; that is, attempts to stabilize the economy may end up creating more instability. We'll describe the long-running debate over macroeconomic policy in later modules. Despite these qualifications, most economists believe that a good case can be made for using macroeconomic policy to offset major negative shocks to the AD curve.

Should policy makers also try to offset positive shocks to aggregate demand? It may not seem obvious that they should. After all, even though inflation may be a bad thing, isn't more output and lower unemployment a good thing? Again, not necessarily. Most economists now believe that any short-run gains from an inflationary gap must be paid back later. So policy makers today usually try to offset positive as well as negative demand shocks. For reasons we'll explain later, attempts to eliminate recessionary gaps and inflationary gaps usually rely on monetary rather than fiscal policy. But how should macroeconomic policy respond to supply shocks?

Responding to Supply Shocks

In panel (a) of Figure 29-3 we showed the effects of a negative supply shock: in the short run such a shock leads to lower aggregate output but a higher aggregate price level. As we've noted, policy makers can respond to a negative *demand* shock by using monetary and fiscal policy to return aggregate demand to its original level. But what can or should they do about a negative *supply* shock?

In contrast to the case of a demand shock, there are no easy remedies for a supply shock. That is, there are no government policies that can easily counter-act the changes in production costs that shift the short-run aggregate supply curve. So the policy response to a negative supply shock cannot aim to simply push the curve that shifted back to its original position.

And if you consider using monetary or fiscal policy to shift the aggregate de-mand curve in response to a supply shock, the right response isn't obvious.

Two bad things are happening simultaneously: a fall in aggregate output, leading to a rise in unemployment, *and* a rise in the aggregate price level. Any policy that shifts the aggregate demand curve helps one problem only by making the other worse. If the government acts to increase aggregate demand and limit the rise in unemployment, it reduces the decline in output but causes even more inflation. If it acts to reduce aggregate demand, it curbs inflation but causes a further rise in unemployment.

It's a trade-off with no good answer. In the end, the United States and other economically advanced nations suffering from the supply shocks of the 1970s eventually chose to stabilize prices even at the cost of higher unemployment. But being an economic policy maker in the 1970s, or in early 2008, meant facing even harder choices than usual.

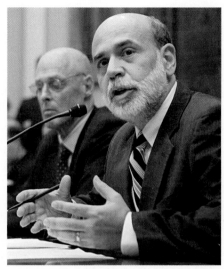

In 2008, stagflation made for difficult policy choices for the Federal Reserve chairman at the time, Ben Bernanke.

29 Review

Check Your Understanding

1. Describe the short-run effects of each of the following shocks on the aggregate price level and on aggregate output.

   a. The government sharply increases the minimum wage, raising the wages of many workers.

   b. Solar energy firms launch a major program of investment spending.

   c. Congress raises taxes and cuts spending.

   d. Severe weather destroys crops around the world.

2. A rise in productivity increases potential output, but some worry that demand for the additional output will be insufficient even in the long run. How would you respond?

3. Suppose someone says, "Using monetary or fiscal policy to pump up the economy is counterproductive—you get a brief high, but then you have the pain of inflation."

   a. Explain what this means in terms of the *AD–AS* model.

   b. Is this a valid argument against stabilization policy? Why or why not?

4. In 2008, in the aftermath of the collapse of the housing bubble and a sharp rise in the price of commodities, particularly oil, there was much internal disagreement within the Fed about how to respond, with some advocating lowering interest rates and others contending that this would set off a rise in inflation. Explain the reasoning behind each of these views in terms of the *AD–AS* model.

Multiple-Choice Questions

1. Which of the following causes a negative supply shock?

   I. a technological advance
   II. increasing productivity
   III. an increase in oil prices

   a. I only
   b. II only
   c. III only
   d. I and III only
   e. I, II, and III

2. Which of the following causes a positive demand shock?

   a. an increase in wealth
   b. pessimistic consumer expectations
   c. a decrease in government spending
   d. an increase in taxes
   e. an increase in the existing stock of capital

3. During stagflation, what happens to the aggregate price level and real GDP?

	Aggregate price level	Real GDP
a.	decreases	increases
b.	decreases	decreases
c.	increases	increases
d.	increases	decreases
e.	stays the same	stays the same

Refer to the graph for questions 4 and 5.

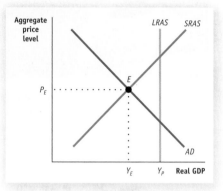

4. Which of the following statements is true if this economy is operating at P_E and Y_E?

I. The level of aggregate output equals potential output.

II. It is in short-run macroeconomic equilibrium.

III. It is in long-run macroeconomic equilibrium.

a. I only

b. II only

c. III only

d. II and III

e. I and III

5. The economy depicted in the graph is experiencing a(n)

a. contractionary gap.

b. recessionary gap.

c. inflationary gap.

d. demand gap.

e. supply gap.

Critical-Thinking Question

Draw a graph to illustrate an economy in the midst of an inflationary gap. Explain and illustrate why the economy will eventually return to long-run equilibrium.

WHERE'S THE DEFLATION?

? The *AD–AS* model tells us that either a negative demand shock or a positive supply shock should lead to a fall in the aggregate price level—that is, it should lead to deflation. But, how often does deflation actually occur?

> RARELY. SINCE 1949, AN ACTUAL FALL IN THE AGGRE- GATE PRICE LEVEL HAS BEEN A RARE OCCURRENCE IN THE UNITED STATES. SIMILARLY, MOST OTHER COUNTRIES HAVE HAD LITTLE OR NO EXPERIENCE WITH DEFLATION. Japan, which experienced sustained mild deflation in the late 1990s and the early part of the next decade, is the big (and much discussed) exception. What happened to deflation?

The basic answer is that since World War II economic fluctuations have largely taken place around a long-run inflationary trend. Before the war, it was common for prices to fall during recessions, but since then negative demand shocks have largely been reflected in a decline in the rate of inflation rather than an actual fall in prices. For example, the rate of consumer price inflation fell from more than 3% at the beginning of the 2001 recession to 1.1% a year later, but it never went below zero. All of this changed during the recession of 2007–2009. The negative demand shock that followed the 2008 financial crisis was so severe that, for most of 2009, consumer prices in the United States indeed fell. But the deflationary period didn't last long: beginning in 2010, prices again rose, at a rate of between 1% and 4% per year.

To learn more, see pages 297–301, especially Figure 29-5.

BUSINESS CASE: United in Pain

BSTAR IMAGES/Alamy

The airline industry is notoriously "cyclical." That is, instead of making profits all through the business cycle, it tends to plunge into losses during recessions, only regaining profitability sometime after recovery begins. Mainly this is because airlines have large fixed costs that remain high even if ticket sales slump. The cost of operating a flight from one city to another is pretty much the same whether the flight is fully booked or two-thirds empty, so when business slumps for whatever reason, even highly profitable routes quickly become money-losers.

It's true that airlines can to some extent adapt to a decline in business by switching to smaller planes, consolidating flights, and so on, but this process takes time and still tends to leave costs per passenger higher than before.

But some recessions are worse for airlines than for other businesses, because operating costs rise even as demand falls. This was very much the case in early 2008. In the spring of that year, the Great Recession of 2007–2009 was still in its early stages, with unemployment just starting to rise. Yet airlines were already, as an article in the *Los Angeles Times* put it, in a "sea of red ink." The article highlighted the case of United Airlines, which had suddenly plunged into large losses and was planning large layoffs.

Why was United in so much trouble? Business travel had started to slacken, but at that point leisure travel, such as flights to Disney World, was still holding up. What was hurting United and its sister airlines was the cost of fuel, which soared in late 2007 and early 2008.

Fuel prices fell back down in late 2008. But by that time United was suffering from a sharp drop in ticket sales. The airline finally returned to profitability in 2010, which was also the year it agreed to merge with Continental. But in early 2011 fuel prices rose again, putting airlines once more in a difficult position.

Questions for Thought

1. How did United's problems in early 2008 relate to our analysis of the causes of recessions?

2. The chairman of the Fed at the time, Ben Bernanke, had to make a choice between fighting two evils in early 2008. How would that choice affect United compared with, say, a company producing a service without expensive raw-material inputs, like health care?

3. In early 2008, business travel was beginning to slacken, but leisure travel was still holding up. Given the situation the overall economy was in, what would you expect to happen to leisure travel as the economy moved further into recession?

SECTION 8 REVIEW

Summary

Aggregate Demand

1. The **aggregate demand curve** shows the relationship between the aggregate price level and the quantity of aggregate output demanded.

2. The aggregate demand curve is downward sloping for two reasons. The first is the **wealth effect of a change in the aggregate price level**—a higher aggregate price level reduces the purchasing power of households' wealth and reduces consumer spending. The second is the **interest rate effect of a change in the aggregate price level**—a higher aggregate price level reduces the purchasing power of households' and firms' money holdings, leading to a rise in interest rates and a fall in investment spending and consumer spending.

3. The aggregate demand curve shifts because of changes in expectations, changes in wealth not due to changes in the aggregate price level, and the effect of the size of the existing stock of physical capital. Policy makers can use *fiscal policy* and *monetary policy* to shift the aggregate demand curve.

Aggregate Supply

4. The **aggregate supply curve** shows the relationship between the aggregate price level and the quantity of aggregate output supplied.

5. The **short-run aggregate supply curve** is upward sloping because **nominal wages** are **sticky** in the short run: a higher aggregate price level leads to higher profit per unit of output and increased aggregate output in the short run.

6. Changes in commodity prices, nominal wages, and productivity lead to changes in producers' profits and shift the short-run aggregate supply curve.

7. In the long run, all prices, including nominal wages, are flexible and the economy produces at its **potential output.** If actual aggregate output exceeds potential output, nominal wages will eventually rise in response to low unemployment and aggregate output will fall. If potential output exceeds actual aggregate output, nominal wages will eventually fall in response to high unemployment and aggregate output will rise. So the **long-run aggregate supply curve** is vertical at potential output.

The *AD–AS* Model

8. In the ***AD–AS* model,** the intersection of the short-run aggregate supply curve and the aggregate demand curve is the point of **short-run macroeconomic equilibrium.** It determines the **short-run equilibrium aggregate price level** and the level of **short-run equilibrium aggregate output.**

9. Economic fluctuations occur because of a shift of the aggregate demand curve (a *demand shock*) or the short-run aggregate supply curve (a *supply shock*). A **demand shock** causes the aggregate price level and aggregate output to move in the same direction as the economy moves along the short-run aggregate supply curve. A **supply shock** causes them to move in opposite directions as the economy moves along the aggregate demand curve. A particularly nasty occurrence is **stagflation**—inflation and falling aggregate output—which is caused by a negative supply shock.

10. Demand shocks have only short-run effects on aggregate output because the economy is **self-correcting** in the long run. In a **recessionary gap,** an eventual fall in nominal wages moves the economy to **long-run macroeconomic equilibrium,** in which aggregate output is equal to potential output. In an **inflationary gap,** an eventual rise in nominal wages moves the economy to long-run macroeconomic equilibrium. We can use the **output gap,** the percentage difference between actual aggregate output and potential output, to summarize how the economy responds to recessionary and inflationary gaps. Because the economy tends to be self-correcting in the long run, the output gap always tends toward zero.

11. The high cost—in terms of unemployment—of a recessionary gap and the future adverse consequences of an inflationary gap lead many economists to advocate active **stabilization policy:** using fiscal or monetary policy to offset demand shocks. There can be drawbacks, however, because such policies may contribute to a long-term rise in the budget deficit, leading to lower long-run growth. Also, poorly timed policies can increase economic instability.

12. Negative supply shocks pose a policy dilemma: a policy that counteracts the fall in aggregate output by increasing aggregate demand will lead to higher inflation, but a policy that counteracts inflation by reducing aggregate demand will deepen the output slump.

Key Terms

Aggregate demand curve,
  p. 274
Wealth effect of a change in
  the aggregate price level,
  p. 276
Interest rate effect of a change
  in the aggregate price level,
  p. 276
Aggregate supply curve,
  p. 284

Nominal wage, p. 285
Sticky wages, p. 285
Short-run aggregate supply
  curve, p. 286
Long-run aggregate supply
  curve, p. 290
Potential output, p. 291
AD–AS model, p. 296

Short-run macroeconomic
  equilibrium, p. 296
Short-run equilibrium
  aggregate price level, p. 296
Short-run equilibrium
  aggregate output, p. 296
Demand shock, p. 297
Supply shock, p. 298
Stagflation, p. 299

Long-run macroeconomic
  equilibrium, p. 300
Recessionary gap, p. 301
Inflationary gap, p. 302
Output gap, p. 302
Self-correcting, p. 302
Stabilization policy, p. 304

Problems

1. A fall in the value of the dollar against other currencies makes U.S. final goods and services cheaper to foreigners even though the U.S. aggregate price level stays the same. As a result, foreigners demand more American aggregate output. Your study partner says that this represents a movement down the aggregate demand curve because foreigners are demanding more in response to a lower price. You, however, insist that this represents a rightward shift of the aggregate demand curve. Who is right? Explain.

2. Your study partner is confused by the upward-sloping short-run aggregate supply curve and the vertical long-run aggregate supply curve. How would you explain this?

3. Suppose that in Wageland all workers sign annual wage contracts each year on January 1. No matter what happens to prices of final goods and services during the year, all workers earn the wage specified in their annual contract. This year, prices of final goods and services fall unexpectedly after the contracts are signed. Answer the following questions using a diagram and assume that the economy starts at potential output.

   a. In the short run, how will the quantity of aggregate output supplied respond to the fall in prices?

   b. What will happen when firms and workers renegotiate their wages?

4. In each of the following cases, in the short run, determine whether the events cause a shift of a curve or a movement along a curve. Determine which curve is involved and the direction of the change.

   a. As a result of an increase in the value of the dollar in relation to other currencies, American producers now pay less in dollar terms for foreign steel, a major commodity used in production.

   b. An increase in the quantity of money by the Federal Reserve increases the quantity of money that people wish to lend, lowering interest rates.

   c. Greater union activity leads to higher nominal wages.

   d. A fall in the aggregate price level increases the purchasing power of households' and firms' money holdings. As a result, they borrow less and lend more.

5. The economy is at point *A* in the accompanying diagram. Suppose that the aggregate price level rises from P_1 to P_2. How will aggregate supply adjust in the short run and in the long run to the increase in the aggregate price level? Illustrate with a diagram.

6. Suppose that all households hold all their wealth in assets that automatically rise in value when the aggregate price level rises (an example of this is what is called an "inflation-indexed bond"—a bond whose interest rate, among other things, changes one-for-one with the inflation rate). What happens to the wealth effect of a change in the aggregate price level as a result of this allocation of assets? What happens to the slope of the aggregate demand curve? Will it still slope downward? Explain.

7. Suppose that the economy is currently at potential output. Also suppose that you are an economic policy maker and that a college economics student asks you to rank, if possible, your most preferred to least preferred type of shock: positive demand shock, negative demand shock, positive supply shock, negative supply shock. How would you rank them and why?

8. Explain whether the following government policies affect the aggregate demand curve or the short-run aggregate supply curve and how.

   a. The government reduces the minimum nominal wage.

   b. The government increases Temporary Assistance to Needy Families (TANF) payments, which are government transfers to families with dependent children.

   c. To reduce the budget deficit, the government announces that households will pay much higher taxes beginning next year.

   d. The government reduces military spending.

9. In Wageland, all workers sign an annual wage contract each year on January 1. In late January, a new computer operating system is introduced that increases labor productivity dramatically. Explain how Wageland will move from one short-run macroeconomic equilibrium to another. Illustrate with a diagram.

10. The Conference Board publishes the Consumer Confidence Index (CCI) every month based on a survey of 5,000 representative U.S. households. It is used by many economists to track the state of the economy. A press release by the Board on June 28, 2011 stated: "The Conference Board Consumer Confidence Index, which had declined in May, decreased again in June. The Index now stands at 58.5 (1985 = 100), down from 61.7 in May."

   a. To an economist, is this news encouraging for economic growth?

   b. Explain your answer to part a with the help of the AD–AS model. Draw a typical diagram showing two equilibrium points (E_1) and (E_2). Label the vertical axis "Aggregate price level" and the horizontal axis "Real GDP." Assume that all other major macroeconomic factors remain unchanged.

   c. How should the government respond to this news? What are some policy measures that could be used to help neutralize the effect of falling consumer confidence?

11. There were two major shocks to the U.S. economy in 2007, leading to the severe recession of 2007–2009. One shock was related to oil prices; the other was the slump in the housing market. This question analyzes the effect of these two shocks on GDP using the AD–AS framework.

   a. Draw typical aggregate demand and short-run aggregate supply curves. Label the horizontal axis "Real GDP" and the vertical axis "Aggregate price level." Label the equilibrium point E_1, the equilibrium quantity Y_1, and equilibrium price P_1.

   b. Data taken from the Department of Energy indicate that the average price of crude oil in the world increased from $54.63 per barrel on January 5, 2007, to $92.93 on December 28, 2007. Would an increase in oil prices cause a demand shock or a supply shock? Redraw the diagram from part a to illustrate the effect of this shock by shifting the appropriate curve.

   c. The Housing Price Index, published by the Office of Federal Housing Enterprise Oversight, calculates that

U.S. home prices fell by an average of 3.0% in the 12 months between January 2007 and January 2008. Would the fall in home prices cause a supply shock or demand shock? Redraw the diagram from part b to illustrate the effect of this shock by shifting the appropriate curve. Label the new equilibrium point E_3, the equilibrium quantity Y_3, and equilibrium price P_3.

   d. Compare the equilibrium points E_1 and E_3 in your diagram for part c. What was the effect of the two shocks on real GDP and the aggregate price level (increase, decrease, or indeterminate)?

12. Using aggregate demand, short-run aggregate supply, and long-run aggregate supply curves, explain the process by which each of the following economic events will move the economy from one long-run macroeconomic equilibrium to another. Illustrate with diagrams. In each case, what are the short-run and long-run effects on the aggregate price level and aggregate output?

   a. There is a decrease in households' wealth due to a decline in the stock market.

   b. The government lowers taxes, leaving households with more disposable income, with no corresponding reduction in government purchases.

13. Using aggregate demand, short-run aggregate supply, and long-run aggregate supply curves, explain the process by which each of the following government policies will move the economy from one long-run macroeconomic equilibrium to another. Illustrate with diagrams. In each case, what are the short-run and long-run effects on the aggregate price level and aggregate output?

   a. There is an increase in taxes on households.

   b. There is an increase in the quantity of money.

   c. There is an increase in government spending.

14. The economy is in short-run macroeconomic equilibrium at point E_1 in the accompanying diagram. Based on the diagram, answer the following questions.

   a. Is the economy facing an inflationary or a recessionary gap?

   b. What policies can the government implement that might bring the economy back to long-run macroeconomic equilibrium? Illustrate with a diagram.

c. If the government did not intervene to close this gap, would the economy return to long-run macroeconomic equilibrium? Explain and illustrate with a diagram.

d. What are the advantages and disadvantages of the government implementing policies to close the gap?

15. In the accompanying diagram, the economy is in long-run macroeconomic equilibrium at point E_1 when an oil shock shifts the short-run aggregate supply curve to $SRAS_2$. Based on the diagram, answer the following questions.

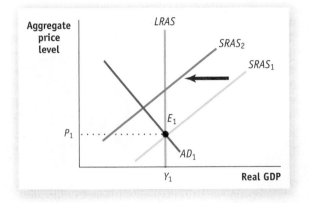

a. How do the aggregate price level and aggregate output change in the short run as a result of the oil shock? What is this phenomenon known as?

b. What fiscal or monetary policies can the government use to address the effects of the supply shock? Use a diagram that shows the effect of policies chosen to address the change in real GDP. Use another diagram to show the effect of policies chosen to address the change in the aggregate price level.

c. Why do supply shocks present a dilemma for government policy makers?

16. The late 1990s in the United States was characterized by substantial economic growth with low inflation; that is, real GDP increased with little, if any, increase in the aggregate price level. Explain this experience using aggregate demand and aggregate supply curves. Illustrate with a diagram.

SECTION 9

Fiscal Policy

TO STIMULATE OR NOT TO STIMULATE?

On February 17, 2009, President Obama signed the American Recovery and Reinvestment Act, a $787 billion package of spending, aid, and tax cuts intended to help the struggling U.S. economy reverse a severe recession that began in December 2007. A week earlier, as the bill neared final passage in Congress, Obama hailed the measure: "It is the right size; it is the right scope. Broadly speaking it has the right priorities to create jobs that will jumpstart our economy and transform it for the twenty-first century."

Others weren't so sure. Some argued that the government should be cutting spending, not increasing it, at a time when American families were suffering. "It's time for government to tighten their belts and show the American people that we 'get' it," said John Boehner, the leader of Republicans in the House of Representatives. Some economic analysts warned that the stimulus bill, as the Recovery Act was commonly called, would drive up interest rates and increase the burden of national debt.

Others had the opposite complaint—that the stimulus was too small given the economy's troubles. For example, Joseph Stiglitz, the 2001 recipient of the Nobel Prize in economics, stated about the stimulus, "First of all that it was not enough should be pretty apparent from what I just said: It is trying to offset the deficiency in aggregate demand and it is just too small."

Nor did the passage of time resolve these disputes. True, some predictions were proved false. On one side, Obama's hope that the bill would "jumpstart" the economy fell short: although the recession officially ended in June 2009, unemployment remained high through 2011 and into 2012, by which time the stimulus had largely run its course. On the other side, the soaring interest rates predicted by stimulus opponents failed to materialize, as U.S. borrowing costs remained low by historical standards. But the net effect of the stimulus remained controversial, with opponents arguing that it had failed to help the economy and defenders arguing that things would have been much worse without the bill.

Whatever the verdict—and this is one of those issues that economists and historians will probably be arguing about for decades to come—the Recovery Act of 2009 was a classic example of *fiscal policy*, the use of government spending and taxes to manage aggregate demand. In this section we'll see how fiscal policy fits into the models of economic fluctuations we studied in the last section. We'll also see why budget deficits and government debt can be a problem and how short-run and long-run concerns can pull fiscal policy in different directions.

30 Fiscal Policy Basics

Shutterstock

Andrew Zarivny/Shutterstock

1 What fiscal policy is

2 Why fiscal policy is an important tool for managing economic fluctuations

3 Which policies constitute expansionary fiscal policy and which constitute contractionary fiscal policy

What Is Fiscal Policy?

Let's begin with the obvious: modern governments in economically advanced countries spend a great deal of money and collect a lot in taxes. Figure 30-1 shows government spending and tax revenue as percentages of GDP for a selection of high-income countries in 2007. We focus on 2007, rather than a more recent year, because it was a largely "normal" year. The numbers for later years were very much affected by the financial crisis of 2008 and its aftermath.

FIGURE 30-1 Government Spending and Tax Revenue for Some High-Income Countries in 2007

We focus on 2007 because it was a "normal" year, not a year of deep economic slump. Government spending and tax revenue are represented as a percentage of GDP. Sweden has a particularly large government sector, representing more than half of its GDP. The U.S. government sector, although sizable, is smaller than those of Canada and most European countries as a percentage of GDP.

Source: OECD.

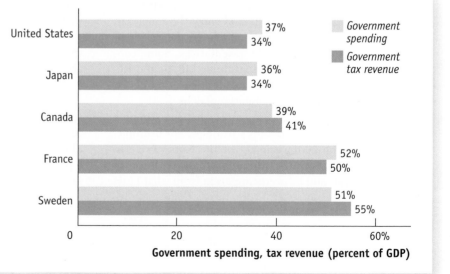

	Government spending	Government tax revenue
United States	37%	34%
Japan	36%	34%
Canada	39%	41%
France	52%	50%
Sweden	51%	55%

Government spending, tax revenue (percent of GDP)

As you can see, the Swedish government sector is relatively large, accounting for more than half of the Swedish economy. The government of the United States plays a smaller role in the economy than those of Canada or most European countries. But that role is still sizable, with the government playing a major role in the U.S. economy. As a result, changes in the federal budget—changes in government spending or in taxation—can have large effects on the American economy.

To analyze these effects, we begin by showing how taxes and government spending affect the economy's flow of income. Then we can see how changes in spending and tax policy affect aggregate demand.

Taxes, Purchases of Goods and Services, Government Transfers, and Borrowing

In Figure 10-2 on page 107 we showed the circular flow of income and spending in the economy as a whole. One of the sectors represented in that figure was the government. Funds flow *into* the government in the form of taxes and government borrowing; funds flow *out* in the form of government purchases of goods and services and government transfers to households.

What kinds of taxes do Americans pay, and where does the money go? Figure 30-2 shows the composition of U.S. tax revenue in 2007. Taxes, of course, are required payments to the government. In the United States, taxes are collected at the national level by the federal government; at the state level by each state government; and at local levels by counties, cities, and towns. At the federal level, the taxes that generate the greatest revenue are income taxes on both personal income and corporate profits as well as *social insurance* taxes, which we'll explain shortly. At the state and local levels, the picture is more complex: these governments rely on a mix of sales taxes, property taxes, income taxes, and fees of various kinds.

Overall, taxes on personal income and corporate profits accounted for 48% of total government revenue in 2007; social insurance taxes accounted for 25%; and a variety of other taxes, collected mainly at the state and local levels, accounted for the rest.

Figure 30-3 shows the composition of total U.S. government spending in 2007, which takes two broad forms. One form is purchases of goods and services. This includes everything from ammunition for the military to the salaries of public school teachers (who are treated in the national accounts as providers of a service—education). The big items here are national defense and education. The large category labeled "Other goods and services" consists mainly of state and local spending

FIGURE 30-2 Sources of Tax Revenue in the United States, 2007

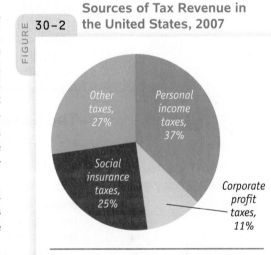

Personal income taxes, taxes on corporate profits, and social insurance taxes account for most government tax revenue. The rest is a mix of property taxes, sales taxes, and other sources of revenue.

Source: Bureau of Economic Analysis.

FIGURE 30-3 Government Spending in the United States, 2007

The two types of government spending are purchases of goods and services and government transfers. The big items in government purchases are national defense and education. The big items in government transfers are Social Security and the Medicare and Medicaid health care programs. (Numbers do not add to 100% due to rounding.)

Source: Bureau of Economic Analysis.

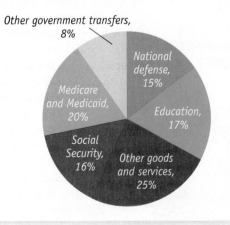

on a variety of services, from police and firefighters, to highway construction and maintenance, to building and operating dams.

The other form of government spending is government transfers, which are payments by the government to households for which no good or service is provided in return. In the modern United States, as well as in Canada and Europe, government transfers represent a very large proportion of the budget. Most U.S. government spending on transfer payments is accounted for by three big programs:

1. **Social Security,** which provides guaranteed income to older Americans, disabled Americans, and the surviving spouses and dependent children of deceased or retired beneficiaries
2. **Medicare,** which covers much of the cost of health care for Americans over age 65
3. **Medicaid,** which covers much of the cost of health care for Americans with low incomes

The term **social insurance** is used to describe government programs that are intended to protect families against economic hardship. These include Social Security, Medicare, and Medicaid, as well as smaller programs such as unemployment insurance and food stamps (also known as the Supplemental Nutrition Assistance Program, or SNAP). In the United States, social insurance programs are largely paid for with special, dedicated taxes on wages—the social insurance taxes we mentioned earlier.

But how do tax policy and government spending affect the economy? The answer is that taxation and government spending have a strong effect on total aggregate spending in the economy.

The Government Budget and Total Spending

Let's recall the basic equation of national income accounting:

$$(30\text{-}1) \quad GDP = C + I + G + X - IM$$

The left-hand side of this equation is GDP, the value of all final goods and services produced in the economy. The right-hand side is aggregate spending, total spending on final goods and services produced in the economy. It is the sum of consumer spending (C), investment spending (I), government purchases of goods and services (G), and the value of exports (X) minus the value of imports (IM). It includes all the sources of aggregate demand.

The government directly controls one of the variables on the right-hand side of Equation 30-1: government purchases of goods and services (G). But that's not the only effect fiscal policy has on aggregate spending in the economy. Through changes in taxes and transfers, it also influences consumer spending (C) and, in some cases, investment spending (I).

To see why the budget affects consumer spending, recall that *disposable income,* the total income households have available to spend, is equal to the total income they receive from wages, dividends, interest, and rent, *minus* taxes, *plus* government transfers.

So either an increase in taxes or a reduction in government transfers *reduces* disposable income. And a fall in disposable income, other things equal, leads to a fall in consumer spending. Conversely, either a decrease in taxes or an increase in government transfers *increases* disposable income. And a rise in disposable income, other things equal, leads to a rise in consumer spending.

The important point to remember is that the government taxes profits, and changes in the rules that determine how much a business owes can increase or reduce the incentive to spend on investment goods.

Because the government itself is one source of spending in the economy, and because taxes and transfers can affect spending by consumers and firms, the government can

GOVERNMENT BUDGET

Government budgets affect consumer spending and, in some cases, investment spending.

Shutterstock

use changes in taxes or government spending to *shift the aggregate demand curve.* And as we saw in the previous module, there are sometimes good reasons to shift the aggregate demand curve. As this section-opening story explained, in 2009, the Obama administration believed it was crucial that the U.S. government act to increase aggregate demand—that is, to move the aggregate demand curve to the right of where it would otherwise be. The 2009 stimulus package was a classic example of *fiscal policy:* the use of taxes, government transfers, or government purchases of goods and services to stabilize the economy by shifting the aggregate demand curve.

Expansionary fiscal policy is fiscal policy that increases aggregate demand.

Expansionary and Contractionary Fiscal Policy

Why would the government want to shift the aggregate demand curve? Because it wants to close either a recessionary gap, created when aggregate output falls below potential output, or an inflationary gap, created when aggregate output exceeds potential output.

Figure 30-4 shows the case of an economy facing a recessionary gap. *SRAS* is the short-run aggregate supply curve, *LRAS* is the long-run aggregate supply curve, and AD_1 is the initial aggregate demand curve. At the initial short-run macroeconomic equilibrium, E_1, aggregate output is Y_1, below potential output, Y_P. What the government would like to do is increase aggregate demand, shifting the aggregate demand curve rightward to AD_2. This would increase aggregate output, making it equal to potential output. Fiscal policy that increases aggregate demand, called **expansionary fiscal policy,** normally takes one of three forms:

1. An increase in government purchases of goods and services

2. A cut in taxes

3. An increase in government transfers

The 2009 American Recovery and Reinvestment Act, or simply, the Recovery Act, was a combination of all three: a direct increase in federal spending and aid to state governments to help them maintain spending, tax cuts for most families, and increased aid to the unemployed.

FIGURE 30-4   Expansionary Fiscal Policy Can Close a Recessionary Gap

The economy is in short-run macroeconomic equilibrium at E_1, where the aggregate demand curve, AD_1, intersects the *SRAS* curve. However, it is not in long-run macroeconomic equilibrium. At E_1, there is a recessionary gap of $Y_P - Y_1$. An expansionary fiscal policy—an increase in government purchases of goods and services, a reduction in taxes, or an increase in government transfers—shifts the aggregate demand curve rightward. It can close the recessionary gap by shifting AD_1 to AD_2, moving the economy to a new short-run macroeconomic equilibrium, E_2, which is also a long-run macroeconomic equilibrium.

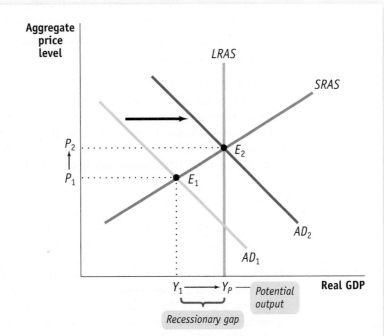

FIGURE 30-5   Contractionary Fiscal Policy Can Close an Inflationary Gap

The economy is in short-run macro-economic equilibrium at E_1, where the aggregate demand curve, AD_1, intersects the *SRAS* curve. But it is not in long-run macroeco-nomic equilibrium. At E_1, there is an inflationary gap of $Y_1 - Y_P$. A con-tractionary fiscal policy—such as reduced government purchases of goods and services, an increase in taxes, or a reduction in government transfers—shifts the aggregate demand curve leftward. It closes the inflationary gap by shifting AD_1 to AD_2, moving the economy to a new short-run macroeconomic equi-librium, E_2, which is also a long-run macroeconomic equilibrium.

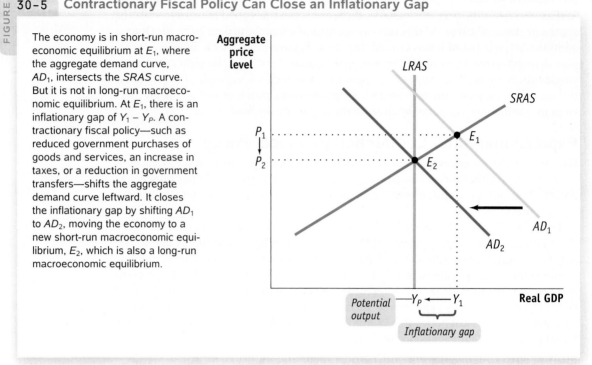

Figure 30-5 shows the opposite case—an economy facing an inflationary gap. Again, *SRAS* is the short-run aggregate supply curve, *LRAS* is the long-run aggregate supply curve, and AD_1 is the initial aggregate demand curve. At the initial equilib-rium, E_1, aggregate output is Y_1, above potential output, Y_P.

Policy makers often try to head off inflation by eliminating inflationary gaps. To eliminate the inflationary gap shown in Figure 30-5, fiscal policy must reduce ag-gregate demand and shift the aggregate demand curve leftward to AD_2. This reduces aggregate output and makes it equal to potential output. Fiscal policy that reduces ag-gregate demand, called **contractionary fiscal policy,** is the opposite of expansionary fiscal policy. It is implemented in three possible ways:

1. A reduction in government purchases of goods and services

2. An increase in taxes

3. A reduction in government transfers

A classic example of contractionary fiscal policy occurred in 1968, when U.S. pol-icy makers grew worried about rising inflation. President Lyndon Johnson imposed a temporary 10% surcharge on taxable income—everyone's income taxes were in-creased by 10%. He also tried to scale back government purchases of goods and ser-vices, which had risen dramatically because of the cost of the Vietnam War.

Can Expansionary Fiscal Policy Actually Work?

In practice, the use of fiscal policy—in particular, the use of expansionary fiscal pol-icy in the face of a recessionary gap—is often controversial. Let's quickly summarize the major points of the debate over expansionary fiscal policy, so we can understand when the critiques are justified and when they are not.

Broadly speaking, there are three arguments against the use of expansionary fiscal policy. We'll examine each in turn.

Contractionary fiscal policy is fis-cal policy that reduces aggregate demand.

1. Government spending always crowds out private spending (this claim, although wrong in principle, has played a prominent role in public debates)

2. Government borrowing always crowds out private investment spending (this claim is valid under some, but not all, circumstances)

3. Government budget deficits lead to reduced private spending (although this claim raises some important issues, it isn't a good reason to believe that expansionary fiscal policy doesn't work).

CLAIM 1: GOVERNMENT SPENDING ALWAYS CROWDS OUT PRIVATE SPENDING Some claim that expansionary fiscal policy can never raise aggregate spending and therefore can never raise aggregate income, with reasons that go something like this: "Every dollar that the government spends is a dollar taken away from the private sector. So any rise in government spending must be offset by an equal fall in private spending." In other words, every dollar spent by the government *crowds out*, or displaces, a dollar of private spending. So what's wrong with this view?

The answer is that the statement is wrong because it assumes that resources in the economy are always fully employed and, as a result, the aggregate income earned in the economy is always a fixed sum—which isn't true. In particular, when the economy is suffering from a recessionary gap, there are unemployed resources in the economy and output, and therefore income, is below its potential level. Expansionary fiscal policy during these periods puts unemployed resources to work and generates higher spending and higher income. So the argument that expansionary fiscal policy always crowds out private spending is wrong in principle.

CLAIM 2: GOVERNMENT BORROWING ALWAYS CROWDS OUT PRIVATE INVESTMENT SPENDING We've discussed the possibility that government borrowing uses funds that would have otherwise been used for private investment spending—that is, it crowds out private investment spending. How valid is that argument?

The answer is it depends on whether the economy is depressed or not. If the economy is not depressed, then increased government borrowing, by increasing the demand for loanable funds, can raise interest rates and crowd out private investment spending. However, if the economy *is* depressed, crowding out is much less likely.

When the economy is at far less than full employment, a fiscal expansion will lead to higher incomes, which in turn lead to increased savings at any given interest rate. This larger pool of savings allows the government to borrow without driving up interest rates. The Recovery Act of 2009 was a case in point: despite high levels of government borrowing, U.S. interest rates stayed near historic lows.

CLAIM 3: GOVERNMENT BUDGET DEFICITS LEAD TO REDUCED PRIVATE SPENDING Other things equal, expansionary fiscal policy leads to a larger budget deficit and greater government debt. And higher debt will eventually require the government to raise taxes to pay it off. So, according to this argument against expansionary fiscal policy, consumers, anticipating that they must pay higher taxes in the future to pay off today's government debt, will cut their spending today in order to save money.

This argument, known as *Ricardian equivalence*, is often taken to imply that expansionary fiscal policy will have no effect on the economy because far-sighted consumers will undo any attempts at expansion by the government. (And will also undo any contractionary fiscal policy.)

In reality, however, it's doubtful that consumers behave with such foresight and budgeting discipline. Most people, when provided with extra cash (generated by the fiscal expansion), will spend at least some of it. So even fiscal policy that takes the form of temporary tax cuts or transfers of cash to consumers probably does have an expansionary effect.

Moreover, it's possible to show that a temporary rise in government spending that involves direct purchases of goods and services—such as a program of road construction—would still lead to a boost in total spending in the near term. That's because even if consumers cut back their current spending in anticipation of higher future taxes, their reduced spending will take place over an extended period as consumers save over time to pay the future tax bill. Meanwhile, the additional government spending will be concentrated in the near future, when the economy needs it.

So although the effects emphasized by Ricardian equivalence may reduce the impact of fiscal expansion, the claim that it makes fiscal expansion completely ineffective is neither consistent with how consumers actually behave nor a reason to believe that increases in government spending have no effect. So, in the end, it's not a valid argument against expansionary fiscal policy.

In sum, then, the extent to which we should expect expansionary fiscal policy to work depends upon the circumstances. When the economy has a recessionary gap—as it did when the 2009 Recovery Act was passed—economics tells us that this is just the kind of situation in which expansionary fiscal policy helps the economy. However, when the economy is already at full employment, expansionary fiscal policy is the wrong policy and will lead to crowding out, an overheated economy, and higher inflation.

Steve Byland/Shutterstock

Time lags create real challenges for policy makers who are considering the use of expansionary fiscal policy to fight a recessionary gap.

A Cautionary Note: Lags in Fiscal Policy

Looking back at Figures 30-4 and 30-5, it may seem obvious that the government should actively use fiscal policy—always adopting an expansionary fiscal policy when the economy faces a recessionary gap and always adopting a contractionary fiscal policy when the economy faces an inflationary gap. But many economists caution against an extremely active stabilization policy, arguing that a government that tries too hard to stabilize the economy—through either fiscal policy or monetary policy—can end up making the economy less spage.

One key reason for caution is that there are important *time lags* between when the policy is decided upon and when it is implemented. To understand the nature of these lags, think about what has to happen before the government increases spending to fight a recessionary gap.

- First, the government has to realize that the recessionary gap exists: economic data take time to collect and analyze, and recessions are often recognized only months after they have begun.

- Second, the government has to develop a spending plan, which can itself take months, particularly if politicians take time debating how the money should be spent and passing legislation.

- Finally, it takes time to spend money. For example, a road construction project begins with activities such as surveying that don't involve spending large sums. It may be quite some time before the big spending begins.

Because of these lags, an attempt to increase spending to fight a recessionary gap may take so long to get going that the economy has already recovered on its own. In fact, the recessionary gap may have turned into an inflationary gap by the time the fiscal policy takes effect. In that case, the fiscal policy will make things worse instead of better.

This doesn't mean that fiscal policy should never be actively used. In early 2009 there was good reason to believe that the slump facing the U.S. economy would be both deep and long and that a fiscal stimulus designed to arrive over the next year or two would almost surely push aggregate demand in the right direction. In fact, the 2009 stimulus arguably faded out too soon, leaving the economy still deeply depressed. But the problem of lags makes the use of both fiscal and monetary policy harder than you might think from a simple analysis like the one we have just given.

ECONOMICS ▶ IN ACTION

WHAT WAS IN THE RECOVERY ACT?

As we've just learned, fiscal stimulus can take three forms: increased government purchases of goods and services, increased transfer payments, and tax cuts. So what form did the Recovery Act of 2009 take? The answer is that it's a bit complicated.

Figure 30-6 shows the composition of the budget impact of the Recovery Act, a measure that adds up the dollar value of tax cuts, transfer payments, and government spending. Here, the numbers are broken down into *four* categories, not three.

"Infrastructure and other spending" means spending on roads, bridges, and schools as well as "nontraditional" infrastructure like research and development, all of which fall under government purchases of goods and services. "Tax cuts" are self-explanatory. "Transfer payments to persons" mostly took the form of expanded benefits for the unemployed. But a fourth category, "transfers to state and local governments," accounted for roughly a third of the funds. Why this fourth category?

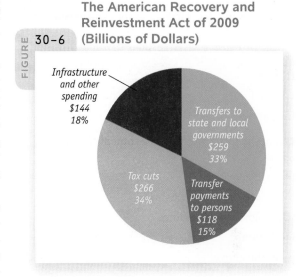

FIGURE 30-6

The American Recovery and Reinvestment Act of 2009 (Billions of Dollars)

Infrastructure and other spending $144 18%

Transfers to state and local governments $259 33%

Tax cuts $266 34%

Transfer payments to persons $118 15%

Because America has multiple levels of government. The authors live in Princeton Township, which has its own budget, which is part of Mercer County, which has its own budget, which is part of the state of New Jersey, which has its own budget, which is part of the United States. One effect of the recession was a sharp drop in revenues at the state and local levels, which in turn forced these lower levels of government to cut spending. Federal aid—those transfers to state and local governments—was intended to mitigate these spending cuts.

Perhaps the most surprising aspect of the Recovery Act was how little direct federal spending on goods and services was involved. The great bulk of the program involved giving money to other people, one way or another, in the hope that they would spend it.

MODULE 30 Review

Solutions appear at the back of the book.

Check Your Understanding

1. In each of the following cases, determine whether the policy is an expansionary or contractionary fiscal policy.

   a. Several military bases around the country, which together employ tens of thousands of people, are closed.

   b. The number of weeks an unemployed person is eligible for unemployment benefits is increased.

   c. The federal tax on gasoline is increased.

2. Explain why federal disaster relief, which quickly disburses funds to victims of natural disasters such as hurricanes, floods, and large-scale crop failures, will stabilize the economy more effectively after a disaster than relief that must be legislated.

3. Suppose someone says, "Using fiscal policy to pump up the economy is counterproductive—you get a brief high, but then you have the pain of inflation."

   a. Explain what this means in terms of the *AD–AS* model.

   b. Is this a valid argument against stabilization policy? Why or why not?

Multiple-Choice Questions

1. Which of the following contributes to the lag in implementing fiscal policy?

   I. It takes time for Congress and the president to pass spending and tax changes.

   II. Current economic data take time to collect and analyze.

   III. It takes time to realize an output gap exists.

   a. I only

   b. II only

   c. III only

   d. I and III only

   e. I, II, and III

2. Which of the following is a government transfer program?

   a. Social Security

   b. Medicare/Medicaid

   c. unemployment insurance

   d. food stamps

   e. all of the above

3. Which of the following is an example of expansionary fiscal policy?

   a. increasing taxes

   b. increasing government spending

   c. decreasing government transfers

   d. decreasing interest rates

   e. increasing the money supply

4. Which of the following is a fiscal policy that is appropriate to combat inflation?

   a. decreasing taxes

   b. decreasing government spending

   c. increasing government transfers

   d. increasing interest rates

   e. expansionary fiscal policy

5. An income tax rebate is an example of

   a. an expansionary fiscal policy.

   b. a contractionary fiscal policy.

   c. an expansionary monetary policy.

   d. a contractionary monetary policy.

   e. none of the above.

Critical-Thinking Questions

Draw a graph showing an economy experiencing a recessionary gap, then answer the following questions.

1. What type of fiscal policy is appropriate in this situation?

2. Give an example of what the government could do to implement the type of policy you listed in question 1.

Fiscal Policy and the Multiplier

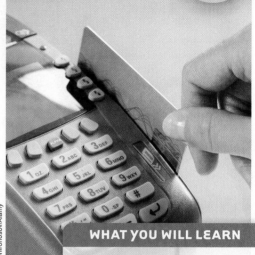

WHAT YOU WILL LEARN

1 Why fiscal policy has a multiplier effect

2 How the multiplier effect is influenced by automatic stabilizers

Multiplier Effects of Fiscal Policy

An expansionary fiscal policy, like the 2009 U.S. stimulus, pushes the aggregate demand curve to the right. A contractionary fiscal policy, like Lyndon Johnson's tax surcharge, pushes the aggregate demand curve to the left. For policy makers, however, knowing the direction of the shift isn't enough: they need estimates of *how much* a given policy will shift the aggregate demand curve. To get these estimates, they use the concept of the *multiplier*, which we learned about in Module 24.

Multiplier Effects of an Increase in Government Purchases of Goods and Services

Suppose that a government decides to spend $50 billion building bridges and roads. The government's purchases of goods and services will directly increase total spending on final goods and services by $50 billion.

But as we learned, there will also be an indirect effect: the government's purchases will start a chain reaction throughout the economy. The firms that produce the goods and services purchased by the government earn revenues that flow to households in the form of wages, profits, interest, and rent. This increase in disposable income leads to a rise in consumer spending. The rise in consumer spending, in turn, induces firms to increase output, leading to a further rise in disposable income, which leads to another round of consumer spending increases, and so on.

As we know, the *multiplier* is the ratio of the change in real GDP caused by an autonomous change in aggregate spending to the size of that autonomous change. An increase in government purchases of goods and services is a prime example of such an autonomous increase in aggregate spending.

In Module 24 we considered a simple case in which there are no taxes or international trade, so that any change in GDP accrues entirely to households. We also assumed that the aggregate price level is fixed, so that any increase in nominal GDP is also a rise in real GDP, and that the interest rate is fixed. In that case the multiplier is $1/(1 - MPC)$. Recall that MPC is the *marginal propensity to consume*, the fraction of an additional dollar in disposable income that is spent.

For example, if the marginal propensity to consume is 0.5, the multiplier is $1/(1 - 0.5) = 1/0.5 = 2$. Given a multiplier of 2, a $50 billion increase in government

Expansionary or contractionary fiscal policy will start a chain reaction throughout the economy.

Ralf Hettler/Getty Images

purchases of goods and services would increase real GDP by $100 billion. Of that $100 billion, $50 billion is the initial effect from the increase in G, and the remaining $50 billion is the subsequent effect arising from the increase in consumer spending.

What happens if government purchases of goods and services are reduced instead? The math is exactly the same, except that there's a minus sign in front: if government purchases of goods and services fall by $50 billion and the marginal propensity to consume is 0.5, real GDP falls by $100 billion.

Multiplier Effects of Changes in Government Transfers and Taxes

Expansionary or contractionary fiscal policy need not take the form of changes in government purchases of goods and services. Governments can also change transfer payments or taxes. In general, however, a change in government transfers or taxes shifts the aggregate demand curve by *less* than an equal-sized change in government purchases, resulting in a smaller effect on real GDP.

To see why, imagine that instead of spending $50 billion on building bridges, the government simply hands out $50 billion in the form of government transfers. In this case, there is no direct effect on aggregate demand, as there was with government purchases of goods and services. Real GDP goes up only because households spend some of that $50 billion—and they probably won't spend it all.

Table 31-1 shows a hypothetical comparison of two expansionary fiscal policies assuming an *MPC* equal to 0.5 and a multiplier equal to 2: one in which the government directly purchases $50 billion in goods and services and one in which the government makes transfer payments instead, sending out $50 billion in checks to consumers. In each case there is a first-round effect on real GDP, either from purchases by the government or from purchases by the consumers who received the checks, followed by a series of additional rounds as rising real GDP raises disposable income.

However, the first-round effect of the transfer program is smaller; because we have assumed that the *MPC* is 0.5, only $25 billion of the $50 billion is spent, with the other $25 billion saved. And as a result, all the further rounds are smaller, too. In the end, the transfer payment increases real GDP by only $50 billion. In comparison, a $50 billion increase in government purchases produces a $100 billion increase in real GDP.

Overall, when expansionary fiscal policy takes the form of a rise in transfer payments, real GDP may rise by either more or less than the initial government outlay—that is, the multiplier may be either more or less than 1 depending upon the size of the *MPC*. In Table 31-1, with an *MPC* equal to 0.5, the multiplier is exactly 1: a $50 billion rise in transfer payments increases real GDP by $50 billion. If the *MPC* is less than 0.5, so that a smaller share of the initial transfer is spent, the multiplier on that transfer is *less* than 1. If a larger share of the initial transfer is spent, the multiplier is *more* than 1.

A tax cut has an effect similar to the effect of a transfer. It increases disposable income, leading to a series of increases in consumer spending. But the overall effect is smaller than that of an equal-sized increase in government purchases of goods and services: the autonomous increase in aggregate spending is smaller because households save part of the amount of the tax cut.

In practice, economists often argue that the size of the multiplier determines *who* among the population should get tax cuts or increases in government transfers. For example, compare the effects of an increase in unemployment benefits with a cut in taxes on profits distributed to shareholders as dividends.

TABLE 31-1

Hypothetical Effects of a Fiscal Policy with Multiplier of 2

Effect on real GDP	$50 billion rise in government purchases of goods and services	$50 billion rise in government transfer payments
First round	$50 billion	$25 billion
Second round	$25 billion	$12.5 billion
Third round	$12.5 billion	$6.25 billion
• • •	• • •	• • •
Eventual effect	$100 billion	$50 billion

Consumer surveys suggest that the average unemployed worker will spend a higher share of any increase in his or her disposable income than would the average recipient of dividend income. That is, people who are unemployed tend to have a higher *MPC* than people who own a lot of stocks because the latter tend to be wealthier and tend to save more of any increase in disposable income. If that's true, a dollar spent on unemployment benefits increases aggregate demand more than a dollar's worth of dividend tax cuts.

How Taxes Affect the Multiplier

When we introduced the analysis of the multiplier, we simplified matters by assuming that a $1 increase in real GDP raises disposable income by $1. In fact, however, government taxes capture some part of the increase in real GDP that occurs in each round of the multiplier process, since most government taxes depend positively on real GDP. As a result, disposable income increases by considerably less than $1 once we include taxes in the model.

The increase in government tax revenue when real GDP rises isn't the result of a deliberate decision or action by the government. It's a consequence of the way the tax laws are written, which causes most sources of government revenue to increase *automatically* when real GDP goes up.

The income taxes individuals pay to the government are a percentage of their income. Therefore, when real GDP rises, this increase in aggregate income leads to an increase in government tax revenue. In the real world, governments rarely impose **lump-sum taxes,** in which the amount of tax an individual owes is independent of his or her income.

In addition, sales tax receipts increase when real GDP rises because people with more income spend more on goods and services. And corporate profit tax receipts increase when real GDP rises because profits increase when the economy expands.

The effect of these automatic increases in tax revenue is to reduce the size of the multiplier. Remember, the multiplier is the result of a chain reaction in which higher real GDP leads to higher disposable income, which leads to higher consumer spending, which leads to further increases in real GDP. The fact that the government siphons off some of any increase in real GDP means that at each stage of this process, the increase in consumer spending is smaller than it would be if taxes weren't part of the picture. The result is to reduce the multiplier.

Many macroeconomists believe it's a good thing that in real life taxes reduce the multiplier. Earlier we argued that most, though not all, recessions are the result of negative demand shocks. The same mechanism that causes tax revenue to increase when the economy expands causes it to decrease when the economy contracts. Since tax receipts decrease when real GDP falls, the effects of these negative demand shocks are smaller than they would be if there were no taxes. The decrease in tax revenue reduces the adverse effect of the initial fall in aggregate demand.

The automatic decrease in government tax revenue generated by a fall in real GDP—caused by a decrease in the amount of taxes households pay—acts like an automatic expansionary fiscal policy implemented in the face of a recession.

Similarly, when the economy expands, the government finds itself automatically pursuing a contractionary fiscal policy—a tax increase. Government spending and taxation rules that cause fiscal policy to be automatically expansionary when the economy contracts and automatically contractionary when the economy expands, without requiring any deliberate action by policy makers, are called **automatic stabilizers.**

The rules that govern tax collection aren't the only automatic stabilizers, although they are the most important ones. Some types of government transfers also play a stabilizing role. For example, more people receive unemployment insurance when the economy is depressed than when it is booming. The same is true of Medicaid and food stamps, or SNAP.

So transfer payments tend to rise when the economy is contracting and fall when the economy is expanding. Like changes in tax revenue, these automatic changes in

Lump-sum taxes are taxes that don't depend on the taxpayer's income.

Automatic stabilizers are government spending and taxation rules that cause fiscal policy to be automatically expansionary when the economy contracts and automatically contractionary when the economy expands.

The Works Progress Administration (WPA), a Depression-era relief measure that put millions of unemployed Americans to work building bridges, roads, and parks, is an example of discretionary fiscal policy.

transfers tend to reduce the size of the multiplier because the total change in disposable income that results from a given rise or fall in real GDP is smaller.

As in the case of government tax revenue, many macroeconomists believe that it's a good thing that government transfers reduce the multiplier. Expansionary and contractionary fiscal policies that are the result of automatic stabilizers are widely considered helpful to macroeconomic stabilization because they blunt the extremes of the business cycle.

But what about fiscal policy that *isn't* the result of automatic stabilizers? **Discretionary fiscal policy** is fiscal policy that is the direct result of deliberate actions by policy makers rather than automatic adjustment. For example, during a recession, the government may pass legislation that cuts taxes and increases government spending in order to stimulate the economy. In general, economists tend to support the use of discretionary fiscal policy only in special circumstances, such as an especially severe recession.

ECONOMICS ▶ *IN ACTION*

MULTIPLIERS AND THE OBAMA STIMULUS

The American Recovery and Reinvestment Act, also known as the Obama stimulus, was the largest example of discretionary fiscal expansion in U.S. history. The total stimulus was $787 billion, although not all of that was spent at once: only about half, or roughly $400 billion, of the stimulus arrived in 2010, the year of peak impact. Still,

"WE'RE GONNA NEED A BIGGER BOAT."

even that was a lot—roughly 2.7% of GDP. But was that enough? From the beginning, there were doubts.

The first description of the planned stimulus and its expected effects came in early January 2009, from two of the incoming administration's top economists. They were explicit about the assumed multipliers: based on models developed at the Federal Reserve and elsewhere, they assumed that government spending would have a multiplier of 1.57 and that tax cuts would have a multiplier of 0.99.

These assumptions yielded an overall multiplier for the stimulus of almost 1.4, implying that the stimulus would, at its peak in 2010, add about 3.7% to real GDP. It would also, they estimated, reduce unemployment by about 1.8 percentage points relative to what it would otherwise have been.

But here's the problem: the slump the Obama stimulus was intended to fight was brought on by a major financial crisis—and such crises tend to produce very deep, prolonged slumps. Around this time, two Harvard economists, Carmen Reinhart and Kenneth Rogoff, circulated a paper with their findings that major crises are followed, on average, by a 7-percentage-point rise in the unemployment rate and that it takes years before unemployment falls to anything like normal levels (based on an analysis of historical episodes).

Compared with the economy's problems, then, the Obama stimulus was actually small: it cut only 1.8 points off the unemployment rate in 2010 and faded out rapidly thereafter. And given its small size relative to the problem, the failure of the stimulus to avert persistently high unemployment should not have come as a surprise.

Discretionary fiscal policy is fiscal policy that is the result of deliberate actions by policy makers rather than automatic adjustments.

31 Review

Solutions appear at the back of the book.

Check Your Understanding

1. Explain why a $500 million increase in government purchases of goods and services will generate a larger rise in real GDP than a $500 million increase in government transfers.

2. Explain why a $500 million reduction in government purchases of goods and services will generate a larger fall in real GDP than a $500 million reduction in government transfers.

3. The country of Boldovia has no unemployment insurance benefits and a tax system using only lump-sum taxes. The neighboring country of Moldovia has generous unemployment benefits and a tax system in which residents must pay a percentage of their income. Which country will experience greater variation in real GDP in response to demand shocks, positive and negative? Explain.

Multiple-Choice Questions

1. The marginal propensity to consume
    I. is inversely related to the multiplier.
    II. is equal to 1.
    III. represents the proportion of consumers' disposable income that is spent.

    a. I only
    b. II only
    c. III only
    d. I and III only
    e. I, II, and III

2. Assume that taxes and interest rates remain unchanged when government spending increases, and that both savings and consumer spending increase when income increases. The ultimate effect on real GDP of a $100 million increase in government purchases of goods and services will be

    a. an increase of $100 million.
    b. an increase of more than $100 million.
    c. an increase of less than $100 million.
    d. an increase of either more than or less than $100 million, depending on the *MPC*.
    e. a decrease of $100 million.

3. Taxes have what effect on the multiplier? They
    a. increase it.
    b. decrease it.
    c. destabilize it.
    d. negate it.
    e. have no effect on it.

4. A lump-sum tax is
    a. higher as income increases.
    b. lower as income increases.
    c. independent of income.
    d. the most common form of tax.
    e. a type of business tax.

5. Which of the following is NOT an automatic stabilizer?
    a. income taxes
    b. unemployment insurance
    c. Medicaid
    d. food stamps
    e. monetary policy

Critical-Thinking Questions

A change in government purchases of goods and services results in a change in real GDP equal to $200 million. Assuming the absence of taxes, international trade, and changes in the aggregate price level, answer the following.

1. Suppose that the *MPC* is equal to 0.75. What was the size of the change in government purchases of goods and services that resulted in the increase in real GDP of $200 million?

2. Now suppose that the change in government purchases of goods and services was $20 million. What value of the multiplier would result in an increase in real GDP of $200 million?

3. Given the value of the multiplier you calculated in the preceding question, what marginal propensity to save would have led to that value of the multiplier?

Marmaduke St. John/Alamy

Headlines about the government's budget tend to focus on just one point: whether the government is running a surplus or a deficit and, in either case, how big. People usually think of surpluses as good: when the federal government ran a record surplus in 2000, many people regarded it as a cause for celebration. Conversely, people usually think of deficits as bad: the record deficits run by the U.S. federal government from 2009–2012 were a cause of concern for many people.

The Budget Balance

How do surpluses and deficits fit into the analysis of fiscal policy? Are deficits ever a good thing and surpluses a bad thing? To answer those questions, let's look at the causes and consequences of surpluses and deficits.

The Budget Balance as a Measure of Fiscal Policy

What do we mean by surpluses and deficits? The budget balance, which we defined earlier, is the difference between the government's revenue, in the form of tax revenue, and its spending, both on goods and services and on government transfers, in a given year. That is, the budget balance—savings by government—is defined by Equation 32-1 (which is the same as Equation 20-7):

(32-1) $S_{Government} = T - G - TR$

where T is the value of tax revenues, G is government purchases of goods and services, and TR is the value of government transfers. A budget surplus is a positive budget balance and a budget deficit is a negative budget balance.

Other things equal, expansionary fiscal policies—increased government purchases of goods and services, higher government transfers, or lower taxes—reduce the budget balance for that year. That is, expansionary fiscal policies make a budget surplus smaller or a budget deficit bigger. Conversely, contractionary fiscal policies—reduced government purchases of goods and services, lower government transfers, or higher taxes—increase the budget balance for that year, making a budget surplus bigger or a budget deficit smaller.

You might think this means that changes in the budget balance can be used to measure fiscal policy. In fact, economists often do just that: they use changes in the budget balance as a "quick-and-dirty" way to assess whether current fiscal policy is expansionary or contractionary. But they always keep in mind two reasons this quick-and-dirty approach is sometimes misleading:

1. Two different changes in fiscal policy that have equal-sized effects on the budget balance may have quite unequal effects on the economy. As we have already seen, changes in government purchases of goods and services have a larger effect on real GDP than equal-sized changes in taxes and government transfers.

2. Often, changes in the budget balance are themselves the result, not the cause, of fluctuations in the economy.

To understand the second point, we need to examine the effects of the business cycle on the budget.

The Business Cycle and the Cyclically Adjusted Budget Balance

Historically there has been a strong relationship between the federal government's budget balance and the business cycle. The budget tends to move into deficit when the economy experiences a recession, but deficits tend to get smaller or even turn into surpluses when the economy is expanding. Figure 32-1 shows the federal budget deficit as a percentage of GDP from 1970 to 2013. Shaded areas indicate recessions; unshaded areas indicate expansions. As you can see, the federal budget deficit increased around the time of each recession and usually declined during expansions. In fact, in the late stages of the long expansion from 1991 to 2000, the deficit actually became negative—the budget deficit became a budget surplus.

FIGURE **32-1**   The U.S. Federal Budget Deficit and the Business Cycle, 1970–2013

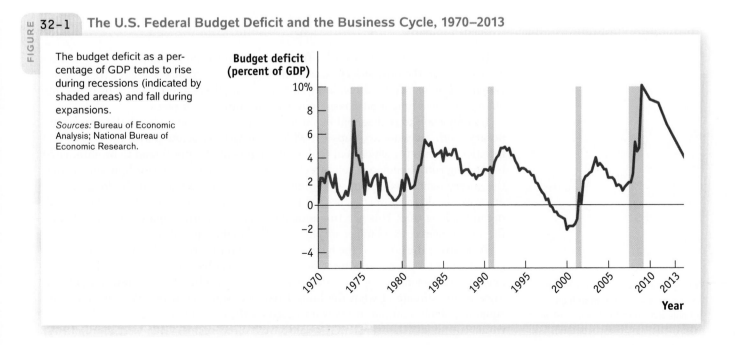

The budget deficit as a percentage of GDP tends to rise during recessions (indicated by shaded areas) and fall during expansions.

Sources: Bureau of Economic Analysis; National Bureau of Economic Research.

The relationship between the business cycle and the budget balance is even clearer if we compare the budget deficit as a percentage of GDP with the unemployment rate, as we do in Figure 32-2. The budget deficit almost always rises when the unemployment rate rises and falls when the unemployment rate falls.

Is this relationship between the business cycle and the budget balance evidence that policy makers engage in discretionary fiscal policy, using expansionary fiscal policy during recessions and contractionary fiscal policy during expansions? Not necessarily. To a large extent the relationship in Figure 32-2 reflects automatic stabilizers at work. As we learned in the discussion of automatic stabilizers, government tax revenue tends to rise and some government transfers, like unemployment benefit payments, tend to fall when the economy expands. Conversely, government tax revenue tends to fall and some government transfers tend to rise when the economy contracts. So the budget balance tends to move toward surplus during expansions and toward deficit during recessions even without any deliberate action on the part of policy makers.

FIGURE 32-2   The U.S. Federal Budget Deficit and the Unemployment Rate

There is a close relationship between the budget balance and the business cycle: a recession moves the budget balance toward deficit, but an expansion moves it toward surplus. Here, the unemployment rate serves as an indicator of the business cycle, and we should expect to see a higher unemployment rate associated with a higher budget deficit. This is confirmed by the figure: the budget deficit as a percentage of GDP moves closely in tandem with the unemployment rate.

Source: Federal Reserve Bank of St. Louis.

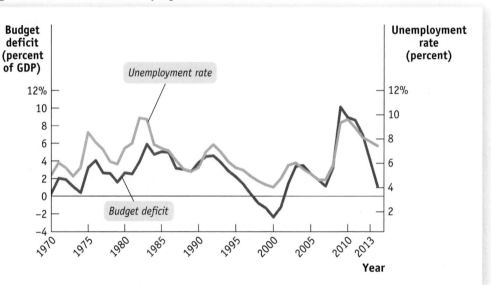

In assessing budget policy, it's often useful to separate movements in the budget balance due to the business cycle from movements due to discretionary fiscal policy changes. The former are affected by automatic stabilizers and the latter by deliberate changes in government purchases, government transfers, or taxes.

It's important to realize that business-cycle effects on the budget balance are temporary: both recessionary gaps (in which real GDP is below potential output) and inflationary gaps (in which real GDP is above potential output) tend to be eliminated in the long run. Removing their effects on the budget balance sheds light on whether the government's taxing and spending policies are sustainable in the long run. In other words, do the government's tax policies yield enough revenue to fund its spending in the long run? This is a fundamentally more important question than whether the government runs a budget surplus or deficit in the current year.

To separate the effect of the business cycle from the effects of other factors, many governments produce an estimate of what the budget balance would be if there were neither a recessionary nor an inflationary gap. The **cyclically adjusted budget balance** is an estimate of what the budget balance would be if real GDP were exactly equal to potential output. It takes into account the extra tax revenue the government would collect and the transfers it would save if a recessionary gap were eliminated—

The **cyclically adjusted budget balance** is an estimate of what the budget balance would be if real GDP were exactly equal to potential output.

or the revenue the government would lose and the extra transfers it would make if an inflationary gap were eliminated.

Figure 32-3 shows the actual budget deficit and the Congressional Budget Office estimate of the cyclically adjusted budget deficit, both as a percentage of GDP, from 1970 to 2013. As you can see, the cyclically adjusted budget deficit doesn't fluctuate as much as the actual budget deficit. In particular, large actual deficits, such as those of 1975, 1983, and 2009, are usually caused in part by a depressed economy.

FIGURE 32-3 The Actual Budget Deficit versus the Cyclically Adjusted Budget Deficit

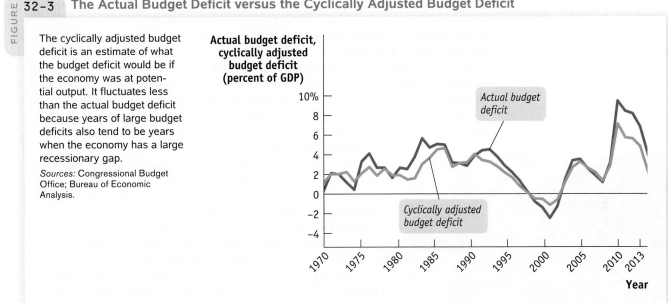

The cyclically adjusted budget deficit is an estimate of what the budget deficit would be if the economy was at potential output. It fluctuates less than the actual budget deficit because years of large budget deficits also tend to be years when the economy has a large recessionary gap.

Sources: Congressional Budget Office; Bureau of Economic Analysis.

Should the Budget Be Balanced?

Persistent budget deficits can cause problems for both the government and the economy. Yet politicians are always tempted to run deficits because this allows them to cater to voters by cutting taxes without cutting spending or by increasing spending without increasing taxes. As a result, there are occasional attempts by policy makers to force fiscal discipline by introducing legislation—even a constitutional amendment—forbidding the government from running budget deficits. This is usually stated as a requirement that the budget be "balanced"—that revenues at least equal spending each fiscal year. Would it be a good idea to require a balanced budget annually?

Most economists don't think so. They believe that the government should only balance its budget on average—that it should be allowed to run deficits in bad years, offset by surpluses in good years. They don't believe the government should be forced to run a balanced budget *every year* because this would undermine the role of taxes and transfers as automatic stabilizers.

As we've learned, the tendency of tax revenue to fall and transfers to rise when the economy contracts helps to limit the size of recessions. But falling tax revenue and rising transfer payments generated by a downturn in the economy push the budget toward deficit. If constrained by a balanced-budget rule, the government would have to respond to this deficit with contractionary fiscal policies that would tend to deepen a recession.

Yet policy makers concerned about excessive deficits sometimes feel that rigid rules prohibiting—or at least setting an upper limit on—deficits are necessary. As the following Economics in Action explains, Europe has had a lot of trouble reconciling rules to enforce fiscal responsibility with the challenges of short-run fiscal policy.

EUROPE'S SEARCH FOR A FISCAL RULE

In 1999 a group of European nations took a momentous step when they adopted a common currency, the euro, to replace their various national currencies, such as the French franc, the German mark, and the Italian lira. Along with the introduction of the euro came the creation of the European Central Bank, which sets monetary policy for the whole region.

As part of the agreement creating the new currency, governments of member countries signed on to the European "stability pact," requiring each government to keep its budget deficit—its actual deficit, not a cyclically adjusted number—below 3% of the country's GDP or face fines.

The pact was intended to prevent irresponsible deficit spending arising from political pressure that might eventually undermine the new currency. The stability pact, however, had a serious downside: in principle, it would force countries to slash spending and/or raise taxes whenever an economic downturn pushed their deficits above the critical level. This would turn fiscal policy into a force that worsens recessions instead of fighting them.

As it turned out, the stability pact proved impossible to enforce: European nations, including France and even Germany, with its reputation for fiscal probity, simply ignored the rule during the 2001 recession and its aftermath.

In 2011 the Europeans tried again, this time against the background of a severe debt crisis. In the wake of the 2008 financial crisis, Greece, Ireland, Portugal, Spain, and Italy lost the confidence of investors worried about their ability and/or willingness to repay all their debt—and the efforts of these nations to reduce their deficits seemed likely to push Europe back into recession.

Yet a return to the old stability pact didn't seem to make sense. Among other things, the stability pact's rule on the size of budget deficits would not have done much to prevent the crisis—in 2007

Although several European nations have adopted a common currency—the euro—many of them have struggled to establish effective fiscal policy.

all of the problem debtors except Greece were running deficits under 3% of GDP. Ireland and Spain were actually running surpluses.

So the agreement reached in December 2011 was framed in terms of the "structural" budget balance, more or less corresponding to the cyclically adjusted budget balance as we defined it in the text. According to the new rule, the structural budget balance of each country should be very nearly zero, with deficits not to exceed 0.5% of GDP. This seemed like a much better rule than the old stability pact.

Yet big problems remained. One was a question about the reliability of the estimates of the structural budget balances. Also, the new rule seemed to ban the use of discretionary fiscal policy, under any circumstances. Was this wise?

Before patting themselves on the back over the superiority of their own fiscal rules, Americans should note that the United States has its own version of the original, flawed European stability pact. The federal government's budget acts as an automatic stabilizer, but 49 of the 50 states are required by their state constitutions to balance their budgets every year. When recession struck in 2008, most states were forced to—guess what?—slash spending and raise taxes, exactly the wrong thing from a macroeconomic point of view.

Long-Run Implications of Fiscal Policy

In 2009 the government of Greece ran into a financial wall. Like most other governments in Europe (and the U.S. government, too), the Greek government was running a large budget deficit, which meant that it needed to keep borrowing more funds, both to cover its expenses and to pay off existing loans as they came due. But governments, like companies or individuals, can only borrow if lenders believe there's a good chance they are willing or able to repay their debts. By 2009 most investors, having lost confidence in Greece's financial future, were no longer willing to lend to the Greek government. Those few who were willing to lend demanded very high interest rates to compensate them for the risk of loss.

Figure 32-4 compares interest rates on 10-year bonds issued by the governments of Greece and Germany. At the beginning of 2007, Greece could borrow at almost the same rate as Germany, widely considered a very safe borrower. By the end of 2013, however, Greece had to pay an interest rate around 10 times the rate Germany paid.

Why was Greece having these problems? Largely because investors had become deeply worried about the level of its debt (in part because it became clear that the Greek government had been using creative accounting to hide just how much debt it had already taken on). Government debt is, after all, a promise to make future payments to lenders. By 2009 it seemed likely that the Greek government had already promised more than it could possibly deliver.

The result was that Greece found itself unable to borrow more from private lenders; it received emergency loans from other European nations and the International Monetary Fund, but these loans came with the requirement that the Greek government make severe spending cuts, which wreaked havoc with its economy, imposed severe economic hardship on Greeks, and led to massive social unrest.

No discussion of fiscal policy is complete if it doesn't take into account the long-run implications of government budget surpluses and deficits, especially for government debt. We now turn to those long-run implications.

Deficits, Surpluses, and Debt

When a family spends more than it earns over the course of a year, it has to raise the extra funds either by selling assets or by borrowing. And if a family borrows year after year, it will eventually end up with a lot of debt.

The same is true for governments. With a few exceptions, governments don't raise large sums by selling assets such as national parkland. Instead, when a government spends more than the tax revenue it receives—when it runs a budget deficit—it almost always borrows the extra funds. And governments that run persistent budget deficits end up with substantial debts.

The severe economic downturn that followed Greece's debt crisis continued into 2014.

FIGURE 32-4   Greek and German Long-Term Interest Rates

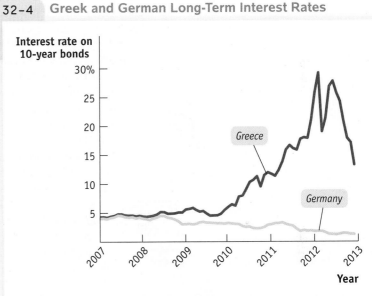

As late as 2008, the government of Greece could borrow at interest rates only slightly higher than those facing Germany, widely considered a very safe borrower. But in early 2009, as it became clear that both Greek debt and Greek deficits were larger than previously reported, investors lost confidence, sending Greek borrowing costs sky-high.

Source: European Central Bank.

To interpret the numbers that follow, you need to know a slightly peculiar feature of federal government accounting. For historical reasons, the U.S. government does not keep books by calendar years. Instead, budget totals are kept by **fiscal years,** which run from October 1 to September 30 and are labeled by the calendar year in which they end. For example, fiscal 2010 began on October 1, 2009, and ended on September 30, 2010.

At the end of fiscal 2013, the U.S. federal government had total debt equal to $16.7 trillion. However, part of that debt represented special accounting rules specifying that the federal government as a whole owes funds to certain government programs, especially Social Security. We'll explain those rules shortly. For now, however, let's

A **fiscal year** runs from October 1 to September 30 and is labeled according to the calendar year in which it ends.

Public debt is government debt held by individuals and institutions outside the government.

focus on **public debt:** government debt held by individuals and institutions outside the government. At the end of fiscal 2013, the federal government's public debt was "only" $12.0 trillion, or 71% of GDP. If we include the debts of state and local governments, total public debt at the end of fiscal 2013 was larger than it was at the end of fiscal 2012 because the federal government ran a budget deficit during fiscal 2013. A government that runs persistent budget deficits will experience a rising level of public debt. Why is this a problem?

Problems Posed by Rising Government Debt

There are two reasons to be concerned when a government runs persistent budget deficits. We described the first reason in an earlier module: when the economy is at full employment and the government borrows funds in the financial markets, it is competing with firms that plan to borrow funds for investment spending. As a result, the government's borrowing may crowd out private investment spending, increasing interest rates and reducing the economy's long-run rate of growth.

But there's a second reason: today's deficits, by increasing the government's debt, place financial pressure on future budgets. The impact of current deficits on future budgets is straightforward. Like individuals, governments must pay their bills, including interest payments on their accumulated debt. When a government is deeply in debt, those interest payments can be substantial. In fiscal 2013, the U.S. federal government paid 1.3% of GDP—$221 billion—in interest on its debt. The more heavily indebted government of Italy paid interest of 5.3% of its GDP in 2013.

Other things equal, a government paying large sums in interest must raise more revenue from taxes or spend less than it would otherwise be able to afford—or it must borrow even more to cover the gap. And a government that borrows to pay interest on its outstanding debt pushes itself even deeper into debt. This process can eventually push a government to the point where lenders question its ability to repay. Like a consumer who has maxed out his or her credit cards, it will find that lenders are unwilling to lend any more funds. The result can be that the government defaults on its debt—it stops paying what it owes. Default is often followed by deep financial and economic turmoil.

Americans aren't used to the idea of government default, but such things do happen. In the 1990s Argentina, a relatively high-income developing country, was widely praised for its economic policies—and it was able to borrow large sums from foreign lenders. By 2001, however, Argentina's interest payments were spiraling out of control, and the country stopped paying the sums that were due. In the end, it reached a settlement with most of its lenders under which it paid less than a third of the amount originally due. By late 2011 investors were placing a fairly high probability on an Argentine-type default by Greece, Ireland, and Portugal—and were seriously worried about Italy and Spain. Each one was forced to pay high interest rates on its debt by nervous lenders, raising the risk of default.

Default creates havoc in a country's financial markets and badly shakes public confidence in the government and the economy. Argentina's debt default was accompanied by a crisis in the country's banking system and a very severe recession.

And even if a highly indebted government avoids default, a heavy debt burden typically forces it to slash spending or raise taxes, politically unpopular measures that can also damage the economy. In some cases, "austerity" measures intended to reassure lenders that the government can indeed pay end up depressing the economy so much that lender confidence continues to fall, a situation faced to varying degrees by Greece, Ireland, Portugal, Spain, and Italy at the end of 2013.

Some may ask, why can't a government that has trouble borrowing just print money to pay its bills? Yes, it can if it has its own currency (which the troubled European nations don't). But printing money to pay the government's bills can lead to another problem: inflation. Governments do not want to find themselves in a position where the choice is between defaulting on their debts and inflating those debts away by printing money.

The **debt–GDP ratio** is the government's debt as a percentage of GDP.

Concerns about the long-run effects of deficits need not rule out the use of expansionary fiscal policy to stimulate the economy when it is depressed. However, these concerns do mean that governments should try to offset budget deficits in bad years with budget surpluses in good years. In other words, governments should run a budget that is approximately balanced over time. Have they actually done so?

Deficits and Debt in Practice

Figure 32-5 shows how the U.S. federal government's budget deficit and its debt evolved from 1940 to 2013. Panel (a) shows the federal deficit as a percentage of GDP. As you can see, the federal government ran huge deficits during World War II. It briefly ran surpluses after the war, but it has normally run deficits ever since, especially after 1980. This seems inconsistent with the advice that governments should offset deficits in bad times with surpluses in good times.

However, panel (b) of Figure 32-5 shows that for most of the period these persistent deficits didn't lead to runaway debt. To assess the ability of governments to pay their debt, we use the **debt–GDP ratio,** the government's debt as a percentage of GDP. We use this measure, rather than simply looking at the size of the debt, because GDP, which measures the size of the economy as a whole, is a good indicator of the potential taxes the government can collect. If the government's debt grows more slowly than GDP, the burden of paying that debt is actually falling compared with the government's potential tax revenue.

What we see from panel (b) is that although the federal debt grew in almost every year, the debt–GDP ratio fell for 30 years after the end of World War II. This shows that the debt–GDP ratio can fall, even when debt is rising, as long as GDP grows faster than debt.

FIGURE 32-5   U.S. Federal Deficits and Debt

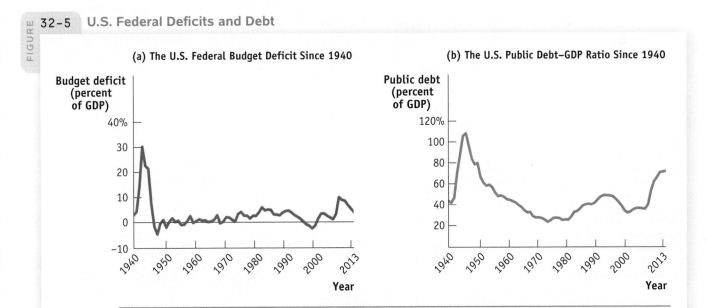

Panel (a) shows the U.S. federal budget deficit as a percentage of GDP from 1940 to 2013. The U.S. government ran huge deficits during World War II and has run smaller deficits, or a surplus, ever since. Panel (b) shows the U.S. debt–GDP ratio. Comparing panels (a) and (b), you can see that in many years the debt–GDP ratio has declined in spite of government deficits. This seeming paradox reflects the fact that the debt–GDP ratio can fall, even when debt is rising, as long as GDP grows faster than debt. The rising debt–GDP ratio in recent years can be attributed to the aftermath of the 2008 financial crisis when deficits were much larger than average and growth in GDP was well below average.

Source: Office of Management and Budget.

Implicit liabilities are spending promises made by governments that are effectively a debt despite the fact that they are not included in the usual debt statistics.

Still, a government that runs persistent *large* deficits will have a rising debt–GDP ratio when debt grows faster than GDP. In the aftermath of the financial crisis of 2008, the U.S. government began running deficits much larger than anything seen since World War II, and the debt–GDP ratio began rising sharply. Similar surges in the debt–GDP ratio could be seen in a number of other countries in 2008.

Economists and policy makers agreed that this was not a sustainable trend, that governments would need to get their spending and revenues back in line. But *when* to bring spending in line with revenue was a source of great disagreement. Some argued for fiscal tightening right away; others argued that this tightening should be postponed until the major economies had recovered from their slump.

Implicit Liabilities

Looking at Figure 32-5, you might be tempted to conclude that until the 2008 crisis struck, the U.S. federal budget was in fairly decent shape: the return to budget deficits after 2001 caused the debt–GDP ratio to rise a bit, but that ratio was still low compared with both historical experience and some other wealthy countries. In fact, however, experts on long-run budget issues view the situation of the United States (and other countries such as Japan and Italy) with alarm. The reason is the problem of *implicit liabilities*. **Implicit liabilities** are spending promises made by governments that are effectively a debt despite the fact that they are not included in the usual debt statistics.

The largest implicit liabilities of the U.S. government arise from two transfer programs that principally benefit older Americans: Social Security and Medicare. The third-largest implicit liability, Medicaid, benefits low-income families. In each of these cases, the government has promised to provide transfer payments to future as well as current beneficiaries. So these programs represent a future debt that must be honored, even though the debt does not currently show up in the usual statistics. Together, these three programs currently account for almost 40% of federal spending.

The implicit liabilities created by these transfer programs worry fiscal experts. Figure 32-6 shows why. It shows actual spending on Social Security and on Medicare, Medicaid, and CHIP (a program that provides health care coverage to uninsured children) as percentages of GDP from 2000 to 2013, together with Congressional Budget Office projections of spending through 2085. According to these projections, spending on Social Security will rise substantially over the next few decades and spending on the three health care programs will soar. Why?

FIGURE 32-6   Future Demands on the Federal Budget

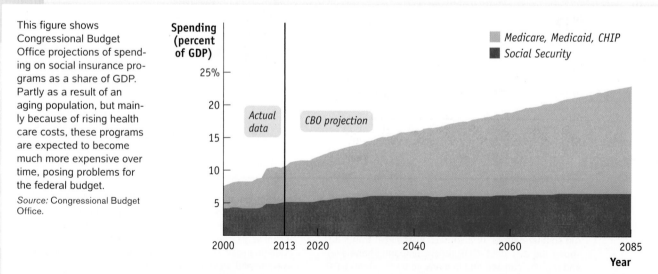

This figure shows Congressional Budget Office projections of spending on social insurance programs as a share of GDP. Partly as a result of an aging population, but mainly because of rising health care costs, these programs are expected to become much more expensive over time, posing problems for the federal budget.

Source: Congressional Budget Office.

In the case of Social Security, the answer is demography. Social Security is a "pay-as-you-go" system: current workers pay payroll taxes that fund the benefits of current retirees. So the ratio of the number of retirees drawing benefits to the number of workers paying into Social Security has a major impact on the system's finances.

There was a huge surge in the U.S. birth rate between 1946 and 1964, commonly called the "baby boom." Most baby boomers are currently of working age—which means they are paying taxes, not collecting benefits. But some are starting to retire, and as more of them do so, they will stop earning taxable income and start collecting benefits. As a result, the ratio of retirees receiving benefits to workers paying into the Social Security system will rise.

In 2013 there were 35 retirees receiving benefits for every 100 workers paying into the system. By 2030, according to the Social Security Administration, that number will rise to 46; by 2050, it will rise to 48; and by 2080, that number will be 51. So as baby boomers move into retirement, benefit payments will continue to rise relative to the size of the economy.

The aging of the baby boomers, by itself, poses only a moderately sized long-run fiscal problem. The projected rise in Medicare and Medicaid spending is a much more serious concern. The main story behind projections of higher Medicare and Medicaid spending is the long-run tendency of health care spending to rise faster than overall spending, both for government-funded and for privately funded health care.

To some extent, the implicit liabilities of the U.S. government are already reflected in debt statistics. We mentioned earlier that the government had a total debt of $16.7 trillion at the end of fiscal 2013 but that only $12.0 trillion of that total was owed to the public. The main explanation for that discrepancy is that both Social Security and part of Medicare (the hospital insurance program) are supported by *dedicated taxes:* their expenses are paid out of special taxes on wages. At times, these dedicated taxes yield more revenue than is needed to pay current benefits.

In particular, since the mid-1980s the Social Security system has been taking in more revenue than it currently needs in order to prepare for the retirement of the baby boomers. This surplus in the Social Security system has been used to accumulate a *Social Security trust fund,* which was $2.7 trillion at the end of fiscal 2013.

The money in the trust fund is held in the form of U.S. government bonds, which are included in the $16.7 trillion in total debt. You could say that there's something funny about counting bonds in the Social Security trust fund as part of government debt. After all, these bonds are owed by one part of the government (the government outside the Social Security system) to another part of the government (the Social Security system itself). But the debt corresponds to a real, if implicit, liability: promises by the government to pay future retirement benefits.

So many economists argue that the gross debt of $16.7 trillion, the sum of public debt and government debt held by Social Security and other trust funds, is a more accurate indication of the government's fiscal health than the smaller amount owed to the public alone.

MODULE 32 Review

Solutions appear at the back of the book.

Check Your Understanding

1. Why is the cyclically adjusted budget balance a better measure of whether government policies are sustainable in the long run than the actual budget balance?

2. Explain why states required by their constitutions to balance their budgets are likely to experience more severe economic fluctuations than states not held to that requirement.

3. Explain how each of the following events would affect the public debt or implicit liabilities of the U.S. government, other things equal. Would the public debt or implicit liabilities be greater or smaller?

   a. A higher growth rate of real GDP

   b. Retirees live longer

   c. A decrease in tax revenue

   d. Government borrowing to pay interest on its current public debt

Multiple-Choice Questions

1. Over the course of the business cycle

   a. the budget deficit tends to increase during expansions.

   b. the budget deficit tends to decrease during expansions.

   c. Congress will take steps to ensure the budget balance does not change.

   d. the budget balance does not change due to automatic stabilizers.

   e. the level of government debt tends to decline.

2. The total debt of the U.S. federal government

   a. is the same as the public debt.

   b. is measured by the difference between the government's revenue and spending for a particular year.

   c. increases when the government runs a budget deficit.

   d. decreases when the government runs a budget deficit.

   e. is measured by the size of its implicit liabilities.

3. The budget balance tends to decline during a recession because

   a. tax revenue automatically declines.

   b. transfer payments automatically decline.

   c. government spending automatically declines.

   d. the government must cut spending as tax revenue automatically declines.

   e. the government is likely to pursue contractionary fiscal policy.

4. During a recession the budget balance tends to _____ because of _____

   a. increase : discretionary fiscal policy

   b. decrease : discretionary fiscal policy

   c. increase : automatic stabilizers

   d. decrease : automatic stabilizers

   e. remain unchanged : discretionary fiscal policy

5. The cyclically adjusted budget balance estimates

   a. the budget balance during a recession.

   b. the budget balance during an expansion.

   c. the change in the budget balance during the business cycle.

   d. the budget balance if real GDP was equal to potential output.

   e. how much tax revenues should change to balance the budget.

Critical-Thinking Question

Suppose the economy is in a slump and the current public debt is quite large. Explain the trade-off of short-run versus long-run objectives that policy makers face when deciding whether or not to engage in fiscal policy.

PITFALLS

DEFICITS AND DEBT DO DIFFER

? What Is the difference between deficit and debt? Confusing deficit and debt is a common mistake—it happens all the time in news reports, for example.

> A *DEFICIT* IS THE DIFFERENCE BETWEEN THE AMOUNT OF MONEY A GOVERNMENT SPENDS AND THE AMOUNT IT RECEIVES IN TAXES OVER A GIVEN PERIOD—USUALLY, THOUGH NOT ALWAYS, A YEAR. A *DEBT* IS THE SUM OF MONEY A GOVERNMENT OWES AT A PARTICULAR POINT IN TIME. Deficit numbers always come with a statement about the time period to which they apply, as in "the U.S. budget deficit *in fiscal 2013* was $683 billion." Debt numbers usually come with a specific date, as in "U.S. public debt *at the end of fiscal 2013* was $17 trillion."

Although deficits and debt are linked, because government debt grows when governments run deficits, they aren't the same thing, and they can even tell different stories. For example, Italy, which found itself in debt trouble in 2011, had a fairly small deficit by historical standards, but it had very high debt, a legacy of past policies.

To learn more, see pages 333–334.

BUSINESS CASE : Priming the Pumps

Courtesy Garney Companies, Inc.

In the old days, when fewer Americans had cars but many more people lived in rural areas and drew their water from wells, advocates of fiscal expansion used different metaphors. Instead of talking, as President Obama did, about giving the economy a "jump start," they'd talk about "priming the pump." You see, it was often necessary to add water to old-fashioned hand pumps before they would work; similarly, people would argue, you need to add funds to the economy before it will get back to producing jobs and income.

In the case of the Obama stimulus, priming the pump was more than a metaphor: some of the most obvious beneficiaries were companies that made . . . pumps. The Recovery Act allocated $7 billion for drinking-water and wastewater projects, creating a number of new opportunities for companies in the business of moving water around.

A case in point was Garney Construction, a Kansas-City-based company specializing in water and sewage projects whose slogan is "Advancing Water." By the summer of 2009, Garney had won contracts to work on nine water- and sewer-related projects that were being financed in whole or in part by the Recovery Act.

None of these infrastructure projects were dreamed up as ways to spend more money; they were all things that state or local governments had been planning to do eventually. "I think most of these projects were sitting on a shelf, waiting for funding," Garney's president told a local business journal.

Although the stimulus was good for Garney, it was not exactly a financial gusher. In 2007, the United States spent about $100 billion on water-supply and wastewater infrastructure; the extra $7 billion coming from the stimulus, not all of it coming in one year, was basically a, well, drop in the bucket by comparison. Indeed, Garney said that only about 10% of its business was coming from stimulus money. And despite the stimulus, the company had less business than it had two years earlier.

Still, Garney and other companies in the water-infrastructure business were clearly getting some benefit from the Recovery Act.

Questions for Thought

1. Some opponents of fiscal expansion have accused it of consisting of make-work projects of little social value. What does the Garney story say about this view?

2. Based on this case, would you say that government spending was competing with the private sector for scarce resources?

3. If a water or sewer project is something we want to do eventually, is the depth of a recession a good or a bad time to undertake that project? Why?

SECTION 9 REVIEW

Summary

Fiscal Policy Basics

1. The government plays a significant role in the economy by collecting a large share of GDP in taxes and spending a large share both to purchase goods and services and to make transfer payments, mainly for **social insurance.**

2. Fiscal policy is the use of taxes, government transfers, or government purchases of goods and services to shift the aggregate demand curve.

3. Government purchases of goods and services directly affect aggregate demand, and changes in taxes and government transfers affect aggregate demand indirectly by changing households' disposable income.

4. **Expansionary fiscal policy** shifts the aggregate demand curve rightward, and leads to an increase in real GDP. **Contractionary fiscal policy** shifts the aggregate demand curve leftward, and leads to a reduction in real GDP.

5. Only when the economy is at full employment is there potential for crowding out of private spending and private investment spending by expansionary fiscal policy.

6. The argument that expansionary fiscal policy won't work because of Ricardian equivalence—that consumers will cut back spending today to offset expected future tax increases—appears to be untrue in practice.

7. Very active fiscal policy may make the economy less stable due to time lags in policy formulation and implementation.

Fiscal Policy and the Multiplier

8. Expansionary and contractionary fiscal policies have a multiplier effect on the economy, the size of which depends on the fiscal policy. Except in the case of **lump-sum taxes,** an increase in taxes will reduce the size of the multiplier.

9. Since part of any change in taxes or transfers is absorbed by savings in the first round of spending, changes in government purchases of goods and services have a more powerful effect on the economy than equal-sized changes in taxes or transfers.

10. Some taxes and transfers act as **automatic stabilizers,** reducing the size of the multiplier and automatically reducing the size of fluctuations in the business cycle. Lump-sum taxes do not change as real GDP changes, and therefore do not act as automatic stabilizers.

11. **Discretionary fiscal policy** arises from deliberate actions by policy makers rather than automatic adjustment caused by the business cycle.

Budget Deficits and Public Debt

12. Some of the fluctuations in the budget balance are due to the effects of the business cycle. In order to separate the effects of the business cycle from the effects of discretionary fiscal policy, governments estimate the **cyclically adjusted budget balance,** an estimate of the budget balance if the economy were at potential output.

13. U.S. government budget accounting is calculated on the basis of **fiscal years.**

14. Persistent budget deficits have long-run consequences because they lead to an increase in **public debt.** This can be a problem for two reasons. Public debt may crowd out investment spending, which reduces long-run economic growth. In extreme cases, rising debt may lead to government default, resulting in economic and financial turmoil.

15. A widely used measure of fiscal health is the **debt–GDP ratio.** This number can remain stable or fall even in the face of moderate budget deficits if GDP rises over time.

16. A stable debt–GDP ratio may give a misleading impression that all is well because modern governments often have large **implicit liabilities.** The largest implicit liabilities of the U.S. government come from Social Security, Medicare, and Medicaid, the costs of which are increasing due to the aging of the population and rising medical costs.

Key Terms

Social insurance, p. 316
Expansionary fiscal policy, p. 317
Contractionary fiscal policy, p. 318

Lump-sum taxes, p. 325
Automatic stabilizers, p. 325
Discretionary fiscal policy, p. 326

Cyclically adjusted budget balance, p. 330
Fiscal year, p. 333
Public debt, p. 334

Debt–GDP ratio, p. 335
Implicit liabilities, p. 336

Problems

1. The accompanying diagram shows the current macroeconomic situation for the economy of Albernia. You have been hired as an economic consultant to help the economy move to potential output, Y_P.

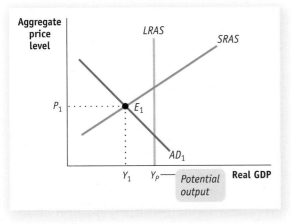

a. Is Albernia facing a recessionary or inflationary gap?

b. Which type of fiscal policy—expansionary or contractionary—would move the economy of Albernia to potential output, Y_P? What are some examples of such policies?

c. Draw a diagram illustrating the macroeconomic situation in Albernia after the successful fiscal policy has been implemented.

2. The accompanying diagram shows the current macroeconomic situation for the economy of Brittania; real GDP is Y_1, and the aggregate price level is P_1. You have been hired as an economic consultant to help the economy move to potential output, Y_P.

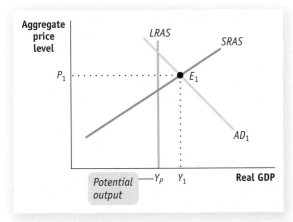

a. Is Brittania facing a recessionary or inflationary gap?

b. Which type of fiscal policy—expansionary or contractionary—would move the economy of Brittania to potential output, Y_P? What are some examples of such policies?

c. Draw a diagram illustrating the macroeconomic situation in Brittania after the successful fiscal policy has been implemented.

3. An economy is in long-run macroeconomic equilibrium when each of the following aggregate demand shocks occurs. What kind of gap—inflationary or recessionary—will the economy face after the shock, and what type of fiscal policies would help move the economy back to potential output? How would your recommended fiscal policy shift the aggregate demand curve?

a. A stock market boom increases the value of stocks held by households.

b. Firms come to believe that a recession in the near future is likely.

c. Anticipating the possibility of war, the government increases its purchases of military equipment.

d. The quantity of money in the economy declines and interest rates increase.

4. During a recent interview, the German finance minister said, "We have to watch out that in Europe and beyond, nothing like a combination of downward economic [growth] and high inflation rates emerges—something that experts call stagflation." Such a situation can be depicted by the movement of the short-run aggregate supply curve from its original position, $SRAS_1$, to its new position, $SRAS_2$, with the new equilibrium point E_2 in the accompanying figure. In this question, we try to understand why stagflation is particularly hard to fix using fiscal policy.

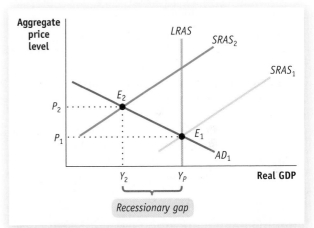

a. What would be the appropriate fiscal policy response to this situation if the primary concern of the government was to maintain economic growth? Illustrate the effect of the policy on the equilibrium point and the aggregate price level using the diagram.

b. What would be the appropriate fiscal policy response to this situation if the primary concern of the government was to maintain price stability? Illustrate the effect of the policy on the equilibrium point and the aggregate price level using the diagram.

c. Discuss the effectiveness of the policies in parts a and b in fighting stagflation.

5. Show why a $10 billion reduction in government purchases of goods and services will have a larger effect on real GDP than a $10 billion reduction in government transfers by completing the following table for an economy with a marginal propensity to consume (MPC) of 0.6.

Rounds	Decrease in G = −$10 billion (Billions of dollars)			Decrease in TR = −$10 billion (Billions of dollars)		
	Change in G or C	Change in real GDP	Change in YD	Change in TR or C	Change in real GDP	Change in YD
1	ΔG = −$10.00	−$10.00	−$10.00	ΔTR = −$10.00	$0.00	−$10.00
2	ΔC = −6.00	−6.00	−6.00	ΔC = −6.00	−6.00	−6.00
3	ΔC = ?	?	?	ΔC = ?	?	?
4	ΔC = ?	?	?	ΔC = ?	?	?
5	ΔC = ?	?	?	ΔC = ?	?	?
6	ΔC = ?	?	?	ΔC = ?	?	?
7	ΔC = ?	?	?	ΔC = ?	?	?
8	ΔC = ?	?	?	ΔC = ?	?	?
9	ΔC = ?	?	?	ΔC = ?	?	?
10	ΔC = ?	?	?	ΔC = ?	?	?

The first and second rows of the table are filled in for you: on the left side of the table, in the first row, the $10 billion reduction in government purchases decreases real GDP and disposable income, YD, by $10 billion, leading to a reduction in consumer spending of $6 billion ($MPC$ × change in disposable income) in row 2. However, on the right side of the table, the $10 billion reduction in transfers has no effect on real GDP in round 1 but does lower YD by $10 billion, resulting in a decrease in consumer spending of $6 billion in round 2.

a. When government purchases decrease by $10 billion, what is the sum of the changes in real GDP after the 10 rounds?

b. When the government reduces transfers by $10 billion, what is the sum of the changes in real GDP after the 10 rounds?

c. Using the formula for the multiplier for changes in government purchases and for changes in transfers, calculate the total change in real GDP due to the $10 billion decrease in government purchases and the $10 billion reduction in transfers. What explains the difference? (*Hint:* The multiplier for government purchases of goods and services is $1/(1 - MPC)$. But since each $1 change in government transfers only leads to an initial change in real GDP of $MPC × 1, the multiplier for government transfers is $MPC/(1 - MPC)$.)

6. In each of the following cases, either a recessionary or inflationary gap exists. Assume that the aggregate supply curve is horizontal, so that the change in real GDP arising from a shift of the aggregate demand curve equals the size of the shift of the curve. Calculate both the change in government purchases of goods and services and the change in government transfers necessary to close the gap.

a. Real GDP equals $100 billion, potential output equals $160 billion, and the marginal propensity to consume is 0.75.

b. Real GDP equals $250 billion, potential output equals $200 billion, and the marginal propensity to consume is 0.5.

c. Real GDP equals $180 billion, potential output equals $100 billion, and the marginal propensity to consume is 0.8.

7. Most macroeconomists believe it is a good thing that taxes act as automatic stabilizers and lower the size of the multiplier. However, a smaller multiplier means that the change in government purchases of goods and services, government transfers, or taxes needed to close an inflationary or recessionary gap is larger. How can you explain this apparent inconsistency?

8. The accompanying table shows how consumers' marginal propensities to consume in a particular economy are related to their level of income.

Income range	Marginal propensity to consume
$0–$20,000	0.9
$20,001–$40,000	0.8
$40,001–$60,000	0.7
$60,001–$80,000	0.6
Above $80,000	0.5

a. Suppose the government engages in increased purchases of goods and services. For each of the income groups in the table, what is the value of the multiplier—that is, what is the "bang for the buck" from each dollar the government spends on government purchases of goods and services in each income group?

b. If the government needed to close a recessionary or inflationary gap, at which group should it primarily aim its fiscal policy of changes in government purchases of goods and services?

9. The government's budget surplus in Macroland has risen consistently over the past five years. Two government policy makers disagree as to why this has happened. One argues that a rising budget surplus indicates a growing economy; the other argues that it shows that the government is using contractionary fiscal policy. Can you determine which policy maker is correct? If not, why not?

10. Figure 32-3 shows the actual budget deficit and the cyclically adjusted budget deficit as a percentage of GDP in the United States from 1970 to 2013. Assuming that potential output was unchanged, use this figure to determine which of the years from 1990 to 2011 the government used expansionary fiscal policy and in which years it used contractionary fiscal policy.

11. You are an economic adviser to a candidate for national office. She asks you for a summary of the economic consequences of a balanced-budget rule for the federal government and for your recommendation on whether she should support such a rule. How do you respond?

12. In 2012, the policy makers of the economy of Eastlandia projected the debt–GDP ratio and the ratio of the budget deficit to GDP for the economy for the next 10 years under different scenarios for growth in the government's deficit. Real GDP is currently $1,000 billion per year and is expected to grow by 3% per year, the public debt is $300 billion at the beginning of the year, and the deficit is $30 billion in 2012.

Year	Real GDP (billions of dollars)	Debt (billions of dollars)	Budget deficit (billions of dollars)	Debt (percent of real GDP)	Budget deficit (percent of real GDP)
2012	$1,000	$300	$30	?	?
2013	1,030	?	?	?	?
2014	1,061	?	?	?	?
2015	1,093	?	?	?	?
2016	1,126	?	?	?	?
2017	1,159	?	?	?	?
2018	1,194	?	?	?	?
2019	1,230	?	?	?	?
2020	1,267	?	?	?	?
2021	1,305	?	?	?	?
2022	1,344	?	?	?	?

a. Complete the accompanying table to show the debt–GDP ratio and the ratio of the budget deficit to GDP for the economy if the government's budget deficit remains constant at $30 billion over the next 10 years. (Remember that the government's debt will grow by the previous year's deficit.)

b. Redo the table to show the debt–GDP ratio and the ratio of the budget deficit to GDP for the economy if the government's budget deficit grows by 3% per year over the next 10 years.

c. Redo the table again to show the debt–GDP ratio and the ratio of the budget deficit to GDP for the economy if the government's budget deficit grows by 20% per year over the next 10 years.

d. What happens to the debt–GDP ratio and the ratio of the budget deficit to GDP for the economy over time under the three different scenarios?

13. Your study partner argues that the distinction between the government's budget deficit and debt is similar to the distinction between consumer savings and wealth. He also argues that if you have large budget deficits, you must have a large debt. In what ways is your study partner correct and in what ways is he incorrect?

14. In which of the following cases does the size of the government's debt and the size of the budget deficit indicate potential problems for the economy?

a. The government's debt is relatively low, but the government is running a large budget deficit as it builds a high-speed rail system to connect the major cities of the nation.

b. The government's debt is relatively high due to a recently ended deficit-financed war, but the government is now running only a small budget deficit.

c. The government's debt is relatively low, but the government is running a budget deficit to finance the interest payments on the debt.

15. How did or would the following affect the current public debt and implicit liabilities of the U.S. government?

a. In 2003, Congress passed and President Bush signed the Medicare Modernization Act, which provides seniors and individuals with disabilities with a prescription drug benefit. Some of the benefits under this law took effect immediately, but others will not begin until sometime in the future.

b. The age at which retired persons can receive full Social Security benefits is raised to age 70 for future retirees.

c. Social Security benefits for future retirees are limited to those with low incomes.

d. Because the cost of health care is increasing faster than the overall inflation rate, annual increases in Social Security benefits are increased by the annual increase in health care costs rather than the overall inflation rate.

16. Unlike households, governments are often able to sustain large debts. For example, in 2011, the U.S. government's total debt reached $14.8 trillion, approximately equal to 102.7% of GDP. At the time, according to the U.S. Treasury, the average interest rate paid by the government on its debt was 2.2%. However, running budget deficits becomes hard when very large debts are outstanding.

a. Calculate the dollar cost of the annual interest on the government's total debt assuming the interest rate and debt figures cited above.

b. If the government operates on a balanced budget before interest payments are taken into account, at what rate must GDP grow in order for the debt–GDP ratio to remain unchanged?

c. Calculate the total increase in national debt if the government incurs a deficit of $600 billion in 2012.

d. At what rate would GDP have to grow in order for the debt–GDP ratio to remain unchanged when the deficit in 2012 is $600 billion?

e. Why is the debt–GDP ratio the preferred measure of a country's debt rather than the dollar value of the debt? Why is it important for a government to keep this number under control?

SECTION 10

Money, Banking, and the Federal Reserve System

FUNNY MONEY

In 2013, police in Lima, Peru, were stunned when they arrested a 13-year-old boy carrying a sack filled with $700,000 in counterfeit U.S. dollars. The boy, along with other children, worked for one of the many highly successful counterfeiting rings in Peru.

In recent years, Peru has become a major source for the production of counterfeit U.S. currency. Workers in these rings meticulously add decorative details to printed bills by hand, creating high-quality fakes that are very hard to detect.

The funny thing is that elaborately decorated pieces of paper have little or no intrinsic value. Indeed, a $100 bill printed with blue or orange ink wouldn't be worth the paper it was printed on.

But if the ink on that piece of paper is just the right shade of green, people will think that it's *money* and will accept it as payment for very real goods and services. Why? Because they believe, correctly, that they can do the same thing: exchange that piece of green paper for real goods and services.

In fact, here's a riddle: If a fake $100 bill from Peru enters the United States and is successfully exchanged for a good or service with nobody ever realizing it's fake, who gets hurt? Accepting a fake $100 bill isn't like buying a car that turns out to be a lemon or a meal that turns out to be inedible; as long as the bill's counterfeit nature remains undiscovered, it will pass from hand to hand just like a real $100 bill.

The answer to the riddle is that the actual victims of the counterfeiting are U.S. taxpayers because counterfeit dollars reduce the revenues available to pay for the operations of the U.S. government. Accordingly, the Secret Service diligently monitors the integrity of U.S. currency, promptly investigating any reports of counterfeit dollars.

The efforts of the Secret Service attest to the fact that money isn't like ordinary goods and services. In this section we'll look at the role money plays, the workings of a modern monetary system, and the institutions that sustain and regulate it, including the *Federal Reserve*.

Shutterstock

The Meaning of Money

People often use the word *money* to mean "wealth." If you ask, "How much money does Bill Gates have?" the answer will be something like, "Oh, $50 billion or so, but who's counting?" That is, the number will include the value of the stocks, bonds, real estate, and other assets he owns.

But the economist's definition of money doesn't include all forms of wealth. The dollar bills in your wallet are money; other forms of wealth—such as cars, houses, and stock certificates—aren't money. What, according to economists, distinguishes money from other forms of wealth?

What Is Money?

Money is defined in terms of what it does: **money** is any asset that can easily be used to purchase goods and services. Earlier, we defined an asset as *liquid* if it can easily be converted into cash. Money consists of cash itself, which is liquid by definition, as well as other assets that are highly liquid.

You can see the distinction between money and other assets by asking yourself how you pay for groceries. The person at the cash register will accept dollar bills in return for milk and frozen pizza—but he or she won't accept stock certificates or a collection of vintage baseball cards. If you want to convert stock certificates or vintage baseball cards into groceries, you have to sell them—trade them for money—and then use the money to buy groceries.

Of course, many stores allow you to write a check on your bank account in payment for goods (or to pay with a debit card that is linked to your bank account).

Money is any asset that can easily be used to purchase goods and services.

Does that make your bank account money, even if you haven't converted it into cash? Yes. **Currency in circulation**—actual cash in the hands of the public—is considered money. So are **checkable bank deposits**—bank accounts on which people can write checks.

Are currency and checkable bank deposits the only assets that are considered money? It depends. As we'll see later, there are two widely used definitions of the **money supply,** the total value of financial assets in the economy that are considered money. The narrower definition considers only the most liquid assets to be money: currency in circulation, traveler's checks, and checkable bank deposits. The broader definition includes these three categories plus other assets that are "almost" checkable, such as savings account deposits that can be transferred into a checking account online with a few mouse clicks. Both definitions of the money supply, however, make a distinction between those assets that can easily be used to purchase goods and services, and those that can't.

Money is the essential channel that links the various parts of the modern economy.

Money plays a crucial role in generating *gains from trade* because it makes indirect exchange possible. Think of what happens when a cardiac surgeon buys a new refrigerator. The surgeon has valuable services to offer—namely, performing heart operations. The owner of the store has valuable goods to offer: refrigerators and other appliances. It would be extremely difficult for both parties if, instead of using money, they had to directly barter the goods and services they sell. In a barter system, a cardiac surgeon and an appliance store owner could trade only if the store owner happened to want a heart operation *and* the surgeon happened to want a new refrigerator.

This is known as the problem of finding a "double coincidence of wants": in a barter system, two parties can trade only when each wants what the other has to offer. Money solves this problem: individuals can trade what they have to offer for money and trade money for what they want.

Because the ability to make transactions with money rather than relying on bartering makes it easier to achieve gains from trade, the existence of money increases welfare, even though money does not directly produce anything.

Let's take a closer look at the roles money plays in the economy.

Roles of Money

Money plays three main roles in any modern economy: it is a *medium of exchange,* a *store of value,* and a *unit of account.*

1. MEDIUM OF EXCHANGE Our cardiac surgeon/refrigerator store owner example illustrates the role of money as a **medium of exchange**—an asset that individuals use to trade for goods and services rather than for consumption. People can't eat dollar bills; rather, they use dollar bills to trade for edible goods and their accompanying services.

In normal times, the official money of a given country—the dollar in the United States, the peso in Mexico, and so on—is also the medium of exchange in virtually all transactions in that country. During troubled economic times, however, other goods or assets often play that role instead. For example, people often turn to other countries' moneys as the medium of exchange in times of economic turmoil: U.S. dollars have played this role in troubled Latin American countries, as have euros in troubled Eastern European countries.

In a famous example, cigarettes functioned as the medium of exchange in World War II prisoner-of-war camps. Even nonsmokers traded goods and services for cigarettes because the cigarettes could in turn be easily traded for other items. During the extreme German inflation of 1923, goods such as eggs and lumps of coal became, briefly, mediums of exchange.

Currency in circulation is cash held by the public.

Checkable bank deposits are bank accounts on which people can write checks.

The **money supply** is the total value of financial assets in the economy that are considered money.

A **medium of exchange** is an asset that individuals acquire for the purpose of trading goods and services rather than for their own consumption.

A **store of value** is a means of holding purchasing power over time.

A **unit of account** is a measure used to set prices and make economic calculations.

Commodity money is a good used as a medium of exchange that has intrinsic value in other uses.

Commodity-backed money is a medium of exchange with no intrinsic value whose ultimate value is guaranteed by a promise that it can be converted into valuable goods.

2. STORE OF VALUE In order to act as a medium of exchange, money must also be a **store of value**—a means of holding purchasing power over time. To see why this is necessary, imagine trying to operate an economy in which ice-cream cones were the medium of exchange. Such an economy would quickly suffer from, well, monetary meltdown: your medium of exchange would often turn into a sticky puddle before you could use it to buy something else.

Of course, money is by no means the only store of value. Any asset that holds its purchasing power over time is a store of value. So the store-of-value role is a necessary but not distinctive feature of money.

3. UNIT OF ACCOUNT Finally, money normally serves as the **unit of account**—the commonly accepted measure individuals use to set prices and make economic calculations. To understand the importance of this role, consider a historical fact: during the Middle Ages, peasants typically were required to provide landowners with goods and labor rather than money. A peasant might, for example, be required to work on the landowner's land one day a week and hand over one-fifth of his harvest.

Today, rents, like other prices, are almost always specified in money terms. That makes things much clearer: imagine how hard it would be to decide which apartment to rent if modern landowners followed medieval practice. Suppose, for example, that Mr. Smith says he'll let you have a place if you clean his house twice a week and bring him a pound of steak every day, whereas Ms. Jones wants you to clean her house just once a week but wants four pounds of chicken every day. Who's offering the better deal? It's hard to say. If, on the other hand, Smith wants $600 a month and Jones wants $700, the comparison is easy. In other words, without a commonly accepted measure, the terms of a transaction are harder to determine, making it more difficult to make transactions and achieve gains from trade.

For centuries, people used goods with value, like gold and silver, as a medium of exchange.

Thinkstock

Types of Money

In some form or another, money has been in use for thousands of years. For most of that period, people used **commodity money:** the medium of exchange was a good, normally gold or silver, that had intrinsic value in other uses. These alternative uses gave commodity money value independent of its role as a medium of exchange. For example, the cigarettes that served as money in World War II prisoner-of-war camps were valuable because many prisoners smoked. Gold was valuable because it was used for jewelry and ornamentation, aside from the fact that it was minted into coins.

By 1776, the year in which the United States declared its independence and Adam Smith published *The Wealth of Nations*, there was widespread use of paper money in addition to gold or silver coins. Unlike modern dollar bills, however, this paper money consisted of notes issued by private banks, which promised to exchange their notes for gold or silver coins on demand. So the paper currency that initially replaced commodity money was **commodity-backed money,** a medium of exchange with no intrinsic value whose ultimate value was guaranteed by a promise that it could always be converted into valuable goods on demand.

Early paper money consisted of bank-issued promissory notes that functioned in a different way than cash does today.

The big advantage of commodity-backed money over simple commodity money, like gold and silver coins, was that it tied up fewer valuable resources. Although a note-issuing bank still had to keep some gold and silver on hand, it had to keep only enough to satisfy demands for redemption of its notes. And it could rely on the fact that on a normal day only a fraction of its paper notes would be redeemed. So the bank needed to keep only a portion of the total value of its notes in circulation in the form of gold and silver in its vaults. It could lend out the remaining gold and silver to those who wished to use it. This allowed society to use the remaining gold and silver for other purposes, all with no loss in the ability to achieve gains from trade.

Fiat money is a medium of exchange whose value derives entirely from its official status as a means of payment.

At this point you may ask, why make any use at all of gold and silver in the monetary system, even to back paper money? In fact, today's monetary system has eliminated any role for gold and silver. A U.S. dollar bill isn't commodity money, and it isn't even commodity-backed. Rather, its value arises entirely from the fact that it is generally accepted as a means of payment, a role that is ultimately decreed by the U.S. government. Money whose value derives entirely from its official status as a means of exchange is known as **fiat money** because it exists by government *fiat*, a historical term for a policy declared by a ruler.

Fiat money has two major advantages over commodity-backed money. First, creating it doesn't use up any real resources, except for the paper it's printed on. Second, the money supply can be adjusted based on the needs of the economy, instead of being determined by the amount of gold and silver prospectors happen to discover.

Fiat money, though, poses some risks. One such risk is counterfeiting, as we saw in the section-opening story. Counterfeiters usurp a privilege of the U.S. government, which has the sole legal right to print dollar bills. And the benefit that counterfeiters get by exchanging fake bills for real goods and services comes at the expense of the U.S. federal government, which covers a small but nontrivial part of its own expenses by issuing new currency to meet growing demand for money.

The larger risk is that governments that can create money whenever they feel like it will be tempted to abuse the privilege by printing so much money that they create inflation.

ECONOMICS ▶ *IN ACTION*

THE HISTORY OF THE DOLLAR

U.S. dollar bills are pure fiat money: they have no intrinsic value, and they are not backed by anything that does. But American money wasn't always like that.

In the early days of European settlement, the colonies that would become the United States used commodity money, partly consisting of gold and silver coins minted in Europe. But such coins were scarce on this side of the Atlantic, so the colonists relied on a variety of other forms of commodity money. For example, settlers in Virginia used tobacco as money and settlers in the Northeast used "wampum," a type of clamshell.

Later in American history, commodity-backed paper money came into widespread use. But this wasn't paper money as we now know it, issued by the U.S. government and bearing the signature of the Secretary of the Treasury. Before the Civil War, the U.S. government didn't issue any paper money. Instead, dollar bills were issued by private banks, which promised that their bills could be redeemed for silver coins on demand.

These promises weren't always credible because banks sometimes failed, leaving holders of their bills with worthless pieces of paper. Understandably, people were reluctant to accept currency from any bank rumored to be in financial trouble. In other words, in this private money system, some dollars were less valuable than others.

A curious legacy of that time was notes issued by the Citizens' Bank of Louisiana, based in New Orleans. They became among the most widely used bank notes in the southern states. These notes were printed in English on one side and French on the other. (At the time, many people in New Orleans, originally a colony of France, spoke French.) Thus, the $10 bill read *Ten* on one side and *Dix*, the French word for "ten," on the other. These $10 bills became known as "dixies," probably the source of the nickname of the U.S. South.

Not until the Civil War did the U.S. government issue official paper money.

During the Civil War, the U.S. government began issuing official paper money, called "greenbacks," as a way to help pay for the war. At first greenbacks had no fixed value in terms of commodities. After 1873, the U.S. government guaranteed the value of a dollar in terms of gold, effectively turning dollars into commodity-backed money.

In 1933, when President Franklin D. Roosevelt broke the link between dollars and gold, his own federal budget director—who feared that the public would lose confidence in the dollar if it wasn't ultimately backed by gold—declared ominously, "This will be the end of Western civilization." It wasn't. The link between the dollar and gold was restored a few years later, and then dropped again—seemingly for good—in August 1971. Despite the warnings of doom, the U.S. dollar is still the world's most widely used currency.

Measuring the Money Supply

The Federal Reserve (an institution we'll talk about shortly) calculates the size of two **monetary aggregates,** overall measures of the money supply, which differ in how strictly money is defined. The two aggregates are known, rather cryptically, as M1 and M2. (There used to be a third aggregate named—you guessed it—M3, but in 2006 the Federal Reserve concluded that measuring it was no longer useful.)

M1, the narrowest definition, contains only currency in circulation (also known as cash), traveler's checks, and checkable bank deposits. M2 starts with M1 and adds several other kinds of assets, often referred to as **near-moneys**—financial assets that aren't directly usable as a medium of exchange but can be readily converted into cash or checkable bank deposits, such as savings accounts. Examples are time deposits such as small denomination CDs, which aren't checkable but can be withdrawn at any time before their maturity date by paying a penalty. Because currency and checkable deposits are directly usable as a medium of exchange, M1 is the most liquid measure of money.

Figure 33-1 shows the actual composition of M1 and M2 in April 2013, in billions of dollars. As you can see, M1 was valued at $2,514.1 billion, with approximately 44%

A **monetary aggregate** is an overall measure of the money supply.

Near-moneys are financial assets that can't be directly used as a medium of exchange but can be readily converted into cash or checkable bank deposits.

FIGURE 33-1   Monetary Aggregates, April 2013

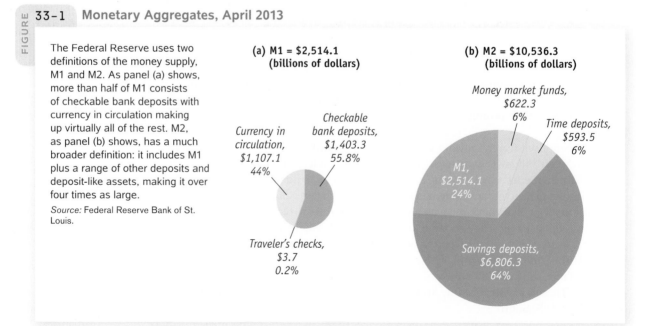

The Federal Reserve uses two definitions of the money supply, M1 and M2. As panel (a) shows, more than half of M1 consists of checkable bank deposits with currency in circulation making up virtually all of the rest. M2, as panel (b) shows, has a much broader definition: it includes M1 plus a range of other deposits and deposit-like assets, making it over four times as large.

Source: Federal Reserve Bank of St. Louis.

(a) M1 = $2,514.1
(billions of dollars)

Currency in circulation, $1,107.1 44%

Checkable bank deposits, $1,403.3 55.8%

Traveler's checks, $3.7 0.2%

(b) M2 = $10,536.3
(billions of dollars)

Money market funds, $622.3 6%

Time deposits, $593.5 6%

M1, $2,514.1 24%

Savings deposits, $6,806.3 64%

accounted for by currency in circulation, approximately 56% accounted for by check-able bank deposits, and a tiny slice accounted for by traveler's checks. In turn, M1 made up 24% of M2, valued at $10,536.3 billion. M2 consists of M1 plus other types of assets: two types of bank deposits, known as savings deposits and time deposits, both of which are considered noncheckable, plus money market funds, which are mutual funds that invest only in liquid assets and bear a close resemblance to bank deposits. These near-moneys pay interest while cash (currency in circulation) does not, and they typically pay higher interest rates than any offered on checkable bank deposits.

MODULE
33 Review

Solutions appear at the back of the book.

Check Your Understanding

1. Suppose you hold a gift certificate, good for certain products at participating stores. Is this gift certificate money? Why or why not?

2. Although most bank accounts pay some interest, depositors can get a higher interest rate by buying a certificate of deposit, or CD. The difference between a CD and a checking account is that the depositor pays a penalty for withdrawing the money before the CD comes due—a period of months or even years. Small CDs are counted in M2, but not in M1. Explain why they are not part of M1.

3. Explain why a system of commodity-backed money uses resources more efficiently than a system of commodity money.

Multiple-Choice Questions

1. When you use money to purchase your lunch, money is serving which role(s)?
   - I. medium of exchange
   - II. store of value
   - III. unit of account
   - a. I only
   - b. II only
   - c. III only
   - d. I and III only
   - e. I, II, and III

2. When you decide you want "$10 worth" of a product, money is serving which role(s)?
   - I. medium of exchange
   - II. store of value
   - III. unit of account
   - a. I only
   - b. II only
   - c. III only
   - d. I and II only
   - e. I, II, and III

3. In the United States, the dollar is
   - a. backed by silver.
   - b. backed by gold and silver.
   - c. commodity-backed money.
   - d. commodity money.
   - e. fiat money.

4. Which of the following is the most liquid monetary aggregate?
   - a. M1
   - b. M2
   - c. M3
   - d. near-moneys
   - e. dollar bills

5. Which of the following is the best example of using money as a store of value?
   - a. A customer pays in advance for $10 worth of gasoline at a gas station.
   - b. A babysitter puts her earnings in a dresser drawer while she saves to buy a bicycle.
   - c. Travelers buy meals on board an airline flight.
   - d. Foreign visitors to the United States convert their currency to dollars at the airport.
   - e. You use $1 bills to purchase soda from a vending machine.

Critical-Thinking Questions

1. The U.S. dollar derives its value from what? That is, what "backs" U.S. currency?

2. What is the term used to describe the type of money used in the United States today?

3. What other two types of money have been used throughout history? Define each.

Banking and Money Creation

Jund Lund/Getty Images

The Monetary Role of Banks

A little less than half of M1, the narrowest definition of the money supply, consists of currency in circulation—$1 bills, $5 bills, and so on. It's obvious where currency comes from: it's printed by the U.S. Treasury. But the rest of M1 consists of bank deposits, and deposits account for the great bulk of M2, the broader definition of the money supply. By either measure, then, bank deposits are a major component of the money supply. And this fact brings us to our next topic: the monetary role of banks.

What Banks Do

A bank is a *financial intermediary* that uses liquid assets in the form of bank deposits to finance the illiquid investments of borrowers. Banks can create liquidity because it isn't necessary for a bank to keep all of the funds deposited with it in the form of highly liquid assets. Except in the case of a *bank run*—which we'll get to shortly—all of a bank's depositors won't want to withdraw their funds at the same time. So a bank can provide its depositors with liquid assets yet still invest much of the depositors' funds in illiquid assets, such as mortgages and business loans.

Banks can't, however, lend out all the funds placed in their hands by depositors because they have to satisfy any depositor who wants to withdraw his or her funds. In order to meet these demands, a bank must keep substantial quantities of liquid assets on hand. In the modern U.S. banking system, these assets take the form either of currency in the bank's vault or deposits held in the bank's own account at the Federal Reserve. The latter can be converted into currency more or less instantly. Currency in bank vaults and bank deposits held at the Federal Reserve are called **bank reserves.** Because bank reserves are in bank vaults and at the Federal Reserve, not held by the public, they are not part of currency in circulation.

Bank reserves are the currency banks hold in their vaults plus their deposits at the Federal Reserve.

To understand the role of banks in determining the money supply, we start by introducing a simple tool for analyzing a bank's financial position: a **T-account.** A business's T-account summarizes its financial position by showing, in a single table, the business's assets and liabilities, with assets on the left and liabilities on the right.

Figure 34-1 shows the T-account for a hypothetical business that *isn't* a bank—Samantha's Smoothies. According to Figure 34-1, Samantha's Smoothies owns a building worth $30,000 and has $15,000 worth of smoothie-making equipment. These are assets, so they're on the left side of the table. To finance its opening, the business borrowed $20,000 from a local bank. That's a liability, so the loan is on the right side of the table. By looking at the T-account, you can immediately see what Samantha's Smoothies owns and what it owes. Oh, and it's called a T-account because the lines in the table make a T-shape.

FIGURE 34-1 A T-Account for Samantha's Smoothies

Assets		Liabilities	
Building	$30,000	Loan from bank	$20,000
Smoothie-making machines	$15,000		

A T-account summarizes a business's financial position. Its assets, in this case consisting of a building and some smoothie-making machinery, are on the left side. Its liabilities, consisting of the money it owes to a local bank, are on the right side.

Samantha's Smoothies is an ordinary, nonbank business. Now let's look at the T-account for a hypothetical bank, First Street Bank, which is the repository of $1 million in bank deposits.

Figure 34-2 shows First Street Bank's financial position. The loans First Street Bank has made are on the left side because they're assets: they represent funds that those who have borrowed from the bank are expected to repay. The bank's only other assets, in this simplified example, are its reserves, which, as we've learned, can take the form either of cash in the bank's vault or deposits at the Federal Reserve. On the right side we show the bank's liabilities, which in this example consist entirely of deposits made by customers at First Street Bank. These are liabilities because they represent funds that must ultimately be repaid to depositors.

Notice, by the way, that in this example First Street Bank's assets are larger than its liabilities. That's the way it's supposed to be! In fact, as we'll see shortly, banks are required by law to maintain assets larger by a specific percentage than their liabilities.

In this example, First Street Bank holds reserves equal to 10% of its customers' bank deposits. The fraction of bank deposits that a bank holds as reserves is its **reserve ratio.**

In the modern American system, the Federal Reserve—which, among other things, regulates banks operating in the United States—sets a **required reserve ratio,** which is the smallest fraction of bank deposits that a bank must hold. To understand why banks are regulated, let's consider a problem banks can face: *bank runs.*

FIGURE 34-2 Assets and Liabilities of First Street Bank

Assets		Liabilities	
Loans	$1,000,000	Deposits	$1,000,000
Reserves	$100,000		

First Street Bank's assets consist of $1,000,000 in loans and $100,000 in reserves. Its liabilities consist of $1,000,000 in deposits—money owed to people who have placed funds in First Street's hands.

The Problem of Bank Runs

A bank can lend out most of the funds deposited in its care because in normal times only a small fraction of its depositors want to withdraw their funds on any given day. But what would happen if, for some reason, all or at least a large fraction of its depositors *did* try to withdraw their funds during a short period of time, such as a couple of days?

If a significant share of its depositors demanded their money back at the same time, the bank wouldn't be able to raise enough cash to meet those demands. The reason is that banks convert most of their depositors' funds into loans made to borrowers; that's how banks earn revenue—by charging interest on loans.

Bank loans, however, are illiquid: they can't easily be converted into cash on short notice. To see why, imagine that First Street Bank has lent $100,000 to Drive-a-Peach Used Cars, a local dealership. To raise cash to meet demands for withdrawals, First Street Bank can sell its loan to Drive-a-Peach to someone else—another bank or an

A **T-account** is a tool for analyzing a business's financial position by showing, in a single table, the business's assets (on the left) and liabilities (on the right).

The **reserve ratio** is the fraction of bank deposits that a bank holds as reserves.

The **required reserve ratio** is the smallest fraction of deposits that the Federal Reserve allows banks to hold.

individual investor. But if First Street Bank tries to sell the loan quickly, potential buyers will be wary: they will suspect that First Street Bank wants to sell the loan because there is something wrong and the loan might not be repaid. As a result, First Street Bank can sell the loan quickly only by offering it for sale at a deep discount— say, a discount of 50%, or $50,000.

The upshot is that if a significant number of First Street Bank's depositors suddenly decided to withdraw their funds, the bank's efforts to raise the necessary cash quickly would force it to sell off its assets very cheaply. Inevitably, this leads to a *bank failure*: the bank would be unable to pay off its depositors in full.

What might start this whole process? That is, what might lead First Street Bank's depositors to rush to pull their money out? A plausible answer is a spreading rumor that the bank is in financial trouble. Even if depositors aren't sure the rumor is true, they are likely to play it safe and get their money out while they still can. And it gets worse: a depositor who simply thinks that *other* depositors are going to panic and try to get their money out will realize that this could "break the bank." So he or she joins the rush. In other words, fear about a bank's financial condition can be a self-fulfilling prophecy: depositors who believe that other depositors will rush to the exit will rush to the exit themselves.

A **bank run** is a phenomenon in which many of a bank's depositors try to withdraw their funds due to fears of a bank failure. Bank runs aren't bad only for the bank in question and its depositors. Historically, they have often proved contagious, with a run on one bank leading to a loss of faith in other banks, causing additional bank runs. The upcoming Economics in Action describes an actual case of just such a contagion, the wave of bank runs that swept across the United States in the early 1930s. In response to that experience and similar experiences in other countries, most modern governments established a system of bank regulations, which we'll look at next.

> A **bank run** is a phenomenon in which many of a bank's depositors try to withdraw their funds due to fears of a bank failure.

ECONOMICS ▶ IN ACTION   WORLD VIEW

IT'S A WONDERFUL BANKING SYSTEM

Next Christmastime, it's a sure thing that at least one TV channel will show the 1946 film *It's a Wonderful Life*, featuring Jimmy Stewart as George Bailey. The movie's climactic scene is a run on Bailey's bank, as fearful depositors rush to take their funds out.

When the movie was made, such scenes were still fresh in Americans' memories. There was a wave of bank runs in late 1930, a second wave in the spring of 1931, and a third wave in early 1933. By the end, more than a third of the nation's banks had failed. To bring the panic to an end, in 1933, the newly inaugurated president, Franklin Delano Roosevelt, closed all banks for a week to give bank regulators time to shut down unhealthy banks and certify healthy ones.

Since then, regulation has protected the United States and other wealthy countries against most bank runs. In fact, the scene in *It's a Wonderful Life* was already out of date when the movie was made. But the last 15 years have seen several waves of bank runs in developing countries. For example, bank runs played a role in an economic crisis that swept Southeast Asia in 1997–1998 and in the severe economic crisis in Argentina, which began in late 2001.

Notice that we said "most bank runs." There are some limits on deposit insurance. As a result, there can still be a rush to pull money out of a bank perceived as troubled. In fact, that's exactly what happened to IndyMac, a California-based lender that had made a large number of questionable home loans. In 2008, as questions about IndyMac's financial soundness were raised, depositors began pulling out funds, forcing federal regulators to step in and close the bank. Unlike in the bank runs of the 1930s, however, most depositors got all their funds back—and the panic at IndyMac did not spread to other institutions.

Panicky IndyMac depositors lined up to pull their money out of the troubled California bank in 2008.

Gabriel Bouys/AFP/Getty Images

Bank Regulation

Should you worry about losing money in the United States due to a bank run? No. After the banking crises of the 1930s, the United States and most other countries put into place a system designed to protect depositors and the economy as a whole against bank runs. This system has three main features: *deposit insurance, capital requirements,* and *reserve requirements.* In addition, banks have access to the *discount window,* a source of cash when it's needed.

The FDIC guarantees that bank deposits up to a certain amount will be paid even if a bank runs short or fails.

1. DEPOSIT INSURANCE Almost all banks in the United States advertise themselves as a "member of the FDIC"—the Federal Deposit Insurance Corporation. The FDIC provides **deposit insurance,** a guarantee that depositors will be paid even if the bank can't come up with the funds, up to a maximum amount per account. Currently, the FDIC guarantees the first $250,000 per depositer, per insured bank.

Deposit insurance doesn't just protect depositors if a bank actually fails. The insurance also eliminates the main reason for bank runs: since depositors know their funds are safe even if a bank fails, they have no incentive to rush to pull them out because of a rumor that the bank is in trouble.

2. CAPITAL REQUIREMENTS Deposit insurance, although it protects the banking system against bank runs, creates a well-known incentive problem. Because depositors are protected from loss, they have no incentive to monitor their bank's financial health, allowing risky behavior by the bank to go undetected. At the same time, the owners of banks have an incentive to engage in overly risky investment behavior, such as making questionable loans at high interest rates. That's because if all goes well, the owners profit; and if things go badly, the government covers the losses through federal deposit insurance.

To reduce the incentive for excessive risk-taking, regulators require that the owners of banks hold substantially more assets than the value of bank deposits. That way, the bank will still have assets larger than its deposits even if some of its loans go bad, and losses will accrue against the bank owners' assets, not the government. The excess of a bank's assets over its bank deposits and other liabilities is called the *bank's capital.* For example, First Street Bank has capital of $100,000, equal to 9% of the total value of its assets. In practice, banks' capital is required to equal at least 7% of the value of their assets.

3. RESERVE REQUIREMENTS Another regulation used to reduce the risk of bank runs is **reserve requirements,** rules set by the Federal Reserve that specify the minimum reserve ratio for banks. For example, in the United States, the required reserve ratio for checkable bank deposits is 10%.

4. THE DISCOUNT WINDOW One final protection against bank runs is the fact that the Federal Reserve, which we'll discuss more thoroughly later, stands ready to lend money to banks in trouble, an arrangement known as the **discount window.** The ability to borrow money means a bank can avoid being forced to sell its assets at fire-sale prices in order to satisfy the demands of a sudden rush of depositors demanding cash. Instead, it can turn to the Federal Reserve and borrow the funds it needs to pay off depositors.

Deposit insurance guarantees that a bank's depositors will be paid even if the bank can't come up with the funds, up to a maximum amount per account.

Reserve requirements are rules set by the Federal Reserve that determine the required reserve ratio for banks.

The discount window is an arrangement in which the Federal Reserve stands ready to lend money to banks.

Determining the Money Supply

Without banks, there would be no checkable deposits, and so the quantity of currency in circulation would equal the money supply. In that case, the money supply would be determined solely by whoever controls government minting and printing presses.

But banks do exist, and through their creation of checkable bank deposits, they affect the money supply in two ways.

1. Banks remove some currency from circulation: dollar bills that are sitting in bank vaults, as opposed to sitting in people's wallets, aren't part of the money supply.

2. Much more importantly, banks create money by accepting deposits and making loans—that is, they make the money supply larger than just the value of currency in circulation.

Next we cover how banks create money and what determines the amount of money they create.

How Banks Create Money

To see how banks create money, let's examine what happens when someone decides to deposit currency in a bank. Consider the example of Silas, a miser, who keeps a shoebox full of cash under his bed. Suppose Silas realizes that it would be safer, as well as more convenient, to deposit that cash in the bank and to use his debit card when shopping. Assume that he deposits $1,000 into a checkable account at First Street Bank. What effect will Silas's actions have on the money supply?

Panel (a) of Figure 34-3 shows the initial effect of his deposit. First Street Bank credits Silas with $1,000 in his account, so the economy's checkable bank deposits rise by $1,000. Meanwhile, Silas's cash goes into the vault, raising First Street Bank's reserves by $1,000 as well.

Money creation begins when cash is deposited into a checkable bank account.

This initial transaction has no effect on the money supply. Currency in circulation, part of the money supply, falls by $1,000; checkable bank deposits, also part of the money supply, rise by the same amount.

But this is not the end of the story because First Street Bank can now lend out part of Silas's deposit. Assume that it holds 10% of Silas's deposit—$100—in reserves and lends the rest out in cash to Silas's neighbor, Mary. The effect of this second stage is shown in panel (b). First Street Bank's deposits remain unchanged, and so does the value of its assets. But the composition of its assets changes: by making the loan, it reduces its reserves by $900, so that they are only $100 larger than they were before Silas made his deposit. In the place of the $900 reduction in reserves, the bank has acquired an IOU, its $900 cash loan to Mary.

FIGURE 34-3

Effect on the Money Supply of Turning Cash into a Checkable Deposit at First Street Bank

(a) Initial Effect Before Bank Makes a New Loan

Assets		Liabilities	
Loans	No change	Checkable deposits	+$1,000
Reserves	+$1,000		

(b) Effect When Bank Makes a New Loan

Assets		Liabilities
Loans	+$900	No change
Reserves	−$900	

When Silas deposits $1,000 (which had been stashed under his bed) into a checkable bank account, there is initially no effect on the money supply: currency in circulation falls by $1,000, but checkable bank deposits rise by $1,000. The corresponding entries on the bank's T-account, depicted in panel (a), show deposits initially rising by $1,000 and the bank's reserves initially rising by $1,000. In the second stage, depicted in panel (b), the bank holds 10% of Silas's deposit ($100) as reserves and lends out the rest ($900) to Mary. As a result, its reserves fall by $900 and its loans increase by $900. Its liabilities, including Silas's $1,000 deposit, are unchanged. The money supply, the sum of checkable bank deposits and currency in circulation, has now increased by $900—the $900 now held by Mary.

The money supply increases when banks lend out a portion of their cash deposits.

So by putting $900 of Silas's cash back into circulation by lending it to Mary, First Street Bank has, in fact, increased the money supply. That is, the sum of currency in circulation and checkable bank deposits has risen by $900 compared to what it had been when Silas's cash was still under his bed. Although Silas is still the owner of $1,000, now in the form of a checkable deposit, Mary has the use of $900 in cash from her borrowings.

And this may not be the end of the story. Suppose that Mary uses her cash to buy a television and a tablet from Acme Electronics. What does Anne Acme, the store's owner, do with the cash? If she holds on to it, the money supply doesn't increase any further. But suppose she deposits the $900 into a checkable bank deposit—say, at Second Street Bank. Second Street Bank, in turn, will keep only part of that deposit in reserves, lending out the rest, creating still more money.

Assume that Second Street Bank, like First Street Bank, keeps 10% of any bank deposit in reserves and lends out the rest. Then it will keep $90 in reserves and lend out $810 of Anne's deposit to another borrower, further increasing the money supply.

Table 34-1 shows the process of money creation we have described so far. At first the money supply consists only of Silas's $1,000. After he deposits the cash into a checkable bank deposit and the bank makes a loan, the money supply rises to $1,900. After the second deposit and the second loan, the money supply rises to $2,710. And the process will, of course, continue from there. (Although we have considered the case in which Silas places his cash in a checkable bank deposit, the results would be the same if he put it into any type of near-money.)

TABLE 34-1

How Banks Create Money

	Currency in circulation	Checkable bank deposits	Money supply
First stage Silas keeps his cash under his bed.	$1,000	$0	$1,000
Second stage Silas deposits cash in First Street Bank, which lends out $900 to Mary, who then pays it to Anne Acme.	900	1,000	1,900
Third stage Anne Acme deposits $900 in Second Street Bank, which lends out $810 to another borrower.	810	1,900	2,710

This process of money creation may sound familiar. Recall the *multiplier process* that we described earlier: an initial increase in real GDP leads to a rise in consumer spending, which leads to a further rise in real GDP, which leads to a further rise in consumer spending, and so on. What we have here is another kind of multiplier—the *money multiplier*. Next, we'll learn what determines the size of this multiplier.

Reserves, Bank Deposits, and the Money Multiplier

In tracing out the effect of Silas's deposit in Table 34-1, we assumed that the funds a bank lends out always end up being deposited either in the same bank or in another bank—so funds disbursed as loans come back to the banking system, even if not to the lending bank itself.

In reality, some of these loaned funds may be held by borrowers in their wallets and not deposited in a bank, meaning that some of the loaned amount "leaks" out of the banking system. Such leaks reduce the size of the money multiplier, just as leaks of real income into savings reduce the size of the real GDP multiplier. (Bear in mind, however, that the "leak" here comes from the fact that borrowers keep some of their funds in currency, rather than the fact that consumers save some of their income.)

But let's set that complication aside for a moment and consider how the money supply is determined in a "checkable-deposits-only" monetary system, where funds are always deposited in bank accounts and none are held in wallets as currency. That is, in our checkable-deposits-only monetary system, any and all funds borrowed from a bank are immediately deposited into a checkable bank account. We'll assume that banks are required to satisfy a minimum reserve ratio of 10% and that every bank lends out all of its **excess reserves,** reserves over and above the amount needed to satisfy the minimum reserve ratio.

Now suppose that for some reason a bank suddenly finds itself with $1,000 in excess reserves. What happens? The answer is that the bank will lend out that $1,000, which will end up as a checkable bank deposit somewhere in the banking system, launching a money multiplier process very similar to the process shown in Table 34-1.

In the first stage, the bank lends out its excess reserves of $1,000, which becomes a checkable bank deposit somewhere. The bank that receives the $1,000 deposit keeps 10%, or $100, as reserves and lends out the remaining 90%, or $900, which again becomes a checkable bank deposit somewhere. The bank receiving this $900 deposit again keeps 10%, which is $90, as reserves and lends out the remaining $810. The bank receiving this $810 keeps $81 in reserves and lends out the remaining $729, and so on.

As a result of this process, the total increase in checkable bank deposits is equal to a sum that looks like:

$$\$1{,}000 + \$900 + \$810 + \$729 + \ldots$$

We'll use the symbol rr for the reserve ratio. More generally, the total increase in checkable bank deposits that is generated when a bank lends out $1,000 in excess reserves is the:

(34-1) Increase in checkable bank deposits from $1,000 in excess reserves = $\$1{,}000 + (\$1{,}000 \times (1 - rr)) + (\$1{,}000 \times (1 - rr)^2) + (\$1{,}000 \times (1 - rr)^3) + \ldots$

As we have seen, an infinite series of this form can be simplified to:

(34-2) Increase in checkable bank deposits from $1,000 in excess reserves = $\$1{,}000/rr$

Given a reserve ratio of 10%, or 0.1, a $1,000 increase in excess reserves will increase the total value of checkable bank deposits by $1,000/0.1 = $10,000. In fact, in a checkable-deposits-only monetary system, the total value of checkable bank deposits will be equal to the value of bank reserves divided by the reserve ratio. Or to put it a different way, if the reserve ratio is 10%, each $1 of reserves held by a bank supports $1/rr = $1/0.1 = $10 of checkable bank deposits.

The Money Multiplier in Reality

In reality, the determination of the money supply is more complicated than our simple model suggests because it depends not only on the ratio of reserves to bank deposits but also on the fraction of the money supply that individuals choose to hold in the form of currency. In fact, we already saw this in our example of Silas depositing the cash under his bed: when he chose to hold a checkable bank deposit instead of currency, he set in motion an increase in the money supply.

To define the money multiplier in practice, it's important to recognize that the Federal Reserve controls the *sum* of bank reserves and currency in circulation, called the *monetary base,* but it does not control the allocation of that sum between bank reserves and currency in circulation. Consider Silas and his deposit one more time: by taking the cash from under his bed and depositing it in a bank, he reduces the quantity of currency in circulation but increases bank reserves by an equal amount— leaving the monetary base, on net, unchanged. The **monetary base,** which is the quantity the monetary authorities control, is the sum of currency in circulation and reserves held by banks.

Excess reserves are a bank's reserves over and above its required reserves.

The **monetary base** is the sum of currency in circulation and bank reserves.

The monetary base is different from the money supply in two ways.

1. Bank reserves, which are part of the monetary base, aren't considered part of the money supply. A $1 bill in someone's wallet is considered money because it's available for an individual to spend, but a $1 bill held as bank reserves in a bank vault or deposited at the Federal Reserve isn't considered part of the money supply because it's not available for spending.

2. Checkable bank deposits, which are part of the money supply because they are available for spending, aren't part of the monetary base.

Figure 34-4 shows the two concepts schematically. The circle on the left represents the monetary base, consisting of bank reserves plus currency in circulation. The circle on the right represents the money supply, consisting mainly of currency in circulation plus checkable or near-checkable bank deposits. As the figure indicates, currency in circulation is part of both the monetary base and the money supply. But bank reserves aren't part of the money supply, and checkable or near-checkable bank deposits aren't part of the monetary base. In normal times, most of the monetary base actually consists of currency in circulation, which also makes up about half of the money supply.

FIGURE 34-4   The Monetary Base and the Money Supply

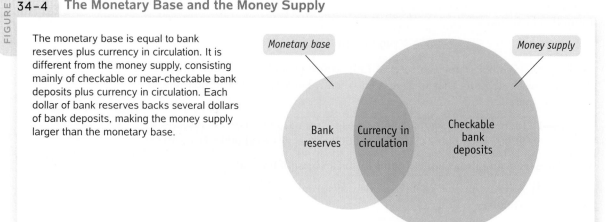

The monetary base is equal to bank reserves plus currency in circulation. It is different from the money supply, consisting mainly of checkable or near-checkable bank deposits plus currency in circulation. Each dollar of bank reserves backs several dollars of bank deposits, making the money supply larger than the monetary base.

Now we can formally define the **money multiplier:** it's the ratio of the money supply to the monetary base. In normal times the money multiplier in the United States, using M1 as our measure of money, has fluctuated between 3.0 and 1.5. During the recession of 2007–2009, it fell to about 0.7. Even in normal times, that's a lot smaller than $1/0.1 = 10$, the money multiplier in a checkable-deposits-only system with a reserve ratio of 10% (the minimum required ratio for most checkable deposits in the United States).

The reason the actual money multiplier is so small arises from the fact that people hold significant amounts of cash, and a dollar of currency in circulation, unlike a dollar in reserves, doesn't support multiple dollars of the money supply. In fact, currency in circulation normally accounts for more than 90% of the monetary base. However, in April 2013, currency in circulation was $1,107 billion, compared with a monetary base of $3,061 billion—just about 36%. What had happened?

Notice that earlier we said "in normal times." As we'll see in upcoming modules, a very abnormal situation developed after Lehman Brothers, a key financial institution, failed in September 2008. Banks, seeing few opportunities for safe, profitable lending, began parking large sums at the Federal Reserve in the form of deposits—deposits that counted as part of the monetary base. As a result, currency in circulation in April 2013 made up only 36% of the monetary base, and the monetary base was actually larger than M1, with the money multiplier therefore less than 1.

The **money multiplier** is the ratio of the money supply to the monetary base.

Module 34 Review

Solutions appear at the back of the book.

Check Your Understanding

1. Suppose you are a depositor at First Street Bank. You hear a rumor that the bank has suffered serious losses on its loans. Every depositor knows that the rumor isn't true, but each thinks that most other depositors believe the rumor. Why, in the absence of deposit insurance, could this lead to a bank run? How does deposit insurance change the situation?

2. A con artist has a great idea: he'll open a bank without investing any capital and lend all the deposits at high interest rates to real estate developers. If the real estate market booms, the loans will be repaid and he'll make high profits. If the real estate market goes bust, the loans won't be repaid and the bank will fail—but he will not lose any of his own wealth. How would modern bank regulation frustrate his scheme?

3. Assume that total reserves are equal to $200 and total checkable bank deposits are equal to $1,000. Also assume that the public does not hold any currency and banks hold no excess reserves. Now suppose that the required reserve ratio falls from 20% to 10%. Trace out how this leads to an expansion in bank deposits.

4. Take the example of Silas depositing his $1,000 in cash into First Street Bank and assume that the required reserve ratio is 10%. But now assume that each recipient of a bank loan keeps half the loan in cash and deposits the rest. Trace out the resulting expansion in the money supply through at least three rounds of deposits.

Multiple-Choice Questions

1. Bank reserves include which of the following?
   I.   currency in bank vaults
   II. bank deposits held in accounts at the Federal Reserve
   III. customer deposits in bank checking accounts
   a. I only
   b. II only
   c. III only
   d. I and II only
   e. I, II, and III

2. The fraction of bank deposits actually held as reserves is the
   a. reserve ratio.
   b. required reserve ratio.
   c. excess reserve ratio.
   d. reserve requirement.
   e. monetary base.

3. Bank regulation includes which of the following?
   I.   deposit insurance
   II. capital requirements
   III. reserve requirements
   a. I only
   b. II only
   c. III only
   d. I and II
   e. I, II, and III

4. Which of the following changes would be the most likely to reduce the size of the money multiplier?
   a. a decrease in the required reserve ratio
   b. a decrease in excess reserves
   c. an increase in cash holding by consumers
   d. a decrease in bank runs
   e. an increase in deposit insurance

5. The monetary base equals
   a. currency in circulation.
   b. reserves held by banks.
   c. currency in circulation − reserves held by banks.
   d. currency in circulation + reserves held by banks.
   e. currency in circulation/reserves held by banks.

Critical-Thinking Questions

Assume that the required reserve ratio is 5% to answer the following.

1. If a bank has deposits of $100,000 and holds $10,000 as reserves, how much are its excess reserves? Explain.

2. If a bank holds no excess reserves and it receives a new deposit of $1,000, how much of that $1,000 can the bank lend out and how much is the bank required to add to its reserves? Explain.

3. By how much can an increase in excess reserves of $2,000 change the money supply in a checkable-deposits-only system? Explain.

Visions of America/JoeSohm/Getty Images

MODULE 35 ⟩ The Federal Reserve System

WHAT YOU WILL LEARN

1. **The structure of the Federal Reserve System**

2. **The history of the Federal Reserve System**

3. **How the Federal Reserve has responded to major financial crises**

Who's in charge of ensuring that banks maintain enough reserves? Who decides how large the monetary base will be? The answer, in the United States, is an institution known as the Federal Reserve (or, informally, as "the Fed"). The Federal Reserve is a **central bank**—an institution that oversees and regulates the banking system and controls the monetary base. Other central banks include the Bank of England, the Bank of Japan, and the European Central Bank, or ECB. The ECB acts as a common central bank for 18 European countries.

The Structure of the Fed

The legal status of the Fed, which was created in 1913, is unusual: it is not exactly part of the U.S. government, but it is not really a private institution either. Strictly speaking, the Federal Reserve System consists two parts: the Board of Governors and the 12 regional Federal Reserve Banks.

The Board of Governors, which oversees the entire system from its offices in Washington, D.C., is constituted like a government agency: its seven members are appointed by the president and must be approved by the Senate. However, they are appointed for 14-year terms.

Although the chair is appointed more frequently—every four years—it is traditional for the chair to be reappointed and serve much longer terms. For example, William McChesney Martin was chair of the Fed from 1951 until 1970. Alan Greenspan, appointed in 1987, served as the Fed's chair until 2006. By comparison, Ben Bernanke's tenure as chair, from 2006 to early 2014, was on the brief side.

The 12 Federal Reserve Banks each serve a region of the country, providing various banking and supervisory services. One of their jobs, for example, is to audit the books of private-sector banks to ensure their financial health. Each regional bank is run by a board of directors chosen from the local banking and business community. The

A **central bank** is an institution that oversees and regulates the banking system and controls the monetary base.

362

FIGURE   35-1 **The Federal Reserve System**

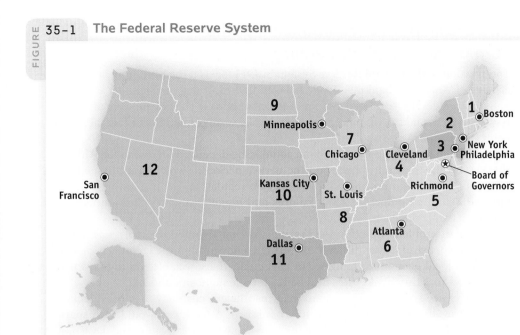

Alaska and Hawaii are part of the San Francisco District

The Federal Reserve System consists of the Board of Governors in Washington, D.C., plus 12 regional Federal Reserve Banks. This map shows each of the 12 Federal Reserve districts.
Source: Board of Governors of the Federal Reserve System.

Federal Reserve Bank of New York plays a special role: it carries out *open-market operations,* usually the main tool of monetary policy. Figure 35-1 shows the 12 Federal Reserve districts and the city in which each regional Federal Reserve Bank is located.

Decisions about monetary policy are made by the Federal Open Market Committee, which consists of the Board of Governors plus five of the regional bank presidents. The president of the Federal Reserve Bank of New York is always on the committee, and the other four seats rotate among the 11 other regional bank presidents. The chair of the Board of Governors normally also serves as the chair of the Federal Open Market Committee.

The effect of this complex structure is to create an institution that is ultimately accountable to the voting public because the Board of Governors is chosen by elected officials. But the long terms served by board members, as well as the indirectness of their appointment process, largely insulate them from short-term political pressures.

The Evolution of the American Banking System

Up to this point in the section, we have been describing the U.S. banking system and how it works. To fully understand that system, however, it is helpful to understand how and why it was created—a story that is closely intertwined with the story of how and when things went wrong. For the key elements of twenty-first-century U.S. banking weren't created out of thin air: efforts to change both the regulations that govern banking and the Federal Reserve System that began in 2008 have propelled financial reform to the forefront. This reform promises to continue reshaping the financial system well into future years.

The Crisis in American Banking at the Turn of the Twentieth Century

The creation of the Federal Reserve System in 1913 marked the beginning of the modern era of American banking. From 1864 until 1913, American banking was dominated by a federally regulated system of national banks. They alone were allowed to issue currency, and the currency notes they issued were printed by the federal government with uniform size and design.

How much currency a national bank could issue depended on its capital. Although this system was an improvement on the earlier period in which banks issued their own notes with no uniformity and virtually no regulation, the national banking regime still suffered numerous bank failures and major financial crises—at least one and often two per decade.

The main problem afflicting the system was that the money supply was not sufficiently responsive: it was difficult to shift currency around the country to respond quickly to local economic changes. (In particular, there was often a tug-of-war between New York City banks and rural banks for adequate amounts of currency.)

As we've seen, rumors that a bank had insufficient currency to satisfy demands for withdrawals would quickly lead to a bank run. A bank run would then spark a contagion, setting off runs at nearby banks, sowing widespread panic and devastation in the local economy. In response, bankers in some locations pooled resources to create local clearinghouses that would guarantee a member's liabilities in the event of a panic, and some state governments began offering deposit insurance on their banks' deposits.

However, the cause of the Panic of 1907 was different from those of previous crises; in fact, its cause was eerily similar to the roots of the 2008 crisis. Ground zero of the 1907 panic was New York City, but the consequences devastated the entire country, leading to a deep four-year recession.

The crisis originated in institutions in New York known as *trusts,* bank-like institutions that accepted deposits but that were originally intended to manage only inheritances and estates for wealthy clients. Because these trusts were supposed to engage only in low-risk activities, they were less regulated, had lower reserve requirements, and had lower cash reserves than national banks.

In both the Panic of 1907 and the financial crisis of 2008, large losses from risky speculation destabilized the banking system.

However, as the American economy boomed during the first decade of the twentieth century, trusts began speculating in real estate and the stock market, areas forbidden to national banks. Less regulated than national banks, trusts were able to pay their depositors higher returns. Yet trusts took a free ride on national banks' reputation for soundness, with depositors considering them equally safe.

As a result, trusts grew rapidly: by 1907, the total assets of trusts in New York City were as large as those of national banks. Meanwhile, the trusts declined to join the New York Clearinghouse, a consortium of New York City national banks that guaranteed one another's soundness; that would have required the trusts to hold higher cash reserves, reducing their profits.

The Panic of 1907 began with the failure of the Knickerbocker Trust, a large New York City trust that failed when it suffered massive losses in unsuccessful stock market speculation. Quickly, other New York trusts came under pressure, and frightened depositors began queuing in long lines to withdraw their funds. The New York Clearinghouse declined to step in and lend to the trusts, and even healthy trusts came under serious assault.

Within two days, a dozen major trusts had gone under. Credit markets froze, the stock market fell dramatically as stock traders were unable to get credit to finance their trades, and business confidence evaporated.

Fortunately, one of New York City's wealthiest men, the banker J. P. Morgan, quickly stepped in to stop the panic. Understanding that the crisis would spread and soon engulf healthy institutions, trusts and banks alike, he worked with other bankers, wealthy men such as John D. Rockefeller, and the U.S. Secretary of the Treasury to shore up the reserves of banks and trusts to withstand the onslaught of withdrawals. Once people were assured that they could withdraw their money, the panic ceased.

Although the panic itself lasted little more than a week, it and the stock market collapse decimated the economy. A four-year recession ensued, with production falling 11% and unemployment rising from 3% to 8%.

Responding to Banking Crises: The Creation of the Federal Reserve

Concerns over frequent banking crises and the unprecedented role of J. P. Morgan in saving the financial system prompted the federal government to initiate banking reform. In 1913 the national banking system was eliminated and the Federal Reserve System was created as a way to compel all deposit-taking institutions to hold adequate reserves and open their accounts to inspection by regulators.

The Panic of 1907 convinced many that the time for centralized control of bank reserves had come. In addition, the Federal Reserve was given the sole right to issue currency in order to make the money supply sufficiently responsive to satisfy economic conditions around the country.

THE EFFECTIVENESS OF THE FEDERAL RESERVE SYSTEM Although the Federal Reserve System standardized and centralized the holding of bank reserves, it did not eliminate the potential for bank runs because banks' reserves were still less than the total value of their deposits. The potential for more bank runs became a reality during the Great Depression. Plunging commodity prices hit American farmers particularly hard, precipitating a series of bank runs in 1930, 1931, and 1933, each of which started at midwestern banks and then spread throughout the country.

After the failure of a particularly large bank in 1930, federal officials realized that the economy-wide effects compelled them to take a less hands-off approach and to intervene more vigorously. In 1932, the Reconstruction Finance Corporation (RFC) was established and given the authority to make loans to banks in order to stabilize the banking sector.

Also, the Glass-Steagall Act of 1933, which increased the ability of banks to borrow from the Federal Reserve System, was passed. A loan to a leading Chicago bank from the Federal Reserve appears to have stopped a major banking crisis in 1932. However, the beast had not yet been tamed. Banks became fearful of borrowing from the RFC because doing so signaled weakness to the public.

During the midst of the catastrophic bank run of 1933, the new U.S. president, Franklin Delano Roosevelt, was inaugurated. He immediately declared a "bank holiday," closing all banks until regulators could get a handle on the problem.

In March 1933, emergency measures were adopted that gave the RFC extraordinary powers to stabilize and restructure the banking industry by providing capital to banks either by loans or by outright purchases of bank shares. With the new regulations, regulators closed nonviable banks and recapitalized viable ones by allowing the RFC to buy preferred shares in banks (shares that gave the U.S. government more rights than regular shareholders) and by greatly expanding banks' ability to borrow from the Federal Reserve.

By 1933, the RFC had invested over $17 billion (2013 dollars) in bank capital—one-third of the total capital of all banks in the United States at that time—and purchased shares in almost one-half of all banks. The RFC loaned more than $34 billion (2013 dollars) to banks during this period.

Economic historians uniformly agree that the banking crises of the early 1930s greatly exacerbated the severity of the Great Depression, rendering monetary policy ineffective as the banking sector broke down and currency, withdrawn from banks and stashed under beds, reduced the money supply.

A **commercial bank** accepts deposits and is covered by deposit insurance.

An **investment bank** trades in financial assets and is not covered by deposit insurance.

A **savings and loan (thrift)** is another type of deposit-taking bank, usually specialized in issuing home loans.

THE GLASS-STEAGALL ACT Although the powerful actions of the RFC stabilized the banking industry, new legislation was needed to prevent future banking crises. The Glass-Steagall Act separated banks into two categories: **commercial banks,** depository banks that accepted deposits and were covered by deposit insurance, and **investment banks,** which engaged in creating and trading financial assets such as stocks and corporate bonds but were not covered by deposit insurance because their activities were considered more risky.

Regulation Q prevented commercial banks from paying interest on checking accounts, in the belief that this would promote unhealthy competition between banks. In addition, investment banks were much more lightly regulated than commercial banks. The most important measure for the prevention of bank runs, however, was the adoption of federal deposit insurance (with an original limit of $2,500 per deposit).

These measures were clearly successful, and the United States enjoyed a long period of financial and banking stability. As memories of the bad old days dimmed, Depression-era bank regulations were lifted. In 1980 Regulation Q was eliminated, and by 1999, the Glass-Steagall Act had been so weakened that offering services like trading financial assets were no longer off-limits to commercial banks.

The Savings and Loan Crisis of the 1980s

Along with banks, the banking industry also included **savings and loans** (also called S&Ls or **thrifts**), institutions designed to accept savings and turn them into long-term mortgages for home-buyers. S&Ls were covered by federal deposit insurance and were tightly regulated for safety. However, trouble hit in the 1970s, as high inflation led savers to withdraw their funds from low-interest-paying S&L accounts and put them into higher-interest-paying money market accounts. In addition, the high inflation rate severely eroded the value of the S&Ls' assets, the long-term mortgages they held on their books.

In order to improve S&Ls' competitive position vis-à-vis banks, Congress eased regulations to allow S&Ls to undertake riskier investments in addition to long-term home mortgages. However, the new freedom did not bring with it increased oversight, leaving S&Ls with less oversight than banks. Unsurprisingly, during the real estate boom of the 1970s and 1980s, S&Ls engaged in overly risky real estate lending. There was also corruption as some S&L executives used their institutions as private piggy banks.

Unfortunately, during the late 1970s and early 1980s, political interference from Congress kept insolvent S&Ls open when a bank in a comparable situation would have been quickly shut down by regulators. By the early 1980s, many S&Ls had failed. Because accounts were covered by federal deposit insurance, the liabilities of a failed S&L became liabilities of the federal government, and depositors had to be paid from taxpayer funds. From 1986 through 1995, the government closed over 1,000 failed S&Ls, costing U.S. taxpayers over $124 billion dollars.

In a classic case of shutting the barn door after the horse has escaped, in 1989 Congress put in place comprehensive oversight of S&L activities. It also empowered Fannie Mae and Freddie Mac to take over much of the home mortgage lending previously done by S&Ls. Fannie Mae and Freddie Mac are quasi-governmental agencies created during the Great Depression to make homeownership more affordable for low- and moderate-income households. It has been calculated that the S&L crisis helped cause a steep slowdown in the finance and real estate industries, leading to the recession of the early 1990s.

Back to the Future: The Financial Crisis of 2008

The financial crisis of 2008 shared features of previous crises. Like the Panic of 1907 and the S&L crisis, it involved institutions that were not as strictly regulated as deposit-taking banks, as well as excessive speculation. Like the crises of the early 1930s, it involved a U.S. government that was reluctant to take aggressive action until the scale of the devastation became clear. In addition, by the late 1990s, advances in technology and financial innovation had created yet another systemic weakness that played a central role in 2008. The story of Long-Term Capital Management, or LTCM, highlights these problems.

LONG-TERM CAPITAL (MIS)MANAGEMENT Created in 1994, LTCM was a *hedge fund*, a private investment partnership open only to wealthy individuals and institutions. Hedge funds are virtually unregulated, allowing them to make much riskier investments than mutual funds, which are open to the average investor. Using vast amounts of **leverage**—that is, borrowed money—in order to increase its returns, LTCM used sophisticated computer models to make money by taking advantage of small differences in asset prices in global financial markets to buy at a lower price and sell at a higher price. In one year, LTCM made a return as high as 40%.

LTCM was also heavily involved in *derivatives,* complex financial instruments that are constructed—derived—from the obligations of more basic financial assets. Derivatives are popular investment tools because they are cheaper to trade than basic financial assets and can be constructed to suit a buyer's or seller's particular needs. Yet their complexity can make it extremely hard to measure their value. LTCM believed that its computer models allowed it to accurately gauge the risk in the huge bets that it was undertaking in derivatives using borrowed money.

However, LTCM's computer models hadn't factored in a series of financial crises in Asia and in Russia during 1997 and 1998. Through its large borrowing, LTCM had become such a big player in global financial markets that attempts to sell its assets depressed the prices of what it was trying to sell. As the markets fell around the world and LTCM's panic-stricken investors demanded the return of their funds, LTCM's losses mounted as it tried to sell assets to satisfy those demands. Quickly, its operations collapsed because it could no longer borrow money and other parties refused to trade with it. Financial markets around the world froze in panic.

The Federal Reserve realized that allowing LTCM's remaining assets to be sold at panic-stricken prices presented a grave risk to the entire financial system through the **balance sheet effect:** as sales of assets by LTCM depressed asset prices all over the world, other firms would see the value of their balance sheets fall as assets held on these balance sheets declined in value.

Moreover, falling asset prices meant the value of assets held by borrowers on their balance sheet would fall below a critical threshold, leading to a default on the terms of their credit contracts and forcing creditors to call in their loans. This in turn would lead to more sales of assets as borrowers tried to raise cash to repay their loans, more credit defaults, and more loans called in, creating a **vicious cycle of deleveraging.**

The Federal Reserve Bank of New York arranged a $3.625 billion bailout of LTCM in 1998, in which other private institutions took on shares of LTCM's assets and obligations, liquidated them in an orderly manner, and eventually turned a small profit. Quick action by the Federal Reserve Bank of New York prevented LTCM from sparking a contagion, yet virtually all of LTCM's investors were wiped out.

SUBPRIME LENDING AND THE HOUSING BUBBLE After the LTCM crisis, U.S. financial markets stabilized. They remained more or less stable even as stock prices fell sharply from 2000 to 2002 and the U.S. economy went into recession. During the recovery from the 2001 recession, however, the seeds for another financial crisis were planted.

The story begins with low interest rates: by 2003, U.S. interest rates were at historically low levels, partly because of Federal Reserve policy and partly because of large inflows of capital from other countries, especially China. These low interest rates helped cause a boom in housing, which in turn led the U.S. economy out of recession. As housing boomed,

A financial institution engages in leverage when it finances its investments with borrowed funds.

The balance sheet effect is the reduction in a firm's net worth from falling asset prices.

A vicious cycle of deleveraging takes place when asset sales to cover losses produce negative balance sheet effects on other firms and force creditors to call in their loans, forcing sales of more assets and causing further declines in asset prices.

"Honey, we're homeless."

Subprime lending is lending to home buyers who don't meet the usual criteria for being able to afford their payments.

In **securitization** a pool of loans is assembled and shares of that pool are sold to investors.

however, financial institutions began taking on growing risks—risks that were not well understood.

Traditionally, people were able to borrow money to buy homes only if they had sufficient income to meet the mortgage payments. Making home loans to people who didn't meet the usual criteria for borrowing, called **subprime lending,** was only a minor part of overall lending. But in the booming housing market of 2003–2006, subprime lending started to seem like a safe bet. Since housing prices kept rising, borrowers who couldn't make their mortgage payments could always pay off their mortgages, if necessary, by selling their homes. As a result, subprime lending exploded.

Who was making these subprime loans? For the most part, it wasn't traditional banks lending out depositors' money. Instead, most of the loans were made by "loan originators," who quickly sold mortgages to other investors. These sales were made possible by a process known as **securitization:** financial institutions assembled pools of loans and sold shares in the income from these pools. These shares were considered relatively safe investments since it was considered unlikely that large numbers of home-buyers would default on their payments at the same time.

But that's exactly what happened. The housing boom turned out to be a bubble, and when home prices started falling in late 2006, many subprime borrowers were unable either to meet their mortgage payments or sell their houses for enough to pay off their mortgages. As a result, investors in securities backed by subprime mortgages started taking heavy losses. Many of the mortgage-backed assets were held by financial institutions, including banks and other institutions playing bank-like roles. Like the trusts that played a key role in the Panic of 1907, these "nonbank banks" were less regulated than commercial banks, which allowed them to offer higher returns to investors but left them extremely vulnerable in a crisis. Mortgage-related losses, in turn, led to a collapse of trust in the financial system.

Figure 35-2 shows one measure of this loss of trust: the TED spread, which is the difference between the interest rate on three-month loans that banks make to each other and the interest rate the federal government pays on three-month bonds. Since government bonds are considered extremely safe, the TED spread shows how much risk banks think they're taking on when lending to each other. Normally, the spread is around a quarter of a percentage point, but it shot up in August 2007 and surged to an unprecedented 4.58 percentage points in October 2008 before returning to more normal levels in mid-2009.

FIGURE 35-2   The TED Spread

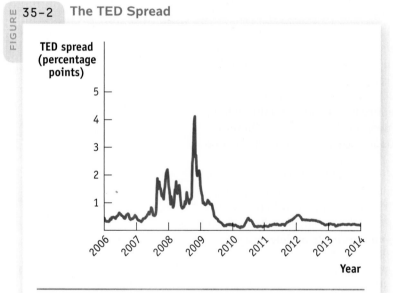

The TED spread is the difference between the interest rate at which banks lend to each other and the interest rate on U.S. government debt. It's widely used as a measure of financial stress. The TED spread soared as a result of the financial crisis of 2007–2008.

Source: Federal Reserve Bank of St. Louis.

CRISIS AND RESPONSE The collapse of trust in the financial system, combined with the large losses suffered by financial firms, led to a severe cycle of deleveraging and a credit crunch for the economy as a whole. Firms found it difficult to borrow, even for short-term operations; individuals found home loans unavailable and credit card limits reduced.

Overall, the negative economic effect of the financial crisis bore a distinct and troubling resemblance to the effects of the banking crisis of the early 1930s, which helped cause the Great Depression. Policy makers noticed the resemblance and tried to prevent a repeat performance. Beginning in August 2007, the Federal Reserve engaged in a series of efforts to provide cash to the financial system, lending funds to a widening range of institutions and buying private-sector debt. The Fed and the

Treasury Department also stepped in to rescue individual firms that were deemed too crucial to be allowed to fail, such as the investment bank Bear Stearns and the insurance company AIG.

In September 2008, however, policy makers decided that one major investment bank, Lehman Brothers, could be allowed to fail. They quickly regretted the decision. Within days of Lehman's failure, widespread panic gripped the financial markets, as illustrated by the late surge in the TED spread shown in Figure 35-2. In response to the intensified crisis, the U.S. government intervened further to support the financial system, as the U.S. Treasury began "injecting" capital into banks. Injecting capital, in practice, meant that the U.S. government would supply cash to banks in return for shares—in effect, partially nationalizing the financial system.

The crisis of 2008 led to major changes in the financial system, the largest changes since the 1930s. The crisis raised new questions about the appropriate scope of safety nets and regulations and, like the crises preceding it, exerted a powerful negative effect on the rest of the economy. There is a detailed discussion of the crisis and its impact in Module 42.

Like FDR, President Obama was faced with a major financial crisis upon taking office.

ECONOMICS ▶ *IN ACTION*

REGULATION AFTER THE 2008 CRISIS

In 2010, President Obama signed the Wall Street Reform and Consumer Protection Act—generally known as Dodd-Frank, after its sponsors in the Senate and House, respectively—into law. It was the biggest financial reform enacted since the 1930s—not surprising given that the nation had just gone through the worst financial crisis since the 1930s. How did Dodd-Frank change regulation?

For the most part, it left regulation of traditional deposit-taking banks more or less as it was. The main change facing these banks was the creation of a new agency, the Bureau of Consumer Financial Protection, whose mission was to protect borrowers from being exploited through seemingly attractive financial deals they didn't understand.

The major changes came in the regulation of financial institutions other than banks—institutions that, as the fall of Lehman Brothers showed, could trigger banking crises.

The new law gave a special government committee, the Financial Stability Oversight Council, the right to designate certain institutions as "systemically important" even if they weren't ordinary deposit-taking banks. These systemically important institutions would be subjected to bank-style regulation, including relatively high capital requirements and limits on the kinds of risks they could take. In addition, the federal government would acquire "resolution authority," meaning the right to seize troubled financial institutions in much the same way that it routinely takes over troubled banks.

Dodd-Frank was an attempt to extend the spirit of old-fashioned bank regulation to today's more complex financial system.

Beyond this, the law established new rules on the trading of derivatives: most derivatives would have to be bought and sold on exchanges, where everyone could observe their prices and the volume of transactions. The idea was to make the risks taken by financial institutions more transparent. Will Dodd-Frank succeed in heading off future banking crises? Stay tuned.

MODULE 35 Review

Solutions appear at the back of the book.

Check Your Understanding

1. What are the similarities between the Panic of 1907, the S&L crisis, and the crisis of 2008?

2. Why did the creation of the Federal Reserve fail to prevent the bank runs of the Great Depression? What measures did stop the bank runs?

3. Describe the balance sheet effect. Describe the vicious cycle of deleveraging. Why is it necessary for the government to step in to halt a vicious cycle of deleveraging?

Multiple-Choice Questions

1. Which of the following contributed to the creation of the Federal Reserve System?

   I. the bank panic of 1907
   II. the Great Depression
   III. the savings and loan crisis of the 1980s

   a. I only
   b. II only
   c. III only
   d. I and II only
   e. I, II, and III

2. Which of the following is a part of both the Federal Reserve System and the federal government?

   a. the Federal Reserve Board of Governors
   b. the 12 regional Federal Reserve Banks
   c. the Reconstruction Finance Corporation
   d. commercial banks
   e. the Treasury Department

3. Which of the following is NOT a role of the Federal Reserve System?

   a. controlling bank reserves
   b. printing currency (Federal Reserve notes)
   c. carrying out monetary policy
   d. supervising and regulating banks
   e. holding reserves for commercial banks

4. Who oversees the Federal Reserve System?

   a. the presidents of the Regional Federal Reserve Banks
   b. the president of the United States
   c. the Federal Open Market Committee
   d. the Board of Governors of the Federal Reserve System
   e. the Reconstruction Finance Corporation

5. Which of the following contributed to the financial crisis of 2008?

   a. subprime lending
   b. securitization
   c. deleveraging
   d. low interest rates leading to a housing boom
   e. all of the above

Critical-Thinking Questions

Answer the following questions about the Board of Governors of the Federal Reserve System.

1. What does the Board of Governors of the Federal Reserve System do?

2. How many members serve on the group?

3. Who appoints members?

4. How long do members serve?

5. Why do they serve a term of this length?

6. How long does the chair serve?

Jeff Greenberg/Alamy

BUSINESS
CASE : ## The Perfect Gift: Cash or a Gift Card?

Over the past few years, more and more people have been buying gift cards, prepaid plastic cards issued by a retailer that can be redeemed for merchandise.

Several websites are now making a profit from the fact that gift card recipients are often willing to sell their cards at a discount—sometimes at a fairly sizable discount. Cashcard.com is one such site. At the time of writing, it offers to pay cash to a seller of a Whole Foods gift card equivalent to 90% of the card's face value (for example, the seller of a card with a value of $100 would receive $90 in cash). But it offers cash equal to only 70% of a Gap card's face value.

Cashcard.com profits by reselling the card for more than what it paid; for example, it buys a Gap card for 70% of its face value and then resells it for 88% of its face value.

Many consumers may be willing to sell at a sizable discount to turn their gift cards into cash, but retailers are eager to promote the use of gift cards over cash. According to GiftCardUSA.com, 5% to 15% of gift cards are never redeemed. Those unredeemed dollars accrue to the retailer, making gift cards a highly profitable line of business. The Tower Group, a financial consulting firm, has estimated that the value of "breakage," the amount of a gift card that accrues to the retailer rather than to the card holder, amounts to billions of dollars annually.

How does breakage occur? People lose cards. Or they spend only $47 of a $50 gift card, figuring it's not worth the effort to return to the store to spend that last $3. Also, retailers impose fees on the use of the card or make cards subject to expiration dates, which customers forget about. And if a retailer goes out of business, the value of any outstanding gift cards disappears with it.

In addition to breakage, retailers benefit when customers intent on using up the value of their gift card find that it is too difficult to spend exactly the amount of the card; instead, they spend more than the card's face value, sometimes even spending more than they would have in the absence of the gift card.

Gift cards are so beneficial to retailers that those which used to reward customer loyalty with rebate checks have largely switched to dispensing gift cards. As one commentator noted in explaining why retailers prefer gift cards to rebate checks, "Nobody neglects to spend cash."

Questions for Thought

1. Why are gift card owners willing to sell their cards for a cash amount less than their face value?

2. Why do gift cards for retailers like Walmart, Home Depot, and Whole Foods sell for a smaller discount than those for retailers like the Gap and Aeropostale?

3. Use your answer from Question 2 to explain why cash never "sells" at a discount.

4. Explain why retailers prefer to reward loyal customers with gift cards instead of rebate checks.

5. Congress has enacted legislation restricting the ability of retailers to impose fees and expiration dates on their gift cards and mandating greater disclosure of their terms. Why do you think Congress did this?

SECTION 10 REVIEW

Summary

Defining and Measuring Money

1. **Money** is any asset that can easily be used to purchase goods and services. **Currency in circulation** and **checkable bank deposits** are both considered part of the **money supply.** Money plays three roles: it is a **medium of exchange** used for transactions, a **store of value** that holds purchasing power over time, and a **unit of account** in which prices are stated.

2. Over time, **commodity money,** which consists of goods possessing value aside from their role as money, such as gold and silver coins, was replaced by **commodity-backed money,** such as paper currency backed by gold. Today the dollar is pure **fiat money,** whose value derives solely from its official role.

3. The Federal Reserve calculates two measures of the money supply. M1 is the narrowest **monetary aggregate;** it contains only currency in circulation, traveler's checks, and checkable bank deposits. M2 includes a wider range of assets called **near-moneys,** mainly other forms of bank deposits, that can easily be converted into checkable bank deposits.

Banking and Money Creation

4. Banks allow depositors immediate access to their funds, but they also lend out most of the funds deposited in their care. To meet demands for cash, they maintain **bank reserves** composed of both currency held in vaults and deposits at the Federal Reserve. The **reserve ratio** is the ratio of bank reserves to bank deposits. A **T-account** summarizes a bank's financial position, with loans and reserves counted as assets, and deposits counted as liabilities.

5. Banks have sometimes been subject to **bank runs,** most notably in the early 1930s. To avert this danger, depositors are now protected by **deposit insurance,** bank owners face capital requirements that reduce the incentive to make overly risky loans with depositors' funds, and banks must satisfy **reserve requirements,** a legally mandated **required reserve ratio.**

6. When currency is deposited in a bank, it starts a multiplier process in which banks lend out **excess reserves,** leading to an increase in the money supply—so banks create money. If the entire money supply consisted of checkable bank deposits, the money supply would be equal to the value of reserves divided by the reserve ratio. In reality, much of the **monetary base** consists of currency in circulation, and the **money multiplier** is the ratio of the money supply to the monetary base.

The Federal Reserve System

7. In response to the Panic of 1907, the Fed was created to centralize holding of reserves, inspect banks' books, and make the money supply sufficiently responsive to varying economic conditions.

8. The Great Depression sparked widespread bank runs in the early 1930s, which greatly worsened and lengthened the depth of the Depression. Federal deposit insurance was created, and the government recapitalized banks by lending to them and by buying shares of banks. By 1933, banks had been separated into two categories: **commercial** (covered by deposit insurance) and **investment** (not covered). Public acceptance of deposit insurance finally stopped the bank runs of the Great Depression.

9. The **savings and loan (thrift)** crisis of the 1980s arose because insufficiently regulated S&Ls engaged in overly risky speculation and incurred huge losses. Depositors in failed S&Ls were compensated with taxpayer funds because they were covered by deposit insurance. However, the crisis caused steep losses in the financial and real estate sectors, resulting in a recession in the early 1990s.

10. During the mid-1990s, the hedge fund LTCM used huge amounts of **leverage** to speculate in global financial markets, incurred massive losses, and collapsed. LTCM was so large that, in selling assets to cover its losses, it caused **balance sheet effects** for firms around the world, leading to the prospect of a **vicious cycle of deleveraging.** As a result, credit markets around the world froze. The New York Fed coordinated a private bailout of LTCM and revived world credit markets.

11. **Subprime lending** during the U.S. housing bubble of the mid-2000s spread through the financial system via **securitization.** When the bubble burst, massive losses by banks and nonbank financial institutions led to widespread collapse in the financial system. To prevent another Great Depression, the Fed and the U.S. Treasury expanded lending to bank and nonbank institutions, provided capital through the purchase of bank shares, and purchased private debt. Because much of the crisis originated in nontraditional bank institutions, the crisis of 2008 raised the question of whether a wider safety net and broader regulation were needed in the financial sector.

Key Terms

Money, p. 346
Currency in circulation, p. 347
Checkable bank deposits, p. 347
Money supply, p. 347
Medium of exchange, p. 347
Store of value, p. 348
Unit of account, p. 348
Commodity money, p. 348

Commodity-backed money, p. 348
Fiat money, p. 349
Monetary aggregate, p. 350
Near-moneys, p. 350
Bank reserves, p. 353
T-account, p. 354
Reserve ratio, p. 354
Required reserve ratio, p. 354

Bank run, p. 355
Deposit insurance, p. 356
Reserve requirements, p. 356
Discount window, p. 356
Excess reserves, p. 359
Monetary base, p. 359
Money multiplier, p. 360
Central bank, p. 362
Commercial bank, p. 366

Investment bank, p. 366
Savings and loan (thrift), p. 366
Leverage, p. 367
Balance sheet effect, p. 367
Vicious cycle of deleveraging, p. 367
Subprime lending, p. 368
Securitization, p. 368

Problems

1. For each of the following transactions, what is the initial effect (increase or decrease) on M1? On M2?

   a. You sell a few shares of stock and put the proceeds into your savings account.

   b. You sell a few shares of stock and put the proceeds into your checking account.

   c. You transfer money from your savings account to your checking account.

   d. You discover $0.25 under the floor mat in your car and deposit it in your checking account.

   e. You discover $0.25 under the floor mat in your car and deposit it in your savings account.

2. There are three types of money: commodity money, commodity-backed money, and fiat money. Which type of money is used in each of the following situations?

   a. Bottles of rum were used to pay for goods in colonial Australia.

   b. Salt was used in many European countries as a medium of exchange.

   c. For a brief time, Germany used paper money (the "Rye Mark") that could be redeemed for a certain amount of rye, a type of grain.

   d. The town of Ithaca, New York, prints its own currency, the Ithaca HOURS, which can be used to purchase local goods and services.

3. The following table shows the components of M1 and M2 in billions of dollars for the month of December in the years 2001 to 2011 as published in the 2012 Economic Report of the President. Complete the table by calculating M1, M2, currency in circulation as a percentage of M1, and currency in circulation as a percentage of M2. What trends or patterns about M1, M2, currency in circulation as a percentage of M1, and currency in circulation as a percentage of M2 do you see? What might account for these trends?

Year	Currency in circulation	Traveler's checks	Checkable deposits	Savings deposits	Time deposits	Money market funds	M1	M2	Currency in circulation as a percentage of M1	Currency in circulation as a percentage of M2
2001	$581.1	$8.0	$592.9	$2,309.5	$974.5	$962.5	?	?	?	?
2002	626.2	7.8	585.7	2,773.4	894.5	887.5	?	?	?	?
2003	662.5	7.7	636.2	3,162.8	817.8	777.0	?	?	?	?
2004	697.7	7.6	671.1	3,508.8	827.9	694.7	?	?	?	?
2005	724.1	7.2	643.5	3,606.0	993.1	699.4	?	?	?	?
2006	749.6	6.7	610.0	3,694.6	1,205.3	799.0	?	?	?	?
2007	759.7	6.3	607.6	3,872.6	1,275.0	972.7	?	?	?	?
2008	815.0	5.5	782.1	4,106.1	1,455.7	1,080.5	?	?	?	?
2009	861.5	5.1	827.0	4,836.9	1,177.4	820.8	?	?	?	?
2010	915.7	4.7	911.7	5,357.6	926.6	700.0	?	?	?	?
2011	$1,000.0	4.3	1,169.7	6,023.2	759.7	683.3	?	?	?	?

Source: 2012 Economic Report of the President.

4. Indicate whether each of the following is part of M1, M2, or neither:

   a. $95 on your campus meal card

   b. $0.55 in the change cup of your car

   c. $1,663 in your savings account

   d. $459 in your checking account

   e. 100 shares of stock worth $4,000

   f. A $1,000 line of credit on your Sears credit card

5. Tracy Williams deposits $500 that was in her sock drawer into a checking account at the local bank.

   a. How does the deposit initially change the T-account of the local bank? How does it change the money supply?

   b. If the bank maintains a reserve ratio of 10%, how will it respond to the new deposit?

   c. If every time the bank makes a loan, the loan results in a new checkable bank deposit in a different bank equal to the amount of the loan, by how much could the total money supply in the economy expand in response to Tracy's initial cash deposit of $500?

   d. If every time the bank makes a loan, the loan results in a new checkable bank deposit in a different bank equal to the amount of the loan and the bank maintains a reserve ratio of 5%, by how much could the money supply expand in response to Tracy's initial cash deposit of $500?

6. Ryan Cozzens withdraws $400 from his checking account at the local bank and keeps it in his wallet.

   a. How will the withdrawal change the T-account of the local bank and the money supply?

   b. If the bank maintains a reserve ratio of 10%, how will it respond to the withdrawal? Assume that the bank responds to insufficient reserves by reducing the amount of deposits it holds until its level of reserves satisfies its required reserve ratio. The bank reduces its deposits by calling in some of its loans, forcing borrowers to pay back these loans by taking cash from their checking deposits (at the same bank) to make repayment.

   c. If every time the bank decreases its loans, checkable bank deposits fall by the amount of the loan, by how much will the money supply in the economy contract in response to Ryan's withdrawal of $400?

   d. If every time the bank decreases its loans, checkable bank deposits fall by the amount of the loan and the bank maintains a reserve ratio of 20%, by how much will the money supply contract in response to a withdrawal of $400?

7. The government of Eastlandia uses measures of monetary aggregates similar to those used by the United States, and the central bank of Eastlandia imposes a required reserve ratio of 10%. Given the following information, answer the questions below.

   Bank deposits at the central bank = $200 million

   Currency held by public = $150 million

   Currency in bank vaults = $100 million

   Checkable bank deposits = $500 million

   Traveler's checks = $10 million

   a. What is M1?

   b. What is the monetary base?

   c. Are the commercial banks holding excess reserves?

   d. Can the commercial banks increase checkable bank deposits? If yes, by how much can checkable bank deposits increase?

8. In Westlandia, the public holds 50% of M1 in the form of currency, and the required reserve ratio is 20%. Estimate how much the money supply will increase in response to a new cash deposit of $500 by completing the accompanying table. (*Hint:* The first row shows that the bank must hold $100 in minimum reserves—20% of the $500 deposit—against this deposit, leaving $400 in excess reserves that can be loaned out. However, since the public wants to hold 50% of the loan in currency, only $400 × 0.5 = $200 of the loan will be deposited in round 2 from the loan granted in round 1.) How does your answer compare to an economy in which the total amount of the loan is deposited in the banking system and the public doesn't hold any of the loan in currency? What does this imply about the relationship between the public's desire for holding currency and the money multiplier?

Round	Deposits	Required reserves	Excess reserves	Loans	Held as currency
1	$500.00	$100.00	$400.00	$400.00	$200.00
2	200.00	?	?	?	?
3	?	?	?	?	?
4	?	?	?	?	?
5	?	?	?	?	?
6	?	?	?	?	?
7	?	?	?	?	?
8	?	?	?	?	?
9	?	?	?	?	?
Total after 10 rounds	?	?	?	?	?

9. What will happen to the money supply under the following circumstances in a checkable-deposits-only system?

   a. The required reserve ratio is 25%, and a depositor withdraws $700 from his checkable bank deposit.

   b. The required reserve ratio is 5%, and a depositor withdraws $700 from his checkable bank deposit.

   c. The required reserve ratio is 20%, and a customer deposits $750 to her checkable bank deposit.

   d. The required reserve ratio is 10%, and a customer deposits $600 to her checkable bank deposit.

10. Although the U.S. Federal Reserve doesn't use changes in reserve requirements to manage the money supply, the central bank of Albernia does. The commercial banks of Albernia have $100 million in reserves and $1,000 million in checkable deposits; the initial required reserve ratio is 10%. The commercial banks follow a policy of holding no excess reserves. The public holds no currency, only checkable deposits in the banking system.

   a. How will the money supply change if the required reserve ratio falls to 5%?

   b. How will the money supply change if the required reserve ratio rises to 25%?

11. Using Figure 35-1, find the Federal Reserve district in which you live. Go to http://www.federalreserve.gov/bios/pres.htm and click on your district to identify the president of the Federal Reserve Bank in your district. Go to http://www.federalreserve.gov/fomc/ and determine if the president of the regional Federal Reserve bank in your district is currently a voting member of the Federal Open Market Committee (FOMC).

12. The Congressional Research Service estimates that at least $45 million of counterfeit U.S. $100 notes produced by the North Korean government are in circulation.

   a. Why do U.S. taxpayers lose because of North Korea's counterfeiting?

   b. As of March 2013, the interest rate earned on one-year U.S. Treasury bills was 0.14%. At a 0.14% rate of interest, what is the amount of money U.S. taxpayers are losing per year because of these $45 million in counterfeit notes?

13. The accompanying figure shows new U.S. housing starts, in thousands of units per month, between January 1980 and August 2011. The graph shows a large drop in new housing starts in 1984–1991 and 2006–2009. New housing starts are related to the availability of mortgages.

   a. What caused the drop in new housing starts in 1984–1991?

   b. What caused the drop in new housing starts in 2006–2009?

   c. How could better regulation of financial institutions have prevented these two instances?

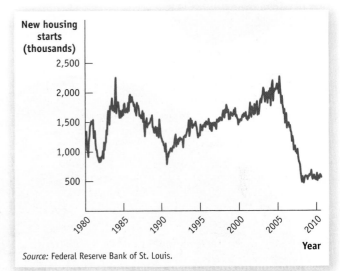

Source: Federal Reserve Bank of St. Louis.

Monetary Policy

PERSON OF THE YEAR

"A bald man with a gray beard and tired eyes is sitting in his oversize Washington office, talking about the economy. He doesn't have a commanding presence. He isn't a mesmerizing speaker. He has none of the look-at-me swagger or listen-to-me charisma so common among men with oversize Washington offices. His arguments aren't partisan or ideological; they're methodical, grounded in data and the latest academic literature. When he doesn't know something, he doesn't bluster or bluff. He's professorial, which makes sense, because he spent most of his career as a professor."

So began *Time* magazine's profile of Ben Bernanke, whom the magazine named Person of the Year for 2009. Who is this mild-mannered man, and why did he matter so much? The answer is that Bernanke was chairman of the Board of Governors of the Federal Reserve System—the body that controls *monetary policy*. In 2014, Bernanke was succeeded in the post by Janet Yellen.

People sometimes say that the Fed chair decides how much money to print. That's not quite true: for one thing, the Fed doesn't literally print money, and beyond that, monetary decisions are actually made by a committee rather than by one person. But, as we will see, the Federal Reserve can use open-market operations and other ac-

tions, such as changes in reserve requirements, to alter the money supply—and, like others who held the job of Fed chair, Ben Bernanke had more influence over these actions than anyone else in America.

And these actions matter a lot. Roughly half of the recessions the United States has experienced since World War II can be attributed, at least in part, to the decisions of the Federal Reserve to tighten policy to fight inflation.

In a number of other cases, the Fed has played a key role in fighting slumps and promoting recovery. The financial crisis of 2008 put the Fed at center stage. Bernanke's aggressive response to the crisis included a tripling of the monetary base, inspiring both praise (including his designation as Person of the Year) and condemnation.

In this section we'll learn how monetary policy works—how the Fed's actions can have a powerful effect on the economy. We'll start by looking at what the Federal Reserve does and the tools it uses. We'll proceed to consider the demand for money from households and firms. And then we'll see how the Fed's ability to change the *supply of money* allows it to move interest rates in the short run and thereby affect real GDP. We conclude by examining U.S. monetary policy and its long-run effects.

Drew Angerer/Bloomberg via Getty Images

WHAT YOU WILL LEARN

1 The functions of the Federal
Reserve System

2 The major tools the Federal
Reserve uses to serve its
functions

In the previous section, we learned that the Federal Reserve System serves as the central bank of the United States. It has two parts: the Board of Governors, which is part of the U.S. government, and the 12 regional Federal Reserve Banks, which are privately owned.

Functions of the Federal Reserve System

The Federal Reserve's functions fall into four categories. We touched on these functions of the Federal Reserve in the previous section. We examine them again here, but then turn our full attention to the fourth function, conducting monetary policy.

1. PROVIDE FINANCIAL SERVICES The 12 regional Federal Reserve Banks provide financial services to depository institutions such as banks and other large institutions, including the U.S. government. The Federal Reserve is sometimes referred to as the "banker's bank" because it holds reserves, clears checks, provides cash, and transfers funds for commercial banks—all services that banks provide for their customers. The Federal Reserve also acts as the banker and fiscal agent for the federal government. The U.S. Treasury has its checking account with the Federal Reserve, so when the federal government writes a check, it is written on an account at the Fed.

2. SUPERVISE AND REGULATE BANKING INSTITUTIONS The Federal Reserve is responsible for ensuring the safety and soundness of the nation's banking and financial system. The regional Federal Reserve Banks examine and regulate commercial banks in their district. The Board of Governors also engages in regulation and supervision of financial institutions.

3. MAINTAIN THE STABILITY OF THE FINANCIAL SYSTEM One of the major reasons the Federal Reserve System was created was to provide the nation with a safe and stable monetary and financial system. As part of this function, Federal Reserve banks provide liquidity to financial institutions to ensure their safety and soundness.

4. CONDUCT MONETARY POLICY One of the Federal Reserve's most important functions is the conduct of *monetary policy,* which involves the Fed using changes in the quantity of money to alter interest rates, which in turn affect the level of overall spending. The goal of monetary policy is to prevent or address extreme macroeconomic fluctuations in the U.S. economy.

How the Fed Conducts Policy

The Federal Reserve has three main policy tools at its disposal: reserve requirements, the discount rate, and, most importantly for the conduct of monetary policy, *open-market operations.* These tools give the Fed the ability to adjust the money supply to achieve its policy goals.

The Reserve Requirement

In our discussion of bank runs, we noted that the Fed sets a minimum required reserve ratio, currently equal to 10% for checkable bank deposits. Banks that fail to maintain at least the required reserve ratio on average over a two-week period face penalties.

What does a bank do if it looks as if it has insufficient reserves to meet the Fed's reserve requirement? Normally, it borrows additional reserves from other banks via the **federal funds market,** a financial market that allows banks that fall short of the reserve requirement to borrow reserves (usually just overnight) from banks that are holding excess reserves. The interest rate in this market is determined by supply and demand but the supply and demand for bank reserves are both strongly affected by Federal Reserve actions. The **federal funds rate,** the interest rate at which funds are borrowed and lent in the federal funds market, plays a key role in modern monetary policy.

In order to alter the money supply, the Fed can change reserve requirements. If the Fed reduces the required reserve ratio, banks will lend a larger percentage of their deposits, leading to more loans and an increase in the money supply via the money multiplier. Alternatively, if the Fed increases the required reserve ratio, banks are forced to reduce their lending, leading to a fall in the money supply via the money multiplier.

Under current practice, however, the Fed doesn't use changes in reserve requirements to actively manage the money supply. The last significant change in reserve requirements was in 1992.

The Discount Rate

Banks in need of reserves can also borrow from the Fed itself via the discount window. The **discount rate** is the interest rate the Fed charges on those loans. Normally, the discount rate is set 1 percentage point above the federal funds rate in order to discourage banks from turning to the Fed when they are in need of reserves.

In order to alter the money supply, the Fed can change the discount rate. Beginning in the fall of 2007, the Fed reduced the spread between the federal funds rate and the discount rate as part of its response to an ongoing financial crisis. As a result, by the spring of 2008 the discount rate was only 0.25 percentage points above the federal funds rate. And by January 2014 the discount rate was still only 0.68 percentage points above the federal funds rate.

If the Fed reduces the spread between the discount rate and the federal funds rate, the cost to banks of being short of reserves falls; banks respond by increasing their lending, and the money supply increases via the money multiplier. If the Fed increases the spread between the discount rate and the federal funds rate, bank lending falls—and so will the money supply via the money multiplier.

The Fed normally doesn't use the discount rate to actively manage the money supply. Although, as we mentioned earlier, there was a temporary surge in lending through the discount window from the middle of 2007 through 2008 in response to a financial crisis.

The Federal Reserve Board of Governors, the main governing body of the Federal Reserve System, oversees Federal Reserve Banks and helps to implement monetary policy.

The **federal funds market** allows banks that fall short of the reserve requirement to borrow funds from banks with excess reserves.

The **federal funds rate** is the interest rate determined in the federal funds market.

The **discount rate** is the interest rate the Fed charges on loans to banks.

An **open-market operation** is a purchase or sale of government debt by the Fed.

Today, normal monetary policy is conducted almost exclusively using the Fed's third policy tool: open-market operations.

Open-Market Operations

Like the banks it oversees, the Federal Reserve has assets and liabilities. The Fed's assets consist of its holdings of debt issued by the U.S. government, mainly short-term U.S. government bonds with a maturity of less than one year, known as U.S. Treasury bills. Remember, the Fed isn't exactly part of the U.S. government, so U.S. Treasury bills held by the Fed are a liability of the government but an asset of the Fed. The Fed's liabilities consist of currency in circulation and bank reserves. Figure 36-1 summarizes the normal assets and liabilities of the Fed in the form of a T-account.

In an **open-market operation** the Federal Reserve buys or sells U.S. Treasury bills, normally through a transaction with *commercial banks*—banks that mainly make business loans, as opposed to home loans. The Fed never buys U.S. Treasury bills directly from the federal government. There's a good reason for this: when a central bank buys government debt directly from the government, it is lending directly to the government—in effect, the central bank is "printing money" to finance the government's budget deficit. This has historically been a formula for disastrous levels of inflation.

The two panels of Figure 36-2 show the changes in the financial position of both the Fed and commercial banks that result from open-market operations. When the Fed buys U.S. Treasury bills from a commercial bank, it pays by crediting the bank's reserve account by an amount equal to the value of the Treasury bills. This is shown in panel (a): the Fed buys $100 million of U.S. Treasury bills from commercial banks, increasing the monetary base by $100 million because it increases bank reserves by $100 million.

FIGURE 36-1

The Federal Reserve's Assets and Liabilities

Assets	Liabilities
Government debt (Treasury bills)	Monetary base (Currency in circulation + bank reserves)

The Federal Reserve holds its assets mostly in short-term government bonds called U.S. Treasury bills. Its liabilities are the monetary base—currency in circulation plus bank reserves.

FIGURE 36-2   Open-Market Operations by the Federal Reserve

(a) An Open-Market Purchase of $100 Million

	Assets		Liabilities	
Federal Reserve	Treasury bills	+$100 million	Monetary base	+$100 million

	Assets		Liabilities
Commercial banks	Treasury bills	−$100 million	No change
	Reserves	+$100 million	

(b) An Open-Market Sale of $100 Million

	Assets		Liabilities	
Federal Reserve	Treasury bills	−$100 million	Monetary base	−$100 million

	Assets		Liabilities
Commercial banks	Treasury bills	+$100 million	No change
	Reserves	−$100 million	

In panel (a), the Federal Reserve increases the monetary base by purchasing U.S. Treasury bills from private commercial banks in an open-market operation. Here, a $100 million purchase of U.S. Treasury bills by the Federal Reserve is paid for by a $100 million increase in the monetary base. This will ultimately lead to an increase in the money supply via the money multiplier as banks lend out some of these new reserves. In panel (b), the Federal Reserve reduces the monetary base by selling U.S. Treasury bills to private commercial banks in an open-market operation. Here, a $100 million sale of U.S. Treasury bills leads to a $100 million reduction in commercial bank reserves, resulting in a $100 million decrease in the monetary base. This will ultimately lead to a fall in the money supply via the money multiplier as banks reduce their loans in response to a fall in their reserves.

When the Fed sells U.S. Treasury bills to commercial banks, it debits the banks' accounts, reducing their reserves. This is shown in panel (b), where the Fed sells $100 million of U.S. Treasury bills. Here, bank reserves and the monetary base decrease.

You might wonder where the Fed gets the funds to purchase U.S. Treasury bills from banks. The answer is that it simply creates them with a stroke of the pen or a click of the mouse, crediting the banks' accounts with extra reserves. (The Fed issues currency to pay for Treasury bills only when banks want the additional reserves in the form of currency.) Remember, the modern dollar is fiat money, which isn't backed by anything. So the Fed can increase the monetary base at its own discretion.

The change in bank reserves caused by an open-market operation doesn't directly affect the money supply. Instead, it sets the money multiplier in motion. After the $100 million increase in reserves shown in panel (a), commercial banks would lend out their additional reserves, immediately increasing the money supply by $100 million. Some of those loans would be deposited back into the banking system, increasing reserves again and permitting a further round of loans, and so on, leading to a rise in the money supply. An open-market sale has the reverse effect: bank reserves fall, requiring banks to reduce their loans, leading to a fall in the money supply.

Economists often say, loosely, that the Fed controls the money supply—checkable deposits plus currency in circulation. In fact, it controls only the monetary base—bank reserves plus currency in circulation. But by increasing or reducing the monetary base, the Fed can exert a powerful influence on both the money supply and interest rates, which is the basis of monetary policy.

The Fed buys or sells U.S. Treasury bills in transactions with commercial banks in an effort to influence the money supply and interest rates.

ECONOMICS ▶ IN ACTION

WHO GETS THE INTEREST ON THE FED'S ASSETS?

As we've just learned, the Fed owns a lot of assets—Treasury bills—which it bought from commercial banks in exchange for the monetary base in the form of credits to banks' reserve accounts. These assets pay interest. Yet the Fed's liabilities consist mainly of the monetary base, liabilities on which the Fed *doesn't* pay interest. So the Fed is, in effect, an institution that has the privilege of borrowing funds at a zero interest rate and lending them out at a positive interest rate. That sounds like a pretty profitable business. Who gets the profits?

You do—or rather, U.S. taxpayers do. The Fed keeps some of the interest it receives to finance its operations but turns most of it over to the U.S. Treasury. For example, in 2012 the Federal Reserve System earned net income of $91.0 billion—largely in interest on its holdings of Treasury bills, of which $88.9 billion was returned to the Treasury.

Consider what happens when a fake $100 bill enters circulation. It has the same economic effect as a real $100 bill printed by the U.S. government. That is, as long as the forgery isn't caught, the fake bill is, for all practical purposes, part of the monetary base.

Meanwhile, the Fed decides on the size of the monetary base based on economic considerations—in particular, the Fed doesn't let the monetary base get too large because that can cause inflation. So every fake $100 bill that enters circulation basically means that the Fed prints one less real $100 bill. When the Fed prints a $100 bill legally, however, it gets Treasury bills in return—and the interest on those bills helps pay for the U.S. government's expenses.

So a counterfeit $100 bill reduces the amount of Treasury bills the Fed can acquire and thereby reduces the interest payments going to the Fed and the U.S. Treasury. In the end, taxpayers bear the real cost of counterfeiting.

Taxpayers profit from interest earned on Fed assets and pay when counterfeit bills enter the money supply, reducing those interest payments.

MODULE

36 Review

Solutions appear at the back of the book.

Check Your Understanding

1. Assume that any money lent by a bank is deposited back in the banking system as a checkable deposit and that the reserve ratio is 10%. Trace out the effects of a $100 million open-market purchase of U.S. Treasury bills by the Fed on the value of checkable bank deposits. What is the size of the money multiplier?

Multiple-Choice Questions

1. Which of the following is a function of the Federal Reserve System?
   I. examine commercial banks
   II. print Federal Reserve notes
   III. conduct monetary policy

   a. I only

   b. II only

   c. III only

   d. I and III only

   e. I, II, and III

2. Which of the following financial services does the Federal Reserve provide for commercial banks?
   I. clearing checks
   II. holding reserves
   III. making loans

   a. I only

   b. II only

   c. III only

   d. I and II

   e. I, II, and III

3. When the Fed makes a loan to a commercial bank, it charges

   a. no interest.

   b. the prime rate.

   c. the federal funds rate.

   d. the discount rate.

   e. the market interest rate.

4. If the Fed purchases U.S. Treasury bills from a commercial bank, what happens to bank reserves and the money supply?

	Bank reserves	*Money supply*
a.	increase	decrease
b.	increase	increase
c.	decrease	decrease
d.	decrease	increase
e.	increase	no change

5. When banks make loans to each other, they charge the

   a. prime rate.

   b. discount rate.

   c. federal funds rate.

   d. CD rate.

   e. mortgage rate.

Critical-Thinking Question

What are the four basic functions of the Federal Reserve System?

The Money Market

WHAT YOU WILL LEARN

1. What the money demand curve is

2. Why the liquidity preference model determines the interest rate in the short run

The Demand for Money

In Module 33 we learned about the various types of monetary aggregates: M1, the most commonly used definition of the money supply, consists of currency in circulation (cash), plus checkable bank deposits, plus traveler's checks; and M2, a broader definition of the money supply, consists of M1 plus deposits that can easily be transferred into checkable deposits. We also learned why people hold money—to make it easier to purchase goods and services. Now we'll go deeper, examining what determines how much money individuals and firms want to hold at any given time.

The Opportunity Cost of Holding Money

Most economic decisions involve trade-offs at the margin. That is, individuals decide how much of a good to consume by determining whether the benefit they'd gain from consuming a bit more of any given good is worth the cost. The same decision process is used when deciding how much money to hold.

Individuals and firms find it useful to hold some of their assets in the form of money because of the convenience money provides: money can be used to make purchases directly, but other assets can't. But there is a price to be paid for that convenience: money normally yields a lower rate of return than nonmonetary assets.

As an example of how convenience makes it worth incurring some opportunity costs, consider the fact that even today—with the prevalence of credit cards, debit cards, and ATMs—people continue to keep cash in their wallets rather than leave the funds in an interest-bearing account. They do this because they don't want to have to go to an ATM to withdraw money every time they want to buy lunch from a place that doesn't accept credit cards or won't accept them for small amounts because of the processing fee. In other words, the convenience of keeping some cash in your wallet is more valuable than the interest you would earn by keeping that money in the bank.

There is a price to be paid for the convenience of holding money.

Even holding money in a checking account involves a trade-off between convenience and earning interest. That's because you can earn a higher interest rate by putting your money in assets other than a checking account. For example, many banks offer certificates of deposit, or CDs, which pay a higher interest rate than ordinary bank accounts. But CDs also carry a penalty if you withdraw the funds before a certain amount of time—say, six months—has elapsed. An individual who keeps funds in a checking account is forgoing the higher interest rate those funds might earn if placed in a CD in return for the convenience of having cash readily available when needed.

So making sense of the demand for money is about understanding how individuals and firms trade off the benefit of holding cash—that provides convenience but no interest—versus the benefit of holding interest-bearing nonmonetary assets—that provide interest but not convenience. And that trade-off is affected by the interest rate. (As before, when we say *the interest rate* it is with the understanding that we mean a nominal interest rate—that is, it's unadjusted for inflation.) Next, we'll examine how that trade-off changed dramatically from June 2007 to June 2008, when there was a big fall in interest rates.

Table 37-1 illustrates the opportunity cost of holding money in a specific month, June 2007. The first row shows the interest rate on one-month certificates of deposit—that is, the interest rate individuals could get if they were willing to tie their funds up for one month. In June 2007, one-month CDs yielded 5.30%. The second row shows the interest rate on interest-bearing demand deposits (specifically, those included in M2, minus small time deposits). Funds in these accounts were more accessible than those in CDs, but the price of that convenience was a much lower interest rate, only 2.30%. Finally, the last row shows the interest rate on currency—cash in your wallet—which was, of course, zero.

Table 37-1 shows the opportunity cost of holding money at one point in time, but the opportunity cost of holding money changes when the overall level of interest rates changes. Specifically, when the overall level of interest rates falls, the opportunity cost of holding money falls, too.

Table 37-2 illustrates this point by showing how selected interest rates changed between June 2007 and June 2008, a period when the Federal Reserve was slashing rates in an (unsuccessful) effort to fight off a rapidly worsening recession.

A comparison between interest rates in June 2007 and June 2008 illustrates what happens when the opportunity cost of holding money falls sharply. Between June 2007 and June 2008, the federal funds rate, which is the rate the Fed controls most directly, fell by 3.25 percentage points. The interest rate on one-month CDs fell almost as much, 2.8 percentage points. These interest rates are **short-term interest rates**—rates on financial assets that come due, or mature, within less than a year.

As short-term interest rates fell between June 2007 and June 2008, the interest rates on money didn't fall by the same amount. The interest rate on currency, of course, remained at zero. The interest rate paid on demand deposits did fall, but by much less than short-term interest rates.

As a comparison of the two columns of Table 37-2 shows, the opportunity cost of holding money fell. The last two rows of Table 37-2 summarize this comparison: they give the differences between the interest rates on demand deposits and on currency and the interest rate on CDs. These differences—the opportunity cost of holding money rather than interest-bearing assets—declined sharply between June 2007 and June 2008. This reflects a general result: *The higher the short-term interest rate, the higher the opportunity cost of holding money; the lower the short-term interest rate, the lower the opportunity cost of holding money.*

TABLE 37-1

Selected Interest Rates, June 2007

One-month certificates of deposit (CDs)	5.30%
Interest-bearing demand deposits	2.30%
Currency	0

Source: Federal Reserve Bank of St. Louis.

TABLE 37-2

Interest Rates and the Opportunity Cost of Holding Money

	June 2007	June 2008
Federal funds rate	5.25%	2.00%
One-month certificates of deposit (CDs)	5.30%	2.50%
Interest-bearing demand deposits	2.30%	1.24%
Currency	0	0
CDs minus interest-bearing demand deposits (percentage points)	**3.00**	**1.26**
CDs minus currency (percentage points)	**5.30**	**2.50**

Source: Federal Reserve Bank of St. Louis.

Short-term interest rates are the interest rates on financial assets that mature within less than a year.

The fact that the federal funds rate in Table 37-2 and the interest rate on one-month CDs fell by almost the same percentage is not an accident: all short-term interest rates tend to move together, with rare exceptions. The reason short-term interest rates tend to move together is that CDs and other short-term assets (like one-month and three-month U.S. Treasury bills) are in effect competing for the same business. Any short-term asset that offers a lower-than-average interest rate will be sold by investors, who will move their wealth into a higher-yielding short-term asset. The selling of the asset, in turn, forces its interest rate up, because investors must be rewarded with a higher rate in order to induce them to buy it.

Conversely, investors will move their wealth into any short-term financial asset that offers an above-average interest rate. The purchase of the asset drives its interest rate down when sellers find they can lower the rate of return on the asset and still find willing buyers. So interest rates on short-term financial assets tend to be roughly the same because no asset will consistently offer a higher-than-average or a lower-than-average interest rate.

Table 37-2 contains only short-term interest rates. At any given moment, **long-term interest rates**—rates of interest on financial assets that mature, or come due, a number of years into the future—may be different from short-term interest rates. The difference between short-term and long-term interest rates is sometimes important as a practical matter.

Moreover, it's short-term rates rather than long-term rates that affect money demand, because the decision to hold money involves trading off the convenience of holding cash versus the payoff from holding assets that mature in the short term—a year or less.

For the moment, however, let's ignore the distinction between short-term and long-term rates and assume that there is only one interest rate.

Long-term interest rates are interest rates on financial assets that mature a number of years in the future.

Short-term interest rates tend to move together.

The Money Demand Curve

Because the overall level of interest rates affects the opportunity cost of holding money, the quantity of money individuals and firms want to hold is, other things equal, negatively related to the interest rate.

In Figure 37-1, the horizontal axis shows the quantity of money demanded and the vertical axis shows the interest rate, *r*, which you can think of as a representative short-term interest rate such as the rate on one-month CDs. (Recall that it is the

FIGURE 37-1   The Money Demand Curve

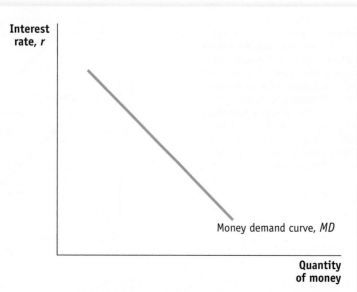

The money demand curve illustrates the relationship between the interest rate and the quantity of money demanded. It slopes downward: a higher interest rate leads to a higher opportunity cost of holding money and reduces the quantity of money demanded. Correspondingly, a lower interest rate reduces the opportunity cost of holding money and increases the quantity of money demanded.

nominal interest rate, not the real interest rate, that influences people's money allocation decisions. Hence, r in Figure 37-1 and all subsequent figures is the nominal interest rate.)

The relationship between the interest rate and the quantity of money demanded by the public is illustrated by the **money demand curve,** MD, in Figure 37-1. The money demand curve slopes downward because, other things equal, a higher interest rate increases the opportunity cost of holding money, leading the public to reduce the quantity of money it demands. For example, if the interest rate is very low—say, 1%—the interest forgone by holding money is relatively small. As a result, individuals and firms will tend to hold relatively large amounts of money to avoid the cost and nuisance of converting other assets into money when making purchases.

By contrast, if the interest rate is relatively high—say, 15%, a level it reached in the United States in the early 1980s—the opportunity cost of holding money is high. People will respond by keeping only small amounts in cash and deposits, converting assets into money only when needed.

You might ask why we draw the money demand curve with the interest rate—as opposed to rates of return on other assets, such as stocks or real estate—on the vertical axis. The answer is that for most people the relevant question in deciding how much money to hold is whether to put the funds in the form of other assets that can be turned fairly quickly and easily into money.

Stocks don't fit that definition because there are significant transaction fees when you sell stock (which is why stock market investors are advised not to buy and sell too often). Real estate doesn't fit the definition either because selling real estate involves even larger fees and can take a long time as well. So the relevant comparison is with assets that are "close to" money—fairly liquid assets like CDs. And as we've already seen, the interest rates on all these assets normally move closely together.

Shifts of the Money Demand Curve

A number of factors other than the interest rate affect the demand for money. When one of these factors changes, the money demand curve shifts. Figure 37-2 shows shifts of the money demand curve: an increase in the demand for money corresponds

FIGURE 37-2   Increases and Decreases in the Demand for Money

The demand curve for money shifts when non-interest rate factors that affect the demand for money change. An increase in money demand shifts the money demand curve to the right, from MD_1 to MD_2, and the quantity of money demanded rises at any given interest rate. A decrease in money demand shifts the money demand curve to the left, from MD_1 to MD_3, and the quantity of money demanded falls at any given interest rate.

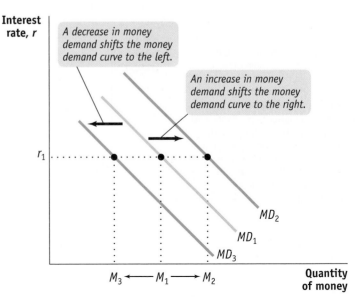

to a rightward shift of the *MD* curve, raising the quantity of money demanded at any given interest rate; a decrease in the demand for money corresponds to a leftward shift of the *MD* curve, reducing the quantity of money demanded at any given interest rate.

The most important factors causing the money demand curve to shift are changes in the aggregate price level, changes in real GDP, changes in credit markets and banking technology, and changes in institutions.

CHANGES IN THE AGGREGATE PRICE LEVEL Americans keep a lot more cash in their wallets and funds in their checking accounts today than they did in the 1950s. One reason is that they have to if they want to be able to buy anything: almost everything costs more now than it did when you could get a burger, fries, and a drink at McDonald's for 45 cents and a gallon of gasoline for 29 cents.

So, other things equal, higher prices increase the demand for money (a rightward shift of the *MD* curve), and lower prices decrease the demand for money (a leftward shift of the *MD* curve).

We can actually be more specific than this: other things equal, the demand for money is *proportional* to the price level. That is, if the aggregate price level rises by 20%, the quantity of money demanded at any given interest rate, such as r_1 in Figure 37-2, also rises by 20%—the movement from M_1 to M_2. Why? Because if the price of everything rises by 20%, it takes 20% more money to buy the same basket of goods and services.

And if the aggregate price level falls by 20%, at any given interest rate the quantity of money demanded falls by 20%—shown by the movement from M_1 to M_3 at the interest rate r_1. As we'll see later, the fact that money demand is proportional to the price level has important implications for the long-run effects of monetary policy.

CHANGES IN REAL GDP Households and firms hold money as a way to facilitate purchases of goods and services. The larger the quantity of goods and services they buy, the larger the quantity of money they will want to hold at any given interest rate. So an increase in real GDP—the total quantity of goods and services produced and sold in the economy—shifts the money demand curve rightward. A fall in real GDP shifts the money demand curve leftward.

CHANGES IN CREDIT MARKETS AND BANKING TECHNOLOGY Credit cards are everywhere in American life today, but it wasn't always so. The first credit card that allowed customers to carry a balance from month to month (called a "revolving balance") was issued in 1959. Before then, people had to either pay for purchases in cash or pay off their balance every month.

The invention of revolving-balance credit cards allowed people to hold less money in order to fund their purchases and decreased the demand for money. In addition, changes in banking technology that made credit cards widely available and widely accepted magnified the effect, making it easier for people to make purchases without having to convert funds from their interest-bearing assets, further reducing the demand for money.

Credit cards allow people to hold less money to fund their purchases, decreasing the demand for money.

CHANGES IN INSTITUTIONS Changes in institutions can increase or decrease the demand for money. For example, until Regulation Q was eliminated in 1980, U.S. banks weren't allowed to offer interest on checking accounts. So the interest you would forgo by holding funds in a checking account instead of an interest-bearing asset made the opportunity cost of holding funds in checking accounts very high. When banking regulations changed, allowing banks to pay interest on checking account funds, the demand for money rose and shifted the money demand curve to the right.

ECONOMICS ▶ IN ACTION

A YEN FOR CASH

Japan, say financial experts, is still a "cash society." Visitors from the United States or Europe are surprised at how little use the Japanese make of credit cards and how much cash they carry around in their wallets. Yet Japan is an economically and technologically advanced country and, according to some measures, ahead of the United States in the use of telecommunications and information technology.

So why do the citizens of this economic powerhouse still do business the way Americans and Europeans did a generation ago? The answer highlights the factors affecting the demand for money.

One reason the Japanese use cash so much is that their institutions never made the switch to heavy reliance on plastic. For complex reasons, Japan's retail sector is still dominated by small mom-and-pop stores, which are reluctant to invest in credit card technology. Japan's banks have also been slow about pushing transaction technology; visitors are often surprised to find that ATMs close early in the evening rather than staying open all night.

Sakarin Sawasdinaka/Shutterstock

No matter what they are shopping for, Japanese consumers tend to pay with cash rather than plastic.

But there's another reason the Japanese hold so much cash: there's little opportunity cost to doing so. Short-term interest rates in Japan have been below 1% since the mid-1990s. It also helps that the Japanese crime rate is quite low, so you are unlikely to have your wallet full of cash stolen. So why not hold cash?

Money and Interest Rates

The Federal Open Market Committee decided today to lower its target for the federal funds rate 75 basis points to 2¼ percent.

Recent information indicates that the outlook for economic activity has weakened further. Growth in consumer spending has slowed and labor markets have softened. Financial markets remain under considerable stress, and the tightening of credit conditions and the deepening of the housing contraction are likely to weigh on economic growth over the next few quarters.

So read the beginning of a press release from the Federal Reserve issued on March 18, 2008. (A basis point is equal to 0.01 percentage point. So the statement implies that the Fed lowered the target from 3% to 2.25%.) Recall that the federal funds rate is the rate at which banks lend reserves to each other to meet the required reserve ratio.

As the statement implies, at each of its eight-times-a-year meetings, a group called the Federal Open Market Committee sets a target value for the federal funds rate. It's then up to Fed officials to achieve that target. This is done by the Open Market Desk at the Federal Reserve Bank of New York, which buys and sells short-term U.S. government debt, known as Treasury bills, to achieve that target.

As we've already seen, other short-term interest rates, such as the rates on CDs, move with the federal funds rate. So when the Fed reduced its target for the federal funds rate from 3% to 2.25% in March 2008, many other short-term interest rates also fell by about three-quarters of a percentage point.

How does the Fed go about achieving a *target federal funds rate*? And more to the point, how is the Fed able to affect interest rates at all?

The Equilibrium Interest Rate

According to the **liquidity preference model of the interest rate**, the interest rate is determined by the supply and demand for money.

Remember that, for simplicity, we're assuming there is only one interest rate paid on nonmonetary financial assets, both in the short run and in the long run. To understand how the interest rate is determined, consider Figure 37-3, which illustrates the **liquidity preference model of the interest rate;** this model says that the interest rate is determined by the supply and demand for money in the market for money.

Figure 37-3 combines the money demand curve, *MD*, with the **money supply curve,** *MS*, which shows how the quantity of money supplied by the Federal Reserve varies with the interest rate.

The **money supply curve** shows how the quantity of money supplied varies with the interest rate.

In the previous module we learned how the Federal Reserve can increase or decrease the money supply: it usually does this through open-market operations, buying or selling Treasury bills, but it can also lend via the discount window or change reserve requirements.

Let's assume for simplicity that the Fed, using one or more of these methods, simply chooses the level of the money supply that it believes will achieve its interest rate target. Then the money supply curve is a vertical line, *MS* in Figure 37-3, with a horizontal intercept corresponding to the money supply chosen by the Fed, $\overline{M}$. The money market equilibrium is at *E*, where *MS* and *MD* cross. At this point the quantity of money demanded equals the money supply, $\overline{M}$, leading to an equilibrium interest rate of r_E.

To understand why r_E is the equilibrium interest rate, consider what happens if the money market is at a point like *L*, where the interest rate, r_L, is below r_E. At r_L the public wants to hold the quantity of money M_L, an amount larger than the actual money supply, $\overline{M}$. This means that at point *L*, the public wants to shift some of its wealth out of interest-bearing assets such as CDs into money.

This has two implications. One is that the quantity of money demanded is *more* than the quantity of money supplied. The other is that the quantity of interest-bearing money assets demanded is less than the quantity supplied. So those trying to sell nonmoney assets will find that they have to offer a higher interest rate to attract buyers. As a result, the interest rate will be driven up from r_L until the public wants to hold the quantity of money that is actually available, $\overline{M}$. That is, the interest rate will rise until it is equal to r_E.

Now consider what happens if the money market is at a point such as *H* in Figure 37-3, where the interest rate r_H is above r_E. In that case the quantity of money demanded, M_H, is less than the quantity of money supplied, $\overline{M}$. Correspondingly, the quantity of interest-bearing nonmoney assets demanded is greater than the quantity supplied. Those trying to sell interest-bearing nonmoney assets will find that they can

FIGURE 37-3   Equilibrium in the Money Market

The money supply curve, *MS*, is vertical at the money supply chosen by the Federal Reserve, $\overline{M}$. The money market is in equilibrium at the interest rate r_E: *the quantity of money demanded by the public is equal to $\overline{M}$, the quantity of money supplied.*

At a point such as *L*, the interest rate, r_L, is below r_E and the corresponding quantity of money demanded, M_L, exceeds the money supply, $\overline{M}$. In an attempt to shift their wealth out of nonmoney interest-bearing financial assets and raise their money holdings, investors drive the interest rate up to r_E. At a point such as *H*, the interest rate r_H exceeds r_E and the corresponding quantity of money demanded, M_H, is less than the money supply, $\overline{M}$. In an attempt to shift out of money holdings into nonmoney interest-bearing financial assets, investors drive the interest rate down to r_E.

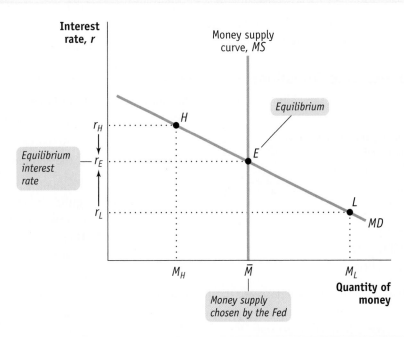

offer a lower interest rate and still find willing buyers. This leads to a fall in the interest rate from r_H. It falls until the public wants to hold the quantity of money that is actually available, $\overline{M}$. Again, the interest rate will end up at r_E.

Two Models of Interest Rates?

You might have noticed that this is the second time we have discussed the determination of the interest rate. In an earlier module, we studied the *loanable funds model* of the interest rate; according to that model, the interest rate is determined by the equalization of the supply of funds from lenders and the demand for funds by borrowers in the market for loanable funds. But here we have described a seemingly different model in which the interest rate is determined by the equalization of the supply and demand for money in the money market.

Which of these models is correct? The answer is both, depending on context. The loanable funds model is focused on the interest rate in the long run. The money market model, however, focuses on the interest rate in the short run.

MODULE 37 Review

Solutions appear at the back of the book.

Check Your Understanding

1. Explain how each of the following would affect the quantity of money demanded, and indicate whether each change would cause a movement along the money demand curve or a shift of the money demand curve.

   a. Short-term interest rates rise from 5% to 30%.

   b. All prices fall by 10%.

   c. New wireless technology automatically charges supermarket purchases to credit cards, eliminating the need to stop at the cash register.

   d. In order to avoid paying taxes, a vast underground economy develops in which workers are paid their wages in cash rather than with checks.

2. Will each of the following increase the opportunity cost of holding cash, reduce it, or have no effect on it? Explain your answers.

   a. Merchants charge a 1% processing fee on debit/credit card transactions for purchases of less than $50.

   b. To attract more deposits, banks raise the interest paid on six-month CDs.

   c. Real estate prices fall significantly.

   d. The cost of food rises significantly.

Multiple-Choice Questions

1. A change in which of the following will shift the money demand curve?

   I. the aggregate price level
   II. real GDP
   III. the interest rate

   a. I only

   b. II only

   c. III only

   d. I and II only

   e. I, II, and III

2. Which of the following will decrease the demand for money?

   a. an increase in the interest rate

   b. inflation

   c. an increase in real GDP

   d. an increase in the availability of ATMs

   e. the adoption of Regulation Q

3. What will happen to the money supply and the equilibrium interest rate if the Federal Reserve sells Treasury securities?

	Money supply	*Equilibrium interest rate*
a.	increase	increase
b.	decrease	increase
c.	increase	decrease
d.	decrease	decrease
e.	decrease	no change

4. Which of the following is true regarding short-term and long-term interest rates?

   a. Short-term interest rates are always above long-term interest rates.

   b. Short-term interest rates are always below long-term interest rates.

   c. Short-term interest rates are always equal to long-term interest rates.

   d. Short-term interest rates are more important for determining the demand for money.

   e. Long-term interest rates are more important for determining the demand for money.

5. The quantity of money demanded rises (that is, there is a movement along the money demand curve) when

   a. the aggregate price level increases.

   b. the aggregate price level falls.

   c. real GDP increases.

   d. new technology makes banking easier.

   e. short-term interest rates fall.

Critical-Thinking Question

Draw a graph showing equilibrium in the money market. Select an interest rate below the equilibrium interest rate and explain what occurs in the market at that interest rate and how the market will eventually return to equilibrium.

MODULE

38 Monetary Policy and the Interest Rate

WHAT YOU WILL LEARN

1 **How the Federal Reserve implements monetary policy, moving the interest rate to affect aggregate output**

2 **Why monetary policy is the main tool for stabilizing the economy**

In the previous module we developed a model of the money market to show how the interest rate is determined in the short run. Now we are ready to use this model to explain how the Federal Reserve can use monetary policy to stabilize the economy in the short run.

The Fed, the Money Supply, and the Interest Rate

Let's examine how the Federal Reserve can use changes in the money supply to change the interest rate. Figure 38-1 shows what happens when the Fed increases the money supply from $\overline{M}_1$ to $\overline{M}_2$.

The economy is originally in equilibrium at E_1, with the equilibrium interest rate r_1 and the money supply $\overline{M}_1$. An increase in the money supply by the Fed to $\overline{M}_2$ shifts the money supply curve to the right, from MS_1 to MS_2, and leads to a fall in the equilibrium interest rate to r_2. Why? Because r_2 is the only interest rate at which the public is willing to hold the quantity of money actually supplied, $\overline{M}_2$.

So an increase in the money supply drives the interest rate down. Similarly, a reduction in the money supply drives the interest rate up. By adjusting the money supply up or down, the Fed can set the interest rate.

In practice, at each meeting the Federal Open Market Committee decides on the interest rate to prevail for the next six weeks, until its next meeting. The Fed sets a **target federal funds rate,** a desired level for the federal funds rate. This target is then enforced by the Open Market Desk of the Federal Reserve Bank of New York, which adjusts the money supply through *open-market operations*—the purchase or sale of Treasury bills—until the actual federal funds rate equals the target rate.

The **target federal funds rate** is the Federal Reserve's desired federal funds rate.

Harrer/Bloomberg via Getty Images

392

FIGURE 38-1   The Effect of an Increase in the Money Supply on the Interest Rate

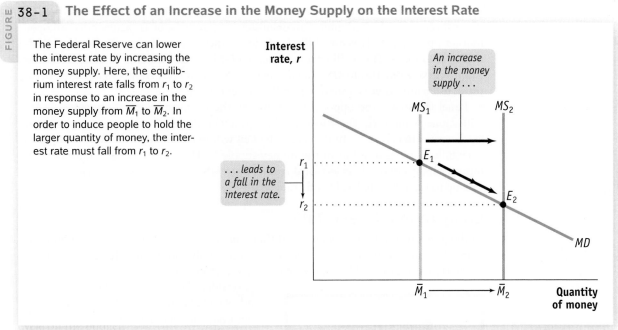

The Federal Reserve can lower the interest rate by increasing the money supply. Here, the equilibrium interest rate falls from r_1 to r_2 in response to an increase in the money supply from $\overline{M}_1$ to $\overline{M}_2$. In order to induce people to hold the larger quantity of money, the interest rate must fall from r_1 to r_2.

The other tools of monetary policy, lending through the discount window and changes in reserve requirements, aren't used on a regular basis, although the Fed used discount window lending in its efforts to address the 2008 financial crisis.

Figure 38-2 shows how the Fed adjusts the money supply in order to change the interest rate and achieve its target federal funds rate. In both panels, r_T is the target federal funds rate. In panel (a), the initial money supply curve is MS_1 with money

FIGURE 38-2   Setting the Federal Funds Rate

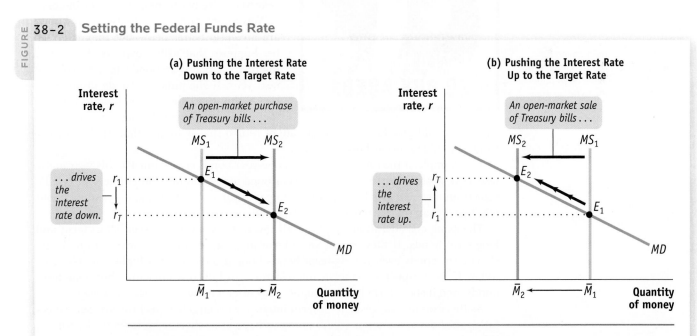

The Federal Reserve sets a target for the federal funds rate and uses open-market operations to achieve that target. In both panels the target rate is r_T. In panel (a) the initial equilibrium interest rate, r_1, is above the target rate. The Fed increases the money supply by making an open-market purchase of Treasury bills, pushing the money supply curve rightward, from MS_1 to MS_2, and

driving the interest rate down to r_T. In panel (b) the initial equilibrium interest rate, r_1, is below the target rate. The Fed reduces the money supply by making an open-market sale of Treasury bills, pushing the money supply curve leftward, from MS_1 to MS_2, and driving the interest rate up to r_T.

supply $\overline{M}_1$, and the equilibrium interest rate, r_1, is above the target rate. To lower the interest rate to r_T, the Fed makes an open-market purchase of Treasury bills. An open-market purchase of Treasury bills leads to an increase in the money supply via the money multiplier. This is illustrated in panel (a) by the rightward shift of the money supply curve from MS_1 to MS_2 and an increase in the money supply to $\overline{M}_2$. This drives the equilibrium interest rate down to the target rate, r_T.

Panel (b) shows the opposite case. Again, the initial money supply curve is MS_1 with money supply $\overline{M}_1$. But this time the equilibrium interest rate, r_1, is below the target federal funds rate, r_T. In this case, the Fed will make an open-market sale of Treasury bills, leading to a fall in the money supply to $\overline{M}_2$ via the money multiplier. The money supply curve shifts leftward from MS_1 to MS_2, driving the equilibrium interest rate up to the target federal funds rate, r_T.

Long-Term Interest Rates

In the previous module we mentioned that *long-term interest rates*—rates on bonds or loans that mature in several years—don't necessarily move with short-term interest rates. How is that possible, and what does it say about monetary policy?

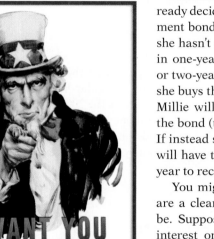

Advertising during the two world wars increased the demand for government long-term bonds from savers who may have been reluctant, at other times, to tie up their funds for several years.

Consider the case of Millie, who has already decided to place $10,000 in U.S. government bonds for the next two years. However, she hasn't decided whether to put the money in one-year bonds, at a 4% rate of interest, or two-year bonds, at a 5% rate of interest. If she buys the one-year bond, then in one year, Millie will receive the $10,000 she paid for the bond (the *principal*) plus interest earned. If instead she buys the two-year bond, Millie will have to wait until the end of the second year to receive her principal and her interest.

You might think that the two-year bonds are a clearly better deal—but they may not be. Suppose that Millie expects the rate of interest on one-year bonds to rise sharply next year. If she puts her funds in one-year bonds this year, she will be able to reinvest the money at a much higher rate next year. And this could give her a two-year rate of return that is higher than if she put her funds into the two-year bonds today.

For example, if the rate of interest on one-year bonds rises from 4% this year to 8% next year, putting her funds in a one-year bond today and in another one-year bond a year from now will give her an annual rate of return over the next two years of about 6%, better than the 5% rate on two-year bonds.

The same considerations apply to all investors deciding between short-term and long-term bonds. If they expect short-term interest rates to rise, investors may buy short-term bonds even if long-term bonds bought today offer a higher interest rate today. If they expect short-term interest rates to fall, investors may buy long-term bonds even if short-term bonds bought today offer a higher interest rate today.

As this example suggests, long-term interest rates largely reflect the average expectation in the market about what's going to happen to short-term rates in the future. When long-term rates are higher than short-term rates, the market is signaling that it expects short-term rates to rise in the future.

This is not, however, the whole story: risk is also a factor. Return to the example of Millie, deciding whether to buy one-year or two-year bonds. Suppose that there is some chance she will need to cash in her investment after just one year—say, to meet an emergency medical bill. If she buys two-year bonds, she would have to sell those bonds to meet the unexpected expense. But what price will she get for those bonds? It depends on what has happened to interest rates in the rest of the economy. Recall that bond prices and interest rates move in opposite directions: if interest rates rise, bond prices fall, and vice versa.

This means that Millie will face extra risk if she buys two-year rather than one-year bonds, because if a year from now bond prices fall and she must sell her bonds in order to raise cash, she will lose money on the bonds.

Owing to this risk factor, long-term interest rates are, on average, higher than short-term rates in order to compensate long-term bond purchasers for the higher risk they face (although this relationship is reversed when short-term rates are unusually high).

The fact that long-term rates don't necessarily move with short-term rates is sometimes an important consideration for monetary policy.

ECONOMICS ▶ IN ACTION

FED REVERSES COURSE

The Fed's decision in March 2008 to cut its target interest rate represented a dramatic reversal of Fed policy that began in September 2007.

Figure 38-3 shows two interest rates from the beginning of 2004 through 2013: the target federal funds rate, decided by the Federal Open Market Committee, and the effective, or actual, rate in the market.

As you can see, the Fed raised its target rate in a series of steps from late 2004 until the middle of 2006; it did this to head off the possibility of an overheating economy and rising inflation.

But the Fed dramatically reversed course beginning in September 2007, as falling housing prices triggered a growing financial crisis and ultimately a severe recession. And in December 2008, the Fed decided to allow the federal funds rate to move inside a target band between 0% and 0.25%. From 2009 through 2013, the Fed funds rate was kept close to zero in response to a very weak economy and high unemployment.

Figure 38-3 also shows that the Fed doesn't always hit its target. There were a number of days, especially in 2008, when the effective federal funds rate was significantly above or below the target rate. But these episodes didn't last long, and overall the Fed got what it wanted, at least as far as short-term interest rates were concerned.

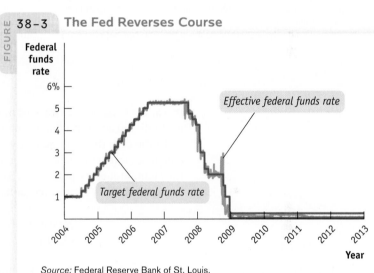

FIGURE 38-3   The Fed Reverses Course

Source: Federal Reserve Bank of St. Louis.

Monetary Policy and Aggregate Demand

In an earlier section we saw how fiscal policy can be used to stabilize the economy. Now we will see how monetary policy—changes in the money supply and the interest rate—can play the same role.

Expansionary and Contractionary Monetary Policy

In Module 27 we learned that monetary policy shifts the aggregate demand curve. We can now explain how that works: through the effect of monetary policy on the interest rate.

Figure 38-4 illustrates the process. Suppose, first, that the Federal Reserve wants to reduce interest rates, so it expands the money supply. As you can see in the top portion of the figure, a lower interest rate, in turn, will lead, other things equal, to more

FIGURE **38-4**   **Expansionary and Contractionary Monetary Policy**

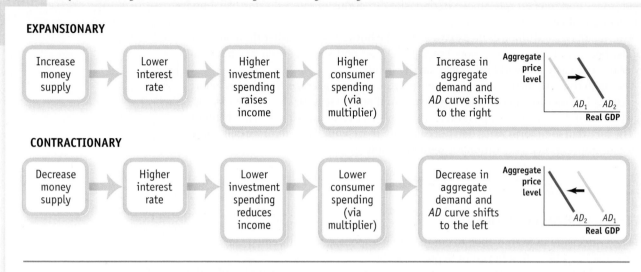

The top portion shows what happens when the Fed adopts an expansionary monetary policy and increases the money supply. Interest rates fall, leading to higher investment spending, which raises income, which, in turn, raises consumer spending and shifts the AD curve to the right. The bottom portion shows what happens when the Fed adopts a contractionary monetary policy and reduces the money supply. Interest rates rise, leading to lower investment spending and a reduction in income. This lowers consumer spending and shifts the AD curve to the left.

investment spending. This will in turn lead to higher consumer spending, through the multiplier process, and to an increase in aggregate output demanded.

In the end, the total quantity of goods and services demanded at any given aggregate price level rises when the quantity of money increases, and the AD curve shifts to the right. Monetary policy that increases the demand for goods and services is known as **expansionary monetary policy.**

Suppose, alternatively, that the Federal Reserve wants to increase interest rates, so it contracts the money supply. You can see this process illustrated in the bottom portion of the diagram. Contraction of the money supply leads to a higher interest rate. The higher interest rate leads to lower investment spending, then to lower consumer spending, and then to a decrease in aggregate output demanded.

So the total quantity of goods and services demanded falls when the money supply is reduced, and the AD curve shifts to the left. Monetary policy that decreases the demand for goods and services is called **contractionary monetary policy.**

Monetary Policy in Practice

How does the Fed decide whether to use expansionary or contractionary monetary policy? And how does it decide how much is enough? As we know, policy makers try to fight recessions, as well as try to ensure *price stability*: low (though usually not zero) inflation. Actual monetary policy reflects a combination of these goals.

In general, the Federal Reserve and other central banks tend to engage in expansionary monetary policy when actual real GDP is below potential output. Panel (a) of Figure 38-5 shows the U.S. output gap, which we've previously defined as the percentage difference between actual real GDP and potential output, versus the federal funds rate since 1985. (Recall that the output gap is positive when actual real GDP exceeds potential output.) As you can see, the Fed has tended to raise interest rates when the

"I told you the Fed should have tightened."

Expansionary monetary policy is monetary policy that increases aggregate demand.

Contractionary monetary policy is monetary policy that decreases aggregate demand.

FIGURE

38-5 Tracking Monetary Policy Using the Output Gap and Inflation

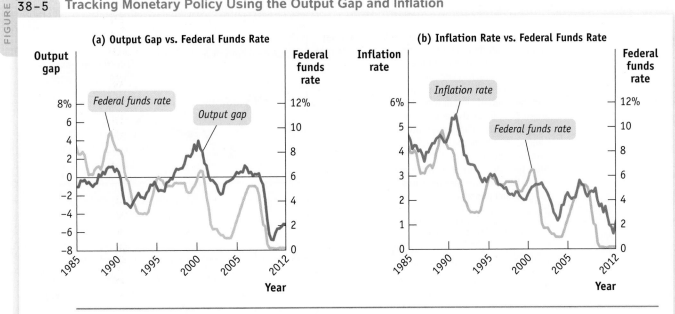

Panel (a) shows that the federal funds rate usually rises when the output gap is positive—that is, when actual real GDP is above potential output—and falls when the output gap is negative. Panel (b) illustrates that the federal funds rate tends to be high when inflation is high and low when inflation is low.

Sources: Bureau of Labor Statistics; Congressional Budget Office; Federal Reserve Bank of St. Louis.

output gap is rising—that is, when the economy is developing an inflationary gap—and cut rates when the output gap is falling.

The big exception was the late 1990s, when the Fed left rates steady for several years even as the economy developed a positive output gap (which went along with a low unemployment rate). One reason the Fed was willing to keep interest rates low in the late 1990s was that inflation was low.

Panel (b) of Figure 38-5 compares the inflation rate, measured as the rate of change in consumer prices excluding food and energy, with the federal funds rate. You can see how low inflation during the mid-1990s, the early 2000s, and the late 2000s helped encourage loose monetary policy in the late 1990s, in 2002–2003, and again beginning in 2008.

The Taylor Rule Method of Setting Monetary Policy

In 1993 Stanford economist John Taylor suggested that monetary policy should follow a simple rule that takes into account concerns about both the business cycle and inflation. He also suggested that actual monetary policy often looks as if the Federal Reserve was, in fact, more or less following the proposed rule. A **Taylor rule for monetary policy** is a rule for setting interest rates that takes into account the inflation rate and the output gap or, in some cases, the unemployment rate.

A widely cited example of a Taylor rule is a relationship among Fed policy, inflation, and unemployment estimated by economists at the Federal Reserve Bank of San Francisco. These economists found that between 1988 and 2008 the Fed's behavior was well summarized by the following Taylor rule:

Federal funds rate = 2.07 + 1.28 × inflation rate – 1.95 × unemployment gap

where the inflation rate was measured by the change over the previous year in consumer prices excluding food and energy, and the unemployment gap was the difference between the actual unemployment rate and Congressional Budget Office estimates of the natural rate of unemployment.

A **Taylor rule for monetary policy** is a rule that sets the federal funds rate according to the level of the inflation rate and either the output gap or the unemployment rate.

38-6   The Taylor Rule and the Federal Funds Rate

The red line shows the federal funds rate predicted by the San Francisco Fed's version of the Taylor rule, which relates the interest rate to the inflation rate and the unemployment rate. The green line shows the actual federal funds rate. The actual rate tracked the predicted rate quite closely through the end of 2008. After that, however, the Taylor rule called for negative interest rates, which aren't possible.

Sources: Bureau of Labor Statistics; Congressional Budget Office; Federal Reserve Bank of St. Louis; Glenn D. Rudebusch, "The Fed's Monetary Policy Response to the Current Crisis," *FRBSF Economic Letter* #2009-17 (May 22, 2009).

Figure 38-6 compares the federal funds rate predicted by this rule with the actual federal funds rate from 1985 to 2012. As you can see, the Fed's decisions were quite close to those predicted by this particular Taylor rule from 1988 through the end of 2008. We'll talk about what happened after 2008 shortly.

Inflation Targeting

Until January 2012, the Fed did not explicitly commit itself to achieving a particular inflation rate. However, in January 2012, the Fed chairman at the time, Ben Bernanke, announced that the Fed would set its policy to maintain an approximately 2% inflation rate per year. With that statement, the Fed joined a number of other central banks that have explicit inflation targets.

So rather than using a Taylor rule to set monetary policy, they instead announced the inflation rate that they want to achieve—the *inflation target*—and set policy in an attempt to hit that target. This method of setting monetary policy, called **inflation targeting,** involves having the central bank announce the inflation rate it is trying to achieve and set policy in an attempt to hit that target. The central bank of New Zealand, which was the first country to adopt inflation targeting, specified a range for that target of 1% to 3%.

Other central banks commit themselves to achieving a specific number. For example, the Bank of England has committed to keeping inflation at 2%. In practice, there doesn't seem to be much difference between these versions: central banks with a target range for inflation seem to aim for the middle of that range, and central banks with a fixed target tend to give themselves considerable wiggle room.

One major difference between inflation targeting and the Taylor rule method is that inflation targeting is forward-looking rather than backward-looking. That is, the Taylor rule method adjusts monetary policy in response to *past* inflation, but inflation targeting is based on a forecast of future inflation.

Advocates of inflation targeting argue that it has two key advantages over a Taylor rule: *transparency* and *accountability*. First, economic uncertainty is reduced because the central bank's plan is transparent: the public knows the objective of an inflation-targeting central bank. Second, the central bank's success can be judged by seeing how closely actual inflation rates have matched the inflation target, making central bankers accountable.

Inflation targeting occurs when the central bank sets an explicit target for the inflation rate and sets monetary policy in order to hit that target.

Critics of inflation targeting argue that it's too restrictive because there are times when other concerns—like the stability of the financial system—should take priority over achieving any particular inflation rate. Indeed, in late 2007 and early 2008 the Fed cut interest rates much more than either a Taylor rule or inflation targeting would have dictated because it feared that turmoil in the financial markets would lead to a major recession. (In fact, it did.)

Many American macroeconomists have had positive things to say about inflation targeting—including Bernanke. And in January 2012 the Fed declared that what it means by the "price stability" it seeks is 2 percent inflation, although there was no explicit commitment about when this inflation rate would be achieved.

The Zero Lower Bound Problem

As Figure 38-6 shows, a Taylor rule based on inflation and the unemployment rate does a good job of predicting Federal Reserve policy from 1988 through 2008. After that, however, things go awry, and for a simple reason: with very high unemployment and low inflation, the same Taylor rule called for an interest rate less than zero, which isn't possible.

Why aren't negative interest rates possible? Because people always have the alternative of holding cash, which offers a zero interest rate. Nobody would ever buy a bond yielding an interest rate less than zero because holding cash would be a better alternative.

The fact that interest rates can't go below zero—called the **zero lower bound for interest rates**—sets limits to the power of monetary policy. In 2009 and 2010, inflation was low and the economy was operating far below potential, so the Federal Reserve wanted to increase aggregate demand. Yet the normal way it does this—open-market purchases of short-term government debt to expand the money supply—had run out of room to operate because short-term interest rates were already at or near zero.

In November 2010 the Fed began an attempt to circumvent this problem, which went by the somewhat obscure name *quantitative easing*. Instead of purchasing only short-term government debt, it began buying longer-term government debt—five-year or six-year bonds, rather than three-month Treasury bills.

As we have already pointed out, long-term interest rates don't exactly follow short-term rates. At the time the Fed began this program, short-term rates were near zero, but rates on longer-term bonds were between 2% and 3%. The Fed hoped that direct purchases of these longer-term bonds would drive down interest rates on long-term debt, exerting an expansionary effect on the economy.

Long-term interest rates did decline to about 1% in 2010, then rose back up to 2% in 2011, before once again returning to 1% where they stayed until mid-2013. Although the Fed's policy may have boosted spending from 2010 to 2013, recovery remained slow.

Since 2012, the Fed has targeted inflation at 2%.

ECONOMICS ▶ IN ACTION

WHAT THE FED WANTS, THE FED GETS

What's the evidence that the Fed can actually cause an economic contraction or expansion? You might think that finding such evidence is just a matter of looking at what happens to the economy when interest rates go up or down. But it turns out that there's a big problem with that approach: the Fed usually changes interest rates in an attempt to tame the business cycle, raising rates if the economy is expanding and reducing rates if the economy is slumping. So in the actual data, it often looks as if low interest rates go along with a weak economy and high rates go along with a strong economy.

The **zero lower bound for interest rates** means that interest rates cannot fall below zero.

FIGURE

38-7   When the Fed Wants a Recession

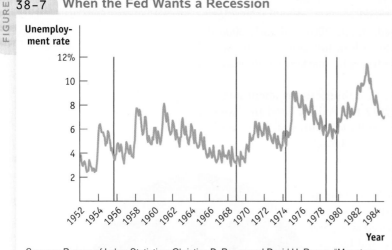

Sources: Bureau of Labor Statistics; Christina D. Romer and David H. Romer, "Monetary Policy Matters," *Journal of Monetary Economics* 34 (August 1994): 75–88.

In a famous paper titled "Monetary Policy Matters," the macroeconomists Christina Romer and David Romer solved this problem by focusing on episodes in which monetary policy wasn't a reaction to the business cycle. Specifically, they used minutes from the Federal Open Market Committee and other sources to identify episodes "in which the Federal Reserve in effect decided to attempt to create a recession to reduce inflation."

Rather than just using monetary policy as a tool of macroeconomic stabilization, sometimes it is used to eliminate *embedded* inflation—inflation that people believe will persist into the future. In such a case, the Fed needs to create a recessionary gap—not just eliminate an inflationary gap—to wring embedded inflation out of the economy.

Figure 38-7 shows the unemployment rate between 1952 and 1984 (orange) and also identifies five dates on which, according to Romer and Romer, the Fed decided that it wanted a recession (vertical red lines). In four out of the five cases, the decision to contract the economy was followed, after a modest lag, by a rise in the unemployment rate. On average, Romer and Romer found, the unemployment rate rises by 2 percentage points after the Fed decides that unemployment needs to go up.

So yes, the Fed gets what it wants.

MODULE

38 Review

Solutions appear at the back of the book.

Check Your Understanding

1. Assume that there is an increase in the demand for money at every interest rate. Draw a diagram that shows what effect this will have on the equilibrium interest rate for a given money supply.

2. Now assume that the Fed is following a policy of targeting the federal funds rate. What will the Fed do in the situation described in Problem 1 to keep the federal funds rate unchanged? Illustrate with a diagram.

3. Suppose the economy is currently suffering from a recessionary gap and the Federal Reserve uses

an expansionary monetary policy to close that gap. Describe the short-run effect of this policy on the following.

  a. the money supply curve

  b. the equilibrium interest rate

  c. investment spending

  d. consumer spending

  e. aggregate output

Multiple-Choice Questions

1. At each meeting of the Federal Open Market Committee, the Federal Reserve sets a target for which of the following?

  I. the federal funds rate

  II. the prime interest rate

  III. the market interest rate

  a. I only

  b. II only

  c. III only

  d. I and III only

  e. I, II, and III

2. Which of the following actions can the Fed take to decrease the equilibrium interest rate?

   a. increase the money supply

   b. increase money demand

   c. decrease the money supply

   d. decrease money demand

   e. both (a) and (d)

3. Contractionary monetary policy attempts to _____ aggregate demand by _____ interest rates.

   a. decrease; increasing

   b. increase; decreasing

   c. decrease; decreasing

   d. increase; increasing

   e. increase; maintaining

Critical-Thinking Questions

1. What can the Fed do with each of its tools to implement expansionary monetary policy during a recession?

2. Use a graph of the money market to explain how the Fed's use of expansionary monetary policy affects interest rates in the short run.

3. Explain how the interest rate changes you graphed in Problem 2 affect aggregate supply and demand in the short run.

4. Use an aggregate demand and supply graph to illustrate how expansionary monetary policy affects aggregate output in the short run.

4. Which of the following is a goal of monetary policy?

   a. zero inflation

   b. deflation

   c. price stability

   d. increased potential output

   e. decreased actual real GDP

5. When implementing monetary policy, the Federal Reserve attempts to achieve

   a. an explicit target inflation rate.

   b. zero inflation.

   c. a low rate of deflation.

   d. a low but positive inflation rate.

   e. between 4% and 5% inflation.

PITFALLS

THE TARGET VERSUS THE MARKET

? Over the years, the Federal Reserve has changed the way in which monetary policy is implemented. In the late 1970s and early 1980s, it set a target level for the money supply and altered the monetary base to achieve that target. Under this way of operating, the federal funds rate fluctuated freely. Today the Fed uses the reverse procedure, setting a target for the federal funds rate and allowing the money supply to fluctuate as it pursues that target. Do these changes in the way the Fed operates alter the way the money market works?

> NOT AT ALL. THE MONEY MARKET WORKS THE SAME WAY AS ALWAYS: THE INTEREST RATE IS DETERMINED BY THE SUPPLY AND DEMAND FOR MONEY. THE ONLY DIFFERENCE IS THAT NOW THE FED ADJUSTS THE SUPPLY OF MONEY TO ACHIEVE ITS TARGET INTEREST RATE Although you may hear people say that the interest rate no longer reflects the supply and demand for money because the Fed sets the interest rate, this is a common misconception. It's important not to confuse a change in the Fed's operating procedure with a change in the way the economy works.

To learn more, see pages 392–394.

Jezper/Shutterstock

In the previous module we discussed how expansionary and contractionary monetary policy can be used to stabilize the economy. The Federal Reserve can use its monetary policy tools to change the money supply and cause the equilibrium interest rate in the money market to increase or decrease.

But what if a central bank pursues a monetary policy that is not appropriate? That is, what if a central bank pursues expansionary policy during an expansion or contractionary policy during a recession? In this module we consider how a counterproductive action by a central bank can actually destabilize the economy in the short run.

We also introduce the long-run effects of monetary policy. As we've seen, the money market (where monetary policy has its effect on the money supply) determines the interest rate only in the short run. In the long run, the interest rate is determined in the market for loanable funds. Now we turn to long-run adjustments and consider the long-run effects of monetary policy.

Money, Output, and Prices

Because of its expansionary and contractionary effects, monetary policy is generally the policy tool of choice to help stabilize the economy. However, not all actions by central banks are productive. Central banks sometimes print money not to fight a recessionary gap but to help the government pay its bills, an action that typically destabilizes the economy.

What happens when a change in the money supply pushes the economy away from, rather than toward, long-run equilibrium? The economy is self-correcting in the long run: a demand shock has only a temporary effect on aggregate output. If the demand shock is the result of a change in the money supply, we can make a stronger statement: in the long run, changes in the quantity of money affect the aggregate price level, but they do not change real aggregate output or the interest rate.

To see why, let's look at what happens if the central bank permanently increases the money supply.

Short-Run and Long-Run Effects of an Increase in the Money Supply

To analyze the long-run effects of monetary policy, it's helpful to think of the central bank as choosing a target for the money supply rather than for the interest rate. In assessing the effects of an increase in the money supply, we return to the analysis of the long-run effects of an increase in aggregate demand.

Figure 39-1 shows the short-run and long-run effects of an increase in the money supply when the economy begins at potential output, Y_1. The initial short-run aggregate supply curve is $SRAS_1$, the long-run aggregate supply curve is $LRAS$, and the initial aggregate demand curve is AD_1. The economy's initial equilibrium is at E_1, a point of both short-run and long-run macroeconomic equilibrium because it is on both the short-run and the long-run aggregate supply curves. Real GDP is at potential output, Y_1.

Now suppose there is an increase in the money supply. Other things equal, an increase in the money supply reduces the interest rate, which increases investment spending, which leads to a further rise in consumer spending, and so on. So an increase in

FIGURE

39-1 The Short-Run and Long-Run Effects of an Increase in the Money Supply

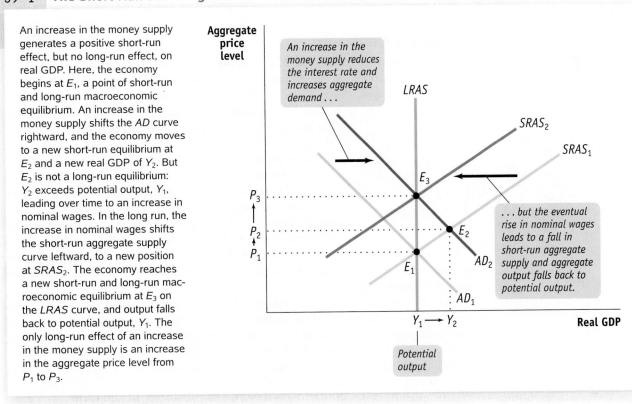

An increase in the money supply generates a positive short-run effect, but no long-run effect, on real GDP. Here, the economy begins at E_1, a point of short-run and long-run macroeconomic equilibrium. An increase in the money supply shifts the AD curve rightward, and the economy moves to a new short-run equilibrium at E_2 and a new real GDP of Y_2. But E_2 is not a long-run equilibrium: Y_2 exceeds potential output, Y_1, leading over time to an increase in nominal wages. In the long run, the increase in nominal wages shifts the short-run aggregate supply curve leftward, to a new position at $SRAS_2$. The economy reaches a new short-run and long-run macroeconomic equilibrium at E_3 on the $LRAS$ curve, and output falls back to potential output, Y_1. The only long-run effect of an increase in the money supply is an increase in the aggregate price level from P_1 to P_3.

the money supply increases the quantity of goods and services demanded, shifting the AD curve rightward to AD_2.

In the short run, the economy moves to a new short-run macroeconomic equilibrium at E_2. The price level rises from P_1 to P_2, and real GDP rises from Y_1 to Y_2. That is, both the aggregate price level and aggregate output increase in the short run.

But the aggregate output level Y_2 is above potential output. As a result, nominal wages will rise over time, causing the short-run aggregate supply curve to shift leftward. This process stops only when the SRAS curve ends up at $SRAS_2$ and the economy ends up at point E_3, a point of both short-run and long-run macroeconomic equilibrium.

The long-run effect of an increase in the money supply, then, is that the aggregate price level has increased from P_1 to P_3, but aggregate output is back at potential output, Y_1. In the long run, a monetary expansion raises the aggregate price level but has no effect on real GDP.

If the money supply decreases, the story we have just told plays out in reverse. Other things equal, a decrease in the money supply raises the interest rate, which decreases investment spending, which leads to a further decrease in consumer spending, and so on. So a decrease in the money supply decreases the quantity of goods and services demanded at any given aggregate price level, shifting the aggregate demand curve to the left.

In the short run, the economy moves to a new short-run macroeconomic equilibrium at a level of real GDP below potential output and a lower aggregate price level. That is, both the aggregate price level and aggregate output decrease in the short run.

But what happens over time? When the aggregate output level is below potential output, nominal wages fall. When this happens, the short-run aggregate supply curve shifts rightward. This process stops only when the SRAS curve ends up at a point of both short-run and long-run macroeconomic equilibrium.

The long-run effect of a decrease in the money supply, then, is that the aggregate price level decreases, but aggregate output is back at potential output. In the long run, a monetary contraction decreases the aggregate price level but has no effect on real GDP.

Monetary Neutrality

How much does a change in the money supply change the aggregate price level in the long run? The answer is that a change in the money supply leads to a proportional change in the aggregate price level in the long run. For example, if the money supply falls 25%, the aggregate price level falls 25% in the long run; if the money supply rises 50%, the aggregate price level rises 50% in the long run.

In the long run, a change in the money supply leads to a proportional change in the aggregate price level.

FeaturePics

According to the concept of monetary neutrality, changes in the money supply have no real effects on the economy in the long run.

How do we know this? Consider the following thought experiment: suppose all prices in the economy—prices of final goods and services and also factor prices, such as nominal wage rates—double. And suppose the money supply doubles at the same time. What difference does this make to the economy in real terms? None. All real variables in the economy—such as real GDP and the real value of the money supply (the amount of goods and services it can buy)—are unchanged. So there is no reason for anyone to behave any differently.

We can state this argument in reverse: if the economy starts out in long-run macroeconomic equilibrium and the money supply changes, restoring long-run macroeconomic equilibrium requires restoring all real values to their original values. This includes restoring the real value of the money supply to its original level. So if the money supply falls 25%, the aggregate price level must fall 25%; if the money supply rises 50%, the price level must rise 50%; and so on.

This analysis demonstrates the concept known as **monetary neutrality,** in which changes in the money supply have no real effects on the economy. In the long run, the only effect of an increase in the money supply is to raise the aggregate price level by an equal percentage. Economists argue that *money is neutral in the long run*.

This is, however, a good time to recall the dictum of John Maynard Keynes: "In the long run we are all dead." In the long run, changes in the money supply don't have any effect on real GDP, interest rates, or anything else except the price level.

But it would be foolish to conclude from this that the Fed is irrelevant. Monetary policy does have powerful real effects on the economy in the short run, often making the difference between recession and expansion. And that matters a lot for society's welfare.

Changes in the Money Supply and the Interest Rate in the Long Run

In the short run, an increase in the money supply leads to a fall in the interest rate, and a decrease in the money supply leads to a rise in the interest rate. We have explained that in the long run it's a different story: changes in the money supply don't affect the interest rate at all. Let's look at why.

Figure 39-2 shows why. It shows the money supply curve and the money demand curve before and after the Fed increases the money supply. We assume that the economy is initially at E_1, in long-run macroeconomic equilibrium at potential output, and with money supply $\overline{M}_1$. The initial equilibrium interest rate, determined by the intersection of the money demand curve MD_1 and the money supply curve MS_1, is r_1.

FIGURE 39-2   The Long-Run Determination of the Interest Rate

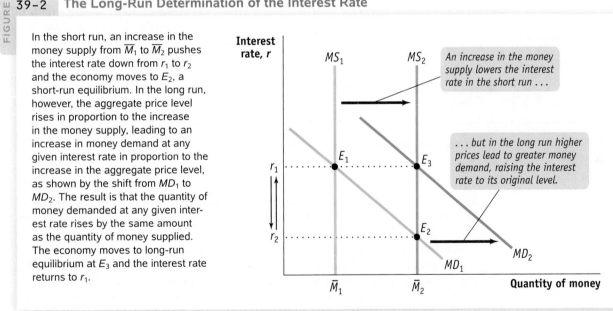

In the short run, an increase in the money supply from $\overline{M}_1$ to $\overline{M}_2$ pushes the interest rate down from r_1 to r_2 and the economy moves to E_2, a short-run equilibrium. In the long run, however, the aggregate price level rises in proportion to the increase in the money supply, leading to an increase in money demand at any given interest rate in proportion to the increase in the aggregate price level, as shown by the shift from MD_1 to MD_2. The result is that the quantity of money demanded at any given interest rate rises by the same amount as the quantity of money supplied. The economy moves to long-run equilibrium at E_3 and the interest rate returns to r_1.

An increase in the money supply lowers the interest rate in the short run . . .

. . . but in the long run higher prices lead to greater money demand, raising the interest rate to its original level.

Now suppose the money supply increases from $\overline{M}_1$ to $\overline{M}_2$. In the short run, the economy moves from E_1 to E_2 and the interest rate falls from r_1 to r_2. Over time, however, the aggregate price level rises, and this raises money demand, shifting the money demand curve rightward from MD_1 to MD_2. The economy moves to a new long-run equilibrium at E_3, and the interest rate rises to its original level at r_1.

And it turns out that the long-run equilibrium interest rate is the original interest rate, r_1. We know this for two reasons.

1. Because of monetary neutrality, in the long run the aggregate price level rises by the same proportion as the money supply; so if the money supply rises by, say, 50%, the price level will also rise by 50%.

2. The demand for money is, other things equal, proportional to the aggregate price level. So a 50% increase in the money supply raises the aggregate price level by 50%, which increases the quantity of money demanded at any given interest rate by 50%. As a result, the quantity of money demanded at the initial interest rate, r_1, rises exactly as much as the money supply—so that r_1 is still the equilibrium interest rate.

In the long run, then, changes in the money supply do not affect the interest rate.

ECONOMICS ▶ IN ACTION   WORLD VIEW

INTERNATIONAL EVIDENCE OF MONETARY NEUTRALITY

These days monetary policy is quite similar among wealthy countries. Each major nation (or, in the case of the euro, the euro area) has a central bank that is insulated from political pressure. All of these central banks try to keep the aggregate price level roughly stable, which usually means inflation of, at most, 2% to 3% per year.

But if we look at a longer period and a wider group of countries, we see large differences in the growth of the money supply. Between 1970 and the present, the money supply rose only a few percent per year in some countries, such as Switzerland and the United States, but rose much more rapidly in some poorer countries, such as South Africa.

These differences allow us to see whether increases in the money supply in the long run really do lead to equal percent rises in the aggregate price level.

Figure 39-3 shows the annual percentage increases in the money supply and average annual increases in the aggregate price level—that is, the average rate of inflation—for a sample of countries during the period 1970–2010, with each point representing a country.

FIGURE 39-3 **The Long-Run Relationship Between Money and Inflation**

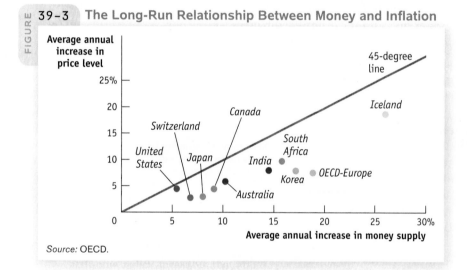

Source: OECD.

If the relationship between increases in the money supply and changes in the aggregate price level were exact, the points would lie precisely on a 45-degree line. In fact, the relationship isn't exact, because other factors besides money affect the aggregate price level.

But the scatter of points clearly lies close to a 45-degree line, showing a more or less proportional relationship between money and the aggregate price level. That is, the data support the concept of monetary neutrality in the long run.

MODULE 39 Review

Solutions appear at the back of the book.

Check Your Understanding

1. Suppose the economy begins in long-run macroeconomic equilibrium. What is the long-run effect on the aggregate price level of a 5% increase in the money supply? Explain.

2. Again supposing the economy begins in long-run macroeconomic equilibrium, what is the long-run effect on the interest rate of a 5% increase in the money supply? Explain.

Multiple-Choice Questions

1. In the long run, changes in the quantity of money affect which of the following?

    I. real aggregate output

    II. interest rates

    III. the aggregate price level

    a. I only

    b. II only

    c. III only

    d. I and II only

    e. I, II, and III

2. An increase in the money supply will lead to which of the following in the short run?

    a. higher interest rates

    b. decreased investment spending

    c. decreased consumer spending

    d. increased aggregate demand

    e. lower real GDP

3. A 10% decrease in the money supply will change the aggregate price level in the long run by

    a. zero.

    b. less than 10%.

    c. 10%.

    d. 20%.

    e. more than 20%.

4. Monetary neutrality means that, in the long run, changes in the money supply

    a. cannot happen.

    b. have no effect on the economy.

    c. have no real effect on the economy.

    d. increase real GDP.

    e. change real interest rates.

5. A graph of percentage increases in the money supply and average annual increases in the price level for various countries provides evidence that

    a. changes in the two variables are exactly equal.

    b. the money supply and aggregate price level are unrelated.

    c. money neutrality holds only in wealthy countries.

    d. monetary policy is ineffective.

    e. money is neutral in the long run.

Critical-Thinking Questions

1. Draw a graph of aggregate demand and supply showing an economy in long-run macroeconomic equilibrium.

2. On your graph, show what happens in the short run if the central bank increases the money supply to pay off a government deficit. Explain.

3. On your graph, show what will happen in the long run. Explain.

BUSINESS CASE: PIMCO Bets on Cheap Money

Pacific Investment Management Company, generally known as PIMCO, is one of the world's largest investment companies. Among other things, it runs PIMCO Total Return, the world's second-largest mutual fund. The head of PIMCO, Bill Gross, is legendary for his ability to predict trends in financial markets, especially bond markets, where PIMCO does much of its investing.

In the fall of 2009, Gross decided to put more of PIMCO's assets into long-term U.S. government bonds. This amounted to a bet that long-term interest rates would fall. This bet was especially interesting because it was the opposite of the bet many other investors were making. For example, in November 2009 the investment bank Morgan Stanley told its clients to expect a sharp rise in long-term interest rates.

What lay behind PIMCO's bet? Gross explained the firm's thinking in his September 2009 commentary. He suggested that unemployment was likely to stay high and inflation low. "Global policy rates," he asserted—meaning the federal funds rate and its equivalents in Europe and elsewhere—"will remain low for extended periods of time."

The Federal Funds Rate and Long-Term Interest Rates, 2009–2011

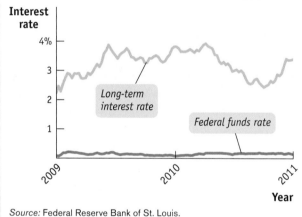

Source: Federal Reserve Bank of St. Louis.

PIMCO's view was in sharp contrast to those of other investors: Morgan Stanley expected long-term rates to rise in part because it expected the Fed to raise the federal funds rate in 2010.

Who was right? PIMCO, mostly. As the accompanying figure shows, the federal funds rate stayed near zero, and long-term interest rates fell through much of 2010, although they rose somewhat very late in the year as investors became somewhat more optimistic about economic recovery.

Morgan Stanley, which had bet on rising rates, actually apologized to investors for getting it so wrong.

Bill Gross's foresight, however, was a lot less accurate in 2011. Anticipating a significantly stronger U.S. economy by mid-2011 that would result in inflation, Gross bet heavily against U.S. government bonds early that year. But this time he was wrong, as weak growth continued. By late summer 2011, Gross realized his mistake as U.S. bonds rose in value and the value of his funds sank. He admitted to the *Wall Street Journal* that he had "lost sleep" over his bet, and called it a "mistake."

Questions for Thought

1. Why did PIMCO's view that unemployment would stay high and inflation low lead to a forecast that policy interest rates would remain low for an extended period?

2. Why would low policy rates suggest low long-term interest rates?

3. What might have caused long-term interest rates to rise in late 2010, even though the federal funds rate was still zero?

SECTION 11 REVIEW

Summary

The Federal Reserve and Monetary Policy

1. The monetary base is controlled by the Federal Reserve, the central bank of the United States. The Fed regulates banks and sets reserve requirements. To meet those requirements, banks borrow and lend reserves in the **federal funds market** at the **federal funds rate.** Through the discount window facility, banks can borrow from the Fed at the **discount rate.**

2. **Open-market operations** by the Fed are the principal tool of monetary policy: the Fed can increase or reduce the monetary base by buying U.S. Treasury bills from banks or selling U.S. Treasury bills to banks.

The Money Market

3. The **money demand curve** arises from a trade-off between the opportunity cost of holding money and the liquidity that money provides. The opportunity cost of holding money depends on **short-term interest rates,** not **long-term interest rates.** Changes in the aggregate price level, real GDP, technology, and institutions shift the money demand curve.

4. According to the **liquidity preference model of the interest rate,** the interest rate is determined in the money market by the money demand curve and the **money supply curve.** The Federal Reserve can change the interest rate in the short run by shifting the money supply curve.

Monetary Policy and the Interest Rate

5. In practice, the Fed uses open-market operations to achieve a **target federal funds rate,** which other short-term interest rates generally track. Although long-term interest rates don't necessarily move with short-term interest rates, they reflect expectations about what's going to happen to short-term rates in the future.

6. **Expansionary monetary policy** reduces the interest rate by increasing the money supply. This increases investment spending and consumer spending, which in turn increases aggregate demand and real GDP in the short run. **Contractionary monetary policy** raises the interest rate by reducing the money supply. This reduces investment spending and consumer spending, which in turn reduces aggregate demand and real GDP in the short run.

7. The Federal Reserve and other central banks try to stabilize the economy, limiting fluctuations of actual output around potential output, while also keeping inflation low but positive. Under a **Taylor rule for monetary policy,** the target federal funds rate rises when there is high inflation and either a positive output gap or very low unemployment; it falls when there is low or negative inflation and either a negative output gap or high unemployment. Some central banks (including the Fed as of January 2012) engage in **inflation targeting,** which is a forward-looking policy rule, whereas the Taylor rule method is a backward-looking policy rule.

8. Because monetary policy is subject to fewer implementation lags than fiscal policy, it is the preferred policy tool for stabilizing the economy. Because interest rates cannot fall below zero—the **zero lower bound for interest rates**—the power of monetary policy is limited.

Money, Output, and Prices in the Long Run

9. In the long run, changes in the money supply affect the aggregate price level but not real GDP or the interest rate. Data show that the concept of **monetary neutrality** holds: changes in the money supply have no real effect on the economy in the long run.

Key Terms

Federal funds market, p. 379
Federal funds rate, p. 379
Discount rate, p. 379
Open-market operations, p. 380
Short-term interest rates, p. 384

Long-term interest rates, p. 385
Money demand curve, p. 386
Liquidity preference model of the interest rate, p. 388
Money supply curve, p. 389

Target federal funds rate, p. 392
Expansionary monetary policy, p. 396
Contractionary monetary policy, p. 396

Taylor rule for monetary policy, p. 397
Inflation targeting, p. 398
Zero lower bound for interest rates, p. 399
Monetary neutrality, p. 404

Problems

1. Show the changes to the T-accounts for the Federal Reserve and for commercial banks when the Federal Reserve buys $50 million in U.S. Treasury bills. If the public holds a fixed amount of currency (so that all loans create an equal amount of deposits in the banking system), the minimum reserve ratio is 10%, and banks hold no excess reserves, by how much will deposits in the commercial banks change? By how much will the money supply change? Show the final changes to the T-account for commercial banks when the money supply changes by this amount.

2. Show the changes to the T-accounts for the Federal Reserve and for commercial banks when the Federal Reserve sells $30 million in U.S. Treasury bills. If the public holds a fixed amount of currency (so that all new loans create an equal amount of checkable bank deposits in the banking system) and the minimum reserve ratio is 5%, by how much will checkable bank deposits in the commercial banks change? By how much will the money supply change? Show the final changes to the T-account for the commercial banks when the money supply changes by this amount.

3. Go to the FOMC page of the Federal Reserve Board's website (http://www.federalreserve.gov/FOMC/) to find the statement issued after the most recent FOMC meeting. (Click on "Meeting calendars and information" and then click on the most recent statement listed in the calendar.)

   a. What is the target federal funds rate?

   b. Is the target federal funds rate different from the target federal funds rate in the previous FOMC statement? If yes, by how much does it differ?

   c. Does the statement comment on current macroeconomic conditions in the United States? How does it describe the U.S. economy?

4. How will the following events affect the demand for money? In each case, specify whether there is a shift of the demand curve or a movement along the demand curve and its direction.

   a. There is a fall in the interest rate from 12% to 10%.

   b. Thanksgiving arrives and, with it, the beginning of the holiday shopping season.

   c. McDonald's and other fast-food restaurants begin to accept credit cards.

   d. The Fed engages in an open-market purchase of U.S. Treasury bills.

5. a. Go to www.treasurydirect.gov. Under "Individuals," go to "Treasury Bills, Notes, Bonds, TIPS, and FRNs." Click on "Treasury Bills." Under "at a glance," click on "rates in recent auctions." What is the investment rate for the most recently issued 26-week T-bills?

   b. Go to the website of your favorite bank. What is the interest rate for six-month CDs?

   c. Why are the rates for six-month CDs higher than for 26-week Treasury bills?

6. Go to www.treasurydirect.gov. Under "Individuals," go to "Treasury Bills, Notes, Bonds, TIPS, and FRNs." Click on "Treasury Notes." Under "at a glance," click on "rates in recent auctions." Use the list of Recent Note, Bond, and TIPS Auction Results to answer the following questions.

   a. What are the interest rates on 2-year and 10-year notes?

   b. How do the interest rates on the 2-year and 10-year notes relate to each other? Why is the interest rate on the 10-year note higher (or lower) than the interest rate on the 2-year note?

7. An economy is facing the recessionary gap shown in the accompanying diagram. To eliminate the gap, should the central bank use expansionary or contractionary monetary policy? How will the interest rate, investment spending, consumer spending, real GDP, and the aggregate price level change as monetary policy closes the recessionary gap?

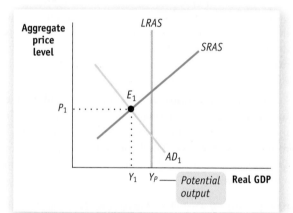

8. An economy is facing the inflationary gap shown in the accompanying diagram. To eliminate the gap, should the central bank use expansionary or contractionary monetary policy? How will the interest rate, investment spending, consumer spending, real GDP, and the aggregate price level change as monetary policy closes the inflationary gap?

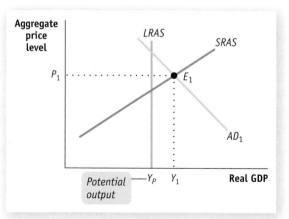

9. In the economy of Eastlandia, the money market is initially in equilibrium when the economy begins to slide into a recession.

   a. Using the accompanying diagram, explain what will happen to the interest rate if the central bank of Eastlandia keeps the money supply constant at $\bar{M}_1$.

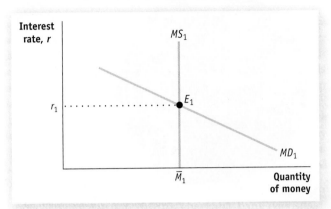

   b. If the central bank is instead committed to maintaining an interest rate target of r_1, then as the economy slides into recession, how should the central bank react? Using your diagram from part a, demonstrate the central bank's reaction.

10. Suppose that the money market in Westlandia is initially in equilibrium and the central bank decides to decrease the money supply.

    a. Using a diagram like the one in Problem 9, explain what will happen to the interest rate in the short run.

    b. What will happen to the interest rate in the long run?

11. An economy is in long-run macroeconomic equilibrium with an unemployment rate of 5% when the government passes a law requiring the central bank to use monetary policy to lower the unemployment rate to 3% and keep it there. How could the central bank achieve this goal in the short run? What would happen in the long run? Illustrate with a diagram.

12. According to the European Central Bank website, the treaty establishing the European Community "makes clear that ensuring price stability is the most important contribution that monetary policy can make to achieve a favourable economic environment and a high level of employment." If price stability is the only goal of monetary policy, explain how monetary policy would be conducted during recessions. Analyze both the case of a recession that is the result of a demand shock and the case of a recession that is the result of a supply shock.

13. The effectiveness of monetary policy depends on how easy it is for changes in the money supply to change interest rates. By changing interest rates, monetary policy affects investment spending and the aggregate demand curve. The economies of Albernia and Brittania have very different money demand curves, as shown in the accompanying diagram. In which economy will changes in the money supply be a more effective policy tool? Why?

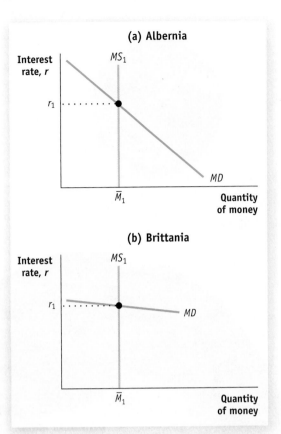

14. During the Great Depression, businesspeople in the United States were very pessimistic about the future of economic growth and reluctant to increase investment spending even when interest rates fell. How did this limit the potential for monetary policy to help alleviate the Depression?

15. Because of the economic slowdown associated with the 2007–2009 recession, the Federal Open Market Committee of the Federal Reserve, between September 18, 2007 and December 16, 2008, lowered the federal funds rate in a series of steps from a high of 5.25% to a rate between zero and 0.25%. The idea was to provide a boost to the economy by increasing aggregate demand.

    a. Use the liquidity preference model to explain how the Federal Open Market Committee lowers the interest rate in the short run. Draw a typical graph that illustrates the mechanism. Label the vertical axis "Interest rate" and the horizontal axis "Quantity of money." Your graph should show two interest rates, r_1 and r_2.

    b. Explain why the reduction in the interest rate causes aggregate demand to increase in the short run.

    c. Suppose that in 2016 the economy is at potential output but that this is somehow overlooked by the Fed, which continues its monetary expansion. Demonstrate the effect of the policy measure on the AD curve. Use the $LRAS$ curve to show that the effect of this policy measure on the AD curve, other things equal, causes the aggregate price level to rise in the long run. Label the vertical axis "Aggregate price level" and the horizontal axis "Real GDP."

SECTION **12**

Policy Responses to Unemployment and Inflation

BRINGING A SUITCASE TO THE BANK   WORLD VIEW

The African nation of Zimbabwe achieved a dubious distinction in 2008: it exhibited one of the highest inflation rates ever recorded, peaking at around 500 billion percent.

Although the government kept introducing ever-larger denominations of the Zimbabwe dollar—for example, in May 2008 it introduced a half-billion-dollar bill—it still took a lot of currency to pay for the necessities of life: a stack of the cash worth $100 U.S. dollars weighed about 40 pounds. The currency was worth so little that some people making bank withdrawals brought suitcases along in order to be able to walk away with enough cash to pay for basic living expenses. In the end, the Zimbabwe dollar lost all value—literally. By October 2008, the currency more or less vanished from circulation, replaced by U.S. dollars and South African rands.

Zimbabwe's experience was shocking, but not unprecedented. In 1994 the inflation rate in Armenia hit 27,000%. In 1991 Nicaraguan inflation exceeded 60,000%. And Zimbabwe's experience was more or less matched by history's most famous example of extreme inflation, which took place in Germany in 1922–1923. Toward the end of the German hyperinflation, prices were rising 16% a *day*, which—through compounding—meant an increase of approximately 500 billion percent over the course of five months. People were so reluctant to hold paper money, which lost value by the hour, that eggs and lumps of coal began to circulate as currency.

German firms would pay their workers several times a day so that they could spend their earnings before they lost value (lending new meaning to the term *hourly wage*). Legend has it that men sitting down at a bar would order two beers at a time, out of fear that the price of a beer would rise before they could order a second round!

The United States has never experienced that kind of inflation. The worst U.S. inflation in modern times took place at the end of the 1970s, when consumer prices were rising at an annual rate of 13%. Yet inflation at even that rate was profoundly troubling to the American public, and the policies the Federal Reserve pursued in order to get U.S. inflation back down to an acceptable rate led to a very deep recession.

In this section we look at the reasons inflation rises and falls. We'll see that the causes of very high inflation, the type of inflation suffered by Zimbabwe, are quite different from the causes of more moderate inflation. We'll also learn about *disinflation*, a reduction in the inflation rate, and the special problems associated with a falling price level, or *deflation*. Finally we'll look at the causes and consequences of banking crises and discuss policy options for helping an economy recover from them.

Thinkstock

Money and Inflation

To understand what causes inflation, we need to revisit the effect of changes in the money supply on the overall price level. Then we'll turn to the reasons why governments sometimes increase the money supply very rapidly.

The Classical Model of Money and Prices

We learned that in the short run an increase in the money supply increases real GDP by lowering the interest rate and stimulating investment spending and consumer spending. However, in the long run, as nominal wages and other sticky prices rise, real GDP falls back to its original level. So in the long run, an increase in the money supply does not change real GDP. Instead, other things equal, it leads to an equal percentage rise in the overall price level; that is, the prices of all goods and services in the economy, including nominal wages and the prices of intermediate goods, rise by the same percentage as the money supply. And when the overall price level rises, the aggregate price level—the prices of all final goods and services—rises as well.

As a result, a change in the *nominal* money supply, M, leads in the long run to a change in the aggregate price level, P, that leaves the *real* quantity of money, M/P, at its original level. There is also no long-run effect on aggregate demand or real GDP. For example, when Turkey dropped six zeros from its currency, the Turkish lira, in 2005, the country's real GDP did not change. The only thing that changed was the number of zeros in prices: instead of something costing 2,000,000 lira, it cost 2 lira.

This is, to repeat, what happens in the long run. When analyzing large changes in the aggregate price level, however, macroeconomists often find it useful to ignore the distinction between the short run and the long run. Instead, they work with a simpli-fied model in which the effect of a change in the money supply on the aggregate price level takes place instantaneously rather than over a long period of time. You might be concerned about this assumption given the emphasis we've placed on the difference between the short run and the long run. However, for reasons we'll explain shortly, this is a reasonable assumption to make in the case of high inflation.

The simplified model in which the real quantity of money, M/P, is always at its long-run equilibrium level is known as the **classical model of the price level** because it was commonly used by "classical" economists prior to the influence of John Maynard Keynes. To understand the classical model and why it is useful in the context of high inflation, let's revisit the AD–AS model and what it says about the effects of an in-crease in the money supply. (Unless otherwise noted, we will always be referring to changes in the *nominal* supply of money.)

Figure 40-1 reviews the effects of an increase in the money supply according to the AD–AS model. The economy starts at E_1, a point of short-run and long-run macroeco-nomic equilibrium. It lies at the intersection of the aggregate demand curve, AD_1, and the short-run aggregate supply curve, $SRAS_1$. It also lies on the long-run aggregate supply curve, $LRAS$. At E_1, the equilibrium aggregate price level is P_1.

Now suppose there is an increase in the money supply. This is an expansionary monetary policy, which shifts the aggregate demand curve to the right, to AD_2, and moves the economy to a new short-run macroeconomic equilibrium at E_2. Over time, however, nominal wages adjust upward in response to the rise in the aggregate price level, and the $SRAS$ curve shifts to the left, to $SRAS_2$. The new long-run macroeco-nomic equilibrium is at E_3, and real GDP returns to its initial level. The long-run in-crease in the aggregate price level from P_1 to P_3 is proportional to the increase in the money supply. As a result, in the long run changes in the money supply have no effect on the real quantity of money, M/P, or on real GDP. In the long run, money—as we learned—is *neutral*.

The classical model of the price level ignores the short-run movement from E_1 to E_2, assuming that the economy moves directly from one long-run equilibrium to another long-run equilibrium. In other words, it assumes that the economy moves directly from E_1 to E_3 and that real GDP never changes in response to a change in the money supply. In effect, in the classical model the effects of money supply changes are analyzed as if the short-run as well as the long-run aggregate supply curves were vertical.

> According to the **classical model of the price level**, the real quantity of money is always at its long-run equilibrium level.

FIGURE **40-1**   The Classical Model of the Price Level

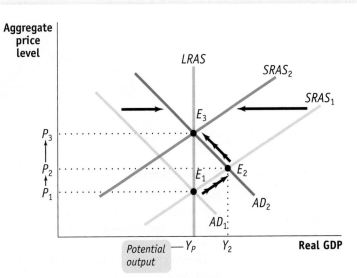

Starting at E_1, an increase in the money supply shifts the aggregate demand curve rightward, as shown by the movement from AD_1 to AD_2. There is a new short-run mac-roeconomic equilibrium at E_2 and a higher price level at P_2. In the long run, nominal wages adjust upward and push the $SRAS$ curve leftward to $SRAS_2$. The total percent increase in the price level from P_1 to P_3 is equal to the percent increase in the money supply. In the *classical model of the price level*, we ignore the transition period and think of the price level as rising to P_3 imme-diately. This is a good approximation under conditions of high inflation.

In reality, this is a poor assumption during periods of low inflation. With a low inflation rate, it may take a while for workers and firms to react to a monetary expansion by raising wages and prices. In this scenario, some nominal wages and the prices of some goods are sticky in the short run. As a result, under low inflation there is an upward-sloping *SRAS* curve, and changes in the money supply can indeed change real GDP in the short run.

But what about periods of high inflation? In the face of high inflation, economists have observed that the short-run stickiness of nominal wages and prices tends to vanish. Workers and businesses, sensitized to inflation, are quick to raise their wages and prices in response to changes in the money supply. This implies that under high inflation there is a quicker adjustment of wages and prices of intermediate goods than occurs in the case of low inflation. So the short-run aggregate supply curve shifts leftward more quickly and there is a more rapid return to long-run equilibrium under high inflation. As a result, the classical model of the price level is much more likely to be a good approximation of reality for economies experiencing persistently high inflation.

The consequence of this rapid adjustment of all prices in the economy is that in countries with persistently high inflation, changes in the money supply are quickly translated into changes in the inflation rate. Let's look at Zimbabwe, which we read about in the story at the start of the section. Figure 40-2 shows the annual rate of growth in the money supply and the annual rate of change of consumer prices from 2003 through April 2008. As you can see, the surge in the growth rate of the money supply coincided closely with a roughly equal surge in the inflation rate. Note that to fit these very large percentage increases—exceeding 100,000 percent—onto the figure, we have drawn the vertical axis using a logarithmic scale that allows us to draw equal sized percent changes as the same size.

What leads a country to increase its money supply so much that the result is an inflation rate in the millions, or even billions, of percent?

FIGURE 40-2 **Money Supply Growth and Inflation in Zimbabwe**

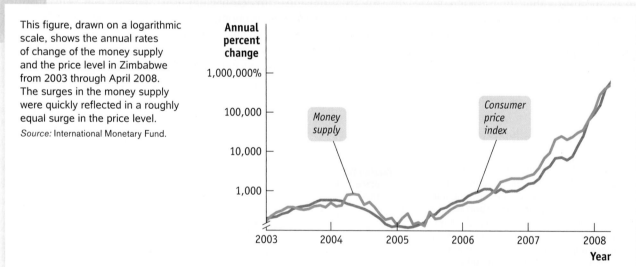

This figure, drawn on a logarithmic scale, shows the annual rates of change of the money supply and the price level in Zimbabwe from 2003 through April 2008. The surges in the money supply were quickly reflected in a roughly equal surge in the price level.

Source: International Monetary Fund.

The Inflation Tax

Modern economies use fiat money—pieces of paper that have no intrinsic value but are accepted as a medium of exchange. In the United States and most other wealthy countries, the decision about how many pieces of paper to issue is placed in the hands of a central bank that is somewhat independent of the political process. However, this independence can always be taken away if politicians decide to seize control of monetary policy.

So what is to prevent a government from paying for some of its expenses not by raising taxes or borrowing but simply by printing money? Nothing. In fact, governments, including the U.S. government, do it all the time. How can the U.S. government do this, given that the Federal Reserve, not the U.S. Treasury, issues money? The answer is that the Treasury and the Federal Reserve work in concert. The Treasury issues debt to finance the government's purchases of goods and services, and the Fed *monetizes* the debt by creating money and buying the debt back from the public through open-market purchases of Treasury bills. In effect, the U.S. government can and does raise revenue by printing money.

For example, in May 2013, the U.S. monetary base—bank reserves plus currency in circulation—was $388 billion larger than it had been a year earlier. This occurred because, over the course of that year, the Federal Reserve had issued $388 billion in money or its electronic equivalent and put it into circulation mainly through open-market operations. To put it another way, the Fed created money out of thin air and used it to buy valuable government securities from the private sector.

It's true that the U.S. government pays interest on debt owned by the Federal Reserve—but the Fed, by law, hands the interest payments it receives on government debt back to the Treasury, keeping only enough to fund its own operations. In effect, then, the Federal Reserve's actions enabled the government to pay off $388 billion in outstanding government debt by printing money.

An alternative way to look at this is to say that the right to print money is itself a source of revenue. Economists refer to the revenue generated by the government's right to print money as *seignorage,* an archaic term that goes back to the Middle Ages. It refers to the right to stamp gold and silver into coins, and charge a fee for doing so, that medieval lords—seigneurs, in France—reserved for themselves.

Seignorage accounts for only a tiny fraction (less than 1%) of the U.S. government's budget. Furthermore, concerns about seignorage don't have any influence on the Federal Reserve's decisions about how much money to print; the Fed is worried about inflation and unemployment, not revenue. But this hasn't always been true, even in the United States: both sides relied on seignorage to help cover budget deficits during the Civil War.

In fact, there have been many occasions in history when governments turned to their printing presses as a crucial source of revenue. According to the usual scenario, a government finds itself running a large budget deficit—and lacks either the competence or the political will to eliminate this deficit by raising taxes or cutting spending. Furthermore, the government can't borrow to cover the gap because potential lenders won't extend loans, given the fear that the government's weakness will continue and leave it unable to repay its debts.

In such a situation, governments end up printing money to cover the budget deficit. But by printing money to pay its bills, a government increases the quantity of money in circulation. And as we've just seen, increases in the money supply translate into equally large increases in the aggregate price level. So printing money to cover a budget deficit leads to inflation.

Who ends up paying for the goods and services the government purchases with newly printed money? The people who currently hold money pay. They pay because inflation erodes the purchasing power of their money holdings. In other words, a government imposes an **inflation tax,** a reduction in the value of the money held by the public, by printing money to cover its budget deficit and creating inflation.

An **inflation tax** is a reduction in the value of money held by the public caused by inflation.

It's helpful to think about what this tax represents. If the inflation rate is 5%, then a year from now $1 will buy goods and services worth only about $0.95 today. So a 5% inflation rate in effect imposes a tax rate of 5% on the value of all money held by the public.

But why would any government push the inflation tax to rates of hundreds or thousands of percent? We turn next to the process by which high inflation turns into explosive hyperinflation.

The Logic of Hyperinflation

Inflation imposes a tax on individuals who hold money. And, like most taxes, it will lead people to change their behavior. In particular, when inflation is high, people will try to avoid holding money and will instead substitute real goods as well as interest-bearing assets for money. During the German hyperinflation, people began using eggs or lumps of coal as a medium of exchange. They did this because lumps of coal maintained their real value over time but money didn't.

In the 1920s, hyperinflation made German currency worth so little that children made kites from banknotes.

Keystone/Getty Images

Indeed, during the peak of German hyperinflation, people often burned paper money, which was less valuable than wood. Moreover, people don't just reduce their nominal money holdings—they reduce their *real* money holdings, cutting the amount of money they hold so much that it actually has less purchasing power than the amount of money they would hold if inflation were low. Why? Because the more real money holdings they have, the greater the real amount of resources the government captures from them through the inflation tax.

We are now prepared to understand how countries can get themselves into situations of extreme inflation. High inflation arises when the government must print a large quantity of money, imposing a large inflation tax, to cover a large budget deficit.

Now, the seignorage collected by the government over a short period—say, one month—is equal to the change in the money supply over that period. Let's use M to represent the money supply and the symbol Δ to mean "monthly change in." Then:

(40-1) Seignorage = ΔM

The money value of seignorage, however, isn't very informative by itself. After all, the whole point of inflation is that a given amount of money buys less and less over time. So it's more useful to look at *real* seignorage, the revenue created by printing money divided by the price level, P:

(40-2) Real seignorage = $\Delta M/P$

Equation 40-2 can be rewritten by dividing and multiplying by the current level of the money supply, M, giving us:

(40-3) Real seignorage = $(\Delta M/M) \times (M/P)$

or

Real seignorage = Rate of growth of the money
supply $\times$ Real money supply

But as we've just explained, in the face of high inflation the public reduces the real amount of money it holds, so that the far right-hand term in Equation 40-3, M/P, gets smaller. Suppose that the government needs to print enough money to pay for a given quantity of goods and services—that is, it needs to collect a given *real* amount of seignorage. Then, as people hold smaller amounts of real money due to a high rate of inflation, the government has to respond by accelerating the rate of growth of the money supply, $\Delta M/M$. This will lead to an even higher rate of inflation. And people will respond to this new higher rate of inflation by reducing their real money holdings, M/P, yet again.

As the process becomes self-reinforcing, it can easily spiral out of control. Although the amount of real seignorage that the government must ultimately collect to pay off its deficit does not change, the inflation rate the government needs to impose to collect that amount rises. So the government is forced to increase the money supply more rapidly, leading to an even higher rate of inflation, and so on.

Here's an analogy: imagine a city government that tries to raise a lot of money with a special fee on taxi rides. The fee will raise the cost of taxi rides, and this will cause people to turn to substitutes, such as walking or taking the bus. As taxi use declines, the government finds that its tax revenue declines and it must impose a higher fee to raise the same amount of revenue as before. You can imagine the ensuing vicious circle: the government imposes fees on taxi rides, which leads to less taxi use, which causes the government to raise the fee on taxi rides, which leads to even less taxi use, and so on.

Substitute the real money supply for taxi rides and the inflation rate for the increase in the fee on taxi rides, and you have the story of hyperinflation. A race develops between the government printing presses and the public: the presses churn out money at a faster and faster rate to try to compensate for the fact that the public is reducing its real money holdings. At some point the inflation rate explodes into hyperinflation, and people are unwilling to hold any money at all (and resort to trading in eggs and lumps of coal). The government is then forced to abandon its use of the inflation tax and shut down the printing presses.

WHAT CAUSED ZIMBABWE'S INFLATION?

As noted in this section's opening story, Zimbabwe offers a recent example of a country experiencing very high inflation. Figure 40-2 showed that surges in Zimbabwe's money supply growth were matched by almost simultaneous surges in its inflation rate. But looking at rates of change doesn't give a true feel for just how much prices went up.

Figure 40-3 shows Zimbabwe's consumer price index from January 2000 to July 2008, with the January 2000 level set equal to 100. As in Figure 40-2, we also use a logarithmic scale. Over the course of just over eight years, consumer prices rose by approximately 80 trillion percent.

Why did Zimbabwe's government pursue policies that led to runaway inflation? The reason boils down to political instability, which in turn had its roots in Zimbabwe's history.

Until the 1970s, Zimbabwe had been ruled by its small white minority; even after the shift to majority rule, many of the country's farms remained in the hands of whites. Eventually Robert Mugabe, Zimbabwe's president, tried to solidify his position by seizing these farms and turning them over to his political supporters. But because this seizure disrupted production, the result was to undermine the country's economy and its tax base. It became impossible for the country's government to balance its budget either by raising taxes or by cutting spending. At the same time, the regime's instability left Zimbabwe unable to borrow money in world markets. Like many others before it, Zimbabwe's government turned to the printing press to cover the gap—leading to massive inflation.

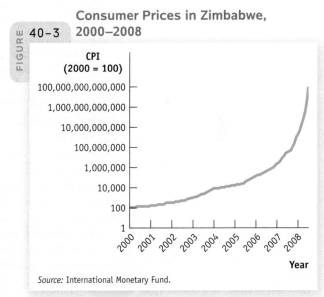

FIGURE 40-3 Consumer Prices in Zimbabwe, 2000–2008

Source: International Monetary Fund.

Moderate Inflation and Disinflation

The governments of wealthy, politically stable countries like the United States and Britain don't find themselves forced to print money to pay their bills. Yet over the past 40 years both countries, along with a number of other nations, have experienced uncomfortable episodes of inflation. In the United States, the inflation rate peaked at

13% in 1980. In Britain, the inflation rate reached 26% in 1975. Why did policy makers allow this to happen?

The answer, in brief, is that in the short run, policies that produce a booming economy also tend to lead to higher inflation, and policies that reduce inflation tend to depress the economy. This creates both temptations and dilemmas for governments.

Imagine yourself as a politician facing an election in a year, and suppose that inflation is fairly low at the moment. You might well be tempted to pursue expansionary policies that will push the unemployment rate down, as a way to please voters, even if your economic advisers warn that this will eventually lead to higher inflation. You might also be tempted to find different economic advisers, who will tell you not to worry: in politics, as in ordinary life, wishful thinking often prevails over realistic analysis.

Conversely, imagine yourself as a politician in an economy suffering from inflation. Your economic advisers will probably tell you that the only way to bring inflation down is to push the economy into a recession, which will lead to temporarily higher unemployment. Are you willing to pay that price? Maybe not.

This political asymmetry—inflationary policies often produce short-term political gains, but policies to bring inflation down carry short-term political costs—explains how countries with no need to impose an inflation tax sometimes end up with serious inflation problems. For example, that 26% rate of inflation in Britain was largely the result of the British government's decision in 1971 to pursue highly expansionary monetary and fiscal policies. Politicians disregarded warnings that these policies would be inflationary and were extremely reluctant to reverse course even when it became clear that the warnings had been correct.

But why do expansionary policies lead to inflation? To answer that question, we need to look first at the relationship between output and unemployment.

Expansionary policies can temporarily reduce unemployment but eventually lead to high inflation.

Grzegorz Knec/Alamy

The Output Gap and the Unemployment Rate

Earlier we introduced the concept of *potential output*, the level of real GDP that the economy would produce once all prices had fully adjusted. Potential output typically grows steadily over time, reflecting long-run growth. However, as we learned from the aggregate demand–aggregate supply model, actual aggregate output fluctuates around potential output in the short run: a recessionary gap arises when actual aggregate output falls short of potential output; an inflationary gap arises when actual aggregate output exceeds potential output.

Recall that the percentage difference between the actual level of real GDP and potential output is called the *output gap*. A positive or negative output gap occurs when an economy is producing more than or less than what would be "expected" because all prices have not yet adjusted. And wages, as we've learned, are the prices in the labor market.

Meanwhile, we learned that the unemployment rate is composed of cyclical unemployment and natural unemployment, the portion of the unemployment rate unaffected by the business cycle. So there is a relationship between the unemployment rate and the output gap. This relationship is defined by two rules:

1. When actual aggregate output is equal to potential output, the actual unemployment rate is equal to the natural rate of unemployment.

2. When the output gap is positive (an inflationary gap), the unemployment rate is *below* the natural rate. When the output gap is negative (a recessionary gap), the unemployment rate is *above* the natural rate.

In other words, fluctuations of aggregate output around the long-run trend of potential output correspond to fluctuations of the unemployment rate around the natural rate.

This makes sense. When the economy is producing less than potential output—when the output gap is negative—it is not making full use of its productive resources. Among the resources that are not fully used is labor, the economy's most important resource. So we would expect a negative output gap to be associated with unusually high unemployment. Conversely, when the economy is producing more than potential output, it is temporarily using resources at higher-than-normal rates. With this positive output gap, we would expect to see lower-than-normal unemployment.

Figure 40-4 confirms this rule. Panel (a) shows the actual and natural rates of unemployment, as estimated by the Congressional Budget Office (CBO). Panel (b) shows two series. One is cyclical unemployment: the difference between the actual unemployment rate and the CBO estimate of the natural rate of unemployment, measured on the left. The other is the CBO estimate of the output gap, measured on the right. To make the relationship clearer, the output gap series is inverted—shown upside down—so that the line goes down if actual output rises above potential output and up if actual output falls below potential output.

As you can see, the two series move together quite closely, showing the strong relationship between the output gap and cyclical unemployment. Years of high cyclical unemployment, like 1982, 1992, or 2009, were also years of a strongly negative output gap. Years of low cyclical unemployment, like the late 1960s or 2000, were also years of a strongly positive output gap.

FIGURE

40-4   Cyclical Unemployment and the Output Gap

Panel (a) shows the actual U.S. unemployment rate from 1950 to early 2013, together with the Congressional Budget Office estimate of the natural rate of unemployment. The actual rate fluctuates around the natural rate, often for extended periods. Panel (b) shows cyclical unemployment—the difference between the actual unemployment rate and the natural rate of unemployment—and the output gap, also estimated by the CBO. The unemployment rate is measured on the left vertical axis, and the output gap is measured with an inverted scale on the right vertical axis. With an inverted scale, it moves in the same direction as the unemployment rate: when the output gap is positive, the actual unemployment rate is below its natural rate; when the output gap is negative, the actual unemployment rate is above its natural rate. The two series track one another closely, showing the strong relationship between the output gap and cyclical unemployment.

Sources: Congressional Budget Office; Bureau of Labor Statistics; Bureau of Economic Analysis.

(a) The Actual Unemployment Rate Fluctuates Around the Natural Rate . . .

(b) . . . and These Fluctuations Correspond to the Output Gap.

MODULE

40 Review

Solutions appear at the back of the book.

Check Your Understanding

1. Suppose there is a large increase in the money supply in an economy that previously had low inflation. As a consequence, aggregate output expands in the short run. What does this say about situations in which the classical model of the price level applies?

2. Suppose that all wages and prices in an economy are indexed to inflation. Can there still be an inflation tax?

Multiple-Choice Questions

1. The real quantity of money is

   I. equal to *M/P*.
   II. the money supply adjusted for inflation.
   III. higher in the long run when the Fed buys government securities.

   a. I only
   b. II only
   c. III only
   d. I and II only
   e. I, II, and III

2. In the classical model of the price level

   a. only the short-run aggregate supply curve is vertical.
   b. both the short-run and long-run aggregate supply curves are vertical.
   c. only the long-run aggregate supply curve is vertical.
   d. both the short-run aggregate demand and supply curves are vertical.
   e. both the long-run aggregate demand and supply curves are vertical.

3. The classical model of the price level is most applicable in

   a. the United States.
   b. periods of high inflation.

   c. periods of low inflation.
   d. recessions.
   e. depressions.

4. An inflation tax is

   a. imposed by governments to offset price increases.
   b. paid directly as a percentage of the sale price on purchases.
   c. the result of a decrease in the value of money held by the public.
   d. generally levied by states rather than the federal government.
   e. higher during periods of low inflation.

5. Revenue generated by the government's right to print money is known as

   a. seignorage.
   b. an inflation tax.
   c. hyperinflation.
   d. fiat money.
   e. monetary funds.

Critical-Thinking Question

Draw a correctly labeled aggregate demand and supply graph showing an economy in long-run macroeconomic equilibrium. On your graph, show the effect of an increase in the money supply, according to the classical model of the price level.

Tom Bonaventure/Photographer's Choice RF/Getty Images

The Phillips Curve

Inflation and Unemployment in the Short Run

We've just seen that expansionary policies lead to a lower unemployment rate. Our next step in understanding the temptations and dilemmas facing governments is to show that there is a short-run trade-off between unemployment and inflation—lower unemployment tends to lead to higher inflation, and vice versa. The key concept is that of the *Phillips curve.*

The Short-Run Phillips Curve

The origins of this concept lie in a famous 1958 paper by the New Zealand–born economist A. W. H. Phillips. Looking at historical data for Britain, he found that when the unemployment rate was high, the wage rate tended to fall, and when the unemployment rate was low, the wage rate tended to rise. Using data from Britain, the United States, and elsewhere, other economists soon found a similar apparent relationship between the unemployment rate and the rate of inflation—that is, the rate of change in the aggregate price level. For example, Figure 41-1 shows the U.S. unemployment rate and the rate of consumer price inflation over each subsequent year from 1955 to 1968, with each dot representing one year's data.

Looking at evidence like Figure 41-1, many economists concluded that there is a negative short-run relationship between the unemployment rate and the inflation rate, represented by the **short-run Phillips curve,** or *SRPC.* (We'll explain the difference between the short-run and the long-run Phillips curve soon.) Figure 41-2 shows a hypothetical short-run Phillips curve.

Early estimates of the short-run Phillips curve for the United States were very simple: they showed a negative relationship between the unemployment rate and the inflation rate, without taking account of any other variables. During the 1950s and 1960s

WHAT YOU WILL LEARN

1 **What the Phillips curve is and the nature of the short-run trade-off between inflation and unemployment**

2 **Why there is no long-run trade-off between inflation and unemployment**

3 **Why expansionary policies are limited due to the effects of expected inflation**

4 **Why deflation is a problem for economic policy**

The **short-run Phillips curve** is the negative short-run relationship between the unemployment rate and the inflation rate.

41-1   Unemployment and Inflation, 1955–1968

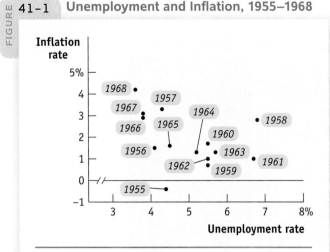

Each dot shows the average U.S. unemployment rate for one year and the percentage increase in the consumer price index over the subsequent year. Data like this lay behind the initial concept of the Phillips curve.

Source: Bureau of Labor Statistics.

this simple approach seemed, for a while, to be adequate. And this simple relationship is clear in the data in Figure 41-1.

Even at the time, however, some economists argued that a more accurate short-run Phillips curve would include other factors. Previously, we discussed the effect of *supply shocks*, such as sudden changes in the price of oil, that shift the short-run aggregate supply curve. Such shocks also shift the short-run Phillips curve: surging oil prices were an important factor in the inflation of the 1970s and also played an important role in the acceleration of inflation in 2007–2008.

In general, a negative supply shock shifts *SRPC* up, as the inflation rate increases for every level of the unemployment rate, and a positive supply shock shifts it down as the inflation rate falls for every level of the unemployment rate. Both outcomes are shown in Figure 41-3.

But supply shocks are not the only factors that can change the inflation rate. In the early 1960s, Americans had little experience with inflation as inflation rates had been low for decades. But by the late 1960s, after inflation had been steadily increasing for a number of years, Americans had come to expect future inflation. In 1968 two economists—Milton Friedman of the University of Chicago and Edmund Phelps of Columbia University—independently set forth a crucial hypothesis: that expectations about future inflation directly affect the present inflation rate. Today most economists accept that the *expected inflation rate*—the rate of inflation that employers and workers expect in the near future—is the most important factor, other than the unemployment rate, affecting inflation.

41-2   The Short-Run Phillips Curve

The short-run Phillips curve, *SRPC*, slopes downward because the relationship between the unemployment rate and the inflation rate is negative.

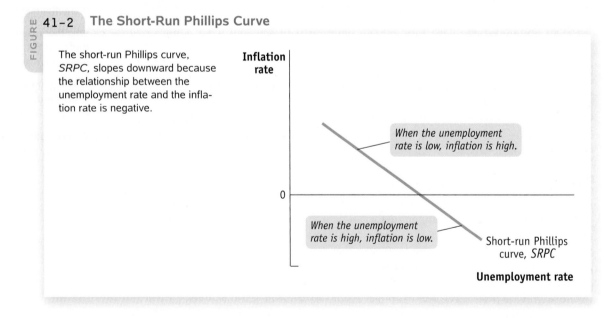

Inflation Expectations and the Short-Run Phillips Curve

The expected rate of inflation is the rate that employers and workers expect in the near future. One of the crucial discoveries of modern macroeconomics is that changes in the expected rate of inflation affect the short-run trade-off between unemployment and inflation and shift the short-run Phillips curve.

Why do changes in expected inflation affect the short-run Phillips curve? Put yourself in the position of a worker or employer about to sign a contract setting the worker's wages over the next year. For a number of reasons, the wage rate they agree

FIGURE

41-3   The Short-Run Phillips Curve and Supply Shocks

A negative supply shock shifts the *SRPC* up, and a positive supply shock shifts the *SRPC* down.

A negative supply shock shifts SRPC up.

A positive supply shock shifts SRPC down.

Inflation rate

Unemployment rate

$SRPC_1$

$SRPC_0$

$SRPC_2$

to will be higher if everyone expects high inflation (including rising wages) than if everyone expects prices to be stable. The worker will want a wage rate that takes into account future declines in the purchasing power of earnings. He or she will also want a wage rate that won't fall behind the wages of other workers. And the employer will be more willing to agree to a wage increase now if hiring workers later will be even more expensive. Also, rising prices will make paying a higher wage rate more affordable for the employer because the employer's output will sell for more.

For these reasons, an increase in expected inflation shifts the short-run Phillips curve upward: the actual rate of inflation at any given unemployment rate is higher when the expected inflation rate is higher. In fact, macroeconomists believe that the relationship between changes in expected inflation and changes in actual inflation is one-to-one. That is, when the expected inflation rate increases, the actual inflation rate at any given unemployment rate will increase by the same amount. When the expected inflation rate falls, the actual inflation rate at any given level of unemployment will fall by the same amount.

Figure 41-4 shows how the expected rate of inflation affects the short-run Phillips curve. First, suppose that the expected rate of inflation is 0%. $SRPC_0$ is the short-run Phillips curve when the public expects 0% inflation. According to $SRPC_0$, the actual inflation rate will be 0% if the unemployment rate is 6%; it will be 2% if the unemployment rate is 4%.

Alternatively, suppose the expected rate of inflation is 2%. In that case, employers and workers will build this expectation into wages and prices: at any given unemployment rate, the actual inflation rate will be 2 percentage points higher than it would be if people expected 0% inflation. $SRPC_2$, which shows the Phillips curve when the expected inflation rate is 2%, is $SRPC_0$ shifted upward by 2 percentage points at every level of unemployment. According to $SRPC_2$, the actual inflation rate will be 2% if the unemployment rate is 6%; it will be 4% if the unemployment rate is 4%.

What determines the expected rate of inflation? In general, people base their expectations about inflation on experience. If the inflation rate has hovered around 0% in the last few years, people will expect it to be around 0% in the near future. But if the inflation rate has averaged around 5% lately, people will expect inflation to be around 5% in the near future.

Since expected inflation is an important part of the modern discussion about the short-run Phillips curve, you might wonder why it was not in the original formulation

PM Images/Getty Images

The expected inflation rate is the most important factor, other than unemployment, that affects inflation.

FIGURE **41-4**   Expected Inflation and the Short-Run Phillips Curve

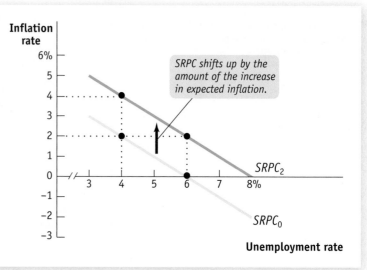

An increase in expected inflation shifts the short-run Phillips curve up. $SRPC_0$ is the initial short-run Phillips curve with an expected inflation rate of 0%; $SRPC_2$ is the short-run Phillips curve with an expected inflation rate of 2%. Each additional percentage point of expected inflation raises the actual inflation rate at any given unemployment rate by 1 percentage point.

of the Phillips curve. The answer lies in history. Think back to what we said about the early 1960s: at that time, people were accustomed to low inflation rates and reasonably expected that future inflation rates would also be low. It was only after 1965 that persistent inflation became a fact of life. So only then did it become clear that expected inflation would play an important role in price-setting.

Inflation and Unemployment in the Long Run

The short-run Phillips curve says that at any given point in time there is a trade-off between unemployment and inflation. According to this view, policy makers have a choice: they can choose to accept the price of high inflation in order to achieve low unemployment, or they can reject high inflation and pay the price of high unemployment. In fact, during the 1960s many economists believed that this trade-off represented a real choice.

However, this view was greatly altered by the later recognition that expected inflation affects the short-run Phillips curve. In the short run, expectations often diverge from reality. In the long run, however, any consistent rate of inflation will be reflected in expectations. If inflation is consistently high, as it was in the 1970s, people will come to expect more of the same; if inflation is consistently low, as it has been in recent years, that, too, will become part of expectations.

So what does the trade-off between inflation and unemployment look like in the long run, when actual inflation is incorporated into expectations? Most macroeconomists believe that there is, in fact, no long-run trade-off. That is, it is not possible to achieve lower unemployment in the long run by accepting higher inflation. To see why, we need to introduce another concept: the *long-run Phillips curve*.

The Long-Run Phillips Curve

Figure 41-5 reproduces the two short-run Phillips curves from Figure 41-4, $SRPC_0$ and $SRPC_2$. It also includes an additional short-run Phillips curve, $SRPC_4$, representing a 4% expected rate of inflation. In a moment, we'll explain the significance of the vertical long-run Phillips curve, $LRPC$.

Suppose that the economy has, in the past, had a 0% inflation rate. In that case, the current short-run Phillips curve will be $SRPC_0$, reflecting a 0% expected inflation rate. If the unemployment rate is 6%, the actual inflation rate will be 0%.

Also suppose that policy makers decide to trade off lower unemployment for a higher rate of inflation. They use monetary policy, fiscal policy, or both to drive the unemployment rate down to 4%. This puts the economy at point *A* on *SRPC*$_0$, leading to an actual inflation rate of 2%.

Over time, the public will come to expect a 2% inflation rate. *This increase in inflationary expectations will shift the short-run Phillips curve upward to* SRPC$_2$. Now, when the unemployment rate is 6%, the actual inflation rate will be 2%. Given this new short-run Phillips curve, policies adopted to keep the unemployment rate at 4% will lead to a 4% actual inflation rate—point *B* on *SRPC*$_2$—rather than point *A* with a 2% actual inflation rate.

Eventually, the 4% actual inflation rate gets built into expectations about the future inflation rate, and the short-run Phillips curve shifts upward yet again to *SRPC*$_4$. To keep the unemployment rate at 4% would now require accepting a 6% actual inflation rate, point *C* on *SRPC*$_4$, and so on. In short, a persistent attempt to trade off lower unemployment for higher inflation leads to *accelerating* inflation over time.

To avoid accelerating inflation over time, the unemployment rate must be high enough that the actual rate of inflation matches the expected rate of inflation. This is the situation at *E*$_0$ on *SRPC*$_0$: when the expected inflation rate is 0% and the unemployment rate is 6%, the actual inflation rate is 0%. It is also the situation at *E*$_2$ on *SRPC*$_2$: when the expected inflation rate is 2% and the unemployment rate is 6%, the actual inflation rate is 2%. And it is the situation at *E*$_4$ on *SRPC*$_4$: when the expected inflation rate is 4% and the unemployment rate is 6%, the actual inflation rate is 4%. As we'll learn shortly, this relationship between accelerating inflation and the unemployment rate is known as the *natural rate hypothesis*.

The unemployment rate at which inflation does not change over time—6% in Figure 41-5—is known as the **nonaccelerating inflation rate of unemployment,** or **NAIRU** for short. Keeping the unemployment rate below the NAIRU leads to ever-accelerating inflation and cannot be maintained. Most macroeconomists believe that there is a NAIRU and that there is no long-run trade-off between unemployment and inflation.

We can now explain the significance of the vertical line *LRPC*. It is the **long-run Phillips curve,** the relationship between unemployment and inflation in the long run, after expectations of inflation have had time to adjust to experience. It is vertical because any unemployment rate below the NAIRU leads to ever-accelerating

The **nonaccelerating inflation rate of unemployment,** or **NAIRU,** is the unemployment rate at which inflation does not change over time.

The **long-run Phillips curve** shows the relationship between unemployment and inflation after expectations of inflation have had time to adjust to experience.

NAIRU is the unemployment rate at which inflation does not change over time.

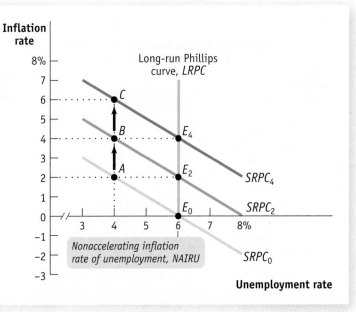

FIGURE 41-5   The NAIRU and the Long-Run Phillips Curve

SRPC$_0$ is the short-run Phillips curve when the expected inflation rate is 0%. At a 4% unemployment rate, the economy is at point *A* with an actual inflation rate of 2%. The higher inflation rate will be incorporated into expectations, and the *SRPC* will shift upward to *SRPC*$_2$. If policy makers act to keep the unemployment rate at 4%, the economy will be at *B* and the actual inflation rate will rise to 4%. Inflationary expectations will be revised upward again, and *SRPC* will shift to *SRPC*$_4$. At a 4% unemployment rate, the economy will be at *C* and the actual inflation rate will rise to 6%. Here, an unemployment rate of 6% is the NAIRU, or nonaccelerating inflation rate of unemployment. As long as unemployment is at the NAIRU, the actual inflation rate will match expectations and remain constant. An unemployment rate below 6% requires ever-accelerating inflation. The long-run Phillips curve, *LRPC*, which passes through *E*$_0$, *E*$_2$, and *E*$_4$, is vertical: no long-run trade-off between unemployment and inflation exists.

inflation. In other words, the long-run Phillips curve shows that there are limits to expansionary policies because an unemployment rate below the NAIRU cannot be maintained in the long run. Moreover there is a corresponding point we have not yet emphasized: any unemployment rate above the NAIRU leads to decelerating inflation.

The Natural Rate of Unemployment, Revisited

Recall the concept of the natural rate of unemployment, the portion of the unemployment rate unaffected by the swings of the business cycle. Now we have introduced the concept of the NAIRU. How do these two concepts relate to each other?

The answer is that the NAIRU is another name for the natural rate. The level of unemployment the economy "needs" in order to avoid accelerating inflation is equal to the natural rate of unemployment.

In fact, economists estimate the natural rate of unemployment by looking for evidence about the NAIRU from the behavior of the inflation rate and the unemployment rate over the course of the business cycle. For example, the way major European countries learned, to their dismay, that their natural rates of unemployment were 9% or more was through unpleasant experience. In the late 1980s, and again in the late 1990s, European inflation began to accelerate as European unemployment rates, which had been above 9%, began to fall, approaching 8%.

ECONOMICS ▶ IN ACTION

THE GREAT DISINFLATION OF THE 1980s

As we've mentioned several times, the United States ended the 1970s with a high rate of inflation, at least by its own peacetime historical standards—13% in 1980. Part of this inflation was the result of one-time events, especially a world oil crisis. But expectations of future inflation at 10% or more per year appeared to be firmly embedded in the economy.

By the mid-1980s, however, inflation was running at about 4% per year. Panel (a) of Figure 41-6 shows the annual rate of change in the "core" consumer price index (CPI)—also called the *core inflation rate*. This index, which excludes volatile energy and food prices, is widely regarded as a better indicator of underlying inflation trends than the overall CPI. By this measure, inflation fell from about 12% at the end of the 1970s to about 4% by the mid-1980s.

How was this disinflation achieved? At great cost. Beginning in late 1979, the Federal Reserve imposed strongly contractionary monetary policies, which pushed the

FIGURE 41-6   The Great Disinflation

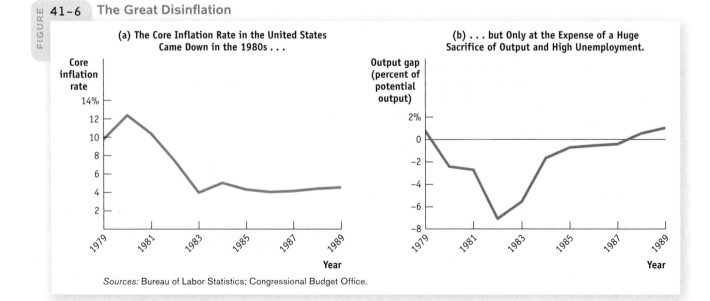

Sources: Bureau of Labor Statistics; Congressional Budget Office.

economy into its worst recession since the Great Depression. Panel (b) shows the Congressional Budget Office estimate of the U.S. output gap from 1979 to 1989: by 1982, actual output was 7% below potential output, corresponding to an unemployment rate of more than 9%. Aggregate output didn't get back to potential output until 1987.

Our analysis of the Phillips curve tells us that a temporary rise in unemployment, like that of the 1980s, is needed to break the cycle of inflationary expectations. Once expectations of inflation are reduced, the economy can return to the natural rate of unemployment at a lower inflation rate. And that's just what happened.

But the cost was huge. If you add up the output gaps over 1980–1987, you find that the economy sacrificed approximately 18% of an average year's output over the period. If we had to do the same thing today, that would mean giving up roughly $2.6 trillion worth of goods and services.

In Figure 41-3 we cited Congressional Budget Office estimates of the U.S. natural rate of unemployment. The CBO has a model that predicts changes in the inflation rate based on the deviation of the actual unemployment rate from the natural rate. Given data on actual unemployment and inflation, this model can be used to deduce estimates of the natural rate—and that's where the CBO numbers come from.

The Costs of Disinflation

Through experience, policy makers have found that bringing inflation down is a much harder task than increasing it. The reason is that once the public has come to expect continuing inflation, bringing inflation down is painful.

A persistent attempt to keep unemployment below the natural rate leads to accelerating inflation that becomes incorporated into expectations. To reduce inflationary expectations, policy makers need to run the process in reverse, adopting contractionary policies that keep the unemployment rate above the natural rate for an extended period of time. The process of bringing down inflation that has become embedded in expectations is known as *disinflation*.

Disinflation can be very expensive. The U.S. retreat from high inflation at the beginning of the 1980s appears to have cost the equivalent of about 18% of a year's real GDP, the equivalent of roughly $2.6 trillion today. The justification for paying these costs is that they lead to a permanent gain. Although the economy does not recover the short-term production losses caused by disinflation, it no longer suffers from the costs associated with persistently high inflation. In fact, the United States, Britain, and other wealthy countries that experienced inflation in the 1970s eventually decided that the benefit of bringing inflation down was worth the required suffering—the large reduction in real GDP in the short term.

Some economists argue that the costs of disinflation can be reduced if policy makers explicitly state their determination to reduce inflation. A clearly announced, credible policy of disinflation, they contend, can reduce expectations of future inflation and so shift the short-run Phillips curve downward. Some economists believe that the clear determination of the Federal Reserve to combat the inflation of the 1970s was credible enough that the costs of disinflation, huge though they were, were lower than they might otherwise have been.

Deflation

Before World War II, *deflation*—a falling aggregate price level—was almost as common as inflation. In fact, the U.S. consumer price index on the eve of World War II was 30% lower than it had been in 1920. After World War II, inflation became the norm in all countries. But in the 1990s, deflation reappeared in Japan and proved difficult to reverse. Concerns about potential deflation played a crucial role in U.S. monetary policy in the early 2000s and again in late 2008. In fact, in late 2008, the U.S. experienced a brief period of deflation.

Why is deflation a problem? And why is it hard to end?

Debt Deflation

Deflation, like inflation, produces both winners and losers—but in the opposite direction. Due to the falling price level, a dollar in the future has a higher real value than a dollar today. So lenders, who are owed money, gain under deflation because the real value of borrowers' payments increases. Borrowers lose because the real burden of their debt rises.

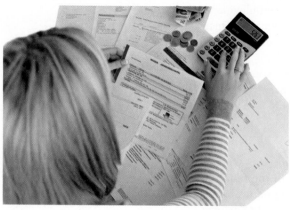

In a famous analysis at the beginning of the Great Depression, economist Irving Fisher claimed that the effects of deflation on borrowers and lenders can worsen an economic slump. Deflation, in effect, takes real resources away from borrowers and redistributes them to lenders. Fisher argued that borrowers, who lose from deflation, are typically short of cash and will be forced to cut their spending sharply when their debt burden rises. Lenders, however, are less likely to increase spending sharply when the values of the loans they own rise. The overall effect, said Fisher, is that deflation reduces aggregate demand, deepening an economic slump, which, in a vicious circle, may lead to further deflation. The effect of deflation in reducing aggregate demand, known as **debt deflation,** probably played a significant role in the Great Depression.

The effects of deflation on borrowers and lenders can worsen an economic slump.

Effects of Expected Deflation

Like expected inflation, expected deflation affects the nominal interest rate. Consider Figure 41-7 (which you may recall seeing in an earlier section). It demonstrates how expected inflation affects the equilibrium interest rate. As shown, the equilibrium nominal interest rate is 4% if the expected inflation rate is 0%. Clearly, if the expected inflation rate is –3%—if the public expects deflation at 3% per year—the equilibrium nominal interest rate will be 1%.

But what would happen if the expected rate of inflation were –5%? Would the nominal interest rate fall to –1%, meaning that lenders are paying borrowers 1% on their debt? No. Nobody would lend money at a negative nominal rate of interest because they could do better by simply holding cash. This illustrates what economists call the **zero bound** on the nominal interest rate: it cannot go below zero.

This zero bound can limit the effectiveness of monetary policy. Suppose the economy is depressed, with output below potential output and the unemployment rate above the natural rate. Normally, the central bank can respond by cutting interest rates so as to increase aggregate demand. If the nominal interest rate is already zero, however, the central bank cannot push it down any further. Banks refuse to lend and consumers and firms refuse to spend because, with a negative inflation rate and a 0%

Debt deflation is the reduction in aggregate demand arising from the increase in the real burden of outstanding debt caused by deflation.

There is a **zero bound** on the nominal interest rate: it cannot go below zero.

 41-7   **The Fisher Effect**

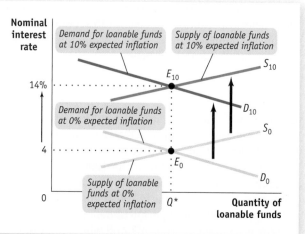

D_0 and S_0 are the demand and supply curves for loanable funds when the expected future inflation rate is 0%. At an expected inflation rate of 0%, the equilibrium nominal interest rate is 4%. An increase in expected future inflation pushes both the demand and supply curves upward by 1 percentage point for every percentage point increase in expected future inflation. D_{10} and S_{10} are the demand and supply curves for loanable funds when the expected future inflation rate is 10%. The 10 percentage point increase in expected future inflation raises the equilibrium nominal interest rate to 14%. The expected real interest rate remains at 4%, and the equilibrium quantity of loanable funds also remains unchanged.

FIGURE **41-8** The Zero Bound in U.S. History

This figure shows U.S. short-term interest rates, specifically the interest rate on three-month Treasury bills, from 1920 to 2013. As shown by the shaded area at left, for much of the 1930s, interest rates were very close to zero, leaving little room for expansionary monetary policy. After World War II, persistent inflation generally kept interest rates well above zero. However, in late 2008, in the wake of the housing bubble bursting and the financial crisis, the interest rate on three-month Treasury bills was again virtually zero.

Source: Federal Reserve Bank of St. Louis.

nominal interest rate, holding cash yields a positive real rate of return. Any further increases in the monetary base will either be held in bank vaults or held as cash by individuals and firms, without being spent.

A situation in which conventional monetary policy to fight a slump—cutting interest rates—can't be used because nominal interest rates are up against the zero bound is known as a **liquidity trap.** A liquidity trap can occur whenever there is a sharp reduction in demand for loanable funds—which is exactly what happened during the Great Depression. Figure 41-8 shows the interest rate on short-term U.S. government debt from 1920 to 2013. As you can see, starting in 1933 and ending when World War II brought a full economic recovery, the U.S. economy was either close to or up against the zero bound. After World War II, when inflation became the norm around the world, the zero bound problem largely vanished as the public came to expect inflation rather than deflation.

However, the recent history of the Japanese economy, shown in Figure 41-9, provides a modern illustration of the problem of deflation and the liquidity trap.

A **liquidity trap** is a situation in which conventional monetary policy is ineffective because nominal interest rates are up against the zero bound.

FIGURE **41-9** Japan's Lost Decade

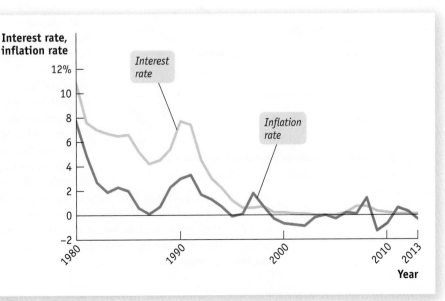

A prolonged economic slump in Japan led to deflation from the late 1990s on. The Bank of Japan responded by cutting interest rates—but eventually ran up against the zero bound.

Source: OECD; Bank of Japan.

Since the 1990s, Japan has been stuck in a deflationary trap.

Japan experienced a huge boom in the prices of both stocks and real estate in the late 1980s, and then saw both bubbles burst. The result was a prolonged period of economic stagnation, the so-called Lost Decade, which gradually reduced the inflation rate and eventually led to persistent deflation.

In an effort to fight the weakness of the economy, the Bank of Japan—the equivalent of the Federal Reserve—repeatedly cut interest rates. Eventually, it arrived at the ZIRP: the zero interest rate policy. The call money rate, the equivalent of the U.S. federal funds rate, was literally set equal to zero. Because the economy was still depressed, it would have been desirable to cut interest rates even further. But that wasn't possible: Japan was up against the zero bound.

In the aftermath of the 2008 financial crisis, the Federal Reserve also found itself up against the zero bound with the interest on short-term U.S. government debt virtually at zero. As the following Economics in Action explains, this led to fears of a Japan-type trap and spurred the Fed to take some unconventional action.

ECONOMICS ▶ IN ACTION   WORLD VIEW

THE DEFLATION SCARE OF 2010

Ever since the financial crisis of 2008, U.S. policy makers have been worried about the possibility of "Japanification"—that is, they have worried that, like Japan since the 1990s, the United States might find itself stuck in a deflationary trap. Indeed, Ben Bernanke, chairman of the Federal Reserve during the crisis, studied Japan intensively before he went to the Fed and sought to do better than his Japanese counterparts.

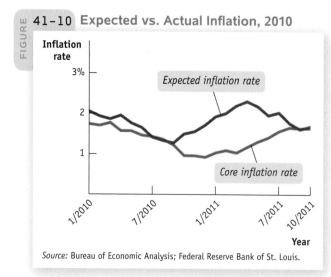

FIGURE **41-10** **Expected vs. Actual Inflation, 2010**

Source: Bureau of Economic Analysis; Federal Reserve Bank of St. Louis.

Fears of deflation were particularly intense in the summer and early fall of 2010. Figure 41-10 shows why, by tracking two numbers the Fed watches carefully when making policy. One of these numbers is the "core" inflation rate over the past year—the percentage rise in a measure of consumer prices (the personal consumption expenditure deflator) that excludes volatile food and energy prices. The Fed normally regards this core inflation rate as its best guide to underlying inflation and tries to keep it at around 2%. The other number is a measure of expected inflation derived by calculating the difference between the interest rate on ordinary government bonds and the rate on government bonds whose yield is protected against inflation.

As you can see, by the late summer of 2010 both actual inflation and expected inflation were sliding to levels well below the Fed's 2% target. Fed officials were worried, and they took action. In August 2010 Bernanke gave a speech at the annual Fed meeting, signaling that he would take special actions to head off the deflationary threat. And in November the Fed, which normally buys only short-term government debt, began a program of long-term bond purchases, hoping to give the economy a boost.

The figure shows that Bernanke's speech and the Fed's action led to a major change in expectations, as investors' fears of deflation ebbed. Actual inflation also picked up significantly.

What was far from clear, however, was whether the Fed had achieved more than a temporary reprieve. A year after Bernanke's big speech, expected inflation was sagging again, and deflation fears were on the rise. And those fears linger, given that core inflation averaged only 1.8% in 2013.

MODULE 41 Review

Solutions appear at the back of the book.

Check Your Understanding

1. Explain how the short-run Phillips curve illustrates the negative relationship between cyclical unemployment and the actual inflation rate for a given level of the expected inflation rate.

2. Why is there no long-run trade-off between unemployment and inflation?

3. Why is disinflation so costly for an economy? Are there ways to reduce these costs?

4. Why won't anyone lend money at a negative nominal rate of interest? How can this pose problems for monetary policy?

Multiple-Choice Questions

1. The long-run Phillips curve is
   I. the same as the short-run Phillips curve.
   II. vertical.
   III. the short-run Phillips curve plus expected inflation.
   a. I only
   b. II only
   c. III only
   d. I and II only
   e. I, II, and III

2. The short-run Phillips curve shows a _____ relationship between _____.
   a. negative; the aggregate price level and aggregate output
   b. positive; the aggregate price level and aggregate output
   c. negative; unemployment and inflation
   d. positive; unemployment and aggregate output
   e. positive; unemployment and the aggregate price level

3. An increase in expected inflation will shift
   a. the short-run Phillips curve downward.
   b. the short-run Phillips curve upward.
   c. the long-run Phillips curve upward.
   d. the long-run Phillips curve downward.
   e. neither the short-run nor the long-run Phillips curve.

4. Bringing down inflation that has become embedded in expectations is called
   a. deflation.
   b. negative inflation.
   c. anti-inflation.
   d. unexpected inflation.
   e. disinflation.

5. Debt deflation is
   a. the effect of deflation in decreasing aggregate demand.
   b. an idea proposed by Irving Fisher.
   c. a contributing factor in causing the Great Depression.
   d. due to differences in how borrowers/lenders respond to inflation losses/gains.
   e. all of the above.

Critical-Thinking Questions

Use the accompanying diagram to answer the questions that follow.

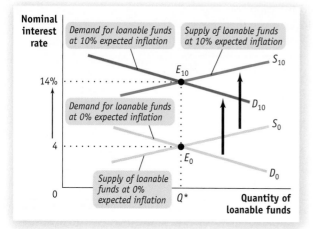

1. What is the nominal interest rate if expected inflation is 0%?

2. What would the nominal interest rate be if the expected inflation rate were −2%? Explain.

3. What would the nominal interest rate be if the expected inflation rate were −6%? Explain.

4. What would a negative nominal interest rate mean for lenders? How much lending would take place at a negative nominal interest rate? Explain.

5. What effect does a nominal interest rate of zero have on monetary policy? What is this situation called?

Crises and Consequences

MODULE 42

Igor Stevanovic/Shutterstock

WHAT YOU WILL LEARN

1. How depository banks and shadow banks differ and why both are subject to bank runs
2. What happens during financial panics and banking crises and why their effects are so severe and long-lasting
3. The causes of the 2008 financial crisis
4. How new regulation seeks to avoid another crisis

Banking: Benefits and Dangers

As we learned earlier, banks perform an essential role in any modern economy. In this module we examine what makes banking vulnerable to a crisis—even to full-blown financial panic. We'll explore the history of such crises, how destructive they are to the economy, and how governments respond to the risks of financial crises.

The Purpose of Banking

We defined commercial banks and savings and loans as financial intermediaries that provide liquid financial assets in the form of deposits to savers and use their funds to finance the illiquid investment spending needs of borrowers. Deposit-taking banks perform the important functions of providing liquidity to savers and directly influencing the level of the money supply.

Banks will accept the savings of individuals, promising to return them on demand, but put most of those funds to work by taking advantage of the fact that not everyone wants access to those funds at the same time. A typical bank account lets you withdraw as much of your funds as you want, anytime you want—but the bank doesn't actually keep everyone's cash in its safe or even in a form that can be turned quickly into cash. Instead, the bank lends out most of the funds, keeping limited reserves to meet day-to-day withdrawals. And because deposits can be put to use, banks don't charge you (or charge very little) for the privilege of keeping your savings safe. Depending on the type of account, they might even pay interest on your deposits.

In contrast, investment banks, hedge funds, and money market funds do not take deposits from consumers. These institutions are sometimes referred to as *shadow banks*. "Shadow" refers to the fact that before the 2008 crisis these financial institutions were neither closely watched nor effectively regulated. Like deposit-taking

435

Maturity transformation is the conversion of short-term liabilities into long-term assets.

A **shadow bank** is a nondepository financial institution that engages in maturity transformation.

A **banking crisis** occurs when a large part of the depository banking sector or the shadow banking sector fails or threatens to fail.

banks, shadow banks are vulnerable to bank runs. From now on, we will use the term *depository banks* for banks that accept deposits (commercial banks and savings and loans) to better distinguish them from shadow banks (investment banks, hedge funds, and money market funds), which do not.

More generally, depository banks borrow on a short-term basis from depositors (who can demand to be repaid at any time) and lend on a long-term basis to others (who cannot be forced to repay until the end date of their loan). This is what economists call **maturity transformation:** converting short-term liabilities (deposits in this case) into long-term assets (bank loans that earn interest).

A **shadow bank** is any financial institution that does not accept deposits but does engage in maturity transformation—borrowing over the short term and lending or investing over the longer term. And just as bank depositors benefit from the liquidity and higher return that banking provides compared to sitting on their money, lenders to shadow banks benefit from liquidity (their loans must be repaid quickly, often overnight) and higher return compared to other ways of investing their funds.

A generation ago, depository banks accounted for most banking. After about 1980, however, there was a steady rise in shadow banking. Shadow banking has grown so popular because it has not been subject to the regulations, such as capital requirements and reserve requirements, that are imposed on depository banking. So, like the unregulated trusts that set off the Panic of 1907, shadow banks can offer their customers a higher rate of return on their funds.

Shadow Banks and the Re-emergence of Bank Runs

Because a depository bank keeps on hand just a small fraction of its depositors' funds, a bank run typically results in a bank failure: the bank is unable to meet depositors' demands for their money and closes its doors. Ominously, bank runs can be self-fulfilling prophecies: although a bank may be in fine financial shape, if enough depositors believe it is in trouble and try to withdraw their money, their beliefs end up dooming the bank.

To prevent such occurrences, after the 1930s the United States (and most countries) adopted wide-ranging banking regulation in the form of regular audits by the Federal Reserve, deposit insurance, capital requirements and reserve requirements, and provisions allowing troubled banks to borrow from the Fed's discount window.

Shadow banks, though, don't take deposits. So how can they be vulnerable to a bank run? The reason is that a shadow bank, like a depository bank, engages in maturity transformation: it borrows short term and lends or invests longer term. If a shadow bank's lenders suddenly decide one day that it's no longer safe to lend it money, the shadow bank can no longer fund its operations. Unless it can sell its assets immediately to raise cash, it will quickly fail. This is exactly what happened in 2008 to the once venerable investment bank Lehman Brothers, which is the topic of the upcoming Economics in Action.

A typical scene outside a bank during the banking crisis of the Great Depression.

FPG/Hulton Archive/Getty Images.

Banking Crises and Financial Panics

Bank failures are common: even in a good year, several U.S. banks typically go under for one reason or another. And shadow banks sometimes fail, too. **Banking crises**—episodes in which a large part of the depository banking sector or the shadow banking sector fails or threatens to fail—are relatively rare by comparison. Yet they do happen, often with severe negative effects on the broader economy. What would cause so many of these institutions to get into trouble at the same time? Let's take a look at the two reasons why many banks—either depository banks or shadow banks—get into trouble. First, many of them could have made similar mistakes, often due to an *asset bubble.* Second, there may be *financial contagion,* in which one institution's problems spread and create trouble for others.

SHARED MISTAKES Banking crises usually owe their origins to many banks making the same mistake of investing in an *asset bubble.* In an **asset bubble,** the price of some kind of asset, such as housing, is pushed to an unreasonably high level by investors' expectations of further price gains. For a while, such bubbles feed on themselves.

A good example of such a bubble is the savings and loan crisis of the 1980s, when there was a huge boom in the construction of commercial real estate, especially office buildings. Many banks extended large loans to real estate developers, believing that the boom would continue indefinitely. By the late 1980s, it became clear that developers had gotten carried away, building far more office space than the country needed. Unable to rent out their space or forced to slash rents, a number of developers defaulted on their loans—and the result was a wave of bank failures.

A similar phenomenon occurred between 2002 and 2006, when rapidly rising housing prices led many people to borrow heavily to buy a house in the belief that prices would keep rising. This process accelerated as more buyers rushed into the market and pushed housing prices up even faster.

Eventually the market runs out of new buyers and the bubble bursts. At this point asset prices fall. This, in turn, undermines confidence in financial institutions that are exposed to losses due to falling asset prices. This loss of confidence, if it's sufficiently severe, can set in motion a financial contagion.

FINANCIAL CONTAGION In especially severe banking crises, an economy-wide vicious downward spiral that occurs among depository banks or shadow banks is known as a **financial contagion.** Each institution's failure worsens depositors' or lenders' fears and increases the odds that another bank will fail. The shadow banking sector, because it is largely unregulated, is especially prone to fear- and rumor-driven contagion.

When a financial institution is under pressure to reduce debt and raise cash, it tries to sell assets. To sell assets quickly, though, it often has to sell them at a deep discount. The contagion comes from the fact that other financial institutions own similar assets, whose prices decline as a result of the "fire sale." This decline in asset prices hurts the other financial institutions' financial positions, too, leading their creditors to stop lending to them. This knock-on effect forces more financial institutions to sell assets, reinforcing the downward spiral of asset prices.

Combine an asset bubble with a huge, unregulated shadow banking system and a vicious cycle of deleveraging and it is easy to see, as the U.S. economy did in 2008, how a full-blown **financial panic**—a sudden and widespread disruption of financial markets that happens when people suddenly lose faith in the liquidity of financial institutions and markets—can arise. A financial panic almost always involves a banking crisis, either in the depository banking sector, or the shadow banking sector, or both.

Because banking provides much of the liquidity needed for trading financial assets like stocks and bonds, severe banking crises almost always lead to disruptions of the stock and bond markets. Disruptions of these markets, along with a headlong rush to sell assets and raise cash, lead to a vicious circle of deleveraging. As the panic unfolds, savers and investors come to believe that the safest place for their money is under their bed, and their hoarding of cash further deepens the distress.

In an **asset bubble,** the price of an asset is pushed to an unreasonably high level due to expectations of further price gains.

A **financial contagion** is a vicious downward spiral among depository banks or shadow banks: each bank's failure worsens fears and increases the likelihood that another bank will fail.

A **financial panic** is a sudden and widespread disruption of the financial markets that occurs when people suddenly lose faith in the liquidity of financial institutions and markets.

ΕCONOMICS ▶ *IN ACTION*

The collapse of Lehman Brothers, the once-venerable investment bank, set off a chain of events that led to a worldwide financial panic.

LIGHTS OUT AT LEHMAN

By 1850, Lehman Brothers had established itself on Wall Street; by 2008, thanks to its skill at trading financial assets, Lehman Brothers was one of the nation's top investment banks. But in September of that year, Lehman's luck ran out.

The firm had invested heavily in subprime mortgages—loans to home-buyers with too little income or too few assets to qualify for standard (also called "prime") mortgages. In the summer and fall of 2008, as the U.S. housing market plunge intensified and investments related to subprime mortgages lost much of their value, Lehman was hit hard.

Lehman had been borrowing heavily in the short-term credit market (also known as the *repo market*)—often using overnight loans that must be repaid the next business day—to finance its ongoing operations and trading. As rumors began to spread about how heavily Lehman was exposed to the tanking housing market, its sources of credit dried up. On September 15, 2008, after being denied a government bailout, the firm declared the largest bankruptcy in history. What happened would shock the world.

When Lehman fell, it set off a chain of events that came close to taking down the entire world financial system. Through securitization (a concept we defined in Module 35) financial institutions throughout the world were exposed to real estate loans that were quickly deteriorating in value as default rates on those loans rose. Credit markets froze because those with funds to lend decided it was better to sit on the funds rather than lend them out and risk losing them to a borrower who might go under like Lehman had.

Around the world, borrowers either lost their access to credit or found themselves forced to pay drastically higher interest rates. Stocks plunged, and within weeks the Dow had fallen almost 3,000 points.

Nor were the consequences limited to financial markets. The U.S. economy was already in recession when Lehman fell, but the pace of the downturn accelerated drastically in the months that followed. By the time U.S. employment bottomed out in early 2010, more than 8 million jobs had been lost. Europe and Japan were also suffering their worst recessions since the 1930s, and world trade plunged even faster than it had in the first year of the Great Depression.

Economists who knew their history quickly recognized what they were seeing: it was a modern version of a financial panic, a sudden and widespread disruption of financial markets.

Financial panics were a regular feature of the U.S. financial system before World War II. The financial panic that hit the United States in 2008 shared many features with the Panic of 1907, whose devastation prompted the creation of the Federal Reserve system. Financial panics almost always include a banking crisis, in which a significant portion of the banking sector ceases to function.

Financial panics and banking crises have happened fairly often, sometimes with disastrous effects on output and employment. Chile's 1981 banking crisis was followed by a 19% decline in real GDP per capita and a slump that lasted through most of the following decade. Finland's 1990 banking crisis was followed by a surge in the unemployment rate from 3.2% to 16.3%. Japan's banking crisis of the early 1990s led to more than a decade of economic stagnation.

The Consequences of Banking Crises

If banking crises affected only banks, they wouldn't be as serious a concern. In fact, however, banking crises are almost always associated with recessions, and severe banking crises are associated with the worst economic slumps. Furthermore, history shows that recessions caused in part by banking crises inflict sustained economic damage, with economies taking years to recover.

Banking Crises, Recessions, and Recovery

A severe banking crisis is one in which a large fraction of the banking system either fails outright (that is, goes bankrupt) or suffers a major loss of confidence and must be bailed out by the government. Such crises almost invariably lead to deep recessions, which are usually followed by slow recoveries.

Figure 42-1 illustrates this phenomenon by tracking unemployment in the aftermath of two banking crises widely separated in space and time: the Panic of 1893 in the United States and the Swedish banking crisis of 1991. In the figure, *t* represents the year of the crisis: 1893 for the United States, 1991 for Sweden. As the figure shows, these crises on different continents, almost a century apart, produced similarly devastating results: unemployment shot up and came down only slowly and erratically so that, even five years after the crisis, the number of jobless remained high by pre-crisis standards.

FIGURE **42-1**   **Unemployment Rates, Before and After a Banking Crisis**

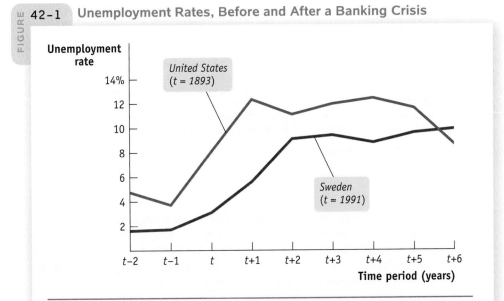

This figure tracks unemployment in the wake of two banking crises: the Panic of 1893 in the United States and the Swedish banking crisis of 1991. *t* represents the year of the crisis—1893 for the United States, 1991 for Sweden. *t* − 2 is the date two years before the crisis hit; *t* + 5 is the date five years after. In both cases, the economy suffered severe damage from the banking crisis: unemployment shot up and came down only slowly and erratically. In both cases, five years after the crisis the unemployment rate remained high compared to pre-crisis levels.

Sources: Christina D. Romer, "Spurious Volatility in Historical Unemployment Data," *Journal of Political Economy* 94, no. 1 (1986): 1–37; Eurostat.

FIGURE 42-2   Episodes of Banking Crises and Unemployment

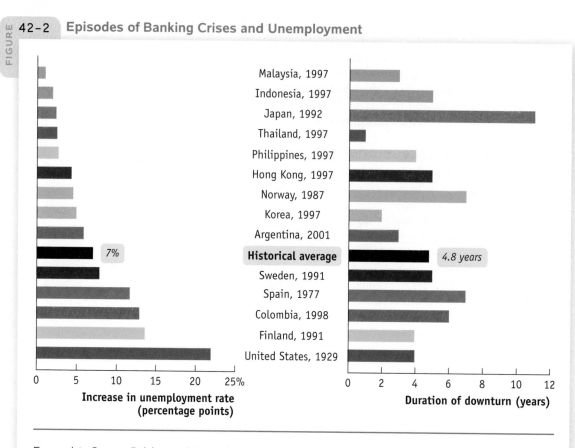

Economists Carmen Reinhart and Kenneth Rogoff have compared employment performance across several countries in the aftermath of a number of severe banking crises. For each country, the bar on the left shows the rise in the unemployment rate during and following the crisis, and the bar on the right shows how long it took for unemployment to begin to fall. On average, severe banking crises have been followed by a 7 percentage point rise in the unemployment rate, and in many cases it has taken four years or more before unemployment even begins to fall, let alone returns to pre-crisis levels.

Source: Carmen M. Reinhart and Kenneth S. Rogoff, "The Aftermath of Financial Crises," *American Economic Review* 99, no. 2 (2009): 466–472.

These historical examples are typical. Figure 42-2, taken from a widely cited study by the economists Carmen Reinhart and Kenneth Rogoff, compares employment performance in the wake of a number of severe banking crises. The bars on the left show the rise in the unemployment rate during and following the crisis; the bars on the right show the time it took before unemployment began to fall.

The numbers in the figure are shocking: on average, severe banking crises have been followed by a 7 percentage point rise in the unemployment rate, and in many cases it has taken four years or more before the unemployment rate even begins to fall, let alone returns to pre-crisis levels.

Why Are Banking-Crisis Recessions So Bad?

It's not difficult to see why banking crises normally lead to recessions. There are three main reasons: a *credit crunch* arising from reduced availability of credit, financial distress caused by a *debt overhang,* and the loss of monetary policy effectiveness.

1. *Credit crunch.* The disruption of the banking system typically leads to a reduction in the availability of credit called a **credit crunch,** in which potential borrowers either can't get credit at all or must pay very high interest rates. Unable to borrow or unwilling to pay higher interest rates, businesses and consumers cut back on spending, pushing the economy into a recession.

In a **credit crunch,** potential borrowers either can't get credit at all or must pay very high interest rates.

2. *Debt overhang.* A banking crisis typically pushes down the prices of many assets through a vicious cycle of deleveraging, as distressed borrowers try to sell assets to raise cash, pushing down asset prices and causing further financial distress. As we have already seen, deleveraging is a factor in the spread of the crisis, lowering the value of the assets banks hold on their balance sheets and so undermining their solvency. It also creates problems for other players in the economy.

   To take an example all too familiar from recent events, falling housing prices can leave consumers substantially poorer, especially because they are still stuck with the debt they incurred to buy their homes. A banking crisis, then, tends to leave consumers and businesses with a **debt overhang:** high debt but diminished assets. Like a credit crunch, this also leads to a fall in spending and a recession as consumers and businesses cut back in order to reduce their debt and rebuild their assets.

3. *Loss of monetary policy effectiveness.* A key feature of banking-crisis recessions is that when they occur, monetary policy—the main tool of policy makers for fighting negative demand shocks caused by a fall in consumer and investment spending—loses much of its effectiveness. The ineffectiveness of monetary policy makes banking-crisis recessions especially severe and long-lasting.

Recall how the Fed normally responds to a recession: it engages in open-market operations, purchasing short-term government debt from banks. This leaves banks with excess reserves, which they lend out, leading to a fall in interest rates and causing an economic expansion through increased consumer and investment spending.

Under normal conditions, this policy response is highly effective. In the aftermath of a banking crisis, though, the whole process tends to break down. Banks, fearing runs by depositors or a loss of confidence by their creditors, tend to hold on to excess reserves rather than lend them out. Meanwhile, businesses and consumers, finding themselves in financial difficulty due to the plunge in asset prices, may be unwilling to borrow even if interest rates fall. As a result, even very low interest rates may not be enough to push the economy back to full employment.

In the previous module we described the problem of the economy's falling into a liquidity trap, when even pushing short-term interest rates to zero isn't enough. In fact, all the historical episodes in which the zero bound on interest rates became an important constraint on policy—the 1930s, Japan in the 1990s, and a number of countries after 2008—have occurred after a major banking crisis.

The inability of the usual tools of monetary policy to offset the macroeconomic devastation caused by banking crises is the major reason such crises produce deep, prolonged slumps. The obvious solution is to look for other policy tools. In fact, governments do typically take a variety of special steps when banks are in crisis.

Governments Step In

Before the Great Depression, policy makers often allowed banks to fail in the belief that market forces should be allowed to work. Since the catastrophe of the 1930s, though, almost all policy makers have believed that it's necessary to take steps to contain the damage from bank failures. In general, central banks and governments take three main kinds of action in an effort to limit the fallout from banking crises:

1. They act as the *lender of last resort.*

2. They offer guarantees to depositors and others with claims on banks.

3. In an extreme crisis, a central bank will step in and provide financing to private credit markets.

1. LENDER OF LAST RESORT An institution, usually a country's central bank, that provides funds to financial institutions when they are unable to borrow from the private credit markets is known as a **lender of last resort.** In particular, the central bank can provide cash to a bank that is facing a run by depositors but is fundamentally solvent, making it unnecessary for the bank to engage in fire sales of its assets to raise cash.

A **debt overhang** occurs when a vicious cycle of deleveraging leaves a borrower with high debt but diminished assets.

A **lender of last resort** is an institution, usually a country's central bank, that provides funds to financial institutions when they are unable to borrow from the private credit markets.

42-3   Total Borrowings of Depository
Institutions from the Federal Reserve

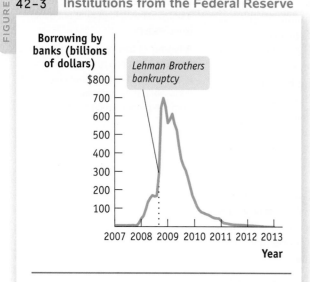

Although commercial banks borrowed negligible
amounts from the Fed before the crisis hit in 2008, in
the months after Lehman's collapse their borrowing
surged to $700 billion—an amount 14 times total bank
reserves before the crisis.

Source: Federal Reserve Bank of St. Louis.

This acts as a lifeline, working to prevent a loss of confidence in
the bank's solvency from turning into a self-fulfilling prophecy.

Did the Federal Reserve act as a lender of last resort in the
2008 financial crisis? Very much so. Figure 42-3 shows borrowing by banks from the Fed: commercial banks borrowed negligible amounts from the central bank before the crisis, but their
borrowing rose to $700 billion in the months following Lehman's
failure. To get a sense of how large this borrowing was, note that
total bank reserves before the crisis were less than $50 billion—
so these loans were 14 times the banks' initial reserves.

2. GOVERNMENT GUARANTEES There are limits, though, to how
much a lender of last resort can accomplish: it can't restore confidence in a bank if there is good reason to believe the bank is fundamentally insolvent. If the public believes that the bank's assets
aren't worth enough to cover its debts even if it doesn't have to
sell these assets on short notice, a lender of last resort isn't going
to help much. And in major banking crises there are often good
reasons to believe that many banks are truly bankrupt.

In such cases, governments often step in to guarantee banks'
liabilities. In 2007, a bank run hit the British bank Northern
Rock, ceasing only when the British government stepped in and
guaranteed all deposits at the bank, regardless of size. Ireland's
government eventually stepped in to guarantee repayment of not
just deposits at all of the nation's banks, but all bank debts. Sweden did the same thing after its 1991 banking crisis.

When governments take on banks' risk, they often take owner-
ship of the banks they are rescuing. Northern Rock was nationalized in 2008. Sweden
nationalized a significant part of its banking system in 1992. In the United States, the
Federal Deposit Insurance Corporation routinely seizes banks that are no longer solvent; it seized 140 banks in 2009. Ireland, however, chose not to seize any of the banks
whose debts were guaranteed by taxpayers.

These government takeovers are almost always temporary. In general, modern governments want to save banks, not run them. So they "reprivatize" nationalized banks,
selling them to private buyers, as soon as they believe they can.

3. PROVIDER OF DIRECT FINANCING During the depths of the 2008 financial crisis the
Federal Reserve expanded its operations beyond the usual measures of open-market
operations and lending to depository banks. It also began lending to shadow banks
and buying commercial paper—short-term bonds issued by private companies—as
well as buying the debt of Fannie Mae and Freddie Mac, the government-sponsored
home mortgage agencies. In this way, the Fed provided credit to keep the economy
afloat when private credit markets had dried up.

The 2008 Crisis and Its Aftermath

As we've just seen, banking crises have typically been followed by major economic
problems. How did the aftermath of the financial crisis of 2008 compare with this historical experience? The answer, unfortunately, is that history has proved a very good
guide: once again, the economic damage from the financial crisis was both large and
prolonged.

Severe Crisis, Slow Recovery

Figure 42-4 shows real GDP in the United States and the European Union, the world's
two largest economies, during the crisis and aftermath, with the peak pre-crisis
quarter—the last quarter of 2007 for the United States, the first quarter of 2008 for
the European Union—set equal to 100. What you can see is that both economies suf-

FIGURE **42-4**   Crisis and Recovery in the United States and the European Union

In the aftermath of the 2008 financial crisis, aggregate output in the European Union and in the United States fell dramatically. Real GDP, shown here as an index with each economy's peak pre-crisis quarter set to 100, declined by more than 5%. As you can see, by 2013, real GDP in the United States had recovered beyond pre-crisis levels, and aggregate output in the European Union had still not reached its pre-crisis peak.

Sources: Bureau of Economic Analysis; Eurostat.

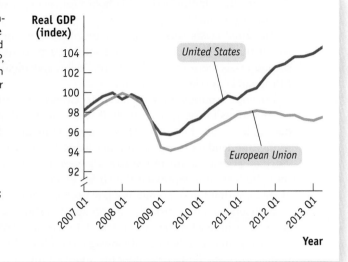

fered severe downturns, shrinking more than 5%, followed by relatively slow recoveries. The United States returned to its pre-crisis level of real GDP in the second quarter of 2011, and managed to exceed it in 2013. While as of late 2013, the European Union had yet to regain its pre-crisis level of output.

The severe slump and the slow recovery were very bad news for workers, since a healthy job market depends on an economy growing fast enough to accommodate both a growing workforce and rising productivity. Figure 42-5 shows two indicators of unemployment in the United States—the overall unemployment rate and the percentage of the unemployed who had been out of work 27 weeks or more. Both measures shot up during the crisis and remained very high through 2012, when the unemployment rate dropped below 8% for the first time in over three years. Nonetheless, it remained well above the pre-crisis level, indicating a labor market in which it was hard to find a job.

This outcome was, sad to say, about what one should have expected given the severity of the initial financial shock and the historical experience with such shocks.

FIGURE **42-5**   Unemployment in the Aftermath of the 2008 Crisis

After 2008, the unemployment rate increased dramatically. Long-term unemployment, measured by the percentage of the unemployed who were out of work for 27 weeks or longer, increased at the same time. By 2011, almost half of all unemployed workers were long-term unemployed. Although the unemployment rate dips slightly starting in late 2012, throughout 2013, both unemployment rates remained above their pre-crisis levels.

Source: Bureau of Labor Statistics.

Aftershocks in Europe

One important factor bedeviling hopes for recovery was the emergence of special difficulties in several European nations.

The 2008 crisis was caused by problems with private debt, mainly home loans, which then triggered a crisis of confidence in banks. In 2011 and 2012, fears of a second crisis were focused on public debt, specifically the public debts of Southern European countries plus Ireland.

Europe's troubles first surfaced in Greece, a country with a long history of fiscal irresponsibility. In late 2009, it was revealed that a previous Greek government had understated the size of the budget deficits and the amount of government debt, prompting lenders to refuse further loans to Greece. Other European countries provided emergency loans to the Greek government in return for harsh budget cuts. But these budget cuts depressed the Greek economy, and by late 2011 there was general agreement that Greece could not pay back its debts in full.

By itself, this was probably a manageable shock for the European economy since Greece accounts for less than 3% of European GDP. Unfortunately, foot-dragging by European officials in confronting Greece's problems and the effects of the harsh budget cuts on the Greek economy spooked investors. By the fall of 2011, the crisis had spread beyond the Greek borders, hitting two major European economies: Spain and Italy.

Spain also ran into trouble, the result of fallout from the 2008 crisis. It suffered a housing bubble between 2000 and 2007 that eventually burst, leading to a deep economic slump that depressed tax receipts and caused large budget deficits. There were worries that the Spanish government might have to spend large amounts bailing out banks. As a result, investors began to worry about the solvency of the government and a possible default, driving up interest rates.

The youth unemployment rate in Spain, shockingly high at almost 58% in late 2013, is one example of the difficulties Europeans face in the aftermath of the 2008 crisis.

Giorgio Fochesato/
Getty Images

Italy's government also faced insolvency fears in 2010 because in the aftermath of the 2008 crisis, investors feared that the Italian economy was growing too slowly to generate enough tax revenue to repay its public debt. These doubts drove up interest rates on Italian public debt, in turn creating a vicious circle: higher interest payments, caused by fears about Italian government solvency, worsened Italy's fiscal position even further and pushed it closer to the edge.

Heading into 2014, the growth rate of real GDP in Greece, Spain, and Italy is forecast to be slightly positive for the first time since the crisis began. However, the level of real GDP in these countries remains well below pre-crisis levels, partly due to the spending cuts and tax increases imposed as a condition of their bailout by the European Union. In addition, unemployment remains high, indicating that recovery is ongoing.

The Stimulus–Austerity Debate

The persistence of economic difficulties after the 2008 financial crisis led to fierce debates about appropriate policy responses. Broadly speaking, economists and policy makers were divided as to whether the situation called for more fiscal stimulus—expansionary fiscal measures such as more government spending and possibly tax cuts to promote spending and reduce unemployment—or for fiscal "austerity," contractionary fiscal measures such as spending cuts and possibly tax increases to reduce budget deficits.

The proponents of more stimulus pointed to the continuing poor performance of major economies, arguing that the combination of high unemployment and relatively low inflation clearly pointed to the need for expansionary policies. And since monetary policy was limited by the zero bound on interest rates, stimulus proponents advocated expansionary fiscal policy to fill the gap.

The austerity camp took a very different view. Strongly influenced by the solvency troubles of Greece, Ireland, Spain, and Italy, they argued that the common source of all the problems were high levels of government deficits and debts. In their view, countries like the United States that continued to run large government deficits several years after the 2008 crisis were at risk of suffering a similar loss of investor confidence in their ability to repay their debts. Moreover, austerity advocates claimed that cuts in government spending would not actually be contractionary because they would improve investor confidence and keep interest rates on government debt low.

Each side of the debate argued that recent experience refuted the other side's claims. Austerity proponents argued that the persistence of high unemployment despite the fiscal stimulus programs adopted by the United States and other major economies in 2009 showed that stimulus doesn't work. Stimulus advocates argued that these programs were simply inadequate in size, pointing out that many economists had warned of their inadequacy from the start.

Stimulus advocates further argued that warnings about the dangers of deficits were overblown, that far from rising, borrowing costs for Japan, the United States, and Britain—nations that, unlike the troubled European debtors, still had their own currencies with all the flexibility that implies—had fallen to record lows. And they dismissed claims that spending cuts would raise confidence as mainly fantasy.

At the time of writing, neither side was giving much ground. Clearly, any resolution of the debate would hinge on future economic developments and how they were interpreted.

The Lesson of the Post-Crisis Slump

Almost all major economies had great difficulty dealing with the aftermath of the 2008 financial crisis—high unemployment, low growth and, for some, solvency concerns, and high interest rates on public debt.

Clearly, then, the best way to avoid the terrible problems that arise after a financial crisis is not to have a crisis in the first place. How can you do that? In part, one might hope, through better regulation of financial institutions.

Regulation in the Wake of the Crisis

By late 2009, interventions by governments and central banks around the world had restored calm to financial markets. However, huge damage had been done to the global economy.

Signed into law in 2010, Dodd-Frank is seen by many on Wall Street as too much regulation, while others wonder if it is enough.

The banking crisis of 2008 demonstrated, all too clearly, that financial regulation is a continuing process—that regulations will and should change over time to keep up with a changing world. The dependence on very short-term loans (called repo), the lack of regulation, and being outside the lender-of-last-resort system made the shadow-banking sector vulnerable to crises and panics.

So what changes will the most recent crisis bring? One thing that became all too clear in the 2008 crisis was that the traditional scope of banking regulation was too narrow. Regulating only depository institutions was clearly inadequate in a world in which a large part of banking, properly understood, is undertaken by the shadow banking sector.

In the aftermath of the crisis, then, an overhaul of financial regulation was clearly needed. And in 2010 the U.S. Congress

AP Photo/Charles Dharapak, File

passed the Wall Street Reform and Consumer Protection Act—often referred to as the Dodd-Frank Act (named for the two legislators who introduced the bill to Congress). President Obama signed Dodd-Frank into law that same year. It represented an effort to respond to the events of the preceding years. These are its four main elements:

1. Consumer protection
2. Derivatives regulation
3. Regulation of shadow banks
4. Resolution authority over nonbank financial institutions that face bankruptcy

1. CONSUMER PROTECTION One factor in the financial crisis was the fact that many borrowers accepted offers they didn't understand, such as mortgages that were easy to pay in the first two years but required sharply higher payments later on. In an effort to limit future abuses, the new law creates a special office, the Consumer Financial Protection Bureau, dedicated to policing financial industry practices and protecting borrowers.

2. DERIVATIVES REGULATION Another factor in the crisis was the proliferation of derivatives, complex financial instruments that were supposed to help spread risk but arguably simply concealed it. Under the new law, most derivatives have to be bought and sold in open, transparent markets, hopefully limiting the extent to which financial players can take on invisible risk.

3. REGULATION OF SHADOW BANKS A key element in the financial crisis, as we've seen, was the rise of institutions that didn't fit the conventional definition of a bank but played the role of banks and created the risk of a banking crisis. How can regulation be extended to such institutions?

Dodd-Frank does not offer an explicit new definition of what it means to be a bank. Instead, it offers a sort of financial version of "you know it when you see it." Specifically, it gives a special panel the ability to designate financial institutions as "systemically important," meaning that their activities have the potential to create a banking crisis. Such institutions will be subject to bank-like regulation of their capital, their investments, and so on.

4. RESOLUTION AUTHORITY The events of 2008 made it clear that governments would often feel the need to guarantee a wide range of financial institution debts in a crisis, not just deposits. Yet how can this be done without creating huge incentive problems, motivating financial institutions to undertake overly risky behavior in the knowledge that they will be bailed out by the government if they get into trouble?

Part of the answer is to empower the government to seize control of financial institutions that require a bailout, the way it already does with failing commercial banks and thrifts. This new power, known as *resolution authority,* should be viewed as solving a problem that seemed acute in early 2009, when several major financial institutions were teetering on the brink. Yet it wasn't clear whether Washington had the legal authority to orchestrate a rescue that was fair to taxpayers.

It has been several years since the crisis ended and Dodd-Frank took effect. But, two questions about the law remain:

1. How will these regulations be worked into the international financial system? Will other nations adopt similar policies? If they do, how will conflicts among different national policies be resolved?

2. Will these regulations do the trick? Post-1930s bank regulation produced decades of stability, but will that happen again? Or will the new system fail in the face of a serious test?

Nobody knows the answers to these questions. We'll just have to continue to wait and see.

42 Review

Solutions appear at the back of the book.

Check Your Understanding

1. Which of the following are examples of maturity transformations? Which are subject to a bank-run-like phenomenon in which fear of a failure becomes a self-fulfilling prophecy? Explain.

   a. You sell tickets to a lottery in which each ticket holder has a chance of winning a $10,000 jackpot.

   b. Dana borrows on her credit card to pay her living expenses while she takes a year-long course to upgrade her job skills. Without a better-paying job, she will not be able to pay her accumulated credit card balance.

   c. An investment partnership invests in office buildings. Partners invest their own funds and can redeem them only by selling their partnership share to someone else.

   d. The local student union savings bank offers checking accounts to students and invests those funds in student loans.

2. In November 2011, the government of France announced that it was reducing its forecast for economic growth in 2012. It was also reducing its estimates of tax revenue for 2012, since a weaker economy would mean smaller tax receipts. To offset the effect of lower revenue on the budget deficit, the government also announced a new package of tax increases and spending cuts. Which side of the stimulus–austerity debate was France taking?

3. Why does the use of short-term borrowing and being outside of the lender-of-last-resort system make shadow banks vulnerable to events similar to bank runs?

4. How do you think the crisis of 2008 would have been mitigated if there had been no shadow banking sector but only the formal depository banking sector?

5. Describe the incentive problem facing the U.S. government in responding to the 2007–2009 crisis with respect to the shadow banking sector. How did the Dodd-Frank Act attempt to address those incentive problems?

Multiple-Choice Questions

1. What makes a shadow bank different from a depository bank?

   a. Shadow banks do not engage in maturity transformation.

   b. Shadow banks do not make loans.

   c. Shadow banks do not accept deposits.

   d. Shadow banks are not vulnerable to bank runs.

   e. Shadow banks are government institutions.

2. The conversion of short-term liabilities into long-term assets is called

   a. an asset bubble.

   b. a shadow bank.

   c. maturity transformation.

   d. financial contagion.

   e. financial panic.

3. People in a coastal community believe housing prices in their area have been pushed to unreasonably high levels due to expectations of rising demand for housing by retiring baby boomers. This situation is termed

   a. an asset bubble.

   b. a shadow bubble.

   c. financial panic.

   d. maturity transformation.

   e. financial contagion.

4. A severe banking crisis typically leads to

   a. a deep recession followed by a quick recovery.

   b. a deep recession followed by a slow recovery.

   c. a shallow recession followed by a quick recovery.

   d. an asset bubble.

   e. an increase in shadow banking.

5. When a borrower is left with high debt but diminished assets this situation is called

   a. an asset bubble.

   b. a credit crunch.

   c. financial contagion.

   d. financial panic.

   e. debt overhang.

Critical-Thinking Question

Why does a banking crisis normally lead to a deep recession?

BUSINESS CASE : Licenses to Print Money   W⊕RLD VIEW

Thinkstock

People sometimes talk about profitable companies as having a "license to print money." Well, the British firm De La Rue actually does. In 1930, De La Rue, printer of items such as postage stamps, expanded into the money-printing business, producing banknotes for the then-government of China. Today it produces the currencies of about 150 countries.

De La Rue's business received some unexpected attention in 2011 when Muammar Gaddafi, who, at the time, was the dictator who had ruled Libya since 1969, was fighting to suppress a fierce popular uprising. To finance his efforts, he turned to seignorage, ordering around $1.5 billion worth of Libyan dinars printed.

But Libyan banknotes weren't printed in Libya; they were printed in Britain at one of De La Rue's facilities. The British Government, an enemy of the Gaddafi regime, seized the new banknotes before they could be flown to Libya, refusing to release them until Gaddafi was overthrown, which happened later that year.

Why do so many countries turn to private companies like De La Rue and its main rival, the German firm Giesecke and Devrient, to print their currencies? The short answer is that printing money isn't as easy as it sounds: producing high-quality banknotes that are hard to counterfeit requires highly specialized equipment and expertise.

Large, wealthy nations like the United States can easily afford to do this for themselves: U.S. currency is printed by the Bureau of Engraving and Printing, a division of the Treasury Department. But smaller, poorer countries do better by turning to experts like De La Rue, which can include high-tech features like security threads and holography to fight counterfeiters.

Actually, De La Rue has had its own problems with quality control: a scandal erupted in 2010, when it emerged that one of its plants had been producing defective security paper and that employees had covered up the problems. Nonetheless, many countries will surely continue relying on expert private firms to produce their currency.

Questions for Thought

1. How can a government obtain revenue by printing money when someone else actually prints the money?

2. Why, exactly, would Gaddafi have resorted to the printing press in early 2011?

3. Were there risks to the Libyan economy in releasing those dinars to its new government?

SECTION 12 REVIEW

Summary

Inflation, Disinflation, Deflation

1. In analyzing high inflation, economists use the **classical model of the price level,** which says that changes in the money supply lead to proportional changes in the aggregate price level even in the short run.

2. Governments sometimes print money in order to finance budget deficits. When they do, they impose an **inflation tax,** generating tax revenue equal to the inflation rate times the money supply, on those who hold money. Revenue from the real inflation tax, the inflation rate times the real money supply, is the real value of resources captured by the government. In order to avoid paying the inflation tax, people reduce their real money holdings and force the government to increase inflation to capture the same amount of real inflation tax revenue. In some cases, this leads to a vicious circle of a shrinking real money supply and a rising rate of inflation, leading to hyperinflation and a fiscal crisis.

3. Countries that don't need to print money to cover government deficits can still stumble into moderate inflation, either because of political opportunism or because of wishful thinking.

The Phillips Curve

4. At a given point in time, there is a downward-sloping relationship between unemployment and inflation known as the **short-run Phillips curve.** This curve is shifted by changes in the expected rate of inflation. The **long-run Phillips curve,** which shows the relationship between unemployment and inflation once expectations have had time to adjust, is vertical. It defines the **nonaccelerating inflation rate of unemployment,** or **NAIRU,** which is equal to the natural rate of unemployment.

5. Once inflation has become embedded in expectations, getting inflation back down can be difficult because *disinflation* can be very costly, requiring the sacrifice of large amounts of aggregate output and imposing high levels of unemployment. However, policy makers in the United States and other wealthy countries were willing to pay that price of bringing down the high inflation of the 1970s.

6. Deflation poses several problems. It can lead to **debt deflation,** in which a rising real burden of outstanding debt intensifies an economic downturn. Also, interest rates are more likely to run up against the **zero bound** in an economy experiencing deflation. When this happens, the economy enters a **liquidity trap,** rendering conventional monetary policy ineffective.

Crises and Consequences

7. Banks engage in **maturity transformation,** transforming short-term liabilities into long-term assets. **Shadow banks** have grown greatly since 1980. Largely unregulated, they can pay savers a higher rate of return than depository banks. Like depository banks, shadow banks engage in maturity transformation, depending on short-term borrowing to operate and investing in long-term assets. Therefore, shadow banks can also be subject to bank runs.

8. Although **banking crises** are rare, they typically inflict severe damage on the economy. They have two main sources: shared mistakes, such as investing in an **asset bubble,** and **financial contagion.** Contagion is spread through bank runs or via a vicious cycle of deleveraging. When unregulated, shadow banking is particularly vulnerable to contagion. In 2008, a **financial panic** hit the United States, arising from the combination of an asset bubble, a huge shadow banking sector, and a vicious cycle of deleveraging.

9. Severe banking crises almost invariably lead to deep and long recessions, with unemployment remaining high for several years after the crisis began. There are three main reasons why banking crises are so damaging to the economy: they result in a **credit crunch,** the vicious cycle of deleveraging leads to a **debt overhang,** and monetary policy is rendered ineffective as the economy falls into a liquidity trap. As a result, households and businesses are either unable or unwilling to spend, deepening the downturn.

10. Unlike during the Great Depression, governments now step in to try to limit the damage from a banking crisis by acting as the **lender of last resort** and by guaranteeing the banks' liabilities. Sometimes, but not always, governments nationalize the banks and then later reprivatize them. In an extreme crisis, the central bank may directly finance commercial transactions.

11. Economic damage from the financial crisis of 2008 was large and prolonged. The world's two largest economies, the United States and the European Union, suffered severe downturns. The persistence of economic difficulties after 2008 led to fierce debates about appropriate policy responses between economists and policy makers calling for more fiscal stimulus—more government spending and possibly tax cuts to promote spending and reduce unemployment—and those favoring fiscal austerity—spending cuts and possibly tax increases to reduce budget deficits.

12. The banking regulatory system put in place during the 1930s has eroded due to the rise of shadow banking. In the aftermath of the crisis, the U.S. Congress enacted the Dodd-Frank Act in the hope of preventing a replay of the crisis. The main elements of the law are stronger consumer protection, greater regulation of derivatives, regulation of shadow banking, and resolution authority for a variety of financial institutions. We have yet to see whether these changes will be adequate or whether they will be adopted by other countries.

Key Terms

Classical model of the price level, p. 415

Inflation tax, p. 417

Short-run Phillips curve, p. 423

Nonaccelerating inflation rate of unemployment (NAIRU), p. 427

Long-run Phillips curve, p. 427

Debt deflation, p. 430

Zero bound, p. 430

Liquidity trap, p. 431

Maturity transformation, p. 436

Shadow bank, p. 436

Banking crisis, p. 436

Asset bubble, p. 437

Financial contagion, p. 437

Financial panic, p. 437

Credit crunch, p. 440

Debt overhang, p. 441

Lender of last resort, p. 441

Problems

1. In the economy of Scottopia, policy makers want to lower the unemployment rate and raise real GDP by using monetary policy. Using the accompanying diagram, show why this policy will ultimately result in a higher aggregate price level but no change in real GDP.

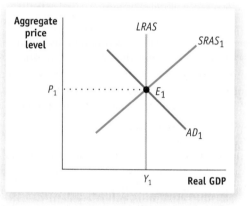

2. In the following examples, would the classical model of the price level be relevant?

a. There is a great deal of unemployment in the economy and no history of inflation.

b. The economy has just experienced five years of hyperinflation.

c. Although the economy experienced inflation in the 10% to 20% range three years ago, prices have recently been stable and the unemployment rate has approximated the natural rate of unemployment.

3. Answer the following questions about the (real) inflation tax, assuming that the price level starts at 1.

a. Maria Moneybags keeps $1,000 in her sock drawer for a year. Over the year, the inflation rate is 10%. What is the real inflation tax paid by Maria for this year?

b. Maria continues to keep the $1,000 in her drawer for a second year. What is the real value of this $1,000 at the beginning of the second year? Over the year, the inflation rate is again 10%. What is the real inflation tax paid by Maria for the second year?

c. For a third year, Maria keeps the $1,000 in the drawer. What is the real value of this $1,000 at the beginning of the third year? Over the year, the inflation rate is again 10%. What is the real inflation tax paid by Maria for the third year?

d. After three years, what is the cumulative real inflation tax paid?

e. Redo parts a through d with an inflation rate of 25%. Why is hyperinflation such a problem?

4. Concerned about the crowding-out effects of government borrowing on private investment spending, a candidate for president argues that the United States should just print money to cover the government's budget deficit. What are the advantages and disadvantages of such a plan?

5. After experiencing a recession for the past two years, the residents of Albernia were looking forward to a decrease in the unemployment rate. Yet after six months of strong positive economic growth, the unemployment rate has fallen only slightly below what it was at the end of the recession. How can you explain why the unemployment rate did not fall as much although the economy was experiencing strong economic growth?

6. Due to historical differences, countries often differ in how quickly a change in actual inflation is incorporated into a change in expected inflation. In a country such as Japan, which has had very little inflation in recent memory, it will take longer for a change in the actual inflation rate to be reflected in a corresponding change in the expected inflation rate. In contrast, in a country such as Zimbabwe, which has recently had very high inflation, a change in the actual inflation rate will immediately be reflected in a corresponding change in the expected inflation rate. What does this imply about the short-run and long-run Phillips curves in these two types of countries? What does this imply about the effectiveness of monetary and fiscal policy to reduce the unemployment rate?

7. a. Go to www.bls.gov. Click on "Subject Areas"; on the left, under "Inflation & Prices," click on the link "Consumer Price Index." Scroll down to the section "CPI Tables," and find the link under the head that reads "Table Containing History of CPI-U U.S." and click on it. What is the value of the percent change in the CPI from 2008 to 2009?

b. Now go to www.treasury.gov and click on "Resource Center." From there, click on "Data and Charts Center." Then click on "Interest Rate Statistics." In the scroll-down windows, select "Daily Treasury Bill Rates" and "2009." Examine the data in "4 Weeks Bank Discount." What is the maximum? The minimum? Then do the same for 2007. How do the data for 2009 and 2007 compare? How would you relate this to your answer in part (a)? From the data on Treasury bill interest rates, what would you infer about the level of the inflation rate in 2007 compared to 2009? (You can check your answer by going back to the www.bls.gov website to find the percent change in the CPI from 2006 to 2007.)

c. How would you characterize the change in the U.S. economy from 2007 to 2009?

8. The economy of Brittania has been suffering from high inflation with an unemployment rate equal to its natural rate. Policy makers would like to disinflate the economy with the lowest economic cost possible. Assume that the state of the economy is not the result of a negative supply shock. How can they try to minimize the unemployment cost of disinflation? Is it possible for there to be no cost of disinflation?

9. Who are the winners and losers when a mortgage company lends $100,000 to the Miller family to buy a house worth $105,000 and during the first year prices unexpectedly fall by 10%? What would you expect to happen if the deflation continued over the next few years? How would continuing deflation affect borrowers and lenders throughout the economy as a whole?

10. Which of the following are examples of debt overhang? Which examples are likely to lead to a cutback in spending? Explain.

a. Your uncle starts a restaurant, borrowing to fund his investment. The restaurant fails, and your uncle must shut down but still must pay his debt.

b. Your parents take out a loan to buy a house. Your father is transferred to a new city, and now your parents must sell the house. The value of the house has gone up during the time your family has lived there.

c. Your friend's parents take out a loan to buy her a condo to live in while she is at college. Meanwhile, the housing market plummets. By the time your friend leaves college, the condo is worth significantly less than the value of the loan.

d. You finish college with an honors degree in a field with many good job prospects and with $25,000 in student loans that you must repay.

11. Which of the following are *not* examples of a vicious cycle of deleveraging? Explain.

a. Your university decides to sell several commercial buildings in the middle of town in order to upgrade buildings on campus.

b. A company decides to sell its large and valuable art collection because other asset prices on its balance sheet have fallen below a critical level, forcing creditors to call in their loans to the company because of provisions written into the original loan contract.

c. A company decides to issue more stock in order to voluntarily pay off some of its debt.

d. A shadow bank must sell its holdings of corporate bonds because falling asset prices have led to a default on the terms of its loans with some creditors.

12. Figure 42-1 tracks the unemployment rate in the years before and after the Panic of 1893 in the United States and the banking crisis of 1991 in Sweden.

a. In Figure 42-1, how many years after the Panic of 1893 did unemployment peak in the United States?

b. In Figure 42-1, how many years after the banking crisis of 1991 did unemployment peak in Sweden?

13. In 2007–2009, the Federal Reserve, acting as a lender of last resort, stepped in to provide funds when private markets were unable to do so. The Fed also took over many banks. In 2007, it seized 3 banks; in 2008, it seized 25 banks; and in 2009, it seized 140 banks. Go to www.fdic.gov; under "Bank Closing Information," click on "Complete Failed Bank List." Then count the number of banks that the Federal Reserve has seized so far this year. Have bank failures decreased since the crisis in 2008?

Open-Economy Macroeconomics

SWITZERLAND DOESN'T WANT YOUR MONEY

WORLD VIEW

Parking your money in a Swiss bank is no way to get rich, given the low interest rates Swiss bankers offer. In fact, Swiss banks have even paid negative interest on deposits, charging customers for the service of keeping their funds.

But for generations, Swiss bank accounts have been seen as a way to *stay* rich, a safe place to store your wealth. In the troubled years that followed the 2008 financial crisis, the Swiss reputation for safety became especially important. European investors, in particular, poured money into Switzerland.

And the Swiss hated it—the result of the inflow of foreign funds was a surge in the value of the Swiss franc that wreaked havoc with Swiss exports.

At the beginning of 2008, one Swiss franc traded for about 0.6 euro. By mid-2011, the franc was trading for around 0.9 euro. That meant that Swiss exports, other things equal, had seen a 50% rise in their labor costs relative to competitors elsewhere in Europe.

Thanks to its reputation for quality, Switzerland has been remarkably successful over the years at selling goods to the world market, despite high labor costs. Nobody expects to get a bargain on Swiss watches or Swiss chocolate. But this was pushing matters to the breaking point.

So what was to be done? Starting in early 2009, the Swiss National Bank, Switzerland's equivalent of the Federal Reserve, began selling francs on the foreign exchange market in an attempt to hold down the franc's value. In

return for these francs, it received other currencies, mainly dollars and euros, which it added to its reserves.

We're talking about a *lot* of sales: over a period of 2½ years, the bank added $180 billion to its foreign exchange reserves, which was about a third of Switzerland's GDP—the equivalent for the United States of selling $5 trillion dollars.

Yet even that wasn't enough to stop the franc's rise. In September 2011, as the franc seemed headed for a value of 1 euro or more, the Swiss National Bank announced that it would do whatever it took—sell an unlimited amount of francs—to keep the franc below a maximum of 0.833 euro per franc (that is, 1.2 francs per euro, which was the way the target was stated). That announcement finally seemed to stop the franc's rise, at least at first.

What the extraordinary efforts of the Swiss National Bank illustrated was the importance of a dimension of macroeconomics that we haven't emphasized so far—the fact that modern national economies are *open economies* that trade goods, services, and assets with the rest of the world. *Open-economy macroeconomics* is a branch of macroeconomics that deals with the relationships between national economies.

In this section we'll learn about some of the key issues in open-economy macroeconomics: the determinants of a country's *balance of payments*, the factors affecting *exchange rates*, the different forms of *exchange rate policy* adopted by various countries, and the relationship between exchange rates and macroeconomic policy.

MODULE 43 — Capital Flows and the Balance of Payments

© Sadik Demiroz/Thinkstock

The Balance of Payments Accounts

In 2012, people living in the United States sold about $3.5 trillion worth of stuff to people living in other countries and bought about $3.5 trillion worth of stuff in return. What kind of stuff? All kinds. Residents of the United States (including employees of firms operating in the United States) sold airplanes, bonds, wheat, and many other items to residents of other countries. Residents of the United States bought cars, stocks, oil, and many other items from residents of other countries.

How can we keep track of these transactions? Earlier we learned that economists keep track of the domestic economy using the national income and product accounts. Economists keep track of international transactions using a different but related set of numbers, the *balance of payments accounts*.

Understanding the Balance of Payments

A country's **balance of payments accounts** are a summary of the country's transactions with other countries.

To understand the basic idea behind the balance of payments accounts, let's consider a small-scale example: not a country, but a family farm. Let's say that we know the following about how last year went financially for the Costas, who own a small artichoke farm in California:

- They made $100,000 by selling artichokes.

- They spent $70,000 on running the farm, including purchases of new farm machinery, and another $40,000 buying food, paying utility bills for their home, replacing their worn-out car, and so on.

- They received $500 in interest on their bank account but paid $10,000 in interest on their mortgage.

- They took out a new $25,000 loan to help pay for farm improvements but didn't use all the money immediately. So they put the extra in the bank.

A country's **balance of payments accounts** are a summary of the country's transactions with other countries.

How could we summarize the Costas' year? One way would be with a table like Table 43-1, which shows sources of cash coming in and money going out, characterized under a few broad headings.

The first row of Table 43-1 shows sales and purchases of goods and services: sales of artichokes; purchases of groceries, heating oil, that new car, and so on. The second row shows interest payments: the interest the Costas received from their bank account and the interest they paid on their mortgage. The third row shows cash coming in from new borrowing versus money deposited in the bank.

In each row we show the net inflow of cash from that type of transaction. So the net in the first row is –$10,000 because the Costas spent $10,000 more than they earned. The net in the second row is –$9,500, the difference between the interest the Costas received on their bank account and the interest they paid on the mortgage. The net in the third row is $19,500: the Costas brought in $25,000 with their new loan but put only $5,500 of that sum in the bank.

The last row shows the sum of cash coming in from all sources and the sum of all cash used. These sums are equal, by definition: every dollar has a source, and every dollar received gets used somewhere. (What if the Costas hid money under the mattress? Then that would be counted as another "use" of cash.)

A country's balance of payments accounts summarize its transactions with the world using a table similar to the one we just used to summarize the Costas' financial year.

Rob MacDougall/Getty Images

TABLE 43-1

The Costas' Financial Year

	Sources of cash	Uses of cash	Net
Purchases or sales of goods and services	Artichoke sales: $100,000	Farm operation and living expenses: $110,000	–$10,000
Interest payments	Interest received on bank account: $500	Interest paid on mortgage: $10,000	–$9,500
Loans and deposits	Funds received from new loan: $25,000	Funds deposited in bank: $5,500	+$19,500
Total	$125,500	$125,500	$0

Table 43-2 on the next page shows a simplified version of the U.S. balance of payments accounts for 2012. Where the Costa family's accounts show sources and uses of cash, the U.S. balance of payments accounts show payments from foreigners—in effect, sources of cash for the United States as a whole—and payments to foreigners.

Row 1 of Table 43-2 shows payments that arise from sales and purchases of goods and services. For example, the value of U.S. wheat exports and the fees foreigners pay to U.S. consulting companies appear in the second column; the value of U.S. oil imports and the fees American companies pay to Indian call centers—the people who often answer your 1-800 calls—appear in the third column.

Row 2 shows *factor income*—payments for the use of factors of production owned by residents of other countries. Mostly this means investment income: interest paid on loans from overseas, the profits of foreign-owned corporations, and so on. For example, the profits earned by Disneyland Paris, which is owned by the U.S.-based Walt Disney Company, appear in the second column; the profits earned by the U.S. operations of Japanese auto companies appear in the third column. Factor income also includes labor income. For example, the wages of an American engineer who works temporarily on a construction site in Dubai are counted in the second column.

Row 3 shows *international transfers*—funds sent by residents of one country to residents of another. The main element here is the remittances that immigrants, such as the millions of Mexican-born workers employed in the United States, send to their families in their country of origin. Notice that Table 43-2 shows only the net value of transfers. That's because the U.S. government provides only an estimate of the net, not a breakdown between payments to foreigners and payments from foreigners.

The next two rows of Table 43-2 show payments resulting from sales and purchases of assets, broken down by who is doing the buying and selling. Row 4 shows transactions that involve governments or government agencies, mainly central banks. As we'll learn later, in 2012 most of the U.S. sales in this category involved the accumulation of *foreign exchange reserves* by the central banks of China and oil-exporting countries. Row 5 shows private sales and purchases of assets. For example, the 2012 purchase

TABLE 43-2

The U.S. Balance of Payments in 2012 (billions of dollars)

		Payments from foreigners	Payments to foreigners	Net
1	**Sales and purchases of goods and services**	2,211	2,745	−534
2	**Factor income**	776	552	224
3	**Transfers**	—	—	−130
	Current account (1 + 2 + 3)			−440
4	**Official asset sales and purchases**	394	−81	475
5	**Private sales and purchases of assets**	150	178	−28
	Financial account (4 + 5)			447
	Total	—	—	7

Source: Bureau of Economic Analysis.

of the American-owned AMC Cinema chain, by the Chinese company Dalian Wanda, showed up in the "Payments from foreigners" column of row 5; purchases of European stocks by U.S. investors show up as positive values in the "Payments to foreigners" column.

In laying out Table 43-2, we have separated rows 1, 2, and 3 into one group and rows 4 and 5 into another. This reflects a fundamental difference in how these two groups of transactions affect the future.

When a U.S. resident sells a good, such as wheat, to a foreigner, that's the end of the transaction. But a financial asset, such as a bond, is different. Remember, a bond is a promise to pay interest and principal in the future. So when a U.S. resident sells a bond to a foreigner, that sale creates a liability: the U.S. resident will have to pay interest and repay principal in the future. The balance of payments accounts distinguish between transactions that don't create liabilities and those that do.

Transactions that don't create liabilities are considered part of the **balance of payments on the current account,** often referred to simply as the **current account:** the balance of payments on goods and services plus factor income and net international transfer payments. The balance of row 1 of Table 43-2, −$534 billion, corresponds to the most important part of the current account: **the balance of payments on goods and services,** the difference between the value of exports and the value of imports during a given period.

If you read news reports on the economy, you may well see references to another measure, the **merchandise trade balance,** sometimes referred to as the **trade balance** for short. This is the difference between a country's exports and imports of goods alone—not including services. Economists sometimes focus on the merchandise trade balance, even though it's an incomplete measure, because data on international trade in services aren't as accurate as data on trade in physical goods, and they are also slower to arrive.

The current account, as we've just learned, consists of international transactions that don't create liabilities. Transactions that involve the sale or purchase of assets, and therefore do create future liabilities, are considered part of the **balance of payments on the financial account,** or the **financial account** for short. (Until a few years ago, economists often referred to the financial account as the *capital account.* We'll use the modern term, but you may run across the older term.)

So how does it all add up? The first two unnumbered rows of Table 43-2 show the bottom lines: the overall U.S. current account and financial account for 2012. As you can see, in 2012, the United States ran a current account deficit: the amount it paid to foreigners for goods, services, factors, and transfers was greater than the amount it

A country's **balance of payments on the current account,** or the **current account,** is its balance of payments on goods and services plus net international transfer payments and factor income.

A country's **balance of payments on goods and services** is the difference between its exports and its imports of both goods and services during a given period.

The **merchandise trade balance,** or **trade balance,** is the difference between a country's exports and imports of goods.

A country's **balance of payments on the financial account,** or simply the **financial account,** is the difference between its sales of assets to foreigners and its purchases of assets from foreigners during a given period.

received. Simultaneously, it ran a financial account surplus: the value of the assets it sold to foreigners was greater than the value of the assets it bought from foreigners.

In the official data, the U.S. current account deficit and financial account surplus almost, but not quite, offset each other: the financial account surplus was $7 billion larger than the current account deficit. But that's just a statistical error, reflecting the imperfection of official data. (And a $7 billion error when you're measuring inflows and outflows of $3.5 trillion isn't bad!) In fact, it's a basic rule of balance of payments accounting that the current account and the financial account must sum to zero:

(43-1) Current account (CA) + Financial account (FA) = 0

or

$$CA = -FA$$

Why must Equation 43-1 be true? We already saw the fundamental explanation in Table 43-1, which showed the accounts of the Costa family: in total, the sources of cash must equal the uses of cash. The same applies to balance of payments accounts. Figure 43-1, a variant on the circular-flow diagram we have found useful in discussing domestic macroeconomics, may help you visualize how this adding up works. Instead of showing the flow of money *within* a national economy, Figure 43-1 shows the flow of money *between* national economies.

Money flows into the United States from the rest of the world as payment for U.S. exports of goods and services, as payment for the use of U.S.-owned factors of production, and as transfer payments. These flows (indicated by the lower yellow arrow) are the positive components of the U.S. current account. Money also flows into the United States from foreigners who purchase U.S. assets (as shown by the lower green arrow)—the positive component of the U.S. financial account.

At the same time, money flows from the United States to the rest of the world as payment for U.S. imports of goods and services, as payment for the use of foreign-owned factors of production, and as transfer payments. These flows, indicated by the upper yellow arrow, are the negative components of the U.S. current account. Money also flows from the United States to purchase foreign assets, as shown by the upper green arrow—the negative component of the U.S. financial account. As in all circular-flow diagrams, the flow into a box and the flow out of a box are equal. This means that the

FIGURE 43-1 The Balance of Payments

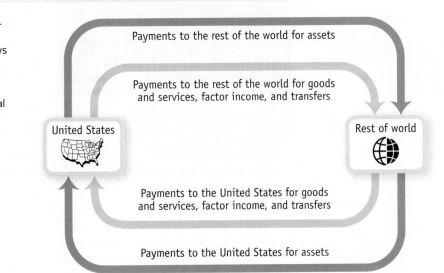

The yellow arrows represent payments that are counted in the current account. The green arrows represent payments that are counted in the financial account. Because the total flow into the United States must equal the total flow out of the United States, the sum of the current account plus the financial account is zero.

Payments to the rest of the world for assets

Payments to the rest of the world for goods and services, factor income, and transfers

United States

Rest of world

Payments to the United States for goods and services, factor income, and transfers

Payments to the United States for assets

sum of the yellow and green arrows going into the United States is equal to the sum of the yellow and green arrows going out of the United States. That is,

(43-2) Positive entries on the current account (lower yellow arrow) + Positive entries on the financial account (lower green arrow) = Negative entries on the current account (upper yellow arrow) + Negative entries on the financial account (upper green arrow)

Equation 43-2 can be rearranged as follows:

(43-3) Positive entries on the current account – Negative entries on the current account + Positive entries on the financial account – Negative entries on the financial account = 0

Equation 43-3 is equivalent to Equation 43-1: the current account plus the financial account—both equal to positive entries minus negative entries—is equal to zero.

But what determines the current account and the financial account?

ECONOMICS ▶ IN ACTION

GDP, GNP, AND THE CURRENT ACCOUNT

When we discussed national income accounting, we derived the basic equation relating GDP to the components of spending:

$$Y = C + I + G + X - IM$$

where X and IM are exports and imports, respectively, of goods and services. But as we've learned, the balance of payments on goods and services is only one component of the current account balance. Why doesn't the national income equation use the current account as a whole?

The answer is that gross domestic product, GDP, is the value of goods and services produced domestically. So it doesn't include international factor income and international transfers, two sources of income that are included in the calculation of the current account balance. The profits of Ford Motors U.K. aren't included in America's GDP, and the funds Latin American immigrants send home to their families aren't subtracted from GDP.

The funds Latin American immigrants send to their home countries aren't subtracted from GDP.

Shouldn't we have a broader measure that does include these sources of income? Actually, gross national product—GNP—does include international factor income. Estimates of U.S. GNP differ slightly from estimates of GDP because GNP adds in items such as the earnings of U.S. companies abroad and subtracts items such as the interest payments on bonds owned by residents of China and Japan. There isn't, however, any regularly calculated measure that includes transfer payments.

Why do economists use GDP rather than a broader measure? Two reasons:

1. The original purpose of the national accounts was to track production rather than income.

2. Data on international factor income and transfer payments are generally considered somewhat unreliable.

So if you're trying to keep track of movements in the economy, it makes sense to focus on GDP, which doesn't rely on these unreliable data.

Modeling the Financial Account

A country's financial account measures its net sales of assets, such as currencies, securities, and factories, to foreigners. Those assets are exchanged for a type of capital called *financial capital,* which is funds from savings that are available for investment spending. We can thus think of the financial account as a measure of *capital inflows* in the form of foreign savings that become available to finance domestic investment spending.

What determines these capital inflows?

Part of our explanation will have to wait for a little while because some international capital flows are created by governments and central banks, which sometimes act very differently from private investors. But we can gain insight into the motivations for capital flows that are the result of private decisions by using the *loanable funds model* we developed previously. In using this model, we make two important simplifications:

1. We simplify the reality of international capital flows by assuming that all flows are in the form of loans. In reality, capital flows take many forms, including purchases of shares of stock in foreign companies and foreign real estate as well as *foreign direct investment,* in which companies build factories or acquire other productive assets abroad.

2. We also ignore the effects of expected changes in *exchange rates,* the relative values of different national currencies. We'll analyze the determination of exchange rates later.

Figure 43-2 recaps the loanable funds model for a closed economy. Equilibrium corresponds to point *E,* at an interest rate of 4%, at which the supply of loanable funds, *S,* intersects the demand for loanable funds curve, *D.* But if international capital flows are possible, this diagram changes and *E* may no longer be the equilibrium. We can analyze the causes and effects of international capital flows using Figure 43-3, which places the loanable funds market diagrams for two countries side by side.

Figure 43-3 illustrates a world consisting of only two countries, the United States and Britain. Panel (a) shows the loanable funds market in the United States, where

FIGURE **43-2** **The Loanable Funds Model Revisited**

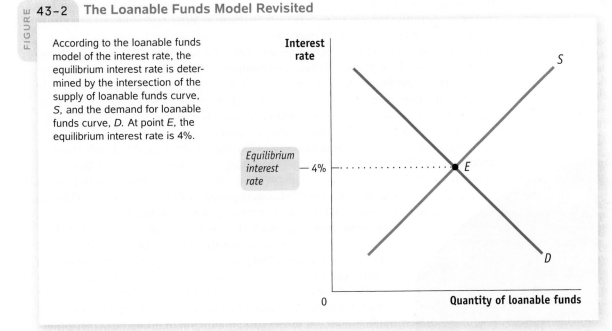

According to the loanable funds model of the interest rate, the equilibrium interest rate is determined by the intersection of the supply of loanable funds curve, *S,* and the demand for loanable funds curve, *D.* At point *E,* the equilibrium interest rate is 4%.

FIGURE 43-3   Loanable Funds Markets in Two Countries

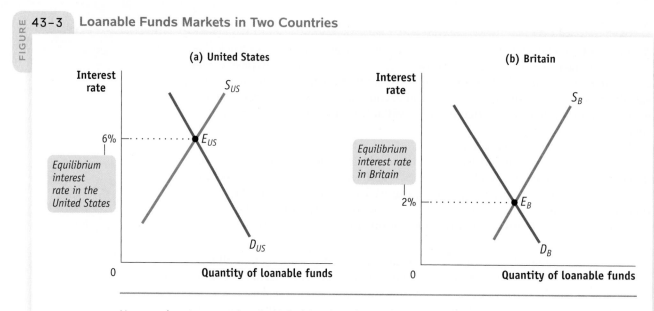

Here we show two countries, the United States and Britain, each with its own loanable funds market. The equilibrium interest rate is 6% in the U.S. market but only 2% in the British market. This creates an incentive for capital to flow from Britain to the United States.

the equilibrium in the absence of international capital flows is at point E_{US} with an interest rate of 6%. Panel (b) shows the loanable funds market in Britain, where the equilibrium in the absence of international capital flows is at point E_B with an interest rate of 2%.

Will the actual interest rate in the United States remain at 6% and that in Britain at 2%? Not if it is easy for British residents to make loans to Americans. In that case, British lenders, attracted by high American interest rates, will send some of their loanable funds to the United States. This capital inflow will increase the quantity of loanable funds supplied to American borrowers, pushing the U.S. interest rate down. At the same time, it will reduce the quantity of loanable funds supplied to British borrowers, pushing the British interest rate up. So international capital flows will narrow the gap between U.S. and British interest rates.

Let's further suppose that British lenders regard a loan to an American as being just as good as a loan to one of their own compatriots, and American borrowers regard a debt to a British lender as no more costly than a debt to an American lender. In that case, the flow of funds from Britain to the United States will continue until the gap between their interest rates is eliminated. In other words, international capital flows will equalize the interest rates in the two countries.

International flows of capital resemble international flows of goods and services.

Figure 43-4 shows an international equilibrium in the loanable funds markets where the equilibrium interest rate is 4% in both the United States and Britain. At this interest rate, the quantity of loanable funds demanded by American borrowers exceeds the quantity of loanable funds supplied by American lenders. This gap is filled by "imported" funds—a capital inflow from Britain.

At the same time, the quantity of loanable funds supplied by British lenders is greater than the quantity of loanable funds demanded by British borrowers. This excess is "exported" in the form of a capital outflow to the United States. And the two markets are in equilibrium at a common interest rate of 4%. At that interest rate, the total quantity of loans demanded by borrowers across the two markets is equal to the total quantity of loans supplied by lenders across the two markets.

FIGURE   **43-4**   International Capital Flows

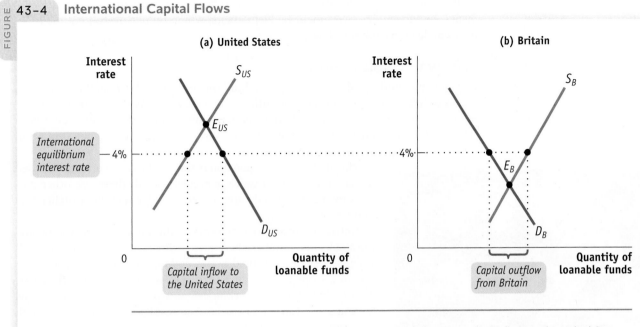

British lenders lend to borrowers in the United States, leading to equalization of interest rates at 4% in both countries. At that rate, American borrowing exceeds American lending; the difference is made up by capital inflows to the United States. Meanwhile, British lending exceeds British borrowing; the excess is a capital outflow from Britain.

In short, international flows of capital are like international flows of goods and services. Capital moves from places where it would be cheap in the absence of international capital flows to places where it would be expensive in the absence of such flows.

Underlying Determinants of International Capital Flows

The open-economy version of the loanable funds model helps us understand international capital flows in terms of the supply and demand for funds. But what underlies differences across countries in the supply and demand for funds? Why, in the absence of international capital flows, would interest rates differ internationally, creating an incentive for international capital flows?

International differences in the demand for funds reflect underlying differences in investment opportunities. In particular, a country with a rapidly growing economy, other things equal, tends to offer more investment opportunities than a country with a slowly growing economy. So a rapidly growing economy typically—though not always—has a higher demand for capital and offers higher returns to investors than a slowly growing economy in the absence of capital flows. As a result, capital tends to flow from slowly growing to rapidly growing economies.

The classic example is the flow of capital from Britain to the United States, among other countries, between 1870 and 1914. During that era, the U.S. economy was growing rapidly as the population increased and spread westward and as the nation industrialized. This created a demand for investment spending on railroads, factories, and so on. Meanwhile, Britain had a much more slowly growing population, was already industrialized, and already had a railroad network covering the country. This left Britain with savings to spare, much of which were lent to the United States and other New World economies.

International differences in the supply of funds reflect differences in savings across countries. These may be the result of differences in private savings rates, which vary widely among countries. For example, in 2012, private savings were 22% of Japan's

GDP but only 17% of U.S. GDP. They may also reflect differences in savings by governments. In particular, government budget deficits, which reduce overall national savings, can lead to capital inflows.

Two-way Capital Flows

The loanable funds model helps us understand the direction of *net* capital flows—the excess of inflows into a country over outflows, or vice versa. As we saw in Table 43-2, however, *gross* flows take place in both directions: for example, the United States both sells assets to foreigners and buys assets from foreigners. Why does capital move in both directions?

Many American companies have opened plants in China for easier access to the growing Chinese market and to take advantage of low labor costs.

The answer to this question is that in the real world, as opposed to the simple model we've just constructed, there are other motives for international capital flows besides seeking a higher rate of interest.

Individual investors often seek to diversify against risk by buying stocks in a number of countries. Stocks in Europe may do well when stocks in the United States do badly, or vice versa, so investors in Europe try to reduce their risk by buying some U.S. stocks, even as investors in the United States try to reduce their risk by buying some European stocks. The result is capital flows in both directions.

Meanwhile, corporations often engage in international investment as part of their business strategy—for example, auto companies may find that they can compete better in a national market if they assemble some of their cars locally. Such business investments can also lead to two-way capital flows, as, say, European carmakers build plants in the United States even as U.S. computer companies open facilities in Europe.

Finally, some countries, including the United States, are international banking centers: people from all over the world put money in U.S. financial institutions, which then invest many of those funds overseas.

The result of these two-way flows is that modern economies are typically both debtors (countries that owe money to the rest of the world) and creditors (countries to which the rest of the world owes money). Due to years of both capital inflows and outflows, at the end of 2012, the United States had accumulated foreign assets worth $20.8 trillion and foreigners had accumulated assets in the United States worth $25.2 trillion.

MODULE 43 Review

Solutions appear at the back of the book.

Check Your Understanding

1. Which of the balance of payments accounts do the following events affect?

   a. Boeing, a U.S.-based company, sells a newly built airplane to China.

   b. Chinese investors buy stock in Boeing from Americans.

   c. A Chinese company buys a used airplane from American Airlines and ships it to China.

   d. A Chinese investor who owns property in the United States buys a corporate jet, which he will keep in the United States so he can travel around America.

2. What effect do you think the collapse of the U.S. housing bubble and the ensuing recession had on international capital flows into the United States?

Multiple-Choice Questions

1. The current account includes which of the following?

    I. payments for goods and services

    II. transfer payments

    III. factor income

    a. I only

    b. II only

    c. III only

    d. I and II only

    e. I, II, and III

2. The balance of payments on the current account plus the balance of payments on the financial account is equal to

    a. zero.

    b. one.

    c. the trade balance.

    d. net capital flows.

    e. the size of the trade deficit.

3. The financial account was previously known as the

    a. gross national product.

    b. capital account.

    c. trade deficit.

    d. investment account.

    e. trade balance.

4. The trade balance includes which of the following?

    I. imports and exports of goods

    II. imports and exports of services

    III. net capital flows

    a. I only

    b. II only

    c. III only

    d. I and II only

    e. I, II, and III

5. Which of the following will increase the demand for loanable funds in a country?

    a. economic growth

    b. decreased investment opportunities

    c. a recession

    d. decreased private savings rates

    e. government budget surpluses

Critical-Thinking Question

Draw two side-by-side graphs of the loanable funds market in the United States and in China to show how a higher interest rate in the United States will lead to capital flows between the two countries. On your graphs, label the starting and ending interest rates and the size of the capital inflows and outflows.

WHAT YOU WILL LEARN

1 The role of the foreign exchange market and the exchange rate

2 The importance of real exchange rates and their role in the current account

The Role of the Exchange Rate

We've just seen how differences in the supply of loanable funds from savings and the demand for loanable funds for investment spending lead to international capital flows. We've also learned that a country's balance of payments on the current account plus its balance of payments on the financial account add up to zero: a country that receives net capital inflows must run a matching current account deficit, and a country that generates net capital outflows must run a matching current account surplus.

The behavior of the financial account—reflecting inflows or outflows of capital—is best described as equilibrium in the international loanable funds market. At the same time, the balance of payments on goods and services, the main component of the current account, is determined by decisions in the international markets for goods and services.

So given that the financial account reflects the movement of capital and the current account reflects the movement of goods and services, what ensures that the balance of payments really does balance? That is, what ensures that the two accounts actually offset each other?

The answer lies in the role of the *exchange rate,* which is determined in the *foreign exchange market.*

Understanding Exchange Rates

In general, goods, services, and assets produced in a country must be paid for in that country's currency. American products must be paid for in dollars; European products must be paid for in euros; Japanese products must be paid for in yen. Occasionally, sellers will accept payment in foreign currency, but they will then exchange that currency for domestic money.

International transactions, then, require a market—the **foreign exchange market**—in which currencies can be exchanged for each other. This market determines **exchange rates,** the prices at which currencies trade. You will not find the foreign exchange market located in any one geographic spot. Rather, it is a global electronic market that traders around the world use to buy and sell currencies.

Table 44-1 shows exchange rates among the world's three most important currencies as of 7:50 A.M., EST, on May 13, 2013. Each entry shows the price of the "row" currency in terms of the "column" currency. For example, at that time US$1 exchanged for €0.7701, so it took €0.7701 to buy US$1. Similarly, it took US$1.2985 to buy €1. These two numbers reflect the same rate of exchange between the euro and the U.S. dollar: 1/1.2985 = €0.7701.

There are two ways to write any given exchange rate. In this case, there were €0.7701 to US$1 and US$1.2985 to €1. Which is the correct way to write it? The answer is that there is no fixed rule. In most countries, people tend to express the exchange rate as the price of a dollar in domestic currency. However, this rule isn't universal, and the U.S. dollar–euro rate is commonly quoted both ways. The important thing is to be sure you know which one you are using!

When discussing movements in exchange rates, economists use specialized terms to avoid confusion. When a currency becomes more valuable in terms of other currencies, economists say that the currency **appreciates.** When a currency becomes less valuable in terms of other currencies, it **depreciates.** Suppose, for example, that the value of €1 went from $1 to $1.25, which means that the value of US$1 went from €1 to €0.80 (because 1/1.25 = 0.80). In this case, we would say that the euro appreciated and the U.S. dollar depreciated.

Movements in exchange rates, other things equal, affect the relative prices of goods, services, and assets in different countries. Suppose, for example, that the price of an American hotel room is US$100 and the price of a French hotel room is €100. If the exchange rate is €1 = US$1, these hotel rooms have the same price. If the exchange rate is €1.25 = US$1, the French hotel room is 20% cheaper than the American hotel room. If the exchange rate is €0.80 = US$1, the French hotel room is 25% more expensive than the American hotel room.

But what determines exchange rates? Supply and demand in the foreign exchange market.

The Equilibrium Exchange Rate

Imagine, for the sake of simplicity, that there are only two currencies in the world: U.S. dollars and euros. Europeans wanting to purchase American goods, services, and assets come to the foreign exchange market to exchange euros for U.S. dollars. That is, Europeans demand U.S. dollars from the foreign exchange market and, correspondingly, supply euros to that market.

Americans wanting to buy European goods, services, and assets come to the foreign exchange market to exchange U.S. dollars for euros. That is, Americans supply U.S. dollars to the foreign exchange market and, correspondingly, demand euros from that market. (International transfers and payments of factor income also enter into the foreign exchange market, but to make things simple, we'll ignore these.)

Figure 44-1 shows how the foreign exchange market works. The quantity of dollars demanded and supplied at any given euro–U.S. dollar exchange rate is shown on the horizontal axis, and the euro–U.S. dollar exchange rate is shown on the vertical axis. The exchange rate plays the same role as the price of a good or service in an ordinary supply and demand diagram.

The figure shows two curves, the demand curve for U.S. dollars and the supply curve for U.S. dollars. The key to understanding the slopes of these curves is that the level of the exchange rate affects exports and imports. When a country's currency

TABLE 44-1

Exchange Rates, May 13, 2013 7:50 A.M.

	U.S. dollars	Yen	Euros
One U.S. dollar exchanged for	1	101.6500	0.7701
One yen exchanged for	0.0098	1	0.0076
One euro exchanged for	1.2985	132.0300	1

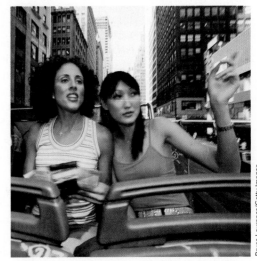

When the dollar appreciates, an American vacation becomes more expensive for European tourists.

Currencies are traded in the **foreign exchange market.**

The prices at which currencies trade are known as **exchange rates.**

When a currency becomes more valuable in terms of other currencies, it **appreciates.**

When a currency becomes less valuable in terms of other currencies, it **depreciates.**

Bruce Laurance/Getty Images

FIGURE **44-1**   The Foreign Exchange Market

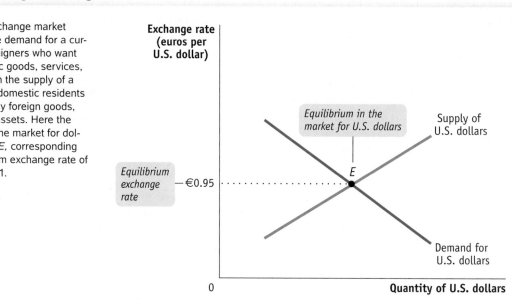

The foreign exchange market matches up the demand for a currency from foreigners who want to buy domestic goods, services, and assets with the supply of a currency from domestic residents who want to buy foreign goods, services, and assets. Here the equilibrium in the market for dollars is at point *E*, corresponding to an equilibrium exchange rate of €0.95 per US$1.

The **equilibrium exchange rate** is the exchange rate at which the quantity of a currency demanded in the foreign exchange market is equal to the quantity supplied.

appreciates (becomes more valuable), exports fall and imports rise. When a country's currency depreciates (becomes less valuable), exports rise and imports fall.

To understand why the demand curve for U.S. dollars slopes downward, recall that the exchange rate, other things equal, determines the prices of American goods, services, and assets relative to those of European goods, services, and assets. If the U.S. dollar rises against the euro (the dollar appreciates), American products will become more expensive to Europeans relative to European products. So Europeans will buy less from the United States and will acquire fewer dollars in the foreign exchange market: the quantity of U.S. dollars demanded falls as the number of euros needed to buy a U.S. dollar rises.

If the U.S. dollar falls against the euro (the dollar depreciates), American products will become relatively cheaper for Europeans. Europeans will respond by buying more from the United States and acquiring more dollars in the foreign exchange market: the quantity of U.S. dollars demanded rises as the number of euros needed to buy a U.S. dollar falls.

A similar argument explains why the supply curve of U.S. dollars in Figure 44-1 slopes upward: the more euros required to buy a U.S. dollar, the more dollars Americans will supply. Again, the reason is the effect of the exchange rate on relative prices. If the U.S. dollar rises against the euro, European products look cheaper to Americans—who will demand more of them. This will require Americans to convert more dollars into euros.

The **equilibrium exchange rate** is the exchange rate at which the quantity of U.S. dollars demanded in the foreign exchange market is equal to the quantity of U.S. dollars supplied. In Figure 44-1, the equilibrium is at point *E*, and the equilibrium exchange rate is 0.95. That is, at an exchange rate of €0.95 per US$1, the quantity of U.S. dollars supplied to the foreign exchange market is equal to the quantity of U.S. dollars demanded.

To understand the significance of the equilibrium exchange rate, it's helpful to consider a numerical example of what equilibrium in the foreign exchange market looks like. A hypothetical example

TABLE **44-2**

A Hypothetical Example of Equilibrium in the Foreign Exchange Market

European purchases of U.S. dollars (trillions of U.S. dollars)	To buy U.S. goods and services: 1.0	To buy U.S. assets: 1.0	Total purchases of U.S. dollars: 2.0
U.S. sales of U.S. dollars (trillions of U.S. dollars)	To buy European goods and services: 1.5	To buy European assets: 0.5	Total sales of U.S. dollars: 2.0
	U.S. balance of payments on the current account: −0.5	U.S. balance of payments on the financial account: +0.5	

is shown in Table 44-2. The first row shows European purchases of U.S. dollars, either to buy U.S. goods and services or to buy U.S. assets. The second row shows U.S. sales of U.S. dollars, either to buy European goods and services or to buy European assets. At the equilibrium exchange rate, the total quantity of U.S. dollars Europeans want to buy is equal to the total quantity of U.S. dollars Americans want to sell.

Remember that the balance of payments accounts divide international transactions into two types. Purchases and sales of goods and services are counted in the current account. (Again, we're leaving out transfers and factor income to keep things simple.) Purchases and sales of assets are counted in the financial account. At the equilibrium exchange rate, then, we have the situation shown in Table 44-2: the sum of the balance of payments on the current account plus the balance of payments on the financial account is zero.

Now let's briefly consider how a shift in the demand for U.S. dollars affects equilibrium in the foreign exchange market. Suppose that for some reason capital flows from Europe to the United States increase—say, due to a change in the preferences of European investors. The effects are shown in Figure 44-2. The demand for U.S. dollars in the foreign exchange market increases as European investors convert euros into dollars to fund their new investments in the United States. This is shown by the shift of the demand curve from D_1 to D_2. As a result, the U.S. dollar appreciates: the number of euros per U.S. dollar at the equilibrium exchange rate rises from XR_1 to XR_2.

FIGURE 44-2 **An Increase in the Demand for U.S. Dollars**

An increase in the demand for U.S. dollars might result from a change in the preferences of European investors. The demand curve for U.S. dollars shifts from D_1 to D_2. So the equilibrium number of euros per U.S. dollar rises—the dollar *appreciates*. As a result, the balance of payments on the current account falls as the balance of payments on the financial account rises.

What are the consequences of this increased capital inflow for the balance of payments? The total quantity of U.S. dollars supplied to the foreign exchange market still must equal the total quantity of U.S. dollars demanded. So the increased capital inflow to the United States—an increase in the balance of payments on the financial account—must be matched by a decline in the balance of payments on the current account. What causes the balance of payments on the current account to decline? The appreciation of the U.S. dollar. A rise in the number of euros per U.S. dollar leads Americans to buy more European goods and services and Europeans to buy fewer American goods and services.

Table 44-3 shows a hypothetical example of how this might work. Europeans are buying more U.S. assets, increasing the balance of payments on the financial account from 0.5 to 1.0 trillion dollars. This is offset by a reduction in European purchases

TABLE 44-3

A Hypothetical Example of Effects of Increased Capital Inflows

European purchases of U.S. dollars (trillions of U.S. dollars)	To buy U.S. goods and services: 0.75 (down 0.25)	To buy U.S. assets: 1.5 (up 0.5)	Total purchases of U.S. dollars: 2.25
U.S. sales of U.S. dollars (trillions of U.S. dollars)	To buy European goods and services: 1.75 (up 0.25)	To buy European assets: 0.5 (no change)	Total sales of U.S. dollars: 2.25
	U.S. balance of payments on the current account: −1.0 (down 0.5)	U.S. balance of payments on the financial account: +1.0 (up 0.5)	

of U.S. goods and services and a rise in U.S. purchases of European goods and services, both the result of the dollar's appreciation. *So any change in the U.S. balance of payments on the financial account generates an equal and opposite reaction in the balance of payments on the current account.* Movements in the exchange rate ensure that changes in the financial account and in the current account offset each other.

Let's briefly run this process in reverse. Suppose there is a reduction in capital flows from Europe to the United States—again due to a change in the preferences of European investors. The demand for U.S. dollars in the foreign exchange market falls, and the dollar depreciates: the number of euros per U.S. dollar at the equilibrium exchange rate falls. This leads Americans to buy fewer European products and Europeans to buy more American products. Ultimately, this generates an increase in the U.S. balance of payments on the current account. So a fall in capital flows into the United States leads to a weaker dollar, which in turn generates an increase in U.S. net exports.

Inflation and Real Exchange Rates

In 1993, one U.S. dollar exchanged, on average, for 3.1 Mexican pesos. By 2013, the peso had fallen against the dollar by more than 75%, with an average exchange rate in early 2013 of 12.1 pesos per dollar. Did Mexican products also become much cheaper relative to U.S. products over that 20-year period? Did the price of Mexican products expressed in terms of U.S. dollars also fall by more than 75%?

The answer is no because Mexico had much higher inflation than the United States over that period. In fact, the relative price of U.S. and Mexican products changed little between 1993 and 2013, although the exchange rate changed a lot.

To take account of the effects of differences in inflation rates, economists calculate **real exchange rates,** exchange rates adjusted for international differences in aggregate price levels. Suppose that the exchange rate we are looking at is the number of Mexican pesos per U.S. dollar. Let P_{US} and P_{Mex} be indexes of the aggregate price levels in the United States and Mexico, respectively. Then the real exchange rate between the Mexican peso and the U.S. dollar is defined as:

(44-1) Real exchange rate = Mexican pesos per U.S. dollar $\times \dfrac{P_{US}}{P_{Mex}}$

To distinguish it from the real exchange rate, the exchange rate unadjusted for aggregate price levels is sometimes called the *nominal* exchange rate.

To understand the significance of the difference between the real and nominal exchange rates, let's consider the following example. Suppose that the Mexican peso depreciates against the U.S. dollar, with the exchange rate going from 10 pesos per U.S. dollar to 15 pesos per U.S. dollar, a 50% change. But suppose that at the same time the price of everything in Mexico, measured in pesos, increases by 50%, so that the

Real exchange rates are exchange rates adjusted for international differences in aggregate price levels.

Javier Correa/Alamy

Mexican price index rises from 100 to 150. We'll assume that there is no change in U.S. prices, so that the U.S. price index remains at 100. Then the initial real exchange rate is:

$$\text{Pesos per dollar} \times \frac{P_{US}}{P_{Mex}} = 10 \times \frac{100}{100} = 10$$

After the peso depreciates and the Mexican price level increases, the real exchange rate is:

$$\text{Pesos per dollar} \times \frac{P_{US}}{P_{Mex}} = 15 \times \frac{100}{150} = 10$$

In this example, the peso has depreciated substantially in terms of the U.S. dollar, but the *real* exchange rate between the peso and the U.S. dollar hasn't changed at all. And because the real peso–U.S. dollar exchange rate hasn't changed, the nominal depreciation of the peso against the U.S. dollar will have no effect either on the quantity of goods and services exported by Mexico to the United States or on the quantity of goods and services imported by Mexico from the United States.

To see why, consider again the example of a hotel room. Suppose that this room initially costs 1,000 pesos per night, which is $100 at an exchange rate of 10 pesos per dollar. After both Mexican prices and the number of pesos per dollar rise by 50%, the hotel room costs 1,500 pesos per night—but 1,500 pesos divided by 15 pesos per dollar is $100, so the Mexican hotel room still costs $100. As a result, a U.S. tourist considering a trip to Mexico will have no reason to change plans.

The same is true for all goods and services that enter into trade: *the current account responds only to changes in the real exchange rate, not the nominal exchange rate.* A country's products become cheaper to foreigners only when that country's currency depreciates in real terms, and those products become more expensive to foreigners only when the currency appreciates in real terms. As a consequence, economists who analyze movements in exports and imports of goods and services focus on the real exchange rate, not the nominal exchange rate.

Figure 44-3 illustrates just how important it can be to distinguish between nominal and real exchange rates. The line labeled "Nominal exchange rate" shows the number of pesos it took to buy a U.S. dollar from November 1993 to December 2011. As you can see, the peso depreciated massively over that period. But the line labeled "Real

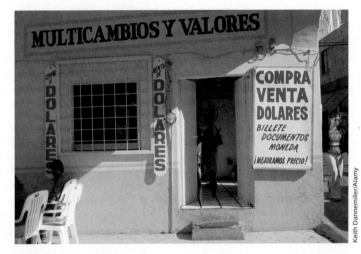

The current account responds only to changes in real exchange rates, which have been adjusted for differing levels of inflation.

44-3 Real versus Nominal Exchange Rates, 1993–2011

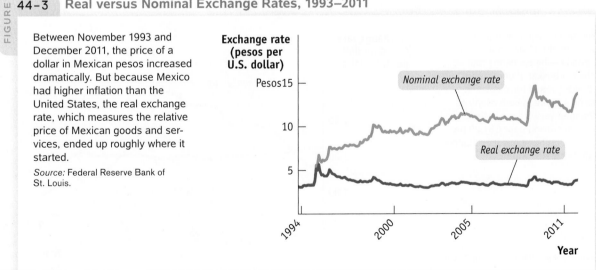

Between November 1993 and December 2011, the price of a dollar in Mexican pesos increased dramatically. But because Mexico had higher inflation than the United States, the real exchange rate, which measures the relative price of Mexican goods and services, ended up roughly where it started.

Source: Federal Reserve Bank of St. Louis.

The **purchasing power parity** between two countries' currencies is the nominal exchange rate at which a given basket of goods and services would cost the same amount in each country.

exchange rate" shows the real exchange rate: it was calculated using Equation 44-1, with price indexes for both Mexico and the United States set so that the value in 1993 was 100. In real terms, the peso depreciated between 1994 and 1995, but not by nearly as much as the nominal depreciation. By the end of 2011, the real peso–U.S. dollar exchange rate was just about back where it started.

Purchasing Power Parity

A useful tool for analyzing exchange rates, closely connected to the concept of the real exchange rate, is known as *purchasing power parity*. The **purchasing power parity** between two countries' currencies is the nominal exchange rate at which a given basket of goods and services would cost the same amount in each country. Suppose, for example, that a basket of goods and services that costs $100 in the United States costs 1,000 pesos in Mexico. Then the purchasing power parity is 10 pesos per U.S. dollar: at that exchange rate, 1,000 pesos = $100, so the market basket costs the same amount in both countries.

Calculations of purchasing power parities are usually made by estimating the cost of buying broad market baskets containing many goods and services—everything from automobiles and groceries to housing and telephone calls. But once a year the magazine *The Economist* publishes a list of purchasing power parities based on the cost of buying a market basket that contains only one item—a McDonald's Big Mac.

Nominal exchange rates almost always differ from purchasing power parities. Some of these differences are systematic: in general, aggregate price levels are lower in poor countries than in rich countries because services tend to be cheaper in poor countries. But even among countries at roughly the same level of economic development, nominal exchange rates vary quite a lot from purchasing power parity.

Figure 44-4 shows the nominal exchange rate between the Canadian dollar and the U.S. dollar, measured as the number of Canadian dollars per U.S. dollar, from 1990 to 2012, together with an estimate of the purchasing power parity exchange rate between the United States and Canada over the same period. The purchasing power parity didn't change much over the whole period because the United States and Canada had about the same rate of inflation.

But at the beginning of the period the nominal exchange rate was below purchasing power parity, so a given market basket was more expensive in Canada than in the United States. By 2002, the nominal exchange rate was far above the purchasing power parity, so a market basket was much cheaper in Canada than in the United States.

Over the long run, however, purchasing power parities are pretty good at predicting actual changes in nominal exchange rates. In particular, nominal exchange rates

FIGURE 44-4 Purchasing Power Parity versus the Nominal Exchange Rate, 1990–2012

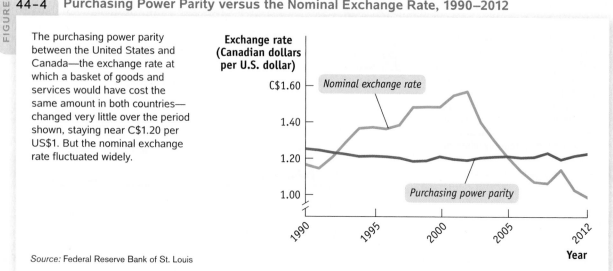

The purchasing power parity between the United States and Canada—the exchange rate at which a basket of goods and services would have cost the same amount in both countries—changed very little over the period shown, staying near C$1.20 per US$1. But the nominal exchange rate fluctuated widely.

Source: Federal Reserve Bank of St. Louis

between countries at similar levels of economic development tend to fluctuate around levels that lead to similar costs for a given market basket. In fact, by July 2005, the nominal exchange rate between the United States and Canada was C$1.22 per US$1—just about the purchasing power parity. And by 2012, the cost of living was once again higher in Canada than in the United States.

ECONOMICS ▶ IN ACTION

BURGERNOMICS

For a number of years the British magazine *The Economist* has produced an annual comparison of the cost in different countries of one particular consumption item that is found around the world—a McDonald's Big Mac.

The magazine finds the price of a Big Mac in local currency, then computes two numbers: the price of a Big Mac in U.S. dollars using the prevailing exchange rate and the exchange rate at which the price of a Big Mac would equal the U.S. price. If purchasing power parity held for Big Macs, the dollar price of a Big Mac would be the same everywhere. If purchasing power parity is a good theory for the long run, the exchange rate at which a Big Mac's price matches the U.S. price should offer some guidance about where the exchange rate will eventually end up.

Table 44-4 shows the *Economist* estimates for selected countries as of July 2013, ranked in increasing order of the dollar price of a Big Mac. The countries with the cheapest Big Macs, and therefore by this measure with the most undervalued currencies, are India and China, both developing countries.

But not all developing countries have low-priced Big Macs: the price of a Big Mac in Brazil, converted into dollars, is considerably higher than in the United States. This reflects a sharp appreciation of the *real*, Brazil's currency, in recent years as the country has become a favorite of international investors. And topping the list, with a Big Mac some 47% more expensive than in the United States, is Switzerland.

TABLE 44-4

Purchasing Power Parity and the Price of a Big Mac

Country	Big Mac price		Local currency per dollar	
	In local currency	In U.S. dollars	Implied PPP	Actual exchange rate
India	Rupee 90	1.50	19.75	59.98
China	Yuan 16	2.61	3.51	6.13
Mexico	Peso 37	2.86	8.12	12.94
Japan	¥ 320	3.20	70.23	100.11
Britain	£ 2.69	4.02	0.59	0.67
United States	$4.56	4.56	1.00	1.00
Euro area	€ 3.62	4.66	0.80	0.78
Brazil	Real 12	5.28	2.63	2.27
Switzerland	SFr 6.5	6.72	1.43	0.97

MODULE 44 Review

Solutions appear at the back of the book.

Check Your Understanding

1. Suppose Mexico discovers huge reserves of oil and starts exporting oil to the United States. Describe how this affects the following:

   a. the nominal peso–U.S. dollar exchange rate

   b. Mexican exports of other goods and services

   c. Mexican imports of goods and services

2. A basket of goods and services that costs $100 in the United States costs 800 pesos in Mexico and the current nominal exchange rate is 10 pesos per U.S. dollar. Over the next five years, the cost of that market basket rises to $120 in the United States and to 1,200 pesos in Mexico, although the nominal exchange rate remains at 10 pesos per U.S. dollar. Calculate the following:

   a. the real exchange rate now and five years from now, if today's price index in both countries is 100

   b. purchasing power parity today and five years from now

Multiple-Choice Questions

1. When the U.S. dollar buys more Japanese yen, the U.S. dollar has

   I. become more valuable in terms of the yen
   II. appreciated
   III. depreciated

   a. I only

   b. II only

   c. III only

   d. I and II only

   e. I and III only

2. The nominal exchange rate at which a given basket of goods and services would cost the same in each country describes

   a. the international consumer price index (ICPI).

   b. appreciation.

   c. depreciation.

   d. purchasing power parity.

   e. the balance of payments on the current account.

3. What happens to the real exchange rate between the euro and the U.S. dollar (expressed as euros per dollar) if the aggregate price levels in Europe and the United States both fall? It

   a. is unaffected.

   b. increases.

   c. decreases.

   d. may increase, decrease, or stay the same.

   e. cannot be calculated.

4. Which of the following would cause the real exchange rate between pesos and U.S. dollars (in terms of pesos per dollar) to decrease?

   a. an increase in net capital flows from Mexico to the United States

   b. an increase in the real interest rate in Mexico relative to the United States

   c. a doubling of prices in both Mexico and the United States

   d. a decrease in oil exports from Mexico to the United States

   e. an increase in the balance of payments on the current account in the United States

5. Which of the following will decrease the supply of U.S. dollars in the foreign exchange market?

   a. U.S. residents increase their travel abroad

   b. U.S. consumers demand fewer imports

   c. Foreigners increase their demand for U.S. goods

   d. Foreigners increase their travel to the United States

   e. Foreign investors see increased investment opportunities in the United States

Critical-Thinking Question

Draw a graph of the foreign exchange market between the United States and Europe. Illustrate what would happen to the value of the U.S. dollar if there were an increase in the U.S. demand for imports from Europe.

PITFALLS

~~~~~~~~~~~~~~~~~~~~~~~~~~~~~~~~~~~~~

WHICH WAY IS UP?

? You are a tourist in Mexico and need to exchange dollars for pesos. You've heard that the U.S. exchange rate is up, which sounds like good news. But, is it?

> IT DEPENDS. TO DETERMINE IF THE DOLLAR HAS AP-PRECIATED OR DEPRECIATED, YOU NEED TO CHECK THE EX-CHANGE RATE DATA TO FIND OUT WHICH WAY THE EXCHANGE RATE IS BEING MEASURED. Sometimes the exchange rate is measured as the price of a dollar in terms of foreign currency, sometimes it's measured as the price of foreign currency in terms of dollars. Most countries, other than the United States, report their exchange rates in terms of the price of a dollar in their domestic currency—for example, Mexican officials will say that the exchange rate is 12, meaning 12 pesos per dollar. But Britain, for historical reasons, usually states its exchange rate the other way. For example, On May 13, 2013, US$1 was worth £0.6514, and £1 was worth US$1.5350. More often than not, this number is reported as an exchange rate of 1.5350. In fact, on occasion, even professional economists and consultants embarrass themselves by getting the direction in which the pound is moving wrong! And Americans generally follow other countries' lead: we usually say that the exchange rate against Mexico is 12 pesos per dollar but that the exchange rate against Britain is 1.53 dollars per pound. But this rule isn't reliable; exchange rates against the euro are often stated both ways.

To learn more about exchange rates, see pages 464–465.

Exchange Rate Policy

Greg Balfour Evans/Alamy

Exchange Rate Regimes

As we saw in the previous module, the nominal exchange rate, like other prices, is determined by supply and demand. Unlike the price of wheat or oil, however, the exchange rate is the price of a country's money (in terms of another country's money). Money isn't a good or service produced by the private sector; it's an asset whose quantity is determined by government policy. As a result, governments have much more power to influence nominal exchange rates than they have to influence ordinary prices.

The nominal exchange rate is a very important price for many countries: the exchange rate determines the price of imports; it determines the price of exports; in economies where exports and imports are large relative to GDP, movements in the exchange rate can have major effects on aggregate output and the aggregate price level. What do governments do with their power to influence this important price?

The answer is, it depends. At different times and in different places, governments have adopted a variety of **exchange rate regimes.** An *exchange rate regime* is a *rule governing policy toward the exchange rate.* Let's talk about these regimes, how they are enforced, and how governments choose a regime. (From now on, we'll adopt the convention that we mean the nominal exchange rate when we refer to the exchange rate.)

Fixed and Floating Exchange Rates

There are two main kinds of exchange rate regimes. A country has a **fixed exchange rate** when the government keeps the exchange rate against some other currency at or near a particular target. For example, Hong Kong has an official policy of setting an exchange rate of HK$7.80 per US$1. A country has a **floating exchange rate** when the government lets the exchange rate go wherever the market takes it. This is the policy followed by Britain, Canada, and the United States.

An **exchange rate regime** is a rule governing policy toward the exchange rate.

A country has a **fixed exchange rate** when the government keeps the exchange rate against some other currency at or near a particular target.

A country has a **floating exchange rate** when the government lets the exchange rate go wherever the market takes it.

Fixed exchange rates and floating exchange rates aren't the only possibilities. At various times, countries have adopted compromise policies that lie somewhere between fixed and floating exchange rates. These include exchange rates that are fixed at any given time but are adjusted frequently, exchange rates that aren't fixed but are "managed" by the government to avoid wide swings, and exchange rates that float within a "target zone" but are prevented from leaving that zone. In this book, however, we'll focus on the two main exchange rate regimes.

The immediate question about a fixed exchange rate is how it is possible for governments to fix the exchange rate when the exchange rate is determined by supply and demand.

How Can an Exchange Rate Be Held Fixed?

To understand how it is possible for a country to fix its exchange rate, let's consider a hypothetical country, Genovia, which for some reason has decided to fix the value of its currency, the geno, at US$1.50.

The obvious problem is that $1.50 may not be the equilibrium exchange rate in the foreign exchange market: the equilibrium rate may be either higher or lower than the target exchange rate. Figure 45-1 shows the foreign exchange market for genos, with the quantities of genos supplied and demanded on the horizontal axis and the exchange rate of the geno, measured in U.S. dollars per geno, on the vertical axis. Panel (a) shows the case in which the equilibrium value of the geno is *below* the target exchange rate. Panel (b) shows the case in which the equilibrium value of the geno is *above* the target exchange rate.

Consider first the case in which the equilibrium value of the geno is below the target exchange rate. As panel (a) shows, at the target exchange rate there is a surplus of genos in the foreign exchange market, which would normally push the value of the geno down. How can the Genovian government support the value of the geno to keep the rate where it wants? There are three possible ways the Genovian government can support the geno, all of which have been used by governments at some point.

1. It can "soak up" the surplus of genos by buying its own currency in the foreign exchange market. Government purchases or sales of currency in the foreign ex-

FIGURE 45-1   Exchange Market Intervention

In both panels, the imaginary country of Genovia is trying to keep the value of its currency, the geno, fixed at US$1.50. In panel (a), there is a surplus of genos on the foreign exchange market. To keep the geno from falling, the Genovian government can buy genos and sell U.S. dollars. In panel (b), there is a shortage of genos. To keep the geno from rising, the Genovian government can sell genos and buy U.S. dollars.

change market are called **exchange market intervention.** To buy genos in the foreign exchange market, of course, the Genovian government must have U.S. dollars to exchange for genos. In fact, most countries maintain **foreign exchange reserves,** stocks of foreign currency (usually U.S. dollars or euros) that they can use to buy their own currency to support its price.

We mentioned earlier that an important part of international capital flows is the result of purchases and sales of foreign assets by governments and central banks. Now we can see why governments sell foreign assets: they are supporting their currency through exchange market intervention. As we'll see in a moment, governments that keep the value of their currency *down* through exchange market intervention must *buy* foreign assets. First, however, let's talk about the other ways governments fix exchange rates.

2. The Genovian government can try to shift the supply and demand curves for the geno in the foreign exchange market. Governments usually do this by changing monetary policy. For example, to support the geno, the Genovian central bank can raise the Genovian interest rate. This will increase capital flows into Genovia, increasing the demand for genos, at the same time that it reduces capital flows out of Genovia, reducing the supply of genos. So, other things equal, an increase in a country's interest rate will increase the value of its currency.

3. It can reduce the supply of genos to the foreign exchange market by requiring domestic residents who want to buy foreign currency to get a license and giving these licenses only to people engaging in approved transactions (such as the purchase of imported goods the Genovian government thinks are essential). Licensing systems that limit the right of individuals to buy foreign currency are called **foreign exchange controls.** Other things equal, foreign exchange controls increase the value of a country's currency.

So far we've been discussing a situation in which the government is trying to prevent a depreciation of the geno. Suppose, instead, that the situation is as shown in panel (b) of Figure 45-1, where the equilibrium value of the geno is *above* the target exchange rate and there is a shortage of genos.

To maintain the target exchange rate, the Genovian government can apply the same three basic options in the reverse direction. It can intervene in the foreign exchange market, in this case *selling* genos and acquiring U.S. dollars, which it can add to its foreign exchange reserves. It can *reduce* interest rates to increase the supply of genos and reduce the demand. Or it can impose foreign exchange controls that limit the ability of foreigners to buy genos. All of these actions, other things equal, will reduce the value of the geno.

As we said, all three techniques have been used to manage fixed exchange rates. But we haven't said whether fixing the exchange rate is a good idea. In fact, the choice of exchange rate regime poses a dilemma for policy makers because fixed and floating exchange rates each have both advantages and disadvantages.

The Exchange Rate Regime Dilemma

Few questions in macroeconomics produce as many arguments as that of whether a country should adopt a fixed or a floating exchange rate. The reason there are so many arguments is that both sides have a case.

To understand the case for a fixed exchange rate, consider for a moment how easy it is to conduct business across state lines in the United States. There are a number of things that make interstate commerce trouble-free, but one of them is the absence of any uncertainty about the value of money: a dollar is a dollar, in both New York City and Los Angeles.

By contrast, a dollar isn't a dollar in transactions between New York City and Toronto. The exchange rate between the Canadian

Government purchases or sales of currency in the foreign exchange market constitute **exchange market intervention.**

Foreign exchange reserves are stocks of foreign currency that governments maintain to buy their own currency on the foreign exchange market.

Foreign exchange controls are licensing systems that limit the right of individuals to buy foreign currency.

Once you cross the border into Canada, a dollar is no longer worth a dollar.

Robert Nickelsberg/Getty Images

dollar and the U.S. dollar fluctuates, sometimes widely. If a U.S. firm promises to pay a Canadian firm a given number of U.S. dollars a year from now, the value of that promise in Canadian currency can vary by 10% or more. This uncertainty has the effect of deterring trade between the two countries. So one benefit of a fixed exchange rate is certainty about the future value of a currency.

There is also, in some cases, an additional benefit to adopting a fixed exchange rate: by committing itself to a fixed rate, a country is also committing not to engage in inflationary policies because such policies would destabilize the exchange rate. For example, in 1991, Argentina, which has a long history of irresponsible policies leading to severe inflation, adopted a fixed exchange rate of US$1 per Argentine peso in an attempt to commit itself to non-inflationary policies in the future. (Argentina's fixed exchange rate regime collapsed disastrously in late 2001. But that's another story.)

The point is that there is some economic value in having a stable exchange rate. Indeed, the presumed benefits of stable exchange rates motivated the international system of fixed exchange rates created after World War II. It was also a major reason for the creation of the euro.

However, there are also costs to fixing the exchange rate.

- To stabilize an exchange rate through intervention, a country must keep large quantities of foreign currency on hand, and that currency is usually a low-return investment. Furthermore, even large reserves can be quickly exhausted when there are large capital flows out of a country.

- If a country chooses to stabilize an exchange rate by adjusting monetary policy rather than through intervention, it must divert monetary policy from other goals, notably stabilizing the economy and managing the inflation rate.

- Finally, foreign exchange controls, like import quotas and tariffs, distort incentives for importing and exporting goods and services. They can also create substantial costs in terms of red tape and corruption.

So there's a dilemma. Should a country let its currency float, which leaves monetary policy available for macroeconomic stabilization but creates uncertainty for everyone affected by trade? Or should it fix the exchange rate, which eliminates the uncertainty but means giving up monetary policy, adopting exchange controls, or both?

Different countries reach different conclusions at different times. Most European countries, except for Britain, have long believed that exchange rates among major European economies, which do most of their international trade with each other, should be fixed. But Canada seems happy with a floating exchange rate with the United States, even though the United States accounts for most of Canada's trade.

In the next module we'll consider macroeconomic policy under each type of exchange rate regime.

ECONOMICS ▶ IN ACTION

CHINA PEGS THE YUAN

In the early years of the twenty-first century, China provided a striking example of the lengths to which countries sometimes go to maintain a fixed exchange rate. Here's the background: China's spectacular success as an exporter led to a rising surplus on current account. At the same time, non-Chinese private investors became increasingly eager to shift funds into China, to invest in its growing domestic economy. These capital flows were somewhat limited by foreign exchange controls—but kept coming in anyway.

As a result of the current account surplus and private capital inflows, China found itself in the position described by panel (b) of Figure 45-1: at the target exchange rate, the demand for yuan exceeded the supply. Yet the Chinese government was determined to keep the exchange rate fixed at a value below its equilibrium level.

To keep the rate fixed, China had to engage in large-scale exchange market intervention, selling yuan, buying up other countries' currencies (mainly U.S. dollars) on the foreign exchange market, and adding them to its reserves. In 2010, China added $450 billion to its foreign exchange reserves, and by the summer of 2011, those reserves had risen to $3.2 trillion.

To get a sense of how big these totals are, in 2010 China's GDP was approximately $5.9 trillion. This means that in 2010 China bought U.S. dollars and other currencies equal to about 7½% of its GDP, making its accumulated reserves equal to more than half its GDP. That's as if the U.S. government had bought well over $1 trillion worth of yen and euros in a single year, even though it was already sitting on an $8 trillion pile of foreign currencies. Not surprisingly, China's exchange rate policy has led to some friction with its trading partners who feel that it has had the effect of subsidizing Chinese exports.

Since late 2011, China has significantly reduced its intervention in the foreign exchange market. In fact, in 2013, the International Monetary Fund declared the yuan to be only moderately undervalued, a big change from past years.

China provides a striking example of the lengths to which countries sometimes go to maintain a fixed exchange rate.

45 Review

Solutions appear at the back of the book.

Check Your Understanding

1. Draw a diagram, similar to Figure 45-1, representing the foreign exchange situation of China when it kept the exchange rate fixed at a target rate of $0.121 per yuan and the market equilibrium rate was higher than the target rate. Then show with a diagram how each of the following policy changes might eliminate the disequilibrium in the market.

a. allowing the exchange rate to float more freely

b. placing restrictions on foreigners who want to invest in China

c. removing restrictions on Chinese who want to invest abroad

d. imposing taxes on Chinese exports, such as clothing

Multiple-Choice Questions

1. Which of the following methods can be used to fix a country's exchange rate at a predetermined level?

   I. using foreign exchange reserves to buy its own currency
   II. using monetary policy to change interest rates
   III. implementing foreign exchange controls

   a. I only
   b. II only
   c. III only
   d. I and II only
   e. I, II, and III

2. Changes in exchange rates affect which of the following?

a. the price of imports

b. the price of exports

c. aggregate demand

d. aggregate output

e. all of the above

3. The United States has which of the following exchange rate regimes?

   a. fixed
   b. floating
   c. fixed, but adjusted frequently
   d. fixed, but managed
   e. floating within a target zone

4. Which of the following interventions would be required to keep a country's exchange rate fixed if the equilibrium exchange rate in the foreign exchange market were below the fixed exchange rate (measured as units of foreign currency per unit of domestic currency)? The government/central bank

a. buys the domestic currency.

b. sells the domestic currency.

c. buys the foreign currency.

d. lowers domestic interest rates.

e. removes foreign exchange controls.

5. Which of the following is a benefit of a fixed exchange rate regime?

a. certainty about the value of domestic currency

b. commitment to inflationary policies

c. no need for foreign exchange reserves

d. allows unrestricted use of monetary policy

e. all of the above

Critical-Thinking Question

List three tools used to fix exchange rates and explain the major costs resulting from their use.

Exchange Rates and Macroeconomic Policy

Millennium Images/SuperStock

When the euro was created in 1999, there were celebrations across the nations of Europe—with a few notabletable exceptions. You see, some countries chose not to adopt the new currency. The most important of these was Britain, but other European countries, such as Switzerland and Sweden, also decided that the euro was not for them.

Why did Britain say no? Part of the answer was national pride: for example, if Britain gave up the pound, it would also have to give up currency that bears the portrait of the queen. But there were also serious economic concerns about giving up the pound in favor of the euro.

British economists who favored adoption of the euro argued that if Britain used the same currency as its neighbors, the country's international trade would expand and its economy would become more productive. But other economists pointed out that adopting the euro would take away Britain's ability to have an independent monetary policy and might lead to macroeconomic problems.

As this discussion suggests, the fact that modern economies are open to international trade and capital flows adds a new level of complication to our analysis of macroeconomic policy. Let's now look at these three policy issues raised by open-economy macroeconomics:

1. Devaluation and revaluation of fixed exchange rates

2. Monetary policy under a floating exchange rate regime

3. International business cycles

Devaluation and Revaluation of Fixed Exchange Rates

Historically, fixed exchange rates haven't been permanent commitments. Sometimes countries with a fixed exchange rate switch to a floating rate. In other cases, they retain a fixed exchange rate but change the target exchange rate. Such adjustments in the target were common during the Bretton Woods era described in the upcoming Economics in Action. For example, in 1967 Britain changed the exchange rate of the pound against the U.S. dollar from US$2.80 per £1 to US$2.40 per £1. Another example is Argentina, which maintained a fixed exchange rate against the dollar from 1991 to 2001, but switched to a floating exchange rate at the end of 2001.

A reduction in the value of a currency that is set under a fixed exchange rate regime is called **devaluation.** As we've already learned, a *depreciation* is a downward move in a currency. A devaluation is a depreciation that is due to a revision in a fixed exchange rate target. An increase in the value of a currency that is set under a fixed exchange rate regime is called a **revaluation.**

A devaluation, like any depreciation, makes domestic goods cheaper in terms of foreign currency, which leads to higher exports. At the same time, it makes foreign goods more expensive in terms of domestic currency, which reduces imports. The effect is to increase the balance of payments on the current account. Similarly, a revaluation makes domestic goods more expensive in terms of foreign currency, which reduces exports, and makes foreign goods cheaper in domestic currency, which increases imports. So a revaluation reduces the balance of payments on the current account.

Devaluations and revaluations serve two purposes under a fixed exchange rate regime. First, they can be used to eliminate shortages or surpluses in the foreign exchange market. For example, in 2010, some economists and politicians were urging China to revalue the yuan because they believed that China's exchange rate policy unfairly aided Chinese exports. China eventually took action at the end of 2011, discontinuing much of their exchange rate intervention and allowing the yuan to gradually appreciate in value.

Second, devaluation and revaluation can be used as tools of macroeconomic policy. A devaluation, by increasing exports and reducing imports, increases aggregate demand. So a devaluation can be used to reduce or eliminate a recessionary gap. A revaluation has the opposite effect, reducing aggregate demand. So a revaluation can be used to reduce or eliminate an inflationary gap.

ECONOMICS ▶ IN ACTION

WORLD VIEW

FROM BRETTON WOODS TO THE EURO

In 1944, while World War II was still raging, representatives of the Allied nations met in Bretton Woods, New Hampshire, to establish a postwar international monetary system of fixed exchange rates among major currencies. The system was highly successful at first, but it broke down in 1971. After a confusing interval during which policy makers tried unsuccessfully to establish a new fixed exchange rate system, by 1973 most economically advanced countries had moved to floating exchange rates.

In Europe, however, many policy makers were unhappy with floating exchange rates, which they believed created too much uncertainty for business. From the late 1970s onward they tried several times to create a system of more or less fixed exchange rates in Europe, culminating in an arrangement known as the Exchange Rate Mechanism. (The Exchange Rate Mechanism was, strictly speaking, a "target zone" system—European exchange rates were free to move within a narrow band, but not outside it.)

And in 1991 they agreed to move to the ultimate in fixed exchange rates: a common European currency, the euro. To the surprise of many analysts, they pulled it off: today most of Europe has abandoned national currencies for the euro.

A **devaluation** is a reduction in the value of a currency that is set under a fixed exchange rate regime.

A **revaluation** is an increase in the value of a currency that is set under a fixed exchange rate regime.

Figure 46-1 illustrates the history of European exchange rate arrangements. It shows the exchange rate between the French franc and the German mark, measured as francs per mark, from 1971 until their replacement by the euro. The exchange rate fluctuated widely at first. The "plateaus" you can see in the data—eras when the exchange rate fluctuated only modestly—are periods when attempts to restore fixed exchange rates were in process.

The Exchange Rate Mechanism, after a couple of false starts, became effective in 1987, stabilizing the exchange rate at about 3.4 francs per mark. (The wobbles in the early 1990s reflect two currency crises—episodes in which widespread expectations of imminent devaluations led to large but temporary capital flows.)

In 1999 the exchange rate was "locked"—no further fluctuations were allowed as the countries prepared to switch from francs and marks to the euro. At the end of 2001, the franc and the mark ceased to exist.

The transition to the euro has not been without costs. Countries that adopted the euro sacrificed some important policy tools: they could no longer tailor monetary policy to their specific economic circumstances or lower their costs relative to other European nations simply by letting their currencies depreciate.

In 2013, the euro area remained under stress as many countries struggled to recover from severe recession following the 2008 financial crisis. Several nations—including Greece, Spain, and Italy, three big economies—were in such serious economic straits that economists and policy makers wondered about their ability to make critically important economic adjustments without defaulting on their debts and abandoning the euro.

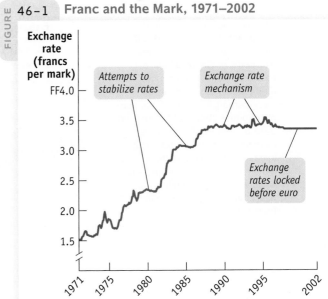

FIGURE 46-1 The Exchange Rate Between the Franc and the Mark, 1971–2002

Monetary Policy Under a Floating Exchange Rate Regime

Under a floating exchange rate regime, a country's central bank retains its ability to pursue independent monetary policy: it can increase aggregate demand by cutting the interest rate or decrease aggregate demand by raising the interest rate. But the exchange rate adds another dimension to the effects of monetary policy. To see why, let's return to the hypothetical country of Genovia as discussed in the preceding module and ask what happens if the central bank cuts the interest rate.

Just as in a closed economy, a lower interest rate leads to higher investment spending and higher consumer spending. But the decline in the interest rate also affects the foreign exchange market. Foreigners have less incentive to move funds into Genovia because they will receive a lower rate of return on their loans. As a result, they have less need to exchange U.S. dollars for genos, so the demand for genos falls. At the same time, Genovians have *more* incentive to move funds abroad because the rate of return on loans at home has fallen, making investments outside the country more attractive. Thus, they need to exchange more genos for U.S. dollars and the supply of genos rises.

Figure 46-2 shows the effect of an interest rate reduction on the foreign exchange market. The demand curve for genos shifts leftward, from D_1 to D_2, and the supply curve shifts rightward, from S_1 to S_2. The equilibrium exchange rate, as measured in U.S. dollars per geno, falls from XR_1 to XR_2. That is, a reduction in the Genovian interest rate causes the geno to *depreciate*.

The depreciation of the geno, in turn, affects aggregate demand. We've already seen that a devaluation—a depreciation that is the result of a change in a fixed exchange rate—increases exports and reduces imports, thereby increasing aggregate demand.

46–2   Monetary Policy and the Exchange Rate

Here we show what happens in the foreign exchange market if Genovia cuts its interest rate. Residents of Genovia have a reduced incentive to keep their funds at home, so they invest more abroad. As a result, the supply of genos shifts rightward, from S_1 to S_2. Meanwhile, foreigners have less incentive to put funds into Genovia, so the demand for genos shifts leftward, from D_1 to D_2. The geno depreciates: the equilibrium exchange rate falls from XR_1 to XR_2.

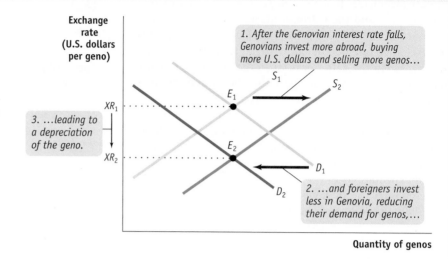

1. After the Genovian interest rate falls, Genovians invest more abroad, buying more U.S. dollars and selling more genos...

3. ...leading to a depreciation of the geno.

2. ...and foreigners invest less in Genovia, reducing their demand for genos,...

Quantity of genos

A depreciation that results from an interest rate cut has the same effect: it increases exports and reduces imports, increasing aggregate demand.

In other words, monetary policy under floating rates has effects beyond those we've described in looking at closed economies.

In a closed economy, a reduction in the interest rate leads to a rise in aggregate demand because it leads to more investment spending and consumer spending.

In an open economy with a floating exchange rate, the interest rate reduction leads to increased investment spending and consumer spending, but it also increases aggregate demand in another way: it leads to a currency depreciation, which increases exports and reduces imports, further increasing aggregate demand.

International Business Cycles

Up to this point, we have discussed macroeconomics, even in an open economy, as if all demand changes or *shocks* originated from the domestic economy. In reality, however, economies sometimes face shocks coming from abroad. For example, recessions in the United States have historically led to recessions in Mexico.

The key point is that changes in aggregate demand affect the demand for goods and services produced abroad as well as at home: other things equal, a recession leads to a fall in imports and an expansion leads to a rise in imports. And one country's imports are another country's exports. This link between aggregate demand in different national economies is one reason business cycles in different countries sometimes— but not always—seem to be synchronized. The prime example is the Great Depression, which affected countries around the world.

For better or worse, trading partners tend to import each other's business cycles as well as each other's goods.

The extent of this link depends, however, on the exchange rate regime. To see why, think about what happens if a recession abroad reduces the demand for Genovia's exports. A reduction in foreign demand for Genovian goods and services is also a reduction in demand for genos on the foreign exchange market. If Genovia has a fixed exchange rate, it responds to this decline with exchange market intervention.

But if Genovia has a floating exchange rate, the geno depreciates. Because Genovian goods and services become cheaper to foreigners when the demand for exports falls, the quantity of goods and services exported doesn't fall by as much as it would under a fixed rate. At the same time, the fall in the geno makes imports more expensive to Genovians, leading to a fall in imports. Both effects limit the decline in Genovia's aggregate demand compared to what it would have been under a fixed exchange rate regime.

One of the virtues of floating exchange rates, according to their advocates, is that they help insulate countries from recessions originating abroad. This theory looked pretty good in the early 2000s: Britain, with a floating exchange rate, managed to stay out of a recession that affected the rest of Europe, and Canada, which also has a floating rate, suffered a less severe recession than the United States.

In 2008, however, the financial crisis that began in the United States produced a recession in virtually every country. In this case, it appears that the international linkages between financial markets were much stronger than any insulation from overseas disturbances provided by floating exchange rates.

MODULE 46 Review

Solutions appear at the back of the book.

Check Your Understanding

1. Look at Figure 46-1. Where do you see devaluations and revaluations of the franc against the mark?

2. In the late 1980s, Canadian economists argued that the high interest rate policies of the Bank of Canada weren't just causing high unemployment—they were also making it hard for Canadian manufacturers to compete with U.S. manufacturers. Explain this complaint, using our analysis of how monetary policy works under floating exchange rates.

Multiple-Choice Questions

1. Devaluation of a currency occurs when which of the following happens?

   I. The supply of a currency with a floating exchange rate increases.
   II. The demand for a currency with a floating exchange rate decreases.
   III. The government decreases the fixed exchange rate.

   a. I only
   b. II only
   c. III only
   d. I and II only
   e. I, II, and III

2. Devaluation of a currency will lead to which of the following?

   a. appreciation of the currency
   b. an increase in exports
   c. an increase in imports
   d. a decrease in exports
   e. floating exchange rates

3. Devaluation of a currency is used to achieve which of the following?

   a. an elimination of a surplus in the foreign exchange market
   b. an elimination of a shortage in the foreign exchange market
   c. a reduction in aggregate demand
   d. a lower inflation rate
   e. a floating exchange rate

4. Monetary policy that reduces the interest rate will do which of the following?

   a. appreciate the domestic currency
   b. decrease exports
   c. increase imports
   d. depreciate the domestic currency
   e. prevent inflation

5. Which of the following will happen in a country if a trading partner's economy experiences a recession?

   a. It will experience an expansion.
   b. Exports will decrease.
   c. The demand for the country's currency will increase.
   d. The country's currency will appreciate.
   e. All of the above will occur.

Critical-Thinking Question

Explain how a floating exchange rate system can help insulate a country from recessions abroad.

BUSINESS CASE: War of the Earthmovers

Philip Lewis/Alamy

Visit a construction site almost anywhere in the world, and odds are that the earthmoving equipment you see—the tractors, dump trucks, excavators, graders, scrapers, and so on—is made by one of two companies, America's Caterpillar or Japan's Komatsu.

Caterpillar and Komatsu both rely heavily on exports, rather than selling only to their domestic markets, and have been fierce competitors for three decades, with first one company, then the other, seemingly on the ropes.

Ask the companies' leaders to explain the course of this see-sawing competitive struggle, and they will tell a tale of corporate cultures and management decisions. Caterpillar, the story goes, entered the 1980s filled with complacency thanks to its longtime dominance of the earthmoving industry, only to face a shock from Komatsu that almost drove it to the brink. Then Caterpillar reformed its management practices, regaining the upper hand in the 1990s, and Komatsu found itself in danger of failing, until reinvigorated management stabilized the company again.

But is this the whole story? Not exactly. Management decisions were no doubt crucial to both firms, but so were movements in the exchange rate. The accompanying figure shows the real exchange rate between the United States and Japan, using consumer prices, from 1980 to 2011.

The figure immediately suggests one reason Caterpillar was able to recover from the shock of competition in the 1980s: a sharp appreciation of the Japanese yen beginning in 1985. And Komatsu's ability to survive Caterpillar's resurgence was surely helped by the slide in the yen after 1995, and especially after 2000.

Recently, the two companies seem to have settled into relatively stable positions, with Caterpillar the bigger firm but Komatsu also doing well thanks in part to rapid growth in demand from China. But Japanese executives at Komatsu (and other firms) are always on the alert for signs that the yen is once again on the rise.

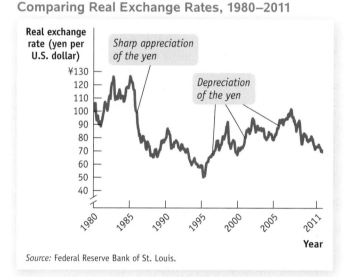

Comparing Real Exchange Rates, 1980–2011

Source: Federal Reserve Bank of St. Louis.

Questions for Thought

1. Why does the yen–dollar exchange rate matter so much for the fortunes of Caterpillar and Komatsu?

2. Why does the figure present the real rather than the nominal exchange rate? Do you think this makes an important difference to the story?

3. In 2011, Japanese policy makers were discussing possible sales of yen on the foreign exchange market. How would this affect the Caterpillar/Komatsu rivalry?

SECTION 13 REVIEW

Summary

Capital Flows and the Balance of Payments

1. A country's **balance of payments accounts** summarize its transactions with the rest of the world. The **balance of payments on the current account,** or the **current account,** includes the **balance of payments on goods and services** together with balances on factor income and transfers. The **merchandise trade balance,** or **trade balance,** is a frequently cited component of the balance of payments on goods and services. The **balance of payments on the financial account,** or **the financial account,** measures capital flows. By definition, the balance of payments on the current account plus the balance of payments on the financial account is zero.

2. Capital flows respond to international differences in interest rates and other rates of return; they can be usefully analyzed using an international version of the loanable funds model, which shows how a country where the interest rate would be low in the absence of capital flows sends funds to a country where the interest rate would be high in the absence of capital flows. The underlying determinants of capital flows are international differences in savings and opportunities for investment spending.

The Foreign Exchange Market

3. Currencies are traded in the **foreign exchange market;** the prices at which they are traded are **exchange rates.** When a currency rises against another currency, it **appreciates;** when it falls, it **depreciates.** The **equilibrium exchange rate** matches the quantity of that currency supplied to the foreign exchange market to the quantity demanded.

4. To correct for international differences in inflation rates, economists calculate **real exchange rates,** which multiply the exchange rate between two countries' respective currencies by the ratio of the countries' price levels. The current account responds only to changes in the real exchange rate, not the nominal exchange rate. **Purchasing power parity** is the exchange rate that makes the cost of a basket of goods and services equal in two countries. While purchasing power parity and the nominal exchange rate almost always differ, purchasing power parity is a good predictor of actual changes in the nominal exchange rate.

Exchange Rate Policy

5. Countries adopt different **exchange rate regimes,** rules governing exchange rate policy. The main types are **fixed exchange rates,** where the government takes action to keep the exchange rate at a target level, and **floating exchange rates,** where the exchange rate is free to fluctuate. Countries can fix exchange rates using **exchange market intervention,** which requires them to hold **foreign exchange reserves** that they use to buy any surplus of their currency. Alternatively, they can change domestic policies, especially monetary policy, to shift the demand and supply curves in the foreign exchange market. Finally, they can use **foreign exchange controls.**

6. Exchange rate policy poses a dilemma: there are economic payoffs to stable exchange rates, but the policies used to fix the exchange rate have costs. Exchange market intervention requires large reserves, and exchange controls distort incentives. If monetary policy is used to help fix the exchange rate, it isn't available to use for domestic policy.

Exchange Rates and Macroeconomic Policy

7. Fixed exchange rates aren't always permanent commitments: countries with a fixed exchange rate sometimes engage in **devaluations** or **revaluations.** In addition to helping eliminate a surplus of domestic currency on the foreign exchange market, a devaluation increases aggregate demand. Similarly, a revaluation reduces shortages of domestic currency and reduces aggregate demand.

8. The fact that one country's imports are another country's exports creates a link between the business cycles in different countries. Floating exchange rates, however, may reduce the strength of that link.

Key Terms

Balance of payments accounts, p. 454

Balance of payments on the current account (the current account), p. 456

Balance of payments on goods and services, p. 456

Merchandise trade balance (trade balance), p. 456

Balance of payments on the financial account (the financial account), p. 456

Foreign exchange market, p. 465

Exchange rates, p. 465

Appreciates, p. 465

Depreciates, p. 465

Equilibrium exchange rate, p. 466

Real exchange rate, p. 468

Purchasing power parity, p. 470

Exchange rate regime, p. 473

Fixed exchange rate, p. 473

Floating exchange rate, p. 473

Exchange market intervention, p. 475

Foreign exchange reserves, p. 475

Foreign exchange controls, p. 475

Devaluation, p. 480

Revaluation, p. 480

Problems

1. How would the following transactions be categorized in the U.S. balance of payments accounts? Would they be entered in the current account (as a payment to or from a foreigner) or the financial account (as a sale of assets to or purchase of assets from a foreigner)? How will the balance of payments on the current and financial accounts change?

   a. A French importer buys a case of California wine for $500.

   b. An American who works for a French company deposits her paycheck, drawn on a Paris bank, into her San Francisco bank.

   c. An American buys a bond from a Japanese company for $10,000.

   d. An American charity sends $100,000 to Africa to help local residents buy food after a harvest shortfall.

2. The accompanying diagram shows foreign-owned assets in the United States and U.S.-owned assets abroad, both as a percentage of foreign GDP. As you can see from the diagram, both increased around fivefold from 1980 to 2010.

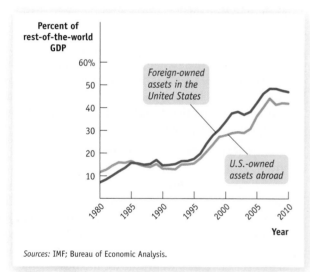

Sources: IMF; Bureau of Economic Analysis.

   a. As U.S.-owned assets abroad increased as a percentage of foreign GDP, does this mean that the United States, over the period, experienced net capital outflows?

   b. Does this diagram indicate that world economies were more tightly linked in 2010 than they were in 1980?

3. In the economy of Scottopia in 2013, exports equaled $400 billion of goods and $300 billion of services, imports equaled $500 billion of goods and $350 billion of services, and the rest of the world purchased $250 billion of Scottopia's assets. What was the merchandise trade balance for Scottopia? What was the balance of payments on current account in Scottopia? What was the balance of payments on financial account? What was the value of Scottopia's purchases of assets from the rest of the world?

4. In the economy of Popania in 2013, total Popanian purchases of assets in the rest of the world equaled $300 billion, purchases of Popanian assets by the rest of the world equaled $400 billion, and Popania exported goods and services equal to $350 billion. What was Popania's balance of payments on financial account in 2013? What was its balance of payments on current account? What was the value of its imports?

5. Suppose that Northlandia and Southlandia are the only two trading countries in the world, that each nation runs a balance of payments on both current and financial accounts equal to zero, and that each nation sees the other's assets as identical to its own. Using the accompanying diagrams, explain how the demand and supply of loanable funds, the interest rate, and the balance of payments on current and financial accounts will change in each country if international capital flows are possible.

6. Based on the exchange rates for the first trading days of 2011 and 2012 shown in the accompanying table, did the U.S. dollar appreciate or depreciate during 2011? Did the movement in the value of the U.S. dollar make American goods and services more or less attractive to foreigners?

January 3, 2011	January 3, 2012
US$1.55 to buy 1 British pound sterling	US$1.57 to buy 1 British pound sterling
29.08 Taiwan dollars to buy US$1	30.28 Taiwan dollars to buy US$1
US$0.99 to buy 1 Canadian dollar	US$1.01 to buy 1 Canadian dollar
81.56 Japanese yen to buy US$1	76.67 Japanese yen to buy US$1
US$1.34 to buy 1 euro	US$1.31 to buy 1 euro
0.93 Swiss franc to buy US$1	0.93 Swiss franc to buy US$1

7. Go to http://fx.sauder.ubc.ca. Using the table labeled "The Most Recent Cross-Rates of Major Currencies," determine whether the British pound (GBP), the Canadian dollar (CAD), the Japanese yen (JPY), the euro (EUR), and the Swiss franc (CHF) have appreciated or depreciated against the U.S. dollar (USD) since January 3, 2012. The exchange rates on January 3, 2012, are listed in the table in Problem 6.

8. Suppose the United States and Japan are the only two trading countries in the world. What will happen to the value of the U.S. dollar if the following occur, other things equal?

   a. Japan relaxes some of its import restrictions.

   b. The United States imposes some import tariffs on Japanese goods.

   c. Interest rates in the United States rise dramatically.

   d. A report indicates that Japanese cars last much longer than previously thought, especially compared with American cars.

9. From January 1, 2001, to June 2003, the U.S. federal funds rate decreased from 6.5% to 1%. During the same period, the marginal lending facility rate at the European Central Bank decreased from 5.75% to 3%.

   a. Considering the change in interest rates over the period and using the loanable funds model, would you have expected funds to flow from the United States to Europe or from Europe to the United States over this period?

   b. The accompanying diagram shows the exchange rate between the euro and the U.S. dollar from January 1, 2001, through September 2008. Is the movement of the exchange rate over the period January 2001 to June 2003 consistent with the movement in funds predicted in part a?

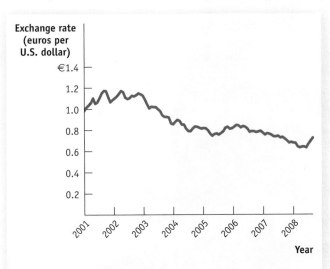

Source: Federal Reserve Bank of St. Louis.

10. In each of the following scenarios, suppose that the two nations are the only trading nations in the world. Given inflation and the change in the nominal exchange rate, which nation's goods become more attractive?

    a. Inflation is 10% in the United States and 5% in Japan; the U.S. dollar–Japanese yen exchange rate remains the same.

    b. Inflation is 3% in the United States and 8% in Mexico; the price of the U.S. dollar falls from 12.50 to 10.25 Mexican pesos.

    c. Inflation is 5% in the United States and 3% in the euro area; the price of the euro falls from $1.30 to $1.20.

    d. Inflation is 8% in the United States and 4% in Canada; the price of the Canadian dollar rises from US$0.60 to US$0.75.

11. Starting from a position of equilibrium in the foreign exchange market under a fixed exchange rate regime, how must a government react to an increase in the demand for the nation's goods and services by the rest of the world to keep the exchange rate at its fixed value?

12. Suppose that Albernia's central bank has fixed the value of its currency, the bern, to the U.S. dollar (at a rate of US$1.50 to 1 bern) and is committed to that exchange rate. Initially, the foreign exchange market for the bern is also in equilibrium, as shown in the accompanying diagram. However, both Albernians and Americans begin to believe that there are big risks in holding Albernian assets; as a result, they become unwilling to hold Albernian assets unless they receive a higher rate of return on them than they do on U.S. assets. How would this affect the diagram? If the Albernian central bank tries to keep the exchange rate fixed using monetary policy, how will this affect the Albernian economy?

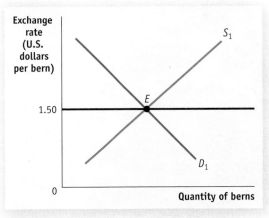

13. Your study partner asks you, "If central banks lose the ability to use discretionary monetary policy under fixed exchange rates, why would nations agree to a fixed exchange rate system?" How do you respond?

Macroeconomics: Events and Ideas

A TALE OF TWO SLUMPS

In November 2002, the Federal Reserve held a special conference to honor Milton Friedman on the occasion of his 90th birthday. Among those delivering tributes was Ben Bernanke, then a member of the Board of Governors, who later served as Fed Chairman. In his tribute, Bernanke surveyed Friedman's intellectual contributions, with particular focus on the argument made by Friedman and his collaborator Anna Schwartz that the Great Depression of the 1930s could have been avoided if only the Fed had done its job properly.

At the close of his talk, Bernanke directly addressed Friedman and Schwartz, who were sitting in the audience: "Let me end my talk by abusing slightly my status as an official representative of the Federal Reserve. I would like to say to Milton and Anna: Regarding the Great Depression. You're right, we did it. We're very sorry. But thanks to you, we won't do it again."

Today, in the aftermath of a devastating financial crisis that continues to inflict high unemployment, those words ring somewhat hollow. Avoiding severe economic downturns, it turned out, wasn't as easy as Friedman, Schwartz, and Bernanke had believed. Yet, as bad as they were, the crisis of 2008 and its aftermath were less devastating than the Great Depression.

It can be reasonably argued that part of the reason was that macroeconomics had evolved in the 78 years from 1930 to 2008. As a result, policy makers knew more about the causes of depressions and how to fight them than they did during the Great Depression.

In this section we'll trace the development of macroeconomic ideas over the past 80 years. As we'll see, this development has been strongly influenced by economic events, from the Great Depression of the 1930s, to the stagflation of the 1970s, to the surprising period of economic stability achieved between 1985 and 2007. And as we'll also see, the process continues, as the economic difficulties since 2008 have spurred many macroeconomists to rethink what they thought they knew.

© Minnesota HistoricalSociety/CORBIS

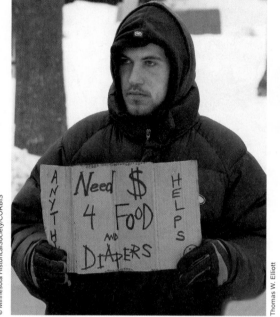

Thomas W. Elliott

Classical Macroeconomics

The term *macroeconomics* appears to have been coined in 1933 by the Norwegian economist Ragnar Frisch. The timing, during the worst year of the Great Depression, was no accident. Still, there were economists analyzing what we now consider macroeconomic issues—the behavior of the aggregate price level and aggregate output—before then.

Money and the Price Level

Previously, we described the *classical model of the price level.* According to the classical model, prices are flexible, making the aggregate supply curve vertical even in the short run. In this model, an increase in the money supply leads, other things equal, to a proportional rise in the aggregate price level, with no effect on aggregate output. As a result, increases in the money supply lead to inflation, and that's all. Before the 1930s, the classical model of the price level dominated economic thinking about the effects of monetary policy.

Did classical economists really believe that changes in the money supply affected only aggregate prices, without any effect on aggregate output? Probably not. Historians of economic thought argue that before 1930 most economists were aware that changes in the money supply affected aggregate output as well as aggregate prices in the short run—or, to use modern terms, they were aware that the short-run aggregate supply curve sloped upward. But they regarded such short-run effects as unimportant, stressing the long run instead. It was this attitude that led John Maynard Keynes to scoff at the focus on the long run, in which, as he said, "we are all dead."

The Business Cycle

Classical economists were, of course, also aware that the economy did not grow smoothly. The American economist Wesley Mitchell pioneered the quantitative study of business cycles. In 1920, he founded the National Bureau of Economic Research, an independent, nonprofit organization that to this day has the official role of declaring the beginnings of recessions and expansions. Thanks to Mitchell's work, the *measurement* of business cycles was well advanced by 1930. But there was no widely accepted *theory* of business cycles.

In the absence of any clear theory, views about how policy makers should respond to a recession were conflicting. Some economists favored expansionary monetary and fiscal policies to fight a recession. Others believed that such policies would worsen the slump or merely postpone the inevitable. When the Great Depression hit, the policy making process was paralyzed by this lack of consensus. In many cases, economists now believe, policy makers took steps in the wrong direction.

Necessity was, however, the mother of invention. As we'll explain next, the Great Depression provided a strong incentive for economists to develop theories that could serve as a guide to policy—and economists responded.

The Great Depression and the Keynesian Revolution

The Great Depression demonstrated, once and for all, that economists cannot safely ignore the short run. Not only was the economic pain severe, it threatened to destabilize societies and political systems.

The whole world wanted to know how this economic disaster could be happening and what should be done about it. But because there was no widely accepted theory of the business cycle, economists gave conflicting and, we now believe, often harmful advice. Some believed that only a huge change in the economic system—such as having the government take over much of private industry and replace markets with a command economy—could end the slump. Others argued that slumps were natural—even beneficial—and that nothing should be done.

Some economists, however, argued that the slump both could have and should have been cured—without giving up on the basic idea of a market economy. In 1930, the British economist John Maynard Keynes compared the problems of the U.S. and British economies to those of a car with a defective alternator. Getting the economy running, he argued, would require only a modest repair, not a complete overhaul.

Nice metaphor. But what was the nature of the trouble?

Tim Gidal/Picture Post/Getty Images

Some people use *Keynesian economics* as a synonym for *left-wing economics*—but, in truth, Keynes's ideas have been accepted across a broad part of the political spectrum.

Keynes's Theory

In 1936, Keynes presented his analysis of the Great Depression—his explanation of what was wrong with the economy's alternator—in a book titled *The General Theory of Employment, Interest, and Money. The General Theory* stands with Adam Smith's *The Wealth of Nations* as one of the most influential books on economics ever written.

Keynes's book is a vast stew of ideas. And Keynesian economics mainly reflected two innovations. First, Keynes emphasized the short-run effects of shifts in aggregate demand on aggregate output, rather than the long-run determination of the aggregate price level. As Keynes's famous remark about being dead in the long run suggests, until his book appeared most economists had treated short-run macroeconomics as a minor issue. Keynes focused the attention of economists on situations in which the short-run aggregate supply curve slopes upward and shifts in the aggregate demand curve affect aggregate output and employment as well as aggregate prices.

47-1 Classical Versus Keynesian Macroeconomics

One important difference between classical and Keynesian economics involves the short-run aggregate supply curve. Panel (a) shows the classical view: the *SRAS* curve is vertical, so shifts in aggregate demand affect the aggregate price level but not aggregate output. Panel (b) shows the Keynesian view: in the short run the *SRAS* curve slopes upward, so shifts in aggregate demand affect aggregate output as well as aggregate prices.

Figure 47-1 illustrates the difference between Keynesian and classical macroeconomics. Both panels of the figure show the short-run aggregate supply curve, *SRAS;* in both it is assumed that for some reason the aggregate demand curve shifts leftward from AD_1 to AD_2—let's say in response to a fall in stock market prices that leads households to reduce consumer spending.

Panel (a) shows the classical view: the short-run aggregate supply curve is vertical. The decline in aggregate demand leads to a fall in the aggregate price level, from P_1 to P_2, but no change in aggregate output. Panel (b) shows the Keynesian view: the short-run aggregate supply curve slopes upward, so the decline in aggregate demand leads to both a fall in the aggregate price level, from P_1 to P_2, and a fall in aggregate output, from Y_1 to Y_2.

As we've already explained, many classical macroeconomists would have agreed that panel (b) was an accurate story in the short run—but they regarded the short run as unimportant. Keynes disagreed. (Just to be clear, there isn't any diagram that looks like panel (b) of Figure 47-1 in Keynes's *General Theory.* But Keynes's discussion of aggregate supply, translated into modern terminology, clearly implies an upward-sloping *SRAS* curve.)

Second, classical economists emphasized the role of changes in the money supply in shifting the aggregate demand curve, paying little attention to other factors. Keynes, however, argued that other factors, especially changes in "animal spirits"—these days usually referred to with the bland term *business confidence*—are mainly responsible for business cycles. Before Keynes, economists often argued that a decline in business confidence would have no effect on either the aggregate price level or aggregate output, as long as the money supply stayed constant. Keynes offered a very different picture.

Keynes's ideas have penetrated deeply into the public consciousness, to the extent that many people who have never heard of Keynes, or have heard of him but think they disagree with his theory, use Keynesian ideas all the time. For example, suppose that a business commentator says something like this: "Because of a decline in business confidence, investment spending slumped, causing a recession." Whether the commentator knows it or not, that statement is pure Keynesian economics.

Policy to Fight Recessions

The main practical consequence of Keynes's work was that it legitimized **macro-economic policy activism**—the use of monetary and fiscal policy to smooth out the business cycle.

Macroeconomic policy activism wasn't something completely new. Before Keynes, many economists had argued for using monetary expansion to fight economic down-turns—though others were fiercely opposed. In fact, many governments followed policies that we would now call Keynesian. In the United States, the administration of Franklin Roosevelt engaged in modest deficit spending in an effort to create jobs. But these efforts were half-hearted. Roosevelt's advisers were deeply divided over the appropriate policies to adopt, and in 1937 Roosevelt gave in to advice from non-Keynesian economists who urged him to balance the budget and raise interest rates, even though the economy was still depressed. The result was a renewed slump.

After World War II, Keynesian ideas were broadly accepted by U.S. economists. There were, however, a series of challenges to those ideas, which led to a consider-able shift in views even among economists who continued to believe that Keynes was broadly right about the causes of recessions. In the upcoming section, we'll learn about those challenges and the schools, *new classical economics* and *new Keynesian economics,* that emerged.

> **Macroeconomic policy activism** is the use of monetary and fiscal policy to smooth out the business cycle.

ECONOMICS ▶ *IN ACTION*

THE END OF THE GREAT DEPRESSION

It would make a good story if Keynes's ideas had led to a change in economic policy that brought the Great Depression to an end. Unfortunately, that's not what happened. Still, the way the Depression ended did a lot to convince economists that Keynes was right.

The basic message many of the young economists who adopted Keynes's ideas in the 1930s took from his work was that economic recovery requires aggressive fiscal expansion—deficit spending on a large scale to create jobs. And that is what they eventually got, but it wasn't because politicians were persuaded. Instead, what happened was a very large and expensive war, World War II.

Figure 47-2 shows the U.S. unemployment rate and the fed-eral budget deficit as a share of GDP from 1930 to 1947. As you can see, deficit spending during the 1930s was on a modest scale. In 1940, as the risk of war grew larger, the United States began a large military buildup, and the budget moved deep into deficit. After the attack on Pearl Harbor on December 7, 1941, the coun-try began deficit spending on an enormous scale: in fiscal 1943, which began in July 1942, the deficit was 30% of GDP. Today that would be a deficit of $5.0 trillion.

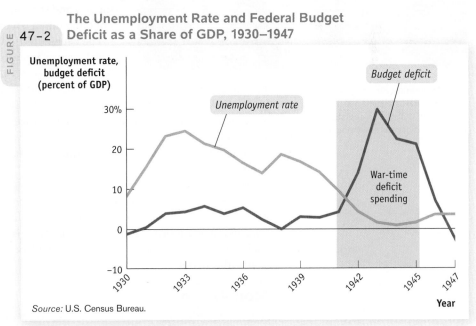

FIGURE 47-2   The Unemployment Rate and Federal Budget Deficit as a Share of GDP, 1930–1947

Source: U.S. Census Bureau.

And the economy recovered. World War II wasn't intended as a Keynesian fiscal policy, but it demonstrated that expansionary fiscal policy can, in fact, create jobs in the short run.

Challenges to Keynesian Economics

Keynes's ideas fundamentally changed the way economists think about business cycles. They did not, however, go unquestioned. In the decades that followed the publication of *The General Theory,* Keynesian economics faced a series of challenges. As a result, the consensus of macroeconomists retreated somewhat from the strong version of Keynesianism that prevailed in the 1950s. In particular, economists became much more aware of the limits to macroeconomic policy activism.

The Revival of Monetary Policy

Keynes's *General Theory* suggested that monetary policy wouldn't be very effective in depression conditions. Many modern macroeconomists agree: earlier we introduced the concept of a *liquidity trap,* a situation in which monetary policy is ineffective because the interest rate is down against the zero bound. In the 1930s, when Keynes wrote, interest rates were, in fact, very close to 0%.

But even when the era of near-0% interest rates came to an end after World War II, many economists continued to emphasize fiscal policy and downplay the usefulness of monetary policy. Eventually, however, macroeconomists reassessed the importance of monetary policy. A key milestone in this reassessment was the 1963 publication of *A Monetary History of the United States, 1867–1960* by Milton Friedman, of the University of Chicago, and Anna Schwartz, of the National Bureau of Economic Research.

Friedman and Schwartz showed that business cycles had historically been associated with fluctuations in the money supply. In particular, the money supply fell sharply during the onset of the Great Depression. Friedman and Schwartz persuaded many, though not all, economists that the Great Depression could have been avoided if the Federal Reserve had acted to prevent that monetary contraction and that monetary policy should play a key role in economic management.

The revival of interest in monetary policy was significant because it suggested that the burden of managing the economy could be shifted away from fiscal policy—meaning that economic management could largely be taken out of the hands of politicians. Fiscal policy, which must involve changing tax rates or government spending, necessarily involves political choices. If the government tries to stimulate the economy by cutting taxes, it must decide whose taxes will be cut. If it tries to stimulate the economy with government spending, it must decide what to spend the money on.

Monetary policy, in contrast, does not involve such choices: when the central bank cuts interest rates to fight a recession, it cuts everyone's interest rate at the same time. So a shift from relying on fiscal policy to relying on monetary policy makes macroeconomics a more technical, less political issue. In fact, monetary policy in most major economies is set by an independent central bank that is insulated from the political process.

Milton Friedman and his co-author Anna Schwartz played a key role in convincing macroeconomists of the importance of monetary policy.

Monetarism

After the publication of *A Monetary History,* Milton Friedman led a movement, called *monetarism,* that sought to eliminate macroeconomic policy activism while maintaining the importance of monetary policy. **Monetarism** asserted that GDP will grow steadily if the money supply grows steadily. The monetarist policy prescription was to have the central bank target a constant rate of growth of the money supply, such as 3% per year, and maintain that target regardless of any fluctuations in the economy.

Monetarism asserts that GDP will grow steadily if the money supply grows steadily.

It's important to realize that monetarism retained many Keynesian ideas. Like Keynes, Friedman asserted that the short run is important and that short-run changes in aggregate demand affect aggregate output as well as aggregate prices. Like Keynes, he argued that policy should have been much more expansionary during the Great Depression.

Monetarists argued, however, that most of the efforts of policy makers to smooth out the business cycle actually make things worse. We have already discussed concerns over the usefulness of *discretionary fiscal policy*—changes in taxes or government spending, or both—in response to the state of the economy. As we explained, government perceptions about the economy often lag behind reality, and there are further lags in changing fiscal policy and in its effects on the economy. As a result, discretionary fiscal policies intended to fight a recession often end up feeding a boom, and vice versa. According to monetarists, **discretionary monetary policy,** changes in the interest rate or the money supply by the central bank in order to stabilize the economy, faces the same problem of lags as fiscal policy, but to a lesser extent.

Friedman also argued that if the central bank followed his advice and refused to change the money supply in response to fluctuations in the economy, fiscal policy would be much less effective than Keynesians believed. Earlier we analyzed the phenomenon of *crowding out*, in which government deficits drive up interest rates and lead to reduced investment spending. Friedman and others pointed out that if the money supply is held fixed while the government pursues an expansionary fiscal policy, crowding out will limit the effect of the fiscal expansion on aggregate demand.

Figure 47-3 illustrates this argument. Panel (a) shows aggregate output and the aggregate price level. AD_1 is the initial aggregate demand curve and $SRAS$ is the short-run aggregate supply curve. At the initial equilibrium, E_1, the level of aggregate output is Y_1 and the aggregate price level is P_1. Panel (b) shows the money market. MS is the money supply curve and MD_1 is the initial money demand curve, so the initial interest rate is r_1.

Discretionary monetary policy is the use of changes in the interest rate or the money supply to stabilize the economy.

FIGURE 47-3   **Fiscal Policy with a Fixed Money Supply**

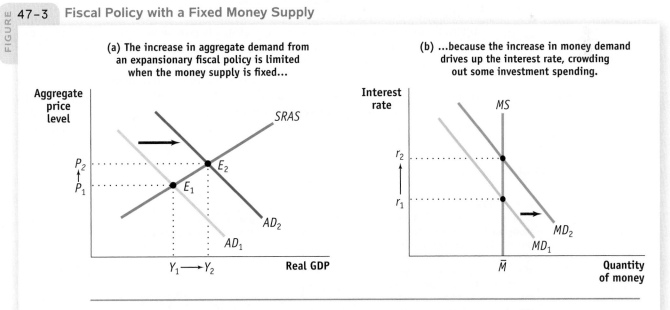

(a) The increase in aggregate demand from an expansionary fiscal policy is limited when the money supply is fixed...

(b) ...because the increase in money demand drives up the interest rate, crowding out some investment spending.

In panel (a) an expansionary fiscal policy shifts the *AD* curve rightward, driving up both the aggregate price level and aggregate output. However, this leads to an increase in the demand for money. If the money supply is held fixed, as in panel (b), the increase in money demand drives up the interest rate, reducing investment spending and offsetting part of the fiscal expansion. So the shift of the *AD* curve is less than it would otherwise be: fiscal policy becomes less effective when the money supply is held fixed.

A **monetary policy rule** is a formula that determines the central bank's actions.

The **Quantity Theory of Money** emphasizes the positive relationship between the price level and the money supply. It relies on the velocity equation ($M \times V = P \times Y$).

The **velocity of money** is the ratio of nominal GDP to the money supply. It is a measure of the number of times the average dollar bill is spent per year.

Now suppose the government increases purchases of goods and services. We know that this will shift the AD curve rightward, as illustrated by the shift from AD_1 to AD_2; that aggregate output will rise, from Y_1 to Y_2; and that the aggregate price level will rise, from P_1 to P_2. Both the rise in aggregate output and the rise in the aggregate price level will, however, increase the demand for money, shifting the money demand curve rightward from MD_1 to MD_2. This drives up the equilibrium interest rate to r_2. Friedman's point was that this rise in the interest rate reduces investment spending, partially offsetting the initial rise in government spending. As a result, the rightward shift of the AD curve is smaller than multiplier analysis indicates. And Friedman argued that with a constant money supply, the multiplier is so small that there's not much point in using fiscal policy, even in a depressed economy.

But Friedman didn't favor activist monetary policy either. He argued that the problem of time lags that limit the ability of discretionary fiscal policy to stabilize the economy also apply to discretionary monetary policy. Friedman's solution was to put monetary policy on "autopilot." The central bank, he argued, should follow a **monetary policy rule,** a formula that determines its actions and leaves it relatively little discretion. During the 1960s and 1970s, most monetarists favored a monetary policy rule of slow, steady growth in the money supply.

Underlying this view was the **Quantity Theory of Money,** which relies on the concept of the **velocity of money,** the ratio of nominal GDP to the money supply. Velocity is a measure of the number of times the average dollar bill in the economy turns over per year between buyers and sellers (e.g., I tip the Starbucks barista a dollar, she uses it to buy lunch, and so on). This concept gives rise to the *velocity equation:*

(47-1) $M \times V = P \times Y$

Where M is the money supply, V is velocity, P is the aggregate price level, and Y is real GDP.

Monetarists believed, with considerable historical justification, that the velocity of money was stable in the short run and changed only slowly in the long run. As a result, they claimed, steady growth in the money supply by the central bank would ensure steady growth in spending, and therefore in GDP.

Monetarism strongly influenced actual monetary policy in the late 1970s and early 1980s. It quickly became clear, however, that steady growth in the money supply didn't ensure steady growth in the economy: the velocity of money wasn't stable enough for such a simple policy rule to work.

Figure 47-4 shows how events eventually undermined the monetarists' view. The figure shows the velocity of money, as measured by the ratio of nominal GDP to M1, from 1960 to 2013. As you can see, until 1980, velocity followed a fairly smooth, seemingly predictable trend. After the Fed began to adopt monetarist ideas in the late 1970s

FIGURE 47-4   The Velocity of Money

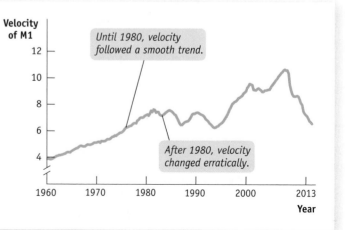

From 1960 to 1980, the velocity of money was stable, leading monetarists to believe that steady growth in the money supply would lead to a stable economy. After 1980, however, velocity began moving erratically, undermining the case for traditional monetarism. As a result, traditional monetarism fell out of favor.

Source: Bureau of Economic Analysis; Federal Reserve Bank of St. Louis.

and early 1980s, however, the velocity of money began moving erratically—probably due to financial market innovations.

Traditional monetarists are hard to find among today's macroeconomists. As we'll see later, however, the concern that originally motivated the monetarists—that too much discretionary monetary policy can actually destabilize the economy—has become widely accepted.

Inflation and the Natural Rate of Unemployment

At the same time that monetarists were challenging Keynesian views about how macroeconomic policy should be conducted, other economists—some, but not all, monetarists—were emphasizing the limits to what activist macroeconomic policy could achieve.

In the 1940s and 1950s, many Keynesian economists believed that expansionary fiscal policy could be used to achieve full employment on a permanent basis. In the 1960s, however, many economists realized that expansionary policies could cause problems with inflation, but they still believed policy makers could choose to trade off low unemployment for higher inflation even in the long run.

In 1968, however, Edmund Phelps of Columbia University and Milton Friedman, working independently, proposed the concept of the *natural rate of unemployment.* Earlier you learned that the natural rate of unemployment is also the nonaccelerating inflation rate of unemployment, or NAIRU. According to the **natural rate hypothesis,** because inflation is eventually embedded in expectations, to avoid accelerating inflation over time, the unemployment rate must be high enough that the actual inflation rate equals the expected rate of inflation. Attempts to keep the unemployment rate below the natural rate will lead to an ever-rising inflation rate.

The natural rate hypothesis limits the role of activist macroeconomic policy compared to earlier theories. Because the government can't keep unemployment below the natural rate, its task is not to keep unemployment low but to keep it *stable*—to prevent large fluctuations in unemployment in either direction.

The Friedman–Phelps hypothesis made a strong prediction: that the apparent trade-off between unemployment and inflation would not survive an extended period of rising prices. Once inflation was embedded in the public's expectations, inflation would continue even in the face of high unemployment. Sure enough, that's exactly what happened in the 1970s. This accurate prediction was one of the triumphs of macroeconomic analysis, and it convinced the great majority of economists that the natural rate hypothesis was correct. In contrast to traditional monetarism, which declined in influence as more evidence accumulated, the natural rate hypothesis has become almost universally accepted among macroeconomists, with a few qualifications. But some macroeconomists believe that at very low or negative rates of inflation the hypothesis doesn't work.

The Political Business Cycle

One final challenge to Keynesian economics focused not on the validity of the economic analysis but on its political consequences. A number of economists and political scientists pointed out that activist macroeconomic policy lends itself to political manipulation.

Statistical evidence suggests that election results tend to be determined by the state of the economy in the months just before the election. In the United States, if the economy is growing rapidly and the unemployment rate is falling in the six months or so before Election Day, the incumbent party tends to be re-elected even if the economy performed poorly in the preceding three years.

This creates an obvious temptation to abuse activist macroeconomic policy: pump up the economy in an election year, and pay the price in higher inflation and/or

According to the **natural rate hypothesis,** to avoid accelerating inflation over time, the unemployment rate must be high enough that the actual inflation rate equals the expected inflation rate.

higher unemployment later. The result can be unnecessary instability in the economy, a **political business cycle** caused by the use of macroeconomic policy to serve political ends.

An often-cited example is the combination of expansionary fiscal and monetary policy that led to rapid growth in the U.S. economy just before the 1972 election and a sharp acceleration in inflation after the election. Kenneth Rogoff, a respected macroeconomist who served as chief economist at the International Monetary Fund, proclaimed Richard Nixon, the president at the time, "the all-time hero of political business cycles."

One way to avoid a political business cycle is to place monetary policy in the hands of an independent central bank, insulated from political pressure. The political business cycle is also a reason to limit the use of discretionary fiscal policy to extreme circumstances.

Rational Expectations, Real Business Cycles, and New Classical Macroeconomics

As we have seen, one key difference between classical economics and Keynesian economics is that classical economists believed that the short-run aggregate supply curve is vertical, but Keynes emphasized the idea that the aggregate supply curve slopes upward in the short run. As a result, Keynes argued that demand shocks—shifts in the aggregate demand curve—can cause fluctuations in aggregate output.

The challenges to Keynesian economics that arose in the 1950s and 1960s—the renewed emphasis on monetary policy and the natural rate hypothesis—didn't question the view that an increase in aggregate demand leads to a rise in aggregate output in the short run nor that a decrease in aggregate demand leads to a fall in aggregate output in the short run.

In the 1970s and 1980s, however, some economists developed an approach to the business cycle known as **new classical macroeconomics,** which returned to the classical view that shifts in the aggregate demand curve affect only the aggregate price level, not aggregate output. The new approach evolved in two steps. First, some economists challenged traditional arguments about the slope of the short-run aggregate supply curve based on the concept of *rational expectations.* Second, some economists suggested that changes in productivity caused economic fluctuations, a view known as *real business cycle theory.*

Rational Expectations

In the 1970s, a concept known as *rational expectations* had a powerful impact on macroeconomics. **Rational expectations,** a theory originally introduced by John Muth in 1961, is the view that individuals and firms make decisions optimally, using all available information.

For example, workers and employers bargaining over long-term wage contracts need to estimate the inflation rate they expect over the life of that contract. Rational expectations says that in making estimates of future inflation, they won't just look at past rates of inflation; they will also take into account available information about monetary and fiscal policy. Suppose that prices didn't rise last year, but that the monetary and fiscal policies announced by policy makers made it clear to economic analysts that there would be substantial inflation over the next few years. According to rational expectations, long-term wage contracts will be adjusted today to reflect this future inflation, even though prices didn't rise in the past.

A **political business cycle** results when politicians use macroeconomic policy to serve political ends.

New classical macroeconomics is an approach to the business cycle that returns to the classical view that shifts in the aggregate demand curve affect only the aggregate price level, not aggregate output.

Rational expectations is the view that individuals and firms make decisions optimally, using all available information.

Rational expectations can significantly alter policy makers' beliefs about the effectiveness of government policy. According to the original version of the natural rate hypothesis, a government attempt to trade off higher inflation for lower unemployment would work in the short run but would eventually fail because higher inflation would get built into expectations.

According to rational expectations, we should remove the word *eventually:* if it's clear that the government intends to trade off higher inflation for lower unemployment, the public will understand this, and expected inflation will immediately rise. So, under rational expectations, government intervention fails in the short run and the long run.

In the 1970s, Robert Lucas of the University of Chicago used this logic to argue that monetary policy can change the level of unemployment only if it comes as a surprise to the public. If his analysis was right, monetary policy isn't useful in stabilizing the economy after all. In 1995 Lucas won the Nobel Prize in economics for this work, which remains widely admired. However, many—perhaps most—macroeconomists, especially those advising policy makers, now believe that his conclusions were overstated.

Why, in the view of many macroeconomists, doesn't the rational expectations hypothesis accurately describe how the economy behaves? **New Keynesian economics,** a set of ideas that became influential in the 1990s, provides an explanation. It argues that market imperfections interact to make many prices in the economy temporarily sticky. For example, one new Keynesian argument points out that monopolists don't have to be too careful about setting prices exactly "right": if they set a price a bit too high, they'll lose some sales but make more profit on each sale; if they set the price too low, they'll reduce the profit per sale but sell more. As a result, even small costs to changing prices can lead to substantial price stickiness and make the economy as a whole behave in a Keynesian fashion.

Over time, new Keynesian ideas combined with actual experience have reduced the practical influence of the rational expectations concept. Nonetheless, the idea of rational expectations served as a useful caution for macroeconomists who had become excessively optimistic about their ability to manage the economy.

Real Business Cycles

Earlier we introduced the concept of *total factor productivity,* the amount of output that can be generated with a given level of factor inputs. Total factor productivity grows over time, but that growth isn't smooth. In the 1980s, a number of economists argued that slowdowns in productivity growth, which they attributed to pauses in technological progress, are the main cause of recessions. **Real business cycle theory** claims that fluctuations in the rate of growth of total factor productivity cause the business cycle.

Believing that the aggregate supply curve is vertical, real business cycle theorists attribute the source of business cycles to shifts of the aggregate supply curve: a recession occurs when a slowdown in productivity growth shifts the aggregate supply curve leftward, and a recovery occurs when a pickup in productivity growth shifts the aggregate supply curve rightward. In the early days of real business cycle theory, the theory's proponents denied that changes in aggregate demand—and likewise, macroeconomic policy activism—had any effect on aggregate output.

This theory was strongly influential, but the current status of real business cycle theory is somewhat similar to that of rational expectations. The theory is widely recognized as having made valuable contributions to our understanding of the economy, and it serves as a useful caution against too much emphasis on aggregate demand.

But many of the real business cycle theorists themselves now acknowledge that their models need an upward-sloping aggregate supply curve to fit the economic data—and that this gives aggregate demand a potential role in determining aggregate output. And as we have seen, policy makers strongly believe that aggregate demand policy has an important role to play in fighting recessions.

According to **new Keynesian economics,** market imperfections can lead to price stickiness for the economy as a whole.

Real business cycle theory claims that fluctuations in the rate of growth of total factor productivity cause the business cycle.

^{MODULE}
47 Review

Solutions appear at the back of the book.

Check Your Understanding

1. When Ben Bernanke, in his tribute to Milton Friedman, said that "Regarding the Great Depression . . . we did it," he was referring to the fact that the Federal Reserve at the time did not pursue expansionary monetary policy. Why would a classical economist have thought that action by the Federal Reserve would not have made a difference in the length or depth of the Great Depression?

2. Consider Figure 47-4.

   a. If the Federal Reserve had pursued a monetarist policy of a constant rate of growth in the money supply, what would have happened to output beginning in 2008 according to the velocity equation?

   b. In fact, the Federal Reserve accelerated the rate of growth in M1 rapidly beginning in 2008, partly in order to counteract a large increase in unemployment. Would a monetarist have agreed with this policy? What limits are there, according to a monetarist point of view, to changing the unemployment rate?

3. What are the limits of macroeconomic policy activism?

4. In late 2008, as it became clear that the United States was experiencing a recession, the Fed reduced its target for the federal funds rate to near zero, as part of a larger aggressively expansionary monetary policy stance (including what the Fed called "quantitative easing"). Most observers agreed that the Fed's aggressive monetary expansion helped reduce the length and severity of the 2007–2009 recession.

   a. What would rational expectations theorists say about this conclusion?

   b. What would real business cycle theorists say?

Multiple-Choice Questions

1. Which of the following was an important point emphasized in Keynes's influential work?

   I. In the short run, shifts in aggregate demand affect aggregate output.

   II. Animal spirits are an important determinant of business cycles.

   III. In the long run we're all dead.

   a. I only

   b. II only

   c. III only

   d. I and II only

   e. I, II, and III

2. Which of the following is a central point of monetarism?

   a. Business cycles are associated with fluctuations in money demand.

   b. Activist monetary policy is the best way to address business cycles.

   c. Discretionary monetary policy is effective while discretionary fiscal policy is not.

   d. The Fed should follow a monetary policy rule.

   e. All of the above.

3. The natural rate hypothesis says that the unemployment rate should be

   a. below the NAIRU.

   b. high enough that the actual rate of inflation equals the expected rate.

   c. as close to zero as possible.

   d. 5%.

   e. left wherever the economy sets it.

4. The main difference between the classical model of the price level and Keynesian economics is that

   a. the classical model assumes a vertical short-run aggregate supply curve.

b. Keynesian economics assumes a vertical short-run aggregate supply curve.

c. the classical model assumes an upward sloping long-run aggregate supply curve.

d. Keynesian economics assumes a vertical long-run aggregate supply curve.

e. the classical model assumes aggregate demand can not change in the long run.

5. That fluctuations in total factor productivity growth cause the business cycle is the main tenet of which theory?

a. Keynesian

b. classical

c. rational expectations

d. real business cycle

e. natural rate

Critical-Thinking Question

For each of the following economic theories, identify its fundamental conclusion.

a. the classical model of the price level

b. Keynesian economics

c. monetarism

d. the natural rate hypothesis

e. rational expectations

f. real business cycle theory

48 The Modern Macroeconomic Consensus

White House Photo/Alamy

WHAT YOU WILL LEARN

1 **The elements of the modern macroeconomic consensus**

2 **The main remaining disputes**

Consensus and Conflict in Modern Macroeconomics

The 1970s and the first half of the 1980s were a stormy period for the U.S. economy (and for other major economies, too). There was a severe recession in 1974–1975, then two back-to-back recessions in 1979–1982 that sent the unemployment rate to almost 11%. At the same time, the inflation rate soared into double digits—and then plunged. As we have seen, these events left a strong mark on macroeconomic thought.

After about 1985, however, the economy settled down. The recession of 1990–1991 was much milder than the 1974–1975 recession or the double-dip slump from 1979 to 1982, and the inflation rate generally stayed below 4%. The period of relative calm in the economy from 1985 to 2007 came to be known as the **Great Moderation.** And the calmness of the economy was to a large extent marked by a similar calm in macroeconomic policy discussion. In fact, it seemed that a broad consensus had emerged about several key macroeconomic issues.

The Great Moderation was, unfortunately, followed by the *Great Recession*, the severe and persistent slump that followed the 2008 financial crisis. We'll talk shortly about the policy disputes caused by the Great Recession. First, however, let's examine the apparent consensus that emerged during the Great Moderation, which we call the **Great Moderation consensus.** It combines a belief in monetary policy as the main tool of stabilization, with skepticism toward the use of fiscal policy, and an acknowledgement of the policy constraints imposed by the natural rate of unemployment and the political business cycle.

The **Great Moderation** is the period from 1985 to 2007 when the U.S. economy experienced relatively small fluctuations and low inflation.

The **Great Moderation consensus** combines a belief in monetary policy as the main tool of stabilization, with skepticism toward the use of fiscal policy, and an acknowledgement of the policy constraints imposed by the natural rate of unemployment and the political business cycle.

To understand where the consensus came from and what still remains in dispute, we'll look at how macroeconomists have changed their answers to five key questions about macroeconomic policy. The five questions and the various answers given by schools of macroeconomics over the decades are summarized in Table 48-1. (In the table, new classical economics is subsumed under classical economics, and new Keynesian economics is subsumed under the Great Moderation consensus.) Notice that classical macroeconomics said no to each question; basically, classical macroeconomists didn't think macroeconomic policy could accomplish very much. But let's go through the questions one by one.

TABLE 48-1

Five Key Questions About Macroeconomic Policy

	Classical macroeconomics	Keynesian macroeconomics	Monetarism	Great Moderation consensus
1. Is expansionary monetary policy helpful in fighting recessions?	No	Not very	Yes	Yes, except in special circumstances
2. Is expansionary fiscal policy effective in fighting recessions?	No	Yes	No	Yes
3. Can monetary and/or fiscal policy reduce unemployment in the long run?	No	Yes	No	No
4. Should fiscal policy be used in a discretionary way?	No	Yes	No	No, except possibly in special circumstances
5. Should monetary policy be used in a discretionary way?	No	Yes	No	Still in dispute

QUESTION 1: IS EXPANSIONARY MONETARY POLICY HELPFUL IN FIGHTING RECESSIONS? As we've seen, classical macroeconomists generally believed that expansionary monetary policy was ineffective or even harmful in fighting recessions. In the early years of Keynesian economics, macroeconomists weren't against monetary expansion during recessions, but they tended to believe that it was of doubtful effectiveness. Milton Friedman and his followers convinced economists that monetary policy is effective after all.

Nearly all macroeconomists now agree that monetary policy can be used to shift the aggregate demand curve and to reduce economic instability. The classical view that changes in the money supply affect only aggregate prices, not aggregate output, has few supporters today. The view held by early Keynesian economists—that changes in the money supply have little effect—has equally few supporters. Now it is generally agreed that monetary policy is ineffective only in the case of a liquidity trap.

QUESTION 2: IS EXPANSIONARY FISCAL POLICY EFFECTIVE IN FIGHTING RECESSIONS? Classical macroeconomists were, if anything, even more opposed to fiscal expansion than monetary expansion. Keynesian economists, on the other hand, gave fiscal policy a central role in fighting recessions. Monetarists argued that fiscal policy was ineffective if the money supply was held constant. But that strong view has become relatively rare.

Most macroeconomists now agree that fiscal policy, like monetary policy, can shift the aggregate demand curve. Most macroeconomists also agree that the government should not seek to balance the budget regardless of the state of the economy: they agree that the role of the budget as an automatic stabilizer helps keep the economy on an even keel.

QUESTION 3: CAN MONETARY AND/OR FISCAL POLICY REDUCE UNEMPLOYMENT IN THE LONG RUN? Classical macroeconomists didn't believe the government could do anything about unemployment. Some Keynesian economists moved to the opposite extreme, arguing that expansionary policies could be used to achieve a permanently low unemployment rate, perhaps at the cost of some inflation. Monetarists believed that unemployment could not be kept below the natural rate.

Almost all macroeconomists now accept the natural rate hypothesis. This hypothesis leads them to accept sharp limits to what monetary and fiscal policy can accomplish. Effective monetary and fiscal policy, most macroeconomists believe, can limit the size of fluctuations of the actual unemployment rate around the natural rate, but they can't be used to keep unemployment below the natural rate.

QUESTION 4: SHOULD FISCAL POLICY BE USED IN A DISCRETIONARY WAY? As we've already seen, views about the effectiveness of fiscal policy have gone back and forth, from rejection by classical macroeconomists, to a positive view by Keynesian economists, to a negative view once again by monetarists. Today most macroeconomists believe that tax cuts and spending increases are at least somewhat effective in increasing aggregate demand.

Many, but not all, macroeconomists, however, believe that *discretionary fiscal policy* is usually counterproductive. They believe that the lags in adjusting fiscal policy mean that, all too often, policies intended to fight a slump end up intensifying a boom.

As a result, the macroeconomic consensus gives monetary policy the lead role in economic stabilization. Some, but not all, economists believe that fiscal policy must be brought back into the mix under special circumstances, in particular when interest rates are at or near the zero lower bound and the economy is in a liquidity trap. As we'll see shortly, the proper role of fiscal policy became a huge point of contention after 2008.

QUESTION 5: SHOULD MONETARY POLICY BE USED IN A DISCRETIONARY WAY? Classical macroeconomists didn't think that monetary policy should be used to fight recessions; Keynesian economists didn't oppose discretionary monetary policy, but they were skeptical about its effectiveness. Monetarists argued that discretionary monetary policy was doing more harm than good. Where are we today? This remains an area of dispute. Today, under the Great Moderation consensus, most macroeconomists agree on these three points:

- Monetary policy should play the main role in stabilization policy.
- The central bank should be independent, insulated from political pressures, in order to avoid a political business cycle.
- Discretionary fiscal policy should be used sparingly, both because of policy lags and because of the risks of a political business cycle.

However, the Great Moderation was up-ended by events that posed very difficult questions. We'll now examine what happened and why the ongoing debate is so fierce.

Crisis and Aftermath

The Great Recession shattered any sense among macroeconomists that they had entered a permanent era of agreement over key policy questions. Given the nature of the slump, however, this should not have come as a surprise. Why? Because the severity of the slump arguably made the policies that seemed to work during the Great Moderation inadequate.

Under the Great Moderation consensus, there had been broad agreement that the job of stabilizing the economy was best carried out by having the Federal Reserve and its counterparts abroad raise or lower interest rates as the economic situation warranted. But what should be done if the economy is deeply depressed, but the interest rates the Fed normally controls are already close to zero and can go no lower (that is, when the economy is in a liquidity trap)? Some economists called for the aggressive use of discretionary fiscal policy and/or unconventional monetary policies that might achieve results despite the zero lower bound. Others strongly opposed these measures, arguing either that they would be ineffective or that they would produce undesirable side effects.

The Debate over Fiscal Policy

In 2009 a number of governments, including that of the United States, responded with expansionary fiscal policy, or "stimulus," generally taking the form of a mix of temporary spending measures and temporary tax cuts. From the start, however, these efforts were highly controversial.

Supporters of fiscal stimulus offered three main arguments for breaking with the normal presumption against discretionary fiscal policy:

1. They argued that discretionary fiscal expansion was needed because the usual tool for stabilizing the economy, monetary policy, could no longer be used now that interest rates were near zero.

2. They argued that one normal concern about expansionary fiscal policy—that deficit spending would drive up interest rates, crowding out private investment spending—was unlikely to be a problem in a depressed economy. Again, this was because interest rates were close to zero and likely to stay there as long as the economy was depressed.

3. Finally, they argued that another concern about discretionary fiscal policy—that it might take a long time to get going—was less of a concern than usual given the likelihood that the economy would be depressed for an extended period.

These arguments generally won the day in early 2009. However, opponents of fiscal stimulus raised two main objections:

1. They argued that households and firms would see any rise in government spending as a sign that tax burdens were likely to rise in the future, leading to a fall in private spending that would undo any positive effect. (As you will recall, this is the *Ricardian equivalence* argument.)

2. They also warned that spending programs might undermine investors' faith in the government's ability to repay its debts, leading to an increase in long-term interest rates despite loose monetary policy.

In fact, by 2010 a number of economists were arguing that the best way to boost the economy was actually to cut government spending, which they argued would increase private-sector confidence and lead to a rise in output and employment. This notion, often referred to as the doctrine of "expansionary austerity," was especially popular in Europe at the time.

One might have hoped that events would resolve this dispute. But the debate continues to rage today. At the time, critics of fiscal stimulus pointed out that the U.S. stimulus had failed to deliver a convincing fall in unemployment; stimulus advocates, however, had warned from the start that this was likely to happen because the stimulus was too small compared with the depth of the slump. Meanwhile, austerity programs in Britain and elsewhere had also failed to deliver an economic turnaround and, in fact, had seemed to deepen the slump; supporters of these programs, however, argued that they were nonetheless necessary to head off a potential collapse of confidence.

One thing that was clear, however, was that those who had predicted a sharp rise in U.S. interest rates due to budget deficits, leading to conventional crowding out, were wrong: by the fall of 2011, U.S. long-term rates were hitting record lows despite continuing large deficits. Interest rates remained low through 2013, even as the budget deficit declined.

The Debate over Monetary Policy

As we've seen, a central bank that wants to increase aggregate demand normally does this by buying short-term government debt, pushing short-term interest rates down and causing spending to rise. By the fall of 2008, however, this conventional form of monetary policy had already reached its limit because the relevant interest rates were close

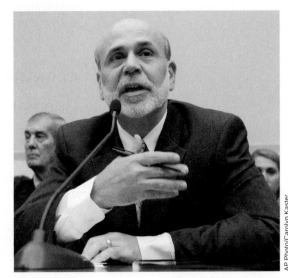

In 2008, the Fed took a series of unconventional monetary policy actions in response to the deepening financial crisis.

AP Photo/Carolyn Kaster

to zero. The question then became whether there were other things the Federal Reserve and other central banks could do.

In 2008–2009 and again in the fall of 2010, the Fed pursued one such alternative, known as *quantitative easing,* which involved buying assets other than short-term government debt, notably long-term debt whose interest rate was still significantly above zero. For example, in November 2010 the Fed began buying $600 billion worth of longer-term U.S. debt in a program generally referred to as "QE2" (quantitative easing 2). The idea was to drive down longer-term interest rates, which arguably matter more for private spending than short-term rates. In September 2011 the Fed announced another program that involved selling shorter-term assets with interest rates already near zero and buying longer-term assets instead.

The policy of quantitative easing was controversial, facing criticisms both from those who believed the Fed was doing too much and from those who believed it wasn't doing enough. Those who thought the Fed was doing too much were concerned about possible future inflation; they argued that the Fed would find its unconventional measures hard to reverse as the economy recovered and that the end result would be a much too expansionary monetary policy.

"I'll pause for a moment so you can let this information sink in."

Critics from the other side argued that the Fed's actions were likely to be ineffective: long-term interest rates, they suggested, mainly reflected expectations about future short-term rates, and even large purchases of long-term bonds by the Fed would have little impact.

Many of those calling for even more active policy advocated an official rise in the Fed's inflation target. Recall the distinction between the nominal interest rate, which is the number normally cited, and the *real* interest rate—the nominal rate minus expected inflation—which is what should matter for investment decisions. Advocates of a higher inflation target argued that by promising to raise prices over, say, the next 10 years by an annual average rate of 3% or 4%, the Fed could push the real interest rate down even though the nominal rate was up against the zero lower bound.

Such proposals, however, led to fierce disputes. Some economists pointed out that the Fed had fought hard to drive inflation expectations down and argued that changing course would undermine hard-won credibility. Others argued that given the enormous economic and human damage being done by high unemployment, it was time for extraordinary measures, and inflation-fighting could no longer be given first priority.

These same debates continue to rage today, and it seems unlikely that a new consensus about macroeconomic policy will emerge any time soon.

ECONOMICS ▶ IN ACTION

AN IRISH ROLE MODEL?

Over the course of 2010 and 2011 a fierce debate raged, among both economists and policy makers, about whether countries suffering large budget deficits should move quickly to reduce those deficits if they were also suffering from high unemployment. Many economists argued that spending cuts and/or tax increases should be delayed until economies had recovered. As we explained in the text, however, others argued that fast action on deficits would actually help the economy even in the short run, by improving confidence—a claim that came to be known as *expansionary austerity.*

How could this dispute be settled? Researchers turned their attention to historical episodes, in particular to cases in which nations had managed to combine sharp reductions in budget deficits with strong economic growth. One case in particular became a major intellectual battleground: Ireland in the second half of the 1980s.

Panel (a) of Figure 48-1 shows why Ireland's experience drew attention. It compares Ireland's cyclically adjusted budget deficit as a percentage of GDP with its growth rate. Between 1986 and 1989 Ireland drastically reduced its underlying deficits with a combination of spending cuts and tax hikes, and the Irish economy's growth sharply accelerated. A number of observers suggested that nations facing large deficits in the aftermath of the 2008 financial crisis should seek to emulate that experience.

FIGURE **48-1**   **Economic Indicators for Ireland**

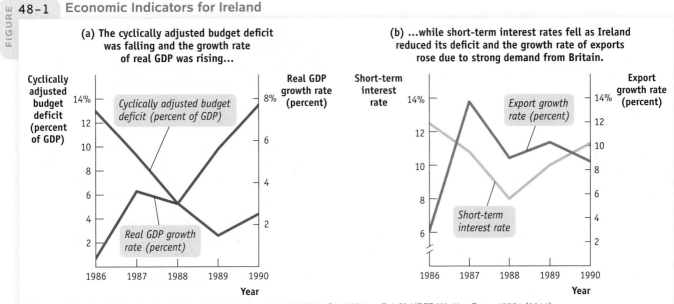

Sources: International Monetary Fund; Roberto Perotti, "The 'Austerity Myth': Gain Without Pain?", NBER Working Paper 17571 (2011).

A closer look, however, suggested that Ireland's situation in the 1980s was very different from that facing Western economies in 2010 and 2011. Panel (b) of Figure 48-1 shows two other economic indicators for Ireland from 1986 to 1990: short-term interest rates and export growth. Ireland entered into fiscal austerity with high interest rates, which fell sharply between 1986 and 1988 as investors gained more confidence in its solvency (although they rose thereafter).

At the same time, Ireland had a major export boom, partly due to rapid economic growth in neighboring Britain. Both factors helped offset any contractionary effects from lower spending and higher taxes.

The point was that these "cushioning" factors would not be available if, say, the United States were to slash spending. Short-term interest rates were already near zero and couldn't fall further, and America had no booming neighbors to export to.

By the end of 2011 careful study of the historical record convinced most, though not all, economists studying the issue that hopes for expansionary austerity were probably misplaced. However, the debate about what the United States and other troubled economies should do raged on.

48 Review

MODULE

Solutions appear at the back of the book.

Check Your Understanding

1. Why did the Great Recession lead to the decline of the Great Moderation consensus? Given events, why is it predictable that a new consensus has not emerged?

Multiple-Choice Questions

1. Which of the following is an example of an opinion on which economists have reached a broad consensus?

   I. The natural rate hypothesis holds true.
   II. Discretionary fiscal policy is usually counterproductive.
   III. Monetary policy is effective, especially in a liquidity trap.

   a. I only
   b. II only
   c. III only
   d. I and II only
   e. I, II, and III

2. Which group of macroeconomists believes that both monetary policy and fiscal policy can be effectively used to keep the unemployment rate below the natural rate?

   a. classical macroeconomists
   b. Keynesian macroeconomists
   c. no macroeconomists believe this
   d. monetarists
   e. Keynesians and monetarists

3. Which of the following policy positions would a monetarist support?

   a. Fiscal policy cannot effectively fight a recession.

   b. Short-run changes in aggregate demand do not affect aggregate output.
   c. Short-run changes in aggregate demand do not affect prices.
   d. Steady growth in the money supply will ensure steady growth in spending and GDP.

4. What is quantitative easing?

   a. The purchase of short-term government debt by the Fed.
   b. The sale of short-term government debt by the Fed.
   c. The purchase of long-term government debt by the Fed.
   d. The sale of long-term government debt by the Fed.
   e. The use of expansionary fiscal policy to stimulate output.

5. Which of the following positions are true under the Great Moderation consensus?

   a. Monetary policy can be used to reduce the unemployment rate in the long run.
   b. Expansionary fiscal policy is not effective in fighting a recession.
   c. Monetary policy is effective in fighting a recession.
   d. Monetary policy and fiscal policy cannot effectively reduce unemployment in the short run.

Critical-Thinking Questions

1. What arguments were made in favor of using expansionary fiscal policy to help the U.S. economy recover from the Great Recession?

2. What arguments were made against the use of fiscal stimulus during the Great Recession?

SECTION 14 REVIEW

Summary

History and Alternative Views of Macroeconomics

1. Classical macroeconomics asserted that monetary policy affected only the aggregate price level, not aggregate output, and that the short run was unimportant. By the 1930s, measurement of business cycles was a well-established subject, but there was no widely accepted theory of business cycles.

2. Keynesian economics attributed the business cycle to shifts of the aggregate demand curve, often the result of changes in business confidence. Keynesian economics also offered a rationale for **macroeconomic policy activism.**

3. In the decades that followed Keynes's work, economists came to agree that monetary policy as well as fiscal policy is effective under certain conditions. **Monetarism,** a doctrine that called for a **monetary policy rule** as opposed to **discretionary monetary policy** and that argued—based on a belief that the **velocity of money** was stable—that GDP would grow steadily if the money supply grew steadily, was influential for a time but was eventually rejected by many macroeconomists.

4. The **natural rate hypothesis** became almost universally accepted, limiting the role of macroeconomic policy to stabilizing the economy rather than seeking a permanently lower unemployment rate. Fears of a **political business cycle** led to a consensus that monetary policy should be insulated from politics.

5. **Rational expectations** claims that individuals and firms make decisions using all available information and only unexpected changes in monetary policy affect aggregate output and employment; expected changes merely alter the price level. **Real business cycle theory** claims that changes in the rate of growth of total factor productivity are the main cause of business cycles. Both of these versions of **new classical macroeconomics** received wide attention and respect, but policy makers and many economists haven't accepted the conclusion that monetary and fiscal policy are ineffective in changing aggregate output.

6. **New Keynesian economics** argues that market imperfections can lead to price stickiness, so that changes in aggregate demand have effects on aggregate output after all.

The Modern Macroeconomic Consensus

7. The **Great Moderation** from 1985 to 2007 generated the **Great Moderation consensus:** belief in monetary policy as the main tool of stabilization; skepticism toward use of fiscal policy, except possibly in exceptional circumstances such as a liquidity trap; and acknowledgement of the policy constraints imposed by the natural rate of unemployment and the political business cycle. But the Great Moderation consensus was challenged by the post-2008 crisis events, as monetary policy lost its effectiveness in the midst of a liquidity trap. As a result, many advocated the use of fiscal policy to address the deep recession.

8. In 2009, a number of governments, including the United States, used fiscal stimulus to support their deeply depressed economies in the face of a liquidity trap. The use of fiscal policy remained highly controversial. In the United States, it failed to significantly reduce unemployment, with critics citing that as proof of its general ineffectiveness, while supporters argued the size of the stimulus was too small. Yet the crowding out predicted by its critics failed to occur.

9. Monetary policy was also hotly debated in the wake of the Great Recession, as the Fed pursued "quantitative easing" and other unconventional monetary policies to address the liquidity trap. Critics claimed the Fed was doing too much and would sacrifice its hard-won credibility as an inflation fighter. Others countered that the Fed was doing too little, yet others claimed the Fed's actions would have little impact. Some proposed the Fed adopt a higher inflation target to push the real interest rate down.

Key Terms

Macroeconomic policy activism, p. 493

Monetarism, p. 494

Discretionary monetary policy, p. 495

Monetary policy rule, p. 496

Quantity Theory of Money, p. 496

Velocity of money, p. 496

Natural rate hypothesis, p. 497

Political business cycle, p. 498

New classical macroeconomics, p. 498

Rational expectations, p. 498

New Keynesian economics, p. 499

Real business cycle theory, p. 499

Great Moderation, p. 502

Great Moderation consensus, p. 502

Problems

1. After the crash of its stock market in 1989, the Japanese economy saw little economic growth and some deflation. The accompanying table from the Organization for Economic Co-operation and Development (OECD) shows some key macroeconomic data for Japan for 1991 (a "normal" year) and 1995–2003.

   a. From the data, determine the type of policies Japan's policy makers undertook at that time to promote growth.

   b. We can safely consider a short-term interest rate that is less than 0.1% to effectively be a 0% interest rate. What is this situation called? What does it imply about the effectiveness of monetary policy? Of fiscal policy?

Year	Real GDP annual growth rate	Short-term interest rate	Government debt (percent of GDP)	Government budget deficit (percent of GDP)
1991	3.4%	7.38%	64.8%	−1.81%
1995	1.9	1.23	87.1	4.71
1996	3.4	0.59	93.9	5.07
1997	1.9	0.60	100.3	3.79
1998	−1.1	0.72	112.2	5.51
1999	0.1	0.25	125.7	7.23
2000	2.8	0.25	134.1	7.48
2001	0.4	0.12	142.3	6.13
2002	−0.3	0.06	149.3	7.88
2003	2.5	0.04	157.5	7.67

2. The National Bureau of Economic Research (NBER) maintains the official chronology of past U.S. business cycles. Go to its website at http://www.nber.org/cycles/cyclesmain.html to answer the following questions.

   a. How many business cycles have occurred since the end of World War II in 1945?

   b. What was the average duration of a business cycle when measured from the end of one expansion (its peak) to the end of the next? That is, what was the average duration of a business cycle in the period from 1945 to 2001?

   c. When was the last announcement by the NBER's Business Cycle Dating Committee, and what was it?

3. The fall of America's military rival, the Soviet Union, in 1989 allowed the United States to significantly reduce its defense spending in subsequent years. Using the data in the following table from the Economic Report of the President, replicate Figure 47-2 for the 1990–2000 period. Given the strong economic growth in the United States during the late 1990s, why would a Keynesian see the reduction in defense spending during the 1990s as a good thing?

Year	Budget deficit (percent of GDP)	Unemployment rate
1990	3.9%	5.6%
1991	4.5	6.8
1992	4.7	7.5
1993	3.9	6.9
1994	2.9	6.1
1995	2.2	5.6
1996	1.4	5.4
1997	0.3	4.9
1998	−0.8	4.5
1999	−1.4	4.2
2000	−2.4	4.0

4. In the modern world, central banks are free to increase or reduce the money supply as they see fit. However, some people harken back to the "good old days" of the gold standard. Under the gold standard, the money supply could expand only when the amount of available gold increased.

   a. Under the gold standard, if the velocity of money were stable when the economy was expanding, what would have had to happen to keep prices stable?

   b. Why would modern macroeconomists consider the gold standard a bad idea?

5. Monetarists believed for a period of time that the velocity of money was stable within a country. However, with financial innovation, the velocity began shifting around erratically after 1980. As would be expected, the velocity of money is different across countries depending upon the sophistication of their financial systems—velocity of money tends to be higher in countries with developed financial systems. The accompanying table provides an example of a single year's money supply and GDP information for six countries.

Country	National currency	M1 (billions in national currency)	Nominal GDP (billions in national currency)
Egypt	Egyptian pounds	101	539
South Korea	Korean won	77,274	806,622
Thailand	Thai baht	863	7,103
United States	U.S. dollars	1,369	12,456
Kenya	Kenyan pounds	231	1,415
India	Indian rupees	7,213	35,314

Source: Datastream.

   a. Calculate the velocity of money for each of the countries. The accompanying table shows an example of a single year's GDP per capita data for each of these countries in U.S. dollars.

Country	Nominal GDP per capita (U.S. dollars)
Egypt	$1,270
South Korea	16,444
Thailand	2,707
United States	41,886
Kenya	572
India	710

Source: IMF.

b. Rank the countries in descending order of per capita income and velocity of money. Do wealthy countries or poor countries tend to "turn over" their money more times per year? Would you expect wealthy countries to have more sophisticated financial systems?

6. Kenneth Rogoff proclaimed Richard Nixon "the all-time hero of political business cycles." Using the following table of data from the Economic Report of the President, explain why Nixon may have earned that title. (*Note:* Nixon entered office in January 1969 and was reelected in November 1972. He resigned in August 1974.)

Year	Government receipts (billions of dollars)	Government spending (billions of dollars)	Government budget balance (billions of dollars)	M1 growth	M2 growth	3-month Treasury bill rate
1969	$186.9	$183.6	$3.2	3.3%	3.7%	6.68%
1970	192.8	195.6	−2.8	5.1	6.6	6.46
1971	187.1	210.2	−23.0	6.5	13.4	4.35
1972	207.3	230.7	−23.4	9.2	13.0	4.07
1973	230.8	245.7	−14.9	5.5	6.6	7.04

7. The economy of Albernia is facing a recessionary gap, and the leader of that nation calls together five of its best economists representing the classical, Keynesian, monetarist, real business cycle, and Great Moderation consensus views of the macroeconomy. Explain what policies each economist would recommend and why.

8. Which of the following policy recommendations are consistent with the classical, Keynesian, monetarist, and/or Great Moderation consensus views of the macroeconomy?

a. Since the long-run growth of GDP is 2%, the money supply should grow at 2%.

b. Decrease government spending in order to decrease inflationary pressure.

c. Increase the money supply in order to alleviate a recessionary gap.

d. Always maintain a balanced budget.

e. Decrease the budget deficit as a percent of GDP when facing a recessionary gap.

9. Using a graph like Figure 47-3, show how a monetarist can argue that a contractionary fiscal policy need not lead to a fall in real GDP given a fixed money supply. Explain.

A Graphs in Economics

Whether you're reading about economics in the news or in your economics textbook, you will see many graphs. Visual presentations can make it easier to understand verbal descriptions, numerical information, or ideas. In economics, graphs are used to facilitate understanding. But to get the full benefit from these visual aids, you need to know how to interpret them. This appendix explains how graphs are constructed, interpreted, and used in economics.

Graphs, Variables, and Economic Models

If you were reading an article about the relationship between educational attainment and income, you would probably see a graph showing the income levels for workers with different levels of education. This graph would depict the idea that, in general, having more education increases a person's income. This graph, like most graphs in economics, would depict the relationship between two economic variables. A **variable** is a quantity that can take on more than one value, such as the number of years of education a person has, the price of a can of soda, or a household's income.

Earlier we discussed how economic analysis relies heavily on *models*, simplified descriptions of real situations. Most economic models describe the relationship between two variables, simplified by holding constant other variables that may affect the relationship. For example, an economic model might describe the relationship between the price of a can of soda and the number of cans of soda that consumers will buy, assuming that everything else that affects consumers' purchases of soda stays constant. This type of model can be described mathematically or verbally, but illustrating the relationship in a graph makes it easier to understand. Next we show how graphs that depict economic models are constructed and interpreted.

How Graphs Work

Most graphs in economics are based on a grid built around two perpendicular lines that show the values of two variables, helping you visualize the relationship between them. So a first step in understanding the use of such graphs is to see how this system works.

Two-Variable Graphs

Figure A-1 shows a typical two-variable graph. It illustrates the data in the accompanying table on outside temperature and the number of sodas a typical vendor can expect to sell at a baseball stadium during one game. The first column shows the values of outside temperature (the first variable) and the second column shows the values of the number of sodas sold (the second variable). Five combinations or pairs of the two variables are shown, denoted by points A through E in the third column.

Now let's turn to graphing the data in this table. In any two-variable graph, one variable is called the *x*-variable and the other is called the *y*-variable. Here we have made outside temperature the *x*-variable and number of sodas sold the *y*-variable.

The solid horizontal line in the graph is called the **horizontal axis** or **x-axis,** and values of the *x*-variable—outside temperature—are measured along it. Similarly, the solid vertical line in the graph is called the **vertical axis** or **y-axis,** and values of the *y*-variable—number of sodas sold—are measured along it. At the **origin,** the point where the two axes meet, each variable is equal to zero. As you move rightward from the origin along the *x*-axis, values of the *x*-variable are positive and increasing. As

A quantity that can take on more than one value is called a **variable**.

The line along which values of the x-variable are measured is called the **horizontal axis** or **x-axis**. The line along which values of the y-variable are measured is called the **vertical axis** or **y-axis**. The point where the axes of a two-variable graph meet is the **origin**.

FIGURE A-1   Plotting Points on a Two-Variable Graph

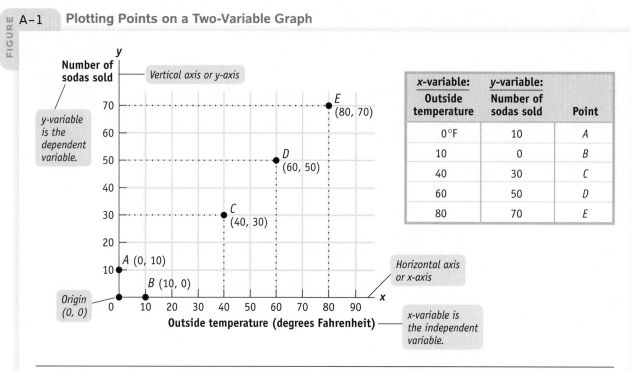

The data from the table are plotted where outside temperature (the independent variable) is measured along the horizontal axis and number of sodas sold (the dependent variable) is measured along the vertical axis. Each of the five combinations of temperature and sodas sold is represented by a point: *A*, *B*, *C*, *D*, and *E*. Each point in the graph is identified by a pair of values. For example, point *C* corresponds to the pair (40, 30)—an outside temperature of 40°F (the value of the *x*-variable) and 30 sodas sold (the value of the *y*-variable).

you move up from the origin along the *y*-axis, values of the *y*-variable are positive and increasing.

You can plot each of the five points *A* through *E* on this graph by using a pair of numbers—the values that the *x*-variable and the *y*-variable take on for a given point. In Figure A-1, at point *C*, the *x*-variable takes on the value 40 and the *y*-variable takes on the value 30. You plot point *C* by drawing a line straight up from 40 on the *x*-axis and a horizontal line across from 30 on the *y*-axis. We write point *C* as (40, 30). We write the origin as (0, 0).

Looking at point *A* and point *B* in Figure A-1, you can see that when one of the variables for a point has a value of zero, it will lie on one of the axes. If the value of the *x*-variable is zero, the point will lie on the vertical axis, like point *A*. If the value of the *y*-variable is zero, the point will lie on the horizontal axis, like point *B*.

Most graphs that depict relationships between two economic variables represent a **causal relationship**, a relationship in which the value taken by one variable directly influences or determines the value taken by the other variable. In a causal relationship, the determining variable is called the **independent variable;** the variable it determines is called the **dependent variable.** In our example of soda sales, the outside temperature is the independent variable. It directly influences the number of sodas that are sold, which is the dependent variable in this case.

By convention, we put the independent variable on the horizontal axis and the dependent variable on the vertical axis. Figure A-1 follows this convention: the independent variable (outside temperature) is on the horizontal axis and the dependent variable (number of sodas sold) is on the vertical axis.

An important exception to this convention is in graphs showing the economic relationship between the price of a product and quantity of the product: although price is generally the independent variable that determines quantity, it is always measured on the vertical axis.

A **causal relationship** exists between two variables when the value taken by one variable directly influences or determines the value taken by the other variable. In a causal relationship, the determining variable is called the **independent variable;** the variable it determines is called the **dependent variable.**

Curves on a Graph

Panel (a) of Figure A-2 contains some of the same information as Figure A-1, with a line drawn through the points *B*, *C*, *D*, and *E*. Such a line on a graph is called a **curve,** regardless of whether it is a straight line or a curved line. If the curve that shows the relationship between two variables is a straight line, or linear, the variables have a **linear relationship.** When the curve is not a straight line, or nonlinear, the variables have a **nonlinear relationship.**

A point on a curve indicates the value of the *y*-variable for a specific value of the *x*-variable. For example, point *D* indicates that at a temperature of 60°F, a vendor can expect to sell 50 sodas. The shape and orientation of a curve reveal the general nature of the relationship between the two variables. The upward tilt of the curve in panel (a) of Figure A-2 suggests that vendors can expect to sell more sodas at higher outside temperatures.

When variables are related in this way—that is, when an increase in one variable is associated with an increase in the other variable—the variables are said to have a **positive relationship.** It is illustrated by a curve that slopes upward from left to right. Because this curve is also linear, the relationship between outside temperature and number of sodas sold illustrated by the curve in panel (a) of Figure A-2 is a positive linear relationship.

When an increase in one variable is associated with a decrease in the other variable, the two variables are said to have a **negative relationship.** It is illustrated by a curve that slopes downward from left to right, like the curve in panel (b) of Figure A-2. Because this curve is also linear, the relationship it depicts is a negative linear relationship. Two variables that might have such a relationship are the outside temperature and the number of hot drinks a vendor can expect to sell at a baseball stadium.

A **curve** is a line on a graph that depicts a relationship between two variables. It may be either a straight line or a curved line. If the curve is a straight line, the variables have a **linear relationship**. If the curve is not a straight line, the variables have a **nonlinear relationship**.

Two variables have a **positive relationship** when an increase in the value of one variable is associated with an increase in the value of the other variable. It is illustrated by a curve that slopes upward from left to right.

Two variables have a **negative relationship** when an increase in the value of one variable is associated with a decrease in the value of the other variable. It is illustrated by a curve that slopes downward from left to right.

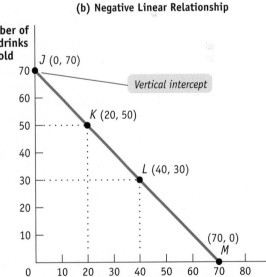

FIGURE A-2   Drawing Curves

The curve in panel (a) illustrates the relationship between the two variables, outside temperature and number of sodas sold. The two variables have a positive linear relationship: positive because the curve has an upward tilt, and linear because it is a straight line. The curve implies that an increase in the *x*-variable (outside temperature) leads to an increase in the *y*-variable (number of sodas sold). The curve in panel (b) is also a straight line, but it tilts downward. The two variables here, outside temperature and number of hot drinks sold, have a negative linear relationship: an increase in the *x*-variable (outside temperature) leads to a decrease in the *y*-variable (number of hot drinks sold). The curve in panel (a) has a horizontal intercept at point *B*, where it hits the horizontal axis. The curve in panel (b) has a vertical intercept at point *J*, where it hits the vertical axis, and a horizontal intercept at point *M*, where it hits the horizontal axis.

The **horizontal intercept** of a curve is the point at which it hits the horizontal axis; it indicates the value of the *x*-variable when the value of the *y*-variable is zero.

The **vertical intercept** of a curve is the point at which it hits the vertical axis; it shows the value of the *y*-variable when the value of the *x*-variable is zero. The slope of a line or curve is a measure of how steep it is.

The **slope** of a line is measured by "rise over run"—the change in the *y*-variable between two points on the line divided by the change in the *x*-variable between those same two points.

Return for a moment to the curve in panel (a) of Figure A-2, and you can see that it hits the horizontal axis at point *B*. This point, known as the **horizontal intercept,** shows the value of the *x*-variable when the value of the *y*-variable is zero. In panel (b) of Figure A-2, the curve hits the vertical axis at point *J*. This point, called the **vertical intercept,** indicates the value of the *y*-variable when the value of the *x*-variable is zero.

A Key Concept: The Slope of a Curve

The **slope** of a curve is a measure of how steep it is; the slope indicates how sensitive the *y*-variable is to a change in the *x*-variable. In our example of outside temperature and the number of cans of soda a vendor can expect to sell, the slope of the curve would indicate how many more cans of soda the vendor could expect to sell with each 1° increase in temperature. Interpreted this way, the slope gives meaningful information.

Even without numbers for *x* and *y*, it is possible to arrive at important conclusions about the relationship between the two variables by examining the slope of a curve at various points.

The Slope of a Linear Curve

Along a linear curve the slope, or steepness, is measured by dividing the "rise" between two points on the curve by the "run" between those same two points. The rise is the amount that *y* changes, and the run is the amount that *x* changes. Here is the formula:

$$\frac{\text{Change in } y}{\text{Change in } x} = \frac{\Delta y}{\Delta x} = \text{Slope}$$

In the formula, the symbol Δ (the Greek uppercase delta) stands for "change in." When a variable increases, the change in that variable is positive; when a variable decreases, the change in that variable is negative.

The slope of a curve is positive when the rise (the change in the *y*-variable) has the same sign as the run (the change in the *x*-variable). That's because when two numbers have the same sign, the ratio of those two numbers is positive.

The curve in panel (a) of Figure A-2 has a positive slope: along the curve, both the *y*-variable and the *x*-variable increase. The slope of a curve is negative when the rise and the run have different signs. That's because when two numbers have different signs, the ratio of those two numbers is negative. The curve in panel (b) of Figure A-2 has a negative slope: along the curve, an increase in the *x*-variable is associated with a decrease in the *y*-variable.

Figure A-3 illustrates how to calculate the slope of a linear curve. Let's focus first on panel (a). From point *A* to point *B* the value of the *y*-variable changes from 25 to 20 and the value of the *x*-variable changes from 10 to 20. So the slope of the line between these two points is

$$\frac{\text{Change in } y}{\text{Change in } x} = \frac{\Delta y}{\Delta x} = \frac{-5}{10} = -\frac{1}{2} = -0.5$$

Because a straight line is equally steep at all points, the slope of a straight line is the same at all points. In other words, a straight line has a constant slope. You can check this by calculating the slope of the linear curve between points *A* and *B* and between points *C* and *D* in panel (b) of Figure A-3.

$$\frac{\Delta y}{\Delta x} = \frac{10}{2} = 5$$

$$\frac{\Delta y}{\Delta x} = \frac{20}{4} = 5$$

FIGURE **A-3**   Calculating the Slope

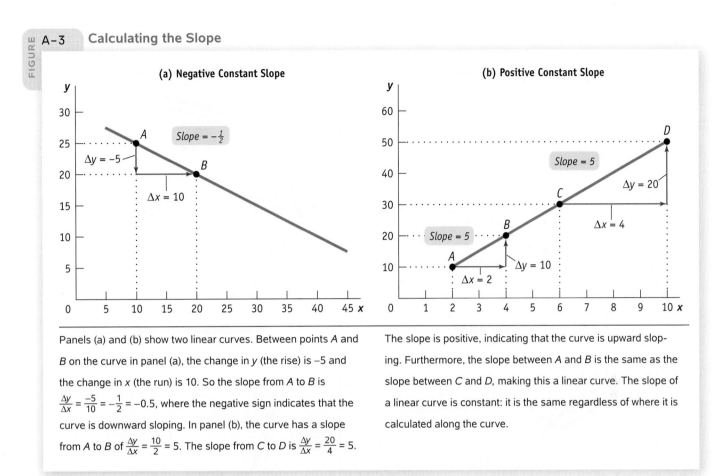

Panels (a) and (b) show two linear curves. Between points A and B on the curve in panel (a), the change in y (the rise) is –5 and the change in x (the run) is 10. So the slope from A to B is

$\frac{\Delta y}{\Delta x} = \frac{-5}{10} = -\frac{1}{2} = -0.5$, where the negative sign indicates that the curve is downward sloping. In panel (b), the curve has a slope from A to B of $\frac{\Delta y}{\Delta x} = \frac{10}{2} = 5$. The slope from C to D is $\frac{\Delta y}{\Delta x} = \frac{20}{4} = 5$.

The slope is positive, indicating that the curve is upward sloping. Furthermore, the slope between A and B is the same as the slope between C and D, making this a linear curve. The slope of a linear curve is constant: it is the same regardless of where it is calculated along the curve.

Horizontal and Vertical Curves and Their Slopes

When a curve is horizontal, the value of y along that curve never changes—it is constant. Everywhere along the curve, the change in y is zero. Now, zero divided by any number is zero. So regardless of the value of the change in x, the slope of a horizontal curve is always zero.

If a curve is vertical, the value of x along the curve never changes—it is constant. Everywhere along the curve, the change in x is zero. This means that the slope of a vertical line is a ratio with zero in the denominator. A ratio with zero in the denominator is equal to infinity—that is, an infinitely large number. So the slope of a vertical line is equal to infinity.

A vertical or a horizontal curve has a special implication: it means that the x-variable and the y-variable are unrelated. Two variables are unrelated when a change in one variable (the independent variable) has no effect on the other variable (the dependent variable). To put it a slightly different way, two variables are unrelated when the dependent variable is constant regardless of the value of the independent variable. If, as is usual, the y-variable is the dependent variable, the curve is horizontal. If the dependent variable is the x-variable, the curve is vertical.

The Slope of a Nonlinear Curve

A **nonlinear curve** is one in which the slope changes as you move along it. Panels (a), (b), (c), and (d) of Figure A-4 show various nonlinear curves. Panels (a) and (b) show nonlinear curves whose slopes change as you follow the line's progression, but the slopes always remain positive.

Although both curves tilt upward, the curve in panel (a) gets steeper as the line moves from left to right in contrast to the curve in panel (b), which gets flatter. A

A **nonlinear curve** is one in which the slope is not the same between every pair of points.

FIGURE **A-4**   Nonlinear Curves

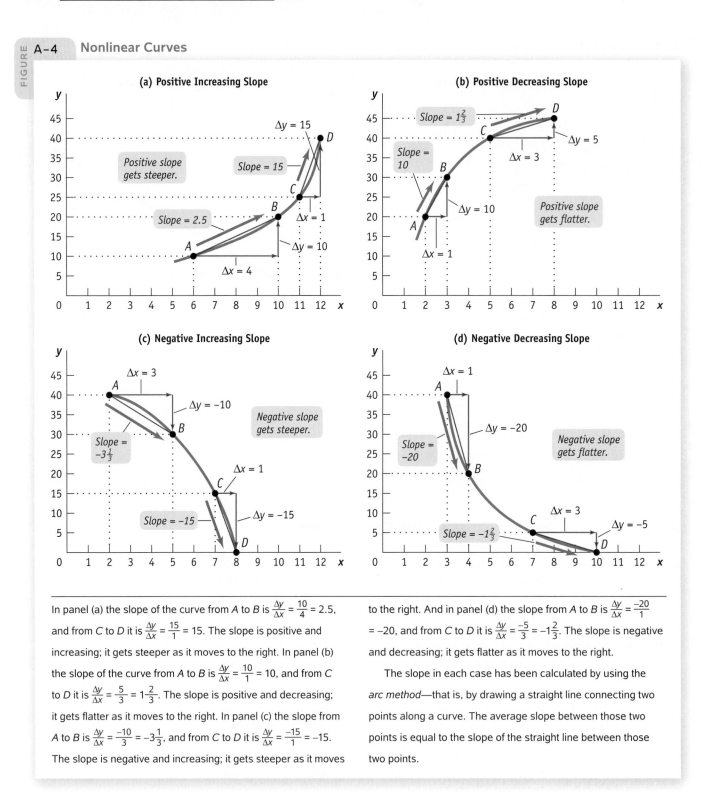

In panel (a) the slope of the curve from A to B is $\frac{\Delta y}{\Delta x} = \frac{10}{4} = 2.5$, and from C to D it is $\frac{\Delta y}{\Delta x} = \frac{15}{1} = 15$. The slope is positive and increasing; it gets steeper as it moves to the right. In panel (b) the slope of the curve from A to B is $\frac{\Delta y}{\Delta x} = \frac{10}{1} = 10$, and from C to D it is $\frac{\Delta y}{\Delta x} = \frac{5}{3} = 1\frac{2}{3}$. The slope is positive and decreasing; it gets flatter as it moves to the right. In panel (c) the slope from A to B is $\frac{\Delta y}{\Delta x} = \frac{-10}{3} = -3\frac{1}{3}$, and from C to D it is $\frac{\Delta y}{\Delta x} = \frac{-15}{1} = -15$. The slope is negative and increasing; it gets steeper as it moves

to the right. And in panel (d) the slope from A to B is $\frac{\Delta y}{\Delta x} = \frac{-20}{1} = -20$, and from C to D it is $\frac{\Delta y}{\Delta x} = \frac{-5}{3} = -1\frac{2}{3}$. The slope is negative and decreasing; it gets flatter as it moves to the right.

The slope in each case has been calculated by using the *arc method*—that is, by drawing a straight line connecting two points along a curve. The average slope between those two points is equal to the slope of the straight line between those two points.

curve that is upward sloping and gets steeper, as in panel (a), is said to have *positive increasing* slope. A curve that is upward sloping but gets flatter, as in panel (b), is said to have *positive decreasing* slope.

When we calculate the slope along these nonlinear curves, we obtain different values for the slope at different points. How the slope changes along the curve determines the curve's shape. For example, in panel (a) of Figure A-4, the slope of the curve is a positive number that steadily increases as the line moves from left to right, whereas in panel (b), the slope is a positive number that steadily decreases.

ABSOLUTE VALUE The slopes of the curves in panels (c) and (d) are negative numbers. Economists often prefer to express a negative number as its **absolute value,** which is the value of the negative number without the minus sign.

In general, we denote the absolute value of a number by two parallel bars around the number; for example, the absolute value of −4 is written as |−4| = 4. In panel (c), the absolute value of the slope steadily increases as the line moves from left to right. The curve therefore has *negative increasing* slope. And in panel (d), the absolute value of the slope of the curve steadily decreases along the curve. This curve therefore has *negative decreasing* slope.

Maximum and Minimum Points

The slope of a nonlinear curve can change from positive to negative or vice versa. When the slope of a curve changes from positive to negative, it creates what is called a *maximum* point of the curve. When the slope of a curve changes from negative to positive, it creates a *minimum* point.

Panel (a) of Figure A-5 illustrates a curve in which the slope changes from positive to negative as the line moves from left to right. When x is between 0 and 50, the slope of the curve is positive. At x equal to 50, the curve attains its highest point—the largest value of y along the curve. This point is called the **maximum** of the curve. When x exceeds 50, the slope becomes negative as the curve turns downward. Many important curves in economics, such as the curve that represents how the profit of a firm changes as it produces more output, are hill-shaped like this one.

The **absolute value** of a negative number is the value of the negative number without the minus sign.

A nonlinear curve may have a **maximum** point, the highest point along the curve. At the maximum, the slope of the curve changes from positive to negative.

A nonlinear curve may have a **minimum** point, the lowest point along the curve. At the minimum, the slope of the curve changes from negative to positive.

FIGURE A-5   **Maximum and Minimum Points**

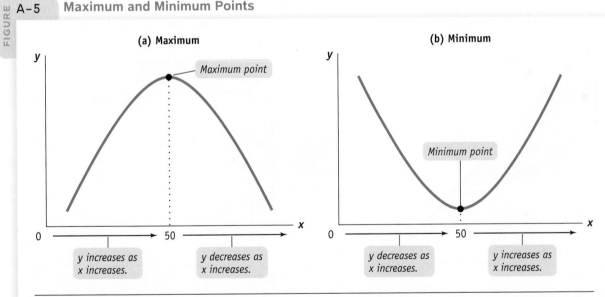

Panel (a) shows a curve with a maximum point, the point at which the slope changes from positive to negative.

Panel (b) shows a curve with a minimum point, the point at which the slope changes from negative to positive.

In contrast, the curve shown in panel (b) of Figure A-5 is U-shaped: it has a slope that changes from negative to positive. At x equal to 50, the curve reaches its lowest point—the smallest value of y along the curve. This point is called the **minimum** of the curve. Various important curves in economics, such as the curve that represents how a firm's cost per unit changes as output increases, are U–shaped like this one.

A **time-series graph** has dates on the horizontal axis and values of a variable that occurred on those dates on the vertical axis.

A **scatter diagram** shows points that correspond to actual observations of the x- and y-variables. A curve is usually fitted to the scatter of points.

Calculating the Area Below or Above a Curve

Sometimes it is useful to be able to measure the size of the area below or above a curve. To keep things simple, we'll only calculate the area below or above a linear curve.

How large is the shaded area below the linear curve in panel (a) of Figure A-6? First, note that this area has the shape of a right triangle. A *right triangle* is a triangle in which two adjacent sides form a 90° angle. We will refer to one of these sides as the *height* of the triangle and the other side as the *base* of the triangle. For our purposes, it doesn't matter which of these two sides we refer to as the base and which as the height.

Calculating the area of a right triangle is straightforward: multiply the height of the triangle by the base of the triangle, and divide the result by 2. The height of the triangle in panel (a) of Figure A-6 is 10 − 4 = 6. And the base of the triangle is 3 − 0 = 3. So the area of that triangle is

$$\frac{6 \times 3}{2} = 9$$

How about the shaded area above the linear curve in panel (b) of Figure A-6? We can use the same formula to calculate the area of this right triangle. The height of the triangle is 8 − 2 = 6. And the base of the triangle is 4 − 0 = 4. So the area of that triangle is

$$\frac{6 \times 4}{2} = 12$$

FIGURE A-6   Calculating the Area Below and Above a Linear Curve

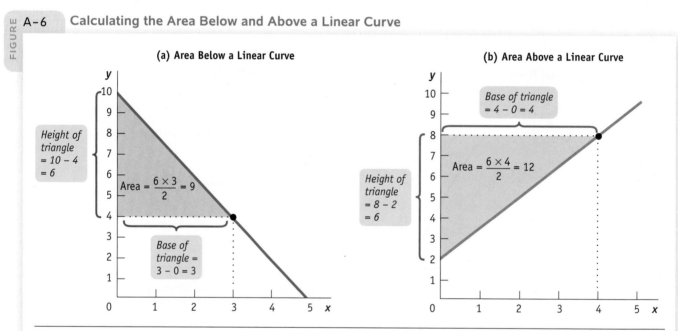

The area below or above a linear curve forms a right triangle. The area of a right triangle is calculated by multiplying the height of the triangle by the base of the triangle, and dividing the result by 2. In panel (a) the area of the shaded triangle is 9. In panel (b) the area of the shaded triangle is 12.

Graphs That Depict Numerical Information

Graphs are also used as a convenient way to summarize and display data without assuming some underlying causal relationship. Graphs that simply display numerical information are called *numerical graphs*.

Here we will consider the four most widely used types of numerical graphs: *time-series graphs*, *scatter diagrams*, *pie charts*, and *bar graphs*. These graphs are used to display real, empirical data about different economic variables and help economists and policy makers identify patterns or trends in the economy.

TIME-SERIES GRAPH You have probably seen graphs that show what happens over time to economic variables such as the unemployment rate or stock prices. A **time-series graph** has successive dates on the horizontal axis and the values of a variable that occurred on those dates on the vertical axis. For example, Figure A-7 shows real gross domestic product (GDP) per capita—a rough measure of a country's standard of living—in the United States from 1947 to late 2010. A line connecting the points that correspond to real GDP per capita for each calendar quarter during those years gives a clear idea of the overall trend in the standard of living over these years.

SCATTER DIAGRAM Figure A-8 is an example of a different kind of numerical graph. It represents information from a sample of 184 countries on the standard of living, measured by GDP per capita, and the amount of carbon emissions per capita, a measure of environmental pollution. This type of graph is a **scatter diagram.** In these graphs, each point corresponds to an actual observation of the *x*-variable and the *y*-variable. Typically, a curve is fitted to the scatter of points; that is, a curve is drawn to approximate, as closely as possible, the general relationship between the variables. Each point in Figure A-8 indicates an average resident's standard of living and his or her annual carbon emissions for a given country.

The points lying in the upper right of the graph, which show combinations of a high standard of living and high carbon emissions, represent economically advanced countries such as the United States. (The country with the highest carbon emissions, at the top of the graph, is Qatar.) Points lying in the bottom left of the graph, which show combinations of a low standard of living and low carbon emissions, represent economically less advanced countries such as Afghanistan and Sierra Leone.

The pattern of points indicates that there is a positive relationship between living standard and carbon emissions per capita:

FIGURE A-7   Time-Series Graph

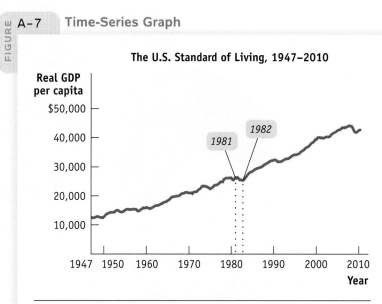

Time-series graphs show successive dates on the *x*-axis and values for a variable on the *y*-axis. This time-series graph shows real gross domestic product per capita, a measure of a country's standard of living, in the United States from 1947 to late 2010.

Source: Bureau of Economic Analysis.

FIGURE A-8   Scatter Diagram

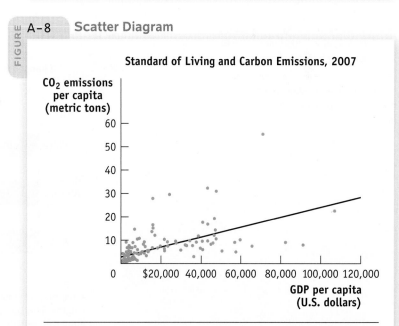

In a scatter diagram, each point represents the corresponding values of the *x*- and *y*-variables for a given observation. Here, each point indicates the GDP per capita and the amount of carbon emissions per capita for a given country for a sample of 184 countries. The upward-sloping fitted line here is the best approximation of the general relationship between the two variables.

Source: World Bank.

A-9   **Pie Chart**

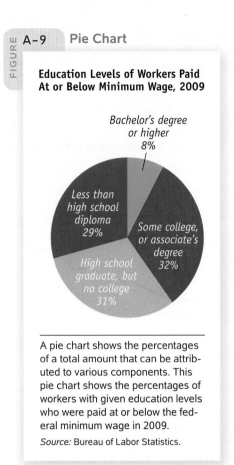

**Education Levels of Workers Paid
At or Below Minimum Wage, 2009**

*Bachelor's degree
or higher*
8%

*Less than
high school
diploma
29%*

*Some college,
or associate's
degree
32%*

*High school
graduate, but
no college
31%*

A pie chart shows the percentages
of a total amount that can be attributed to various components. This
pie chart shows the percentages of
workers with given education levels
who were paid at or below the federal minimum wage in 2009.

Source: Bureau of Labor Statistics.

A **pie chart** shows how some total is
divided among its components, usually expressed in percentages.

A **bar graph** uses bars of varying
height or length to show the comparative sizes of different observations of
a variable.

on the whole, people create more pollution in countries with
a higher standard of living. As you can see, the fitted line in
Figure A-8 is upward sloping, indicating the underlying positive relationship between the two variables.

Scatter diagrams are often used to show how a general relationship can be inferred from a set of data.

PIE CHART A **pie chart** shows the share of a total amount
that is accounted for by various components, usually expressed in percentages. Figure A-9 is a pie chart that depicts
the education levels of workers who in 2009 were paid the
federal minimum wage or less. As you can see, the majority
of workers paid at or below the minimum wage had no college degree. Only 8% of workers who were paid at or below
the minimum wage had a bachelor's degree or higher.

BAR GRAPH A graph that uses bars of various heights or
lengths to indicate values of a variable is a **bar graph**. In the
bar graph in Figure A-10, the bars show the percent change
in the number of unemployed workers in the United States
from 2009 to 2010, separately for White, Black or African-
American, and Asian workers. Exact values of the variable
that is being measured may be written at the end of the bar,
as in this figure. For instance, the number of unemployed
Black or African-American workers in the United States increased by 9.4% between 2009 and 2010. But even without
the precise values, comparing the heights or lengths of the
bars can give useful insight into the relative magnitudes of
the different values of the variable.

A-10   **Bar Graph**

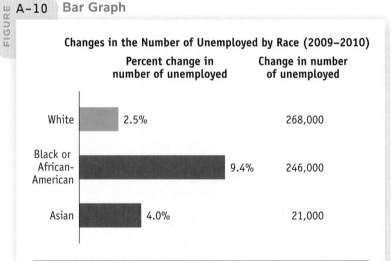

Changes in the Number of Unemployed by Race (2009–2010)

	Percent change in number of unemployed	Change in number of unemployed
White	2.5%	268,000
Black or African-American	9.4%	246,000
Asian	4.0%	21,000

A bar graph measures a variable by using bars of various heights or
lengths. This bar graph shows the percent change in the number of unemployed workers between 2009 and 2010, separately for White, Black
or African-American, and Asian workers.

Source: Bureau of Labor Statistics.

APPENDIX B Macroeconomic Data

This appendix includes the following data tables:

Table 1.
MACROECONOMIC DATA FOR THE UNITED STATES 1929–2012[1]

	1929	1933	1939	1945	1950	1955	1960
Nominal GDP and Its Components							
1. + Consumer spending (C)	77.4	45.9	67.2	120	192.2	258.7	331.6
2. + Investment spending (I)	17.2	2.3	10.2	12.4	56.5	73.8	86.5
3. + Government purchases of goods and services (G)	9.6	8.9	15.2	96.6	50.7	93.3	121
4. + Exports (X)	5.9	2	4	6.8	12.4	17.7	27
5. − Imports (IM)	5.6	1.9	3.1	7.5	11.6	17.2	22.8
6. = **Gross domestic product (GDP)**	**104.6**	**57.2**	**93.5**	**228.2**	**300.2**	**426.2**	**543.3**
7. + Income from abroad earned by Americans	1.1	0.4	0.7	0.8	2.2	3.5	4.9
8. − Income paid to foreigners	0.4	0.1	0.3	0.5	0.7	1.1	1.8
9. = **Gross national product**	**105.3**	**57.5**	**93.9**	**228.5**	**301.7**	**428.6**	**546.4**
10. National income	94.2	49	82.5	201.4	267	377.6	479.9
11. Government transfers	1.2	1.7	2.5	5.6	14	15.7	25.7
12. Taxes	1.7	0.8	1.5	19.4	18.9	32.9	46.1
13. Disposable income	83.5	46.4	72.1	156.3	215	291.7	376.5
14. Private savings	3.9	−0.4	3.9	35.2	20	28.2	37.8
Real GDP and Growth Measures							
15. Real GDP (billions of 2009 dollars)	1055.6	777.6	1162.6	2215.9	2181.9	2736.4	3105.8
16. Real GDP growth (percent change from previous year)	-	−1.3	8	−1	8.7	7.1	2.6
17. Real GDP per capita (2009 dollars)	8661	6187	8873	15836	14384	16557	17182
18. Real GDP per capita growth (percent change from previous year)	-	−1.8	7.1	−2.0	6.9	5.3	0.5
Prices and Inflation							
19. Consumer Price Index (1982 − 1984 = 100)	17.1	13.0	13.9	18.0	24.1	26.8	29.6
20. CPI inflation rate	-	−5.1	−1.4	2.3	1.3	-0.4	1.7
21. Producer Price Index (all commodities, 1982 = 100)	16.4	11.4	13.3	18.2	27.3	29.4	31.7
22. PPI inflation rate (%)		1.8	−2.2	1.7	3.8	0.3	0.0
23. GDP deflator (2009 = 100)	9.9	7.4	8.0	10.3	13.8	15.6	17.5
24. GDP deflator inflation rate (%)		−2.8	−0.9	2.6	1.2	1.7	1.4
Population and Employment							
25. Population (thousands)	121,878	125,690	131,028	139,928	151,684	165,872	180,639
26. Labor force (thousands)[2]	49,180	51,590	55,230	53,860	62,122	64,964	69,659
27. Unemployed (thousands)[2]	1,550	12,830	9,480	1,040	3,230	2,834	3,874
28. Unemployment rate	3.2	24.9	17.2	1.9	5.2	4.4	5.6
Government Finance and Money							
29. Government (federal, state and local) budget balance	2.1	−0.9	−0.8	−31	2.2	1.6	2.8
30. Budget balance (percent of GDP)	2.0	−1.6	−0.9	−13.6	0.7	0.4	0.5
31. M1	-	-	-	-	-	-	140.3
32. M2	-	-	-	-	-	-	304.3
33. Federal funds rate (yearly average)	-	-	-	-	-	1.8	3.2
International Trade							
34. Current account balance	0.8	0.2	1	−1.3	−1.8	0.4	3.2

Sources: Bureau of Economic Analysis, Bureau of Labor Statistics, Federal Reserve Bank of St. Louis.

1. Data in billions of current dollars unless otherwise stated. Only select dates shown for 1929 through 1965; annual data supplied for 1965 through 2012.
2. Until 1947, includes workers 14 years and older; 1948 and after, includes workers 16 years and older.

1965	1966	1967	1968	1969	1970	1971	1972	1973	1974	1975
443.6	480.6	507.4	557.4	604.5	647.7	701	769.4	851.1	932	1032.8
129.6	144.2	142.7	156.9	173.6	170.1	196.8	228.1	266.9	274.5	257.3
164.9	186.4	208.1	226.8	240.4	254.2	269.3	288.2	306.4	343.1	382.9
37.1	40.9	43.5	47.9	51.9	59.7	63	70.8	95.3	126.7	138.7
31.5	37.1	39.9	46.6	50.5	55.8	62.3	74.2	91.2	127.5	122.7
743.7	**815**	**861.7**	**942.5**	**1019.9**	**1075.9**	**1167.8**	**1282.4**	**1428.5**	**1548.8**	**1688.9**
7.9	8.1	8.7	10.1	11.8	12.8	14	16.3	23.5	29.8	28
2.6	3	3.3	4	5.7	6.4	6.4	7.7	10.9	14.3	15
749	**820.1**	**867.1**	**948.6**	**1026**	**1082.3**	**1175.4**	**1291**	**1441.1**	**1564.3**	**1701.9**
660.3	719.7	760.2	832.1	899.5	940.1	1017	1123	1257	1350.8	1451.1
36.2	39.6	48	56.1	62.3	74.7	88.1	97.9	112.6	133.3	170
57.7	66.4	73	87	104.5	103.1	101.7	123.6	132.4	151	147.6
513.2	554.2	592.8	643.8	695.8	761.5	830.4	899.9	1006.1	1098.3	1219.3
58.3	61.4	72.2	72.1	75	96.1	110.1	109.2	131.8	141.7	159
3972.9	4234.9	4351.2	4564.7	4707.9	4717.7	4873	5128.8	5418.2	5390.2	5379.5
6.5	6.6	2.7	4.9	3.1	0.2	3.3	5.2	5.6	−0.5	−0.2
20442	21541	21893	22739	23222	23003	23463	24432	25565	25200	24907
5.2	5.4	1.6	3.9	2.1	−0.9	2.0	4.1	4.6	−1.4	−1.2
31.5	32.4	33.4	34.8	36.7	38.8	40.5	41.8	44.4	49.3	53.8
1.6	2.9	3.1	4.2	5.5	5.7	4.4	3.2	6.2	11.0	9.1
32.3	33.3	33.4	34.2	35.6	36.9	38.1	39.8	45.0	53.5	58.4
2.2	3.1	0.3	2.4	4.1	3.7	3.3	4.5	13.1	18.9	9.2
18.7	19.2	19.8	20.6	21.7	22.8	24.0	25.0	26.4	28.7	31.4
1.8	2.8	2.9	4.3	4.9	5.3	5.1	4.3	5.4	9.0	9.3
194,250	196,508	198,664	200,664	202,649	204,982	207,589	209,838	211,857	213,815	215,891
74,424	75,745	77,348	78,710	80,705	82,796	84,376	87,011	89,411	91,976	93,770
3,354	2,867	2,972	2,797	2,830	4,127	5,022	4,876	4,359	5,173	7,940
4.5	3.8	3.8	3.6	3.5	5.0	6.0	5.6	4.9	5.6	8.5
−1.4	−1.8	−14.8	−9.5	−1	−31.8	−50.2	−40.5	−28	−38.3	−102.5
−0.2	−0.2	−1.7	−1.0	−0.1	−3.0	−4.3	−3.2	−2.0	−2.5	−6.1
163.5	171.0	177.7	190.1	201.4	209.1	223.2	239.0	256.4	269.2	281.4
442.5	471.4	503.6	545.3	578.7	601.4	674.4	758.1	831.8	880.7	963.7
4.1	5.1	4.2	5.7	8.2	7.2	4.7	4.4	8.7	10.5	5.8
6.2	3.8	3.5	1.5	1.6	3.7	0.3	-4	8.9	6	19.8

(continued on next page)

	1976	1977	1978	1979	1980	1981	1982
Nominal GDP and Its Components							
1. + Consumer spending (C)	1150.2	1276.7	1426.2	1589.5	1754.6	1937.5	2073.9
2. + Investment spending (I)	323.2	396.6	478.4	539.7	530.1	631.2	581
3. + Government purchases of goods and services (G)	405.8	435.8	477.4	525.5	590.8	654.7	710
4. + Exports (X)	149.5	159.4	186.9	230.1	280.8	305.2	283.2
5. – Imports (IM)	151.1	182.4	212.3	252.7	293.8	317.8	303.2
6. = Gross domestic product (GDP)	**1877.6**	**2086**	**2356.6**	**2632.1**	**2862.5**	**3210.9**	**3345**
7. + Income from abroad earned by Americans	32.4	37.2	46.3	68.3	79.1	92	101
8. – Income paid to foreigners	15.5	16.9	24.7	36.4	44.9	59.1	64.5
9. = Gross national product	**1894.5**	**2106.3**	**2378.2**	**2664**	**2896.7**	**3243.8**	**3381.5**
10. National income	1614.8	1798.7	2029.9	2248.2	2426.8	2722.1	2840.4
11. Government transfers	184	194.2	209.6	235.3	279.5	318.4	354.8
12. Taxes	172.3	197.5	229.4	268.7	298.9	345.2	354.1
13. Disposable income	1325.8	1456.7	1630.1	1809.3	2018	2250.7	2424.7
14. Private savings	147.3	148.2	166.6	177.5	213.2	252.5	277.7
Real GDP and Growth Measures							
15. Real GDP (billions of 2009 dollars)	5669.3	5930.6	6260.4	6459.2	6443.4	6610.6	6484.3
16. Real GDP growth (percent change from previous year)	5.4	4.6	5.6	3.2	–0.2	2.6	–1.9
17. Real GDP per capita (2009 dollars)	25996	26922	28120	28694	28295	28741	27923
18. Real GDP per capita growth (percent change from previous year)	4.4	3.6	4.4	2.0	–1.4	1.6	–2.8
Prices and Inflation							
19. Consumer Price Index (1982 – 1984 = 100)	56.9	60.6	65.2	72.6	82.4	90.9	96.5
20. CPI inflation rate	5.8	6.5	7.6	11.3	13.5	10.3	6.2
21. Producer Price Index (all commodities, 1982 = 100)	61.1	64.9	69.9	78.7	89.8	98.0	100.0
22. PPI inflation rate (%)	4.6	6.2	7.7	12.6	14.1	9.1	2.0
23. GDP deflator (2009 = 100) (%)	33.1	35.2	37.6	40.8	44.4	48.6	51.6
24. GDP deflator inflation rate (%)	5.5	6.2	7.0	8.3	9.0	9.3	6.2
Population and Employment							
25. Population (thousands)	217,999	220,193	222,525	225,003	227,622	229,916	232,128
26. Labor force (thousands)[2]	96,151	98,984	102,233	104,961	106,974	108,676	110,244
27. Unemployed (thousands)[2]	7,398	6,967	6,187	6,135	7,671	8,276	10,715
28. Unemployment rate	7.7	7.0	6.1	5.8	7.2	7.6	9.7
Government Finance and Money							
29. Government (federal, state and local) budget balance	–77.1	–63.5	–46.4	–36.3	–80.9	–81.7	–169.7
30. Budget balance (percent of GDP)	–4.1	–3.0	–2.0	–1.4	–2.8	–2.5	–5.1
31. M1	297.2	320.0	346.3	372.7	395.7	424.9	453.0
32. M2	1086.6	1221.4	1322.4	1425.8	1540.4	1679.6	1831.4
33. Federal funds rate (yearly average)	5.1	5.5	7.9	11.2	13.4	16.4	12.3
International Trade							
34. Current account balance	7.1	–10.9	–12.6	–1.2	8.5	3.4	–3.3

Sources: Bureau of Economic Analysis, Bureau of Labor Statistics, Federal Reserve Bank of St. Louis.

1. Data in billions of current dollars unless otherwise stated. Only select dates shown for 1929 through 1965; annual data supplied for 1965 through 2012.
2. Until 1947, includes workers 14 years and older; 1948 and after, includes workers 16 years and older.

1983	1984	1985	1986	1987	1988	1989	1990	1991	1992	1993
2286.5	2498.2	2722.7	2898.4	3092.1	3346.9	3592.8	3825.6	3960.2	4215.7	4471
637.5	820.1	829.6	849.1	892.2	937	999.7	993.5	944.3	1013	1106.8
765.7	825.2	908.4	974.5	1030.8	1078.2	1151.9	1238.4	1298.2	1345.4	1366.1
277	302.4	303.2	321	363.9	444.6	504.3	551.9	594.9	633	654.8
328.6	405.1	417.2	452.9	508.7	554	591	629.7	623.5	667.8	720
3638.1	**4040.7**	**4346.7**	**4590.1**	**4870.2**	**5252.6**	**5657.7**	**5979.6**	**6174**	**6539.3**	**6878.7**
101.9	121.9	112.7	111.3	123.3	152.1	177.7	188.8	168.4	152.1	155.6
64.8	85.6	87.3	94.4	105.8	129.5	152.9	154.2	136.8	121	123.6
3675.2	**4077**	**4372.1**	**4607**	**4887.7**	**5275.2**	**5682.5**	**6014.2**	**6205.6**	**6570.4**	**6910.7**
3060.5	3444	3684.2	3848.2	4119.2	4493.4	4782.2	5036.1	5186.1	5499.7	5754.8
383.7	400.1	424.9	451	467.6	496.5	542.6	594.9	665.9	745.8	790.8
352.3	377.4	417.3	437.2	489.1	504.9	566.1	592.7	586.6	610.5	646.5
2617.4	2903.9	3098.5	3287.9	3466.3	3770.4	4052.1	4311.8	4484.5	4800.3	5000.2
247	312.1	265.1	269.4	252.1	294.7	316.5	335.4	365.9	426	367.6
6784.7	7277.2	7585.7	7852.1	8123.9	8465.4	8777	8945.4	8938.9	9256.7	9510.8
4.6	7.3	4.2	3.5	3.5	4.2	3.7	1.9	−0.1	3.6	2.7
28953	30784	31805	32624	33453	34544	35479	35756	35258	36029	36540
3.7	6.3	3.3	2.6	2.5	3.3	2.7	0.8	−1.4	2.2	1.4
99.6	103.9	107.6	109.6	113.6	118.3	124.0	130.7	136.2	140.3	144.5
3.2	4.3	3.6	1.9	3.6	4.1	4.8	5.4	4.2	3.0	3.0
101.3	103.7	103.2	100.2	102.8	106.9	112.2	116.3	116.5	117.2	118.9
1.3	2.4	−0.5	−2.9	2.6	4.0	5.0	3.7	0.2	0.6	1.5
53.6	55.5	57.3	58.5	59.9	62.0	64.5	66.8	69.1	70.6	72.3
3.9	3.5	3.2	2.0	2.6	3.5	3.9	3.7	3.3	2.3	2.4
234,247	236,307	238,416	240,593	242,751	244,968	247,286	250,047	253,392	256,777	260,146
111,515	113,532	115,467	117,846	119,853	121,671	123,851	125,857	126,352	128,099	129,185
10,694	8,529	8,313	8,245	7,414	6,697	6,524	7,061	8,640	9,611	8,927
9.6	7.5	7.2	7.0	6.2	5.5	5.3	5.6	6.8	7.5	6.9
−203.7	−171.4	−175.4	−192.2	−151.1	−140.4	−149.2	−207.4	−271.3	−370.2	−349
−5.6	−4.2	−4.0	−4.2	−3.1	−2.7	−2.6	−3.5	−4.4	−5.7	−5.1
503.2	538.6	587.0	666.4	743.5	774.8	782.2	810.6	859.0	965.9	1078.5
2054.8	2219.3	2416.7	2613.5	2783.8	2933.4	3056.1	3223.6	3342.2	3403.6	3438.0
9.1	10.2	8.1	6.8	6.7	7.6	9.2	8.1	5.7	3.5	3.0
−35.1	−90.1	−114.3	−142.7	−154.1	−115.7	−92.4	−74.9	7.9	−45.6	−78.6

(continued on next page)

	1994	1995	1996	1997	1998	1999	2000
Nominal GDP and Its Components							
1. + Consumer spending (C)	4741	4984.2	5268.1	5560.7	5903	6316.9	6801.6
2. + Investment spending (I)	1256.5	1317.5	1432.1	1595.6	1735.3	1884.2	2033.8
3. + Government purchases of goods and services (G)	1403.7	1452.2	1496.4	1554.2	1613.5	1726	1834.4
4. + Exports (X)	720.9	812.8	867.6	953.8	952.9	989.2	1094.3
5. − Imports (IM)	813.4	902.6	964	1055.8	1115.7	1250.6	1474.4
6. = **Gross domestic product (GDP)**	**7308.7**	**7664**	**8100.2**	**8608.5**	**9089.1**	**9665.7**	**10289.7**
7. + Income from abroad earned by Americans	184.5	229.8	246.4	280.1	286.8	321.4	382.7
8. − Income paid to foreigners	160.7	201.1	214.6	256	268.5	294.3	345.7
9. = **Gross national product**	**7332.5**	**7692.7**	**8132**	**8632.6**	**9107.4**	**9692.8**	**10326.7**
10. National income	6140.2	6479.5	6899.4	7380.4	7857.3	8324.4	8907
11. Government transfers	826.4	878.9	924.1	949.2	977.9	1021.6	1083
12. Taxes	690.5	743.9	832	926.2	1026.4	1107.5	1232.3
13. Disposable income	5244.2	5532.6	5829.9	6148.9	6561.3	6876.3	7400.5
14. Private savings	331.4	352.9	345.2	352.2	405.3	293	297.9
Real GDP and Growth Measures							
15. Real GDP (billions of 2009 dollars)	9894.7	10163.7	10549.5	11022.9	11513.4	12071.4	12565.2
16. Real GDP growth (percent change from previous year)	4	2.7	3.8	4.5	4.4	4.8	4.1
17. Real GDP per capita (2009 dollars)	37557	38125	39114	40383	41692	43216	44495
18. Real GDP per capita growth (percent change from previous year)	2.8	1.5	2.6	3.2	3.2	3.7	3.0
Prices and Inflation							
19. Consumer Price Index (1982 − 1984 = 100)	148.2	152.4	156.9	160.5	163.0	166.6	172.2
20. CPI inflation rate (%)	2.6	2.8	3.0	2.3	1.6	2.2	3.4
21. Producer Price Index (all commodities, 1982 = 100)	120.5	124.8	127.7	127.6	124.4	125.5	132.7
22. PPI inflation rate (%)	1.3	3.6	2.3	−0.1	−2.5	0.9	5.7
23. GDP deflator (2009 = 100)	73.9	75.4	76.8	78.1	78.9	80.1	81.9
24. GDP deflator inflation rate	2.1	2.1	1.8	1.7	1.1	1.4	2.3
Population and Employment							
25. Population (thousands)	263,325	266,458	269,581	272,822	276,022	279,195	282,296
26. Labor force (thousands)[2]	131,047	132,315	133,951	136,301	137,680	139,380	142,586
27. Unemployed (thousands)[2]	7,976	7,407	7,231	6,729	6,204	5,879	5,685
28. Unemployment rate	6.1	5.6	5.4	4.9	4.5	4.2	4.0
Government Finance and Money							
29. Government (federal, state and local) budget balance	−280.7	−272.4	−191	−89.5	18.1	75.8	165.8
30. Budget balance (percent of GDP)	−3.8	−3.6	−2.4	−1.0	0.2	0.8	1.6
31. M1	1145.2	1143.1	1106.5	1070.1	1080.6	1102.3	1103.6
32. M2	3482.1	3552.7	3722.8	3909.8	4188.9	4496.9	4769.3
33. Federal funds rate (yearly average)	4.2	5.8	5.3	5.5	5.4	5.0	6.2
International Trade							
34. Current account balance	−114.7	−105.1	−114.1	−129.3	−204.5	−291.9	−409.1

Sources: Bureau of Economic Analysis, Bureau of Labor Statistics, Federal Reserve Bank of St. Louis.

1. Data in billions of current dollars unless otherwise stated. Only select dates shown for 1929 through 1965; annual data supplied for 1965 through 2012.
2. Until 1947, includes workers 14 years and older; 1948 and after, includes workers 16 years and older.

2001	2002	2003	2004	2005	2006	2007	2008	2009	2010	2011	2012
7106.9	7385.3	7764.4	8257.8	8790.3	9297.5	9744.4	10005.5	9842.9	10201.9	10711.8	11149.6
1928.6	1925	2027.9	2276.7	2527.1	2680.6	2643.7	2424.8	1878.1	2100.8	2232.1	2475.2
1958.8	2094.9	2220.8	2357.4	2493.7	2642.2	2801.9	3003.2	3089.1	3174	3158.7	3167
1028.8	1004.7	1043.4	1183.1	1310.4	1478.5	1665.7	1843.1	1583.8	1843.5	2101.2	2195.9
1397.8	1429.7	1544.3	1797.9	2026.1	2240.9	2375.5	2556.4	1976	2362	2669.9	2743.1
10625.3	**10980.2**	**11512.2**	**12277**	**13095.4**	**13857.9**	**14480.3**	**14720.3**	**14417.9**	**14958.3**	**15533.8**	**16244.6**
325.3	315.8	356.1	451.4	575.8	724.2	875.5	856.8	643.7	720	802.8	818.6
273.5	267.2	288.1	361.4	482.3	655.7	749.1	683.8	496.5	514.1	542.1	565.7
10677.1	**11028.8**	**11580.2**	**12367**	**13188.9**	**13926.4**	**14606.7**	**14893.3**	**14565.1**	**15164.2**	**15794.5**	**16497.5**
9184.6	9436.8	9865.1	10541.9	11240.8	12005.6	12322.3	12430.8	12124.5	12739.5	13395.7	13971.6
1188.1	1280.3	1342.9	1416.7	1512	1609.6	1722.8	1884	2140.2	2276.9	2306.9	2358.3
1234.8	1050.3	1000.9	1046	1208.5	1352.1	1487.9	1435.2	1144.9	1191.5	1404	1498
7752.3	8099.2	8486.7	9003.2	9401.8	10037.7	10507.9	10995.4	10937.2	11243.7	11787.4	12245.8
331.2	403.9	410.8	413.2	242.7	336.9	317.2	551.3	670.7	634.2	668.2	687.4
12684.4	12909.7	13270	13774	14235.6	14615.2	14876.8	14833.6	14417.9	14779.4	15052.4	15470.7
1	1.8	2.8	3.8	3.4	2.7	1.8	−0.3	−2.8	2.5	1.8	2.8
44472	44832	45660	46968	48094	48910	49311	48708	46927	47710	48239	49226
−0.1	0.8	1.8	2.9	2.4	1.7	0.8	−1.2	−3.7	1.7	1.1	2.0
177.1	179.9	184.0	188.9	195.3	201.6	207.342	215.303	214.537	218.056	224.939	229.594
2.8	1.6	2.3	2.7	3.4	3.2	2.8	3.8	−0.4	1.6	3.2	2.1
134.2	131.1	138.1	146.7	157.4	164.8	172.7	189.6	172.9	184.7	201.1	202.2
1.1	−2.3	5.3	6.2	7.3	4.7	4.8	9.8	−8.8	6.8	8.9	0.5
83.8	85.1	86.8	89.1	92.0	94.8	97.3	99.2	100.0	101.2	103.2	105.0
2.3	1.5	2.0	2.7	3.2	3.1	2.7	2.0	0.8	1.2	2.0	1.7
285,216	288,019	290,733	293,389	296,115	298,930	301,903	304,718	307,374	309,733	311,943	314,184
143,769	144,856	146,500	147,380	149,289	151,409	153,123	154,322	154,189	153,888	153,619	154,966
6,830	8,375	8,770	8,140	7,579	6,991	7,073	8,948	14,295	14,810	13,737	12,497
4.8	5.8	6.0	5.5	5.1	4.6	4.6	5.8	9.3	9.6	8.9	8.1
−51.3	−391.9	−524.9	−508.1	−372	−267.5	−339.4	−800.2	−1521.7	−1566.8	−1461.3	−1362.3
−0.5	−3.6	−4.6	−4.1	−2.8	−1.9	−2.3	−5.4	−10.6	−10.5	−9.4	−8.4
1140.3	1196.7	1273.8	1344.3	1371.6	1374.7	1372.6	1434.9	1637.7	1742.3	2010.0	2310.9
5179.4	5562.4	5950.1	6236.0	6504.3	6845.3	7267.1	7763.7	8385.3	8593.4	9221.3	10006.9
3.9	1.7	1.1	1.4	3.2	5.0	5.0	1.9	0.2	0.2	0.1	0.1
−389.8	−449.9	−513.5	−621.7	−737.1	−795.7	−709.1	−678.5	−381.2	−454.5	−457	−439

Table 2.
MACROECONOMIC DATA FOR SELECT COUNTRIES
GDP (Billions of U.S. Dollars)

Country	1985	1986	1987	1988	1989	1990	1991	1992	1993
Argentina	88.18	106.04	108.72	127.34	81.70	141.33	189.58	228.76	236.49
Australia	176.88	183.57	216.18	274.38	310.98	328.20	328.79	321.64	312.89
Austria	68.03	96.53	120.71	132.41	132.06	165.26	172.78	193.52	188.39
Bangladesh	21.34	22.37	24.68	26.64	29.34	30.50	31.43	31.44	32.95
Belgium	85.76	118.88	147.79	160.47	162.45	203.31	208.53	231.79	222.26
Brazil	253.08	293.58	319.55	356.98	490.05	507.78	445.24	426.52	478.62
Bulgaria	27.39	24.24	28.10	45.92	46.77	20.62	2.02	8.20	4.45
Canada	355.71	368.87	421.53	498.16	555.52	582.74	598.20	579.52	563.68
Chile	16.49	17.72	20.90	24.64	28.39	31.56	36.43	44.47	47.69
China	307.02	297.59	323.97	404.15	451.31	390.28	409.17	488.22	613.22
Colombia	48.68	48.75	50.75	54.71	55.17	56.19	57.54	68.75	77.85
Cyprus	2.43	3.09	3.71	4.27	4.56	5.59	5.77	6.91	6.61
Czech Republic	n/a	n/a	n/a	n/a	n/a	n/a	n/a	n/a	n/a
Denmark	61.20	86.37	107.37	113.23	110.06	135.84	136.70	150.20	140.63
Dominican Republic	6.49	7.88	8.30	7.60	8.58	7.99	9.79	11.49	12.95
Ecuador	16.18	11.87	11.10	10.55	10.36	10.52	11.80	12.90	15.07
Egypt	46.45	51.43	73.57	88.00	109.71	91.38	46.06	42.01	47.10
Estonia	n/a	n/a	n/a	n/a	n/a	n/a	n/a	n/a	1.73
Finland	55.25	72.33	90.12	107.26	116.73	139.12	125.66	110.72	87.39
France	547.90	761.35	923.68	1,004.44	1,009.84	1,248.56	1,249.22	1,374.07	1,292.12
Germany	639.70	913.64	1,136.93	1,225.73	1,216.80	1,547.03	1,815.06	2,066.73	2,005.56
Ghana	5.33	6.03	4.76	5.15	5.94	6.53	6.85	6.66	5.97
Greece	45.13	53.10	61.78	71.95	74.56	92.20	99.42	109.56	102.61
Guatemala	10.39	5.62	6.50	7.04	8.12	7.07	8.70	9.60	10.46
Hungary	21.14	24.35	26.77	29.29	29.90	33.89	34.27	38.19	39.57
Iceland	2.94	3.93	5.44	6.02	5.59	6.36	6.80	6.97	6.12
India	229.56	252.45	278.20	304.46	302.14	325.93	289.36	291.86	285.33
Ireland	20.99	28.14	33.36	36.55	37.70	47.77	48.42	54.44	50.44
Israel	25.32	31.17	37.23	46.06	46.81	55.09	62.10	69.03	69.19
Italy	437.10	619.08	777.01	860.86	895.34	1,135.54	1,198.99	1,271.91	1,022.66
Jamaica	2.16	2.57	2.90	3.46	4.01	5.06	4.75	4.25	5.92
Japan	1,352.06	2,003.32	2,429.60	2,950.00	2,951.77	3,030.05	3,464.93	3,781.78	4,340.89
Kenya	8.75	10.39	11.39	11.81	11.71	12.18	11.50	11.33	7.87
Korea	98.50	113.74	143.38	192.11	236.23	270.41	315.58	338.17	372.21
Latvia	n/a	n/a	n/a	n/a	n/a	n/a	n/a	1.55	2.47
Lithuania	n/a	n/a	n/a	n/a	n/a	n/a	n/a	1.99	2.81
Luxembourg	4.57	6.65	8.26	9.36	9.96	12.71	13.77	15.42	15.81
Malaysia	31.77	28.24	32.18	35.27	38.85	44.03	49.88	60.05	67.90
Mexico	211.52	146.45	160.60	196.48	239.44	282.56	338.74	392.84	436.13
Netherlands	133.17	185.60	226.44	241.38	238.18	295.46	303.46	334.65	324.39
New Zealand	22.38	27.23	36.29	44.67	43.07	44.68	42.79	40.62	43.94
Nigeria	25.97	20.56	21.91	24.31	23.49	31.48	28.34	25.52	15.79
Norway	64.26	77.20	92.45	100.06	100.77	117.62	119.67	128.32	118.17
Peru	17.21	25.82	42.64	33.73	41.63	28.98	34.55	35.95	34.82
Philippines	30.73	29.87	33.20	37.89	42.65	44.16	45.32	52.98	54.37
Poland	70.78	73.68	63.71	68.61	66.90	62.08	80.45	88.71	90.37
Portugal	26.78	37.25	46.61	54.52	58.82	78.13	88.43	106.34	93.57
Romania	47.80	51.77	57.89	59.93	53.69	38.24	28.85	19.58	26.36
Russia	n/a	n/a	n/a	n/a	n/a	n/a	n/a	85.59	183.82
Saudi Arabia	103.89	86.95	85.70	88.26	95.34	116.78	131.34	136.30	132.15
Singapore	18.46	18.73	21.55	26.48	31.41	38.84	45.19	52.01	60.47
South Africa	57.27	65.42	85.79	92.24	95.98	112.00	120.24	130.53	130.45
Spain	176.69	244.48	309.75	363.91	401.39	520.71	560.80	613.02	514.95
Sweden	106.38	140.79	171.61	193.88	204.45	244.55	257.90	267.17	202.04
Switzerland	99.47	142.60	178.58	193.20	186.53	238.22	241.00	250.98	244.09
Thailand	38.90	43.10	50.54	61.67	72.25	85.64	96.19	109.43	121.80
Turkey	90.38	101.80	117.18	122.13	144.03	202.38	202.72	213.58	242.14
Ukraine	n/a	n/a	n/a	n/a	n/a	n/a	n/a	20.78	32.71
United Arab Emirates	27.35	21.67	23.80	24.19	27.92	35.99	33.19	33.49	36.72
United Kingdom	468.96	570.88	702.54	852.40	861.29	1,017.79	1,059.26	1,098.30	982.62
United States	4,217.48	4,460.05	4,736.35	5,100.43	5,482.13	5,800.53	5,992.10	6,342.30	6,667.33
Vietnam	15.00	33.87	42.05	23.23	6.29	6.47	7.64	9.87	13.18

Sources: International Monetary Fund, World Economic Outlook Database, April 2013.

1994	1995	1996	1997	1998	1999	2000	2001	2002	2003	2004
257.43	258.02	272.22	292.99	299.08	283.76	284.41	268.96	97.40	127.55	151.82
356.64	382.25	428.03	428.44	382.28	413.57	399.60	376.65	423.69	539.17	654.98
201.64	238.55	234.23	207.13	212.44	211.21	192.63	191.84	208.27	254.43	291.81
35.80	39.58	41.52	43.39	44.76	46.53	47.05	47.19	49.56	54.48	59.12
242.62	284.79	275.17	249.76	255.57	254.38	233.35	232.69	253.69	312.29	362.16
596.76	769.74	840.05	871.52	841.30	573.12	644.28	554.41	505.71	552.24	663.55
7.82	13.11	9.90	10.37	12.85	12.98	12.94	13.88	16.03	20.71	25.32
564.48	590.50	613.78	637.53	616.78	661.25	739.66	732.90	752.63	887.81	1018.12
55.16	71.35	75.77	82.81	79.37	72.99	78.00	71.29	70.11	76.10	99.29
559.22	727.95	856.08	952.65	1,019.48	1,083.28	1198.48	1324.81	1453.83	1640.96	1931.65
97.87	110.81	120.00	112.70	109.12	96.89	99.90	98.21	97.82	94.70	118.80
7.45	9.25	9.35	8.9	9.56	9.78	9.20	9.61	10.48	13.18	15.66
n/a	55.26	62.01	57.14	61.85	60.19	58.80	64.38	78.43	95.29	113.98
153.59	181.99	184.44	170.44	173.65	173.94	160.08	160.48	173.88	212.62	244.73
13.99	15.52	17.07	19.19	20.08	21.48	23.66	24.51	24.91	20.21	21.56
18.59	20.22	21.29	23.66	23.28	16.69	18.69	24.79	28.77	32.39	37.21
51.88	60.16	67.63	75.87	84.82	89.94	99.16	95.40	87.51	81.38	78.80
2.42	3.78	4.73	5.05	5.59	5.71	5.70	6.25	7.35	9.86	12.04
100.99	130.85	128.28	123.07	129.84	130.39	122.15	124.75	135.66	164.57	189.31
1,366.16	1,572.38	1,574.32	1,425.80	1,474.24	1,458.37	1330.22	1339.49	1457.14	1795.64	2058.41
2,151.03	2,524.95	2,439.35	2,163.23	2,187.48	2,146.43	1891.93	1882.51	2013.69	2428.45	2729.92
5.45	6.46	6.93	6.89	7.48	7.72	7.36	7.44	9.48	11.19	14.56
109.82	128.90	136.27	133.13	133.87	137.83	127.60	131.14	147.91	194.99	230.34
11.84	13.32	14.20	16.09	17.31	16.49	17.19	18.70	20.78	21.92	23.97
42.55	45.79	46.59	47.18	48.75	49.13	46.39	52.72	66.39	83.54	101.93
6.29	7.01	7.31	7.42	8.27	8.73	8.68	7.90	8.91	10.97	13.25
323.94	367.73	378.99	424.14	427.55	456.52	476.35	487.80	510.29	590.97	689.03
55.35	67.13	74.09	81.29	88.12	96.42	97.74	105.36	123.60	159.25	186.74
78.37	96.06	105.37	108.39	109.89	110.79	124.89	122.94	112.97	118.67	126.57
1,054.90	1,126.63	1,259.95	1,193.62	1,218.67	1,202.40	1107.25	1124.67	1229.52	1517.40	1737.80
7.66	5.81	7.84	8.20	8.62	8.76	9.07	9.20	9.72	9.43	10.17
4,778.99	5,264.38	4,642.55	4,261.84	3,857.03	4,368.73	4731.20	4159.86	3980.82	4302.94	4655.82
9.42	11.94	12.05	13.28	13.77	12.88	12.32	13.06	13.19	15.04	16.09
435.59	531.14	573	532.24	357.51	461.81	533.39	504.58	575.93	643.76	721.98
4.15	4.96	5.68	6.25	6.73	7.29	7.78	8.22	9.23	11.15	13.74
4.40	6.47	8.17	9.96	11.23	10.97	11.50	12.22	14.24	18.70	22.66
17.59	20.70	20.59	18.54	19.38	21.22	20.33	20.22	22.65	29.20	34.12
75.61	90.17	102.38	101.68	73.27	80.34	93.79	92.78	100.85	110.20	124.75
456.12	310.10	360.06	434.23	455.59	520.45	671.87	709.98	721.79	700.32	759.56
348.91	419.35	418.11	387.01	403.20	412.00	386.20	401.00	439.36	539.34	610.69
51.77	61.06	67.80	67.69	55.60	57.61	53.44	52.55	61.40	81.64	100.68
18.09	36.95	46.02	35.39	32.75	35.94	46.39	44.14	59.12	67.66	87.85
124.48	148.92	160.00	158.23	151.14	159.05	168.29	170.92	191.93	224.88	260.03
44.92	53.66	55.85	59.14	56.76	51.53	51.53	53.36	53.96	56.78	61.36	69.70
64.08	75.53	84.37	83.74	66.60	76.16	81.02	76.26	81.36	83.91	91.37
103.68	139.10	156.66	157.08	172.00	167.79	171.26	190.42	198.21	216.81	253.02
98.05	116.24	121.01	115.67	122.73	126.28	117.64	120.44	132.75	162.24	185.64
30.07	35.48	35.32	35.29	42.12	35.59	37.33	40.59	45.99	59.47	75.80
276.90	313.45	391.78	404.95	271.04	195.91	259.72	306.62	345.13	430.35	590.94
134.33	142.46	157.74	164.99	145.97	161.17	194.81	189.36	194.88	221.47	258.74
73.24	87.06	95.18	99.30	85.01	84.88	94.31	87.70	90.64	95.96	112.70
135.82	151.12	143.83	148.84	134.22	133.11	132.97	118.56	111.36	168.22	219.42
516.72	597.28	622.65	573.38	601.63	618.69	582.05	609.38	688.73	885.53	1045.98
217.55	253.68	276.46	253.18	254.72	258.81	247.53	227.89	251.61	315.98	361.78
270.22	315.95	304.75	264.58	272.63	268.22	256.04	262.65	286.66	334.59	374.23
144.31	168.02	181.95	150.89	111.86	122.63	122.73	115.54	126.88	142.64	161.34
174.45	227.51	243.90	255.07	269.13	249.82	266.44	195.55	232.28	303.26	392.21
36.76	37.01	44.56	50.15	41.88	31.58	31.26	38.01	42.39	50.13	64.88
37.44	40.73	48.01	51.22	48.51	55.18	103.89	103.31	109.82	124.35	147.82
1,061.38	1,157.44	1,220.85	1,359.44	1,456.16	1,502.89	1478.65	1468.53	1604.24	1857.62	2197.94
7,085.15	7,414.63	7,838.48	8,332.35	8,793.48	9,353.50	9951.48	10286.18	10642.30	11142.23	11853.25
16.28	20.80	24.69	26.89	27.23	28.70	31.18	32.52	35.10	39.56	45.45

(continued on next page)

MACROECONOMIC DATA FOR SELECT COUNTRIES
GDP (Billions of U.S. Dollars)

Country	2005	2006	2007	2008	2009	2010	2011	2012
Argentina	181.36	212.51	260.07	324.41	305.76	367.57	444.61	474.95
Australia	730.75	777.94	945.38	1051.26	993.24	1247.11	1490.52	1541.80
Austria	305.51	325.26	375.58	416.12	384.62	380.02	418.41	398.59
Bangladesh	61.13	65.28	73.99	84.47	94.87	106.23	113.89	122.72
Belgium	378.01	400.34	460.28	509.77	474.63	472.54	514.60	484.69
Brazil	881.75	1089.16	1366.22	1650.39	1622.31	2142.93	2492.91	2395.97
Bulgaria	28.97	33.25	42.18	52.14	48.65	47.84	53.58	51.02
Canada	1164.21	1309.92	1457.98	1542.47	1368.90	1616.02	1781.08	1819.08
Chile	123.07	154.71	173.06	179.52	172.11	217.31	250.99	268.18
China	2256.92	2712.92	3494.24	4519.95	4990.53	5930.39	7321.99	8227.04
Colombia	146.59	160.69	210.57	235.26	231.60	284.88	327.63	366.02
Cyprus	16.92	18.42	21.77	25.25	23.47	23.10	25.02	23.01
Czech Republic	130.07	148.37	180.48	225.43	197.19	198.95	217.08	196.07
Denmark	257.68	274.38	311.42	343.88	310.55	313.14	333.70	313.64
Dominican Republic	33.53	35.67	40.99	45.52	46.71	51.67	55.64	59.00
Ecuador	41.77	46.80	51.01	60.75	57.86	63.75	73.04	80.93
Egypt	89.79	107.38	130.35	162.44	188.61	218.46	235.58	256.73
Estonia	13.93	16.82	22.02	23.87	19.18	19.02	22.20	21.86
Finland	196.12	208.14	246.48	273.25	240.00	237.24	263.66	250.13
France	2140.21	2257.78	2586.12	2845.12	2626.54	2570.59	2778.09	2608.70
Germany	2771.06	2905.45	3328.59	3640.73	3307.20	3312.19	3607.36	3400.58
Ghana	17.41	20.41	24.76	28.53	25.80	32.19	38.39	38.94
Greece	240.49	261.96	305.87	343.20	321.85	294.77	290.15	249.20
Guatemala	27.21	30.23	34.11	39.14	37.73	41.34	46.98	49.88
Hungary	110.32	112.53	136.09	154.22	126.65	127.96	138.97	126.87
Iceland	16.32	16.73	20.43	16.83	12.12	12.56	14.06	13.65
India	806.78	909.47	1160.15	1275.73	1259.07	1614.83	1838.17	1824.83
Ireland	203.10	223.17	258.68	263.26	224.62	207.64	221.22	210.42
Israel	133.70	145.14	166.34	201.51	194.79	217.69	243.65	240.89
Italy	1789.38	1874.72	2130.24	2318.16	2116.63	2059.19	2196.33	2014.08
Jamaica	11.23	11.94	12.88	13.85	12.28	13.49	14.78	15.25
Japan	4571.87	4356.75	4356.35	4849.19	5035.14	5495.39	5897.02	5963.97
Kenya	18.74	22.50	27.24	30.47	30.60	32.18	34.06	41.12
Korea	844.87	951.77	1049.24	931.41	834.06	1014.89	1116.25	1155.87
Latvia	15.94	19.85	28.65	33.45	25.85	24.10	28.48	28.38
Lithuania	26.10	30.24	39.32	47.48	37.12	36.63	42.87	42.16
Luxembourg	37.71	42.58	51.39	55.00	50.19	52.95	59.31	56.74
Malaysia	143.54	162.75	193.61	231.07	202.28	246.83	287.94	303.53
Mexico	848.57	951.68	1035.03	1093.74	882.83	1034.15	1158.30	1177.12
Netherlands	639.58	678.32	783.69	874.91	798.40	781.20	837.59	773.12
New Zealand	112.32	108.66	132.70	133.06	118.80	142.02	161.84	169.68
Nigeria	112.25	145.43	165.92	207.12	168.59	228.64	243.99	268.71
Norway	304.06	340.04	393.48	453.89	378.85	420.95	490.66	501.10
Peru	79.39	92.32	107.25	126.87	126.95	153.88	178.49	199.00
Philippines	103.07	122.21	149.36	173.60	168.49	199.59	224.77	250.44
Poland	303.98	341.67	425.32	529.43	430.89	469.80	514.02	487.67
Portugal	192.18	201.98	232.08	253.11	234.69	229.33	237.99	212.72
Romania	99.17	122.70	170.62	204.34	164.34	164.79	182.61	169.38
Russia	764.02	989.93	1299.70	1660.85	1222.65	1525.35	1899.06	2021.96
Saudi Arabia	328.46	376.90	415.97	519.80	429.10	526.81	669.51	727.31
Singapore	125.43	145.64	177.87	190.59	188.83	231.70	265.62	276.52
South Africa	246.95	261.18	285.81	273.45	285.22	363.20	402.25	384.32
Spain	1132.76	1237.50	1443.50	1600.91	1459.74	1391.76	1479.56	1352.06
Sweden	370.17	399.62	463.63	486.61	406.41	462.46	538.62	526.19
Switzerland	384.76	405.18	450.53	524.29	509.47	550.69	660.76	632.40
Thailand	176.35	207.09	246.98	272.58	263.71	318.91	345.67	365.56
Turkey	482.69	529.19	649.13	730.32	614.42	731.29	774.34	794.47
Ukraine	86.18	107.75	142.72	180.12	117.23	136.42	163.42	176.24
United Arab Emirates	180.62	221.97	257.92	314.45	259.73	283.92	341.96	358.94
United Kingdom	2298.64	2456.52	2826.61	2670.40	2193.18	2267.48	2431.53	2440.51
United States	12622.95	13377.20	14028.68	14291.55	13973.65	14498.93	15075.68	15684.75
Vietnam	52.93	60.93	71.11	90.30	93.17	103.58	122.72	138.07

Sources: International Monetary Fund, World Economic Outlook Database, April 2013.

Table 3.
MACROECONOMIC DATA FOR SELECT COUNTRIES
GDP PER PERSON (1985–2012)

Country	1985	1986	1987	1988	1989	1990	1991	1992	1993
Argentina	2,928.87	3,477.26	3,525.01	4,079.01	2,584.99	4,379.50	5,796.41	6,900.12	7,028.62
Australia	10,964.10	11,241.64	12,994.53	16,241.83	18,157.93	18,858.22	18,668.05	18,089.07	17,429.52
Austria	8,988.26	12,740.75	15,911.50	17,431.46	17,309.05	21,511.83	22,259.58	24,678.01	23,847.20
Bangladesh	226.296	230.972	248.09	260.802	280.059	283.992	285.918	279.626	286.814
Belgium	8,464.36	11,729.28	14,561.04	15,813.79	15,902.22	19,875.05	20,313.44	22,545.24	21,459.22
Brazil	1,710.10	1,942.66	2,072.19	2,270.25	3,058.46	3,113.03	2,683.78	2,529.35	2,793.36
Bulgaria	3,130.67	2,777.17	3,232.54	5,313.24	5,449.81	2,422.35	239.505	981.877	538.524
Canada	14,060.69	14,438.27	16,291.17	19,001.44	20,828.27	21,518.68	21,809.72	20,877.26	20,074.52
Chile	1,448.02	1,529.42	1,772.85	2,054.62	2,327.48	2,545.46	2,876.74	3,442.28	3,618.89
China	290.046	276.81	296.408	364.013	400.439	341.353	353.268	416.675	517.414
Colombia	1,573.62	1,543.74	1,573.96	1,662.06	1,641.85	1,638.97	1,644.09	1,926.10	2,140.21
Cyprus	4,390.66	5,512.95	6,541.58	7,466.26	7,858.91	9,428.03	9,476.93	11,064.83	10,322.07
Czech Republic	n/a	n/a	n/a	n/a	n/a	n/a	n/a	n/a	n/a
Denmark	11,974.67	16,880.56	20,950.32	22,075.41	21,454.88	26,451.46	26,560.90	29,095.51	27,144.62
Dominican Republic	1,061.73	1,258.73	1,292.91	1,156.44	1,277.82	1,166.21	1,404.34	1,611.67	1,768.14
Ecuador	2,109.31	1,508.40	1,374.50	1,273.93	1,220.13	1,210.42	1,327.52	1,419.45	1,622.85
Egypt	997.959	1,077.02	1,507.61	1,767.07	2,155.49	1,779.26	878.615	785.038	862.411
Estonia	n/a	n/a	n/a	n/a	n/a	n/a	n/a	n/a	1,145.29
Finland	11,259.11	14,696.74	18,262.52	21,666.93	23,486.11	27,854.86	25,006.32	21,920.30	17,223.04
France	9,932.14	13,713.16	16,501.33	17,924.31	17,912.96	22,046.99	21,984.99	24,090.71	22,632.31
Germany	8,397.49	11,985.43	14,911.90	15,979.26	15,705.89	19,592.68	22,692.73	25,671.42	24,742.34
Ghana	638.019	521.185	506.054	531.591	531.463	617.604	757.762	748.149	575.869
Greece	4,543.24	5,325.20	6,174.13	7,163.58	7,387.05	9,073.88	9,702.81	10,585.18	9,807.41
Guatemala	1,431.50	754.669	852.191	900.109	1,012.37	860.29	1,034.15	1,112.25	1,181.10
Hungary	1,985.30	2,295.26	2,534.76	2,785.72	2,855.53	3,250.63	3,287.86	3,663.94	3,799.05
Iceland	12,211.18	16,228.24	22,274.72	24,289.84	22,154.55	25,077.03	26,568.62	26,825.10	23,336.04
India	312.036	324.955	357.042	369.101	362.165	386.193	318.628	333.21	315.951
Ireland	5,863.83	7,861.61	9,304.87	10,239.26	10,624.69	13,478.01	13,583.60	15,147.74	13,959.02
Israel	6,529.38	7,910.34	9,297.91	11,316.35	11,271.15	12,957.64	14,247.65	15,373.02	14,897.07
Italy	7,882.06	11,161.62	14,009.86	15,517.72	16,127.82	20,111.95	21,226.03	22,512.31	18,087.21
Jamaica	879.434	1,036.04	1,160.02	1,374.42	1,590.50	1,974.11	1,800.91	1,803.94	2,279.03
Japan	11,464.24	16,890.81	20,367.18	24,604.40	24,522.43	25,139.58	28,541.69	30,972.98	35,376.66
Kenya	444.559	509.703	539.628	540.668	518.42	522.332	478.464	457.953	309.76
Korea	2,413.94	2,759.70	3,444.79	4,570.73	5,565.10	6,307.66	7,288.84	7,729.98	8,422.05
Latvia	n/a	n/a	n/a	n/a	n/a	n/a	n/a	582.078	928.28
Lithuania	n/a	n/a	n/a	n/a	n/a	n/a	n/a	n/a	n/a
Luxembourg	12,442.97	18,021.25	22,237.43	24,974.22	26,331.00	33,198.13	35,486.78	39,216.06	39,639.77
Malaysia	1,978.11	1,711.46	1,900.58	2,032.66	2,185.66	2,374.17	2,649.14	3,102.25	3,412.71
Mexico	2,960.57	2,008.52	2,159.17	2,590.36	3,096.75	3,586.12	4,219.65	4,804.19	5,801.94
Netherlands	9,189.30	12,736.41	15,501.24	16,471.39	16,132.50	19,767.94	20,201.82	22,191.00	21,430.99
New Zealand	6,891.89	8,310.97	11,093.14	13,532.61	12,943.73	13,278.32	12,331.48	11,635.06	12,389.85
Nigeria	331.052	254.845	263.86	284.384	266.904	347.625	304.172	266.615	160.529
Norway	15,449.40	18,495.98	22,020.51	23,706.38	23,805.28	27,677.12	27,996.21	29,842.34	27,323.22
Peru	881.63	1,293.11	2,088.09	1,616.27	1,952.82	1,331.72	1,557.49	1,599.87	1,542.74
Philippines	620.246	590.895	640.726	715.079	784.881	796.274	797.084	911.418	914.073
Poland	1,896.08	1,961.68	1,687.80	1,815.82	1,768.61	1,625.84	2,101.35	2,311.09	2,347.12
Portugal	2,673.63	3,713.00	4,644.16	5,438.16	5,873.52	7,815.76	8,868.07	10,670.24	9,380.55
Romania	2,083.00	2,243.90	2,495.19	2,569.62	2,293.82	1,631.94	1,233.00	839.917	1,137.13
Russia	n/a	n/a	n/a	n/a	n/a	n/a	n/a	575.99	1,238.65
Saudi Arabia	8,714.81	6,940.77	6,510.77	6,385.68	6,569.77	7,683.59	8,267.14	8,063.88	7,953.12
Singapore	6,748.29	6,853.03	7,767.00	9,303.40	10,715.16	12,745.06	14,412.55	16,099.09	18,250.52
South Africa	1,735.62	1,937.54	2,485.04	2,614.36	2,662.24	3,039.44	3,192.05	3,389.85	3,315.64
Spain	4,597.63	6,343.30	8,017.91	9,400.09	10,347.54	13,400.01	14,393.43	15,681.87	13,132.27
Sweden	12,643.39	16,689.33	20,253.00	22,761.72	23,805.06	28,273.05	29,645.84	30,523.05	23,102.87
Switzerland	15,783.83	22,524.91	28,045.15	30,136.76	28,863.83	36,564.25	36,540.67	37,559.36	36,184.71
Thailand	750.973	813.604	938.093	1,122.03	1,306.77	1,521.05	1,688.66	1,893.55	2,087.83
Turkey	1,837.97	2,024.85	2,281.01	2,416.97	2,810.15	3,862.75	3,795.75	3,920.70	4,373.52
Ukraine	n/a	n/a	n/a	n/a	n/a	n/a	n/a	415.009	652.902
United Arab Emirates	27,036.00	20,533.02	21,644.07	18,435.20	20,478.53	26,621.51	25,847.41	25,960.97	25,654.37
United Kingdom	8,292.23	10,071.38	12,395.15	15,035.66	15,171.88	17,900.11	18,626.91	19,325.67	17,298.24
United States	18,231.83	19,078.41	20,062.55	21,442.13	22,878.98	23,913.66	24,365.53	25,466.73	26,441.65
Vietnam	251.202	556.019	674.88	365.892	97.158	98.032	113.654	144.149	189.261

Sources: International Monetary Fund, World Economic Outlook Database, 2013.

1994	1995	1996	1997	1998	1999	2000	2001	2001	2003	2004
7,576.83	7,531.45	7,862.15	8,381.06	8,478.20	7,970.20	7,917.15	7,417.62	2,656.23	3,439.37	4,048.33
19,725.52	20,929.85	23,201.57	23,017.57	20,340.85	21,778.63	20,876.31	19,457.24	21,610.11	27,193.09	32,673.23
25,439.40	30,043.89	29,497.01	26,113.72	26,780.11	26,598.11	24,044.50	23,854.31	25,769.47	31,340.72	35,720.10
305.035	330.191	339.18	347.256	351.097	358.01	355.392	350.287	361.732	391.388	418.594
23,336.92	28,111.96	27,199.40	24,589.22	25,111.41	24,950.44	22,790.54	22,671.37	24,606.76	30,155.42	34,835.03
3,428.43	4,755.95	5,111.60	5,222.80	4,982.75	3,413.60	3,696.33	3,133.16	2,822.49	3,041.20	3,609.73
956.589	1,617.78	1,232.72	1,300.59	1,622.99	1,647.47	1,588.37	1,758.27	2,042.61	2,654.15	3,261.87
19,888.86	20,572.16	21,202.83	21,795.99	20,961.72	22,205.35	24,127.69	23,658.81	24,037.51	28,094.78	31,923.94
4,103.67	5,199.27	5,322.60	5,734.23	5,437.33	4,951.66	5,065.26	4,578.24	4,452.59	4,780.29	6,169.16
466.603	601.008	699.478	770.59	817.147	861.212	945.597	1,038.04	1,131.80	1,269.83	1,486.02
2,642.68	2,942.08	3,134.98	2,906.21	2,770.85	2,429.31	2,479.97	2,406.64	2,366.90	2,262.95	2,803.95
11,398.57	14,011.84	13,922.15	13,056.25	13,829.80	13,996.55	13,185.64	13,615.20	14,676.35	18,226.81	21,360.22
n/a	5,592.28	6,287.48	5,768.12	6,200.85	6,041.60	5,721.18	6,270.45	7,683.91	9,339.41	11,161.65
29,556.47	34,891.59	35,123.93	32,309.50	32,796.45	32,735.71	30,033.99	29,999.90	32,389.91	39,495.21	45,339.84
1,898.15	2,052.67	2,210.62	2,455.39	2,564.03	2,641.34	2,862.80	2,914.30	2,909.36	2,318.37	2,430.18
1,917.41	2,043.34	2,101.90	2,324.87	2,329.65	1,649.60	1,508.31	1,971.96	2,254.87	2,525.33	2,808.91
930.632	1,057.35	1,162.07	1,277.18	1,397.39	1,450.67	1,566.42	1,474.48	1,301.79	1,210.20	1,148.71
1,641.19	2,609.58	3,317.06	3,596.63	4,021.33	4,147.08	4,151.15	4,568.35	5,397.58	7,273.07	8,914.16
19,822.50	25,592.36	25,013.86	23,928.37	25,184.63	25,234.25	23,576.21	24,013.85	26,057.31	31,528.53	36,151.81
23,810.08	27,238.24	27,152.86	24,487.66	25,230.31	24,930.36	22,600.49	22,600.48	24,413.99	29,876.70	34,019.75
26,439.46	30,920.73	29,767.35	26,323.24	26,589.97	25,994.91	23,019.52	22,862.72	24,413.62	29,428.65	33,089.57
496.58	517.757	551.547	621.73	680.683	705.42	399.838	393.731	489.639	563.211	714.67
10,387.83	12,352.02	12,949.18	12,664.05	12,654.18	12,966.90	11,702.85	11,997.21	13,484.68	17,716.15	20,863.05
1,301.69	1,425.39	1,480.48	1,633.57	1,711.32	1,588.07	1,530.34	1,625.48	1,761.78	1,812.72	1,933.15
4,091.42	4,408.84	4,450.22	4,517.35	4,664.55	4,706.43	4,537.82	5,168.72	6,524.77	8,236.87	10,074.70
23,729.08	26,255.31	27,280.43	27,479.36	30,355.48	31,678.60	31,094.08	27,879.06	31,106.72	38,026.10	45,602.99
363.025	391.987	419.31	435.418	432.829	459.82	461.111	470.168	491.244	572.129	657.521
15,266.86	18,860.13	20,516.34	22,209.16	23,841.08	25,847.66	25,759.86	27,359.37	31,515.30	39,959.31	46,110.44
16,418.21	18,890.55	20,120.06	20,186.90	19,911.59	19,576.84	21,514.03	20,761.78	18,806.43	19,413.38	20,302.71
18,648.74	19,919.85	22,282.90	21,096.53	21,547.92	21,257.87	19,451.50	19,744.64	21,572.80	26,471.98	30,019.91
2,262.90	2,655.30	2,975.14	3,347.37	3,467.54	3,473.44	3,510.58	3,529.72	3,700.06	3,562.46	3,816.38
38,758.66	42,516.46	37,424.79	34,307.37	30,981.06	35,014.33	37,303.81	32,711.10	31,241.17	33,717.88	36,444.19
361.756	448.134	441.811	476.342	483.632	442.43	426.344	426.351	419.139	461.269	483.442
9,757.50	11,778.76	12,586.61	11,582.11	7,723.84	9,906.50	11,346.66	10,654.82	12,093.73	13,451.10	15,028.82
1,584.66	1,988.82	2,293.81	2,568.52	2,858.36	3,056.42	3,264.81	3,493.18	3,974.67	4,847.76	6,033.31
n/a	n/a	n/a	n/a	n/a	3,113.15	3,286.36	3,510.15	4,104.12	5,413.15	6,594.32
43,478.77	50,532.67	49,664.00	44,157.70	45,572.68	49,184.07	46,513.81	45,745.09	50,712.10	64,559.68	74,420.64
3,697.94	4,295.15	4,752.05	4,601.40	3,231.71	3,454.84	3,991.91	3,846.24	4,078.35	4,352.36	4,815.65
5,964.93	3,810.38	4,339.67	5,175.12	5,332.32	6,072.74	7,063.98	7,354.31	7,436.01	7,079.74	7,519.94
22,881.25	27,126.46	26,922.47	24,791.02	25,670.20	26,055.94	24,249.91	24,990.55	27,206.45	33,241.45	37,507.13
14,415.37	16,737.11	18,285.63	18,012.92	14,702.99	15,175.99	13,832.93	13,501.87	15,503.65	20,224.41	24,584.17
178.953	355.757	431.264	322.73	290.675	309.855	389.951	361.112	470.703	524.261	662.472
28,635.64	34,078.34	36,459.94	35,851.38	34,036.02	35,554.23	37,390.55	37,819.98	42,206.93	49,176.47	56,537.85
1,956.72	2,302.93	2,361.12	2,459.80	2,324.91	2,078.00	2,116.95	2,107.94	2,184.22	2,324.51	2,600.53
1,051.68	1,200.43	1,311.13	1,273.33	960.71	1,080.95	1,055.12	970.377	1,014.94	1,024.77	1,093.48
2,687.41	3,605.31	4,057.58	4,065.33	4,448.94	4,339.24	4,475.91	4,977.81	5,182.89	5,672.93	6,625.21
9,813.67	11,602.51	12,048.14	11,480.82	12,146.45	12,445.05	11,504.58	11,700.72	12,803.71	15,538.76	17,676.71
1,305.21	1,548.97	1,550.50	1,557.48	1,868.29	1,586.44	1,671.53	1,817.91	2,061.24	2,742.19	3,502.87
1,864.66	2,113.63	2,641.77	2,739.83	1,837.54	1,333.61	1,775.13	2,095.58	2,376.90	2,967.51	4,096.86
7,889.53	8,157.46	8,795.62	8,976.16	7,790.87	8,359.73	9,515.06	9,027.49	9,067.84	10,057.69	11,469.08
21,419.97	24,702.00	25,929.64	26,158.10	21,647.26	21,441.38	23,413.77	21,194.09	21,705.06	23,319.87	27,047.14
3,382.24	3,684.84	3,439.25	3,495.07	3,100.05	3,029.06	2,986.51	2,632.86	2,445.22	3,656.12	4,722.68
13,141.99	15,155.44	15,762.76	14,477.11	15,137.33	15,486.74	14,455.74	14,964.58	16,670.51	21,081.77	24,500.85
24,675.35	28,705.08	31,257.62	28,615.37	28,768.35	29,206.66	27,835.73	25,519.75	28,069.13	35,062.93	40,181.34
39,707.59	46,157.58	44,184.22	38,450.50	39,304.06	38,399.27	35,739.31	36,488.59	39,506.20	45,746.13	50,818.24
2,441.95	2,825.72	3,026.60	2,481.11	1,819.86	1,988.75	1,983.32	1,835.78	1,999.30	2,228.26	2,479.03
3,115.00	3,961.64	4,167.43	4,281.13	4,310.68	3,941.70	4,148.66	3,009.34	3,522.76	4,531.10	5,790.59
710.711	721.409	875.865	995.07	838.095	637.416	636.497	781.055	878.771	1,048.30	1,367.74
25,762.53	26,394.42	29,058.86	29,535.55	25,897.65	27,321.04	34,688.98	32,621.29	32,790.71	35,017.31	39,304.51
18,679.57	20,353.52	21,373.35	23,742.74	25,275.24	25,875.93	25,415.29	25,132.28	27,370.06	31,520.54	37,129.76
27,755.48	28,762.68	30,047.22	31,553.44	32,928.95	34,619.90	36,450.14	37,253.44	38,123.18	39,597.37	41,845.61
229.847	288.874	337.524	361.908	360.925	374.722	401.567	413.342	440.209	489.034	603.668

(continued on next page)

Country	2005	2006	2007	2008	2009	2010	2011	2012
Argentina	4,781.86	5,540.64	6,705.04	8,270.21	7,707.99	9,162.21	10,958.90	11,582.48
Australia	35,976.04	37,713.29	44,982.82	48,951.34	45,429.71	56,250.57	66,201.52	67,304.47
Austria	37,143.21	39,339.41	45,245.56	49,915.00	46,003.57	45,111.55	49,444.29	46,642.88
Bangladesh	427.061	450.089	505.053	570.804	634.593	702.83	747.12	797.159
Belgium	36,187.16	38,086.06	43,486.09	47,789.59	44,134.37	43,585.79	46,796.78	43,615.17
Brazil	4,742.50	5,795.20	7,201.62	8,632.72	8,395.03	10,992.27	12,583.64	11,358.54
Bulgaria	3,753.28	4,329.16	5,520.39	6,854.99	6,432.50	6,374.12	7,311.80	7,006.25
Canada	36,149.39	40,290.98	44,336.26	46,372.50	40,709.04	47,367.38	51,645.22	52,299.76
Chile	7,565.31	9,414.66	10,426.27	10,709.21	10,166.62	12,712.54	14,551.69	15,410.12
China	1,726.05	2,063.87	2,644.56	3,403.53	3,739.62	4,422.66	5,434.36	6,071.47
Colombia	3,417.82	3,702.09	4,793.63	5,292.55	5,149.15	6,273.01	7,182.36	7,919.17
Cyprus	22,742.03	24,305.65	28,039.01	31,685.54	28,657.35	27,501.53	29,021.34	26,388.99
Czech Republic	12,725.94	14,474.00	17,544.02	21,715.05	18,837.96	18,891.89	20,603.29	18,624.30
Denmark	47,617.12	50,553.49	57,171.43	62,800.30	56,345.41	56,576.98	60,010.50	56,426.45
Dominican Republic	3,712.24	3,879.11	4,378.36	4,776.56	4,815.83	5,233.14	5,535.34	5,766.16
Ecuador	3,140.91	3,490.61	3,749.19	4,473.93	4,464.10	4,752.81	5,324.55	5,742.65
Egypt	1,282.77	1,505.96	1,771.00	2,160.04	2,452.63	2,775.85	2,930.12	3,111.87
Estonia	10,333.63	12,510.63	16,404.50	17,800.95	14,522.92	14,237.81	16,836.13	16,720.16
Finland	37,316.14	39,443.69	46,501.68	51,302.50	44,848.61	44,118.26	48,605.15	45,634.93
France	35,107.47	36,772.17	41,849.57	45,789.29	42,046.84	40,943.40	44,140.20	41,223.31
Germany	33,603.03	35,274.92	40,463.14	44,334.37	40,388.15	40,493.05	44,405.33	41,865.52
Ghana	833.397	952.739	1,126.86	1,266.11	1,116.45	1,358.16	1,594.43	1,622.24
Greece	21,699.72	23,546.25	27,379.01	30,605.23	28,582.40	26,074.16	25,654.78	22,072.45
Guatemala	2,140.94	2,320.30	2,554.52	2,859.65	2,690.09	2,875.31	3,236.13	3,325.68
Hungary	10,925.11	11,166.95	13,519.92	15,352.90	12,625.81	12,777.74	13,916.32	12,652.04
Iceland	55,590.44	55,786.89	66,390.20	53,354.20	37,933.65	39,556.32	44,163.99	42,725.04
India	748.85	839.927	1,080.70	1,052.67	1,158.91	1,432.25	1,546.55	1,500.76
Ireland	49,090.31	52,675.44	59,405.71	59,146.02	49,858.39	46,056.37	49,452.99	45,984.37
Israel	20,984.22	22,339.21	25,330.42	30,190.17	28,523.42	31,420.31	34,264.73	33,432.68
Italy	30,607.34	31,909.23	36,025.61	38,882.76	35,250.64	34,126.26	36,227.33	33,115.01
Jamaica	4,186.20	4,429.58	4,754.77	5,053.91	4,436.94	4,838.49	5,251.25	5,358.30
Japan	35,780.57	34,076.75	34,038.35	37,865.07	39,321.22	42,916.74	46,101.82	46,706.72
Kenya	546.57	637.226	748.701	813.052	792.75	810.995	839.158	966.587
Korea	17,550.88	19,676.11	21,590.17	19,028.07	16,958.65	20,540.18	22,388.40	22,588.92
Latvia	7,084.34	8,911.82	12,971.07	15,262.65	11,953.72	11,364.95	13,728.02	13,899.89
Lithuania	7,644.31	8,909.56	11,647.88	14,139.73	11,094.68	11,127.45	14,148.40	14,009.01
Luxembourg	80,971.13	90,049.03	106,915.85	112,428.82	100,741.58	104,335.44	114,186.25	106,406.42
Malaysia	5,421.34	6,065.61	7,121.82	8,390.27	7,203.34	8,658.67	9,979.39	10,344.87
Mexico	8,366.99	9,166.16	9,736.17	10,111.47	8,085.20	9,158.24	10,033.52	10,058.50
Netherlands	39,189.91	41,497.70	47,838.63	53,198.73	48,300.07	46,861.68	49,932.22	46,010.95
New Zealand	27,118.27	25,918.65	31,329.09	31,119.79	27,470.50	32,459.07	36,687.08	38,254.62
Nigeria	823.824	1,038.76	1,153.40	1,401.24	1,110.04	1,465.15	1,521.66	1,640.11
Norway	65,646.21	72,784.95	83,335.71	94,815.85	78,231.37	85,764.72	98,664.44	99,170.20
Peru	2,916.68	3,340.24	3,800.44	4,427.11	4,362.46	5,204.83	5,943.85	6,525.36
Philippines	1,208.93	1,405.21	1,683.69	1,918.26	1,851.48	2,155.41	2,378.93	2,611.50
Poland	7,962.95	8,954.31	11,155.83	13,890.16	11,313.67	12,308.93	13,383.56	12,709.27
Portugal	18,217.25	19,082.78	21,876.73	23,827.95	22,076.37	21,562.45	22,334.04	20,037.74
Romania	4,589.37	5,686.89	7,916.74	9,496.90	7,649.49	7,683.84	8,539.55	7,939.30
Russia	5,310.88	6,912.93	9,101.56	11,630.58	8,567.94	10,671.21	13,335.23	14,302.09
Saudi Arabia	14,078.90	15,624.75	16,677.92	20,157.30	16,095.19	19,413.05	23,599.11	24,523.92
Singapore	29,403.39	33,088.75	38,762.59	39,382.95	37,859.79	45,639.35	51,241.74	52,051.81
South Africa	5,266.81	5,511.09	5,851.56	5,544.53	5,732.84	7,244.72	7,971.62	7,525.39
Spain	26,101.60	28,081.47	32,168.13	35,112.83	31,746.74	30,113.76	31,563.40	28,670.09
Sweden	40,958.21	43,790.68	50,366.61	52,521.66	43,442.55	49,180.46	56,523.12	54,814.80
Switzerland	51,888.75	54,321.34	59,998.62	69,049.02	65,442.05	69,771.89	82,834.72	78,880.93
Thailand	2,707.51	3,172.30	3,756.87	4,110.00	3,943.07	4,740.33	5,114.73	5,390.41
Turkey	7,044.10	7,650.66	9,216.55	10,272.53	8,529.77	10,015.27	10,477.01	10,526.80
Ukraine	1,829.76	2,304.92	3,071.49	3,899.27	2,550.45	2,979.67	3,583.97	3,877.28
United Arab Emirates	43,988.56	44,283.30	41,472.29	39,074.84	31,073.63	34,778.05	40,951.45	43,773.84
United Kingdom	38,584.96	41,043.58	46,866.34	44,131.12	35,885.37	36,891.37	39,286.35	39,160.58
United States	44,224.13	46,358.36	47,963.56	48,307.78	46,906.90	48,294.19	49,796.95	51,703.95
Vietnam	699.682	796.928	920.463	1,154.49	1,181.51	1,297.85	1,532.06	1,752.62

Sources: International Monetary Fund, World Economic Outlook Database, 2013.

absolute advantage the advantage conferred by the ability to produce more of a good or service with a given amount of time and resources; not the same as comparative advantage.

accelerator principle the proposition that a higher rate of growth in real GDP results in a higher level of planned investment spending, and a lower growth rate in real GDP leads to lower planned investment spending.

actual investment spending the sum of planned investment spending and unplanned inventory investment.

AD–AS model the basic model used to understand fluctuations in aggregate output and the aggregate price level. It uses the aggregate demand curve and the aggregate supply curve together to analyze the behavior of the economy in response to shocks or government policy.

aggregate consumption function the relationship for the economy as a whole between aggregate current disposable income and aggregate consumer spending.

aggregate demand curve a graphical representation of the relationship between the aggregate price level and the quantity of aggregate output demanded by households, businesses, the government, and the rest of the world.

aggregate output the economy's total production of final goods and services for a given time period, usually a year. Real GDP is the numerical measure of aggregate output typically used by economists.

aggregate price level a measure of the overall level of prices in the economy.

aggregate production function a hypothetical function that shows how productivity (real GDP per worker) depends on the quantities of physical capital per worker and human capital per worker as well as the state of technology.

aggregate spending the total spending on domestically produced final goods and services; the sum of consumer spending (*C*), investment spending (*I*), government purchases of goods and services (*G*), and exports minus imports (*X – IM*).

aggregate supply curve a graphical representation of the relationship between the aggregate price level and the total quantity of aggregate output supplied.

appreciation (of currency) a rise in the value of one currency in terms of other currencies.

asset bubble a phenomenon in which the price of a particular good or service is pushed to an unreasonably high level due to expectations of further price gains.

autarky a situation in which a country does not trade with other countries.

automatic stabilizers government spending and taxation rules that cause fiscal policy to be automatically expansionary when the economy contracts and automatically contractionary when the economy expands. Taxes that depend on disposable income are the most important example of automatic stabilizers.

autonomous consumer spending the amount of money a household would spend if it had no disposable income.

balance of payments accounts a summary of a country's transactions with other countries, including two main elements: the balance of payments on the current account and the balance of payments on the financial account.

balance of payments on the current account (current account) a country's balance of payments on goods and services plus net international transfer payments and factor income.

balance of payments on the financial account (financial account) the difference between a country's sales of assets to foreigners and its purchases of assets from foreigners during a given period.

balance of payments on goods and services the difference between the value of exports and the value of imports during a given period.

balance sheet effect the reduction in a firm's net worth from falling asset prices.

bank a financial intermediary that provides liquid assets in the form of bank deposits to lenders and uses those funds to finance the illiquid investments or investment spending needs of borrowers.

bank deposit a claim on a bank that obliges the bank to give the depositor his or her cash when demanded.

bank reserves currency held by banks in their vaults plus their deposits at the Federal Reserve.

bank run a phenomenon in which many of a bank's depositors try to withdraw their funds due to fears of a bank failure.

banking crisis an episode in which a large part of the depository banking sector or the shadow banking sector fails or threatens to fail.

black market a market in which goods or services are bought and sold illegally, either because it is illegal to sell them at all or because the prices charged are legally prohibited by a price ceiling.

bond a loan in the form of an IOU that pays interest.

budget balance the difference between tax revenue and government spending. A positive budget balance is referred to as a budget surplus; a negative budget balance is referred to as a budget deficit.

budget deficit the difference between tax revenue and government spending when government spending exceeds tax revenue.

budget surplus the difference between tax revenue and government spending when tax revenue exceeds government spending.

business cycle the short-run alternation between economic downturns, known as recessions, and economic upturns, known as expansions.

business-cycle peak the point in time at which the economy shifts from expansion to recession.

business-cycle trough the point in time at which the economy shifts from recession to expansion.

central bank an institution that oversees and regulates the banking system and controls the monetary base.

chained dollars describes a method of calculating real GDP that splits the difference between growth rates calculated using early base years and the growth rates calculated using late base years.

change in demand a shift of the demand curve, which changes the quantity demanded at any given price.

change in supply a shift of the supply curve, which changes the quantity supplied at any given price.)

checkable bank deposits bank accounts on which people can write checks.

circular-flow diagram a diagram that represents the transactions in an economy by two kinds of flows around a circle: flows of physical things such as goods or labor in one direction and flows of money to pay for these physical things in the opposite direction.

classical model of the price level a model of the price level in which the real quantity of money is always at its long-run equilibrium level. This model ignores the distinction between the short run and the long run but is useful for analyzing the case of high inflation.

commercial bank a bank that accepts deposits and is covered by deposit insurance.

commodity money a medium of exchange that is a good, normally gold or silver, that has intrinsic value in other uses.

commodity-backed money a medium of exchange that has no intrinsic value whose ultimate value is guaranteed by a promise that it can be converted into valuable goods on demand.

comparative advantage the advantage conferred if the opportunity cost of producing the good or service is lower for another producer.

competitive market a market in which there are many buyers and sellers of the same good or service, none of whom can influence the price at which the good or service is sold.

complements pairs of goods for which a rise in the price of one good leads to a decrease in the demand for the other good.

consumer price index (CPI) a measure of the cost of a market basket intended to represent the consumption of a typical urban American family of four. It is the most commonly used measure of prices in the United States.

consumer spending household spending on goods and services from domestic and foreign firms.

consumption function an equation showing how an individual household's consumer spending varies with the household's current disposable income.

contractionary fiscal policy fiscal policy that reduces aggregate demand by decreasing government purchases, increasing taxes, or decreasing transfers.

contractionary monetary policy monetary policy that, through the raising of the interest rate, reduces aggregate demand and therefore output.

convergence hypothesis a theory of economic growth that holds that international differences in real GDP per capita tend to narrow over time because countries with low GDP per capita generally have higher growth rates.

credit crunch a time during which potential borrowers either can't get credit at all or must pay very high interest rates.

crowding out the negative effect of budget deficits on private investment, which occurs because government borrowing drives up interest rates.

currency in circulation actual cash held by the public.

cyclical unemployment unemployment resulting from the business cycle; equivalently, the difference between the actual rate of unemployment and the natural rate of unemployment.

cyclically adjusted budget balance an estimate of what the budget balance would be if real GDP were exactly equal to potential output.

deadweight loss losses associated with quantities of output that are greater than or less than the efficient level, as can result from market intervention such as taxes, or from externalities such as pollution.

debt deflation the reduction in aggregate demand arising from the increase in the real burden of outstanding debt caused by deflation; occurs because borrowers, whose real debt rises as a result of deflation, are likely to cut spending sharply, and lenders, whose real assets are now more valuable, are less likely to increase spending.

debt–GDP ratio government debt as a percentage of GDP, frequently used as a measure of a government's ability to pay its debts.

debt overhang high debt but diminished assets, resulting from a vicious cycle of deleveraging.

default the failure of a borrower to make payments as specified by the bond contract.

deflation a fall in the overall level of prices.

demand curve a graphical representation of the demand schedule, showing the relationship between quantity demanded and price.

demand price the price of a given quantity at which consumers will demand that quantity.

demand schedule a list or table showing how much of a good or service consumers will want to buy at different prices.

demand shock any event that shifts the aggregate demand curve. A positive demand shock is associated with higher demand for aggregate output at any price level and shifts the curve to the right. A negative demand shock is associated with lower demand for aggregate output at any price level and shifts the curve to the left.

deposit insurance a guarantee that a bank's depositors will be paid even if the bank can't come up with the funds, up to a maximum amount per account.

depreciation (of currency) a fall in the value of one currency in terms of other currencies.

devaluation a reduction in the value of a currency that is set under a fixed exchange rate regime.

diminishing returns to physical capital describes the effect on an aggregate production function when the amount of human capital per worker and the state of technology are held fixed: each successive increase in the amount of physical capital per worker leads to a smaller increase in productivity.

discount rate the interest rate the Fed charges on loans to banks in trouble.

discount window an arrangement in which the Federal Reserve stands ready to lend money to banks in trouble.

discouraged workers nonworking people who are capable of working but have given up looking for a job due to the state of the job market.

discretionary fiscal policy fiscal policy that is the direct result of deliberate actions by policy makers rather than rules.

discretionary monetary policy the use of changes in the interest rate or the money supply to stabilize the economy.

disinflation the process of bringing down inflation that has become embedded in expectations.

disposable income income plus government transfers minus taxes; the total amount of household income available to spend on consumption and saving.

diversification investment in several different assets with unrelated, or independent, risks, so that the possible losses are independent events.

domestic demand curve a demand curve that shows how the quantity of a good demanded by domestic consumers depends on the price of that good.

domestic supply curve a supply curve that shows how the quantity of a good supplied by domestic producers depends on the price of that good.

economic aggregates economic measures that summarize data across different markets for goods, services, workers, and assets.

economics the study of scarcity and choice.

economy a system for coordinating a society's productive and consumptive activities.

efficiency wages wages that employers set above the equilibrium wage rate as an incentive for workers to deliver better performance.

efficient describes a market or economy that takes all opportunities to make some people better off without making other people worse off.

employed refers to people currently holding a job in the economy, either full time or part time.

equilibrium an economic situation in which no individual would be better off doing something different.

equilibrium exchange rate the exchange rate at which the quantity of a currency demanded in the foreign exchange market is equal to the quantity supplied.

equilibrium price the price at which the market is in equilibrium, that is, the quantity of a good or service demanded equals the quantity of that good or service supplied; also referred to as the market-clearing price.

equilibrium quantity the quantity of a good or service bought and sold at the equilibrium (or market-clearing) price.

excess reserves a bank's reserves over and above the reserves required by law or regulation.

exchange market intervention government purchases or sales of currency in the foreign exchange market.

exchange rate the price at which currencies trade, determined by the foreign exchange market.

exchange rate regime a rule governing policy toward the exchange rate.

expansion a period of economic upturn in which output and employment are rising; most economic numbers are following their normal upward trend; also referred to as a recovery.

expansionary fiscal policy fiscal policy that increases aggregate demand by increasing government purchases, decreasing taxes, or increasing transfers.

expansionary monetary policy monetary policy that, through the lowering of the interest rate, increases aggregate demand and therefore output.

exporting industries industries that produce goods or services that are sold abroad.

exports goods and services sold to other countries.

factor markets markets in which resources, especially capital and labor, are bought and sold.

federal funds market the financial market that allows banks that fall short of reserve requirements to borrow funds from banks with excess reserves.

federal funds rate the interest rate at which funds are borrowed and lent in the federal funds market.

fiat money a medium of exchange whose value derives entirely from its official status as a means of payment.

final goods and services goods and services sold to the final, or end, user.

financial asset a paper claim that entitles the buyer to future income from the seller. Loans, stocks, bonds, and bank deposits are types of financial assets.

financial contagion a vicious downward spiral among depository banks as well as shadow banks: each institution's failure increases the likelihood that another will fail.

financial intermediary an institution, such as a mutual fund, pension fund, life insurance company, or bank, that transforms the funds it gathers from many individuals into financial assets.

financial markets the banking, stock, and bond markets, which channel private savings and foreign lending into investment spending, government borrowing, and foreign borrowing.

financial panic a sudden and widespread disruption of the financial markets that occurs when peope lose faith in the liquidity of financial institutions and markets.

financial risk uncertainty about future outcomes that involve financial losses and gains.

firm an organization that produces goods and services for sale.

fiscal year the time period used for much of government accounting; the U.S. fiscal year runs from October 1 to September 30. Fiscal years are labeled by the calendar year in which they end.

Fisher effect the principle by which an increase in expected future inflation drives up the nominal interest rate, leaving the expected real interest rate unchanged.

fixed exchange rate an exchange rate regime in which the government keeps the exchange rate against some other currency at or near a particular target.

floating exchange rate an exchange rate regime in which the government lets the exchange rate go wherever the market takes it.

foreign exchange controls licensing systems that limit the right of individuals to buy foreign currency.

foreign exchange market the market in which currencies are traded.

foreign exchange reserves stocks of foreign currency that governments can use to buy their own currency on the foreign exchange market.

free trade trade that is unregulated by government tariffs or other artificial barriers; the levels of exports and imports occur naturally, as a result of supply and demand.

frictional unemployment unemployment due to time workers spend in job search.

gains from trade an economic principle that states that by dividing tasks and trading, people can get more of what they want through trade than they could if they tried to be self-sufficient.

GDP deflator a price measure for a given year that is equal to 100 times the ratio of nominal GDP to real GDP in that year.

GDP per capita GDP divided by the size of the population; equivalent to the average GDP per person.

globalization the phenomenon of growing economic linkages among countries.

government borrowing the amount of funds borrowed by the government in financial markets to buy goods and services.

government purchases of goods and services total purchases by federal, state, and local governments on goods and services.

government transfers payments by the government to individuals for which no good or service is provided in return.

Great Moderation the period from 1985 to 2007 when the U.S. economy experienced small fluctuations and low inflation.

Great Moderation consensus a belief in monetary policy as the main tool of stabilization combined with skepticism toward the use of fiscal policy and an acknowledgment of the policy constraints imposed by the natural rate of unemployment and the political business cycle.

gross domestic product (GDP) the total value of all final goods and services produced in the economy during a given period, usually a year.

growth accounting estimation of the contribution of each of the major factors (physical and human capital, labor, and technology) in the aggregate production function.

household a person or a group of people who share income.

human capital the improvement in labor created by the education and knowledge embodied in the workforce.

illiquid describes an asset that cannot be quickly converted into cash without much loss of value.

implicit liabilities spending promises made by governments that are effectively a debt despite the fact that they are not included in the usual debt statistics. In the United States, the largest implicit liabilities arise from Social Security and Medicare, which promise transfer payments to current and future retirees (Social Security) and to the elderly (Medicare).

import quota a legal limit on the quantity of a good that can be imported.

import-competing industries industries that produce goods or services that are also imported.

imports goods and services purchased from other countries.

income–expenditure equilibrium a situation in which aggregate output, measured by real GDP, is equal to planned aggregate spending and firms have no incentive to change output.

income–expenditure equilibrium GDP the level of real GDP at which real GDP equals planned aggregate spending.

individual choice the decision by an individual of what to do, which necessarily involves a decision of what not to do.

individual demand curve a graphical representation of the relationship between quantity demanded and price for an individual consumer.

individual supply curve a graphical representation of the relationship between quantity supplied and price for an individual producer.

inefficient allocation of sales among sellers a form of inefficiency in which sellers who would be willing to sell a good at the lowest price are not always those who actually manage to sell it; often the result of a price floor.

inefficient allocation to consumers a form of inefficiency in which people who want a good badly and are willing to pay a high price don't get it, and those who care relatively little about the good and are only willing to pay a low price do get it; often a result of a price ceiling.

inefficiently high quality a form of inefficiency in which sellers offer high-quality goods at a high price even though buyers would prefer a lower quality at a lower price; often the result of a price floor.

inefficiently low quality a form of inefficiency in which sellers offer low-quality goods at a low price even though buyers would prefer a higher quality at a higher price; often a result of a price ceiling.

inferior good a good for which a rise in income decreases the demand for the good.

inflation a rise in the overall level of prices.

inflation rate the annual percent change in a price index—typically the consumer price index. The inflation rate is positive when the aggregate price level is rising (inflation) and negative when the aggregate price level is falling (deflation).

inflation targeting an approach to monetary policy that requires that the central bank try to keep the inflation rate near a predetermined target rate.

inflation tax the reduction in the value of money held by the public caused by inflation.

inflationary gap the gap that exists when aggregate output is above potential output.

infrastructure physical capital, such as roads, power lines, ports, information networks, and other parts of an economy, that provides the underpinnings, or foundation, for economic activity.

input a good or service used to produce another good or service.

interest rate effect of a change in the aggregate price level the effect on consumer spending and investment spending caused by a change in the purchasing power of consumers' money holdings when the aggregate price level changes. A rise (fall) in the aggregate price level decreases (increases) the purchasing power of consumers' money holdings. In response, consumers try to increase (decrease) their money holdings, which drives up (down) interest rates, thereby decreasing (increasing) consumption and investment.

intermediate goods and services goods and services, bought from one firm by another firm, that are inputs for production of final goods and services.

inventories stocks of goods and raw materials held to satisfy future sales.

inventory investment the value of the change in total inventories held in the economy during a given period. Unlike other types of investment spending, inventory investment can be negative, if inventories fall.

investment bank a bank that creates and trades in financial assets and is not covered by deposit insurance.

investment spending spending on productive physical capital, such as machinery and construction of structures, and on changes to inventories.

invisible hand a phrase used by Adam Smith to refer to the way in which an individual's pursuit of self-interest can lead, without the individual's intending it, to good results for society as a whole.

job search the period in which workers spend time looking for employment.

jobless recovery a period in which GDP growth rate is positive but the unemployment rate is still rising.

Keynesian cross a diagram that identifies income–expenditure equilibrium as the point where the planned aggregate spending line crosses the 45-degree line.

Keynesian economics a school of thought emerging out of the works of John Maynard Keynes; according to Keynesian economics, a depressed economy is the result of inadequate spending and government intervention can help a depressed economy through monetary policy and fiscal policy.

labor the effort of workers.

labor force the number of people who are either actively employed for pay or unemployed and actively looking for work; the sum of employment and unemployment.

labor force participation rate the percentage of the population age 16 or older that is in the labor force.

labor productivity output per worker; also known simply as productivity.

law of demand the principle that a higher price for a good or service, other things equal, leads people to demand a smaller quantity of that good or service.

law of supply the proposition that, other things equal, the price and quantity supplied of a good are positively related.

lender of last resort an institution, usually a country's central bank, that provides funds to financial institutions when they are unable to borrow from the private credit markets.

leverage the degree to which a financial institution is financing its investments with borrowed funds.

liability a requirement to pay income in the future.

license the right, conferred by the government or an owner, to supply a good or service.

life insurance company a financial intermediary that sells policies guaranteeing a payment to a policyholder's beneficiaries when the policyholder dies.

liquid describes an asset that can be quickly converted into cash without much loss of value.

liquidity preference model of the interest rate a model of the market for money in which the interest rate is determined by the supply and demand for money.

liquidity trap a situation in which monetary policy is ineffective because nominal interest rates are up against the zero bound.

loan a lending agreement between an individual lender and an individual borrower. Loans are usually tailored to the individual borrower's needs and ability to pay but carry relatively high transaction costs.

loanable funds market a hypothetical market in which the demand for funds is generated by borrowers and the supply of funds is provided by lenders. The market equilibrium determines the quantity and price, or interest rate, of loanable funds.

loan-backed securities assets created by pooling individual loans and selling shares in that pool.

long-run aggregate supply curve a graphical representation of the relationship between the aggregate price level and the quantity of aggregate output supplied if all prices, including nominal wages, were fully flexible. The long-run aggregate supply curve is vertical because the aggregate price level has no effect on aggregate output in the long run; in the long run, aggregate output is determined by the economy's potential output.

long-run economic growth the sustained rise in the quantity of goods and services the economy produces.

long-run macroeconomic equilibrium a situation in which the short-run macroeconomic equilibrium is also on the long-run aggregate supply curve; so short-run equilibrium aggregate output is equal to potential output.

long-run Phillips curve a graphical representation of the relationship between unemployment and inflation in the long run after expectations of inflation have had time to adjust to experience.

long-term interest rate the interest rate on financial assets that mature a number of years into the future.

lump-sum taxes taxes that don't depend on the taxpayer's income.

macroeconomic policy activism the use of monetary policy and fiscal policy to smooth out the business cycle.

macroeconomics the branch of economics that is concerned with the overall ups and downs in the economy.

marginal propensity to consume (*MPC*) the increase in consumer spending when income rises by $1. Because consumers normally spend part but not all of an additional dollar of disposable income, *MPC* is between 0 and 1.

marginal propensity to save (*MPS*) the increase in household savings when disposable income rises by $1.

marginally attached workers nonworking individuals who say they would like a job and have looked for work in the recent past but are not currently looking for work.

market basket a hypothetical consumption bundle of consumer purchases of goods and services, used to measure changes in overall price level.

market economy an economy in which decisions of individual producers and consumers largely determine what, how, and for whom to produce, with little government involvement in the decisions.

market-clearing price the price at which the market is in equilibrium, that is, the quantity of a good or service demanded equals the quantity of that good or service supplied; also referred to as the equilibrium price.

maturity transformation the conversion of short-term liabilities into long-term assets.

medium of exchange an asset that individuals acquire for the purpose of trading for goods and services rather than for their own consumption.

menu cost the real cost of changing a listed price.

merchandise trade balance (trade balance) the difference between a country's exports and imports of goods alone—not including services.

microeconomics the branch of economics that studies how people make decisions and how those decisions interact.

minimum wage a legal floor on the wage rate. The wage rate is the market price of labor.

model a simplified representation of a real situation that is used to better understand real-life situations.

monetarism a theory of business cycles, associated primarily with Milton Friedman, that asserts that GDP will grow steadily if the money supply grows steadily.

monetary aggregate an overall measure of the money supply. The most common monetary aggregates in the United States are M1, which includes currency in circulation, traveler's checks, and checkable bank deposits, and M2, which includes M1 as well as near-moneys.

monetary base the sum of currency in circulation and bank reserves.

monetary neutrality the concept that changes in the money supply have no real effects on the economy in the long run and only result in a proportional change in the price level.

monetary policy rule a formula that determines the central bank's actions.

money any asset that can easily be used to purchase goods and services.

money demand curve a graphical representation of the negative relationship between the quantity of money demanded and the interest rate. The money demand curve slopes downward because, other things equal, a higher interest rate increases the opportunity cost of holding money.

money multiplier the ratio of the money supply to the monetary base; indicates the total number of dollars created in the banking system by each $1 addition to the monetary base.

money supply the total value of financial assets in the economy that are considered money.

money supply curve a graphical representation of the relationship between the quantity of money supplied by the Federal Reserve and the interest rate.

movement along the demand curve a change in the quantity demanded of a good that results from a change in the price of that good.

movement along the supply curve a change in the quantity supplied of a good that results from a change in the price of that good.

multiplier the ratio of total change in real GDP caused by an autonomous change in aggregate spending to the size of that autonomous change.

mutual fund a financial intermediary that creates a stock portfolio by buying and holding shares in companies and then selling shares of this portfolio to individual investors.

national income and product accounts (national accounts) an accounting of consumer spending, sales of producers, business investment spending, and other flows of money between different sectors of the economy. Calculated by the Bureau of Economic Analysis.

national savings the sum of private savings and the government's budget balance; the total amount of savings generated within the economy.

natural rate hypothesis the hypothesis that the unemployment rate is stable in the long run at a particular natural rate. According to this hypothesis, attempts to lower the unemployment rate below the natural rate of unemployment will cause an ever-rising inflation rate.

natural rate of unemployment the unemployment rate that arises from the effects of frictional plus structural unemployment.

near-money a financial asset that can't be directly used as a medium of exchange but can be readily converted into cash or checkable bank deposits.

net exports the difference between the value of exports and the value of imports. A positive value for net exports indicates that a country is a net exporter of goods and services; a negative value indicates that a country is a net importer of goods and services.

net present value the present value of current and future benefits minus the present value of current and future costs.

new classical macroeconomics an approach to the business cycle that returns to the classical view that shifts in the aggregate demand curve affect only the aggregate price level, not aggregate output.

new Keynesian economics a theory that argues that market imperfections can lead to price stickiness for the economy as a whole.

nominal GDP the value of all final goods and services produced in the economy during a given year, calculated using the prices current in the year in which the output is produced.

nominal interest rate the interest rate actually paid for a loan, not adjusted for inflation.

nominal wage the dollar amount of any given wage paid.

nonaccelerating inflation rate of unemployment (NAIRU) the unemployment rate at which, other things equal, inflation does not change over time.

normal good a good for which a rise in income increases the demand for that good—the "normal" case.

normative economics the branch of economic analysis that makes prescriptions about the way the economy should work.

open economy an economy that trades goods and services with other countries.

open-market operation a purchase or sale of U.S. Treasury bills by the Federal Reserve, undertaken to change the monetary base, which in turn changes the money supply.

opportunity cost the real cost of an item: what you must give up in order to get it.

other things equal assumption in the development of a model, the assumption that all relevant factors except the one under study remain unchanged.

output gap the percentage difference between actual aggregate output and potential output.

pension fund a type of mutual fund that holds assets in order to provide retirement income to its members.

physical asset a claim on a tangible object that gives the owner the right to dispose of the object as he or she wishes.

physical capital human-made goods such as buildings and machines used to produce other goods and services.

planned aggregate spending the total amount of planned spending in the economy; includes consumer spending and planned investment spending.

planned investment spending the investment spending that firms intend to undertake during a given period. Planned investment spending may differ from actual investment spending due to unplanned inventory investment.

political business cycle a business cycle that results from the use of macroeconomic policy to serve political ends.

positive economics the branch of economic analysis that describes the way the economy actually works.

potential output the level of real GDP the economy would produce if all prices, including nominal wages, were fully flexible.

present value the amount of money needed at the present time to produce, at the prevailing interest rate, a given amount of money at a specified future time.

price ceiling the maximum price sellers are allowed to charge for a good or service; a form of price control.

price controls legal restrictions on how high or low a market price may go.

price floor the minimum price buyers are required to pay for a good or service; a form of price control.

price index a measure of the cost of purchasing a given market basket in a given year, where that cost is normalized so that it is equal to 100 in the selected base year; a measure of overall price level.

price stability a period in which the aggregate price level is changing only slowly.

private savings disposable income minus consumer spending; disposable income that is not spent on consumption but rather goes into financial markets.

producer price index (PPI) a measure of the cost of a typical basket of goods and services purchased by producers. Because these commodity prices respond quickly to changes in demand, the PPI is often regarded as a leading indicator of changes in the inflation rate.

product markets markets where goods and services are bought and sold.

production possibility frontier (PPF) a model that illustrates the trade-offs facing an economy that produces only two goods; shows the maximum quantity of one good that can be produced for each possible quantity of the other good produced.

productivity output per worker; an alternative term for labor productivity.

protection policies that limit imports; an alternative term for trade protection.

public debt government debt held by individuals and institutions outside the government.

purchasing power parity (between two countries' currencies) the nominal exchange rate at which a given basket of goods and services would cost the same amount in each country.

quantity control an upper limit, set by the government, on the quantity of some good that can be bought or sold; also referred to as a quota.

quantity demanded the actual amount of a good or service consumers are willing to buy at some specific price.

quantity supplied the actual amount of a good or service producers are willing to sell at some specific price.

Quantity Theory of Money a theory that emphasizes the positive relationship between the price level and the money supply. It relies on the equation ($M \times V = P \times Y$).

quota an upper limit, set by the government, on the quantity of some good that can be bought or sold; also referred to as a quantity control.

quota rent the earnings that accrue to the license-holder from ownership of the right to sell the good.

rational expectations a theory of expectation formation that holds that individuals and firms make decisions optimally, using all available information.

real business cycle theory a theory of business cycles that asserts that fluctuations in the growth rate of total factor productivity cause the business cycle.

real exchange rate the exchange rate adjusted for international differences in aggregate price levels.

real GDP the total value of all final goods and services produced in the economy during a given year, calculated using the prices of a selected base year.

real GDP per capita the average GDP per person.

real income income divided by the price level.

real interest rate the nominal interest rate minus the inflation rate.

real wage the wage rate divided by the price level.

recession a period of economic downturn when output and unemployment are falling; also referred to as a contraction.

recessionary gap exists when aggregate output is below potential output.

required reserve ratio the smallest fraction of deposits that the Federal Reserve allows banks to hold.

research and development (R&D) spending to create and implement new technologies.

reserve ratio the fraction of bank deposits that a bank holds as reserves. In the United States, the minimum required reserve ratio is set by the Federal Reserve.

reserve requirements rules set by the Federal Reserve that set the minimum reserve ratio for banks. For checkable bank deposits in the United States, the minimum reserve ratio is set at 10%.

resource anything, such as land, labor, and capital, that can be used to produce something else; includes natural resources (from the physical environment) and human resources (labor, skill, intelligence).

revaluation an increase in the value of a currency that is set under a fixed exchange rate regime.

Rule of 70 a mathematical formula that states that the time it takes real GDP per capita, or any other variable that grows gradually over time, to double is approximately 70 divided by that variable's annual growth rate.

savings and loans (thrifts) deposit-taking banks, usually specialized in issuing home loans.

savings–investment spending identity an accounting fact that states that savings and investment spending are always equal for the economy as a whole.

scarce in short supply; a resource is scarce when there is not enough of the resource available to satisfy all the various ways a society wants to use it.

securitization the pooling of loans and mortgages made by a financial institution and the sale of shares in such a pool to other investors.

self-correcting describes the economy, referring to the fact that in the long run, shocks to aggregate demand affect aggregate output in the short run, but not in the long run.

self-regulating describes an economy in which problems such as unemployment are resolved without government intervention, through the working of the invisible hand, and in which government attempts to improve the economy's performance would be ineffective at best, and would probably make things worse.

shadow bank a nondepository financial institution that engages in maturity transformation.

shoe-leather costs (of inflation) the increased costs of transactions caused by inflation.

shortage the insufficiency of a good or service that occurs when the quantity demanded exceeds the quantity supplied; shortages occur when the price is below the equilibrium price.

short-run aggregate supply curve a graphical representation of the relationship between the aggregate price level and the quantity of aggregate output supplied that exists in the short run, the time period when many production costs can be taken as fixed. The short-run aggregate supply curve has a positive slope because a rise in the aggregate price level leads to a rise in profits, and therefore output, when production costs are fixed.

short-run equilibrium aggregate output the quantity of aggregate output produced in short-run macroeconomic equilibrium.

short-run equilibrium aggregate price level the aggregate price level in short-run macroeconomic equilibrium.

short-run macroeconomic equilibrium the point at which the quantity of aggregate output supplied is equal to the quantity demanded.

short-run Phillips curve a graphical representation of the negative short-run relationship between the unemployment rate and the inflation rate.

short-term interest rate the interest rate on financial assets that mature within less than a year.

social insurance government programs—like Social Security, Medicare, unemployment insurance, and food stamps—intended to protect families against economic hardship.

specialization a situation in which different people each engage in the different task that he or she is good at performing.

stabilization policy the use of government policy to reduce the severity of recessions and to rein in excessively strong expansions. There are two main tools of stabilization policy: monetary policy and fiscal policy.

stagflation the combination of inflation and falling aggregate output.

sticky wages nominal wages that are slow to fall even in the face of high unemployment and slow to rise even in the face of labor shortages.

stock a share in the ownership of a company held by a shareholder.

store of value an asset that is a means of holding purchasing power over time.

structural unemployment unemployment that results when there are more people seeking jobs in a labor market than there are jobs available at the current wage rate.

subprime lending lending to home buyers who don't meet the usual criteria for borrowing.

substitutes pairs of goods for which a rise in the price of one of the goods leads to an increase in the demand for the other good.

supply and demand model a model of how a competitive market works.

supply curve a graphical representation of the supply schedule, showing the relationship between quantity supplied and price.

supply price the price of a given quantity at which producers will supply that quantity.

supply schedule a list or table showing how much of a good or service producers will supply at different prices.

supply shock an event that shifts the short-run aggregate supply curve. A negative supply shock raises production costs and reduces the quantity supplied at any aggregate price level, shifting the curve leftward. A positive supply shock decreases production costs and increases the quantity supplied at any aggregate price level, shifting the curve rightward.

surplus the excess of a good or service that occurs when the quantity supplied exceeds the quantity demanded; surpluses occur when the price is above the equilibrium price.

sustainable long-run economic growth long-run growth that can continue in the face of the limited supply of natural resources and the impact of growth on the environment.

T-account a simple tool that summarizes a business's financial position by showing, in a single table, the business's assets and liabilities, with assets on the left and liabilities on the right.

target federal funds rate the Federal Reserve's desired level for the federal funds rate. The Federal Reserve adjusts the money supply through the purchase and sale of Treasury bills until the actual rate equals the desired rate.

tariff a tax levied on imports.

Taylor rule for monetary policy a rule for setting the federal funds rate that takes into account both the inflation rate and the output gap.

technological progress an advance in the technical means of the production of goods and services.

technology the technical means for the production of goods and services.

total factor productivity the amount of output that can be produced with a given amount of factor inputs.

trade the practice, in a market economy, in which individuals provide goods and services to others and receive goods and services in return.

trade deficit describes the situation in which the value of the goods and services bought from foreigners is more than the value of the goods and services sold to consumers abroad.

trade protection policies that limit imports; also known simply as protection.

trade surplus describes the situation in which the value of goods and services bought from foreigners is less than the value of the goods and services sold to them.

trade-off the giving up of something in order to have something else.

transaction costs the expenses of negotiating and executing a deal.

underemployed refers to people who work part time because they cannot find full-time jobs.

unemployed refers to people who are actively looking for work but are not currently employed.

unemployment rate the percentage of the total number of people in the labor force who are unemployed, calculated as unemployment/(unemployment + employment).

unit of account a measure used to set prices and make economic calculations.

unit-of-account costs (of inflation) costs arising from the way inflation makes money a less reliable unit of measurement.

unplanned inventory investment unplanned changes in inventories, which occur when actual sales are more or less than businesses expected; sales in excess of expectations result in negative unplanned inventory investment.

value added (of a producer) the value of a producer's sales minus the value of input purchases.

velocity of money the ratio of nominal GDP to the money supply.

vicious cycle of deleveraging describes the sequence of events that takes place when a firm's asset sales to cover losses produce negative balance sheet effects on other firms and force creditors to call in their loans, forcing sales of more assets and causing further declines in asset prices.

wasted resources a form of inefficiency in which people expend money, effort, and time to cope with the shortages caused by a price ceiling.

wealth (of a household) the value of accumulated savings.

wealth effect of a change in the aggregate price level the effect on consumer spending caused by the change in the purchasing power of consumers' assets when the aggregate price level changes. A rise in the aggregate price level decreases the purchasing power of consumers' assets, so they decrease their consumption; a fall in the aggregate price level increases the purchasing power of consumers' assets, so they increase their consumption.

wedge the difference between the demand price of the quantity transacted and the supply price of the quantity transacted for a good when the supply of the good is legally restricted. Often created by a quota or a tax.

world price the price at which a good can be bought or sold abroad.

zero bound the lower bound of zero on the nominal interest rate.

zero lower bound for interest rates statement of the fact that interest rates cannot fall below zero.

SOLUTIONS TO MODULE REVIEW QUESTIONS

This section offers suggested answers to the Review Questions that appear at the end of each module.

MODULE 1

1. **a.** Yes. The increased time spent commuting is a cost you will incur if you accept the new job. That additional time spent commuting—or equivalently, the benefit you would get from spending that time doing something else—is an opportunity cost of the new job.

   b. Yes. One of the benefits of the new job is that you will be making $50,000. But if you take the new job, you will have to give up your current job; that is, you have to give up your current salary of $45,000, so $45,000 is one of the opportunity costs of taking the new job.

   c. No. A more spacious office is an additional benefit of your new job and does not involve forgoing something else, so it is not an opportunity cost.

2. **a.** This is a microeconomic question because it addresses decisions made by consumers about a particular product.

   b. This is a macroeconomic question because it addresses consumer spending in the overall economy.

   c. This is a macroeconomic question because it addresses changes in the overall economy.

   d. This is a microeconomic question because it addresses changes in a particular market, in this case the market for geologists.

   e. This is a microeconomic question because it addresses choices made by consumers and producers about which mode of transportation to use.

   f. This is a microeconomic question because it addresses changes in a particular market.

   g. This is a macroeconomic question because it addresses changes in a measure of the economy's overall price level.

3. **a.** This is a normative statement because it stipulates what should be done. In addition, it may have no "right" answer. That is, should people be prevented from all dangerous personal behavior if they enjoy that behavior—like skydiving? Your answer will depend on your point of view.

   b. This is a positive statement because it is a description of fact.

Multiple-Choice Questions

1. d
2. d
3. b
4. b
5. b
6. a

Critical-Thinking Question

In positive economics there is a "right" or "wrong" answer. In normative economics there is not necessarily a "right" or "wrong" answer. There is more disagreement in normative economics because there is no "right" or "wrong" answer. Economists disagree because of (1) differences in values and (2) disagreements about models and about which simplifications are appropriate.

MODULE 2

Check Your Understanding

1. **a.** False. An increase in the resources available to Boeing for use in producing Dreamliners and small jets changes the production possibility curve by shifting it outward. This is because Boeing can now produce more small jets and Dreamliners than before. In the accompanying figure, the line labeled "Boeing's original *PPF*" represents Boeing's original production possibility curve, and the line labeled "Boeing's new *PPF*" represents the new production possibility curve that results from an increase in resources available to Boeing.

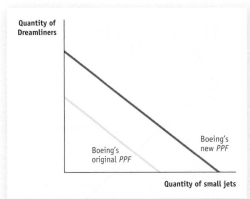

   b. True. A technological change that allows Boeing to build more small jets for any amount of Dreamliners built results in a change in its production possibility curve. This is illustrated in the accompanying figure: the new production possibility curve is represented by the line labeled "Boeing's new *PPF*," and the original production curve is represented by the line labeled "Boeing's original *PPF*." Since the maximum quantity of Dreamliners that Boeing can build is the same as before, the new production possibility curve intersects the vertical axis at the same point as the original curve. But since the maximum possible quantity of small jets is now greater than before, the new curve intersects the horizontal axis to the right of the original curve.

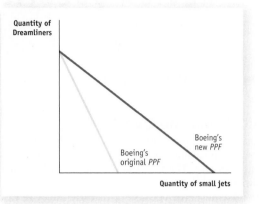

c. False. The production possibility frontier illustrates how much of one good an economy must give up to get more of another good only when resources are used efficiently in production. If an economy is producing inefficiently—that is, inside the frontier—then it does not have to give up a unit of one good in order to get another unit of the other good. Instead, by becoming more efficient in production, this economy can have more of both goods.

Multiple-Choice Questions

1. c
2. d
3. d
4. e
5. a

Critical-Thinking Question

Your graph should look like this.

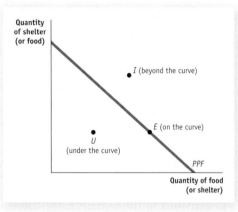

MODULE 3

Check Your Understanding

1. a. The United States has an absolute advantage in automobile production because it takes fewer Americans (6) to produce a car in one day than it takes Italians (8). The United States also has an absolute advantage in washing machine production because it takes fewer Americans (2)

to produce a washing machine in one day than it takes Italians (3).

b. In Italy the opportunity cost of a washing machine in terms of an automobile is ⅜. In other words, ⅜ of a car can be produced with the same number of workers and in the same time it takes to produce 1 washing machine. In the United States the opportunity cost of a washing machine in terms of an automobile is ⅔ = ⅓. In other words, ⅓ of a car can be produced with the same number of workers and in the same time it takes to produce 1 washing machine. Since ⅓ < ⅜, the United States has a comparative advantage in the production of washing machines: to produce a washing machine, only ⅓ of a car must be given up in the United States but ⅜ of a car must be given up in Italy. This means that Italy has a comparative advantage in automobiles. This can be checked as follows. The opportunity cost of an automobile in terms of a washing machine in Italy is ⁸⁄₃, equal to 2⅔. In other words, 2⅔ washing machines can be produced with the same number of workers and in the time it takes to produce 1 car in Italy. And the opportunity cost of an automobile in terms of a washing machine in the United States is ⁶⁄₂, equal to 3. In other words, 3 washing machines can be produced with the same number of workers and in the time it takes to produce 1 car in the United States.

c. The greatest gains are realized when each country specializes in producing the good for which it has a comparative advantage. Therefore, based on this example, the United States should specialize in washing machines and Italy should specialize in automobiles.

2. At a trade of 10 U.S. large jets for 15 Brazilian small jets, Brazil gives up less for a large jet than it would if it were building large jets itself. Without trade, Brazil gives up 3 small jets for each large jet it produces. With trade, Brazil gives up only 1.5 small jets for each large jet from the United States. Likewise, the United States gives up less for a small jet than it would if it were producing small jets itself. Without trade, the United States gives up ¾ of a large jet for each small jet. With trade, the United States gives up only ⅔ of a large jet for each small jet from Brazil.

Multiple-Choice Questions

1. a
2. a
3. a
4. d
5. d

Critical-Thinking Questions

1. Country A: opportunity cost of 1 bushel of wheat = 4 units of textiles

   Country B: opportunity cost of 1 bushel of wheat = 6 units of textiles

2. Country A has an absolute advantage in the production of wheat (15 versus 10)

3. Country A: opportunity cost of 1 unit of textiles = ¼ bushel of wheat

Country B: opportunity cost of 1 unit of textiles = ⅙ bushel of wheat

Country B has the comparative advantage in textile production because it has a lower opportunity cost of producing textiles. (Alternate answer: Country B has the comparative advantage in the production of textiles because Country A has a comparative advantage in the production of wheat based on opportunity costs shown in part a.)

MODULE 4

Check Your Understanding

1. a. The quantity of umbrellas demanded is higher at any given price on a rainy day than on a dry day. This is a rightward *shift* of the demand curve, since at any given price the quantity demanded rises. This implies that any specific quantity can now be sold at a higher price.

   b. The quantity of weekend calls demanded rises in response to a price reduction. This is a *movement along* the demand curve for weekend calls.

   c. The demand for roses increases the week of Valentine's Day. This is a rightward *shift* of the demand curve.

   d. The quantity of gasoline demanded falls in response to a rise in price. This is a *movement along* the demand curve.

Multiple-Choice Questions

1. e
2. a
3. c
4. d
5. a

Critical-Thinking Question

Your graph would look like this.

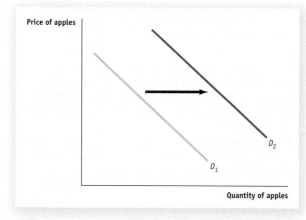

MODULE 5

Check Your Understanding

1. a. The quantity of houses supplied rises as a result of an increase in prices. This is a *movement along* the supply curve.

   b. The quantity of strawberries supplied is higher at any given price. This is an *increase* in supply, which shifts the supply curve to the right.

c. The quantity of labor supplied is lower at any given wage. This is a *decrease* in supply, which shifts the supply curve leftward compared to the supply curve during school vacation. So, in order to attract workers, fast-food chains have to offer higher wages.

d. The quantity of labor supplied rises in response to a rise in wages. This is a *movement along* the supply curve.

e. The quantity of cabins supplied is higher at any given price. This is an *increase* in supply, which shifts the supply curve to the right.

2. a. This is an increase in supply, so the supply curve shifts rightward. At the original equilibrium price of the year before, the quantity of grapes supplied exceeds the quantity demanded, and the result is a surplus. The price of grapes will fall.

   b. This is a decrease in demand, so the demand curve shifts leftward. At the original equilibrium price, the quantity of hotel rooms supplied exceeds the quantity demanded. The result is a surplus. The rates for hotel rooms will fall.

   c. Demand increases, so the demand curve for second-hand snowblowers shifts rightward. At the original equilibrium price, the quantity of second-hand snowblowers demanded exceeds the quantity supplied. This is a case of shortage. The equilibrium price of second-hand snowblowers will rise.

Multiple-Choice Questions

1. d
2. d
3. c
4. b
5. d

Critical-Thinking Question

Your graph would look like this.

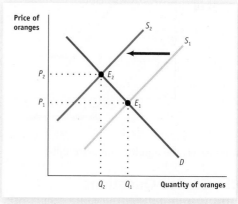

MODULE 6

Check Your Understanding

1. a. The decrease in the price of gasoline caused a rightward shift in the demand for large cars. As a result of the shift, the equilibrium price of large cars rose and the equilibrium quantity of large cars bought and sold also rose.

   b. The technological innovation has caused a rightward shift in the supply of fresh paper made from recycled stock. As a result of this shift, the equilibrium price of fresh paper made from recycled stock has fallen and the equilibrium quantity bought and sold has risen.

c. The fall in the price of pay-per-view movies causes a leftward shift in the demand for movies at local movie theaters. As a result of this shift, the equilibrium price of movie tickets falls and the equilibrium number of people who go to the movies also falls.

2. Upon the announcement of the new chip, the demand curve for computers using the earlier chip shifts leftward (demand decreases), and the supply curve for these computers shifts rightward (supply increases).

a. If demand decreases relatively more than supply increases, then the equilibrium quantity falls, as shown here:

b. If supply increases relatively more than demand decreases, then the equilibrium quantity rises, as shown here:

In both cases, the equilibrium price falls.

Multiple-Choice Questions

1. d
2. b
3. a
4. a
5. c

Critical-Thinking Question

Your graph would look like this.

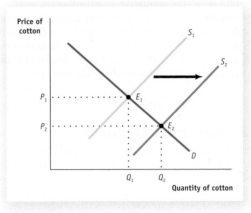

MODULE 7

Check Your Understanding

1.

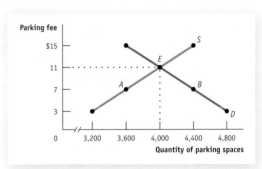

a. Fewer homeowners are willing to rent out their driveways because the price ceiling has reduced the payment they receive. This is an example of a fall in price leading to a fall in the quantity supplied. This is shown in the accompanying diagram by the movement from point E to point A along the supply curve, a reduction in quantity of 400 parking spaces.

b. The quantity demanded increases by 400 spaces as the price decreases. At a lower price, more fans are willing to drive and rent a parking space. It is shown in the diagram by the movement from point E to point B along the demand curve.

c. Under a price ceiling, the quantity demanded exceeds the quantity supplied; as a result, shortages arise. In this case, there will be a shortage of 800 parking spaces. It is shown by the horizontal distance between points A and B.

d. Price ceilings result in wasted resources. The additional time fans spend to secure a parking space is wasted time.

e. Price ceilings lead to the inefficient allocation of goods— here, the parking spaces—to consumers. If less serious fans with connections end up with the parking spaces, diehard fans have no place to park.

f. Price ceilings lead to black markets.

2.

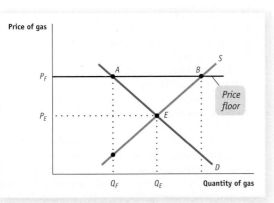

a. Some gas station owners will benefit from getting a higher price. Q_F indicates the sales made by these owners. But some will lose; there are those who make sales at the market equilibrium price of P_E but do not make sales at the regulated price of P_F. These missed sales are indicated on the graph by the fall in the quantity demanded along the demand curve, from point E to point A.

b. Those who buy gas at the higher price of P_F will probably receive better service; this is an example of *inefficiently high quality* caused by a price floor as gas station owners compete on quality rather than price. But opponents are correct to claim that consumers are generally worse off—those who buy at P_F would have been happy to buy at P_E, and many who were willing to buy at a price between P_E and P_F are now unwilling to buy. This is indicated on the graph by the fall in the quantity demanded along the demand curve, from point E to point A.

c. Proponents are wrong because consumers and some gas station owners are hurt by the price floor, which creates "missed opportunities"—desirable transactions between consumers and station owners that never take place. Moreover, the inefficiency of wasted resources arises as consumers spend time and money driving to other states. The price floor also tempts people to engage in black market activity. With the price floor, only Q_F units are sold. But at prices between P_E and P_F, there are drivers who together want to buy more than Q_F and owners who are willing to sell to them, a situation likely to lead to illegal activity.

3. a. The price of a ride is $7 since the quantity demanded at this price is 6 million: $7 is the *demand price* of 6 million rides. This is represented by point A in the accompanying figure.

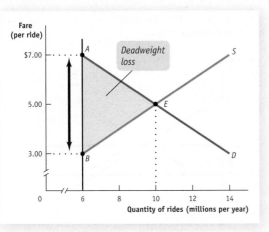

b. At 6 million rides, the supply price is $3 per ride, represented by point B in the figure. The wedge between the demand price of $7 per ride and the supply price of $3 per ride is the quota rent per ride, $4. This is represented in the figure above by the vertical distance between points A and B.

c. The quota discourages 4 million mutually beneficial transactions. The shaded triangle in the figure represents the deadweight loss.

d. At 9 million rides, the demand price is $5.50 per ride, indicated by point C in the following figure, and the supply price is $4.50 per ride, indicated by point D. The quota rent is the difference between the demand price and the supply price: $1. The deadweight loss is represented by the shaded triangle in the figure. Compare that area to the figure in part a, and you can see that the deadweight loss is smaller when the quota is set at 9 million rides than when it is set at 6 million rides.

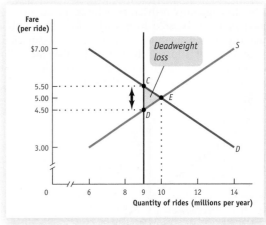

Multiple-Choice Questions

1. a

2. d

3. b

4. e

5. d

Critical-Thinking Questions

1. A binding price ceiling sets the maximum price that can be charged at a level below the market equilibrium price. This lower price will reduce quantity supplied and increase quantity demanded, resulting in a shortage.

2. A binding price floor sets the minimum price that can be charged at a level above the market equilibrium price. This higher price will reduce quantity demanded and increase quantity supplied, resulting in a surplus.

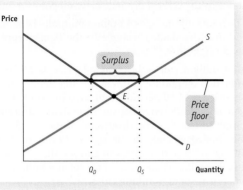

3. A binding quantity restriction reduces the quantity of the good that can be sold to a level below the equilibrium quantity. Given quantity is limited, firms can charge a price (P_D) that is higher than the price they are willing to sell for (P_S). The difference in these two prices results in quota rent, or extra profit, to the sellers of the good.

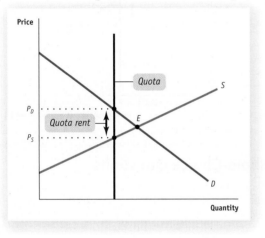

MODULE 8

Check Your Understanding

1. The United States will import tomatoes if the price of Mexican tomatoes is below the U.S. autarky price. This will cause the price of tomatoes to fall in the United States and rise in Mexico. The United States will export chicken to Mexico if the price of chicken in Mexico is above the U.S. autarky price. This will cause the price of chicken to rise in the United States and fall in Mexico.

    a. U.S. tomato consumers are better off and Mexican tomato consumers are worse off.

    b. U.S. tomato producers are worse off and Mexican tomato producers are better off.

    c. U.S. tomato workers are worse off and Mexican tomato workers are better off.

    d. U.S. poultry consumers are worse off and Mexican poultry consumers are better off.

    e. U.S. poultry producers are better off and Mexican poultry producers are worse off.

    f. U.S. poultry workers are better off and Mexican poultry workers are worse off.

2. a. If the tariff is $0.50, the price paid by domestic consumers for a pound of imported butter is $0.50 + $0.50 = $1.00, the same price as a pound of domestic butter. Imported butter will no longer have a price advantage over domestic butter, imports will cease, and domestic producers will capture all the feasible sales to domestic consumers, selling amount Q_A in the accompanying figure. But if the tariff is less than $0.50—say, only $0.25—the price paid by domestic consumers for a pound of imported butter is $0.50 + $0.25 = $0.75, $0.25 cheaper than a pound of domestic butter. American butter producers will gain sales in the amount of $Q_2 - Q_1$ as a result of the $0.25 tariff. But this is smaller than the amount they would have gained under the $0.50 tariff, the amount $Q_A - Q_1$.

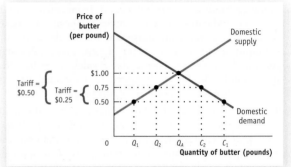

    b. As long as the tariff is at least $0.50, increasing it more has no effect. At a tariff of $0.50, all imports are effectively blocked.

3. All imports are effectively blocked at a tariff of $0.50. So such a tariff corresponds to an import quota of 0.

Multiple-Choice Questions

1. d
2. e
3. a
4. a
5. d

Critical-Thinking Questions

1. In the proposed scenario, the domestic price of the good will fall to the world price of $8. As a result, quantity demanded will increase and domestic quantity supplied will decrease.

2. The country will become an importer of the good because it can buy the good for a lower price from another country.

3. The answers to the previous two questions are supported by the following graph.

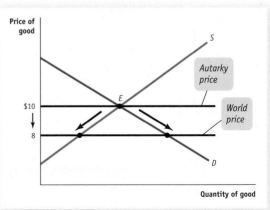

MODULE 9

Check Your Understanding

1. We talk about business cycles for the economy as a whole because recessions and expansions are not confined to a few industries—they reflect downturns and upturns for the economy as a whole. In downturns, almost every sector of the economy reduces output and the number of people employed. Moreover, business cycles are an international phenomenon, sometimes moving in rough synchrony across countries.

2. Countries with high rates of population growth will have to maintain higher growth rates of overall output than countries with low rates of population growth in order to achieve an increased standard of living per person because aggregate output will have to be divided among a larger number of people.

3. **a.** As some prices have risen but other prices have fallen, there may be overall inflation or deflation. The answer is ambiguous.

   b. As all prices have risen significantly, this sounds like inflation.

   c. As most prices have fallen and others have not changed, this sounds like deflation.

Multiple-Choice Questions

1. a
2. c
3. e
4. c
5. a

Critical-Thinking Question

No, Argentina is not poorer than it was in the past. Both Argentina and Canada have experienced long-run growth. However, after World War II, Argentina did not make as much progress as Canada, perhaps because of political instability and bad macroeconomic policies. Canada's economy grew much faster than Argentina's. Although Canada is now about three times as rich as Argentina, Argentina still had long-run growth of its economy.

MODULE 10

Check Your Understanding

1. **a.** Households are linked to firms through the sale of factors of production to firms, through purchases from firms of final goods and services, and through lending funds to firms in the financial markets.

   b. Households are linked to the government through their payment of taxes, their receipt of transfers, and their lending of funds to the government to finance government borrowing via the financial markets.

   c. Finally, households are linked to the rest of the world through their purchases of imports and transactions with foreigners in financial markets.

2. The four types of income received by households are wages, profit, interest, and rent. Wage income is received as payment for selling labor hours to firms. Some of the profit earned by firms is distributed to households who own stock in a company. Interest income is paid to households who hold bonds. In the case of bonds, some households have elected to lend money to firms in return for interest income. Finally, households receive rental income from firms when they rent land or physical structures they own to a firm. Households use their income to pay for consumption spending, taxes, and private savings.

Multiple-Choice Questions

1. a
2. b
3. e
4. c
5. d

Critical-Thinking Question

In the market for goods and services, firms sell the goods and services they produce to households. Firms buy the resources they need to produce the goods and services in factor markets. The banking, stock, and bond markets are collectively known as the financial market. The financial market links lenders (those with savings) and borrowers (such as firms that require funds to pay for investment spending).

MODULE 11

Check Your Understanding

1. Let's start by considering the relationship between the total value added of all domestically produced final goods and services, and aggregate spending on domestically produced final goods and services. These two quantities are equal because every final good and service produced in the economy is either purchased by someone or added to inventories, and additions to inventories are counted as spending by firms. Next, consider the relationship between aggregate spending on domestically produced final goods and services and total factor income. These two quantities are equal because all spending that is channeled to firms to pay for purchases of domestically produced final goods and services is revenue for firms. Those revenues must be paid out by firms to their factors of production in the form of wages, profit, interest, and rent. Taken together, this means that all three methods of calculating GDP are equivalent.

2. The investment spending category of GDP measures purchases of new capital by firms, changes to the stock of firm's inventories, and residential investment (the value of new houses constructed during the given time period).

3. You would be counting the value of the steel twice—once as it was sold by American Steel to American Motors and once as part of the car sold by American Motors.

Multiple-Choice Questions

1. e
2. a
3. c
4. b
5. a

Critical-Thinking Questions

1. Some of the new goods and services produced are intermediate goods. We do not want to count intermediate goods separately because they are part of the value of the final goods.

2. The concept of value added allows the government to measure GDP by counting only the value added by each firm as opposed to the total value of the firm's output. Value added by definition is the value of the firm's output minus the value of any purchased intermediate goods used in production.

MODULE 12

Check Your Understanding

1. a. In 2012 nominal GDP was $(1,000,000 \times \$0.40) + (800,000 \times \$0.60) = \$400,000 + \$480,000 = \$880,000$. The total value of sales of french fries in 2013 was $900,000 \times \$0.50 = \$450,000$. The total value of sales of onion rings in 2013 was $840,000 \times \$0.51 = \$428,400$. Nominal GDP in 2013 was $\$450,000 + \$428,400 = \$878,400$. To find real GDP in 2013, we must calculate the value of sales in 2013 using 2012 prices: $(900,000 \times \$0.40) + (840,000 \times \$0.60) = \$360,000 + \$504,000 = \$864,000$.

   b. A comparison of nominal GDP in 2012 to nominal GDP in 2013 shows a decline of $((\$880,000 - \$878,400) / \$880,000) \times 100 = 0.18\%$. But a comparison using real GDP shows a decline of $((\$880,000 - \$864,000) / \$880,000) \times 100 = 1.8\%$. That is, a calculation based on real GDP shows a drop 10 times larger (1.8%) than a calculation based on nominal GDP (0.18%): in this case, the calculation based on nominal GDP underestimates the true magnitude of the change because it incorporates both quantity changes and price changes.

2. A price index based on 1990 prices will contain a relatively low price of housing compared to a price index based on 2000 prices. This means that a 2000 price index used to calculate real GDP in 2010 will magnify the value of housing production in the economy and increase the relative size of the housing sector as a component of real GDP.

Multiple-Choice Questions

1. d
2. b
3. c
4. c
5. c

Critical-Thinking Questions

1. Country A: $(4,000–2,000/2,000) \times 100 = 100\%$
   Country B: $(6,000–2,000/2,000) \times 100 = 200\%$

2. Country A: It stayed the same.
   Country B: It doubled.

3. Country A: $4,000 (There was no price increase so it is the same.)
   Country B: $6,000/2 = \$3,000 (Prices doubled.)

4. Country A: $(4,000–2,000/2,000) \times 100 = 100\%$
   Country B: $(3,000–2,000/2,000) \times 100 = 50\%$

5. Country A: $4,000/20 = \$200$ versus
   Country B: $3,000/15 = \$200$. It is the same.

MODULE 13

Check Your Understanding

1. The advent of websites that enable job-seekers to find jobs more quickly will reduce the unemployment rate over time. However, websites that induce discouraged workers to begin actively looking for work again will lead to an increase in the unemployment rate over time.

2. a. Not counted as unemployed because not actively looking for work, but counted in broader measures of labor underutilization as a discouraged worker.

   b. Not counted as unemployed—considered employed because the teacher has a job.

   c. Unemployed: not working, actively looking for work.

   d. Not unemployed, but underemployed: working part-time for economic reasons. Counted in broader measures of labor underutilization.

   e. Not unemployed, but considered "marginally attached." Counted in broader measures of labor underutilization.

3. Items (a) and (b) are consistent with the observed relationship between growth in GDP and changes in the unemployment rate. Item (c) is not.

Multiple-Choice Questions

1. e
2. b
3. a
4. d
5. b

Critical-Thinking Questions

1. Employed (underemployed); she is not working up to her full potential.

2. Not in the labor force (discouraged). Once a worker stops actively seeking work, he or she falls out of the labor force.

3. Employed (part-time); individuals are classified as employed if they work full or part time.

4. Not in the labor force; he is not actively seeking employment.

MODULE 14

Check Your Understanding

1. a. Frictional unemployment is unemployment due to the time workers spend searching for jobs. It is inevitable because workers may leave one job in search of another for a variety of reasons. Furthermore, there will always be new entrants into the labor force who are seeking a first job. During the search process, these individuals will be counted as part of the frictionally unemployed.

   b. When the unemployment rate is low, frictional unemployment will account for a larger share of total unemployment because other sources of unemployment will be diminished. So the share of total unemployment composed of the frictionally unemployed will rise.

2. A binding minimum wage represents a price floor below which wages cannot fall. As a result, actual wages cannot move toward equilibrium. So a minimum wage causes

the quantity of labor supplied to exceed the quantity of labor demanded. Because this surplus of labor reflects unemployed workers, it affects the unemployment rate. Collective bargaining has a similar effect—unions are able to raise the wage above the equilibrium level. This will act like a minimum wage by causing the number of job seekers to be larger than the number of workers firms are willing to hire. Collective bargaining causes the unemployment rate to be higher than it otherwise would be, as shown in the accompanying figure.

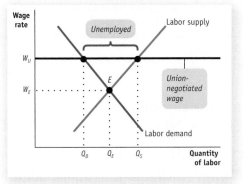

3. An increase in unemployment benefits reduces the cost to individuals of being unemployed, causing them to spend more time searching for a new job. So the natural rate of unemployment would increase.

Multiple-Choice Questions

1. a
2. c
3. b
4. d
5. e

Critical-Thinking Question

This statement is true only if there is no change in the size of the labor force. The size of the labor force will decrease if some employed people quit their jobs and leave the labor force. An example would be people who decide to retire. The size of the labor force will increase if some people who are currently not in the labor force decide to enter the labor force and either become employed or unemployed. An example would be full-time students who graduate and enter the labor force. The size of the labor force will decrease if some unemployed people give up looking for work and exit the labor force.

MODULE 15
Check Your Understanding

1. Shoe-leather costs as a result of inflation will be lower because it is now less costly for individuals to manage their assets in order to economize on their money holdings. ATM machines, for example, give customers 24-hour access to cash in thousands of locations. This reduction in the cost of obtaining money translates into lower shoe-leather costs.

2. If inflation came to a complete stop for several years, the inflation rate of zero would be less than the expected inflation rate of 2–3%. Because the real interest rate is the nominal interest rate minus the inflation rate, the real

interest rates on loans would be higher than expected, and lenders would gain at the expense of borrowers. Borrowers would have to repay their loans with funds that had a higher real value than had been expected.

Multiple-Choice Questions

1. e
2. c
3. b
4. d
5. c

Critical-Thinking Questions

1. 0%

2. You borrowed enough money to buy a couch and paid back just enough to buy the same couch (after inflation). Therefore, you gained the benefit of the loan without paying any real interest for it.

3. Whoever gave you the loan lost. The loan was paid back after prices unexpectedly increased, so the lender received a real interest rate of 0% for letting you use the money for a year.

MODULE 16
Check Your Understanding

1. Pre–frost, this market basket costs $(100 \times \$0.20) + (50 \times \$0.60) + (200 \times \$0.25) = \$20 + \$30 + \$50 = \$100$. The same market basket, post-frost, costs $(100 \times \$0.40) + (50 \times \$1.00) + (200 \times \$0.45) = \$40 + \$50 + \$90 = \$180$. So the price index is $(\$100/\$100) \times 100 = 100$ before the frost and $(\$180/\$100) \times 100 = 180$ after the frost, implying a rise in the price index of 80%. This increase in the price index is less than the 84.2% increase calculated in the text. The reason for this difference is that the new market basket of 100 oranges, 50 grapefruit, and 200 lemons contains proportionately more of an item that has experienced a relatively small price increase (the lemons, the price of which has increased by 80%) and proportionately fewer of an item that has experienced a relatively large price increase (the oranges, the price of which has increased by 100%). This shows that the price index can be very sensitive to the composition of the market basket. If the market basket contains a large proportion of goods whose prices have risen faster than the prices of other goods, it will lead to a higher estimate of the increase in the price level. If it contains a large proportion of goods whose prices have risen more slowly than the prices of other goods, it will lead to a lower estimate of the increase in the price level.

2. a. A market basket determined 10 years ago will contain fewer cars than at present. Given that the average price of a car has grown faster than the average prices of other goods, this basket will underestimate the true increase in the price level because it contains relatively too few cars.

   b. A market basket determined 10 years ago will not contain Internet access, so it cannot track the fall in prices of Internet access over the past few years. As a result, it will overestimate the true increase in the price level.

3. Using Equation 16-2, the inflation rate from 2011 to 2012 is $(229.6 - 224.9)/224.9 \times 100 = 2.1\%$.

Multiple-Choice Questions

1. d
2. c
3. e
4. b
5. b

Critical-Thinking Question

To calculate the inflation rate from 2010 to 2011 using either the GDP deflator or the CPI, start with the 2011 price index value and subtract the 2010 price index value to find the change in the price index. Divide this change in the price index by the 2011 value and then multiply by 100. Do the same to calculate the inflation rate from 2011 to 2012. The results are shown in the following table.

Year	GDP Deflator	CPI
2010–2011	$(2.4/111.0) \times 100 = 2.2\%$	$(6.8/218.1) \times 100 = 3.1\%$
2011–2012	$(2.0/113.4) \times 100 = 1.8\%$	$(4.7/224.9) \times 100 = 2.1\%$

MODULE 17

Check Your Understanding

1. Economists want a measure of economic progress that rises with increases in the living standard of the average resident of a country. An increase in overall real GDP does not accurately reflect an increase in an average resident's living standard because it does not account for growth in the number of residents. If, for example, real GDP rises by 10% but population grows by 20%, the living standard of the average resident falls: after the change, the average resident has only $(110/120) \times 100 = 91.6\%$ as much real income as before the change. Similarly, an increase in nominal GDP per capita does not accurately reflect an increase in living standards because it does not account for any change in prices. For example, a 5% increase in nominal GDP per capita generated by a 5% increase in prices results in no change in living standards. Real GDP per capita is the only measure that accounts for both changes in the population and changes in prices.

2. Using the Rule of 70, the amount of time it will take China to double its real GDP per capita is $(70/8.9) = 7.9$ years; India, $(70/4.2) = 16.7$ years; Ireland, $(70/3.1) = 22.6$ years; the United States, $(70/1.7) = 41.2$ years; France, $(70/1.3) = 53.8$ years; and Argentina $(70/1.2) = 58.3$ years. Since the Rule of 70 can be applied to only a positive growth rate, we cannot apply it to the case of Zimbabwe, which experienced negative growth. If India continues to have a higher growth rate of real GDP per capita than the United States, then India's real GDP per capita will eventually surpass that of the United States.

3. The United States began growing rapidly over a century ago, but China and India have begun growing rapidly only recently. As a result, the living standard of the typical Chinese or Indian household has not yet caught up with that of the typical American household.

Multiple-Choice Questions

1. d
2. c
3. c
4. b
5. b

Critical-Thinking Question

Increases in real GDP per capita result mostly from changes in productivity (or labor productivity). Productivity is defined as output per worker or output per hour. Increased labor force participation could also lead to higher real GDP per capita, but the rate of employment growth is rarely very different from the rate of population growth, meaning that the corresponding increase in output does not lead to an increase in output per capita.

MODULE 18

Check Your Understanding

1. **a.** Significant technological progress will result in a positive growth rate of productivity even though physical capital per worker and human capital per worker are unchanged.

   b. Productivity will grow, but due to diminishing marginal returns, each successive increase in physical capital per worker results in a smaller increase in productivity than the one before it.

2. **a.** If the economy has grown 3% per year and the labor force has grown 1% per year, then productivity—output per worker—has grown at approximately 3% − 1% = 2% per year.

   b. If physical capital has grown 4% per year and the labor force has grown 1% per year, then physical capital per worker has grown at approximately 4% − 1% = 3% per year.

   c. According to estimates, each 1% rise in physical capital, other things equal, increases productivity by 0.3%. So, as physical capital per worker has increased by 3%, productivity growth that can be attributed to an increase in physical capital per worker is $0.3 \times 3\% = 0.9\%$. As a percentage of total productivity growth, this is 0.9%/2% × 100% = 45%.

   d. If the rest of productivity growth is due to technological progress, then technological progress has contributed 2% − 0.9% = 1.1% to productivity growth. As a percentage of total productivity growth, this is 1.1%/2% × 100% = 55%.

3. It will take time for workers to learn how to use the new computer system and to adjust their routines. And because there are often setbacks in learning a new system, such as accidentally erasing your computer files, productivity at Multinomics may decrease for a period of time.

4. Growth increases a country's greenhouse gas emissions. The current best estimates are that a large reduction in emissions will result in only a modest reduction in growth. The international burden sharing of greenhouse gas emissions reduction is contentious because rich countries are reluctant to pay the costs of reducing their emissions only to see newly emerging countries like China rapidly increase their emissions. Yet most of the current accumulation of gases is due to the past actions of rich countries. Poorer countries like China are equally reluctant to sacrifice their growth to pay for the past actions of rich countries.

Multiple-Choice Questions

1. e
2. a
3. a
4. c
5. b

Critical-Thinking Questions

1. Growing physical capital per worker is responsible for 1% productivity growth per year. 2% × 0.5 = 1%

2. There was no growth in total factor productivity because there was no technological progress. According to the Rule of 70, over 70 years (from 1942 to 2012), a 1% growth rate would cause output to double. Real GDP per capita in this case doubled, as would be expected from a 1% productivity growth rate alone; therefore, there was no change in technological progress.

MODULE 19

Check Your Understanding

1. A country that has high domestic savings is able to achieve a high rate of investment spending as a percentage of GDP. This, in turn, allows the country to achieve a high growth rate.

2. Although it is important in determining the growth rate for some countries (such as those of Western Europe), the initial level of GDP per capita isn't the only factor. High rates of saving and investment appear to be better predictors of future growth than today's standard of living.

3. The evidence suggests that both sets of factors matter: better infrastructure is important for growth, but so is political and financial stability. Policies should try to address both areas.

Multiple-Choice Questions

1. e
2. e
3. d
4. e
5. b

Critical-Thinking Question

The convergence hypothesis says a country grows more slowly, other things equal, when its real GDP per capita is relatively higher. This points to lower future growth for East Asian countries. However, other things might not be equal: if Asian economies continue investing in human capital, if savings rates continue to be high, if governments invest in infrastructure, and so on, growth might continue to accelerate.

MODULE 20

Check Your Understanding

1. a. False. In an open economy, investment spending is equal to national savings plus net capital inflow. If the budget balance is zero, then government savings is zero and national savings is equal to private savings. In this case, investment is equal to private savings plus net capital inflow. Investment spending is being financed by private savings and from funds flowing into the country from abroad.

 b. True. In an open economy, investment spending is equal to national savings plus net capital inflow, so investment spending minus national savings equals net capital inflow. If national savings is less than investment spending then investment spending minus national savings is positive, and therefore so is net capital inflow. Investment spending is being financed by national savings and from funds flowing into the country from abroad.

2. $I = GDP - C - G - X + M = \$2,081$

 $S_{National} = GDP - C - G = \$1,548$

 $T = S_{Government} + G = \$1,822$

 $NCI = IM - X = \$533$

 $S_{Private} = I - S_{Government} - NCI = \$2,775$

 Note that the budget balance is the same as government saving.

Multiple-Choice Questions

1. a
2. a
3. e
4. a
5. a

Critical-Thinking Question

Investment spending is equal to national savings plus net capital inflow. This means investment spending can be financed with funds saved by national residents of the country, or by funds that flow into the country from abroad.

MODULE 21

Check Your Understanding

1. a. As capital flows into the economy, the supply of loanable funds increases. This is illustrated by the shift of the supply curve from S_1 to S_2 in the accompanying diagram. As the equilibrium moves from E_1 to E_2, the equilibrium interest rate falls from r_1 to r_2, and the equilibrium quantity of loanable funds increases from Q_1 to Q_2.

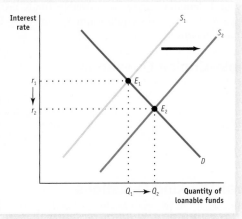

b. Savings fall due to the higher proportion of retired people, and the supply of loanable funds decreases. This is illustrated by the leftward shift of the supply curve from S_1 to S_2 in the accompanying diagram. The equilibrium moves from E_1 to E_2, the equilibrium interest rate rises from r_1 to r_2, and the equilibrium quantity of loanable funds falls from Q_1 to Q_2.

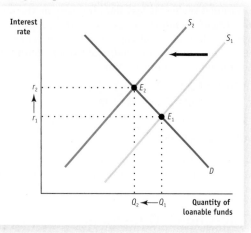

2. We know from the loanable funds market that as the interest rate rises, households want to save more and consume less. But at the same time, an increase in the interest rate lowers the number of investment spending projects with returns at least as high as the interest rate. The statement "households will want to save more money than businesses will want to invest" cannot represent an equilibrium in the loanable funds market because it says that the quantity of loanable funds offered exceeds the quantity of loanable funds demanded. If that were to occur, the interest rate would fall to make the quantity of loanable funds offered equal to the quantity of loanable funds demanded.

3. a. The real interest rate will not change. According to the Fisher effect, an increase in expected inflation drives up the nominal interest rate, leaving the real interest rate unchanged.

b. The nominal interest rate will rise by 3%. Each additional percentage point of expected inflation drives up the nominal interest rate by 1 percentage point.

c. As long as inflation is expected, it does not affect the equilibrium quantity of loanable funds. Both the supply and demand curves for loanable funds are pushed upward, leaving the equilibrium quantity of loanable funds unchanged.

Multiple-Choice Questions

1. e
2. b
3. b
4. c
5. a

Critical-Thinking Questions

1. This causes an increase (rightward shift) in the supply of loanable funds.

2. This causes a decrease (leftward shift) in the demand for loanable funds.

3. This causes an increase (rightward shift) in the demand for loanable funds.

4. This causes a decrease (leftward shift) in the supply of loanable funds.

MODULE 22
Check Your Understanding

1. a. The net present value of project A is unaffected by the interest rate since it is money received today; its present value is still $100. The net present value of project B is now $-\$10 + \$115/1.02 = \$102.75$. The net present value of project C is now $\$119 - \$20/1.02 = \$99.39$. Project B is now preferred.

b. When the interest rate is lower, the cost of waiting for money that arrives in the future is lower. For example, at a 10% interest rate, $1 arriving one year from today is worth only $\$1/1.10 = \$0.91$. But when the interest rate is 2%, $1 arriving one year from today is worth $\$1/1.02 = \$0.98$, a sizable increase. As a result, project B, which has a benefit one year from today, becomes more attractive. And project C, which has a cost one year from today, becomes less attractive.

Multiple-Choice Questions

1. e
2. b
3. c
4. d
5. b

Critical-Thinking Questions

1. $\$1,000 \times (1.05)^3 = \$1,000 \times 1.16 = \$1,157.63$
2. $\$1,000/(1.05)^3 = \$863.84$

MODULE 23
Check Your Understanding

1. The transaction costs for (a) a bank deposit and (b) a share of a mutual fund are approximately equivalent because each can typically be accomplished by making a phone call, going online, or visiting a branch office. Transaction costs are highest for (c) a share of a family business since finding a buyer for the share consumes time and resources. The level of risk is lowest for (a) a bank deposit, since these deposits are insured by the Federal Deposit Insurance Corporation (FDIC) up to $250,000; somewhat higher for (b) a share of a mutual fund since despite diversification, there is still risk associated with holding stocks; and highest for (c) a share of a family business since this investment is not diversified. The level of liquidity is the lowest for (c) a share of a family business, since it can be sold only with the unanimous agreement of other members and it will take some time to find a buyer; higher for (b) a share of a mutual fund, since it will take only a few days between selling your shares and the payment being processed; and highest for (a) a bank deposit, since withdrawals can usually be made immediately.

2. Economic development and growth are the result of, among other factors, investment spending on physical capital. Since investment spending is equal to savings, the greater the amount saved, the higher investment spending will be, and so the higher growth and economic development will be. So the existence of institutions that facilitate savings will help a country's growth and economic development. As a result, a country with a financial system that provides low transaction costs, opportunities for diversification of risk, and high liquidity to its savers will experience faster growth and economic development than a country that doesn't.

Multiple-Choice Questions

1. d

2. a

3. c

4. d

5. b

Critical-Thinking Question

1) **Mutual fund**—a financial intermediary that creates a stock portfolio by buying and holding shares in companies and then selling shares of the stock portfolio to individual investors.

2) **Life insurance company**—a firm that guarantees a payment to the policyholder's beneficiaries (typically, the family) when the policyholder dies.

3) **Bank**—an institution that helps resolve the conflict between lenders' needs for liquidity and the illiquid financing needs of borrowers who don't want to use the stock or bond markets.

4) **Pension fund**—a nonprofit institution that collects the savings of its members and invests those funds in a variety of assets, providing its members with income when they retire.

MODULE 24
Check Your Understanding

1. A decline in investment spending, like a rise in investment spending, has a multiplier effect on real GDP—the only difference in this case is that real GDP falls instead of rises. The fall in I leads to an initial fall in real GDP, which leads to a fall in disposable income, which leads to lower consumer spending, which leads to another fall in real GDP, and so on. So consumer spending falls as an indirect result of the fall in investment spending.

2. When the MPC is 0.5, the multiplier is equal to $1/(1 - 0.5)$ $= 1/0.5 = 2$. When the MPC is 0.8, the multiplier is equal to $1/(1 - 0.8) = 1/0.2 = 5$.

3. The greater the share of GDP that is saved rather than spent, the lower the MPC. Disposable income that goes to savings is like a "leak" in the system, reducing the amount of spending that fuels a further expansion. So it is likely that Amerigo will have the larger multiplier.

Multiple-Choice Questions

1. e

2. a

3. b

4. b

5. c

Critical-Thinking Question

An autonomous change in aggregate spending, such as a $100 million increase in investment spending, has a multiple effect on real GDP. In other words, real GDP will in this example increase by more than $100 million. The initial $100 million increase in investment spending leads to an increase in real GDP, which leads to an increase in disposable income and more consumption spending. This increase in consumption spending is what causes real GDP to increase by an amount larger than the initial increase in autonomous aggregate spending.

MODULE 25
Check Your Understanding

1. a. Angelina's autonomous consumer spending is $8,000. When her current disposable income rises by $10,000, her consumer spending rises by $12,000 − $8,000 = $4,000. So her MPC is $4,000/$10,000 = 0.4 and her consumption function is $c = \$8,000 + 0.4 \times yd$. Felicia's autonomous consumer spending is $6,500. When her current disposable income rises by $10,000, her consumer spending rises by $14,500 − $6,500 = $8,000. So her MPC is $8,000/$10,000 = 0.8 and her consumption function is $c = \$6,500 + 0.8 \times yd$. Marina's autonomous consumer spending is $7,250. When her current disposable income rises by $10,000, her consumer spending rises by $14,250 − $7,250 = $7,000. So her MPC is $7,000/$10,000 = 0.7 and her consumption function is $c = \$7,250 + 0.7 \times yd$.

b. The aggregate autonomous consumer spending in this economy is $8,000 + $6,500 + $7,250 = $21,750. A $30,000 increase in disposable income (3 × $10,000) leads to a $4,000 + $8,000 + $7,000 = $19,000 increase in consumer spending. So the economy-wide MPC is $19,000/$30,000 = 0.63 and the aggregate consumption function is $C = \$21,750 + 0.63 \times YD$.

2. If you expect your future disposable income to fall, you would like to save some of today's disposable income to tide you over in the future. But you cannot do this if you cannot save. If you expect your future disposable income to rise, you would like to spend some of tomorrow's higher income today. But you cannot do this if you cannot borrow. If you cannot save or borrow, your expected future disposable income will have no effect on your consumer spending today. In fact, your MPC must always equal 1: you must consume all your current disposable income today, and you will be unable to smooth your consumption over time.

3. a. An unexpected increase in consumer spending will result in a reduction in inventories as producers sell items from their inventories to satisfy this short-term increase in demand. This is negative unplanned inventory investment: it reduces the value of producers' inventories.

b. A rise in the cost of borrowing is equivalent to a rise in the interest rate: fewer investment spending projects are now profitable to producers, whether they are financed through borrowing or retained earnings. As a result, producers will reduce the amount of planned investment spending.

c. A sharp increase in the rate of real GDP growth leads to a higher level of planned investment spending by producers, according to the accelerator principle, as they increase production capacity to meet higher demand.

d. As sales fall, producers sell less, and their inventories grow. This leads to positive unplanned inventory investment.

4. When consumer spending is sluggish, firms with excess production capacity will cut back on planned investment spending because they think their existing capacities are sufficient for expected future sales. Similarly, when consumer spending is sluggish and firms have a large amount of unplanned inventory investment, they are likely to cut back their production of output because they think their existing inventories are sufficient for expected future sales. So an inventory overhang is likely to depress current economic activity as firms cut back on their planned investment spending and on their output.

Multiple-Choice Questions

1. d
2. c
3. b
4. d
5. a

Critical-Thinking Question

The three most important factors are these:

1. The interest rate is the price (or opportunity cost) of investing, thus they are negatively related.

2. Expected future real GDP—if a firm expects its sales to grow rapidly in the future, it will invest in expanded production capacity.

3. Production capacity—if a firm finds its existing production capacity insufficient for its future production needs, it will undertake investment spending to meet those needs.

MODULE 26

Check Your Understanding

1. A slump in planned investment spending will lead to a fall in real GDP in response to an unanticipated increase in inventories. The fall in real GDP will translate into a fall in households' disposable income, and households will respond by reducing consumer spending. The decrease in consumer spending leads producers to further decrease output, further lowering disposable income and leading to further reductions in consumer spending. So although the slump originated in investment spending, it will cause a reduction in consumer spending.

2. a. After an autonomous fall in planned aggregate spending, the economy is no longer in equilibrium: real GDP is greater than planned aggregate spending. The accompanying figure shows this autonomous fall in planned aggregate spending by the shift of the aggregate spending curve from AE_1 to AE_2. The difference between the

two results in positive unplanned inventory investment: there is an unanticipated increase in inventories. Firms will respond by reducing production. This will eventually move the economy to a new equilibrium. In the accompanying figure, this is illustrated by the movement from the initial income–expenditure equilibrium at E_1 to the new income–expenditure equilibrium at E_2. As the economy moves to its new equilibrium, real GDP falls from its initial income–expenditure equilibrium level at Y_1^* to its new lower level, Y_2^*.

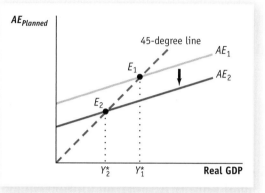

b. We know that the change in income–expenditure equilibrium GDP is given by Equation 62-7: $\Delta Y^* =$ Multiplier $\times \Delta AAE_{Planned}$. Here, the multiplier $= 1/(1 - 0.5) = 1/0.5 = 2$. So a $300 million autonomous reduction in planned aggregate spending will lead to a $2 \times \$300$ million $= \$600$ million ($0.6 billion) fall in income–expenditure equilibrium GDP. The new Y^* will be $500 billion – $0.6 billion = $499.4 billion.

Multiple-Choice Questions

1. c
2. b
3. c
4. b
5. c

Critical-Thinking Question

In income–expenditure equilibrium, unplanned inventory investment is equal to zero. Firms have produced enough output to match expected sales, and to adjust inventories to their desired level. When sales are above or below expected levels, then there will be unplanned inventory changes and the economy will not be in income–expenditure equilibrium.

MODULE 27

Check Your Understanding

1. a This is a shift of the aggregate demand curve. A decrease in the quantity of money raises the interest rate, since people now want to borrow more and lend less. A higher interest rate reduces investment and consumer spending at any given aggregate price level, so the aggregate demand curve shifts to the left.

b. This is a movement up along the aggregate demand curve. As the aggregate price level rises, the real value of money holdings falls. This is the interest rate effect of a change in the aggregate price level: as the value of money falls, people want to hold more money. They do so by borrowing more and lending less. This leads to a rise in the interest rate and a reduction in consumer and investment spending. So it is a movement along the aggregate demand curve.

c. This is a shift of the aggregate demand curve. Expectations of a poor job market, and so lower average disposable incomes, will reduce people's consumer spending today at any given aggregate price level. So the aggregate demand curve shifts to the left.

d. This is a shift of the aggregate demand curve. A fall in tax rates raises people's disposable income. At any given aggregate price level, consumer spending is now higher. So the aggregate demand curve shifts to the right.

e. This is a movement down along the aggregate demand curve. As the aggregate price level falls, the real value of assets rises. This is the wealth effect of a change in the aggregate price level: as the value of assets rises, people will increase their consumption plans. This leads to higher consumer spending. So it is a movement along the aggregate demand curve.

f. This is a shift of the aggregate demand curve. A rise in the real value of assets in the economy due to a surge in real estate values raises consumer spending at any given aggregate price level. So the aggregate demand curve shifts to the right.

Multiple-Choice Questions

1. d
2. c
3. c
4. a
5. a

Critical-Thinking Question

The two effects that cause the aggregate demand curve to have a downward slope are the wealth effect and the interest rate effect of a change in the aggregate price level.

The wealth effect: When the price level increases, the purchasing power of money decreases, causing consumers to scale back on spending. Because consumer spending is a component of aggregate demand, increases in the aggregate price level lead to decreases in the quantity of aggregate output demanded. The opposite is true for decreases in the price level. This negative relationship between the price level and the quantity of aggregate output demanded results in a downward-sloping aggregate demand curve.

The interest rate effect: Increases in the aggregate price level cause people to want to hold more money, which increases the demand for money and drives interest rates up. Higher interest rates reduce investment spending because it costs more to borrow money. Thus, a rise in the price level leads to less investment spending, which is a component of aggregate demand, and causes the quantity of aggregate output demanded to decrease (and vice versa). The result is a downward-sloping aggregate demand curve.

MODULE 28
Check Your Understanding

1. a. This represents a movement along the *SRAS* curve because the CPI—like the GDP deflator—is a measure of the aggregate price level, the overall price level of final goods and services in the economy.

b. This represents a shift of the *SRAS* curve because oil is a commodity. The *SRAS* curve will shift to the right because production costs are now lower, leading to a higher quantity of aggregate output supplied at any given aggregate price level.

c. This represents a shift of the *SRAS* curve because it involves a change in nominal wages. An increase in legally mandated benefits to workers is equivalent to an increase in nominal wages. As a result, the *SRAS* curve will shift leftward because production costs are now higher, leading to a lower quantity of aggregate output supplied at any given aggregate price level.

2. You would need to know what happened to the aggregate price level. If the increase in the quantity of aggregate output supplied was due to a movement along the *SRAS* curve, the aggregate price level would have increased at the same time as the quantity of aggregate output supplied increased. If the increase in the quantity of aggregate output supplied was due to a rightward shift of the *LRAS* curve, the aggregate price level might not rise. Alternatively, you could make the determination by observing what happened to aggregate output in the long run. If it fell back to its initial level in the long run, then the temporary increase in aggregate output was due to a movement along the *SRAS* curve. If it stayed at the higher level in the long run, the increase in aggregate output was due to a rightward shift of the *LRAS* curve.

Multiple-Choice Questions

1. e
2. a
3. c
4. d
5. e

Critical-Thinking Questions

1. If there is a fall in the aggregate price level, then the price received by the perfectly competitive firm for its output will also fall. Since many production costs are fixed in the short run, the price will fall by more than production costs will fall. This will reduce profit per unit and, therefore, the perfectly competitive firm will reduce output.

2. An imperfectly competitive firm is not a price taker and can change price in response to changes in demand. If there is an increase in demand, then the firm can sell more output. The imperfectly competitive firm is likely to increase the price it charges in order to increase profit per unit.

MODULE 29
Check Your Understanding

1. a. An increase in the minimum wage raises the nominal wage and, as a result, shifts the short-run aggregate supply curve to the left. As a result of this negative supply shock, the aggregate price level rises and aggregate output falls.

b. Increased investment spending shifts the aggregate demand curve to the right. As a result of this positive demand shock, both the aggregate price level and aggregate output rise.

c. An increase in taxes and a reduction in government spending both result in negative demand shocks, shifting the aggregate demand curve to the left. As a result, both the aggregate price level and aggregate output fall.

d. This is a negative supply shock, shifting the short-run aggregate supply curve to the left. As a result, the aggregate price level rises and aggregate output falls.

2. As long-run growth increases potential output, the long-run aggregate supply curve shifts to the right. If, in the short run, there is now a recessionary gap (aggregate output is less than potential output), nominal wages will fall, shifting the short-run aggregate supply curve to the right. This results in a fall in the aggregate price level and a rise in aggregate output. As prices fall, we move along the aggregate demand curve due to the wealth and interest rate effects of a change in the aggregate price level. Eventually, as long-run macroeconomic equilibrium is reestablished, aggregate output will rise to be equal to potential output, and the aggregate price level will fall to the level that equates the quantity of aggregate output demanded with potential output.

3. a. An economy is overstimulated when an inflationary gap is present. This will arise if an expansionary monetary or fiscal policy is implemented when the economy is currently in long-run macroeconomic equilibrium. This shifts the aggregate demand curve to the right, in the short run raising the aggregate price level and aggregate output and creating an inflationary gap. Eventually nominal wages will rise and shift the short-run aggregate supply curve to the left, and aggregate output will fall back to potential output. This is the scenario envisaged by the speaker.

b. No, this is not a valid argument. When the economy is not currently in long-run macroeconomic equilibrium, an expansionary monetary or fiscal policy does not lead to the outcome described. Suppose a negative demand shock has shifted the aggregate demand curve to the left, resulting in a recessionary gap. An expansionary monetary or fiscal policy can shift the aggregate demand curve back to its original position in long-run macroeconomic equilibrium. In this way, the short-run fall in aggregate output and deflation caused by the original negative demand shock can be avoided. So, if used in response to demand shocks, fiscal or monetary policy is an effective policy tool.

4. Those within the Fed who advocated lowering interest rates were focused on boosting aggregate demand in order to counteract the negative demand shock caused by the collapse of the housing bubble. Lowering interest rates will result in a rightward shift of the aggregate demand curve, increasing aggregate output but raising the aggregate price level. Those within the Fed who advocated holding interest rates steady were focused on the fact that fighting the slump in aggregate demand in the face of a negative supply shock could result in a rise in inflation. Holding interest rates steady relies on the ability of the economy to self-correct in the long run, with the aggregate price level and aggregate output only gradually returning to their levels before the negative supply shock.

Multiple-Choice Questions

1. c

2. a

3. d

4. b

5. b

Critical-Thinking Question

Since output Y_1 is above potential output, there is an inflationary gap. The low level of unemployment will cause nominal wages to rise, causing production cost to rise. This will shift the $SRAS$ curve up and to the left. As the price level rises, there is a movement along the AD curve and output returns to its potential level.

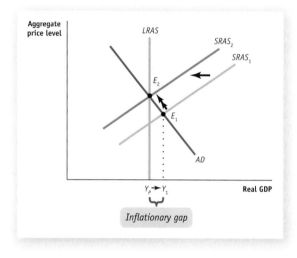

MODULE 30
Check Your Understanding

1. a. This is a contractionary fiscal policy because it is a reduction in government purchases of goods and services.

b. This is an expansionary fiscal policy because it is an increase in government transfers that will increase disposable income.

c. This is a contractionary fiscal policy because it is an increase in taxes, which will reduce disposable income.

2. Federal disaster relief that is quickly disbursed is more effective at stabilizing the economy than legislated aid because there is very little time lag between the time of the disaster and the time when relief is received by victims. In contrast, the process of creating new legislation is relatively slow, so legislated aid is likely to entail a time lag in its disbursement, potentially destabilizing the economy.

3. a. An economy is overstimulated when an inflationary gap is present. This will arise if expansionary fiscal policy is implemented when the economy is currently in long-run macroeconomic equilibrium. This shifts the aggregate demand curve to the right, in the short run raising the aggregate price level and aggregate output and creating an inflationary gap. Eventually, nominal wages will rise and shift the short-run aggregate supply curve to the left, and aggregate output will fall back to potential output. This is the scenario envisaged by the speaker.

b. No, this is not a valid argument. When the economy is not currently in long-run macroeconomic equilibrium, expansionary fiscal policy does not lead to the outcome just described. Suppose a negative demand shock has shifted the aggregate demand curve to the left, resulting in a recessionary gap. Expansionary fiscal policy can shift the aggregate demand curve back to its original position in long-run macroeconomic equilibrium. In this way, the short-run fall in aggregate output and deflation caused by the original negative demand shock can be avoided. So, if used in response to demand shocks, fiscal policy is an effective policy tool.

Multiple-Choice Questions

1. e
2. e
3. b
4. b
5. a

Critical-Thinking Questions

Your graph should look like this.

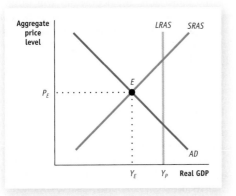

1. Expansionary
2. Decrease taxes, increase government purchases of goods and services, or increase government transfers

MODULE 31
Check Your Understanding

1. A $500 million increase in government purchases of goods and services directly increases aggregate spending by $500 million, which then starts the multiplier in motion. It will increase real GDP by $500 million × $1/(1 − MPC)$. A $500 million increase in government transfers increases aggregate spending only to the extent that it leads to an increase in consumer spending. Consumer spending rises by $MPC × \$1$ for every $1 increase in disposable income, where MPC is less than 1. So a $500 million increase in government transfers will cause a rise in real GDP only MPC times as much as a $500 million increase in government purchases of goods and services. It will increase real GDP by $500 million × $MPC/(1 − MPC)$.

2. If government purchases of goods and services fall by $500 million, the initial fall in aggregate spending is $500 million. If there is a $500 million tax increase, the initial fall in aggregate spending is $MPC × \$500$ million, which is less than $500 million because some of the tax payments

are made with money that would otherwise have been saved rather than spent.

3. Boldovia will experience greater variation in its real GDP than Moldovia because Moldovia has automatic stabilizers while Boldovia does not. In Moldovia the effects of slumps will be lessened by unemployment insurance benefits, which will support residents' incomes, while the effects of booms will be diminished because tax revenues will go up. In contrast, incomes will not be supported in Boldovia during slumps because there is no unemployment insurance. In addition, because Boldovia has lump-sum taxes, its booms will not be diminished by increases in tax revenue.

Multiple-Choice Questions

1. c
2. b
3. b
4. c
5. e

Critical-Thinking Questions

1. $50 million
    multiplier = $1/(1 − MPC) = 1/(1 − 0.75) = 1/0.25 = 4$
    change in $G × 4 = \$200$ million
    change in $G = \$50$ million

2. 10
    $20 million × multiplier = $200 million
    multiplier = $200/20 = 10$

3. 0.1
    $1/(1 − MPC) = 1/MPS = 10$
    $MPS = 0.1$

MODULE 32

1. The actual budget balance takes into account the effects of the business cycle on the budget deficit. During recessionary gaps, it incorporates the effect of lower tax revenues and higher transfers on the budget balance; during inflationary gaps, it incorporates the effect of higher tax revenues and reduced transfers. In contrast, the cyclically adjusted budget balance factors out the effects of the business cycle and assumes that real GDP is at potential output. Since, in the long run, real GDP tends to potential output, the cyclically adjusted budget balance is a better measure of the long-run sustainability of government policies.

2. In recessions, real GDP falls. This implies that consumers' incomes, consumer spending, and producers' profits also fall. So in recessions, states' tax revenue (which depends in large part on consumers' incomes, consumer spending, and producers' profits) falls. In order to balance the state budget, states have to cut spending or raise taxes. But that deepens the recession. Without a balanced-budget requirement, states could use expansionary fiscal policy during a recession to lessen the fall in real GDP.

3. a. A higher growth rate of real GDP implies that tax revenue will increase. If government spending remains constant and the government runs a budget surplus, the size of the public debt will be less than it would otherwise have been.

b. If retirees live longer, the average age of the population increases. As a result, the implicit liabilities of the government increase because spending on programs for older Americans, such as Social Security and Medicare, will rise.

c. A decrease in tax revenue without offsetting reductions in government spending will cause the public debt to increase.

d. Public debt will increase as a result of government borrowing to pay interest on its current public debt.

Multiple-Choice Questions

1. b
2. c
3. a
4. c
5. d

Critical-Thinking Question

To stimulate the economy in the short run, the government can use fiscal policy to increase real GDP. This entails borrowing, which runs the risk of increasing the debt even more and, in extreme cases, of forcing the government to default on its debts. Even in less extreme cases, a large public debt is undesirable because government borrowing crowds out borrowing for private investment spending. The result is a decrease in investment spending and reduced long-run growth of the economy.

MODULE 33
Check Your Understanding

1. The defining characteristic of money is its liquidity: how easily it can be used to purchase goods and services. Although a gift certificate can easily be used to purchase a very defined set of goods or services (the goods or services available at the store issuing the gift certificate), it cannot be used to purchase any other goods or services. A gift certificate is therefore not money since it cannot easily be used to purchase all goods or services.

2. Again, the important characteristic of money is its liquidity: how easily it can be used to purchase goods and services. M1, the narrowest definition of the money supply, consists only of currency in circulation, traveler's checks, and checkable bank deposits. CDs aren't checkable—and they can't be made checkable without incurring a cost because there's a penalty for early withdrawal. This makes them less liquid than the assets counted in M1.

3. Commodity-backed money uses resources more efficiently than simple commodity money, like gold and silver coins, because commodity-backed money ties up fewer valuable resources. Although a bank must keep some of the commodity—generally gold and silver—on hand, it has to keep only enough to satisfy demand for redemptions. It can then lend out the remaining gold and silver, which allows society to use these resources for other purposes, with no loss in the ability to achieve gains from trade.

Multiple-Choice Questions

1. d
2. c

3. e
4. a
5. b

Critical-Thinking Questions

1. its official status given by the U.S. government
2. fiat money
3. i. commodity money—money that has intrinsic value in other uses
   ii. commodity-backed money—money that has no intrinsic value but can be converted into valuable goods on demand

MODULE 34
Check Your Understanding

1. Even though you know that the rumor about the bank is not true, you are concerned about other depositors pulling their money out of the bank. And you know that if enough other depositors pull their money out, the bank will fail. In that case, it is rational for you to pull your money out before the bank fails. All depositors will think like this, so even if they all know that the rumor is false, they may still rationally pull their money out, leading to a bank run. Deposit insurance leads depositors to worry less about the possibility of a bank run. Even if a bank fails, the FDIC will currently pay each depositor up to $250,000 per account. This will make you much less likely to pull your money out in response to a rumor. Since other depositors will think the same, there will be no bank run.

2. The aspects of modern bank regulation that would frustrate this scheme are *capital requirements* and *reserve requirements*. Capital requirements mean that a bank has to have a certain amount of capital—the difference between its assets (loans plus reserves) and its liabilities (deposits). So the con artist could not open a bank without putting any of his own wealth in because his bank would need the required amount of capital—that is, it needs to hold more assets (loans plus reserves) than deposits. So the con artist would be at risk of losing his own wealth if his loans turn out badly.

3. Since they have to hold only $100 in reserves, instead of $200, banks now lend out $100 of their reserves. Whoever borrows the $100 will deposit it in a bank (or spend it, and the recipient will deposit it in a bank), which will lend out $100 × (1 − rr) = $100 × 0.9 = $90. The borrowed $90 will likewise find its way into a bank, which will lend out $90 × 0.9 = $81, and so on. Overall, deposits will increase by $100/0.1 = $1,000.

4. Silas puts $1,000 in the bank, of which the bank lends out $1,000 × (1 − rr) = $1,000 × 0.9 = $900. Whoever borrows the $900 will keep $450 in cash and deposit $450 in the bank. The bank will lend out $450 × 0.9 = $405. Whoever borrows the $405 will keep $202.50 in cash and deposit $202.50 in the bank. The bank will lend out $202.50 × 0.9 = $182.25, and so on. Overall this leads to an increase in deposits of $1,000 + $450 + $202.50 + . . . But it decreases the amount of currency in circulation: the amount of cash is reduced by the $1,000 Silas puts into the bank. This is offset, but not fully, by the amount of cash held by each borrower. The amount of currency in circulation therefore changes

by −$1,000 + $450 + $202.50 + . . . The money supply therefore increases by the sum of the increase in deposits and the change in currency in circulation, which is $1,000 − $1,000 + $450 + $450 + $202.50 + $202.50 + . . . and so on.

Multiple-Choice Questions

1. d
2. a
3. e
4. c
5. d

Critical-Thinking Questions

1. The bank must hold $5,000 as required reserves (5% of $100,000). It is holding $10,000, so $5,000 must be excess reserves.

2. The bank must hold an additional $50 as reserves because that is the reserve requirement multiplied by the deposit: 5% of $1,000. The bank can lend out $950.

3. The money multiplier is 1/0.05 = 20. An increase of $2,000 in excess reserves can increase the money supply by $2,000 × 20 = $40,000.

MODULE 35
Check Your Understanding

1. The Panic of 1907, the S&L crisis, and the crisis of 2008 all involved losses by financial institutions that were less regulated than banks. In the crises of 1907 and 2008, there was a widespread loss of confidence in the financial sector and collapse of credit markets. Like the crisis of 1907 and the S&L crisis, the crisis of 2008 exerted a powerful negative effect on the economy.

2. The creation of the Federal Reserve failed to prevent bank runs because it did not eradicate the fears of depositors that a bank collapse would cause them to lose their money. The bank runs eventually stopped after federal deposit insurance was instituted and the public came to understand that their deposits were protected.

3. The balance sheet effect occurs when asset sales cause declines in asset prices, which then reduce the value of other firms' net worth as the value of the assets on their balance sheets declines. In the vicious cycle of deleveraging, the balance sheet effect on firms forces their creditors to call in their loan contracts, forcing the firms to sell assets to pay back their loans, leading to further asset sales and price declines. Because the vicious cycle of deleveraging occurs across different firms and no single firm can stop it, it is necessary for the government to step in to stop it.

Multiple-Choice Questions

1. a
2. a
3. b
4. d
5. e

Critical-Thinking Questions

1. oversee the Federal Reserve System and serve on the Federal Open Market Committee
2. 7
3. the president of the United States
4. 14-year terms
5. to insulate appointees from political pressure
6. 4 years; may be reappointed

MODULE 36
Check Your Understanding

1. An open-market purchase of $100 million by the Fed increases banks' reserves by $100 million as the Fed credits their accounts with additional reserves. In other words, this open-market purchase increases the monetary base (currency in circulation plus bank reserves) by $100 million. Banks lend out the additional $100 million. Whoever borrows the money puts it back into the banking system in the form of deposits. Of these deposits, banks lend out $100 million × (1 − rr) = $100 million × 0.9 = $90 million. Whoever borrows the money deposits it back into the banking system. And banks lend out $90 million × 0.9 = $81 million, and so on. As a result, bank deposits increased by $100 million + $90 million + $81 million + . . . = $100 million/rr = $100 million/0.1 = $1,000 million = $1 billion. Since in this simplified example all money lent out is deposited back into the banking system, there is no increase of currency in circulation, so the increase in bank deposits is equal to the increase in the money supply. In other words, the money supply increases by $1 billion. This is greater than the increase in the monetary base by a factor of 10: in this simplified model in which deposits are the only component of the money supply and in which banks hold no excess reserves, the money multiplier is 1/rr = 10.

Multiple-Choice Questions

1. d
2. e
3. d
4. b
5. c

Critical-Thinking Question

1. provide financial services to depository institutions
2. supervise and regulate banking institutions
3. maintain the stability of the financial system
4. conduct monetary policy

MODULE 37
Check Your Understanding

1. a. By increasing the opportunity cost of holding money, a high interest rate reduces the quantity of money demanded. This is a movement up and to the left along the money demand curve.

b. A 10% fall in prices reduces the quantity of money demanded at any given interest rate, shifting the money demand curve leftward.

c. This technological change reduces the quantity of money demanded at any given interest rate, so it shifts the money demand curve leftward.

d. Payments in cash require employers to hold more money, increasing the quantity of money demanded at any given interest rate. So it shifts the money demand curve rightward.

2. a. A 1% processing fee on debit/credit card transactions for purchases less than $50 reduces the opportunity cost of holding cash because consumers will save money by paying with cash.

b. An increase in the interest paid on six-month CDs raises the opportunity cost of holding cash because holding cash requires forgoing the higher interest paid.

c. A fall in real estate prices has no effect on the opportunity cost or benefit of holding cash because real estate is an illiquid asset and therefore isn't relevant in the decision of how much cash to hold. Also, real estate transactions are generally not carried out using cash.

d. Because many purchases of food are made in cash, a significant increase in the cost of food reduces the opportunity cost of holding cash.

Multiple-Choice Questions

1. d
2. d
3. b
4. d
5. e

Critical-Thinking Question

Your graph should look like the following. At an interest rate below equilibrium, the quantity of money demanded exceeds the quantity of money supplied. People want to shift more of their wealth out of interest-bearing assets such as CDs and hold it as money instead. Because the quantity of interest-bearing nonmoney assets demanded is less than the quantity supplied, those trying to sell these assets will have to offer a higher interest rate to attract buyers. As the interest rate rises, the quantity of money demanded decreases. This process continues until the market returns to equilibrium.

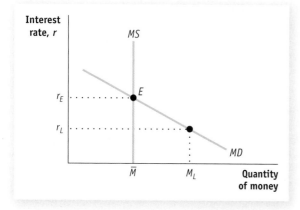

MODULE 38
Check Your Understanding

1. In the accompanying diagram, the increase in the demand for money is shown as a rightward shift of the money demand curve, from MD_1 to MD_2. This raises the equilibrium interest rate from r_1 to r_2.

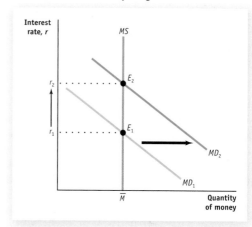

2. In order to prevent the interest rate from rising, the Federal Reserve must make an open-market purchase of Treasury bills, shifting the money supply curve rightward. This is shown in the accompanying diagram as the move from MS_1 to MS_2.

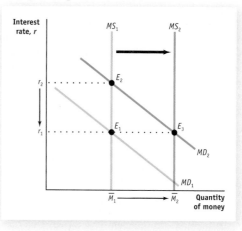

3. a. The money supply curve shifts to the right.

b. The equilibrium interest rate falls.

c. Investment spending rises, due to the fall in the interest rate.

d. Consumer spending rises, due to the multiplier process.

e. Aggregate output rises because of the rightward shift of the aggregate demand curve.

Multiple-Choice Questions

1. a
2. a
3. a
4. c
5. a

Critical-Thinking Questions

1. decrease the discount rate, decrease the reserve requirement, open-market purchases

2. Your graph should look like this.

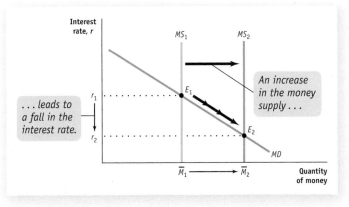

3. There is no change in aggregate supply; aggregate demand increases. Lower interest rates lead to greater investment spending (and more interest-sensitive consumer spending). Aggregate demand is made up of $C + I + G + (X - IM)$, so an increase in I and C increases AD. Interest rate changes don't affect short-run aggregate supply.

4. As shown in the accompanying figure, aggregate output increases in the short run.

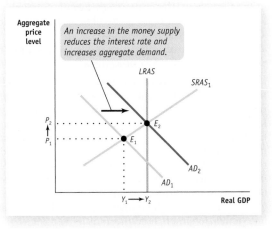

MODULE 39

Check Your Understanding

1. A 5% increase in the money supply will cause a 5% increase in the aggregate price level in the long run. The process begins in the short run, when the larger money supply decreases the interest rate and promotes investment spending. Investment spending is a component of aggregate demand, so the increase in investment spending leads to an increase in aggregate demand, which causes real GDP to increase beyond potential output. The resulting upward pressure on nominal wages and other input prices shifts aggregate supply to the left until a new long-run equilibrium is reached. Although real GDP returns to its original level, both the increase in aggregate demand and the decrease in aggregate supply cause the aggregate price level to increase. The end result is 5% more money being spent on the same quantity of goods and services, which could only mean a 5% increase in the aggregate price level.

2. A 5% increase in the money supply will have no effect on the interest rate in the long run. As explained in the previous answer, a 5% increase in the money supply is matched by a 5% increase in the aggregate price level in the long run. Changes in the aggregate price level, in turn, cause proportional changes in the demand for money. So a 5% increase in the aggregate price level increases the quantity of money demanded at any given interest rate by 5%. This means that at the initial interest rate, the quantity of money demanded rises exactly as much as the money supply, and the new, long-run interest rate is therefore no different from the initial interest rate.

Multiple-Choice Questions

1. c
2. d
3. c
4. c
5. e

Critical-Thinking Questions

1. Your graph should look like this.

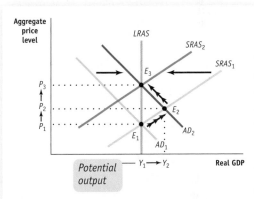

2. The aggregate demand curve shifts to the right, creating a new equilibrium price level and real GDP. The higher money supply leads to a lower interest rate, which increases investment spending and consumer spending, and in turn aggregate demand.

3. Wages rise over time, shifting short-run aggregate supply to the left. This brings equilibrium back to potential output with a higher price level.

MODULE 40

Check Your Understanding

1. The inflation rate is more likely to quickly reflect changes in the money supply when the economy has had an extended period of high inflation. That's because an extended period of high inflation sensitizes workers and firms to raise nominal wages and prices of intermediate goods when the aggregate price level rises. As a result, there will be little or no increase in real output in the short run after an increase in the money supply, and the increase in the money supply will simply be reflected in a proportional increase in prices. In an economy where people are not sensitized to high inflation because of low inflation in the past, an increase in the money supply will

lead to an increase in real output in the short run. This illustrates the fact that the classical model of the price level best applies to economies with *persistently* high inflation, not those with little or no history of high inflation even though they may currently have high inflation.

2. Yes, there can still be an inflation tax because the tax is levied on people who hold money. As long as people hold money, regardless of whether prices are indexed or not, the government is able to use seignorage to capture real resources from the public.

Multiple-Choice Questions

1. d
2. b
3. b
4. c
5. a

Critical-Thinking Question

Your diagram should look like this.

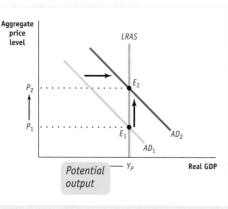

MODULE 41

Check Your Understanding

1. When real GDP equals potential output, cyclical unemployment is zero and the unemployment rate is equal to the natural rate. This is the case at point E_1 in the figure assuming a natural rate of 6%. Any unemployment in excess of this 6% rate represents cyclical unemployment. An increase in aggregate demand leads to a fall in the unemployment rate below the natural rate (negative cyclical unemployment) and an increase in the inflation rate. This is given by the movement from E_1 to E_2 in the figure and traces a movement upward along the short-run Phillips curve. A reduction in aggregate demand leads to a rise in the unemployment rate above the natural rate (positive cyclical unemployment) and a fall in the inflation rate. This would be represented by a movement down along the short-run Phillips curve from point E_1. So for a given expected inflation rate, the short-run Phillips curve illustrates the relationship between cyclical unemployment and the actual inflation rate.

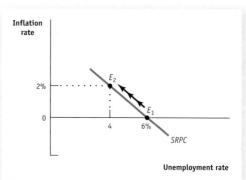

2. There is no long-run trade-off between inflation and unemployment because after expectations of inflation change, wages will adjust to the change, returning employment and the unemployment rate to their equilibrium (natural) levels. This implies that once expectations of inflation fully adjust to any change in actual inflation, the unemployment rate will return to the natural rate of unemployment, or NAIRU. This also implies that the long-run Phillips curve is vertical.

3. Disinflation is costly because to reduce the inflation rate, aggregate output in the short run must typically fall below potential output. This, in turn, results in an increase in the unemployment rate above the natural rate. In general, we would observe a reduction in real GDP. The costs of disinflation can be reduced by not allowing inflation to increase in the first place. The costs of any disinflation will also be lower if the central bank is credible and it announces in advance its policy to reduce inflation. In this situation, the adjustment to the disinflationary policy will be more rapid, resulting in a smaller loss of aggregate output.

4. If the nominal interest rate is negative, an individual is better off simply holding cash, which has a 0% nominal rate of return. If the options facing an individual are to lend and receive a negative nominal interest rate or to hold cash and receive a 0% nominal rate of return, the individual will hold cash. Such a scenario creates the possibility of a liquidity trap, in which monetary policy is ineffective because the nominal interest rate cannot fall below zero. Once the nominal interest rate falls to zero, further increases in the money supply will lead firms and individuals to simply hold the additional cash.

Multiple-Choice Questions

1. b
2. c
3. b
4. e
5. e

Critical-Thinking Questions

1. 4%

2. 2%, because 4% − 2% = 2%

3. 0%, because although 4% − 6% = −2%, nominal interest rates can't go below zero

4. Lenders would effectively have to pay people to borrow money, in that what the lenders received back would be less than what they lent out. No lending would take place. It is better to hold cash than to pay people to borrow money.

5. Conventional monetary policy (decreasing interest rates) can't happen if the nominal interest rate is already zero. This is called the zero bound or a liquidity trap.

MODULE 42

Check Your Understanding

1. **a.** This is not an example of maturity transformation because no short-term liabilities are being turned into long-term assets. So it is not subject to a bank run.

   b. This is an example of maturity transformation: Dana incurs a short-term liability, credit card debt, to fund the acquisition of a long-term asset, better job skills. It can result in a bank-run-like phenomenon if her credit card lender becomes fearful of her ability to repay and stops lending to her. If this happens, she will not be able to finish her course and, as a result, will not be able to get the better job that would allow her to pay off her credit card loans.

   c. This is not an example of maturity transformation because there are no short-term liabilities. The partnership itself has no obligation to repay an individual partner's investment and so has no liabilities, short term or long term.

   d. This is an example of maturity transformation: the checking accounts are short-term liabilities of the student union savings bank, and the student loans are long-term assets.

2. According to standard macroeconomics, a government should adopt expansionary policies to increase aggregate demand to address an economic slump. France, however, did just the opposite, responding to a weaker economy with a contractionary fiscal policy that would make the economy even weaker. This shows that the French government had adopted the austerity view, believing that it was more important to try to assure markets of its solvency than to support the economy.

3. Because shadow banks like Lehman relied on short-term borrowing to fund their operations, fears about their soundness could quickly lead lenders to immediately cut off their credit and force them into failure. And without membership in the lender-of-last-resort system, shadow banks like Lehman could not borrow from the Federal Reserve to make up for the short-term loans it had lost.

4. If there had been only a formal depository banking sector, several factors would have mitigated the potential and scope of a banking crisis. First, there would have been no repo financing; the only short-term liabilities would have been customers' deposits, and these would have been largely covered by deposit insurance. Second, capital requirements would have reduced banks' willingness to take on excessive risk, such as holding onto subprime mortgages. Also, direct oversight by the Federal Reserve would have prevented so much concentration of risk within the banking sector. Finally, depository banks are within the lender-of-last-resort system; as a result, depository banks had another layer of protection against the fear of depositors and other creditors that they couldn't meet their obligations. All of these factors would have reduced the potential and scope of a banking crisis.

5. Because the shadow banking sector had become such a critical part of the U.S. economy, the crisis of 2008 made it clear that in the event of another crisis, the government would need to guarantee a wide range of financial institution debts, including those of shadow banks (in addition to those of depository banks). The result was an incentive problem: shadow banks would be able to take more risk, knowing that the government would bail them out in the event of a meltdown. To counteract this, the Dodd-Frank Act gave the government the power to regulate "systemically important" shadow banks (those likely to wreak havoc on the economy should they fail) in order to reduce their risk taking. It also gave the government the power to seize control of failing shadow banks in a way that was fair to taxpayers and and that did not enrich the bankers involved.

Multiple-Choice Questions

1. c
2. c
3. a
4. b
5. e

Critical-Thinking Question

A banking crisis occurs when a large part of the banking sector is in danger of failing. A banking crisis normally leads to a deep recession because of a credit crunch, debt overhang, and a loss of monetary policy effectiveness. A credit crunch occurs when borrowers either cannot get credit or must pay very high interest rates. The reduction in borrowing will reduce spending and output. Debt overhang occurs when a vicious cycle of deleveraging pushes down asset prices. Consumers and businesses are left with high debt but diminished assets. Monetary policy becomes ineffective when financial institutions are unwilling to lend and/or businesses and consumers are unwilling to borrow. The overall disruption of financial markets typically leads to a deep recession.

MODULE 43

Check Your Understanding

1. **a.** The sale of the new airplane to China represents an export of a good to China and so enters the current account.

   b. The sale of Boeing stock to Chinese investors is a sale of a U.S. asset and so enters the financial account.

   c. Even though the plane already exists, when it is shipped to China it is an export of a good from the United States. So the sale of the plane enters the current account.

   d. Because the plane stays in the United States, the Chinese investor is buying a U.S. asset. So this is identical to the answer in part b: the sale of the jet enters the financial account.

2. The collapse of the U.S. housing bubble and the ensuing recession led to a dramatic fall in interest rates in the United States because of the deeply depressed economy. Consequently, capital inflows into the United States dried up.

Multiple-Choice Questions

1. e
2. a
3. b
4. a
5. a

Critical-Thinking Question

Your graphs should look like the following.

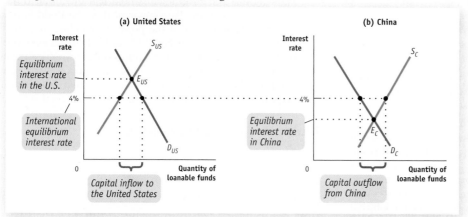

MODULE 44

Check Your Understanding

1. a. The increased purchase of Mexican oil would cause U.S. individuals (and firms) to increase their demand for the peso. To purchase pesos, individuals would increase their supply of U.S. dollars to the foreign exchange market, causing a rightward shift in the supply curve of U.S. dollars. This would cause the peso price of the dollar to fall (the amount of pesos per dollar would fall). The peso would appreciate and the U.S. dollar would depreciate as a result.

b. With the appreciation of the peso it would take more U.S. dollars to obtain the same quantity of Mexican pesos. If we assume that the price level (measured in Mexican pesos) of other Mexican goods and services would not change, other Mexican goods and services would become more expensive to U.S. households and firms. The dollar cost of other Mexican goods and services would rise as the peso appreciated. So Mexican exports of goods and services other than oil would fall.

c. U.S. goods and services would become cheaper in terms of pesos, so Mexican imports of goods and services would rise.

2. a. The real exchange rate equals pesos per U.S. dollar × aggregate price level in the U.S./aggregate price level in Mexico. Today, the aggregate price level in both countries is 100. The real exchange rate today is: $10 \times (100/100)$ = 10. The aggregate price level in five years in the U.S. will be $100 \times (120/100)$ = 120, and in Mexico it will be $100 \times (1,200/800)$ = 150. Thus, the real exchange rate in five years, assuming the nominal exchange rate does not change, will be $10 \times (120/150)$ = 8.

b. Today, a basket of goods and services that costs $100 costs 800 pesos, so the purchasing power parity is 8 pesos per U.S. dollar. In five years, a basket that costs $120 will cost 1,200 pesos, so the purchasing power parity will be 10 pesos per U.S. dollar.

Multiple-Choice Questions

1. d

2. d

3. d

4. b

5. b

Critical-Thinking Question

In order to purchase more imports from Europe, U.S. consumers must supply more dollars in exchange for euros. As shown in the diagram, the increase in the supply of dollars shifts the dollar supply curve to the right and decreases the exchange rate from XR_1 to XR_2.

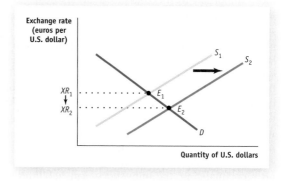

MODULE 45

Check Your Understanding

1. The accompanying diagram shows the supply of and demand for the yuan, with the U.S. dollar price of the yuan on the vertical axis. In 2005, prior to the revaluation, the exchange rate was pegged at 8.28 yuan per U.S. dollar or, equivalently, 0.121 U.S. dollars per yuan ($0.121). At the target exchange rate of $0.121, the quantity of yuan demanded exceeded the quantity of yuan supplied, creating the shortage depicted in the diagram.

Without any intervention by the Chinese government, the U.S. dollar price of the yuan would be bid up, causing an appreciation of the yuan. The Chinese government, however, intervened to prevent this appreciation.

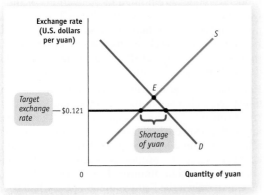

a. If the exchange rate were allowed to float more freely, the U.S. dollar price of the exchange rate would move toward the equilibrium exchange rate (labeled *XR** in the accompanying diagram). This would occur as a result of the shortage, when buyers of the yuan would bid up its U.S. dollar price. As the exchange rate increased, the quantity of yuan demanded would fall and the quantity of yuan supplied would increase. If the exchange rate were allowed to increase to *XR**, the disequilibrium would be entirely eliminated.

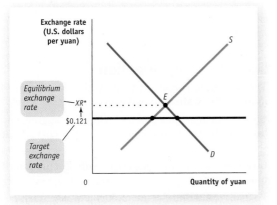

b. Placing restrictions on foreigners who want to invest in China would reduce the demand for the yuan, causing the demand curve to shift in the accompanying diagram from D_1 to something like D_2. This would cause a reduction in the shortage of the yuan. If demand fell to D_3, the disequilibrium would be completely eliminated.

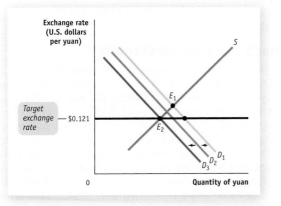

c. Removing restrictions on Chinese who wish to invest abroad would cause an increase in the supply of the yuan and a rightward shift of the supply curve. This increase in supply would reduce the size of the shortage. If, for example, supply increased from S_1 to S_2, the disequilibrium would be eliminated completely, as shown in the accompanying diagram.

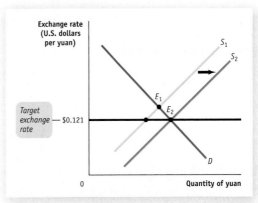

d. Imposing a tax on exports (Chinese goods sold to foreigners) would raise the price of these goods and decrease the amount of Chinese goods purchased. This would also decrease the demand for yuan with which to purchase those goods. The graphical analysis here is virtually identical to that found in the figure accompanying part b.

Multiple-Choice Questions

1. e
2. e
3. b
4. a
5. a

Critical-Thinking Question

1) Use foreign exchange reserves. To stabilize an exchange rate through exchange market intervention (e.g., buying its own currency), a country must keep large quantities of foreign currency on hand, which is usually a low-return investment. And large reserves can be quickly exhausted when there are large capital flows out of a country.

2) Shifting supply and demand curves for currency through monetary policy. If a country chooses to stabilize an exchange rate by adjusting monetary policy rather than through intervention, it must divert monetary policy from other goals, notably stabilizing the economy and managing the inflation rate.

3) Foreign exchange controls. These regulations distort incentives for importing and exporting goods and services. They can also create substantial costs in terms of red tape and corruption.

MODULE 46
Check Your Understanding

1. The devaluations and revaluations most likely occurred in those periods when there was a sudden change in the franc–mark exchange rate: 1974, 1976, the early 1980s, 1986, and 1993–1994.

2. The high Canadian interest rates caused an increase in capital inflows to Canada. To obtain assets that yielded a relatively high interest rate in Canada, investors first had to obtain Canadian dollars. The increase in the demand for the Canadian dollar caused the Canadian dollar to appreciate. This appreciation of the Canadian currency raised the price of Canadian goods to foreigners (measured in terms of the foreign currency). This made it more difficult for Canadian firms to compete in other markets.

Multiple-Choice Questions

1. c
2. b
3. a
4. d
5. b

Critical-Thinking Question

The decrease in aggregate demand that occurs during a recession includes the demand for goods and services produced abroad as well as at home. When a trading partner experiences a recession, it leads to a fall in their imports. The trading partner's imports are the country's exports.

A reduction in foreign demand for the country's domestic goods and services leads to a reduction in demand for the domestic currency. With a floating exchange rate, the currency depreciates. This makes domestic goods and services cheaper, so exports don't fall by as much as they would have, and it makes imports more expensive, leading to a fall in imports. Both effects limit the decline in domestic aggregate demand.

MODULE 47
Check Your Understanding

1. A classical economist would have said that although expansionary monetary policy would probably have some effect in the short run, the short run was unimportant. Instead, a classical economist would have stressed the long run, claiming expansionary monetary policy would result only in an increase in the aggregate price level without affecting aggregate output.

2. a. According to the velocity equation, $M \times V = P \times Y$, where M is the money supply, V the velocity of money, P the aggregate price level, and Y real GDP. If the Federal Reserve had pursued a monetary policy rule of constant money supply growth, the collapse in the velocity of money beginning in 2008 and visible in Figure 47-4 would have resulted in a dramatic decline in aggregate output.

   b. Although monetarists generally believe that monetary policy is not only effective but, in fact, more effective than fiscal policy, they also generally do not favor macroeconomic policy activism. Instead, monetarists generally advocate monetary policy rules, such as a low but constant rate of money supply growth. In addition, the natural rate hypothesis states that although monetary policy may be effective in helping return unemployment to its natural rate, it cannot permanently reduce unemployment below the natural rate.

3. Fiscal policy is limited by time lags in recognizing economic problems, forming a response, passing legislation, and implementing the policies. Monetary policy is also limited by time lags, but these lags are not as severe as those for fiscal policy because the Federal Reserve tends to act more quickly than Congress. Attempts to reduce unemployment below the natural rate via both fiscal and monetary policy are limited by predictions of the natural rate hypothesis: that these attempts will result in accelerating inflation. Also, both fiscal and monetary policy are limited by concerns about the political business cycle: that they will be used to satisfy political ends and will end up destabilizing the economy.

4. a. Rational expectations theorists would argue that only unexpected changes in the money supply would have any short-run effect on economic activity. They would also argue that expected changes in the money supply would affect only the aggregate price level, with no short-run effect on aggregate output. So such theorists would give credit to the Fed for limiting the severity of the 2007–2009 recession only if the Fed's monetary policy had been more aggressive than individuals expected during this period.

   b. Real business cycle theorists would argue that the Fed's policy had no effect on ending the 2007–2009 recession because they believe that fluctuations in aggregate output are caused largely by changes in total factor productivity.

Multiple-Choice Questions

1. e
2. d
3. b
4. a
5. d

Critical-Thinking Question

a. The aggregate supply curve is vertical so changes in the money supply affect only the aggregate price level.

b. Changes in aggregate demand will affect aggregate output because the short-run aggregate supply curve is upward sloping.

c. Business cycles are associated with fluctuations in the money supply.

d. To avoid inflation, the unemployment rate must be set so that actual inflation equals expected inflation.

e. Individuals and firms make optimal decisions using all available information.

f. Fluctuations in total factor productivity growth cause the business cycle by causing the vertical aggregate supply curve to shift.

MODULE 48
Check Your Understanding

The liquidity trap brought on by the Great Recession greatly diminished the Great Moderation consensus because it considered monetary policy to be the main policy tool and monetary policy was now largely ineffective. The continuing disagreements over fiscal policy were now brought to the forefront as fiscal policy was used by policy makers to support their deeply depressed economies. A new consensus is unlikely to emerge anytime soon because results of the various policies have been unclear or disappointing: fiscal stimulus has failed to bring down unemployment substantially (although some say the stimulus was too small); conventional monetary policy does not work; and the Fed's unconventional monetary policy seemed to have relatively little effect.

Multiple-Choice Questions

1. d
2. c
3. d
4. c
5. c

Critical-Thinking Questions

1. Supporters of expansionary fiscal policy, or fiscal stimulus, offered three main arguments:

   • Monetary policy was not effective due to interest rates being near zero.

   • Given the already near zero interest rates, expansionary fiscal policy was unlikely to result in crowding out of investment.

   • Even if fiscal policy took time to implement, the economy was still likely to be in need of stimulus.

2. Opponents of fiscal stimulus offered two main arguments:

   • People would see any increase in government spending as a sign that taxes were sure to rise in the future. This would reduce spending now and negate the effects of the increase in government spending.

   • People might lose faith in the government's ability to repay its debt if the level of debt continued to rise.